Encyclopedia of Medieval Literature

Encyclopedia of Medieval Literature

Edited by **Robert Thomas Lambdin**
and **Laura Cooner Lambdin**

GREENWOOD PRESS
Westport, Connecticut • London

Library of Congress Cataloging-in-Publication Data

Encyclopedia of medieval literature / edited by Robert Thomas Lambdin and
   Laura Cooner Lambdin.
     p. cm.
   Includes bibliographical references and index.
   ISBN 0–313–30054–2 (alk. paper)
    1. Literature, Medieval—Encyclopedias.   I. Lambdin, Robert Thomas.
   II. Lambdin, Laura Cooner.
   PN669.E53   2000
   809′.02—dc21   97–13713

British Library Cataloguing in Publication Data is available.

Library of Congress Catalog Card Number: 97–13713
ISBN: 0–313–30054–2

First published in 2000

Greenwood Press, 88 Post Road West, Westport, CT 06881
An imprint of Greenwood Publishing Group, Inc.
www.greenwood.com

Printed in the United States of America

The paper used in this book complies with the
Permanent Paper Standard issued by the National
Information Standards Organization (Z39.48–1984).

10 9 8 7 6 5 4 3 2 1

*To our dear
Mary Nell*

Contents

Introduction

The *Encyclopedia of Medieval Literature* describes topics related to medieval literature, including literary works, authors, historical figures, events, themes, and genres. This text is intended as a reference tool to serve university and advanced high school students; it is also concise and convenient enough for use as a quick desk reference book for all medievalists.

Entries cover the span of time from c. 500 A. D. to 1500 A. D. (from "Caedmon's Hymn" to *Everyman* in English). While the emphasis is upon early British Literature, also included are entries reflecting the literature written concurrently in many other major countries; these essays concerning the medieval period in other lands are included primarily for comparison and contrast, and are in no way intended to be exhaustive.

The topics are arranged simply and logically in alphabetical order with appropriate cross references indicated by an asterisk (*). An author's last name will generally be the best starting point for locating information. While the stress is upon primary information rather than the critical interpretation of a work, important scholarship is mentioned in the expanded essays in a manner providing clarity for student readers. All entries are followed by a brief bibliography containing standard critical texts, as well as a few recent examinations.

There are two types of entries. The first type are the expanded entries that concern major authors, entire genres, or the literature of another country besides England. In a comprehensive, but not exhaustive fashion, these entries provide necessary information, offer examples, and explain critical analysis. Mentioned in these expanded entries are works preceded by an asterisk (*) that have their own entry--either short or long-- elsewhere listed alphabetically. The second type of entries are brief, informative essays usually consisting of two or three paragraphs including a definition of the entry, a description or plot outline and--where appropriate--a concise analysis of critical importance. As with the expanded entries, these short entries are also followed by a "Selected Bibliography" section. Authorship of all entries is indicated at the end of each entry. Included at the back of this text is a "About the Contributors" section which provides a short summary of each author's professional background.

Although our emphasis has been upon literature, other related topics are briefly mentioned to further the student's overall understanding of the medieval period. Hence, included are short entries for important political and religious leaders; various movements, such as scholasticism; explorers; artists; and major wars and military exercises such as the Crusades, and the Wars of the Roses. The coverage of theses topics is meant as supplements to foster understanding of the literary movements of the Middle Ages.

A

ABELARD, PETER (1079-1142). A philosopher and theologian, Peter Abelard openly disagreed with many of the foremost contemporary scholars, generating some innovative ideas and dialectic techniques. Abelard was born in Pallet, a village about ten miles east of Nantes in Brittany. He began his career as a wanderer, gathering knowledge from scholars he encountered during his travels, most notably Roscelin the Nominalist. He became a permanent pupil of William of Champeaux at the Cathedral School in Paris, but soon separated from him because of a heated difference of opinion. This argument effectively banished him from Paris. After returning to his native land to recover his failing health, he returned to France and established schools at Melun and later at Corbeil in 1101. His next project was to found a school at Mont Sainte-Geneviève in 1108. His fame as a teacher spread after he accepted a position at the Cathedral School in Paris. He detailed this situation in his Historia Calamitatum, or the Story of my calamities. People flocked to hear him speak, but his ego grew in proportion to his renown. Abelard's divergent doctrines and his opinionated personality led him to many disputes with authority throughout his career. These disagreements only enhanced his reputation.

As a result of his outspoken nature, Abelard's next controversy involved the Benedictine monks at the Abbey of St. Denis; he had taken the vow of this order after his doomed love affair with a woman named Heloise. Abelard criticized the name of their patron saint, and the astonished monks banished him to a "branch" monastery. There he again challenged the authorities, especially on the doctrine of the Holy Trinity. Abelard was finally summoned to appear before a papal council at Soissons in 1121. This council, headed by the bishop of Prantoac, sentenced Abelard to burn his book on the Holy Trinity and to subsequent imprisonment in the Abbey of St. Medard. Instead, Abelard fled to a desert near Troyes and successfully resumed his teachings.

In 1125, Abelard's stature as a monk was renewed, and he accepted a post as the abbot of the Abbey of St. Gildas de Rhuys in Brittany. The monks there were unaccepting of Abelard and even allegedly attempted to poison him. Driven from the monastery, Abelard began to teach in Paris again, reviving some of the fame and popularity he had experienced twenty years earlier. Some of his more famous pupils included Arnold of Brescia and *John of Salisbury.

Yet Abelard's teachings were too controversial for him to escape opposition--this time St. *Bernard of Clairvaux disputed his trinitarian theory. A hearing was held at Sens in 1141, in which Abelard was condemned. Peter of Cluny defended Abelard to the papal authorities and invited Abelard to reside safely at Cluny. He died there in 1142.

Peter Abelard's biographical information is taken primarily from the *Story of My Calamities* and also his letters to his lover Heloise. He was the author of many theological and philosophical works, including *Dialectica*, an important four-volume philosophical treatise. His other philosophical works include *Glossulae in Porphyrium, De Generibus et Speciebus, Scito Teipsum, seu Ethica, Tractatus de Unitate et Trinitate Divina,* and *Theologia Christiana.* In these and other writings his mode of philosophical inquiry most often rests on the discussion of *Aristotle's theories and those of Aristotle's pupils. Abelard's argumentative essay *Sic et Non* is his most famous work; it presents evidence both for and against various theological opinions without reaching a definitive conclusion. This method influenced Abelard's successors, including Alexander of Hales and St. Thomas *Aquinas.

Abelard used this dialectic technique of "pro" and "con" to express his controversial theories of morality. In regard to the concept of sin, Abelard emphasized the intention behind the "sinful" act. The psychological element--the notion that the thought of sinning is actually worse than the sin itself--confused the traditional distinctions between good and evil. Abelard held that the "intention of sinning was a formal contempt of God." This belief also obscured the link between faith and good works. Abelard's definition of faith was a source of further debate, for he dismissed theologians such as St. Bernard who advocated blind and unquestioning faith, instead stressing reason as the key to faith. Abelard's view negated the necessity for "mysteries of the faith," a concept freely and conveniently used by the Catholic clergy. Yet although his teachings angered his contemporaries, Abelard was not particularly influential in his time, contributing only minimally to popular ecclesiastical thought.

After Abelard's death, however, philosophers and theologians began to subject his writings to closer scrutiny. His former pupil *Peter Lombard was chiefly responsible for this change. Peter Abelard is now widely regarded as a significant contributor to scholastic theory in the early Middle Ages.

SELECTED BIBLIOGRAPHY

Ferguson, Chris D. "Autobiography as Therapy: Guibert de Nogent, Peter Abelard, and the Making of Medieval Autobiography." *Journal of Medieval and Renaissance Studies* 13:2 (Fall 1983), 187-212; Jussila, Paivi. *Peter Abelard on Imagery: Theory and Practice, with Special Reference to his Hymns.* Helsinki: Suomalainen Tiedeakatemia, 1995; C. J. Mews. "The Sententie of Peter Abelard." *Reserches de Theologie Ancienne et Medievale* 53 (1986), 130-84.

                                                                    Anna Shealy

ACROSTIC. An acrostic is a composition in which a set of letters, usually the first but also in the middle or at the end of each line, spells out a coded word. One of the best examples of this is the Old Testament's 119th Psalm. *Cynewulf, an Old English poet, signed his name in acrostic runes.

SELECTED BIBLIOGRAPHY

Indictor, Nyr. "Alphabet Poems: A Brief History." *Word Ways* 28:3 (August 1995), 131-35; Stephenson, William. "The Acrostic 'Fictio' in Robert Henryson's 'The Testament of Cresseid' (Lines 58-63)." *Chaucer Review* 29:2 (1994), 163-65.

Robert T. Lambdin

ADAM. A twelfth-century *Anglo-Norman play of three scenes, *Adam* serves as a cusp in the evolution of Middle English Dramas. The first scene illustrates Adam and Eve's fall from Paradise, while the second concentrates upon the antics of Cain and Abel; the third is the Prophets' Play. *Adam* is important for the development of the English mystery play cycles (*see* **Drama, Medieval**) because its lines are composed in both the vernacular and Latin. Thus *Adam* is clearly one of the earliest examples of the church reaching out to the people and presenting homiletic notions in a language to which they could relate. Of additional interest is the idea that this play was known to be performed at the church door which further indicates the progression of medieval drama.

SELECTED BIBLIOGRAPHY

Beadle, Richard ed. *The Cambridge Companion to Medieval English Theatre.* Cambridge: Cambridge University Press, 1994; Bevington, David. "Castles in the Air: The Morality Plays." in *The Theatre of Medieval Europe.* Eckehard Simon, ed. Cambridge: Cambridge University Press, 1993. 97-116; Bevington, David. *Medieval Drama.* Boston: Houghton Mifflin, 1975; Diller, Hans Jurgen. *The Middle English Mystery Play: A Study in Dramatic Speech and Form.* Frances Wessels, Trans. Cambridge: Cambridge University Press, 1992; Hardison, O. B. *Christian Rite and Christian Drama in the Middle Ages.* Westport, CT: Greenwood Press, 1965; Ricks, Christopher, ed. *English Drama to 1710.* New York: Peter Bedrick, 1987; Simon, Echehard, ed. *The Theatre of Medieval Europe.* Cambridge: Cambridge University Press,1993; Taylor, Jerome, and Alan H. Nelson, eds. *Medieval English Drama: Essays Critical and Contextual.* Chicago: University of Chicago Press, 1972; Young, Karl. *The Drama of the Medieval Church.* 2 vols. Oxford: Clarendon Press, 1933.

Robert T. Lambdin

ÆLFRIC (955-1010). In largely illiterate tenth-century England, Abbot Ælfric was an outstanding source of didactic literature during his eighteen years at the monastery at Cerne and his last five years at the monastery at Eynsham. His work was part of a long-range plan to institute the Benedictine Rule in the monastic system and to equip the boys in the monastic schools, the monks, and the secular clergy with adequate knowledge for teaching and living the Christian faith. One of the means essential to this purpose was to furnish priests with homilies to be read on appropriate Sundays in the church calendar. Hence Ælfric's first work was a collection of forty *Catholic Homilies* (989), arranged according to the church year. The second series, of forty-five homilies, was completed in 992. About two-thirds of the eighty-five sermons are strictly homiletic; the rest are narratives, topical discourses, or simple exegeses of scripture. Of the homilies, fifty-six are indebted to such church fathers as *Augustine, *Jerome, *Bede, *Gregory the Great, Smaragdus, and Haymo. However, seldom did Ælfric produce a straightforward translation; rather, he wove together material from several sources and added his own commentary.

He was hesitant to translate the Bible into the vernacular (outside his homilies) for fear the texts would be misinterpreted by the poorly educated. He did however, at the urging of his ealdorman Æthelweard and his son Æthemaer, translate twenty-four chapters of Genesis, a section of Numbers, summaries of Joshua, and Judges, and portions of Esther, Judith, the Maccabees, and Job. Late editors added other translators' versions of the rest of Genesis, Exodus, Leviticus and Deuteronomy to produce the so-called Old English Heptateuch. Also while at Cerne, he translated St. Basil's *Hexameron* and *Admonitio* and wrote the *Letter for Wulfsige*. The *Hexameron* is an account of the week of Creation. Ælfric added material from Bede's commentaries on Genesis. The *Admonitio* was intended for the instruction of new monks. It presents such virtues as chastity, love of God and one's neighbor, and the avoidance of worldliness and avarice. The *Letter for Wulfsige* was written at the request of the bishop of Sherborne as a pastoral letter on the duties of the clergy. The main body of the *Letter* explains the need for celibacy, the divisions of the orders, the behavior of a good priest, and the Eucharist.

Additionally the *Grammar*, a *Colloquy*, *Interrogationes*, *De Falsis Deis*, *De XII Abusivis*, *De Temporibus Anni*, and *Lives of the Saints* must be added to th e list. The *Grammar* was the first such grammar of any language to be written in English. Ælfric's chief contribution was the invention of a complete set of English equivalents for the traditional terms of Greek and Latin grammarians. The Latin-English glossary appended to the grammar arranged its items according to subject, beginning with words having to do with God and Creation, followed by words on the parts of the body, society, and family, and on the birds, fish, animals, and so on. The *Colloquy* is a textbook in the form of a Latin dialogue, using a rare series of brief descriptions of the daily lives of common people. The *Interrogationes Sigewulfi in Genesin* is an English translation of a catechetical handbook on Genesis written by the eighth-century scholar Alcuin. *De Temporibus Anni* is a treatise on chronology and astronomy, concerned chiefly with the divisions of the solar year, a major difference between the Celtic and Roman church calendars. Some of his homilies are hagiological, but the collection of *Lives* (998) was intended for private reading.

Some of the saints are biblical characters; most are Roman martyrs or famous clergy; a number are English, several drawn from Bede's hagiographic accounts.

Ælfric as homilist, hagiographer, translator, linguist, and teacher reveals a mastery of English prose that makes him the central figure in Old English literary prose. Both his rhythmical style, characteristic of the *Lives* and other later works, and the non-rhythmical style of the earlier homilies are marked by clarity, balance, and carefully controlled variety. In the preface to the second collection of homilies he stated that he sought to avoid verbosity and strange expressions, using instead the plain words and simple speech of the people. Recent studies have shown that the best Old English prose had significant influence on later English literature.

SELECTED BIBLIOGRAPHY

Clayton, Mary. "Ælfric's 'Judith': Manipulative or Manipulated?" *Anglo-Saxon England* 23 (1994), 215-27; Fausboll, Else. "More Ælfric Fragments." *English Studies* 76:4 (July 1995), 302-06; Hurt, James. *Ælfric*. New York: Twayne Publishers, Inc., 1972; Magennis, Hugh. "Contrasting Narrative Emphases in the Old English Poem 'Judith' and Ælfric's Paraphrase of the *Book of Judith*." *Neuphilologische Mitteilungen* 96:1 (1995), 61-66; Pope, John C. "Introduction" to *Homilies of Ælfric: A Supplementary Collection*. Early English Text Society 259. London: Oxford University Press, 1967; Powell, Timothy E. "The 'Three Orders' of Society in Anglo-Saxon England." *Anglo-Saxon England* 23 (1994), 103-32; White, Caroline L. *Ælfric: A New Study of His Life and Writings*. Yale Studies in English, 2. Boston: Lamson, Wolffe and Company, 1898.

Esther Smith

ÆTHELWOLD (c. 908-94). Æthelwold of Winchester was admitted to the monastery at Glastonbury under *Dunstan; There he favored the Benedictine Rule that had worked its way over from Fleury in France. In 963, upon Dunstan's ascension to the position of archbishop of Canterbury, Æthelwold was appointed bishop of Winchester. Æthelwold along with Dunstan and Oswald developed the Benedictine reforms; as a result of their efforts, secular clergy from various monasteries in and around Winchester were expelled and replaced with monks. In this way Æthelwold was at least partly responsible for a great shift in monastic thought in the late tenth century. Æthelwold was the mentor of *Ælfric, and he contributed to Britain's learning revival with his translation of the *Rule of St. Benedict* (c. 960) as well as his own *Regularis Concordia*.

SELECTED BIBLIOGRAPHY

Hofstetter, Walter. "Winchester and the Standardization of Old English Vocabulary." *Anglo-Saxon England*. 17 (1988), 139-61; Schipper, W. "Dry Point Compilation Notes in the Benedictional of St. Aethelwold." *British Library Journal* 20:1 (Spring 1994), 17-34; Speed, Diane. "Text and Meaning in the South English Legendary Lives of Æthelwold." *Notes and Queries* 41(239):3 (September 1994), 295-301.

Robert T. Lambdin

ALFONSO X ("El Sabio"). King of Castile from 1252 until his death in 1284, Alfonso X was also known as the learned or wise monarch. Although he failed to sustain the efforts of his father, Ferdinand III, to oust the occupying Moors, Alfonso was Spain's greatest medieval patron of arts and letters. Under his sponsorship two massive histories were undertaken: *La primera crónica general* and the *General estoria*. Alfonso consolidated and updated the legal system of Castile with the document known as the *Siete Partidas*. He also sponsored the translation of numerous scientific and technical writings from the Arabic and other eastern languages, thus continuing Spain's position as the gateway linking Eastern and Middle Eastern thought and knowledge with Western Europe. Alfonso X was also the foremost lyric poet of his time.

SELECTED BIBLIOGRAPHY

Chandler, Richard E. and Kessel Schwartz. *A New History of Spanish Literature.* Baton Rouge: Louisiana State University Press, 1961; Deyermond, A.D. *A Literary History of Spain: The Middle Ages.* London: Ernest Benn Limited, 1971; Gerli, E. Michael, and Harvey L. Sharrer, eds. *Hispanic Medieval Studies in Honor of Samuel G. Armistead.* Madison, WI: Hispanic Seminary of Medieval Studies, 1992; Northup, George Tyler. *An Introduction to Spanish Literature.* Chicago: University of Chicago Press, 1965.

Rebecca Stephens

ALFRED THE GREAT (849-899). Alfred was the youngest of the four sons of King Æthelwulf of Wessex. His career as soldier, king, Christian, and scholar earned him the title "the Great," the only English monarch so honored. Despite the chronic challenge of Danish invasions, he won for much of England order and peace that enabled him to promote an outstanding period of education and literary development. While modern scholarship debunks some of the legends associated with Alfred, such as his earliest biographer's claim that he suffered from recurrent and debilitating illness throughout his life, or that he did not begin learning Latin until his mature years, no one doubts that his contributions to the political and spiritual character of his people are significant. Sincerely religious, he sought to improve the quality of the knowledge and devotion of his clergy and lay leaders by translating or having translated from Latin into *Anglo-Saxon (Old English) such works as *Gregory the Great's *Pastoral Care* and *Dialogues*, St. *Augustine's *Soliloquies*, *Boethius's *Consolation of Philosophy*, Orosius's *Histories against the Pagans*, and *Bede's *Ecclesiastical History of the English People*. He personally translated the first fifty biblical

Psalms and wrote, compiled, or supervised, with occasional editorial additions, a *Will*, several charters, a code of Law, and the **Anglo- Saxon Chronicle*.

Pastoral Care was a practical handbook for bishops written by Gregory the Great shortly after he became pope in 590. It dealt with administrative problems, both interpersonal and educational, in the highly structured and powerful Church of the period. Gregory's *Dialogues* presented, in a didactic manner, the lives of saints. Augustine's *Soliloquies* and Boethius's *Consolation* are philosophical treatises dealing with such complex theological issues as the differing roles of human reason and divine revelation, and the implications of the time of the creation of individual souls--at the primal Creation or after the birth of each body. Bede's *History* portrays the same victorious struggle for England, from Caesar's invasion to his own times, and the *Chronicle* seeks to complete this view of history to Alfred's time. Both Bede and Alfred sought to restore the idealized characteristics of England before the Danish invasions,and to strengthen the consciousness of a national entity. Alfred's Law code selected useful traditions and added rules that strengthened his centralized government.

Some of these works are fairly mechanically translated from Latin, but progressively Alfred introduced not only vernacular idioms but allusions that were appropriate to his English readers. He excised references to charioteers, racecourses, and wrestling and substituted for *histriones* or "actors" in the Roman theater the Anglo-Saxon *gligmonna* or "jester." The Roman consul Fabricius became Weland, the Germanic smith-god, whose smithy was believed to have been in Wessex, because Fabricius's name suggested fabricator or craftsman. While the translator of Orosius's *Histories* maintained the Latin *senatus* for Roman senators, Alfred used in his translations the Anglo-Saxon *wetan* or *thegn*. In place of Gregory's Byzantine court metaphors, Alfred used the cunning of hedgehogs, the lack of wisdom of young birds, the flapping of wings of crowing roosters, and other details of the agrarian culture familiar to his readers. He employs universal symbols, such as water and boats, with appropriate adaptations to his own experience. In his translations of the *Consolation* and the *Soliloquies* his additions and commentary sometimes served to complicate rather than elucidate difficult concepts, in part because Anglo Saxon was not a language that had evolved a philosophical vocabulary. Despite this and the handicap of a limited intellectual background for his readership, Alfred's interests argue not only for his unusually broad personal interests and education, but also his genius in promoting religious and cultural principles in the vernacular centuries ahead of its time.

SELECTED BIBLIOGRAPHY

Frantzen, Allen J. *King Alfred*. Boston: Twayne, 1986; Smyth, Alfred P. *King Alfred the Great*. Oxford: Oxford University Press, 1995; Woodruff, Douglas. *The Life and Times of Alfred the Great*. London: Weidenfeld and Nicolson, 1974.

Esther Smith

ALLEGORY. This is a form of extended metaphor that was prevalent in the Middle Ages. In allegories objects, persons, and actions are equated with meanings that lie outside the obvious narrative meaning. Thus an allegorical symbol represents one thing in the guise of another. This means that the order of words conveys actions and characters that represent varying ideas.

In allegory characters are often personifications of abstractions, like the characters of *Everyman*. The action and settings often represent the relationships among these abstractions. Thus allegory presents a dual interest: one of the actual characters and another that portrays further significance. Allegorical characters may be historical or fictitious; their meaning may be religious, moral, political, personal, or satirical.

SELECTED BIBLIOGRAPHY

Braswell, Laurel. "The Visionary Voyage in Science Fiction and Medieval Allegory." *Mosaic* 14:1 (Winter 1981), 125-42; Holman, C. Hugh, and William Harmon. *A Handbook to Literature*. 5th ed. New York, Macmillan, 1986; Kurtz, Barbara E. "The Castle Motif and the Medieval Allegory of Love: Diego de San Pedro's *Carcel de amor*." *Fifteenth Century Studies* 11 (1985), 37-49; Wetherbee, Winthrop. "*The Romance of the Rose* and Medieval Allegory." In *European Writers: The Middle Ages and the Renaissance*. William T. H. Jackson and George Stade, eds. New York: Scribner's, 1983. 309-35.

Robert T. Lambdin

ALLITERATIVE REVIVAL. This term corresponds to a collection of late fourteenth-century English poems, all of which contain heavy alliteration. Previously, authors such as *Layamon, had introduced alliteration into their works. Additionally, the five works of the *Katherine Group are composed in alliterative prose that is so well constructed that it is often confused with verse. Thus alliteration had never truly disappeared from English literature.

However, in west and northwest England during the late fourteenth-century, alliterative verse became the rage. In this movement alliteration, the repetition for effect of consonant sounds in a line of poetry, one of the constant components of *Old English poetry, was again featured in some of the greatest poetry from this era, including *Piers the Plowman* and *Sir Gawain and the Green Knight*. These works, along with *The Parliament of the Three Ages*, demonstrate that politics engrossed many of the authors of this movement.

SELECTED BIBLIOGRAPHY

Blake, N. F. "Middle English Alliterative Revivals." *Review* 1 (1979), 205-14; Lawton, David, ed. *Middle English Alliterative Poetry and Its Literary Background: Seven Essays*. Cambridge: Brewer, 1982; Riddy, Felicity. "The Alliterative Revival." In *The*

History of Scottish Literature, I: Origins to 1660 (Mediaeval and Renaissance). R.D.S.
Jack and Cairns Craig, eds. Aberdeen: Aberdeen University Press, 1988. 39-54.

Robert T. Lambdin

ALLITERATIVE VERSE. Alliterative verse is a form in which many of the
words repeat the same sound at the beginning of two or more stressed syllables.
Alliterative verse was typical in *Old English poetry and reemerged in
fourteenth-century Middle English verse. In *Anglo-Saxon poetry each line is
divided into two short lines by a pause or a *caesura. The short lines hold one or
two stressed syllables or words; the first stressed word in the second half-line
indicates the letter or sound of alliteration. The second stressed word usually
does not alliterate, and there may be up to three or four alliterating words in
longer lines. Unaccented word numeration is not fixed, and in Old English
poetry lines were usually unrhymed. Especially during the Middle English
*alliterative revival, poems were composed with much less restraint. This form
was used in heroic *lais, sung by *minstrels, and it appeared in proverbs, spells,
chants, and *riddles.

The use of unrhymed alliterative meter continued until after the
Teutons were converted to Christianity. After fading away for a short while, the
technique was passionately revived in the fourteenth century.

SELECTED BIBLIOGRAPHY

Fein, Susanna. "The Ghoulish and the Ghastly: A Moral Aesthetic in Middle English
Alliterative Verse." *Modern Language Quarterly* 48:1 (March 1987), 3-19; 1-108;
Lawton, David, ed. *Middle English Alliterative Poetry and Its Literary Background:
Seven Essays*. Cambridge: Brewer, 1982; Moorman, Charles. "The English Alliterative
Revival and the Literature of Defeat." *Chaucer Review* 16:1 (Summer 1981), 85-100;
Riddy, Felicity. "The Alliterative Revival." in *The History of Scottish Literature, I:
Origins to 1660 (Mediaeval and Renaissance)*. R.D.S. Jack and Cairns Craig, eds.
Aberdeen: Aberdeen University Press, 1988, 39-54

Robert T. Lambdin

ALYSOUN. *Alysoun* is one of the most frequently anthologized short *lyric
poems from the Middle English period. The lyric consists of four stanzas, each
followed by a refrain that mentions the name Alysoun. The lines consist of
three or four stresses and end with the rhyme pattern *ababbbbc dddc*.

The first stanza establishes the setting of spring with new plant growth
and songs of "litel fowl." The speaker is a man who, amidst the signs of spring,
suffers from "love longinge" for the best "of alle thinge." In the refrain he
clarifies that the source of his happiness and suffering is the woman Alysoun.
Although he feels completely within her thrall, he also says she is a blessing

sent from heaven, and he has no interest in other women because he loves her. The second stanza provides a physical description of Alysoun with some conventional details (hair, brows, eyes, slender waist). Alysoun is described as cheerful and smiling. In the third stanza the speaker details his insomnia and other suffering because of his love. The final stanza continues the description of his painful longing.

This lyric demonstrates the courtly traditional convention of the lover in pain and uses the setting of spring to establish a contrast between the joyful season and the suffering of the lover. Alysoun is good natured, though, and not disdainful. Critics disagree over the amount of the speaker's suffering, some seeing the refrain as an abrupt, dramatic "outcry," while others describe it as having a "tone of utter joy." Douglas Gray in J. A. Bennett's *Middle English Literature* argues that the lack of continuity reflects the complex nature of the love between the two--the speaker goes "from bliss to grief"--which results in "a kind of unresolved balance at the end." Lewis and Nancy Owen pointed out that the use of the word "make" [mate] in the second stanza indicates that the speaker is courting Alysoun not as a mistress but as a wife, and they felt that the melancholy in stanzas three and four is normal apprehension, not suicidal despair.

SELECTED BIBLIOGRAPHY

Barratt, Alexandra, ed. *Women's Writing in Middle English.* London and New York: Longman, 1992; Bennett, J. A. *Middle English Literature.* Douglas Gray, ed. and completer. Oxford: Clarendon Press, 1986; Owen, Lewis, and Nancy Owen, eds. *Middle English Poetry: An Anthology.* Indianapolis: Bobbs-Merrill, 1971; Sigal, Gale. *Erotic Dawn-Songs of the Middle Ages: Voicing the Lyric Lady.* Gainesville: University Press of Florida, 1996; Stevick, Robert D., ed. *One Hundred Middle English Lyrics.* Revised. Urbana: University of Illinois Press, 1994.

Sigrid King

ANCRENE WISSE. Also known as the *Ancrene Riwle* or the "Rule for Anchoresses," the *Ancrene Wisse* is a prose treatise that is considered to be one of the finest English vernacular prose works composed between *Wulfstan and Richard *Rolle of Hampole. The work is a manual of devotional works created for three nuns around 1230. Its thought must have been prevalent because within fifty years it was revised to benefit any nun who wished to withdraw into the world of the Church. Seventeen manuscripts survive, mainly in English, although there are versions in French and Latin.

Noted for its prosody, the *Ancrene Wisse* is similar to the works of the *Katherine Group. Expressive and clear, the work is divided into eight "deals," each of which concentrates upon one portion of the religious rule. It is theorized that the work was written after 1215 and was subsequently revised, growing into its final form. One manuscript lists the name of Simon of Ghent as the author, but he was probably simply the author of a Latin version. Also identified in one manuscript is the acrostic "Brian of Lingen." From this, some have theorized that an Augustinian priest composed the work for the Limebrook nuns, although it has never been established that the work was originally composed in French, Latin, or English.

SELECTED BIBLIOGRAPHY

Breeze, Andrew. "Welsh Baban 'Baby' and 'Ancrene Wisse.'" *Notes and Queries* 40 (238):1 (March 1993), 12-13; Demoto, Fuminobu. "A Mode of Speech in 'Ancrene Wisse.'" *Hiroshima Studies in English Language and Literature* 32 (1987), 17-27; Kerling, Johan. "The Ancrene Wisse." *Companion to Early Middle English Literature*. N. H. G. E. Veldhoen, ed. Amsterdam: VU University Press, 1995. 133-43.

Robert T. Lambdin

ANDREAS. *Andreas* is an Old English poem that seems to have been based upon a Greek story, *The Acts of St. Andrew and St. Matthew*, which probably had an intervening Latin version. In the work St. Andrew is called by God to rescue St. Matthew and others from the cannibalistic Mermedonians. Andrew, broke and distraught, sees no way to reach his peer in time. However, he secures passage upon a ship that is piloted by God and two angels. Andrew survives the voyage, which includes a terrible storm, awaking on the Mermedonian shore; here he realizes that God was his captain and that his initial hesitation demonstrated a lack of faith in God. Andrew proceeds to rescue Matthew and then converts the Mermedonians, in spite of Satan's efforts to doom his mission.

The only extant copy of Andreas is the version in fifteen fits found in the *Vercelli Book. Its rich heroic atmosphere is reminiscent of pre-Christian *Anglo-Saxon works. For years critics named *Cynewulf or one of his followers as the author because of the great similarities of *Andreas* to many of Cynewulf's works. However, upon further review, critics now date the work to the later ninth century, which eliminates Cynewulf and his followers as authors because they date to the early ninth century. Perhaps it is safer to infer that the survival of *Andreas* demonstrates simply the popularity of Cynewulf's style inasmuch as it continued to be emulated well after his death. The content of *Andreas* seems to have been directly influenced by *Beowulf*.

SELECTED BIBLIOGRAPHY

Brooks, K. R., ed. *Andreas and the Fates of the Apostles*. 1906. Oxford: Clarendon Press, 1961; Scragg, D. G. "The Compilation of the Vercelli Book." *Anglo-Saxon Manuscripts: Basic Readings*. Mary P. Richards, ed. New York: Garland, 1994. 317-43.

Robert T. Lambdin

ANDREAS CAPELLANUS (c. 1180). Andreas Capellanus claims to have been a royal chaplain, perhaps attached to Marie de Champagne at Troyes. In medieval literature, he is important as the otherwise unknown author of the Latin treatise *De Arte Honeste Amandi*. This work reflects upon the nature and the practice of human love and became a primer for the art of *courtly love.

Capellanus felt that true love between a husband and a wife was impossible, but he added that being married did not exempt one from loving. The courtly lover was required to worship at the shrine of a beautiful lady, usually someone else's wife. After being singled out by his beloved, the lover should swoon in her presence, send her tokens of his affection, and be available to her every whim. It was up to this courtly lover to do anything possible, including risking his life, to protect her honor. The major influences upon the *De Arte* are the classical authors, especially Ovid.

Perhaps the most important contribution of Capellanus's work is his detailed definition and description of courtly love. He provides the rules and regulations of an art that would play great roles in works such as *Sir Gawain and the Green Knight* and portions of *Chaucer's writings. Today Capellanus's work is regarded as seminal by many in the field of medieval literature, mainly because critics such as C. S. Lewis noted the great impact this work had upon the grand social implications of this fleeting medieval trend. The magnitude of Lewis's work helped elevate the status of Capellanus to one of the most influential of the Middle Ages.

SELECTED BIBLIOGRAPHY

Carlson, David. "Religion and Romance: The Languages of Love in the Treatises of Gerard of Liege and the Case of Andreas Capellanus." *Poetics of Love in the Middle Ages: Texts and Contexts.* Moshe Lazar and Norris J. Lacy, eds. Fairfax, VA: George Mason University Press, 1989. 81-92; Lewis, C. S. *The Allegory of Love.* 1936. Oxford: Oxford University Press, 1977; Monson, Donald A. "Andreas Capellanus and the Problem of Irony." *Speculum* 63:3 (July 1988), 539-72; Monson, Donald A. "Auctoritas and Intertextuality in Andreas Capellanus' *De Amore*." *Poetics of Love in the Middle Ages: Texts and Contexts.* Moshe Lazar and Norris J. Lacy, eds. Fairfax, VA: George Mason University Press, 1989. 69-79; Williams, Andrew. "Clerics and Courtly Love in Andreas Capellanus' *The Art of Courtly Love* and Chaucer's *Canterbury Tales*." *Revista Alicantina de Estudios Ingleses* 3 (November1990), 127-36.

Robert T. Lambdin

ANELIDA AND ARCITE. Composed by Geoffrey *Chaucer, *Anelida and Arcite* is a fragment. It resembles somewhat Chaucer's *"The Knight's Tale" in the *Canterbury Tales* in its presentation of the Thebes legend. Its opening demonstrates that it was to be a *romance concerning the faithless love between

Arcite and Anelida. Anelida, forsaken by her love, delivers an unextraordinary pseudo complaint.

In *Anelida and Arcite*, Statius and Corinna are stated to be sources, yet it is obvious that Chaucer relied more upon the *Teseida* of *Boccaccio when he composed this work. *Anelida and Arcite* is one of Chaucer's more complicated works in terms of arrangement. Its stanzaic form contains strophes with answering antistrophes.

The poem begins with 210 lines of rhyme-royal and tells of Arcite's cuckolding Queen Anelida. The final 147 lines begin the *Compleynt* of Anelida, an incomplete and puzzling section. It is not known why Chaucer failed to complete this work, but it is clear that the poem was also influenced by the *Heroides* of Ovid.

SELECTED BIBLIOGRAPHY

David, Alfred. "Recycling *Anelida and Arcite*: Chaucer as a Source for Chaucer." *Studies in the Age of Chaucer* 1 (1984), 105-15; Favier, Dale A. "*Anelida and Arcite*: Anti-Feminist Allegory, Pro-Feminist Complaint." *Chaucer Review* 26:1 (1991), 83-94; Peck, Russell, compiler. *Chaucer's Lyrics and* "Anelida and Arcite": *An Annotated Bibliography 1900 to 1980*. Toronto: University of Toronto Press, 1983; Stallcup, Stephen "With the 'Poynte of Remembraunce': Re-Viewing the Complaint in *Anelida and Arcite*." *Representations of the Feminine in the Middle Ages*. Bonnie Wheeler, ed. Dallas: Academia Press, 1993. 43-67.

Robert T. Lambdin

ANGLO-LATIN LITERATURE. For the majority of the Middle Ages in Europe, the language of the educated was Latin. It is possible to trace Latin as the dominant literary language from as far back as the time of St. Augustine the first bishop of Canterbury to the late 1300s. Extant manuscripts and fragments of Anglo-Latin texts of the Old English period demonstrate that these works were often didactic; they existed solely for religious instruction or inspiration. However, other writings from this genre stray into the secular. Prominent theological writers in this field include Alcuin, who wrote a commentary on the Book of Genesis, and Aldhelm, who wrote verse, English songs, and prose works. Historians such as *Gildas and *Nennius produced works that although only semihistorical, provide key insight into the politics of their day. Perhaps the greatest author of this time was *Bede.

*Geoffrey of Monmouth's *Historia Regum Brittaniae* (1135) establishes the *Arthurian tradition, oddly based upon the Classical tale of the fall of Troy. The popularity of his works is evident because adaptations of his efforts are found throughout the Continent. Geoffrey's success paved the way for other English authors to find their niche in the literature of the Continent. Among the most prominent of these are Walter *Map and *John of Salisbury, both of whom were active during the reign of *Henry II (1154-89). By the end of the twelfth-century the courtier authors had incorporated satire into their treatises; the most popular works attacked the courts. For the most part, the treatises directed their assaults against human vices, but it was not out of the ordinary for the authors to also make personal attacks. Most of the works were composed in hexameter, but others incorporated elegaic couplets; Thomas *Becket's martyrdom in 1170 created a flurry of compositions in couplets. A master writer from this period is *Geoffrey de Vinsauf.

By the thirteenth-century the themes of the genre had shifted from sin to the topical. Events such as the Wars of the Barons caught the fancy of both the authors and the readers. Perhaps the most popular stories in this regard dealt with the fall of Gaveston, Edward II's lover. By the late thirteenth century English was making headway into the written literatures. When Geoffrey *Chaucer composed his famous works in the English vernacular, the demise of Anglo-Latin was eminent. For several decades Anglo-Latin continued to be used by historians and critics; however, for all intents and purposes, this genre waned into oblivion.

SELECTED BIBLIOGRAPHY

Clayton, Mary. "*Assumptio Mariae*: An Eleventh Century Anglo-Latin Poem from Abingdon." *Analecta Bollandiana* 104: 3-4 (1986), 419-26; Greenfield, Stanley B., Daniel Calder, and Michael Lapidge. *A New Critical History of Old English Literature: With a Survey of the Anglo-Latin Background*. New York: New York University Press, 1986; Hill, Thomas. "The Cross as Symbolic Body: An Anglo-Latin Liturgical Analogue to the'Dream of the Rood.'" *Neophilologus* 77:2 (April 1993), 297-301. Rigg, A, G. *A History of Anglo-Latin Literature, 1066-1422*. Cambridge: Cambridge University Press, 1992.

Robert T. Lambdin

ANGLO-NORMAN. From the Norman Conquest of 1066 until the fourteenth-century, the French language thrived in England. As is natural in the progression of a language, derivations from the native French evolved, a point not hidden from the character of Geoffrey *Chaucer's Prioress in his *Canterbury Tales. The Voyage of St. Brendan*, an early example written sometime in the twelfth-century, is a precursor to this genre. French was the language of the courts and the learned, so literature of this type was aimed at the affluent. This continued until the fourteenth-century when few works were composed in the French vernacular in English literature.

However, continental French continued to be used in English works, as seen in John Gower's *Mirour de l'omme*. French was no longer used in the courts, but it was still the language often studied by the scholars of the fourteenth-century. *Chronicles and other works translated from Latin sources were popular additions into Anglo-Norman works. This may seem an odd twist:

the notion of Anglo-Norman was reciprocated by the French. One of the first French dramas of merit, the *Mystère d'Adam*, probably was composed in England. Even after the demise of French as a spoken entity in England, it remained the language for legal and official written documents.

SELECTED BIBLIOGRAPHY

Blacker, Jean. *The Faces of Time: Portrayal of the Past in Old French and Latin Historical Narrative of the Anglo-Norman "Regnum."* Austin: University of Texas Press, 1994; Masters, Bernadette A. "Anglo-Norman in Context: The Case for the Scribes."*Exemplaria* 6:1 (Spring 1994), 167-203; Sinclair, Keith. "On the Text of the Anglo-Norman Poem 'The Walling of New Ross." *Romanische Forschungen* 106:1 (1994), 225-35; Wogan-Browne, Jocelyn. "Wreaths of Thyme: The Female Translator in Anglo-Norman Hagiography." *Medieval Translator IV.* Roger Ellis and Ruth Evans, eds. Binghampton, NY: Medieval and Renaissance Texts, 1994. 46-65.

Robert T. Lambdin

ANGLO-SAXON. The Angles and the Saxons, along with the Jutes, invaded and conquered Britain in the fifth and sixth centuries. The name "Anglo-Saxon" refers to the tribal group they formed after the invasion. *Alfred the Great, who was king of the West Saxons, obtained the Anglian territory belonging to the Danish-English people in the ninth- century. His name for his subjects was *Angli et Saxones.* England derives its name from the word "Angle" (Angle-land). In contemporary times the term is used to identify people of English descent who live not only in England but around the world. The literary term "Anglo-Saxon versification" denotes the verse written by Anglo-Saxon authors from the seventh to the twelfth-centuries. It is characterized by an accentual alliterative quality.

SELECTED BIBLIOGRAPHY

Doane, A. N. "The Ethnography of Scribal Writing and Anglo-Saxon Poetry: Scribe as Performer." *Oral Tradition* 9:2 (October 1994), 420-39; Magennis, Hugh. "Treatments of Treachery and Betrayal in Anglo-Saxon Texts." *English Studies* 76:1 (January 1995), 1-19; McNamara, John. "Bede's Role in Circulating Legend in the *Historia Ecclesiastica.*" *Anglo-Saxon Studies in Archaeology* 7 (1994), 61-69; Pasternack, Carol Braun. *The Textuality of Old English Poetry.* Cambridge: Cambridge University Press, 1995.

Anna Shealy

ANGLO-SAXON CHRONICLES. The *Anglo-Saxon Chronicle* or *Annales Saxonici* is one of the earliest historical records to have been kept in a vernacular language. The *Chronicle* exists today in seven distinct manuscripts and two fragments. A wide range of styles is found in every version of the chronicle, ranging from brief *annals to historical legends and stories including transcribed documents, like charters, and narratives with speeches.

The *Chronicle* starts with pre-Roman Britain and extends into the twelfth century in some manuscripts. For the early years of the *Chronicle*, the writers relied on sources such as *Bede's *Ecclesiastical History* and some West Saxon chronicles and genealogies of *Anglo-Saxon kings. The entries are sparse for the period before A. D. 400, but are consistently in chronological order and often repeat information found in Bede. As in Bede's work, there are numerous attempts to establish the history of place names by associating a particular town's name with an event in the life of a local hero. Although the entries, are often short and lacking in detail, those entries probably were evocative of stories and historical events with which the writer and his audience would have been familiar. The earliest installment of the *Chronicle* covers the time period from 54 B. C. to A. D. 891 and was most likely done by a scribe in King *Alfred's court, although there is no definitive proof that Alfred commissioned the piece. This Alfredian version of the *Chronicle* was copied and sent to monasteries throughout England for copying. The document was updated from a central source several times; entries were circulated for the period 894-924, and later for 925-975 and 983-1018, in addition to a section for the years 902-924 known as the Mercian Register. Those who updated the manuscripts of the *Chronicle* typically tailored the additions to suit their own needs, including information important to their own locale.

Although the *Chronicle* was able to compete with the scholarly predisposition to write in Latin, after the Norman Invasion in 1066, and the resulting shift in the vernacular of the ruling class from Anglo-Saxon to French, many of the manuscripts were discontinued, but the *Peterborough Chronicle* manuscript continued chronicling English history, in Anglo-Saxon, up until 1154. The *Chronicle*, was able to preserve many historical events of England, particularly aspects of the Viking invasions, which might otherwise have been lost forever. The *Anglo-Saxon Chronicle* has the distinction of being the first continuous history of a Western country in its own language and is ranked alongside Bede's *Ecclesiastical History* for its usefullness to English history. (*See also **Chronicles and Annals**.*)

Richard McDonald

SELECTED BIBLIOGRAPHY

Frantzen, Allen J. *King Alfred*. Boston: Twayne, 1986; Garmonsway, G. N., trans and ed. *Anglo-Saxon Chronicle*. London: Dent, 1990. Gransden, Antonia. *Historical Writing In England c. 550 to c. 1307*. Ithaca: Cornell University Press, 1974. ; Smalley, Beryl. *Historians in the Middle Ages*. New York: Scribner's, 1974; Smyth, Alfred P. *King Alfred the Great*. Oxford: Oxford University Press, 1995; Sterns, Indrikis. *The Greater*

Medieval Historians: An Interpretation and a Bibliography. Lanham, MD: University Press of America, 1980; Woodruff, Douglas. *The Life and Times of Alfred the Great.* London: Weidenfeld and Nicolson, 1974.

Richard McDonald

ANNALES CAMBRIAE. The *Annales Cambriae (Welsh Annals)* date from the mid-tenth century. They span the years 447-954 and are often attached to *Nennius's *Historia Brittonum*. They corroborate some of the occurrences reported by Nennius and set specific dates for a number of historically questionable events. For example, the entry for 516 states that Arthur (King Arthur) (*See also* **Arthurian Legend**) carried a cross on his shoulders at the Battle of Badon for three days, and the Britons were victorious. In typical *annal's format, each entry is a short sentence, and entries are made for less than one-third of the possible 507 years. Its laconic, notational style is reminiscent of its forerunner the Easter table.

SELECTED BIBLIOGRAPHY

British History and the Welsh Annals. John Morris, ed. and trans. Totowa, N. J.: Rowman and Littlefield, 1980; Gransden, Antonia. *Historical Writing in England c. 550 to c. 1307.* Ithaca: Cornell University Press, 1974; Smalley, Beryl. *Historians in the Middle Ages.* New York: Scribner's, 1974; Sterns, Indrikis. *The Greater Medieval Historians: An Interpretation and a Bibliography.* Lanham, MD: University Press of America, 1980.

Richard McDonald

ANNALS. Annals were the simplest method of historical record keeping maintained during the early Middle Ages. They evolved from the interlinear notations made on monasteries' Easter tables. They typically consist of one-line entries for given years placed in chronological order. Often a collection of annals will have numerous years for which nothing was recorded. Some annals recount important national events, but events are included primarily for their importance to the monastery.

SELECTED BIBLIOGRAPHY

Gransden, Antonia. *Historical Writing in England c. 550 to c. 1307.* Ithaca: Cornell University Press, 1974; Smalley, Beryl. *Historians in the Middle Ages.* New York: Scribner's, 1974; Sterns, Indrikis. *The Greater Medieval Historians: An Interpretation and a Bibliography.* Lanham, MD: University Press of America, 1980.

Richard McDonald

ANSELM, ST. (1033-1109). Anselm was born into an aristocratic family. He was educated at the Bec abbey in Normandy, where he later replaced *Lanfranc, his mentor, as the prior. Anselm acquired a great amount of prestige and was asked to go to Canterbury to become the archbishop, a position vacated in 1089 after Lanfranc's death. He had reservations about the position, yet was compelled by his abbey to venture to England. There a series of events forced him into the see against his will. The reason he gave for his resistance was that he was an old man, but he really did not want the job because he felt that he was a political pawn.

Anselm was one of the finest philosophers of his day, and he refused to be a puppet to King William II. Anselm vacated the office of archbishop of Canterbury in 1097 to protest the king's control of the position. In 1100 he returned to England after the coronation of Henry I. During this time he composed a portfolio of theological and philosophic treatises, including his *Monologion*.

A standard in Anselm's writings was the Augustinian tradition (**see Augustine**) concerning the import of Faith in the quest for Reason. His *Proslogion* posited the homiletic debate: if the Almighty is a Being than which no greater can be imagined, then he must exist in actuality. This is true, Anselm argued, because a Being with identical attributes and with the additional concept of existence would be greater a greater being. Since none could be greater than God, this could not occur. This ontological proof of God's existence was later harshly criticized by Descartes, Hegel, and Locke, among other prominent philosophers.

SELECTED BIBLIOGRAPHY

Baumstein, Paschal. "Benedictine Education: Principles of Anselm's Patronage." *American Benedictine Review* 43:1 (March 1992), 3-11; Berthold, George C. "St. Anselm and the Filioque: Selected Papers from the Symposium and Convocation Celebrating the St. Anselm College Centennial." *Faith Seeking Understanding: Learning and the Catholic Tradition.* George C. Berthold, ed. Manchester: St. Anselm College Press, 1991; Kobialka, Michal. "Historic Time, Mythical Time, and Mimetic Time: The Impact of the Humanistic Philosophy of St. Anselm on Early Medieval Drama." *Medieval Perspectives* 3:1 (Spring 1988), 172-90.

Robert T. Lambdin

AQUINAS, ST. THOMAS (c.1225-74). Perhaps the greatest of the medieval scholastic theologians, Thomas Aquinas, often referred to as the "Doctor Angelicus," was born into a noble family in Aquino, Italy. His family was perturbed and opposed to his decision to enter the Dominican order in 1243; for one year he was forcibly detained from the order. Eventually his family acceded to his wishes.

In 1243 Aquinas reached Paris, where he studied under Albertus Magnus. Aquinas began teaching in 1252; for the most part his career fluctuated between Paris and Italy. In 1259 he began composing his commentaries on a range of authors, including *Boethius and *Peter Lombard. His writings demonstrated the influences of Peter *Abelard and St. *Augustine on him.

He then began composing his greatest work, the *Summa Theologica, a composition that represents the highwater mark of Scholastic philosophy in regard to its concerns with the harmony of Faith and Reason. His Summa [de Veritate Catholicae Fide,] contra Gentiles, composed from 1259 to 1264, defends what Aquinas saw as the truths of the Catholic faith against the pagans. Here he distinguished between reason and faith, noting that reason seeks knowledge from experimental or logical evidence. Conversely, faith depends upon revelation for understanding and also uses the knowledge provided by reason. The Summa Theologica uses this background to illustrate all that is known about God and man as it is derived from faith and reason. Aquinas's work influenced many of the Medieval authors, including *Dante in his *Divine Comedy. The Thomists, as Aquinas's followers are still called today, remain an active school in philosophy.

SELECTED BIBLIOGRAPHY

Burrell, David B. "Aquinas and Islamic Jewish Thinkers." The Cambridge Companion to Aquinas. Norman Kretzmann and Eleonore Stump, eds. Cambridge: Cambridge University Press, 1993, 60-84; Jordan, Mark D. "Aquinas Reading Aristotle's Ethics." Ad Litteram: Authoritative Texts and Their Medieval Readers. Mark Jordan and Emery Kent, Jr. eds. Notre Dame: University of Notre Dame Press, 1992. 229-49.

Anna Shealy

ARISTOTLE (384-322 B.C.). Aristotle was born in Macedonia and was the son of the royal physician to King Amyntas II. When he was eighteen, Aristotle went to Athens to study at Plato's Academy, where he stayed for some twenty years until the death of his teacher. He then moved to Assos and then to Mytilene before he returned to Macedonia. Once back home, Aristotle was hired by Philip of Macedonia to teach his son, Alexander the Great. Aristotle remained with Alexander for seven years and then opened his school in the Lyceum at Athens. At Alexander's death in 323 b. c., Aristotle left Athens, which was swept up in an anti-Macedonian frenzy, and retired to Chalcis, where he died one year later.

The works for which Aristotle was most widely known to the ancients are long lost; fragments indicate that they were probably highly polished rhetorical dialogues. These documents are known as the exoteric, or those designed for the general public. A second set of writings, the esoteric, does survive. The more familiar name for these writings is the treatises of Aristotle. The writings of a third group, the hypomnematic, or memoranda, are also lost.

His extant works discuss a wide range of topics that worked their way throughout the medieval world in translations. Islamic countries first were open to his teaching (see **Islamic Literature**). After their commentaries, the works soon became standards in the schools of the Continent and, finally, in Britain. As his stature grew, Aristotle's notions became known as the seminal root of all knowledge. With this spurt of popularity, his ideas impacted the twelfth century academic curriculum. After a short-lived philosophical conflict among the clerics, the bulk of his canon was found to be amicable with Christianity. This allowed for it to become the cornerstone of many of the subjects of later scholars. These treatises influenced the great minds of this time.

His ideas remained popular until the end of the seventeenth century. At this time, ironically, the *Poetics* became important. This work, whose surviving part deals with the construction of tragedy, was virtually unknown during the Middle Ages. Its growing popularity in the Renaissance played a large role in the emergence of the seventeenth century Neoclassical movement. Evidence of the effect of this treatise is found in the critical compositions of authors such as Philip Sidney and John Dryden. Thus, Aristotle's ideas played a seminal role in the creation of Western thought.

SELECTED BIBLIOGRAPHY

Golden, Leon. "On Discovering What Aristotle Really Meant." *Hypotheses* 7 (Fall 1993), 5-7; Hamarnah, Walid. "The Reception of Aristotle's Theory of Poetry in the Arab-Islamic Medieval Thought." *Poetics East and West*. Velingerova Milena Dalezelova, ed. Toronto: University of Toronto, 1988-89. 183-201; Kelly, Henry Ansgar. *Ideas and Forms of Tragedy from Aristotle to the Middle Ages*. Cambridge: Cambridge University Press, 1993; Knuuttila, Sima. "Remarks on Induction in Aristotle's 'Dialectic' and 'Rhetoric.'" *Revue Internationale de Philosophie* 47:1(184) (1993), 78-88; Murnaghan, Shiela. "Sucking the Juice without Biting the Rind: Aristotle and Tragic Mimesis." *New Literary History* 26:4 (Fall 1995), 755-73.

Robert T. Lambdin

ARTHURIAN LEGEND. The *Matter of Britain or the Arthurian legend, as stories of King Arthur and the members of his court are called, had an enormous impact upon the customs and culture of medieval England. The stories came from either Welsh or French sources and are an odd intermingling of the customs of both countries. The English Arthur is generally a more rugged, fighting hero than his smooth-talking, charming counterpart from France. What remains the same is that the king is attractive in ways worth emulating, and the characters of Camelot, such as Lancelot, Guinevere, Merlin, Morgan, Gawain, Mordred, and Tristrain, are some of the most compelling in all literature. When Merlin shows Arthur the sword in the stone, when the Lady of the Lake gives

Arthur his sword Excalibur, when Galahad beholds the Holy Grail at the end of his quest, and when Arthur is taken to Avalon, land of the Blessed Dead, by three queens--these are all unforgettable moments that particularly moved and influenced the British people at a time when they were searching for historical consciousness.

If there was a real King Arthur, he probably lived in the sixth or the seventh century A. D.--a period from which we have collected little reliable data. The early information we have does not clearly mean "that he ever became 'king' of any part of Britain. His achievements as a warrior alone are mentioned, and all that we can gather besides from Welsh tradition only serves to emphasize the fact that his renown among the British people rested mainly upon his warlike prowess" (Jones 11). He may have been a Welsh guerrilla fighter who defended the English or one of the last Roman generals of Britain. The name Arthur is not Welsh, but transliterates from the common Roman name Arthurius, so it seems likely that he was a Roman who helped the Celts against the Anglo-Saxons.

Arthur is first mentioned by name in a ninth century chronicle, *Historia Brittonum* (c. 800), attributed to a Welsh historian named *Nennius. In this revival of Welsh nationalism Arthur is not a king but a great warlord, who pushes the British force to victory in twelve great battles; in one, the Battle of Badon, Arthur kills 960 of the enemy by his own hand.

A later work, *Annales Cambriae* (c. 950), is a brief, anonymous account that adds that Arthur fought in the Battle of Badon for three days while bearing a cross of Christ on his shoulders. This chronicle also mentions that Arthur was killed at the Battle of Camlann (c. 539) along with a certain Medraut (who later becomes Mordred, the patricide).

There are other histories of this type that give little information about Arthur and read like newspaper headlines or outlines. *Chronicles in the early twelfth-century elaborated Arthur's story, using details from the firmly established Welsh and Irish folklore concerning the hero. The legend was also known by this time in France and northern Italy.

It was *Geoffrey of Monmouth's *Historia Regum Britanniae (History of the Kings of England) (1136) that solidified the Arthurian legends and claimed an important place for them, as this fiction was taken as history by many generations of later writers well into the Renaissance. Geoffrey's work is a patriotic history that gives the *Anglo-Norman aristocracy a British hero/ruler as noble as *Charlemagne. Geoffrey claimed to have translated an ancient book written in the English language, which had been given to him by Walter, Archdeacon of Oxford. Scholars believe in this source, inasmuch as citing such authorities was a standard ploy of medieval writers, although it is possible that the author may have had a written copy of ancient oral folklore. Many of the details, like the characters' names and the names of Arthur's weapons, can be traced to Welsh oral tradition. England is traced from the fall of Troy until Brutus flees to Britain.

For the first time we see contemporary politics involved in an English chronicle: the Norman's interest in bringing Brittany into their sphere of influence is reflected in the large part that the Bretons play (Barber 10). There is also the possibility that Geoffrey intended Arthur's Roman expedition to reflect Henry's conquest of France, as Rosemary Morris notes:

> Henry was challenged in his own court by an insolent message; his counselors urged him to take up the challenge which he joyfully did; he crossed the channel, landing at Harfleur, swept through Northern France, fought a great battle and was hailed as king, but died before he could be crowned--all this Geoffrey's Arthur does--in the 1130's. (1)

Geoffrey was the first to record Arthur's conception as the product of Merlin's disguising Uther Pendragon as the Duke of Cornwall, the husband of Igerna. This echoes a similar tale in the romances about Alexander the Great. Arthur became a symbol of British national spirit and a practical model for medieval and Renaissance kings as well as an ideal for the people, a hero in touch with the latest fashions of courtly behavior.

Despite the many anachronisms this currency demanded, between 1150 and 1420 some fifty chroniclers used *Historia Regum Britanniae* as the basis for other histories of England. A Norman clerk, Wace, wrote a poem in French based on Geoffrey's work; Wace called it the *Roman de Brut* (1154) and presented it to the wife of *Henry II of England, *Eleanor of Aquitaine. The poem contains the first extant mention of the Round Table, a piece of furniture introduced because Arthur's followers could not agree on a proper order of precedence as they sat down to meet.

The first English copy of Wace's translation was *Layamon's Brut* (c.1190), written by a Worcestershire priest. Layamon substituted the native alliterative meter for Wace's continental poetic form of octosyllabic couplets. The theme is the glory of Celtic Britain rather than Saxon England. Parts of the *Mabinogion* (1100-1250), a collection of early Welsh *romances (*see* **Welsh Literature**), elaborate Arthurian legend with two features typical of all the later stories: Arthur is ruler of the noblest court in the world, and he is involved, with his brave followers, in an assortment of marvelous adventures. The society depicted here is much more primitive than that of Geoffrey of Monmouth; the men hunt and fight on foot, rather than jousting in armor on enormous steeds. This Arthurian romance, untouched by the ideals of *chivalry, deals only indirectly with the noble Arthur. It is, however, very important, as so little native Welsh storytelling has survived, because their bards were reciting performers who did not record their work.

Although the Bretons were known for their talented *minstrels, we have even less surviving material from them than we do from the Welsh. Breton lais are charming short fairy tales often set in Arthur's court, but barely mentioning him by name except as the "Breton hope," referring to the possible return of an Arthur who never died. These works involve much magic with some chivalry, as in the *Lay of Sir Launful* by Marie de France (1175), author of twelve Breton lays. Launful is one of her few Arthurian stories and reflects the reality of the court as a world of strife and jealousy, not nearly as appealing as the beautiful world of fairies.

The earliest extant long Arthurian romances are the elegant, artificial verses of the twelfth-century Frenchman *Chrétien de Troyes, who was associated with the court of Champagne and especially with the Countess Marie, the daughter of Eleanor of Aquitaine. Chrétien was concerned with the interlacing of court life, *courtly love, and chivalry; he moved the exotic fairy tales of Welsh heroes into the castles of England and France. His surviving Arthurian works include *Erec et Enide* (c. 1170), *Lancelot* (c.1179), *Yvain* (c.1179), and *Perceval* (1180-90), all of which contain models of courtly behavior and polite conversation. For the first time Chrétien combined all the essential ingredients of Arthurian romance. In England, French influence of this type resulted in the tale of *Sir Gawain and the Green Knight* (c.1350). This poem represents the climax of English alliterative poetry and is the first poem to present Gawain, Arthur's nephew, as the primary hero.

From verse romances about individual heroes of Arthur's court, the French writers moved to prose, attempting to tell the whole history of Arthur, from his miraculous birth to his uncertain death. These writers became so caught up in complex digressions, frequently moral, that the story lines became difficult or impossible to follow or were even dropped entirely. Sir Thomas *Malory's *Le Morte Darthur* was the first coherent, abbreviated version. This work reduces the French Arthurian legends, which had by this point become rambling, separate stories about each particular character, into one text that clarifies an overall plot that includes all the known Arthurian figures. This last flowering of Arthurian legend in the literature of the Middle Ages was written in English in the late 1460s and published as a book by William *Caxton in 1485.

Malory begins his text with the miraculous birth of Arthur, fruit of the adulterous union of the warlike Uther Pendragon and the chaste Igrayne. This is closely followed by the other important aspects of Arthur's early career: his coronation, his acquisition of the sword Excalibur from the Lady of the Lake, and his incestuous coupling with his sister Morgawse. Arthur attempts to cover this last mistake by ruthlessly drowning all the babies born around the same time (cf. Matthew 2:16). This brutality earns for Arthur the hatred of many powerful families, but does not kill the infant Mordred.

For some time Arthur escapes the repercussions of his guilt as he wages triumphant campaigns against the Romans and the Saracens. By aiding her father, Lodegraunce, Arthur wins the fair Gwenyvere, who brings Uther's Round Table as her dowry. Arthur surrounds the table with knights of unmatched prowess, like Launcelot, Trystrame, and Galahad, who fight to remove evil from the world. All goes well for some time until the early seeds blossom into evil.

The final disintegration of the once-indomitable Order of the Round Table is caused, in the *Morte*, by many factors: Launcelot is Arthur's greatest knight and best friend, but he loves the King's wife, just as Trystrame loves La Beale Isode, wife of King Mark. The sainted Galahad is conceived when Launcelot is tricked into unfaithfulness to the Queen by Elayne; the bastard child becomes a knight so pure that the Holy Grail (the vessel used at the Last Supper and later to collect the blood of Christ as he hung on the cross) again visits earth because of Galahad's presence; thus begins a quest from which most of the knights do not return. Simultaneously, Aggravayne and Gawayne succeed in a plot to trap Launcelot and Gwenyvere together. When the knight arrives to save his lady, he accidentally kills the brothers of Aggravayne and Gawayne. Gawayne demands vengeance from Arthur, his uncle, so they leave to wage war on Launcelot across the sea. While Arthur is away, Mordred seizes the kingdom and the queen. Arthur returns to reprimand Mordred in a battle that begins through a mere accident when a soldier steps on a snake. This war leaves only Arthur, Mordred, and Bedyvere standing.

Arthur kills Mordred, receives a mortal wound, and is taken away in a barge by mourning women in black hoods. Bedyvere returns Excaleber to the lake and laments his lonely position. Gwenyvere dies soon after as an abbess in the nunnery of Almysburye, and Launcelot, another newcomer to the monastic life, also dies shortly.

Malory greatly simplified the form for his English audience, dropping most of the magic and religious mysteries, while adding realism. His method is a swift presentation of action that avoids complicated emotional analysis. Whereas Chrétien excelled at psychological passages showing the inner life of a character, Malory relied upon showing rather than telling. Many times there is a message, but it is rarely direct; one must decipher the carefully contrived layering of scenes. In the *Morte* the characters are not interested in word puns, and there is much more direct conversation with few narrative interventions, so the dialogue must be assessed by the reader (LaFarge 227).

Malory did not tantalize, but seems intent on clarifying the events for himself and his readers (Vinaver 1545). The work can be viewed as composed of eight sections: the first two concentrate on Arthur's rise to power; the next three show him at his height; and the final three concentrate on the downfall of Camelot. This configuration, according to D. S. Brewer, "makes sense in itself because it describes a general chronological progression, just like life, and is also comprehensible to medieval views of life. Growth, flowering and decay; rise, supremacy and fall not only completely accord with normal experience, but can easily be imagined in such medieval terms as Fortune's wheel" (241).

Malory's work, with its frequent contradictions in detail and often confusing arrangement, is by no means perfect, but the story retains its beauty and dissolution, and most of Malory's embroidery is an improvement. Much of what Malory discarded from French writers involved Merlin and Morgan le Fay, as the author was clearly concerned with the political ramifications of Arthur's decisions; possibly this interest in battle over magic, and especially the civil strife that ends Arthur's kingdom, reflects Malory's perception of the *Wars of the Roses (1455-85), which were ravaging England as he wrote. Malory was a knight himself, but apparently one not interested in outmoded concepts of courtly love; possibly for this reason he eliminated many of the love scenes between Launcelot and Gwenyvere, while concentrating on Launcelot as a Christian warrior. Chrétien's *Lancelot* portrays this knight as the Queen's willing pawn who is often made to look foolish for his love. Malory removed from Launcelot's character most aspects of the fawning courtly lover and substitutes a warrior of great courage. Malory also increased Arthur's knightly prowess.

Arthur was not merely an English king, but a British one, so his name was used as a political tool by the Welsh Tudors from the ascension of Henry VII in 1485, the same year in which Caxton published the *Morte*. Caxton's preface claims Arthur's historicity as "the most renomed Crysten kyng . . . whyche ought moost to be remembred emonge us Englysshemen tofore Crysten kynges" (cxlii), but the evidence was too flimsy; the Tudors eventually chose *Alfred the Great for their hero, because his existence was indisputable and most of his actions had been carefully documented.

There are many theories suggesting different kings whom Malory may have intended Arthur to reflect. William Matthews believed that Malory wrote against *Edward III, "whose military successes, like Arthur's, had brought him within reach of the emperor's crown, but whose ambition combined with ill luck had resulted in a senseless and profitless campaign which had made him widely unpopular" (188). R. M. Lumiansky found in the work a sympathy for Edward IV (882), while *The Arthurian Encyclopedia* (1986) noted that a passage near the end of *Morte* suggests that Malory sympathized with the ousted Lancastrian King Henry VI (Lacy 532).

By far the most comprehensive argument for the work as a parallel to other military triumphs and disasters is Eugene Vinaver's discussion of the idealized portrait of Arthur as a tribute to Henry V. Malory altered the section about Arthur and Emperor Lucius to make Arthur's expedition against the Romans resemble Henry V's triumphant campaign in France. Both kings follow the same route, appoint two leaders to rule while they are away, and are called rulers of two kingdoms "Whether as a Lancastrian or as a follower of Warwick who had sworn allegiance to Henry VI while fighting his advisors and even resisted the Duke of York's attempt to assume the crown, Malory had every reason to remember Henry V as the model of the 'crowned knight.'" (Vinaver xxxii).

D. S. Brewer agreed with Vinaver that Malory's work may be a tribute to Henry V, but adds that it is more likely a tribute to Arthur himself and all that he stood for in the author's imagination. Brewer suggested that Malory postponed Arthur's fall so that the king can become established in greatness (239). It would seem likely also that Malory added this postponement, which allowed Arthur to be crowned emperor of Rome and rise to further glory, to elevate the tragedy, making the ultimate fall greater.

Malory's devotion to the chivalric past is evident, and he expressed scorn for the system's disintegration because "the people were soo new fangill"

(1229; bk. 21, chap 1). This is especially touching, when we recall that Malory wrote in an age of great change "when the art of printing, the new learning and the reformation were soon to sweep away all outgrowths of chivalric romance and devoted naive, primitive faith and religion" (Ven-Ten Bensel 154). There seems to have been a fifteenth-century reversion to the Middle Ages in several important, but mostly negative, aspects that Malory may have resented: "the *Lollard heresy was repressed, the real authority of Parliament declined, the Wars of the Roses restored the anarchy of feudalism" (MacCallum 89).

The source of Malory's chapter called "The Tale of the Sankgreall" uses the French Vulgate Quest for the outline of the Holy Grail: Malory did little to alter the basic material, but again his skill is shown in omitting selected expositions on the doctrines of grace and salvation. In the French version a multitude of hermits sermonize to various questing knights. Malory diminished the distinction between religious and secular chivalry, making the distance less apparent between saintly Galahad and his more earthly father, Launcelot. The result is not always sound theology, but it does serve to integrate the Grail quest, a part of the work that had always seemed separate from the rest of the legend because of its intense moralizing.

Malory's conclusion, the aftermath of the battle between Arthur and Mordred, seems the most brilliant and majestic part of the *Morte*. Whereas violence and magic dominate early Arthurian tales, Malory's work is more concerned with feudal laws of loyalty and setting forth a coherent definition of chivalry:

> At his greatest, in the final passages dealing with the last battle and death of Arthur, he seems to reflect in an enlarged form all the troubles of his own society, the ruin which civil strife had brought upon him and his kind. This is imaginatively seen in the dissolution of the Table Round, the bond and fellowship of knighthood. Conquest, like true and faithful love, belongs to the past: the first and last campaigns of Arthur represent for Malory a youthful hope of the past contrasted with a tragic present. (Bradbrook 395-96)

Without gratuitous moralizing, Malory expanded the nobility of Arthur and the enduring love of Launcelot and Gwenyvere for each other and the king. This devotion restores the story's unrelenting tragedy and adds a climax of befitting grandeur never before attained. The entire tale becomes a grim vision with relevance to any civilization as Malory explores the forces, both internal and external, that ruin a kingdom.

While Launcelot does feel contrition for his sins when he confesses to a priest that he has "loved a quene unmesurably and oute of measure longe" (897; bk. 13, chap 20), Malory does not blame this love, nor the love of Tristram and Isode, for the fall. Caxton asserted in his preface that Malory's work is moral in tone because it teaches readers "the noble actes of chyvalrye, the jentyl and vertuous dedes that somme knyghtes used in tho dayes, by whyche they came to honour, and how they that were vycious were punysshed and ofte put out to shame and rebuke" (cxlv). The consensus among critics, however, is that Malory's work is not intended to be didactic. Many note that the fall seems caused by conflicting loyalties: Launcelot owes allegiance to Arthur, but loves Gweyvere (Zesmer 109); Arthur admires Launcelot, but his ties of kinship with Gawain are stronger (Harrington 66); and as Arthur's illegitimate and unacknowledged son, Mordred feels that he owes the king no special loyalty (Kendrick 65)

This concern with loyalty seems explainable as a key aspect of chivalry. Most of the knights become disloyal because of their great ambitions, especially in the Grail quest and the backing of Mordred. It is understandable that the knights are untrue to Arthur and the chivalric code: "Since they cannot understand the meaning and purpose of the King's ideals, his followers fail to keep the vows of the high order of knighthood" (Ven-Ten Bensel 154). Beyond virtue, true chivalry depends upon blind obedience and loyalty to a cause--a rule of conduct that establishes order in times of disorder (Vinaver xxxiii). It is in times of struggle that chivalry is tested, and, as Malory clearly shows (possibly despite himself), it does not always work. Most of the knights are neither virtuous nor unambitious enough to follow the strict code. The Round Table fellowship fails "and this was the fate of chivalry, because as a guiding principle, it was unequal to the problem which it undertook, and men soon saw that it merely professed to give the answer" (MacCallum 95-96). Arthur may have had the best of intentions, but he was surrounded by ordinary men of lesser standards. This is one of the main problems addressed in Tennyson's *Idylls of the King*.

Malory's work was followed by an almost total eclipse of interest in the legends, which were nearly forgotten until the latter half of the eighteenth-century. Arthur rarely appears in the intervening period when advocates of classical learning and of the Reformation were alike hostile to the medieval splendors of Arthur's court. Wisely, many historians of Tudor England questioned the truth of Geoffrey of Monmouth's chronicle; therefore, many historians of the period deleted Arthur's name.

Arthur as prince is a central figure of Edmund Spenser's *Faerie Queene* (1590-96), but this is invented material about the blank period in the character's life from his birth to his accession to the throne. The name is traditional, but the character is not the same.

Between 1639 and 1641 Milton considered writing an Arthurian epic, but decided instead to write *Paradise Lost* (1667). In 1684 John Dryden wrote the libretto for the composer Henry Purcell's *King Arthur*, which was not performed until 1691. This work is not actually about Arthurian legend and uses Arthur only as a symbol of chivalry and kingship.

With the Gothic Revival and the romantics came some interest in the Arthurian cycle. In 1813 Sir Walter Scott published *The Bridal of Triermain*, an Arthurian poem. William Wordsworth's "The Egyptian Maid" (1835) refers to Sir Galahad, although here he is married, while all previous Grail stories refer to

Galahad as the "virgin knight." There were, of course, during these two centuries, other stories of Arthurian characters, but none of great significance until Alfred Tennyson published his first Arthurian poem in 1832.

SELECTED BIBLIOGRAPHY

Barber, Richard, ed. *The Arthurian Legend*. London: Dorset, 1979; Bradbrook, M. C. "Malory and the Heroic Tradition." *Arthur, King of Britain*. Richard Brengle, ed. New York: Prentice, 1964. 392-96; Brewer, D. S. "'the hoole booke.'" *Middle English Survey*. Edward Vasta, ed. London: University of Notre Dame Press, 1965. 233-58; Bryden, Inga. "Arthur as Artefact: Concretizing the Fictions of the Past." *Angelaki* 1:2 (Winter 193-94), 149-57; Fletcher, Alan J. "King Arthur's Passing in the *Morte D'Arthur*. *English Language Notes* 31:4 (June 1994), 19-24; Harrington, David V. "The Conflicting Passions of Malory's 'Sir Gawain' and 'Sir Lancelot.'" *Arthurian Interpretations* 2 (1987). 64-69; Jones, W. Lewis. *King Arthur in History and Legend*. Cambridge: Cambridge University Press, 1911; Kindrick, Robert L. "The Administration of Justice in Malory's Works." *Arthurian Interpretations* 2:1 (1987), 63-82; Lacy, Norris J., ed. *The Arthurian Encyclopedia*. New York: Bedrick, 1986; LaFarge, Catherine. "Conversation in Malory's *Morte Darthur*." *Medium Evum* 55 (1984), 225-38; Lumiansky, R. M. "Sir Thomas Malory's *Le Morte Darthur*, 1947-1987: Author, Title, Text." *Speculum* 62 (1987), 878-97; MacCallum, Sir Mungo William. *Tennyson's "Idylls of the King" and Arthurian Story from the XVIth Century*. New York: Books for Libraries, 1971; Matthews, William. *The Tragedy of Arthur*. Berkeley: University of California Press, 1960; Morris, Rosemary. *The Character of King Arthur in Medieval Literature*. Totowa, NJ: Rowman & Littlefield, 1982; Ven-ten Bensel, Elise Francisca Wilhelmina Maria van der. *The Character of King Arthur in English Literature*. New York: Haskell House, 1966; Vinaver, Eugene, ed. *The Works of Thomas Malory*. 3 vols., continuously paged. Clarendon: Oxford University Press, 1990; Wilhelm, James J., ed. *The Romance of Arthur: An Anthology of Medieval Texts in Translation*. New York: Garland, 1994; Wood, Juliette. "The Selling of Arthur: Popular Culture and the Arthurian Legend." *Folklore in Use* 2:1 (1994), 115-29; Zesmer, David M. *Guide to English Literature--From "Beowulf" through Chaucer and Medieval Drama*. New York: Barnes, 1965.

Laura Cooner Lambdin

ATHELSTON. An English *romance from about 1350, *Athelston* should not be confused with the true Athelstan, *Alfred's grandson. The romance's only link with this historical figure is its mention of the ascension of Edmund. It is likely that this, like other romances, finds its roots in the *chansons de geste* of the previous three centuries.

Athelston differs from other romances in that it is often terse and somewhat melodramatic. In the romance four messengers meet by coincidence in the forest. One is the title character, Athelston. The four come to prominence, and the romance focuses upon Athelston, the king of Wessex, and his relationship with his archbishop of Canterbury, another of the messengers.

This conflict summarily resembles that of Thomas *Becket and *Henry II. Another of the messengers becomes the earl of Dover and plots against Athelston. Before his plan can come to fruition, he is discovered and executed. The final messenger becomes the earl of Stane, and, later, Edmund's father. Perhaps the greatest contribution this work gives to medieval literature is its illustration of the significant struggle between church and state during this period.

SELECTED BIBLIOGRAPHY

Frakes, Jerold C. "Metaphysical Structure as Narrative Structure in the Medieval Romance." *Neophilologus* 69:4 (1985), 481-89; Lapidge, Michael. "Some Latin Poems as Evidence for the Reign of Athelstan." *Anglo-Saxon England* 9 (1981), 61-98; Lindahl, Carl. "The Oral Undertones of Late Medieval Romance." in *Oral Tradition in the Middle Ages*. W.F.H. Nicolaisen, ed. Binghamton, NY: Medieval and Renaissance Texts and Studies, 1995. 59-75.

Robert T. Lambdin

AUCASSIN ET NICOLETTE. One of the best medieval love *romances, *Aucassin et Nicolette* is a thirteenth-century French *chantefable*, or a work told in alternating prose and verse. The author was probably from northern France, a hypothesis derived from his obvious unfamiliarity with the setting of the story.

In the romance Aucassin, the son of the count of Beaucaire, falls in love with Nicolette, a captive Saracen girl. To keep the couple apart, the count incarcerates them, but the lovers escape. The couple then spend three blissful years together until they are captured again, this time by the Saracens. Aucassin is shipwrecked near his home; upon his return he learns of his father's death and becomes the count.

Nicolette is taken to Carthage, where she is identified as the king's daughter. He betroths her to another, but she flees in search of Aucassin, her true love. She finds her way to Beaucaire, where, disguised as a minstrel, she is reunited with her lover. The couple are then married and become the count and countess of Beaucaire.

SELECTED BIBLIOGRAPHY

Cobby, Anne Elizabeth. *Ambivalent Conventions: Formula and Parody in Old French*. Amsterdam: Rodopi, 1995; Green, Virginia M. "*Aucassin et Nicolette*: The Economics of Desire." *Neophilologus* 79:2 (Apr 1995), 197-206; Thomas, Patrick Michael. "The Diminutive World of *Aucassin et Nicolette*." *Language and Literature* 16 (1991), 55-64.

Rebecca Chalmers

AUGUSTINE, ST. (354-430). Augustine was a noted cleric and philosopher whose Latin name is Aurelius Augustinus. Born to a Christian mother and a pagan father in North Africa, Augustine was initially educated in Latin literature. He later earned a living from 374 to 387 as a rhetoric teacher in Carthage, Rome, and Milan. In his quest for knowledge, he joined the Manichaeans for several years, but became disillusioned and left the sect. This was followed by several years of skepticism until he was converted to Christianity by St. Ambrose. Augustine was baptized in 387. He then returned to Africa and set up a monastery. In 396 Augustine was promoted to bishop of Hippo. The intense internal struggle of Augustine during this period became the basis for his *Confessions*, a work that expounds his spiritual experiences and development.

For the next thirty years until his death, Augustine preached and wrote an abundant corpus of tracts. These works mainly sought to define points of Christian doctrine. Often the works attacked the teachings of the Manichaeans, as well as the Donatists and the *Pelagians. Throughout his work Augustine maintained the significance of the idea of a solitary, unified church. In this resolve he developed a philosophy of sin, grace, and predestination that became seminal to the doctrines of the Roman Catholic Church. This dogma was later adopted by the followers of Luther and Calvin.

Among Augustine's other works are *De Trinitate* (On the Trinity), composed from 400 to 416; *The *City of God*, 413-26; and *De natura et gratia* (On Nature and Grace), 415. He also wrote his famous *Retractiones* (Retractions) in 426. This work revised many of his more exaggerated earlier statements.

SELECTED BIBLIOGRAPHY

Donnelly, Dorothy F., ed. "The City of God": *A Collection of Critical Essays*. New York: Peter Lang, 1995; Horn, Christoph. *Augustinus*. Munich: Beck, 1995; Schnaubelt, Joseph C., and Frederick Van Fleteren, eds. *Collectanea Augustiniana: Augustine: Second Founder of Faith*. New York: Peter Lang, 1990.

Robert T. Lambdin

AWNTYRS OF ARTHURE. The *Awntyrs of Arthure* survives complete in five medieval manuscripts. Its language and meter indicate northern composition, but the five copies were made in different parts of England, including Yorkshire, the Midlands, and the London area. The number of surviving copies indicates that *Awntyrs* enjoyed a remarkable popularity inside and outside the region in which it originated. Its supernatural and chivalric story lines are similar to those of popular oral compositions, but the complex rhyme scheme, narrative structure, and content demonstrate that *Awntyrs* was a distinctively literary effort.

Until fairly recently, critics have regarded *Awntyrs* as deficient in structural and thematic unity. The poem divides neatly into two halves. The first part (lines 1-338) changes a popular legend, the Mass of Saint Gregory, into a chivalric episode. It begins with a standard opening for a Gawain *romance: Arthur (*see **Arthurian Legend***) and his companions go to hunt in Inglewood Forest. A ghost, who turns out to be the tormented soul of Guenevere's mother, appears to Gawain and Guenevere. The ghost suffers for the hidden sins of the flesh that she committed on earth, laments the split within her life, and believes that her condition should be a warning to the entire court. She warns Gawain and Guenevere that the conduct of knights and ladies must conform to Christian law, and that the court must narrow the schism between its lavish consumption and the poverty that besets others. In this way spiritual and material concerns must coincide.

The apparition passes, the hunt ends, and the second part (lines 339-702) follows a scenario familiar in chivalric romance. As the Round Table members are seated at dinner, a strange knight, Sir Galeron of Galloway, enters; he accuses Arthur and Gawain of falsely owning his lands and demands a combat. His challenge is to Sir Gawain. The narrative focuses on the courage and skill of the fight; neither knight can gain victory, and each does great damage to his opponent. Just as Gawain seems at the point of triumph, Galeron's lady and then Guenevere intervene, and Arthur halts the combat. Galeron submits, and the dispute is ended by Arthur assigning other lands to Gawain and restoring lands to Galeron. Galeron marries his lady and becomes a knight of the Round Table. In the last stanza of *Awntyrs* Guenevere arranges the Masses for her mother.

Awntyrs is composed of thirteen-lined stanzas with the rhyme scheme *ababababbcddc*. The first nine lines are long, alliterative, and structurally bound by four stresses and the end rhyme. In the last four verses of each stanza, each line contains two or three stresses, while the first three rhyme of the same sound, and the last line rhymes with the long ninth line. The density of alliteration of *Awntyrs* is higher than that of any other Middle English poem. The first line of every stanza incorporates a word or phrase from the last line of the previous stanza. Finally, the last lines of *Awntyrs* repeat the first line, linking these two stanzas and thereby imposing a circular structure on the entire poem. The structure of *Awntyrs* is obviously one of the most demanding forms in the English language.

SELECTED BIBLIOGRAPHY

Allen, Rosemund. "Some Sceptical Observations of the Editing of *The Awntyrs off Arthure*: Essays from 1985." *Manuscripts and Texts. Editorial Problems in Later Middle English Literature*. Derek Pearsall, ed. Cambridge: Brewer, 1987. 5-25.

Rebecca Chalmers

AYMON, THE FOUR SONS OF. The medieval French *romance, "The Four Sons of Aymon" concerns *Charlemagne's conflict with four noblemen. The eldest and most prominent of these is Rinaldo. The work is found in an English prose version printed by William *Caxton around 1489-91. Other than Caxton's edition, there is no other known original version which survives.

SELECTED BIBLIOGRAPHY

Renoir, Alain. "Bayard and Troilus: Chaucerian Non-Paradox in the Reader." *Orbis Litterarum* 36:2 (1981), 116-40.

Rebecca Chalmers

B

BACON, ROGER (c. 1214-1294?). In the early thirteenth-century the long struggle between orthodox theology and "natural philosophy" or experimental science began to trouble the schools. In 1210 the papacy banned the reading or teaching of *Aristotle's works on natural philosophy at the University of Paris. By 1240 the university decided to ignore the ban and sought a master in the field; Roger Bacon, a lay master of arts at Oxford, was invited to begin lecturing on the complete works of Aristotle. From then until his return to England (1250-52) he produced an impressive number of Commentaries, Questions, and appropriate textbooks on grammar and logic.

Sometime after his return to England Bacon joined the Franciscan order, possibly in part for financial security, since his once-prosperous family could no longer support him. He did not fear the personal poverty required, and he admired much of the order's discipline toward holiness. The Franciscans reputation for learning encouraged him to believe that they would approve of his growing conviction that theology must be supported by all kinds of knowledge. However, in 1257 the order placed restrictions on his freedom, sending him to a convent in France where he was under close observation.

When Cardinal Guy de Foulquois became Pope Clement IV in 1265, Bacon's second appeal for support of his proposal for the unity of knowledge brought encouragement to proceed--privately. Bacon sent the pope the first of his great works, *Opus Majus*. Whether or not Clement saw the following treatises, *Opus Secundum*, or *Opus Minus*, and *Opus Tertium*, is unknown, since he died in November 1268. By this time Bacon had been given comparative freedom and had returned to England, where he continued to write challenging works on medicine, alchemy, astrology, mathematics, and metaphysics. His interest in alchemy may have led to his legendary reputation as a worker in magic. His real-life troubles stemmed chiefly from his somewhat abrasive personality and his support of radical reform in his order. Three of Bacon's best-known works deal with the philosophical search for an understanding of universals. The *Quaestiones* and *Quaestiones Altere* deal with Aristotle's *Metaphysics*, with increasing allusions to other works and authors. The format follows the traditional *scholastic pattern of pro and con statements, endeavoring to define and distinguish common or species entities and the individual or particular examples relevant to each class. The third treatise,

Communia Naturalium, is less Scholastic, abandoning the rigid pro and con format, but the basic issues are still being debated. The following translated quotation suggests the syntactic complexity of these debates:

Particular nature is the governing force of species (*virtus regitiva speciei*) with its individuals, and is thus twofold, namely, the governing force of species and the governing force of an individual, because in every [act of] generation there arises one species and likewise one individual, because an individual does not exst without a species, nor the converse (*Communia Naturalium*, chapter 7, 4, Maloney, *Three Treatments*, 86)

The *Opus Majus* discusses the obstacles in the way of true science, rejects authority and verbal subtleties, and sketches in broad outline the essentials of the great branches of knowledge: grammar and logic, mathematics, physics or optics, experimental research, and moral philosophy. *Opus Minus* contains a brief review of *Opus Majus*, criticism of the errors of theological study, and a detailed treatment of speculative and practical alchemy. *Opus Tertium* continues the discussion of alchemy, adds more mathematics, and asserts that optics are in essence the power of the soul.

In his writing on medicine Bacon considered astrology, alchemy, and metaphysics essential tools. He did not in his *De Secretis Operibus Naturae* claim to have invented flying machines and self-propelled boats himself, but attributed these technical marvels to others, assuring the reader that they would be found useful in the future. The one field in which he conducted his own experiments was optics. He observed the stars and paid special attention to the rainbow, which he analyzed by observing that bubbles reflect different colors and that hexagonal stones and crystals refract light.

Bacon was learned in Hebrew, Greek, and possibly Arabic. He considered mathematics the key to other sciences and observation essential to verification of any theory. That which was beyond such methods, matters of spiritual significance, could be reasoned from accepted premises Nature was reasonable and universals were consistent. Bacon's claim to fame as a scientist does not rest upon his technical work but on his attempts to think through the implications of the work of others. His vision of the synthesis of all knowledge continues to challenge philosophy and scholarship.

SELECTED BIBLIOGRAPHY

Easton, Stewart C. *Roger Bacon and His Search for a Universal Science*. Oxford: Basil Blackwell, 1952. Reprint. New York: Russell and Russell, 1971; Hackett, Jeremiah M. G. "Moral Philosophy and Rhetoric in Roger Bacon." *Philosophy and Rhetoric* 20:1 (1987), 18-40; Linden, Stanton J. "Roger Bacon in the Age of Francis: The Mirror of Alchimy and the Mirror of Nature." *Cauda Pavonis* 10:1 (Spring 1991), 10-13; Maloney, Thomas S. "The Semiotics of Roger Bacon." *Mediaeval Studies* 45 (1983), 120-54.

Esther Smith

BALLADS (BALLADRY). Standing among the most significant poetic developments of the medieval period, balladry alone, aside from a few isolated *lyrics, brings us the unmitigated voice of the British medieval commoner. Its influence on subsequent English literature is immense. Rooted in the earlier *Anglo-Saxon epic tradition, often adopting and subverting aristocratic ideals and literary conventions to express the very different world view of the middle and lower classes, and influencing later poets from Christopher Marlowe to Thomas Hardy to C. Day Lewis, the ballad at once provides a unifying influence and a means of measuring the changing perceptions and concerns of the general populace. Nonetheless, no poetic form has been so unfairly maligned. As the original vehicle for the *vox populi*, it has always been associated with social unrest, and this, combined with its essentially parodic mode and frequently sardonic tone, removes it from the realm of "polite" literature. At best, balladry has been considered simplistic folk song; at worst, vulgar and propagandistic. Only in recent years, with the growth of appreciation for popular culture and the democratization of the arts in general, have the medieval ballad's special qualities begun to receive the serious consideration they deserve.

Of all poetic forms, the ballad alone has enjoyed uninterrupted popularity from the early Middle Ages to the present. Both as a term and a genre it derives from the tenth century, reaching its heyday between the thirteenth and seventeenth centuries and again, after a brief hiatus, with the Romantic poets of the nineteenth century and continuing into the present. In the broadest sense, balladry connotes popular folk song, anonymous and pervasive, and frequently with very ancient roots. All agree that it is an oral tradition, that is, one in which the poems are produced, experienced, and transmitted orally, without the aid of the written word. Moreover, three general classifications of ballads--traditional, broadside, and literary--are generally accepted.

The traditional, or folk, ballad is the earliest form, deriving from the general populace, primarily in rural areas or small villages and towns. It arises from the common farm worker, laborer, or tradesperson, many of whom in the Middle Ages were the descendants of the displaced *Anglo-Saxons conquered in 1066 by *William I's Norman armies. Thus the folk ballad has at heart the epic tradition (by definition, also oral) of the earlier English people. This is important, as the discussion of ballad perceptions and themes here indicates, since the medieval commoners, with their very different racial and cultural heritage, embraced a profoundly different way of viewing the world from that of the primarily Norman-French aristocracy.

The traditional ballad functioned for the nonliterate of the Middle Ages in many of the same ways popular writing functions in contemporary society. It offered them a means of recording their opinions, perceptions, history, and world views; usually set to popular folk tunes, it also provided entertainment. Sometimes it became a kind of "oral newspaper," recording events and concerns (local, regional, and national) in song and passing them from area to area and even to nations abroad via traveling tradespeople and the crews of merchant ships. The subject occurrences may have been major, such as those recorded in the so-called historical ballads *Chevy Chase* and *The Battle of Otterburn*, or they may have been more of household or clan tragedies, like the bride stealing of *The Douglas Tragedy* or the child murders in *The Cruel Mother*. The story of **Sir Patrick Spens* shows how, over time, historical events can enter the realm of quasiepic fiction. Also like a newspaper, the songs included their share of editorials, where the actions of public figures might be condemned or satirized (e.g. *Queen Eleanor's Confession, Lamkin*). They functioned as a political forum and vehicle for propaganda and as such drew attention and censure from those bastions of medieval feudal society, the aristocracy and the church. But most often ballads functioned simply to record the world views, behavioral codes, and aspirations of the non-elite of medieval society.

Broadside balladry, too, began in the Middle Ages, although several centuries later than the traditional, originating in the cities with laborers and the new middle classes represented by trade guilds, shopkeepers, entrepreneurs, and civic leaders. Also commoners, and often originally migrants from the countryside, these people nonetheless developed concerns and aspirations diverging from those of their rural counterparts in the same way as rural and urban perceptions have always differed. Thus, while traditional folk song continued to flourish in the urban areas there arose alongside of it a distinctly new form of balladry more immediately concerned with politics, economics, commerce, and class relations. Such ballads tended more to the harshly satirical and propagandistic, so much so that they quickly became associated with rabble-rousing and general social unrest. Indeed, Warton (46) credited a political ballad with instigating a statute against libel as early as 1275, and under Elizabeth I ballads were reviewed as a matter of course for the purposes of determining and manipulating public opinion. By the early 1700s the broadside was generally considered, in the words of Daniel Defoe (59), "a useful incentive to mischief." Later in the same century Horace Walpole went so far as to suggest government composition of ballads ridiculing the French Revolution with the purpose of swaying public opinion in favor of the monarchy and his own political party.

As broadside balladry grew to become a major form of propaganda, it was not only employed by social reformers and general rabble-rousers associated with the lower and middle classes, but it was also appropriated by establishment strategists and publicists who thought it better to adopt and manipulate that which they could not eliminate. It is from these later specimens that the broadside type receives its name, for by the early Renaissance the practice of printing such ballads on broadsheets and selling or publicly posting them had been established. Nonetheless, while more topical (and hence more short-lived) and more politically motivated than the traditional ballad, the broadside at least shares with the former the quality of being generally a product of and for the commoner. The third type of ballad--the literary--is a different creature indeed.

The earliest literary ballads were religious, represented, in fact, by the first ballad to be written down in its entirety, the thirteenth-century *Judas*.

Indeed, only one religious ballad of true popular origin, *The Bitter Withy*, survives from the medieval period, and it evokes the same bitter world view as the main body of traditional song. The other three are believed to be products of the clergy, who sought to "rehabilitate" an offensive tradition--rebellious, satiric, and often bawdy--by composing alternate lyrics for established popular tunes. Occasionally the upper classes did likewise. Literacy being the province of these elite segments of the population, such imitations were more likely to be recorded in medieval manuscripts and were probably composed in writing. In contrast, folk ballads continued for centuries to depend upon communal memory and entertainment for their survival. Nonetheless, as befits a form associated with the commoners and generally scorned by the poets of the elite, the popular ballads that we can trace back to the Middle Ages far outnumber literary specimens.

During the Renaissance, as class boundaries continued to break down, the ballad entered mainstream literature with such writers as Christopher Marlowe, Walter Ralegh, and John Donne, and their famous related trio of poems, *The Passionate Shepherd to His Love*, *The Nymph's Reply to the Shepherd*, and *The Bait*. However, as a glance at these examples confirms, the ballad retained its satiric mode and pragmatic outlook even as it entered the world of literacy. Moreover, it continued to be scorned as a form for "serious" poetic endeavors. Both characteristics and reputation persisted in later literary ballads. The Victorian poet Thomas Hardy, for example, openly drew upon old traditional songs when he produced such sardonic pieces as *Ah, Are You Digging on My Grave?* and *The Ruined Maid*. Similarly, C. Day Lewis's *Song* represents yet another paraphrase of Marlowe's famous poem in updated form, this time expressing the dismal economic and social conditions of the 1930s, and X. J. Kennedy took potshots at everything from romantic love to drug abuse in his ballad *In a Prominent Bar in Secaucus One Day*.

Despite its adoption as a mainstream literary poetic form, the ballad has also remained strong in oral tradition, although, with the growth over the centuries to almost universal literacy in English-speaking countries, the oral tradition itself has declined considerably. Not only do ancient songs such as *Barbara Allen* and *I Gave My Love a Cherry* still survive in the nursery and coffee house, but popular music of the twentieth century continues to adapt old ballads and create new ones. American folk singer Woody Guthrie produced scores of ballads in which he immortalized the hard conditions of middle America in the 1930s and 1940s, with his son Arlo following his lead in singing about the hippie culture of the 1960s; popular 1960s and 1970s musical duo Paul Simon and Art Garfunkel directly adapted one of the oldest of English ballads in writing *Scarborough Fair*; within the last decade, a popular British singing group revived the ancient *Sir Patrick Spens* in a new musical version; and contemporary American country and western music produces more ballads than any other form of song. The ballad, then, rather than disappearing or surviving only as a specialized literary exercise in the manner of the roundel or the sonnet, remains a very strong and consistent influence in poetry. Its major formal and thematic characteristics have changed little since the Middle Ages, although the continuing democratic impulse has allowed it to establish itself in literary as well as oral tradition, and in "high" as well as popular culture.

In formal terms the ballad is a slippery animal. Purists insist upon highly regulated rhyme and metrics, but in actuality, medieval as well as later ballads varied greatly from such strictures. Stanzas tended to be two or four lines, although certain medieval specimens stretch to eight or ten lines; meters tended to be between three and seven stresses per line (four being the most common), and individual poems might combine several; the primary rhyme scheme tended to be either the couplet or alternating rhyme (*abab*). In other words, loose rules existed but embraced broad variations and were not infrequently broken.

The most notable of mechanical matters in balladry is the vocabulary of stock lines held in common by the genre as a whole. These are formulaic phrases, usually descriptive, any one of which may appear in scores of completely unrelated ballads. For example, *Robin Hood, Johnnie Cock, and any number of star-crossed lovers meet "under the greenwood tree." Many a hero or heroine rides on a "milk-white steed," even though he or she may have instructed the servants to "saddle me the black, the black / Or saddle me the brown." In folk song everything from a maiden's hair to the towers of a castle may shine "like the gold so red." Such stock lines perform a number of functions. They may help to maintain rhyme schemes (as is reflected by their usual appearance in the second or fourth line of a stanza) or offer the balladeer time to think during a performance, whether he is calling upon memory for an old song or composing a new one. On the other hand, formulaic phrases may simply act as a shorthand to express a commonplace that bears no real import in the story. In any event, they clearly exist as a by-product of oral composition. Composing and singing poems without the aid of writing necessarily involves extensive memorization; stock lines and phrases considerably ease the burden. An associated feature also resulting from the oral nature of folk song is the profusion of ballad analogues. These are varying versions of what is clearly the same song. As Albert Lord proves in his unsurpassed study of oral composition, *The Singer of Tales*, two performances of a ballad, even by the same singer, will virtually never be identical; and this, combined with the imperfection of human memory, accounts for the minor changes effected in a ballad over time. As time or distance lengthens, such changes become more significant. The multiple versions of *Barbara Allen* or *Sir Patrick Spens* are examples of this. In contrast, some analogues represent a deliberate re-working of a story, changing emphasis or outcome to reflect a different purpose or opinion. The related ballads *The *Three Ravens*, *The Twa Corbies*, and *The Corpus Christi Carol* exemplify this latter type. Nonetheless, in both kinds of analogues, plot and characters generally remain the same.

While most formal characteristics of balladry are somewhat hard to pin down, those related to semantics are much more consistent. Medieval ballads are famed for their "impersonal" stance, that is, the lack of moral commentary on the actions of ballad characters. Indeed, the narrator is not often an obvious presence; when he does intrude, it is usually to call for attention from the audience or to assert the truth of his story. Such a presence reflects the relationship of balladry to the earlier epic tradition, where the Anglo-Saxon *scop (bard) held the important and dignified position as the guardian of history and social mores and the commentator on current events within his non-literate society. In keeping with this apparent "reporter" stance, ballads also concentrate upon action and result rather than motive. It has been frequently observed that ballads enter the drama of their story "in the fifth act": they present the crisis and the denouement, but ignore the events that lead up to them. As has already been hinted, simple description for the sake of painting a scene or delineating characters is nonexistent, dismissed with a formulaic vocabulary so widely used as to make it almost meaningless. Explanations and extenuating circumstances carry no weight in the ballad universe.

It is nonetheless a mistake to assume that the ballads offer no judgement on the behavior of their characters. It is merely that their value system is implicit, shown in the concrete cause-and-effect relations of their action. Their mode is ironic and satiric, letting the absurdity or disaster of a situation direct the audience to the obvious conclusion: rejection of that which leads to the undesirable result. Consider the following stanzas from *Sir Patrick Spens*, describing the aftermath of the shipwreck in which all of the crew, led by Sir Patrick, are drowned:

> O ours Scots nobles were right loath
> To wet their cork-heeled shoes,
> But long before the play was done,
> Their hats, they swam above.
>
> . . . .
>
> Half over, half over to Aberdour
> It's fifty fathoms deep,
> And there lies good Sir Patrick Spens
> With the Scots lords at his feet.

The voyage was ill considered in the first place, as both Spens and a common shipman indicate earlier in the ballad, yet Spens was bound by his honor and feudal obligation to the king (who ordered the voyage) to undertake it anyway, even though he knew that his monarch had been directed by a rival who wished him out of the way. Rather than painting a sympathetic or tragic portrait, however, the ballad presents us with comedy. The image of the nobles' hats floating on the surface of the water after the owners have drowned might have come straight from a cartoon; calling the endeavor a "play" suggests the artificiality, or perhaps the absurdity, of the system (chivalric feudalism) that dictates such ridiculous behavior over common sense. The final stanza takes the parody to its ultimate degree, depicting the drowned Scots lords at the feet of the heroic, but very dead, Sir Patrick in a parody of feudal obligation.

Indeed, such rejection of the ideal is precisely what constitutes the value system propounded by the ballads. Heroism is rejected as foolish or destructive, and canniness is exalted in its place. Romanticism is at best an unrealistic dream, but more frequently a misleading and destructive force. Only pragmatism, seeing to the essential needs of everyday life, leads to success in medieval folk song. The mothers of *Lord Randal* and *Edward, Edward*, for example, do not concern themselves with the imminent deaths of their sons--the deaths are unavoidable--but with the inheritance portions for the family left behind. The various discarded mistresses do not waste time mourning broken hearts, but rather worry about lost means of support; in the words of *The Lass of Rock Royal*,

> O, who will shoe my bonny foot,
> Or who will glove my hand?
> Or who will bind my middle slim
> With the broad lily band?
>
> Or who will comb my bonny head
> With the red river comb?
> Or who will be my babe's father
> Ere Gregory, he come home?

So it continues throughout the ballads, this obsession with the basic needs of survival and a tacit or explicit rejection of idealism and the gentler emotions.

The reason for such a coldly pragmatic outlook is not hard to find in the ballads. Quite simply, the universe is a cold, unfriendly, dangerous place that makes no special allowances for humanity. Consider the following definition of existence offered by a ballad maiden from the thirteenth-century *Riddles Wisely Expounded*:

> Hunger is sharper than is the thorn,
> Thunder is louder than is the horn.
>
> Longing is longer than is the way,
> Sin is more ready than is the day.
>
> God's flesh is better than is the bread,
> Pain is more fearful than is death.
>
> Grass is greener than is the wood,
> Love is sweeter than is the nut.
>
> Thought is swifter than is the wind,
> Jesus is richer than is the king.

> Sulphur is yellower than is the wax,
> Silk is softer than is the flax.

The natural world here is not beautiful: it is filled with thorns, thunder, and wind, and the human lot with hunger, pain, death, and unfulfilled longing. The apparent religious consolations of "God's flesh" and Jesus' promise are undercut by their comparisons, for clearly this maiden knows flax, not silk, and sees the king as so rich that only a deity can be more so. Likewise, human behavior is far from admirable, for "sin" is more frequent than the sun rising.

This maiden's perceptions, though bittersweet, are nonetheless pessimistic in the extreme, concentrating on an unfriendly nature and the most basic of human needs under its conditions. She is echoed several centuries later by the lady of *The Gardener*, who presents the case in a much less gentle fashion:

> The hail stones shall be on thy head,
> And the snow upon thy breast,
> And the east wind shall be for a shirt
> To cover thy body next.
>
> Thy boots shall be of the tangle
> That nothing can betide;
> Thy steed shall be of the wan water:
> Leap on, young man, and ride.

Throughout the ballad universe humanity is generally cruel, untrustworthy, and dangerous. Around every corner is one--often an aristocrat--who would lie or cheat, rape a girl, steal another's belongings, unjustly maim or kill, or refuse to pay for good services rendered. The best one can do, in the ballads, is look to one's own survival and trust nobody. It is a bitter vision indeed.

Sadly for the medieval commoner, religious consolation is lacking. The near absence of ballads on religious themes was mentioned earlier. Four ballads survive, and only one a folk product. *The Bitter Withy* suggests no reward, earthly or heavenly, for virtuous behavior; indeed, it implies the opposite. Concentrating on a fictional incident in the childhood of Jesus, the ballad depicts the Savior as a vengeful commoner who, rejected as a playmate by the "lords' and ladies' sons" because he was "a poor maid's child / born in an ox's stall," repays the insult by drowning his tormenters. Moreover, the murders go unpunished except for a spanking from his mother with the withy (willow), and even the tree is then cursed. Says the child Jesus, since the withy hurt his behind, "It shall be the very first tree / That perishes from the heart." Not for the commoner's Savior meek Christian tolerance or forgiveness, but rather a satisfying revenge that distinctly smacks of class jealousy and resentment.

Perhaps the chivalric ballads offer the most significant windows into the commoner's mind, for they demolish the misconception of a period of idyllic feudalism or cohesive ideology, and certainly of a monolithic age of faith. A number of ballads draw upon tales of *chivalry or *courtly love, and substantially more adopt motifs and themes from the *romances produced by the nobility. However, such are not simply adopted without question. Rather, the balladeers twisted and undercut the symbols of aristocratic ideology, deliberately juxtaposing them upon the pragmatism and the bleak universe they inhabited. A brief study of three related medieval ballads will suffice to illustrate the divergence of the commoners' view from that of the aristocracy and the church, as well as demonstrate the practice of creating deliberate analogues. *The Three Ravens* and *The Twa Corbies* reflect, respectively, the aristocratic and commoner's views of the same subject: a knight slain in combat.

> Down in yonder green field,
> There lies a knight slain under his shield.
> His hounds they lie down at his feet,
> So well they can their master keep.
>
> His hawks, they fly so eagerly,
> There's no fowl dare come him nigh.
> Down there comes a fallow doe,
> As great with young as she might go.
>
> She lifted up his bloody head
> And kissed his wounds that were so red.
> She got him up upon her back
> And carried him to the earthen lake.
>
> She buried him before the prime,
> She was dead herself ere evensong time.
> God send every gentleman
> Such hawks, such hounds, and such a leman.

Here the knight's animal companions, themselves symbols of nobility, behave with appropriate loyalty, protecting his body (the speakers are ravens who would devour it) until his metamorphosed beloved buries him decently. Similarly, in the tradition of true love, the lady subsequently dies of heartbreak. The imagery of the poem--green fields and an "earthen lake" reminiscent of rebirth for a grave--along with the religious hours and final apostrophe to God, romanticize the deaths and underscore the "rightness" of the chivalric ideal. The spokesman for the commoner, however, takes a different view of the same situation:

> "In behind yon old foul ditch

I know there lies a new slain knight,
And nobody knows that he lies there
But his hawk, his hound, and lady fair.

"His hound is to the hunting gone,
His hawk to fetch the wild foul home,
His lady's taken another mate,
So we may make our dinner sweet.

"Ye'll sit on his white neck bone,
And I'll pick out his bonny blue eyes;
With a lock of his golden hair,
We'll thatch our nest when it grows bare.

"Many a one for him makes moan,
But none shall know where he is gone;
O'er his white bones, when they are bare,
The wind shall blow for ever more."

Obviously, a different value system is at work in this second poem. Not only is there a suggestion of treachery, both in the hidden and defiled body and the inconstancy of the lady, but all participants in the drama exude the commoner's pragmatism by simply getting on with their lives. Hounds hunt, hawks prey on smaller fowl, and ladies get married. Moreover, the corbies are in tune with the bleak universe of the ballads--a dirty ditch, the cold wind blowing over naked bones--for they make use of that which chance has brought them, mindful of empty bellies and the threat of a winter coming upon them in a bare nest. No room for sentimentality exists.

The third medieval analogue, *The Corpus Christ Carol*, adapts the tale to religious ends. The ravens are eliminated, and the falcon becomes a metaphor for the soul, traveling to a fruitful orchard by grace of the sacrifice of the knight (Christ), whose eternally bleeding body recalls both the magnitude of his sacrifice and the eternity of heaven. The lady becomes a maid, or virgin, kneeling and weeping beside the bed upon which the body lies. Interestingly, the courtly and religious ballads thus borrow from each other's imagery to reinforce an idealism in which church and aristocracy work together to reinforce a feudal system that rests so heavily on the shoulders of the deprived commoner.

In such manipulation of the nobility's symbols and ideologies, as well as in carefully crafted vision of a mournful and unfriendly universe, lies the greatest art of the ballad. From the sardonic to the lyric, the medieval ballads prove that non-literate does not equate to unskilled or unintelligent. Moreover, the overall view of life and living conditions that they offer should dispel any notions we may still have of the Middle Ages as a period unified by faith and courtly idealism. Here we find instead the impulse which led to the great peasant and laborer uprisings of the thirteenth and fourteenth centuries, to the

*Lollard movement toward a more accessible religion, and eventually to the democratic impulse that broke down feudal barriers in the fifteenth through the seventeenth centuries.

That the traditional ballads concern themselves as much with arguing for a different world view and an alternate value system as with the stories they relate, that they operate on a philosophical level as well as provide entertainment, accounts for their quite amazing survival. In contrast, the lack of the same in the broadsides ensured their demise shortly after the situation prompting their composition dissipated or changed. Only scholars of the medieval period have ever heard of *London Lickpenny*, but any folksong enthusiast can hum a few bars of *Barbara Allen, Greensleeves*, or *Scarborough Fair*. But songs passed on from one generation to another are not the only way in which a ballad can survive. When a particular set of conditions ceases to exist, the same general outlook and attitude can transfer itself to a new situation.

Billie McGee Magar, a mid-twentieth-century American ballad from the Midwest, provides a fascinating study of changes in balladry. Still dimly recognizable as the tale of *The Twa Corbies*, this song transforms the dead knight into a dead horse, which "some cruel butcher's slain," lying on the great plains of middle America instead of the fields or ditches of England. Nonetheless, as in its medieval antecedent, the carrion birds--this time, crows-- make use of the meat it provides, still sitting on a neck bone and picking out eyes. The pragmatic and pessimistic perceptions of the medieval commoner resurface in the songs of rural America during the dust-bowl era . . . as they do today in the parodic and tragic ballads of Montana, Wyoming, and Idaho in the West, and of Tennessee, Kentucky, and Louisiana in the South.

Thus far, mention has been made of several thematic divisions in the medieval ballads. As one would expect, classifications are inexact tools, and a single ballad may operate primarily in one arena while exhibiting characteristics of one or several others. This being said, along with the chivalric, the religious, the romantic, and the domestic (the catch-all classification for the majority of ballads that do not fall under any other), two other types merit consideration here. The supernatural ballads are particularly interesting for their preservation of pre-Norman practices and beliefs. That superstition dies hard, and hardest among country folk, is a banality borne out by balladry of the Middle Ages. Fairies and elves, doors to the underworld (or otherworld), dwarves, giants, and demons, enchantments of every variety--all find a home in the folk song of the period. Underlying their entertainment value, however, is a system of belief that predates Christianity and coexisted with that faith for centuries after the British Isles were supposedly converted. Here we find ancestors dwelling as corporeal dead in a parallel world, the gates to which open more easily at some times than others (the origins of our modern *Halloween). We know that the dead are sentient and physical, disturbed by too much mourning (e.g. *The Unquiet Grave*) or by calling their names (*Earl Bran*), and that, for some reason, they have ill intentions toward even those they loved in life (*The Demon Lover*). We also find remnants of a nature religion, in which trees, plants, streams, and places have spirits (*Young Aiken*), and where fairies dance, luring mortals to magical worlds where time passes differently and the unconscious reigns (*Thomas Rhymer*). In short, an entire folk wisdom based upon the spiritual truths of an earlier period can be found in the supernatural ballads of medieval times.

Just as the ballads offer us a glimpse into the past beyond the Middle Ages, so do they foreshadow those to come. The so-called yeoman ballads-- produced by the rural class of that name dividing the peasant from the nobility-- exhibit a peculiar hybrid of the commoners' and the aristocracy's views. The yeomenry rose from the ranks of the peasants, finally acquiring their own land and, with it, some wealth. They slowly acquired a level of education and a higher status in the employment of the nobility, even establishing a level of a sort in the feudal military hierarchy. Thus they aspired to (and after a few centuries attained) a near equality with the lesser nobility. Not surprisingly, such people required a certain level of conformity with the ideology of their social betters. Nonetheless, the yeomen never entirely lost the sensibilities of the class from that they arose, and the odd mixture of the two manifested itself in the outlaw hero archetype which dominates their song. Ballads of Robin Hood and Johnnie Cock and Adam Bell exalt heroes as much for their canniness (they are all, for example, masters of disguise, puns, and the shady deal) and their pure physical prowess as for their honor and piety. They are loyal to the king and conform, even in their outlaw groups, to a kind of feudal hierarchy. Nonetheless, they *are* outlaws, at war with the aristocracy, the high church officials, and public servants such as sheriffs and foresters. Most notably, they all poach the king's deer, which is itself a handy metaphor for the social position of the class as a whole. Caught in the middle, aspiring to the ranks of the nobility and thereby domination over the class from which it arose, on the one hand, and abhorring the abuse of the commoners by greedy and selfish abbots and aristocrats, on the other, dreaming of honor and romance yet bound by the pragmatism of generations, the yeomanry was neither fish nor fowl nor good red herring. Such is reflected in the yeoman ballads. The unifying force underlying these diverse perceptions is, again, the democratic tendency that eventually led to the crumbling of the feudal system and the ability of the middle classes, rural and urban alike, to break through class barriers, so that by the reign of Elizabeth I the sons of tradesmen could occupy positions of influence such as those held by Christopher Marlowe, Walter Ralegh, and John Donne.

Medieval balladry, then, far from being the inexpert poetry of docile imitators of a paternal aristocracy, represents the voice of the majority in the England of the Middle Ages. As art, it raised irony and parody to new levels of sophistication; as a document of social history, it reveals the inequities and abuses of the feudal system; as philosophy, it recognizes with piercing clarity the weaknesses of the complex aristocratic ideology and the inadequacies of the medieval church. Above all, the ballad represents change--in ideals and approaches, in social structure, in poetics. In it the Middle Ages survive in all their diversity and discovery, and in it the past and the future are met.

SELECTED BIBLIOGRAPHY

Buchan, David. *The Ballad and the Folk*. London: Routledge and Kegan Paul, 1972; Cantor, Norman. *The Medieval Reader*. New York: HarperCollins, 1994; Child, Francis. *The English and Scottish Popular Ballads*. 5 vols. Boston: Houghton Mifflin, 1882-98; Defoe, Daniel. "The Ballad Maker's Plea." *Daniel Defoe: His Life and Recently Discovered Writings*. William Lee, ed. New York: Franklin, 1969; Fowler, David C. *A Literary History of the Popular Ballad*. Durham: Duke University Press, 1968; Garb<ty, Thomas J. "Rhyme, Romance, Ballad, Burlesque, and the Confluence of Form." In *Fifteenth-Century Studies: Recent Essays*. Robert F. Yeager, ed. Hamden, CT: Archon, 1984. 283-301; Hodgart, M. J. C. *The Ballads*. 2nd ed. London: Hutchinson, 1962; Lewis, W.S. *The Yale Edition of Horace Walpole's Correspondence*. New Haven: Yale UP, 1947. Lord, Albert B. *The Singer of Tales*. Cambridge: Harvard University Press, 1960; Morgan, Gwendolyn. *Medieval Balladry and the Courtly Tradition*. New York: Peter Lang, 1993. Morgan, Gwendolyn. *Medieval Ballads: Chivalry, Romance, and Everyday Life*. New York: Peter Lang, 1996; Moore, Arthur K. "The Literary Status of the English Popular Ballad." *Comparative Literature* 10 (1958) 1-20; Oates, Joyce Carol. "The English and Scottish Traditional Ballads." *Southern Review* 15 (1979) 560-66; Pearsall, Derek. *Old and Middle English Poetry*. London: Routledge and Kegan Paul, 1977; Percy, Thomas. *Reliques of Ancient English Poetry*. 1765. Reprint. London: Bickers and Sons, 1876; Pinto, Vivian de Solo, and Allan Edwin Rodway, eds. *The Common Muse*. London: Chatto and Windus, 1957; Richmond, Edson. *Ballad Scholarship: An Annotated Bibliography*. New York: Garland Press, 1989; Warton, Thomas. *History of English Poetry*. 1774. Rpt. Ed. Rene Wellek. New York: Johnson Reprint Corps. 1968; Wimberley, L.C. *Folklore in the English and Scottish Popular Ballads*. New York: Frederick Ungar, 1959.

Gwendolyn Morgan

BALLADE. A popular artificial medieval French verse form, the ballade is not to be confused with the *ballad. Early usage of the ballade form dictated that the work contain three stanzas and an *envoy. The number of lines per stanza and syllables per line varied.

Ballades typically contained refrains that repeated the motif of the poem. These occurred regularly at the end of each stanza and envoy. The envoy was, logically, of import due to its perorative position and was usually addressed to the poet's patron or some other esteemed individual. Additionally, ballades usually incorporated only three rhymes in the entire poem; the only place that a rhyme was repeated was in the refrain. The most common rhyme scheme of the ballade was *ababbcbc*, with the envoy having the scheme *bcbc*. The most noted use of the ballade is Geoffrey *Chaucer's "Balade de Bon Conseyl."

SELECTED BIBLIOGRAPHY

Cropp, Glynnis M. "Fortune and the Poet in Ballades of Eustache Deschamps, Charles d'Orleans, and François Villon." *Medium Ævum* 58:1 (1989), 125-32; Phillips, Helen.

"Literary Allusion in Chaucer's Ballade 'Hyd, Absalon, Thy Gilte Tresses Clere.'" *Chaucer Review* 30:2 (1995), 134-49.

Robert T. Lambdin

BARBARA ALLEN. Still popular today, the *ballad *Barbara Allen* dates from at least the fifteenth century, for it was already in broadside by the sixteenth, and its use of a variety of medieval motifs (notably the sympathetic grave plants) associates it with even earlier *romances. It has a number of extant versions, differing mainly in the motivation of the heroine. Although considered a "romantic ballad," the song is atypical of this classification in that the sympathies lie with the romantic and idealistic, rather than the pragmatic.

The song describes the purportedly "cruel" response of the heroine to a young noble dying of love for her. At his request, she goes to see him but refuses to offer any vows of devotion. Her reason is always simple: either he has insulted her in the past and she is exacting revenge, or she sees that there is no way to save him and so will not waste her time. The young man dies, and seeing his corpse (in one version) or at the behest of her friends (in others), Barbara Allen repents of her cold response and herself dies of remorse.

Barbara Allen is notable not only for its remarkable longevity, but also for its typical gender specific attitudes, where the male is idealistic and romantic, usually to his injury or demise, and the female solidly pragmatic in attitude and in actions and concerns. Surprisingly, though, the practical heroine relents and condemns herself to the same tragic fate as her admirer.

SELECTED BIBLIOGRAPHY

Edson, Richmond.   *Ballad Scholarship: An Annotated Bibliography*. New York: Garland, 1989; Fowler, David C.   *A Literary History of the Popular Ballad*. Durham: Duke University Press, 1968; Moore, Arthur K.   "The Literary Status of the English Popular Ballad." *Comparative Literature* 10 (1958), 1-20; Morgan, Gwendolyn. *Medieval Balladry and the Courtly Tradition*. New York: Peter Lang, 1993; Morgan, Gwendolyn.   *Medieval Ballads: Chivalry, Romance, and Everyday Life*.   New York: Peter Lang, 1996; Oates, Joyce Carol.   "The English and Scottish Traditional Ballads." *Southern Review* 15 (1979), 560-66; Pearsall, Derek.   *Old and Middle English Poetry*. London: Routledge and Kegan Paul, 1977; Wimberley, L.C.   *Folklore in the English and Scottish Ballads*. Chicago: University of Chicago Press, 1928.

Gwendolyn Morgan

BARBOUR, JOHN (c. 1320-95). Of all of the so-called "Scottish Chaucerians," John Barbour is probably the most renowned. More is known about his life than is actually known about Geoffrey *Chaucer. Barbour was probably educated both at Oxford and Paris. He was also the archbishop at

Aberdeen (1357) as well as one of the royal auditors. More importantly, Barbour composed The *Bruce, a work of more than 13,00 lines in octosyllabic couplets. The work is broken into 20 books which chronicle the renowned Scot, Robert Bruce.

This is the only work that can be certainly linked to him. The work is novel because it is presented more from the perspective of a historian than that of a teller of tales. Critics debate whether or not John Ramsey, who composed both manuscripts in which The Bruce appears, emended the poem in any way. Ramsey's manuscripts are dated 1487 and 1489. The work contains graphic descriptions of the battle at Bannockburn where Bruce's army defeated Edward II's, and Bruce was named king of Scotland. The work is a precursor to those of Walter Scott, especially in its contents, which include humor, gore, and an innate understanding of the history it presents. Three other works are often ascribed to Barbour: The Troy Book, The Lives of the Saints, and The Buik of Alexander, a translation of two French *romances.

SELECTED BIBLIOGRAPHY

Purdon, Liam O., and Julian Wasserman. "Chivalry and Feudal Obligation in Barbour's Bruce." in The Rusted Hauberk: Feudal Ideals of Order and Their Decline. Liam O. Purdon and Cindy L. Vitto, eds. Gainesville: University Press of Florida, 1994; 77-95. Watt, Diane. "Nationalism in Barbour's Bruce." Parergon 12:1 (July 1994), 89-107; Wilson, Grace G. "Barbour's Bruce and Hary's Wallace: Complements, Compensations, and Conventions." Studies in Scottish Literature 25 (1990), 189-201.

Robert T. Lambdin

BARD. The term "bard" historically refers to the poets who recited verses that glorified the deeds of heroes, leaders, and people of repute; usually the bards are associated with the Celts. These recitations were often accompanied by musical instruments such as lutes and harps. Bards were similar to the Norman *trouvéres, the Scandinavian *skald, and the *Provençal troubadours.

SELECTED BIBLIOGRAPHY

Holman, C. Hugh, and William Harmon. A Handbook to Literature. 5th ed. New York, Macmillan, 1986.

Robert T. Lambdin

BARLAAM AND JOSAPHAT. Apparently a Christianized version of the Buddha legend, the twelfth-century * Anglo-Norman *romance Barlaam and Josaphat tells of the hermit Barlaam's conversion of Josaphat, the son of Abenner, an Italian king and a Saracen. Upon Josephat's conversion, Abenner becomes extremely irate, but after his initial ill will he reconsiders his attitude toward his son's changed theology and is eventually converted himself. After Abenner's death Josaphat ascends to the throne, only to abdicate and leave his people so that he may become a hermit, for he prefers to emulate the life of his mentor.

SELECTED BIBLIOGRAPHY

Drabble, Margaret, ed. *The Oxford Companion to English Literature.* 1932. 5th ed. Oxford: Oxford University Press, 1985; Swanton, Michael. *English Literature before Chaucer.* New York: Longman, 1987.

Robert T. Lambdin

BATTLE OF BRUNNANBURGH, THE. The Old English poem *The Battle of Brunnanburgh* appears in the **Anglo-Saxon Chronicle* under the year A. D. 937. More than half of the half-lines are exact quotations from other **Anglo-Saxon poems, making it an early form of anthology.

The narrative describes a conspiracy of Danes who lived north of the Humber River with their kin in Ireland, the Scottish king Constantius, and the Strathclyde Britons under the leadership of King Eugenius against Ethelstan, king of Wessex. The conspirators gathered in the south of Northumbria. In the pitched battle at Brunnanburg they were met on the field by Ethelstan and soundly defeated. Although the site of the battle has never been exactly identified, a great hoard of silver ingots and coins from no later than A. D. 950 were dug up near Preston as early as 1840. Scholars suggest that this may have been the war chest of the conspiracy.

Ethelstan the King and Edmund the Etheling won honor at Brunnanburg, "Defending their firesides. . . . against foeman invaders." On the other hand, five chieftains, seven earls of Anlaf, and unnumbered Norsemen and Scots perished in the battle. Silver-haired Constantius, "Full of age and evil," crept back northward. The defeated returned to Dublin in Ireland; victorious Ethelstan and Edmund the Etheling, "warriors exultant," to the wide land of Wessex. The hyperbolic claim is made that

> Not worse was the slaughter
> Ever on this island . . . . at any time,
> Or more folk felled . . . . as is said in old books
> In ancient authors, . . . since from the east hither
> The Angles and Saxons . . . eagerly sailed
> Over the salt sea . . . . in search of Britain.

This familiar convention breathes life into the poem and intensifies the greediness of the creatures, including the eagle, wolf, and raven, that feast upon the defeated conspirators.

SELECTED BIBLIOGRAPHY

Alexander, Michael. Trans. *The Earliest English Poems: A Bilingual Edition.* Berkeley and Los Angeles: University of California Press, 1970; Campbell, Jackson J. ed. *The Advent Lyrics of the Exeter Book.* Princeton: Princeton University Press, 1959; Clemoes, Peter. *Interactions of Thought and Language in Old English Poetry.* Cambridge: Cambridge University Press, 1995; Clemoes, Peter. "Language in Context: 'Her' in the 890 *Anglo-Saxon Chronicle.*" *Leeds Studies in English* 16(1985), 27-36; Conybeare, John Josias. *Illustrations of Anglo-Saxon Poetry.* William Daniel Conybeare, ed. New York: Haskell House, 1964; Faust, Cosette and Stith Thompson. *Old English Poems: Translated into the Original Meter Together with Short Selections from Old English Prose.* Norwood Editions, 1977; Garmonsway, G. N., trans. *The Anglo-Saxon Chronicle.* London: Dent, 1990; Hamer, Richard. *A Choice of Anglo-Saxon Verse, Selected, with an Introduction and Parallel Verse Translation.* London: Faber, Ltd, 1970; Kaiser, Rolf. *Medieval English: An Old English and Middle English Anthology.* West Berlin: Markobrunner Str. 21, 1961; Kennedy, Charles. *Old English Elegies: Translated into Alliterative Verse with a Critical Introduction.* Princeton: Princeton University Press, 1936; Kennedy, Charles. *An Anthology of Old English Poetry: Translated into Alliterative Verse.* New York: Oxford University Press, 1960; Lehnert, Martin. *Poetry and Prose of the Anglo-Saxons.* Vol. 1: *Texts.* Halle: Veb Max Niemayer Verlag, 1960; Niles, John D. "Sign and Psyche in Old English Poetry." *The American Journal of Semiotics* 9:4 (1992), 11-25; Spaeth, J. Duncan. *Old English Poetry: Translations into Alliterative Verse with Introduction and Notes.* New York: Gordian Press, 1967.

Karl Hagen

"BATTLE OF FINNSBURGH." The "Battle of Finnsburgh" relates an episode in *Old English literature of which two versions survive: as one of the *scop's stories in *Beowulf* (ll. 1063-1159) and as an independent story, of which only one short fragment survives. This fragment, a single manuscript folio containing forty-eight lines of verse, was discovered and printed in the early eighteenth-century, but the original has since been lost.

The full story relates how a Danish princess Hildeburh, sister of Hnæf, was married to Finn, king of the Frisians, in the attempt to end an old feud. While Hnæf is visiting his sister, the feud breaks out again and Hnæf is slain. After a long and inconclusive fight, Hengest, leader of the surviving Danes arranges a truce with Finn. Winter, however, forces Hengest and the other Danes to remain at Finn's hall, and eventually the desire to avenge Hnæf causes Hengest to break the truce and kill Finn and his retainers.

The Finnsburg Fragment describes a period during the first of the fights, while Hnæf is still alive. The Danes have barricaded themselves in the hall and are holding it against assault for five days. The Fragment has generally been read as an explanatory gloss upon the rather allusive episode described in *Beowulf*. It testifies to a body of Germanic stories which we can now only glimpse fragmentarily but which must have been well known to an *Anglo-Saxon audience.

SELECTED BIBLIOGRAPHY

Breeze, Andrew. "'Finnsburgh' and 'Maldon': 'Celaes Bord, Cellod Bord.'" *Notes and Queries* 39(237):3 (September 1992), 267-69; O'Keeffe, Katherine O'Brien, ed. *Old English Shorter Poems: Basic Readings*. New York: Garland, 1994.

Karl Hagen

BATTLE OF MALDON, THE. The *Battle of Maldon* is an *Old English poem about an actual battle between Viking raiders and the men of Essex, led by Byrhtnoth, that took place in A. D. 991. The original manuscript was destroyed in the Cotton Library fire of 1731, and the poem only survived thanks to a copy made a few years earlier. The beginning and the end of the poem were missing when the copy was made, but the story of the battle is virtually complete.

Vikings have landed on the island of Northey in the river Pante (Essex), near the town of Maldon. Byrhtnoth marshals his troops on the river bank, and the Vikings demand tribute, which Byrhtnoth refuses scornfully. After some initial skirmishing, Byrhtnoth agrees to allow the Vikings to cross a narrow causeway exposed at low tide so that the battle can be joined in full. In the course of battle, Byrhtnoth is killed, and the rest of the poem charts the reactions of his followers. On seeing their lord slain, a number of the English flee. Godric takes Byrhtnoth's horse, which causes others to retreat, convinced that it is Byrhtnoth himself who withdraws. The remaining retainers dedicate themselves to avenging their lord or dying in the effort.

Critics are generally agreed that the poem's principal theme is heroism in the face of defeat, and that the poem draws on the traditional Germanic expectations of loyalty shown by retainers toward their lord. The treatment of heroism has been disputed. Much discussion has centered around the term *ofermod*, "pride," which is used to describe Byrhtnoth's decision to allow the Vikings over the causeway. Some critics argue that Byrhtnoth's rashness in pursuit of glory ultimately undermines the traditional warrior's code of heroic conduct. Others have argued that confidence, even overconfidence, is a natural part of the heroic ethic and part of what makes heroes admirable and worthy of their followers' devotion.

SELECTED BIBLIOGRAPHY

Bravo, Antonio. "Prayer as a Literary Device in "The Battle of Maldon" and in the Poem of the *Cid*." *SELIM: Journal of the Spanish Society for Medieval English*

Language and Literature 2 (1992), 31-46; O'Keeffe, Katherine O'Brien, ed. *Old English Shorter Poems: Basic Readings*. New York: Garland, 1994; Scragg, Donald, ed. *The Battle of Maldon, AD 991*. Oxford: Blackwell, 1991; Stork, Nancy Porter. "Maldon, the Devil, and the Dictionary." *Exemplaria* 5:1 (Spring 1993), 111-34.

Karl Hagen

BEAST EPIC. (BEAST FABLE). The medieval literary form of the beast epic consists of a series of linked stories grouped around animal characters. The beast epic often presents a satirical commentary about events related to the church or the court. The work was novel in that it gave human qualities to beast characters, for example, Chanticleer in Geoffrey *Chaucer's *"Nun's Priest's Tale."

It is believed that the stories originated in popular tradition and were given literary form by monastic scholars and *trouvères, or that later *Scholastics were the originators. The oldest author of beast epics seems to be Paulus Diacinus, who was a cleric at Charlemagne's court; he composed these works around 780.

It is not clear whether the form first developed in Germany or France. However, the genre flourished in the twelfth and thirteenth-centuries in northern France, western Germany, and Flanders. The beast epic typically has an episode that forms the nucleus of the story. An example of this is the sick lion being healed by wrapping himself in a wolf's skin, as prescribed by the fox. Other animals common to the form are the cat, the hare, the camel, and the badger. Among the best-known beast epics are those dealing with *Reynard the Fox.

SELECTED BIBLIOGRAPHY

Holman, C. Hugh, and William Harmon. *A Handbook to Literature*. 5th ed. New York: Macmillan, 1986; Needler, Howard. "The Animal Fable Among Other Medieval Literary Genres." *New Literary History* 22:2 (Spring 1991), 423-39; Varty, Kenneth. "Renart through the Looking Glass: The Passage of the Fox from One Fictitious World to Another in the *Roman de Renart*." *Bestia* 3 (May 1991), 68-73; Ziolkowski, Jan M. *Talking Animals: Medieval Latin Beast Poetry, 750-1150*. Philadelphia: University of Pennsylvania Press. 1993.

Robert T. Lambdin

BECKET, ST. THOMAS (c. 1118-1170). Thomas Becket was born to Gilbert Becket, who saw to it that his son was well educated, as Thomas attended universities at London and Paris and eventually studied canon law at both Bologna and Auxerre. He was later appointed chancellor by *Henry II, an action that resulted in a very close friendship between the two. In 1162, Henry named Thomas archbishop of Canterbury, a position that placed Thomas in direct conflict with his friend. Henry had placed him in the position hoping that Becket would give in to the king's every whim. However, the opposite occurred. Becket found himself leaning more toward the role of an ascetic monk and determined that he would become the people's spiritual leader. This led to a feeling of insecurity by Henry, who, as king, attempted to curtail the rights of the church which he saw as an imposition upon his rule. Thus the two had a series of disputes that quickly escalated into a major conflict. Becket especially opposed the Constitutions of Clarendon (1164), in which Henry attempted to force the church to recognize the king's power over everything in his kingdom. Becket responded to this strong-arm tactic by reimposing the relations of the church and state from the time of *William I (1066-87).

Becket was especially upset over the maverick point that no clerical appeal could be made to Rome without the authority of the English monarch. At first Becket acceded to this, but he quickly repented and appealed to the pope for mercy. The misgivings between Henry and Thomas grew until Becket finally fled to the Continent and asked the pope for assistance. This directly usurped the tenets of the Clarendon Constitutions. He returned in 1170 after the pope assured him that no cleric would be tried twice (by the state and by the church) for the same crime, a scenario made possible by Henry's bequest. The pair had a brief reconciliation, but animosity soon ruled again, and further arguments ensued. Henry felt betrayed by Becket, whom he had trusted implicitly; by breaking his oath to the king, Becket was conceived by Henry to be a traitor. Henry ordered Becket assassinated on December 29, 1170. Henry claimed that his orders were misinterpreted; nevertheless, he fell into disfavor with the church. The pope restored Henry only after he was appropriately humiliated.

Becket's shrine at Canterbury became a popular site for pilgrims. This was the goal of Geoffrey *Chaucer's pilgrims in his *Canterbury Tales, composed in the late fourteenth century, some two hundred years after the murder.

SELECTED BIBLIOGRAPHY

Gullick, Michael. "A Twelfth-Century Manuscript of the Letters of Thomas Becket." *English Manuscript Studies 1100 1700.* 2 (1990), 1-31; O'Reilly, Jennifer. "'Candidus et Rubicundus': An Image of Martyrdom in the 'Lives' of Thomas Becket." *Analecta Bollandiana* 99.3-4 (1981), 303-14; Peters, Timothy. "Elements of the *Chanson de Geste* in an Old French *Life of Becket*: Garnier's *Vie de Saint Thomas le Martyr*." *Olifhant* 18: 3-4 (Fall 1994), 278-88; Roberts, Phyllis B. "Archbishop Stephen Langton and His Preaching on Thomas Becket in 1220." in *De Ore Domini: Preacher and the Word in the Middle Ages*. Thomas Amos, Eugene Green, et al, eds. Kalamazoo, MI: Medieval Institution Publications, 1989. 75-92.

Robert T. Lambdin

BEDE, ST., THE VENERABLE (673?-735). Although Christianity had been brought to Northumbria only fifty years earlier, the twin monasteries of Wearmouth and Jarrow were well established in 680 when Bede, at age seven, was brought by kinsmen to Wearmouth and consecrated to lifelong service to God. The rest of his life was spent at Wearmouth and Jarrow, where his writing, virtually a summary of the learning of his day, earned him the reputation of being the greatest scholar in Western Europe. His genius and goodness so impressed his peers that he was ordained at nineteen although the usual age for holy orders was twenty-five. He was beatified in 1899. He was early set to teach younger boys, and his first works were textbooks on orthography (spelling) and meter. *De Orthographia* consists of several hundred words, each the subject of comment intended to aid beginning students of Latin. *De Arte Metrica* and *De Schematibus et Tropis* were intended for more advanced pupils ready to try Latin verse and the use of figures of speech.

Nearly all of his writing--theological, historical, or scientific--was didactic, aimed at strengthening the knowledge and faith of both clergy and laity. *De Natura Rerum* (The nature of things) is a book of elementary science for his pupils and fellow monks. It presents the universe as described in the Bible and explained by the church fathers and his own keen observations. One of its now-outdated concepts is that the global earth lay at the center of the universe, surrounded by seven heavens: air, ether, Olympus, fiery space, firmament, heaven of angels, and heaven of Trinity. His two widely used books on time, *De Temporibus* (703) and *De Temporum Ratione* (725), were also written as manuals for use in the schoolrooms of Wearmouth and Jarrow. In addition to the everyday need to establish time for monastic schedules and lay festivals, Bede's theological world was concerned with past and future ages. Leading church fathers conceived of the temporal world as having six ages: Creation, the Flood, Abraham, David, the Captivity of Judah, and the birth of Christ.

Chronographers reached differing conclusions about the year in which the first age began, but most chose a figure between 5,000 and 5,500 years before Advent. Bede asserted that no one but God knew how much of the sixth age remained, but when his careful calculations greatly shortened two of the ages and hence the time from Creation to the Birth of Christ, he was, to his horror, accused of heresy. He successfully defended himself, and in his masterpiece, *The Ecclesiastical History of the English People* (731), he abandoned the use of *annus mundi* (the year of the world), standard with Eusebius, *Jerome and *Isidore, and used instead *annus domini* (the year of the Lord). This was the first major historical work to use this latter term, yet we have now become so used to it that we find it difficult to appreciate the magnitude of Bede's achievement.

Bede wrote thirty-five prose and some verse works, in Latin, including Bible commentary, the lives of saints, science, and history. The most famous is *The Ecclesiastical History*, which reviews British history from Caesar's invasion in 55 B. C. to Bede's day and is considered the indispensable primary source for English history from 597 to 731. Bede gathered his information from all the written records at his disposal, from oral tradition, and from travelers and eye witnesses. Bede cited many of his sources, not a common practice.

While books were laboriously produced and scarce, the emphasis on education was paramount with Bede and his two great abbots, Benedict Biscop, founder of Wearmouth and Jarrow, and Bede's mentor, Ceolfrith, also a recognized scholar. Hence the library at Jarrow was impressive, but the greatness of Bede's work is due to his broad logic and his perception of significant incidents and concepts. *Ecclesiastical History* has been translated and studied from the days of *Charlemagne and *Alfred the Great to modern times.

SELECTED BIBLIOGRAPHY

Colgrave, B., and R.A.B. Mynors, eds. *Bede's Ecclesiastical History of the English People*. Oxford: Clarendon Press, 1969; Holder, Arthur G. "The Venerable Bede and the Mysteries of Our Salvation." *American Benedictine Review* 42:2 (June 1991), 140-62; McNamara, John. "Bede's Role in Circulating Legend in *Historia Ecclesiastica. Anglo-Saxon Studies in Archaeology* 7 (1994), 61-69; O'Hare, Colman. "The Story of Caedmon: Bede's Account of the First English Poet." *American Benedictine Review* 43:3 (September 1992), 345-57.

Esther Smith

BEOWULF. The most famous of all *Old English poems, *Beowulf* survives in a single manuscript, now partly damaged by fire, written around the year 1000. The poem chronicles the deeds of Beowulf as a youth and an old man. It opens in Denmark at the hall of king Hrothgar. For twelve years this hall, Heorot, has been invaded each evening by the monster Grendel, who seizes and eats the thegns sleeping there. Beowulf, the nephew of Hygelac, king of the Geats (in the southeast of present-day Sweden), hears of Grendel's depredations and sails to Hrothgar to offer his aid. After an evening of speeches and feasting where he vows to fight the monster without benefit of weapons, Beowulf and his companions go to sleep in the hall. True to his pattern, Grendel bursts into the hall and fights with Beowulf, who proves to be too strong for the monster. As Grendel attempts to flee, Beowulf tears off his arm, leaving the monster to run back to its lair to die. After a day of celebration Hrothgar's men once again sleep in the hall, only to find that the terror is not over. Grendel's mother comes to the hall and seizes Hrothgar's chief advisor in vengeance for her son's death. Beowulf pursues Grendel's mother to her lair under a foreboding mere where he fights and kills her thanks to a sword, the work of giants, that hangs on the wall of the cave.

After still more feasting during which Hrothgar gives Beowulf both lavish gifts and sage advice, Beowulf and his companions return home, where he tells his adventures to his uncle Hygelac. Then the poem shifts with only a rapid transition to Beowulf's old age, after he has become king and ruled for fifty years. A thief discovers a dragon's barrow and steals a costly cup, in revenge for which the dragon rampages through Beowulf's realm, burning even Beowulf's own hall. Although now quite old, Beowulf arms himself and sets out with a band of retainers to fight the dragon. When the battle is joined, however, all his retainers except one Wiglaf flee in terror. Despite this desertion, Beowulf and Wiglaf manage to kill the dragon, although Beowulf is mortally wounded in the fight. The poem concludes with Beowulf's funeral.

Much about *Beowulf* remains under dispute, in large measure because critics have been unable to agree on a particular context in which to place the poem. Traditionally, most scholars were agreed that the poem dated from the eighth century. The poem was thus read in the context of the flourishing Latin culture in the age of *Bede. More recently, arguments have been made to date the poem later, perhaps to the period after *Alfred had established English as a medium for serious literature. Whatever the poem's date, however, its focus is retrospective in nature, as it is set several hundred years in the past and in the ancestral home of the *Anglo-Saxons before their migration. Equally controversial is the attitude expressed toward Beowulf and the heroic ethic generally. That the *Beowulf* poet was Christian is undoubted, but some have argued that the narrator censures the poem's characters as pagans and critiques the heroic ethic as vainglorious. Others have seen the poet as taking a more tolerant position recognizing the pre-Christian nature of the characters but admiring them for their heroic achievements.

SELECTED BIBLIOGRAPHY

Bammesberger, Alfred. "Beowulf's Last Will." *English Studies* 77:4 (July 1996), 305-10; Bjork, Robert E. "Speech as Gift in Beowulf." *Speculum* 69:4 (October 1994), 993-1022; Davis, Craig R. *"Beowulf" and the Demise of Germanic Legend in England."* New York: Garland, 1996; Hill, John M. *The Cultured World in "Beowulf."* Toronto: University of Toronto Press, 1995; Lionarons, Joyce Tally. "*Beowulf*: Myth and Monsters." *English Studies* 77:1 (January 1996), 1-14; Niles, John D. "'Editing' *Beowulf*: What Can Study of Ballads Tell Us?" *Oral Traditions* 9:2 (October1994), 440-67; Niles, John D. "Sign and Psyche in Old English Poetry." *American Journal of Semiotics* 9:4 (1992), 11-25.

Karl Hagen

BERNARD OF CLAIRVAUX, ST. (1090-1153). A French cleric, Bernard became a member of the Cistercian Abbey in 1113. Two years later, at age twenty-four, he founded and became abbot of a new monastery at Clairvaux, where he remained until his death.

Bernard gained a reputation as a preacher, and crowds of pilgrims flocked to Clairvaux to hear his speeches. He played a major role in the development of the Augustinian contemplative theological tradition, stressing the importance of faith rather than reason. His beliefs put him at odds with Peter *Abelard's dialectical theological method, a technique Bernard condemned at Soissons and Sens in 1141.

Bernard espoused the role of a personal mysticism in his thoughts; this led to his presentation of the "Cistercian Program" which explicated a progression from carnal to spiritual love. This component of his thought influenced writers, including *Dante, for centuries. His mysticism emphasizes God's forgiveness and Augustinian dogma. This was also a direct assault on the Neoplatonists' emphasis upon the intentional feats of man's contemplative labors. Bernard was a key figure in Pope Innocent II's triumph over the claims of the antipope Peter of Leon. In 1146 he called on his people to crusade in the name of Pope Eugenius II; this caused Louis VII of France to organize the Second *Crusade. Bernard was canonized in 1175.

SELECTED BIBLIOGRAPHY

Billy, Dennis J. "Redemption and the Order of Love in Bernard of Clairvaux's 'Sermon 20' on 'The Canticles of Canticles.'" *Downside Review* 112:387 (April 1994), 88-102; Guzzardo, John. "'Paradiso XXXIII': St. Bernard's Prayer." *Italian Culture* 12 (1994), 45-57; McGinn, Bernard "Freedom, Formation, and Reformation: The Anthropological Roots of St. Bernard's Spiritual Teaching." *Analecta Cisterciensia* 46:1-2 (January-December 1990), 91-114; Renna, Thomas. "Bernard and Bede." *American Benedictine Review* 44:3 (September 1993), 223-35.

Robert T. Lambdin

BESTIARIES. A series of short poems that allegorize various animals with a Christian application or moral, the medieval Bestiaries were derived from the ancient Greek *Physiologus* or *Book of Nature*, composed around a. d. 200. The Middle English *Bestiary* is more detailed than its source, which included only three sketches. The medieval version contains beasts adopted from the eleventh-century Latin *Physiologus* of Theobaldus. Although they were usually perused solely for their fictitious natural history, these works aimed to teach moral and religious lessons. The Whale stood for Satan, the Panther for the three days before Christ's ascension from the dead, and the Elephant for Adam's fall.

Those composed in twelfth and thirteenth-century England were usually grandly illustrated, and they must have been popular for many of these manuscripts are extant. Coupled with their moral overtones, the animals became influential on much medieval literature, as their very mention in texts immediately elicited meaning. Bestiaries differed from the beast fables (see **Beast Epic**), as exemplified by the famous *Reynard the Fox, which presented a more satirical delivery or moral, unlike the allegorical examinations of the bestiaries.

SELECTED BIBLIOGRAPHY

Cole, Roger L. "Beast Allegory in the Late Medieval Sermon in Strasbourg: The Example of John Von den vier Lewengeschrei." *Bestia* 3 (May 1991), 115-24; Duncan, Edwin. "The Middle English *Bestiary*: Missing Link in the Alliterative Long Line?" *Studia Neophilologica* 64:1 (1992), 25-33; Houwen, L.A. "Animal Parallelism in Medieval Literature and the *Bestiaries*: A Preliminary Investigation." *Neophilologus* 78:3 (July 1994), 483-96.

Robert T. Lambdin

BEVIS OF HAMPTON.   Based on the twelfth-century *Anglo-Norman *chanson de geste Beuves de Hanstone, Bevis of Hampton* was a popular 4,620 line Middle English verse romance; it is sometimes paralleled with Shakespeare's *Hamlet*. In the romance Bevis's mother, who is married to the earl of Southampton, Guy, has her lover murder the earl. She then marries the murderer, and sells Bevis into servitude.

Bevis converts Josian, daughter of the king of Arabia, before marrying her. The two embark on a series of adventures that take them to Europe, England, and the East. While in England, Bevis kills the emperor of Germany, who happened to be his father's murderer. Other noteworthy components of this romance include the naming of Bevis's sword, Morglay, and his horse, Arundel.

SELECTED BIBLIOGRAPHY

Brownrigg, Linda. "The Taymouth Hours and the Romance of Beves of Hampton." *English Manuscript Studies 1100-1700* 1 (1989), 222-41; Jacobs, Nicholas. "Sir Degare, Lay le Freine, Beves of Hamtoun, and the 'Auchinleck Bookshop.'" *Notes and Queries* 29 (227):4 (August 1982), 294-301.

Robert T. Lambdin

BOCCACCIO, GIOVANNI (1313-1375). One of the most influential authors and literary theorists of the Italian *trecento* was Giovanni Boccaccio. A prolific writer of both poetic and prose fiction, he is widely acknowledged by scholars to have shaped the development of vernacular prose fiction in Italy and across Europe. Boccaccio's biography represented a vexed question for scholars until the middle of the twentieth century. Before the detailed historical studies of scholars, including Vittore Branca, many critics falsely attributed a legitimacy to pseudo biographical information contained in some of Boccaccio's literary works, leading to a romanticized and inaccurate portrait of the Florentine poet.

Although Boccaccio is traditionally associated with *Dante and *Petrarch as one of the three great poets of the Italian vernacular renaissance, both scholarly and popular audiences tended to discount his literary accomplishment. As Bergin suggested Boccaccio's reputation as a salacious poet interfered with his acceptance as an important author until more recent times. Boccaccio's literary works, then, were often published in expurgated editions or suppressed altogether. This late-nineteenth-century scholarly skepticism was fueled by such scholars as De Sanctis, who dismissed Boccaccio's early poetry as cynical, immature, and unimportant. Therefore, scholarly attention focused primarily on his acknowledged masterpiece, *The Decameron*, and on his Latin poetry. Only recently have definitive editions of Boccaccio's earlier works been issued in Italy. In the United States and England translations of these early works as well as his Latin text *Genealogy of the Gentile Gods* into English have gotten underway only recently. This renewed interest in the Boccaccian canon indicates the growing appreciation by scholars of the complex and inventive genius of this Italian author.

Boccaccio was born in Certaldo, a tiny village outside of Florence, in June or July 1313. His father, Boccaccino, was a prominent merchant in the Tuscan city and actively participated in the emergence of Florence as a prominent mercantile and banking power during the early fourteenth century. Boccaccio was born out of wedlock; we have no historical documents that could shed light on the identity of his mother. Boccaccino legitimized Boccaccio, giving him the name Giovanni in honor of his brother, and records indicate that the family moved to the San Piero Maggiore quarter of Florence, a prosperous bourgeois neighborhood.

The Italian chronicler Filippo Villani suggested that Boccaccio received a good education, and by the age of six he could read and write. He was trained in Latin grammar and was no doubt introduced to Latin authors such as Ovid during this period, a typical pedagogical method that simultaneously instructed students in mythology, Roman history, and Latin grammar. Florentine literary culture was also approaching its height during this period, and Boccaccio probably was introduced to the works of Dante and other poets of the *dolce stil nuovo* during this period. His stepmother, Margherita de' Mardoli was related to the family of Beatrice, and, as Branca suggested, may have been one of the first to speak with Boccaccio about Beatrice and her relationship to Dante himself. In addition to this humanistic aspect of Boccaccio's education, his father expected his son to acquire the practical skills that would allow him to contribute to the family business. By the time he was eleven, Boccaccio's education focused on mathematics and commercial activity.

During this period Boccaccio's business interests led him to establish an association with the illustrious Acciaiuoli banking family in Florence; he was transferred to Naples to pursue their interests with the Angevin kingdom of Naples in 1327. In the early days of his adolescence Boccaccio attempted to serve as an apprentice in banking at the Bardi. Naples at this time was an important trading port and enjoyed a lively and famous court life, filled with intrigue, high literary culture, tournaments, and other spectacles. In this setting Boccaccio forged key friendships and ultimately abandoned his apprenticeship to devote himself exclusively to vernacular culture.

During the fourteenth century Naples enjoyed an era of relative prosperity under the Angevins. The court of King Robert was a vital and glittering one, and writing about stylized love experiences was central to much of the traditional love literature of the time. Boccaccio, straddling the mercantile and aristocratic worlds during this period, began to write his own early vernacular love poetry in this tradition. Of particular importance remains the myth he created about an imaginary love affair he pretended to enjoy with an illegitimate daughter of King Robert, Maria d'Aquino, whom he designated with the metaphorical name "Fiammetta" or "little flame." Despite some early confusion over the historical validity of Maria's existence, ultimately no historical record exists to attest to her existence as anything more than a Boccaccian fantasy, perhaps invented to relieve anxiety about his own illegitimate birth.

Boccaccio learned how to write vernacular love poetry in the Studio Napoletano under the tutelage of Cino da Pistoia, who was, following in the steps of Dante's *De vulgari eloquentia*, an important early champion of the value of vernacular poetry. In addition, Boccaccio could indulge his life-long dedication to reading and books by visiting the great royal library in Naples. According to Branca, at the royal library Boccaccio no doubt met Paolo da Perugia. From Paolo, Boccaccio learned to appreciate the Greek and Byzantine cultural traditions, which he incorporated into much of the Hellenic mythographic imagery that characterizes his early poetry, especially in the *Filostrato* and the *Teseida*. Robert's royal library housed a significant collection of literary, medical, and astrological texts. The information that Boccaccio gleaned from these editions surfaces repeatedly in all of his literary works. A large circle of learned men, including Bertrando del Balzo, an early commentator on Dante, the theologian Dionigi of Borgo San Sepolcro, and Pietro Canigiani, a relative of Petrarch, among others, had great influence on him.

Between 1330 and 1340, then, Boccaccio began to pursue his literary career in a more purposeful way. The four significant poems he completed during this period are the *Caccia di Diana* (1334?), *Il Filostrato* (1335?), *Il *Filocolo* (1336-38), and *Il Teseida* (1339-41). All four reflect Boccaccio's growing dexterity with the so-called "sweet new style," or *dolce stil nuovo*, introduced late in the thirteenth century by writers such as Dante and Guido *Cavalcanti. The *Caccia*, the earliest of these formative works, describes a group of Neapolitan ladies thinly allegorized as mythical rebels fighting against the chaste rule of the goddess Diana in favor of the eroticism of Venus. *Il Filostrato*, in contrast, whose title indicates Boccaccio's efforts to create an etymological play on Greek roots--one can render the title roughly as "he who is leveled by love"--draws more heavily on popular versions of Trojan history and employs an elaborate octave verse structure.

Composed in nine books, *Il Filostrato* relates the story of faithless Cressida, who betrays Troilo, son of Priam. The despair and anguish generated by her betrayal eventually result in Troilo's death at the hands of Achilles.

Boccaccio borrowed extensively from Benoît de Sainte-Maure's *Roman de Troie* as well as Guido delle Colonne's *Historia Troiana*. *Il Filostrato*, dedicated to a lady Boccaccio named as Filomena, foreshadows the more mature *Il Filocolo*, the first Boccaccian poem written to the mythical Fiammetta. This latter poem's title derives again from a rough transcription of Greek roots and means, basically, "love-wearied." This is a long prose *romance in five books. Of French origin, it tells of the adventures of Florio and Biancifiore, tracing their complex love story from its origins in childhood, and describes a painful separation, Florio's quest to recover his beloved, their happy wedding celebrations, their conversion to Christianity, and finally their triumphant return to their home. It is filled with long learned digressions and pseudo-autobiographical allusions; two of the short episodes related here appear again in Boccaccio's masterpiece, the *Decameron*.

In the *Teseida* Boccaccio returns to the octave verse form and the classical materials of the *Filostrato*. Drawn predominantly from Statius and the author of the *Roman de Thèbes*, the *Teseida* relates the potentially tragic story of two friends, Palamones and Arcita, prisoners in Athens, who fight to the death for the love of Emilia, the young sister of Hippolita, Amazon queen and consort of Theseus (*see* "**The Knight's Tale**"). All of these early poems demonstrate Boccaccio's fascination with and love for erudition and learnedness. These works represent considerable achievement and ambition for the young Florentine poet; however, sometime soon after the completion of the *Teseida*, political relations between Naples and Florence deteriorated, and after thirteen years Boccaccio returned to Florence by the middle of 1341.

The transition from the glittering and cosmopolitan life Boccaccio enjoyed in Naples to the more constrictive situation in Florence, recently ravaged by plague (not yet the Black Death of 1348) as well as by political and economic difficulties, proved especially troubling for the young poet. His domestic life, according to some of his letters also indicates a tension between himself and his father, Boccaccino, who was no doubt disappointed in his son's failure to follow in the footsteps of the family business. This tension was further exacerbated by Boccaccino's subsequent remarriage to Bice de' Bostichi. Nevertheless, Florence held some attractions for Boccaccio, principally in the developing cult of Dante.

Boccaccio's interest in vernacular and mercantile style increased; the popularity of mercantile and other less aristocratic types of literature that emphasized moral and allegorical themes is shown by his assembling of a large collection of Dantean texts, although his imitations of the *Divine Comedy* are already present in the *Teseida*. Moreover, Boccaccio became interested in disseminating classical mythographic materials to a larger Florentine reading public; to this end, for example, he added his glosses and commentary to the *Teseida*. The Tuscan literary tradition appears in Boccaccio's first Florentine works, the *Comedia delle Ninfe* (1341-42), and the *Amorosa Visione* (1342). The former, a beautiful pastoral poem that imitates both *Boethius's *Consolatio Philosophiae* and Dante's the *Vita nuova*, is written in the lovely *terza rima*;

the latter is an allegorical dream vision, also in tercets, that exploits figures of mythology, classical history, and contemporary political leaders as examples of virtue. Boccaccio paid particular attention to Dantean style, thereby helping to install Dante as the foremost literary figure of Tuscan and indeed Italian writing. Simultaneously, Boccaccio developed a deep and abiding admiration for Petrarch, poet laureate.

Boccaccio's next work, the *Elegia della donna Fiammetta* (1343-44), represents a radical departure from all of his previous literary efforts. Told from the point of view of Fiammetta, this prose work is set in Florence, and in it Boccaccio related the despair of the erstwhile fickle lover of his Neapolitan period after she is abandoned by her lover. Branca, in a view widely accepted by scholars, described *Fiammetta* as the first modern psychological novel. Written after a period of great social and civic unrest in Florence, scholars remain puzzled about the radical shift in this poem's style. Thomas Bergin, speculating about the loss of the ornamented style that characterized so much of Boccaccio's earlier works, suggested that *Fiammetta* is a novel of disillusionment, perhaps connected with the collapse of Florentine politics. At any rate, the years between 1344 and 1348 proved difficult for Florence; the relationship between Angevin Naples and Florence remained troubled.

Boccaccio may have written the *Ninfale Fiesolano* between 1344 and 1346, a rustic work that details the love story of the nymph Mensola, who betrays her vows of chastity to the goddess Diana with Africo, a simple shepherd. Mensola is killed by the angry goddess, and Africo kills himself in despair. Their child, Pruneo, in turn grows up and proves his worth in a variety of adventures linked to the founding of Florence and the nearby town of Fiesole.

The collapse of relations between Florence and Naples stymied Boccaccio's efforts to seek a political post in Florence, and in 1345 he travelled to Ravenna, where he met and talked with many learned men of letters who still revered the memory of Dante and his exile there. Among these the most significant was probably Donato degli Albanzani, a friend of Petrarch's. By 1348, however, the Black Death had begun its ravages across Europe, and historical documents indicate that Boccaccio, unsuccessful in his quest for a political post, had returned to Florence.

The terrible plague and its effects on the city are described by the chronicler Villani and incorporated into the introduction to Boccaccio's *Decameron* (1349-51). Boccaccio lost some of his dearest friends to this devastating pestilence, including Matteo Frescobaldi, Villani, Ventura Monachi, Bruno Casini, and a host of others. He also lost his father and stepmother Bice and was left with the responsibility for his family and his inheritance. The *Decameron*, then, was written in the context of tragedy, death, and, perhaps paradoxically, hope for those who were spared the ravages of disease.

The *Decameron*, whose title is drawn from the Greek for "ten days" is a framed narrative of one hundred stories told by the aristocratic company who assemble outside of Florence to escape the plague. This "brigata" of narrators, seven young women and three young men, each relate one story for each day of their sojourn under a rubric designated by a "queen" or "king" of the day. The narratives related within this miscellany are varied in genre, tone, and style, from the farcical to the tragic, interspersed with authorial intrusions that function as commentary to the reception of the text by its readers. Certainly the most important of Boccaccio's works in terms of its influence on literary history, the *Decameron* is arguably the starting point from which all novelistic fiction stems.

As the ravages of the plague receded, Boccaccio's involvement in foreign politics continued, and as part of these duties Boccaccio made another trip to Ravenna in August and September 1350. Upon his return to Florence one of Boccaccio's most dearly held dreams materialized: a meeting with Petrarch, who had decided to come to Florence. Boccaccio met him outside the gates of the city, gave him a traditional gift of a ring, and invited him to stay at his home as his guest. This meeting led to a close friendship that would span twenty-five years, survive intellectual and political disagreements, and generate a large correspondence recorded by Petrarch in his collections of letters, *Familiares* and *Seniles*. In this way one of the most important literary relationships in Western literary history flowered. Petrarch's influence on Boccaccio was enormous and should not be underestimated. Under Petrarch's example Boccaccio turned to the serious study of humanism that led, ultimately, to the establishment of a series of lectures on Dante at the newly instituted University of Florence, where Boccaccio eventually would teach and lecture on Dante.

The years between 1352 and 1360, however, found Boccaccio both actively involved in the political unrest that had troubled the Italian peninsula for so long and enjoying an ever-increasing reputation for literary and intellectual genius at home. In 1354 Boccaccio was entrusted with a diplomatic mission to the pope in an attempt to reconcile the city of Florence with the papacy. Petrarch's journey to Milan, where he worked for the dreaded house of Visconti, the tyrants of Lombardy, resulted in some strain in the relationship between the two poets. Nevertheless, letters of introduction from Petrarch must have assisted Boccaccio in his trip across the Alps to the Court of Avignon.

Successful in this mission, Boccaccio returned to Florence and continued to serve the city in other diplomatic matters, one of which involved a return to Naples in 1355. In fact, Boccaccio had high hopes for a post in Naples when he set out in September; however, his hopes were frustrated, no doubt in part due to the tension between his support of the papacy and the interests of his patrons, the Acciaiuoli. This antagonism continued throughout Boccaccio's lifetime. Nevertheless, his visit, as Branca reminded us, was fruitful in a different way. Boccaccio was afforded the opportunity to visit the fabulous library at Montecassino, and his interest in classical texts was revived with new urgency.

The years between 1355 and 1360 found Boccaccio with more leisure time back in Florence or in Certaldo. During this period he found time to finish his *Vita di Dante* and to revise his *Amorosa Visione*. Following up on his experiences at Montecassino, Boccaccio began his largest and most erudite work: *Genealogie deorum gentilium,* or *Genealogy of the Gentile Gods,* a Latin work devoted to recording the texts of antiquity for the growing reading public. This interest in humanistic concerns led Boccaccio, for the most part, to abandon his interest in fiction, except for his *Corbaccio,* a short text written sometime after 1360.

The reasons for this shift in focus remain obscure and are undoubtedly complex. To be sure, a good deal of the impetus for this change can be attributed to the influence of Petrarch, as their correspondence indicates. Further, a serious illness in 1355, followed by a growing anxiety about death, may also have contributed to the increased seriousness with which Boccaccio approached his writing. Finally, his growing interest in literary theory, cultivated since his youth, may have led him to consider the wider philosophical ramifications of the moral and didactic function of literature and its relationship to a reading public. For these and no doubt other reasons, the rest of Boccaccio's career was devoted largely to humanist concerns.

Among these concerns the revival of Greek studies figured prominently. Eager to have access to the works of such authors as Homer, Boccaccio engaged Leontius Pilatus to come to Florence to work on a translation of Homer and to teach at the university. Although the appointment lapsed after two years, Boccaccio learned a great deal from Leontius and incorporated much of this learning into his *Genealogy.* During this time Boccaccio also began his *De casibus virorum illustrium* (The Fates of Famous Men), a work that he would eventually finish in 1373 and a text that remains a standard model for the medieval definition of tragedy and its relationship to fortune.

However, in October 1362, Boccaccio decided to abandon this comfortable life in Florence to return again to Naples in hopes of a position of prominence in the South, despite his unfortunate reception there seven years earlier. Again, Boccaccio's hopes were destroyed. Accompanied by his younger half-brother, he was treated disgracefully by the Acciaiuoli, even to the extent of being housed in filthy lodgings. Mainardo Cavalcanti, another official of the court, eventually took pity on Boccaccio and invited him to stay in his home. The situation, however, continued to deteriorate, and Boccaccio returned to Florence in March 1363.

After 1365 the political upheavals that had characterized so much of Florentine political life appeared to calm after a victory over the Pisans. Boccaccio again held office and was sent on another diplomatic mission to Pope Urban V in August of that year. By this time both age and obesity made it difficult for Boccaccio to travel, but he left eagerly for Avignon, stopping at Genoa to dispatch other business. His mission was apparently successful, and he enjoyed his time in Avignon, talking and visiting with friends. Returning to Florence in November, he left again by the following May to visit with Petrarch in Venice.

By October of 1367, Urban V was reinstalled in Rome, and Boccaccio went on a short mission there in November before he went back to Florence to carry out other duties for the city. Always restless during these years, Boccaccio soon journeyed to visit with Petrarch in Padua, where the laureate had moved a few months earlier. Here Boccaccio spent a good deal of time copying, in his fine hand, some of Petrarch's works, and returned to Tuscany in October 1368. No historical record of Boccaccio's activities attests to the years between this period and the spring of 1370. The friendship between Urban and Florence, for which Boccaccio had worked so long, had soured, and by September 1370, for unknown reasons, he returned to Naples for his final visit, remaining this time until the spring of 1371.   Again, Boccaccio was disappointed with this nostalgic visit to the city of his youth, although his reception was certainly more generous on this trip. A large group of intellectuals gathered to celebrate his vast literary achievements, but despite this recognition, he returned to Certaldo.

Back in Florence, Boccaccio's continued his long correspondence with Petrarch, and he spent some of his time revising the *Decameron*.   In turn, Petrarch was inspired to translate Boccaccio's tale of Griselda, which closes the *Decameron*, into Latin, thereby increasing and validating the reputation of its author. Unfortunately, the political situation in Florence shifted, and Boccaccio's influence waned permanently. Also around this time, the author's health took a turn for the worse; he did not fully recover until the autumn of 1372.   Further, Boccaccio considered this last illness a warning that his life would soon end, and he devoted his last years to revising his *Genealogy*, working on minor poetic works addressing spiritual concerns, and studying Dante. His attention to Dante was rewarded by his appointment by the city council to teach and interpret Dante's complex works in an open debate. His first public reading and *explication de texte* occurred on October 23, 1373 in the church of Santo Stefano di Badia, close to Dante's ancestral home; these readings continued until October 1374, when ill health prevented Boccaccio from continuing his lectures. During this same period he learned to his great grief of the death of Petrarch, notice of which he received on October 19. He returned to Certaldo, but continued to meet with exponents of Florentine culture until his death on December 21, 1375.

SELECTED BIBLIOGRAPHY

Bergin, Thomas. *Boccaccio*. New York:Viking Press, 1981; Branca, Vittore. *Boccaccio: The Man and His Works*. Richard Monges, tr. and Dennis McAuliffe, ed. New York: New York University Press, 1976; De Sanctis, Francesco. *History of Italian Literature*. 1931. New York: Barnes and Noble, 1968; Hollander, Robert.   *Boccaccio's Two Venuses*. New York: Columbia University Press, 1977; Kirkham, Victoria. *The Sign of Reason in Boccaccio's Fiction*. Florence: Olschki, 1993; Rimanelli, Giose, and Kenneth Achity, eds. *Italian Literature: Roots and Branches*. New Haven: Yale University Press, 1976; Smarr, Janet L. "Boccaccio's Elegia on the Use of Classics." *Italian Culture* 11 (1993), 127-34.

Theresa Kennedy

BOETHIUS (c. 480-525). Anicius Manlius Severinus Boethius was born near Rome around A. D. 480. Orphaned young, he was brought up in the house of one of the richest aristocrats of that time, Symmachus.   He married Symmachus's daughter and pursued a career for a senatorial scion, alternating between ceremonial public office and private leisure. He was a Roman philosopher who was appointed consul in 510, where he served under Theodoric the Great, a Goth. He was accused of treason for allegedly plotting against the Gothic rule, imprisoned, and executed around 525 in Padua.

Boethius was by far the best-educated Roman of his age. He had a command of the Greek language adequate to make him a student, translator, and commentator of the Platonic philosophies of his age (to which is given the name "Neoplatonism"). He undertook the project of translating all the works of Plato and *Aristotle. Only a few pieces of this undertaking were complete before his life was cut short.

In the early 520s, he served as magister officiorum in the half-Roman regime of the Ostrogothic king Theodoric. Theodoric had taken Italy at the command of the emperors in Constantinople; but political fashions had changed in the thirty years since Theodoric entered Italy. In the reign of Emperor Justin the aging Theodoric fell out with Constantinople; Boethius came to be suspected by Theoderic of disloyal sympathies;   sometime around 525 Boethius was executed.

The *Consolation of Philosophy* is apparently the fruit of Boethius's spell of imprisonment awaiting execution. Its genre is Menippean satire, after the Roman models. It has a regular alternation of prose and verse sections. The dialogue between the two characters is carefully structured according to the best classical models. Its language is classical, but some of the qualities that would come to characterize medieval Latin are already discernible. The verse often is a story as told by Ovid or Horace and is used to illustrate the philosophy being expounded. The style of the *Consolation* itself was an influence on the medieval moral narratives. Geoffrey *Chaucer's fifteenth-century followers were greatly influenced by the work.

The *Consolation* was translated into English in 890 by *Alfred; later, Geoffrey Chaucer composed his famous *Boece*. The work was translated into French by Jean de Muen. Thus it was also one of the most influential books of the Middle Ages. While the *Consolation* is neoplatonic, it is believed that Boethius was a Christian. Before the Middle Ages Boethius was known for his translations of Aristotle, including the *Topics*. He provided the bulk of extant Aristotle before the twelfth-century recovery of his works. Boethius also translated the Neoplatonist Porphyry and wrote many philosophical treatises used by the *scholastics of the Middle Ages.

SELECTED BIBLIOGRAPHY

Frakes, Jerold C. "The Ancient Concept of *Casus* and Its Early Medieval Interpretations." *Vivarium* 22:1 (May 1984), 1-34; Frakes, Jerold C. *The Fate of Fortune in the Early Middle Ages: The Boethian Tradition.* New York: E. J. Brill, 1988; Swanton, Michael. *English Literature before Chaucer.* New York: Longman, 1987.

Rebecca Chalmers

BOOK OF THE DUCHESS, THE. Geoffrey *Chaucer's *Book of the Duchess* is a *dream vision composed around 1369 that laments the death on September 12, 1369 of Blanche, the Duchess of Lancaster and *John of Gaunt's wife. Chaucer and John had a close relationship, and the poet wrote the work to pay homage to his friend's sorrow. Among the sources are the *Roman de la Rose* and several of Guillaume de Machaut's works.

In the first portion of *The Book of the Duchess* the narrator-poet seeks diversion by reading Ovid's heart-wrenching work about Ceyx and Alcyone. He nods off and dreams of a splendid hunt during which he encounters a mysterious black knight who recites a sorrowful verse for his departed lady. The black knight condemns Fortune, who introduced him to the perfect woman, and allowed him to marry her before stealing her away from him in death. The narrator questions the knight, allowing him to espouse his frustrations. When the narrator learns of the knight's lady's death, the hunters reappear at twelve o'clock. The poet awakes, looks at the copy of Ovid's poem, which he still holds, and decides to write a poem about his experience.

The poem, one of Chaucer's earliest, is not considered to be his greatest. Its construction highlights three specific griefs: the poet's unrequited love, Ceyx and Alcyone's tempestuous relationship, and the black knight's sorrow. Chaucer here advances the character of the dreamer by expanding his role in the work. Instead of the narrator playing the traditional role as simple observer, this character interacts with the black knight and questions his sorrow. The work has also been seen as an *allegory which bemoans the loss of the ideals of *courtly love.

SELECTED BIBLIOGRAPHY

Burger, Glenn. "Reading Otherwise: Recovering the Subject in *The Book of the Duchess.*" *Exemplaria* 5:2 (Fall 1993), 325-41; Connolly, Margaret. "Chaucer and Chess." *Chaucer Review* 29:1 (1994), 40-44; Drabble, Margaret, ed. *The Oxford Companion to English Literature.* 5th ed. Oxford: Oxford University Press, 1985; Ellis, Steve. "The Death of *The Book of the Duchess.*" *Chaucer Review* 29:3 (1995), 249-58; Hardman, Phillipa. "*The Book of the Duchess* as a Memorial Monument." *Chaucer Review* 28:3 (1994), 205-15; Martin, Carol A. N. "Mercurial Translation in *The Book of the Duchess.*" *Chaucer Review* 28:2 (1993), 95-116.

Robert T. Lambdin

BOURCHIER, JOHN (1467-1533). John Bourchier, later known as Lord Berners, was the English translator of Jean *Froissant's *Chronicles*. A member of *Henry VIII's court, Bourchier was asked by Henry to translate several other French romances, including mid-sixteenth-century *Huon de Bordeaux* and *The Castell of Love*. Additionally, Bourchier translated into English the French editions of the Spanish works of Antonio de Guerva and Diego de San Pedro.

SELECTED BIBLIOGRAPHY

Kane, George. "An Accident of History: Lord Berner's Translation of Froissart's *Chronicles*." *Chaucer Review* 21:2 (1986), 217-225; O'Brien, Dennis J. "Lord Berner's 'Huan of Burdeux': The Survival of Medieval Ideals in the Reign of Henry VIII. *Studies in Medievalism* 4 (1992), 36-64.

Robert T. Lambdin

BRUCE, THE. *The Bruce*, composed in 1375 by poet-historian John *Barbour (1316?-1396), is the truest national epic of early Scotland. A poem of 13,550 lines of octosyllabic couplets, it is the first major work written in the language of the Lowland Scots and helped to carve and shape the character and temper of that region. Barbour chronicled with reasonable historical accuracy the ascension of *Robert the Bruce (Robert I) to the Scottish throne during the nation's tumultuous war of liberation from England. The historical verse narrative follows the Scottish patriot from his ascension in 1306 until his death in 1329. Of even more importance than the work's literary virtue was Barbour's political purpose of reinvigorating the patriotism of previous generations in a time when the state of the nation was perilous. Robert the Bruce, the hero of the work, is dramatized as a model of courage, valor, and moral and physical strength, but above all, a defender of freedom and independence.

As far as historical accuracy is concerned, Barbour was careful and deliberate, but without leaving his narrative stripped of interest and artistic effect. Of the few errors that have been attributed to him, the ones that are rightly so are minor or justifiable, such as the sequencing of some events and the exclusion of some other historical figures of the period, notably William *Wallace. Barbour's piece is valuable for purely historical reasons because it is the only source for several key facts about the life of the title character. Judging from his detailed depictions, it is probable that he also had experience from eyewitness accounts. Many of the events of the poem actually happened during Barbour's lifetime, while the rest were likely composed from extensive collections of oral histories and detailed chronicles.

In an episodic rather than thorough or comprehensive fashion, Barbour traced in twenty books the trials of Robert the Bruce, his friend James

Douglas, his brother Edward, and his nephew Randolph. As the poem opens, Bruce has refused an offer of titular kingship as vassal to *Edward I of England, determined instead to claim his rightful rule of an independent Scotland. Barbour carefully characterized his hero through detailed episodes and the reiteration of his virtues. Choosing freedom over an empty title, Bruce is outlawed, and after his small army is defeated, they are forced to seek refuge in the mountains and hills. His wife and daughter, whom he had hidden in a castle, are captured and imprisoned. Bruce gains gradual support when others witness his bravery and prowess in battle, as he leads sieges of castles, including the recapture of Kildrummy Castle, where he rescues his wife and daughter. During the years of war England sees its king die and his son *Edward II take command. The biggest victory for Bruce was at the battle of Bannockburn, which is recounted in one of the poem's most memorable passages. Crowned in 1306, Robert the Bruce continued to wage war and rid his land of the English. He eventually succeeded, sacking the few remaining English castles, including the one at Stirling. A truce in the war called for by the Pope did not yet declare Scotland an independent land, so Bruce did not resign his campaign and continued to siege. When he died at age fifty, Robert the Bruce was finally king of an independent Scotland.

The Bruce laid a solid foundation for future literature of the Scottish Lowlands, marking a departure from earlier unrhymed *alliterative verse and a beginning of continental rhymed forms. As a national work, Barbour's piece is important historically and as a contribution that helped shape the national character. As a work of literature, The Bruce is unparalleled as a commemoration of Scottish chivalry and patriotism. The work is not quite as unified or dignified as an epic, and the rhyme is more regular and correct than musical. The plot structure is not as intricate as that of great epic works. As a history, it does not observe the same veracity a modern historian would insist upon. But overall, the work's value as a cultural contribution, a political affirmation, a historical preservation, and a stirring work of literature is unmistakable.

SELECTED BIBLIOGRAPHY

Barrow, G.W.S. Robert Bruce and the Community of the Realm of Scotland. Berkeley: University of California Press, 1965; Ebin, Lois A. "John Barbour's 'Bruce': Poetry, History, and Propaganda." Studies in Scottish Literature 9 (April 1972), 218-42; Purdon, Liam, and Julian Wasserman. "Chivalry and Feudal Obligation in Barbour's 'Bruce.'" The Rusted Hauberk: Feudal Ideals of Order and Their Decline. Liam Purdon and Cindy Vitto, eds. Gainesville: University Press of Florida, 1994. 77-95; Watt, Diane. "Nationalism in Barbour's 'Bruce.'" Parergon 12:1 (July 1994), 89-107; Wilson, Grace G. "Barbour's 'Bruce' and Harry's 'Wallace': Complements, Compensations, and Conventions." Studies in Scottish Literature 25 (1990), 189-201.

J. Scott Plaster

C

CABALERO ZIFAR, EL. Written around 1300, *El Cabalero Zifar* is the first full-length Spanish novel. The work combines chivalric *romance with the hagiographic tale of Saint Eustace and a more general didactic and moral prose. The chivalric plot line recounts the adventures of a knight-errant named Cifar, or Zifar, his wife Grima, and his sons Garfin and Roboan. The novel's realism, the oriental sources of its didactic sections, and a strain of popular language make it uniquely Spanish. *El Cabalero Zifar* is most noted for its character type, el Ribaldo, who evolved into the picaro of Golden Age fiction, the gracioso of Golden Age drama, and eventually Don Quixote's Sancho Panza.

SELECTED BIBLIOGRAPHY

Gonzalez-Casanovas, Roberto J. "Ethical Poetics in the 'Counsels' of the *Caballero Zifar*: The Exemplification of Wisdom as Power." *Romance Languages Annual* 5 (1993), 419-25; Harney, Michael. "More on the Geography of the *Libro del Cauallero Zifar*." *La Coronica* 16:2 (Spring 1988), 76-85; Northup, George Tyler. *An Introduction to Spanish Literature*. Chicago: University of Chicago Press, 1960.

Rebecca Stephens

CABOT, JOHN (d. 1498?). John Cabot was a native of Genoa who traveled the world extensively in the fifteenth century. Because he saw lessening opportunities for economic activity at home, in 1490 he moved his family to England and, using his wealth, sent out expeditions for several years. His great interest was Brazil, where there were vast sources of raw materials needed in the dyeing industry. With Columbus's success as a model, he led an expedition from Bristol on May 2, 1497. He found the coast of Newfoundland, in particular Cape Breton Island. Cabot returned to England and set out on successive voyages, again hoping to locate Brazil. On the second of these expeditions, he led six ships to the north and sailed the coast of Greenland, Labrador, and New England, probably as far south as Delaware. Cabot and his crews were never successful in reaching the elusive Brazil of their earliest explorations.

SELECTED BIBLIOGRAPHY

Howard, Richard Christopher. *Bristol and the Cabots*. Toronto: Clarke, 1967; Winship, George Parker. *Cabot Bibliography with an Introductory Essay on the Careers of the Cabots Based upon an Independent Examination of the Sources of Information*. New York: Franklin, 1967.

R. Churchill Curtis

CÆDMON (c. 670). The Venerable *Bede provided a brief background for Cædmon in his *Ecclesiastical History*. In a monastery with Hilda as abbess, Cædmon lived a layman's life, with no particular gift for sacred song. On an evening when he had slunk from the hall because he observed the approach of a harp and had no talent for singing, in the cattle barn he slept and heard in his dreams the voice of a stranger: "Cædmon, sing me something." When he protested that he could not, the dream figure suggested that his song should be about "the beginning of things." To his own amazement, he immediately composed and sang. When he told the story to Hild, she assigned a selection from Christian doctrine, and the next morning he sang an "excellent poem" to her. She was so impressed that she urged him to take monastic vows and assigned sacred teachers for his instruction. From this there developed the tradition that he had celebrated in song portions of the Old and New Testaments. Later scholarship contends that all these passages are simply paraphrases by different authors, the only certainly genuine selection being *"Cædmon's Hymn," which is found in both Northumbrian and West Saxon texts, as well as being repeated *in toto* in Bede's *History*. Like much of *Old English poetry, the translation is made difficult by the piling up of compound adjectives known as *"kennings."

The structure of the short poem of praise is made even more intricate by shifts of the subject. Thus line 1 puts "the Prince of heaven" in the second part of the line; however, in lines 2, 3, and 4, "the Might of the Maker," "the work of the Father," and "the Lord Everlasting" are at the beginning of each line. In lines 6 and 7, "holy Ruler" and "Wards of mankind" appear in the second half-line. The last two lines place "the Lord everlasting" at the beginning and "the Almighty Lord" at the end. The brief canticle of Christian praise was originally in Latin as *Primo cantavit Cædmon istud carmen*.

As part of this same contested opus, the *Selections from Genesis* can be divided into the bulk of the poem and a B section (lines 235-852) that was itself a translation from Old Saxon. These selections include "The Offering of Isaac" (lines 2845-2935), with its resolution of the contest between paternal love and obedience to God: "his friendship shall be / More sacred than thy son . . . ." (2920-2921). *Selections from Exodus* includes "The Crossing of the Red Sea," generally assumed to be by a different hand than Genesis A or B.

SELECTED BIBLIOGRAPHY

Abraham, Lenore. "'Cædmon's Hymn' and the 'Gethwærnysse' ('Fitness') of Things." *American Benedictine Review* 43:4 (September 1992), 331-44; Lees, Clare A., and Gillian R. Overing. "Birthing Bishops and Fathering Poets: Bede, Hilda, and the Relations of Cultural Production." *Exemplaria* 6:1 (Spring 1994), 35-65; O'Hare, Colman. "The Story of *Cædmon*: Bede's Account of the First English Poet." *American Benedictine Review* 43:3 (September 1992), 345-57.

Elton E. Smith

"CÆDMON'S HYMN." "Cædmon's Hymn" is one of the earliest extant *Old English poems, and the only one where we know both the author and something of the circumstances of its composition. According to the story *Bede tells in his *Historia ecclesiastica* (4 24), Cædmon was a stable hand with no knowledge of poetry. Embarrassed by his ignorance, Cædmon would generally avoid parties where it was the custom for everyone to sing songs in turn. After one such party a figure came to Cædmon in a dream, commanding him to sing about the world's creation. In the morning Cædmon awoke not merely remembering the song, but able to compose more verse in the same fashion. He related this hymn to his reeve, who brought him to the abbess Hilda (d. 680). Convinced that his poem was the gift of God, Hilda convinced Cædmon to become a brother at her monastery of Streoncshealh (Whitby), where he produced many other poems in English, all on religious topics. Although Bede gives a list of topics upon which Cædmon composed, no other extant poems can be convincingly attributed to him.

Bede's story is generally taken to describe the *fons et origo* of religious poetry in English, and Cædmon as the first to adapt the pagan medium of vernacular poetry to Christian purposes. Significantly, however, Bede gives not the Old English text of the poem but a Latin paraphrase. The hymn itself was added later as a marginal gloss, a fact that has led to the suggestion that the Old English version we have might in fact be a paraphrase of the Latin, although the variant versions found in different manuscripts have been argued to reflect oral transmission independent of the Latin manuscripts, which would tend to undermine the idea of a retranslation.

SELECTED BIBLIOGRAPHY

Abraham, Lenore. "'Cædmon's Hymn' and the 'Gethwærnysse' ('Fitness') of Things." *American Benedictine Review* 43:3 (September 1992), 331-44; O'Keeffe, Katherine O'Brien. "Orality and Developing Text of *Cædmon's Hymn*." *Anglo-Saxon Manuscripts: Basic Readings*. Mary P. Richards, ed. New York: Garland, 1994. 221-50.

Karl Hagen

CAESURA. A break or pause in a line of poetry, the caesura provides rhetorical effect. This technique, derived from Greek and Latin prosody, is found often in *Old English poetry. The break, which usually, but not always, occurs in the middle of a line, generally indicates a sentence pause.

SELECTED BIBLIOGRAPHY

Garmonsway, G. N., trans. and ed. *The Anglo-Saxon Chronicle*. London: Dent, 1990; Hamer, Richard. *A Choice of Anglo-Saxon Verse, Selected, with an Introduction and Parallel Verse Translation*. London: Faber and Faber, 1970.

Robert T. Lambdin

"CANON'S YEOMAN'S TALE, THE." "The Canon's Yeoman's Tale" from Geoffrey *Chaucer's *Canterbury Tales* (c. 1387-1400) concerns a fraudulent alchemist. The Canon and his Yeoman ride furiously in order to join the pilgrims traveling to the shrine of Thomas *Becket at Canterbury Cathedral, only to have the Canon leave after he is scrutinized by the Host. The Yeoman begins a confession of the graft involved in being an alchemist, beginning with a confused but complete list of alchemical recipes, ingredients, and utensils.

In the actual tale a priest is conned by a canon/alchemist. The canon pretends to allow a priest to help with the conversion of quicksilver and copper into silver. The canon exchanges the minerals by sleight of hand when the priest is not paying close-enough attention. The priest asks to purchase the recipe and gladly gives the canon forty pounds for it. The canon takes the money and disappears.

SELECTED BIBLIOGRAPHY

Brown, Dorothy H. "The Unreliable Narrator: The Canon's Yeoman." *New Laurel Review* 12:1-2 (Spring-Fall 1982), 6-16; Bush, Douglas. *English Poetry*. New York: Oxford University Press, 1963; Campbell, Jackson J. "The Canon's Yeoman as Imperfect Paradigm." *Chaucer Review* 17:2 (Fall 1982), 171-81; Cook, Robert. "The Canon's Yeoman and His Tale." *Chaucer Review* 22:1 (1987), 28-40; Garbáty, Thomas J. *Medieval English Literature*. Toronto: Heath, 1984; Lambdin, Laura C., and Robert T. Lambdin, eds. *Chaucer's Pilgrims: An Historical Guide to the Pilgrims in the "Canterbury Tales."* Westport, CT: Greenwood Press, 1996.

Laura Cooner Lambdin

CANTAR DE MIO CID. The epic poem *Cantar de Mio Cid* is the oldest surviving work of literature written completely in Spanish (*See **Hispanic Literature***). Its author is unknown, but it seems likely that he was a juglar, a traveling performer. Composed around 1140, this work is based upon the eleventh-century hero Rodrigo Díaz de Vivar, who led a series of campaigns against the Moors. The existing manuscript consists of 3,735 lines; the opening episode is missing, but is available in historical documents.

The *Cid* recounts the life of Rodrigo, beginning with his exile from the court of the Castillian king Alfonso VI. In exile Rodrigo carries out numerous campaigns against the Moors and the Christians, possibly for personal gain. He is never known to lose a battle. The poem details the conquest of Valencia, El Cid's most significant victory. Subsequent episodes cover the marriage of the hero's daughters to the Infantes de Carrion, the beating of the daughters by their husbands that results in the women's deaths, and El Cid's revenge upon the brothers.

In contrast to the more fantastic German and French epics of the period, the *Cid* is realistic and objective. A note of antifeudalism resounds as El Cid, a caballero or baron, defeats the nobly born Infantes de Carrion. The characters speak for themselves through dialogue, adding a dramatic quality to the otherwise stark, dry language and descriptive detail. The story of El Cid has been inspirational to Spanish writers throughout history.

SELECTED BIBLIOGRAPHY

England, John. "'Comed, Conde': The *Cid's* Use of Parody." *Medium Ævum* 63:1 (1994), 101-03; Thompson, Billy Russell. "Chivalric Transformations of the *Cid*." in *Studies on Medieval Spanish Literature in Honor of Charles F. Fraker*. Mercedes Vaquero and Alan Deyermañ, eds. Madison, WI: Hispanic Seminary of Medieval Studies, 1995. 259-64; Torres, Isabel. "The *Cid* in the Shade in Gala's *Anillos para una Dama*." *Romance Studies* 26 (Autumn 1995), 77-97.

Rebecca Stephens

CANTERBURY TALES. The collection of the *Canterbury Tales* was evidently undertaken soon after Geoffrey *Chaucer ceased to serve as controller of customs in 1386, when he was relieved from tending an office six days a week and thought that he would have more time for writing. At this time, he completed *Troilus and Criseyde*, his most "finished" production, and began to collect into a frame the short narrative poems with which he had no doubt been entertaining the royal household and civic groups for more than twenty-five years. Anthologies of prose and poetry were a favorite form of pedagogic literature in Latin. Popular collections were the *Gesta Romanorum* and the *Legenda Aurea*, but there are many other collections of miracles of the Virgin, saints' lives, and didactic anecdotes in both prose and verse intended as source material for sermons. In the vernaculars, there are collections of fables and *fabliaux, the *lais and *isopets*. The idea of collecting independent compositions in a narrative frame appears in the *Vita nuova* into whose story of Beatrice *Dante collected lyrics that he had composed before the story was imagined. In

Chaucer's own time *Boccaccio had created *Ameto*, *Filocolo*, and *The Decameron* (1336-51) as frames into which he could insert a variety of moral and comic tales, and Giovanni Sercambi in his *Novelliero* of 1374--which Chaucer could have seen on one of his trips to Italy--devised a pilgrimage frame for a collection of stories that could have suggested a similar frame to Chaucer.

None of these collections features the stylistic innovation that made *Canterbury Tales* so influential: the contrasting voices, personalities, and points of view of the narrators produces a drama of persons and styles in a collection of stories. This innovation we may attribute to Chaucer's training in the Inns of Chancery. The writing masters trained clerks in the *ars dictaminis*, the art of taking down in Latin a missive or writ that a "dictator" might dictate in any language. This composition would be transmitted to the "auditor," whose clerk would read it out to him in his own language. Handbooks taught that the composition was to be appropriate to the "conditions" (in the medieval sense) of the dictator and auditor and to the context of the occasion. We recall that in introducing the pilgrims at the beginning of the *"General Prologue" Chaucer promises to tell us "al the condicioun / Of ech of hem, so as it semed me, / And whiche [what] they weren, and of what degree" (17-40).

The textbooks for teaching *ars dictaminis* were "formularies." These were collections of model letters appropriate for various speakers and situations. The earliest collection, compiled in 1119, has sixteen models, among them were

> *A papa ad imperatorem* (from pope to emperor)
> *A subditor ad episcopum* (from subordinate to bishop)
> *Ad magistrum* (to a teacher)
> *Ad patrem* (to a father).

The formularies provided models that the students imitated. More information about the pedagogical method may be found in *The Importance of Chaucer* (Fisher 63-65). Chaucer's education in the Inns of Chancery must have involved imitating formulary models, learning to write sundry letters to sundry individuals in sundry styles. This had been the mode of clerical training for centuries, as it is in college composition classes today, but Chaucer was the first to take the imaginative step from creating letters in different registers to imagining the composers speaking their letters in their own voices. This is a dramatic innovation found in neither Boccaccio nor Sercambi.

The "General Prologue" and the headlink to the *"Parson's Tale" provide a dramatic framework for the collection of individual stories. We may suppose that these two parts were created shortly after 1386, when Chaucer was looking forward to an extended leisure for writing. Skeat's hypothesis of April 17, 1386, the week after *Easter, as the date on which the pilgrimage began has been generally accepted. This date is indicated by the zodiacal reference at "General Prologue" 8 and the date at Man of Law's headlink 5. The marks of ingress and egress in the "General Prologue" and in the Parson's headlink calibrate so closely that we must suppose that they were composed together and adapted as the collection took shape. Much has been surmised about the evolution of the "General Prologue" and the dates and arrangements of the stories. A group of rascals, including the Miller and the Reeve, was evidently added to the end of the prologue (542 ff.), and the Miller and the Reeve tell the first bawdy *fabliaux in contrast to the genteel *"Knight's Tale." This suggests the sort of adaptation that could have taken place as the conception of dramatic interplay developed in Chaucer's mind. In the Prologue the Host proposes 2 tales going and 2 returning for each pilgrim (I.792), some 120 tales in all. By the Squire's headlink this has been reduced to "A tale or two" (V.698), and at the end the Host says to the Parson, "every man save thou hath toold his tale" (X.25). Even that is not true; we have 24 tales for 30 pilgrims, 2 of them by the Chaucer persona, and several tales betray evidence of adaptation: the Man of Law says that he will tell a tale in prose and goes on to tell one in rhymed stanzas; the Shipman refers to himself as a "wyf" whose "sely housbonde. . . moot us clothe" (VII.3); the Second Nun calls herself an "unworthy sone of Eve" (VIII.62). The Man of Law's and Nun's Priest's tales are followed in many manuscripts by epilogues that connect with nothing, and the *Physician's, Shipman's, and Second Nun's Tales have no prologues.

Within the frame of the *Canterbury Tales* are ten parts that appear in different orders in different manuscripts. Most scholars believe that Chaucer never made a final arrangement of the parts and that the various arrangements are all scribal. The arrangement that has met with the most acceptance is that preserved in the Ellesmere manuscript. Five parts contain references to towns along the Canterbury Way. In Part I, the "General Prologue" begins in Southwark, just across London Bridge (I.20), and the Host refers to Depford, five miles from Southwark toward Canterbury (I.3906). In Part III the Summoner refers to Siittingbourn, *forty* miles from London (III.847). In Part VII the Host refers to Rochester, *thirty* miles from London (VII.1926). In Part VIII the Canon and his Yeoman catch up with the pilgrims in Blean Forest, four miles from Canterbury (VIII.556), and the *"Manciple's Tale" begins at Harbledown, just outside of Canterbury (IX.2). The apparent error in the Ellesmere order led F. J. Furnivall to place Part VII after Part II, in what has been called the Chaucer Society order. But this order is not found in any manuscript and it raises problems with the dramatic progress of the tales. The Ellesmere order is aesthetically very satisfactory. Its evolution has been discussed by N. F. Blake, *The Textual Tradition of the Canterbury Tales* (1985).

Chaucer was the first English secular writer after a thousand years in which writing had been regarded as an ecclesiastical monopoly. He was the first writer in England to broaden the subject matter of poetry beyond the cloister and the court as Dante and Boccaccio were doing on the Continent. He was the first to treat in English the bawdy and naturalistic materials that have become the favorite subject matter of modern literature. Chaucer was the first English writer to create realistic characters and situations. The medieval view of society was strictly corporate. Its concept of the community was the *corpus Christi* described by St. Paul in I Corinthians 12:12-27, in which each part of the body has a specific function without which the whole could not survive. This corporate view of the community is by definition hierarchic and totalitarian. An eye must not try to be a hand, a foot must not try to be a head. The head directs the hands and the feet, which in turn sustain the head. The organism and its functions are created and sustained by God, not by the consent of its members. The elective process in the "General Prologue" by which the pilgrims select the Host as their leader (I.761-87) is a negation of the *corpus Christi* corporate ideal. The triumph of the *Canterbury Tales* is the way in which it converts the medieval corporate view into the modern individualized world view. Chaucer's pilgrims are presented as representatives of the medieval corporate estates, a knight, a monk, a nun, a miller, a carpenter, a lawyer, a wife, and so on. Medieval social criticism, "satire on the estates," turns on complaints about how the estates failed to live up to the responsibilities assigned to them in the divine plan of the universe, but modern social criticism turns on appraisal of individual behavior in the context of psychological and communal verities. The triumph of the Canterbury stories is the way that they convert personifications of the medieval estates into genuine personalities. We can discuss the Knight, the Prioress, the Man of Law and their stories like Hamlet and Macbeth and their stories, as individuals and narratives that have an existence beyond the cameos that appear in the *Canterbury* composition.

Parts I through V, the General Prologue through *"The Franklin's Tale" in the Ellesmere order, appear to represent the sort of structure Chaucer was working toward as his composition took shape. Parts I and II present dramatic contrasts in style and subject, very like the social contrasts detailed in John of Garland's *Poetria* (see *Chaucer Review* 8 (1973) 119-27), the courtly *"Knight's Tale," the bourgeois *"Miller's Tale," the rustic *"Reeve's Tale," the potentially coarse *"Cook's Tale," and then back to the virtuous *"Man of Law's Tale." References in the connecting links show that these tales were composed or adapted to form a series. The serial references are even more pronounced in the "marriage group" in Parts III through V, the *"Wife of Bath's Tale" through the *"Franklin's Tale," which explore various attitudes and situations in marriage. There has been much discussion of why *"The Friar's Tale" and the *"Summoner's Tale" appear in this series, but they do in all the manuscripts so all we can do is wonder. Parts VI through IX have nothing like the stylistic and topical unity of the first five parts. Indeed, we can see the dramatic structure beginning to emerge in the post-V parts, especially Part VII, which leads me to believe that these parts were composed before I-V, and that I-V represent the sort of revision that Chaucer had in process when he stopped working on the collection. However we may arrange the tales, the sense of completeness of the *Canterbury* collection--which has been recognized by readers since the beginning--derives from the brilliant opening of the "General Prologue," with its images of spring, germination, and commencement, and the equally brilliant conclusion in the Parson's headlink, with its images of sunset, death, and completion, and the final farewell in the "Retraction." The passage from birth to death in the *Canterbury* collection demonstrates the structure that Northrop Frye identified in the Bible as the archetype of narrative completeness.

For text and bibliography to 1987, see *The Complete Poetry and Prose of Geoffrey Chaucer*, ed. John H. Fisher (New York: Holt, Rinehart, and Winston, 2nd ed., 1989). There is an annual annotated bibliography in *Studies in the Age of Chaucer.*

SELECTED BIBLIOGRAPHY

Allen, Mark, and John H. Fisher. *The Essential Chaucer: An Annotated Bibliography of Major Modern Studies.* Boston, G.K. Hall, 1987; Baird-Lange, Lorrayne Y., and Hildegard Schnuttgen. *A Bibliography of Chaucer, 1974-1985.* Hamden, CT: Archon Books, 1988; Blake, N. F. *The Textual Tradition of the Canterbury Tales.* London: Arnold, 1985; Chance, Jane. *The Mythographic Chaucer: The Fabulation of Sexual Politics.* Minneapolis: University of Minnesota Press, 1995; Fisher, John H. *The Importance of Chaucer.* Carbondale: Southern Illinois University Press, 1992; Lerer, Seth. *Chaucer and His Readers: Imagining the Author in Late Medieval England.* Princeton: Princeton University Press, 1993; Pearsall, Derek Albert. *The Life of Geoffrey Chaucer: A Critical Biography.* Oxford: Blackwell, 1992.

John H. Fisher

CANUTE (CNUT) (994-1035). Canute was a king of England who later also became king of Denmark; with his English queen Emma, he helped usher in a period of peace and prosperity. According to legend, Canute, who felt that he was being held too highly in esteem by his followers, commanded the waves to be still. The waves continued to roll in, thereby reinforcing to all the witnesses that Canute was merely human.

An early twelfth-century Middle English lyric, *The Song of Canute* may actuall have been composed earlier by Canute, himself. It is alleged that he composed the work because he was greatly moved by the music he heard as he rowed past the Abbey at Ely. In these ways Canute demonstrates that literature is often the result of an intellectual spark. Through his curious nature Canute shows that even kings are affected by literature.

SELECTED BIBLIOGRAPHY

Heslop, T. A. "The Production of de Luxe Manuscripts and the Patronage of King Cnut and Queen Emma." *Anglo-Saxon England* 19 (1990), 151-95.

Robert T. Lambdin

CANZONE. An Italian lyric form of verse, the canzone was a popular form from the Middle Ages to the Renaissance. The canzone is derived from the ProvenHal *canso*, normally composed in five to seven stanzas, each copying the first stanza in rhyme and lines.

The *comrato*, a first short stanza, similar to the French **envoi*, relates to the poem itself or is addressing some person. The subject of the canzone was usually love, but it could also be political, satirical, or humorous. Among the most noted authors of canzoni were *Petrarch, Leopardi, and *Boccaccio. In English, Spenser's *Epithalamion* is among the best examples.

SELECTED BIBLIOGRAPHY

Alcorn, John, and Dario Del Puppo. "Leopardi's Historical Poetics in the Canzone 'Ad Angelo Mai.'" *Italica* 72:1 (Spring 1995) 21-39; Drabble, Margaret, ed. *The Oxford Companion to English Literature*. 5th ed. Oxford: Oxford University Press, 1985; Jones, F. J. "An Analyses of Petrarch's Eleventh Canzone: 'Mai non vo' piu cantar com'io soleva.'" *Italian Studies* 41 (1986), 24-44; Schiesari, Juliana. "The Victim's Discourse: Torquato Tasso's 'Canzone al Metauro.'" *Stanford Italian Review* 5:2 (Fall 1985), 189-203.

Robert T. Lambdin

CAPET, HUGH (940?-996), King of France. Hugh, supported by the Dukes of Normandy and Anjou, was crowned at Nayon and recognized by the Holy Roman Emperor, Otto III, in return for Hugh's claim to Lorraine. This installation marked the beginning of the Capetian House which controlled the future of the French Monarchy until the execution of Louis XVI in 1792.

SELECTED BIBLIOGRAPHY

Brown, Elizabeth A. R. *Politics and Institutions on Capetian France*. Brookefield, VT: Gower, 1991; Duby, Georges. *France in the Middle Ages 987-1460: From Hugh Capet to Joan of Arc*. Oxford: Blackwell, 1991.

R. Churchill Curtis

CAPGRAVE, JOHN (1393-1464). John Capgrave was born near Lynn in Norfolk in 1393. He probably joined the monastery at Lynn and was ordained as a priest in 1417. In 1422 he became a lector in theology and went to study at Cambridge, where he received his doctor of theology degree in 1425. Capgrave was an earnest student and a prodigious writer in both Latin and Middle English, finishing numerous lives of saints and histories within his lifetime. Of particular note, he completed his best-known historical work, *Abbreviacion of Chronicles*, in Middle English sometime between 1461 and his death in 1464.

The work is comprised of three main sections: Part I (from Creation to Christ), part II (Roman and Holy Roman emperors, and Part III the kings of England). He used no known source directly for Part I, although some of its passages and arrangement are reminiscent of *Isidore of Seville's chronicle of world history. For the second part he relied heavily on Martin Polonus's *Chronicon Pontificum*. For his dual history of the Roman Church and the Roman Empire, Capgrave used a dual text structure, where events concerning Roman emperors are recorded in one column while information concerning popes is included in a separate column. But Capgrave's desire to abridge his sources often leads to oversimplification and misinformation. In the final section of the history Capgrave relied on Thomas Walsingham's highly derivative *Historia Anglicana*. The *Abbreviacion of Chronicles* brings together what Capgrave felt were the most important events in world and later British history. He often moralized historical incidents, and consistently revealed a bias for Christians and later Englishmen in his depiction of events.

SELECTED BIBLIOGRAPHY

Brandt, William J. *The Shape of Medieval History*. New Haven: Yale University Press, 1966; Gransden, Antonia. *Historical Writing in England II: c. 1307 to the Early Sixteenth Century*. Ithaca: Cornell University Press, 1982; Lucas, Peter J., ed. *John Capgrave's Abbreviacion of Chronicles*. Oxford: Oxford University Press, 1983; Lucas, Peter J. "Towards a Standard Written English? Continuity and Change in the Orthographic Usage of John Capgrave, O.S.A. (1393-1464)." in *English Historical Linguistics 1992*. Amsterdam: Benjamins, 1994, 91-104; Winstead, Karen A. "Piety, Politics, and Social Commitment in Capgrave's 'Life of St. Katherine.'" *Medievalia et Humanistica* 17 (1991), 59-80.

Richard McDonald

CARMINA BURANA. Discovered in 1803, the *Carmina Burana* or "Benediktbeuern Manuscript," composed around 1230, is perhaps the best collection of thirteenth-century goliardic verse. As is normal in Goliardic verse, most of the works were composed in Latin, although some were written in German and French. The *Carmina Burana* includes a variety of types, such as moral-satirical poems, love poems, and drinking poems; thus it has been suggested that they were written by the troubadours. Some of the known poets found in the work include Walter of Chatillon, Hugh of Orleans, and Philip the Chancellor.

SELECTED BIBLIOGRAPHY

Walsh, P. G., ed. and trans. *Love Lyrics from the "Carmina Burana."* Chapel Hill: University of North Carolina Press. 1993; Wright, Stephen K. "The Play of the King of

Egypt: An Early Thirteenth Century Music-Drama from the *Carmina Burana* Manuscript." *Allegorica* 16 (1995), 47-71.

Robert T. Lambdin

CASTLE OF PERSEVERANCE, THE (c. 1425). The Morality Play *The Castle of Perseverance* (see **Drama, Medieval**) has within its 3,600 lines almost all the themes found in other individual morality plays. The hero, Humanum Genus (Mankind), is seduced by the Bad Angel into the service of the world. He is attended by his servants Lust and Folly until Shrift and Penance place him in the Castle of Perseverance, guarded by the Seven Moral Virtues. The evil forces of the World, Flesh, and the Devil unsuccessfully attack the castle. Later, however, Covetousness tempts Mankind with promises of wealth, but Death suddenly appears and kills Covetousness with a dart. Mankind prays to God to deliver his soul, and the play ends with Mankind instructing the audience to think on their own Judgment Day before committing sinful acts.

      The manuscript of the play is unique in that it contains an appendage that explains the staging. Five scaffolds are to be erected, representing the World, Flesh, the Devil, Covetousness, and God. The Castle of Perseverance is at the center of these scaffolds. This setup visually clarifies the morals that are to be stated within the text of the play.

SELECTED BIBLIOGRAPHY

Fletcher, Alan J. "'Coveytyse Copbord Schal Be at the Ende of the Castel Be the Beddys Feet': Staging the Death of Mankind in *The Castle of Perseverance*." *English Studies* 68:4 (August 1987), 305-12; Holbrook, S. E. "Covetousness, Contrition, and the Town in *The Castle of Perseverance*." *Fifteenth Century Studies* 13:213 (1988), 275-89; Scherb, Victor I. "The Parable of the Talents in *The Castle of Perseverance*." *English Language Notes* 28:1 (1990), 20-25.

Anna Shealy

CAVALCANTI, GUIDO (1250-1300). While little is known about his youth and education, except that he was taught by Brunetto Latini who employed rhetoric and classical literature, Guido Cavalcanti is clearly ranked as the best poet of the early Italian Renaissance next to *Dante. Guido was the son of Cavalcante Cavalcanti, head of a distinguished, wealthy, and politically engaged Florentine family. Dante, in *Inferno* X, 58-63, meets the elder Cavalcanti in the sixth circle where heretics abide in the burning tombs of the intellectually obstinate and spiritually deficient. Cavalcanti's shade queries Dante as to why, if poetical art enabled him to make the journey to Hell, his own brilliant artist son did not accompany his Florentine friend. Dante's much-discussed response suggests possibly that Guido had an aversion for classical poetry, Roman imperialism, and the Roman virtue of *pietas*, all of which, of course, Virgil, Dante's revered guide, represents. Dante's hesitant response causes Cavalcanti to assume that his son is dead, and thus he falls backward into his eternally burning tomb. Later in the canto, ll. 110-14, Dante receives clarifying knowledge about the awareness of the damned about the living world, after which he asks Farinata degli Uberti, the famous Florentine Ghibelline and major speaking shade of the canto, to inform Cavalcante Cavalcanti that his son lives. Another contested mention of Guido, to whom Dante refers in his *Vita Nuova* as "the first of my friends," appears in *Purgatory* XI, 97. Their friendship began when Guido wrote a reply to one of Dante's sonnets. Also, it was Guido who accompanied Dante to the famous party where he saw Beatrice after a long time, and she mocked him.

Guido Cavalcanti supported the Guelfs, but although he did not hold public office, he became embroiled in the complicated party struggles between the White Guelfs, who supported constitutional government against the emperor, and the Black Ghibellines, who supported the emperor against the pope. In a compromising attempt to reconcile the factions, Guido married Bice degli Uberti, the daughter of the head of the Black Ghibelline faction. But Guido, an intelligent and passionate individual, soon became the bitter enemy of the Guelf Corso Donati, who tried to have Guido assassinated while he was on a pilgrimage in Spain. The political battles reached a point where Dante, a White himself, participated in the Florentine priors' decision to exile Guido to Sarzana in May 1300 where he became ill with malaria, was allowed to return to Florence, and died in August 1300. Dante's hesitation in responding to the elder Cavalcanti's query about his son thus becomes more understandable. Guido left one son, Andrea, who died in 1340.

Guido was well versed in the *Provençal, Sicilian, and classical poets, but his poetry reflects a fresh approach to the formulaic conventions of medieval traditions. It came to be known as *dolce stil nuovo*, a lyricized philosophical inquiry into the nature of love. This inquiry was expressed in a newly created "illustrious vernacular" that was simple, natural, clear, and elegant, and aimed at articulating the immediacy of passions and intellectually probing the nature, scope, and origin of love and strife in human relationships. It represents the first completely native Italian vernacular poetry.

Guido's extant canon consists of 52 poems, including 6 sonnets, 2 songs, 11 *ballade, 1 motteto, and 2 independent stanzas. Some of the poems show how he borrowed the idiom of Provençal and Sicilian poets while advancing the new stilnovistic idea of using language close to practical, common words of daily life to explore the idealized quest for a perfect love. Guido's conclusions about the possible achievement of the ideal love are pessimistic since he believed that a balanced, moderate satisfaction of the earthly desire for love was impossible. His *canzone "Donna me prega" is a difficult exploration of the immoderate demands of love as it confronts the requirement of reason. While several of his poems offer great praise of an idealized image of feminine beauty,

Guido mostly sees love as a malign, dark influence that diminishes reason and degrades the intellectual faculties.

SELECTED BIBLIOGRAPHY

Cirigliano, Marc A., ed. *Guido Cavalcanti: The Complete Poems.* New York: Italica, 1992; Enders, Jody. "Rhetoric and Dialectic in Guido Cavalcanti's 'Donna mi prega.'" *Stanford Italian Review* 5:2 (Fall 1985), 161-74; Fogli, Giovanna. "Tragedy, Laughter, and Cavalcantian Lovers: Boccaccio's Criticism of the Sweet New Style." *NEMLA Italian Studies* 18 (1994), 13-29.

Silvia R. Fiore

CAXTON, WILLIAM (c.1422-1491). William Caxton was the first English printer and also a renowned translator. Caxton spent some thirty years dealing in textiles and served from 1465-69 as the Governor of the English Association of Merchant Adventurers in Bruges. Caxton's first translation, *The Recuyell of the Historyes of Troye,* took three years (1469-71), and was delayed in part because Caxton became Margaret of Burgundy's secretary. His translation was so well received that he learned the new art of printing, perhaps at a local house in Bruges. Around 1471 his work became the first book ever printed in English. The following year he published *The Game and Playe of the Chesse,*.

In 1476 Caxton relocated and opened a press at Westminster where his first printed text was *The Dictes or Sayengis of the Philosophres* (1477). He went on to print nearly one hundred books; of particular interest are Thomas *Malory's *Morte d'Arthur,* Geoffrey *Chaucer's *Canterbury Tales,* and the works of *Boethius and John Gower. He also continued to print many of his own translations, including Carolingian and *Arthurian legends and *romances.

Caxton used eight different types of print and was one of the originators of the inclusion of added woodcut illustrations to editions. Perhaps his best-known illustrated version was his edition of the *Canterbury Tales.* Caxton's writing tends to be elaborate, almost excessive. His works exemplify the problems of courtly literature, a genre that had become passé. Caxton rose to such prominence that whatever he printed became essential reading. After Caxton's death in 1491, his assistant *Wynken de Worde became his successor.

SELECTED BIBLIOGRAPHY

Drabble, Margaret, ed. *The Oxford Companion to English Literature.* 5th ed. Oxford: Oxford University Press. 1985; Hullen, Werner. " A Close Reading of Caxton's Dialogues: '. . . to Lerne Shortly Frenssh and Englyssh.'" *Historical Pragmatics: Pragmatic Developments in the History of English.* Andreas Jucker, ed. Amsterdam: Benjamins, 1995. 99-124; Koster, Patricia. "Caxon, Caxton: A Predating, a Definition, and a Supposed Derivation." *Notes and Queries* 40 (238): 1 (March 1993), 34-35; Warvik, Brita. "The Ambiguous Adverbial/Conjunctions 'Tha' and 'Thonne' in Middle

English: A Discourse-Pragmatic Study of 'Then' and 'When' in Early English Saints'
Lives." *Historical Pragmatics: Pragmatic Developments in the History of English*.
Andreas Jucker, ed. Amsterdam: Benjamins, 1995. 345-57.

Robert T. Lambdin

CELTIC LITERATURE. By 800 B. C., the Celts had emerged in eastern
Europe as a distinct cultural and linguistic group. During the next several
centuries Celtic tribes moved westward, spreading their culture across much of
Europe and the British Isles. The language they spoke belonged to the Indo-
European Family of languages and was closely related to other Indo-European
sub-groups such as Germanic and Italic. During the millennium preceding the
birth of Christ, the Celtic culture of Europe passed through two major phases, the
Hallstatt culture (before 500 B. C. and the La Tène culture (after 500 B. C.). But
the rise of the Roman empire and the growing importance of Christianity proved
destructive to the Celts; in many places Celtic culture was assimilated into
Roman culture, and in others it was vigorously rooted out. By the end of the first
millennium A. D., Celtic culture persisted only in a few isolated areas,
particularly in Europe's "Celtic fringe" of Brittany, Cornwall, Wales, Scotland,
and Ireland. In Ireland and Wales, remnants of the early literary culture of the
Celts survived, recorded either in the Celtic dialect of Goidelic, the ancester of
modern Irish, Scottish, and Manx Gaelic, or in Brythonic, the ancester of Welsh,
Cornish, and Breton.

Scholars believe that within early Celtic society the responsibility for
cultivating and preserving learning and literature rested with three important
professional groups: the druids, the bards, and an intermediate group known as
the *fili*. The druids, who enjoyed the highest social status of the three, oversaw
Celtic religious knowledge and practices--the druidic arts. The bards, who were
chiefly court poets, composed and performed songs praising the lives of kings
and the deeds of heroes. The *fili* stood somewhere between the other two. While
they might serve as seers, teachers, or advisors to rulers, the *fili* were also
concerned with literature. In Ireland they were responsible for preserving Celtic
literary traditions in general, and more specifically for preserving the "lore of
places," one of richest sources of traditional materials passed down orally from
story-teller to story-teller.

The literary works of the insular Celts survive in a small number of Irish
and Welsh manuscripts compiled during the twelfth to the fifteenth centuries.
The earliest is a fragmentary Irish manuscript is known as the *Book of the Dun
Cow; it dates to the first half of the twelfth century, this *ms* contains thirty-seven
Irish tales, including an incomplete version of the *Tain Bó Cuailnge*, a work that
is usually called *The Tain* or "The Cattle Raid of Cooley." Another work,
composed as early, is the Book of Leinster, which contains a wide variety of tales
and a complete and more polished version of *The Tain*. Among the earliest Welsh
manuscripts are included the thirteenth-century Black Book of Carmarthen, the

Book of Aneirin, and the Book of Taliesin, which contain important Welsh poems; and the early fourteenth-century *mss* the White Book of Rhydderch and the Red Book of Hergest, which contain the prose tales known as *The *Mabinogion*.

The earliest examples of Celtic literature have much in common with the heroic literatures of Greece, Scandinavia, and *Anglo-Saxon England, for many of these songs and tales depict warfare and celebrate the valor and prowess of individual heroes. But while the earliest Celtic works share many traits with other heroic literatures, they often possess attributes that seem more distinctly Celtic. Many of the early Irish and Welsh narratives, for example, blend realism and fantasy in a peculiarly Celtic fashion, sometimes creating a dream-like surrealism. Many of them also have greater amounts of sentimentality and humor than is found in works such as *Beowulf*, the *Iliad*, or the Norse *sagas. Celtic writers often delighted in the whimsical and the fantastic, and were fond of outrageous exaggeration; thus the feats of heroes such as Cú Chulainn or Fionn mac Cumhall seem far more astonishing and far less realistic than those performed by figures such as Beowulf or Achilles. (*See **Irish Literature***).

SELECTED BIBLIOGRAPHY

Translations: Cross, T. P., and C. H. Slover, eds. *Ancient Irish Tales*. New York: Henry Holt, 1936. Reprint. New York: Barnes and Noble, 1969; Gantz, Jeffrey, trans. *Early Irish Myths and Sagas*. New York: Penguin, 1981; Jackson, Kenneth H. trans. *A Celtic Miscellany*. New York: Penguin, 1971; Kinsella, Thomas, trans. *The T<in*. Oxford:Oxford University Press, 1969; Background: Beach, Sarah. "Breaking the Pattern: Alan Garner's 'The Owl Service' and the *Mabinogion*." *Mythlore*. 20:1(75) (Winter 1994), 10-14; Carney, James. *Studies in Irish Literature and History*, Dublin: Dublin Institute for Advanced Studies. 1955; Chadwick, Nora. *The Celts*. New York: Penguin, 1970; Cunliffe, Barry. *The Celtic World*. New York: McGraw-Hill, 1979; Dillon, Myles. *Early Irish Literature*. Chicago: University of Chicago Press, 1948; Flower, Robin. *The Irish Tradition*. Oxford: Clarendon Press, 1947; Jones, Gwyn and Thomas Gwyn, trans. *The Mabinogion* London: Dent, 1989; Mac Cana, Proinsias. *Celtic Mythology*. 2nd ed. New York: P. Bedrick, 1985; Murphy, Gerard. *Saga and Myth in Ancient Ireland*. Dublin: Dublin Institute for Advanced Studies, 1961; O'Rahilly, T. F. *Early Irish History and Mythology*. Dublin, Dublin Institute for Advanced Studies, 1946; Rees, Alwyn, and Brinley Rees, *Celtic Heritage*. London: Thames and Hudson, 1961; Ward, Charlotte. "A Formulaic Consideration of the *Mabinogion*, Branch I, 'Pwyll Pendeuic Dyuet.'" *Etudes Celtiques* 29 (1992), 423-39.

John Conlee

CHANDOS HERALD (*fl.* 1360s). The Chandos Herald is the only name by which we know the author of *Vie du Prince Noir* (The Life of the Black Prince), a biography of Edward, Prince of Wales. The Herald probably began service to Sir John Chandos sometime around 1360. His history is devoted to the chivalric virtues of Edward and to a lesser extent, the herald's patron, Sir John Chandos. The accounts, although often historically accurate in many details, are significantly biased in favor of presenting the Black Prince and his supporters (i.e. Sir John Chandos) in the best possible light. The Herald is known to have acted on his patron's behalf as a messenger for certain business surrounding Edward's campaign and probably had firsthand knowledge of some of the battles and locales. His description of the Battle of Najera is among the best written from an English perspective. (*See Chronicles and Annals.*)

SELECTED BIBLIOGRAPHY

Brandt, William J. *The Shape of Medieval History.* New Haven: Yale University Press, 1966; Chandos Herald. *The Life and Campaign of the Black Prince.* New York: St. Martin's Press, 1986; Gransden, Antonia. *Historical Writing in England II: c. 1307 to Early Sixteenth Century.* Ithaca: Cornell University Press, 1982.

Richard McDonald

CHANSON DE GESTE. The term *chanson de geste* refers to a "song of great deeds" and applies to the early French epic. One of the earliest examples of this form is *La *Chanson de Roland,* which dates from around 1100. The early *chansons de geste* were composed in decasyllabic lines. They often were marked by assonance and grouped in strophes of varying length. Cycles of these works developed; the most noted of these concern *Charlemagne, the *Geste du roi.* There are also *chansons* for William of Orange, ones that glorify the efforts of Christian heroes against the Saracens, and others that deal with the strife between the northern barons. *Chansons de Geste* usually demonstrate chivalric ideals, but rely little upon the theme of love. This form was popular for several centuries; there are about eighty existing examples. These tales later supplied much of the material for the medieval *romances; thus their importance in the canon of medieval literature is assured.

SELECTED BIBLIOGRAPHY

Balfour, Mark. "Moses and the Princess: Josephus' *Antiquitates Judaicae* and the *Chansons de Geste.*" *Medium Evum* 64:1 (1995), 1-16; Holman, C. Hugh, and William Harmon. *A Handbook to Literature.* 5th ed. New York: Macmillan, 1986; Kay, Sarah. "The Life of the Dead Body: Death and the Sacred in the *Chansons de Geste.*" *Yale French Studies* 86 (1994), 94-108.

Robert T. Lambdin

CHANSON DE ROLAND, LA. *La Chanson de Roland* is the earliest of the more than one hundred extant Old French epics. It survives in seven complete manuscripts; the oldest is in the Bodleian Library in Oxford and is dated 1130-50. The Oxford manuscript is a copy, but the questions that arise as to when, where, by whom, and in what form the original poem was composed present problems for scholars.

The poem was composed in assonating stanzas of irregular length as a song to be sung by a *minstrel. It tells the story of *Charlemagne's wars against the Saracens of Spain. The French choose the paladin Ganelon as their ambassador. He quarrels with Roland and in his anger betrays Roland and his rear guard of 20,000 men to the enemy. The French are attacked by overwhelming numbers of Saracens in the Pyrenees. They fight magnificently, and the Saracens are stayed. One by one the twelve peers fall, the last to resist being Archbishop Turpin and the companions Oliver and Roland. When Roland dies, he is victor on a field from which the last enemy has fled. Charlemagne, summoned by the urgent call of Roland's horn, returns too late to save him and his comrades, but is in time to destroy the remnants of the Saracens. He then leads his army against the emir, Baligant, who has assembled against him Saracen forces. Baligant is defeated and slain, and Ganelon is led home, tried, condemned, and put to death.

Several conflicts interweave within the narrative and its heroic characters, including Christian opposing pagan views, Frenchman opposing Saracens, and in the protagonists themselves, the deeper and more obscure conflict between incompatible ideals. The final victory of Christian over pagan is won both on the battlefield and in the minds of men through action, as befits an epic poem. The scenes and portraits created in the poem live for the senses. The style is laconic and suited to an audience unschooled in rhetoric, which has a direct and moving effect. Characters are portrayed in strong and simple strokes, creating an impression of their strength and simplicity.

The date of the poem seems to be the last few years of the eleventh century, probably before the First *Crusade, of which much of the spirit but none of the facts are reflected in the poem. Linguistic evidence suggests that the poem was composed somewhere to the southwest of Paris. *La Chanson de Roland* was very popular throughout the Middle Ages as is evidenced by the later manuscripts and the many foreign translations. The poem early became popular in Germany as well as in Spain, where it gave rise to a cycle of ballads. In Italy it was a source for the great romancers Pulci, Boiardo, and Ariosto.

SELECTED BIBLIOGRAPHY

Olifant 15:2 (Summer 1990), 137-55; Reed, J. "The 'Bref' in the *Chanson de Roland*." *French Studies Bulletin* 39 (Summer 1991), 3-7; Reed, J. "The Passage of Time in *La Chanson de Roland*." *Modern Language Review* 87:3 (July 1992), 555-66; Vance, Eugene, "Style and Value: From Soldier to Pilgrim in *The Song of Roland*." *Yale French Studies* (1991), 75-96.

Rebecca Chalmers

CHARLEMAGNE (742-814), Frankish emperor. Physically huge by the standards of the time, Charlemagne, at six feet, seven inches, understood Greek and spoke Latin, but he never learned to write. He preferred to dress and conduct himself as a Frankish prince. In general, he continued the policies of earlier Frankish leaders: expansion of Frankish rule to include all of Germany, Lombardy, Venetia Istria, Dalmatia, Corsica, Bavaria, and Saxony. Christianity was forcibly introduced, with the close understanding of and support from the papacy. Charlemagne also supported church reform, which settled the unity of medieval Christianity.

After 782 Charlemagne was able to bring control to his far flung holdings by establishing the Marches of the Danes: Altmearts, Thuringia, Bohemia, Ostmarks; and, finally, the Spanish March. By 801 he had accomplished the suppression of Islam in northeast Spain.

Charlemagne had very little contact with the papacy, but held it to be his duty to defend the church and the pope as he did the Frankish bishops; he also recognized the pope's unique spiritual prestige. During his 774 visit to Rome, the first by any Frankish leader, the Donation of Pepin was confirmed and the pope crowned Charlemagne's sons—Pepin as king of Italy and Louis as king of Aquitaine. Charlemagne himself was crowned emperor on Christmas Day in 800 at St. Peter's. His coronation marked a return to the dualism of Theodosius I (two emperors over one empire). The Frankish Empire was more German than Roman in population as well as institutions.

In the eyes of the Byzantine Empire, the coronation of Charlemagne by the pope in Rome marked a definite break between Rome and Constantinople. The Byzantines considered this event an act of rebellion. In 812 the Byzantine emperor was finally forced to recognize Charlemagne's title in the west in return for sovereignty in VenetPa, Istria and Dalmatia.

Charlemagne had a lasting impact on the institutions of society. In the church his rule was a theocracy: he insisted on supremacy over the Frankish Church, and the right to legislate on all matters—settling questions of dogma, making appointments, and presiding at synods.

In matters of state Charlemagne insisted on centralization of authority, and taxation in the Roman sense, although this system was eventually replaced by one in which service was rendered in return for land grants, which became the economic basis of Carolinian society. Such service included forced labor by the lower ranks, the provision of food for the court and public officials on duty, and judicial and military obligations. Charlemagne's constant campaigns reduced the number of small farmers, accentuating the tendency to serfdom. He attempted to offset this tendency by allowing groups of poorer farmers to cooperate in sending a single soldier to the campaigns and by excusing the poorest from ordinary field service. Systemization of the army and of military service began to develop. The basis of future feudal development was firmly established.

To prevent hereditary tenure and to limit local abuses, the *missi dominici* were introduced in 802 as officers on circuit. These *missi* held their own courts, had power to remove a count for cause, and were charged with supervising financial, judicial, and clerical functions. They formed an essential link between local and central government. Under Charlemagne, efforts at education were revived. Clerics were also given grants to open local schools.

SELECTED BIBLIOGRAPHY

Banfield, Susan. *Charlemagne*. New York: Chelsea House, 1986; Cobby, Anne Elizabeth. *Ambivalent Conventions: Formula and Parody in Old French*. Amsterdam: Rodopi, 1995; Farrier, Susan E. *The Medieval Charlemagne Legend: An Annotated Bibliography; Dutch Materials Treated by Geert H. M. Claassens*. New York: Garland, 1993.

R. Churchill Curtis

CHARLES V (1338-1380), Capetian, king of France (1364-1380). Charles's reign opened with a bad harvest, plague, and the pillage of large areas by free companies of infantry. The king dominated the new financial machinery set up by the Estates-General, continued the war levies, and utilized the peace for general reform and reconstruction. Castles were rebuilt, royal control was re-established, and permanent companies of cavalry and infantry were reinstituted; artillery was supported by pioneers and sappers were organized. A military staff and hierarchy of command were established; the changes were done by 1374.

The government and finance were reorganized, and the general frame of the financial structure, which lasted virtually unchanged until 1789, was set. Charles was able to persuade the Estates-General to agree to the general principle that the king was free of control until he needed new taxes. The Estates-General was no longer vital, and financial control passed to the chambre de comptes.

SELECTED BIBLIOGRAPHY

Laird, Edgar. "Astrology in the Court of Charles V of France as Reflected in Oxford, St. John's College, MS 164." *Manuscripta* 34:3 (November 1990), 167-76; Sherman, Claire Richter. *The Portraits of Charles V of France (1338-1380)*. New York: New York University Press, 1969.

R. Churchill Curtis

CHARMS. Among the most fascinating forms of medieval literature are mystical charms that are filled with archaic language of great pagan beauty and supernaturalism. Some of the most interesting relics of old heathen practices incongruously mixed with Christian ritual may be found in the texts and stage directions of *Old English charms. Their ritual directions are obviously an important condition of their efficacy. Felix Grendon, in his analysis of such magical formulae in American folklore, listed five classes of such spells: (1) exorcisms of diseases and disease spirits, (2) herbal charms, (3) charms for transferring diseases, (4) amulet charms, and (5) charm remedies.

One of the most carefully articulated charms in *Anglo-Saxon literature is addressed to the relief of a bewitched land. This remedy, without change of form or language may be applied to fields that are non-productive, thus suggesting the activity of sorcery or witchcraft. It is notable that in charms Erce, the old Teutonic deity, is still remembered as the Mother of Men. One might easily separate the pagan from the Christian elements by considering all the instructions to physical action as the residue of oral magic and the repeated text of prayers as the overlay of Christianity. The medieval suspicion that malign influences come through the female gender is made explicit in line 71 "no woman of witchcraft," although the added codicil "no worker of magic" by its gender-free form softens the anti-feminism.

The whole charm makes it quite clear that Anglo-Saxon religion assumes a material return for piety, in contrast to the many references in the Gospels that we are not to lay up treasures in barns but in heaven. The importance of magic ritual must be akin to the ceremonial exactitude of the Mass. Only in the words of the mouth and the desires of the heart, but also in the precise motions of hand and body.

SELECTED BIBLIOGRAPHY

Bozoky, Edina. "From Matter of Devotion to Amulets." *Medieval Folklore* 3 (Fall 1994), 91-107; Bragg, Lois. "The Modes of the Old English Metrical Charms." *Comparatist* 16 (May 1992), 3-23; Grambo, Ronald. "Mythical Thought in Norwegian Charms." *Acta Ethnographica Hungarica* 38:1 (1993), 271-85; Olsan, Lea. "Latin Charms of Medieval England: Verbal Healing in a Christian Oral Tradition." *Oral Tradition* 7:1 (March 1992), 116-42.

Elton E. Smith

CHAUCER, GEOFFREY (c.1343/44-1400). Geoffrey Chaucer was the first person to be recognized as an English "author." There had been important compositions in English before Chaucer, from *Beowulf* to *Sir Gawain and the Green Knight,* but these pieces are all anonymous, and there is no evidence that they were ever circulated. They are extant in unique manuscripts that were not rediscovered until the nineteenth century. From the Norman Conquest in 1066 until the usurpation of the throne by *Henry IV in 1399, French and Latin were the official languages of England, and English was a domestic patois. All of the population except the *Anglo-Norman aristocracy continued to speak English dialects, but nearly everything written was in Latin or French. After 1340, with the effort by King *Edward III to assert dominance over France, English nationalism began to make its appearance, and authors like Chaucer, *Gower, *Wycliffe, and others began to compose in English. But there was no evidence yet of a reading public for English. Virtually all compositions in English before 1400 are extant in manuscripts produced after 1400.

After usurping the throne from *Richard II in 1399, Henry IV and his Lancastrian court began trying to secure political support from Parliament by reintroducing English as the official written language. They cited Chaucer's poems as the prototypes of polished expression partly because they were so well written, but also because of Chaucer's social prestige--he was, after all, first cousin to the king and a leading figure in the government and business community. Thus from 1400 onwards Chaucer was constantly referred to as the "firste fyndere of our faire langage," "the noble rethor poete of Breteine," and his style and language provided a model for expression that has extended to the present day. Combining the native idiom with Latin and French rhetoric and poetic, he originated the melody and idiom of English poetry.

All of the records cited in this biographical account are printed and discussed in *Chaucer Life Records*, edited by M. M. Crow and C. C. Olson. On October 15, 1386, Geoffrey Chaucer gave a deposition in a trial about a contested coat of arms in which he gave his age as "xl ans et plus, armeez par xxvii ans" (forty years and more, having borne arms for twenty-seven years). This is the best evidence we have about the date of Geoffrey's birth. Forty years and more places his birth date before 1346. In 1876 F. J. Furnivall discovered a deed of conveyance of a house on Thames Street, just below St. Paul's Cathedral, in which the seller identified himself as "me Galfridum Chaucer filiuum Johannis Chaucer Vintenarii Londonie" (I Geoffrey Chaucer, son of John Chaucer, vintner of London). This identifies Geoffrey as the son of a prosperous London citizen associated with the court of Edward III about whom there is much information in the records. Geoffrey probably began his education at St. Paul's School, a few minute walk from John's home on Thames Street. St. Paul's had an exceptionally fine library where Geoffrey could have begun his broad acquaintance with the Latin classics.

Geoffrey soon transferred to service in the household of Elizabeth, countess of Ulster, wife of Lionel, the second son of Edward III. Fragments of the countess's household accounts for 1356-59 were found within the lining of the covers of a volume purchased by the British Museum in 1851. These accounts record allowances of clothing and other gratuities to various members of her household, including the page Geoffrey Chaucer. This appointment demonstrates the considerable influence of John Chaucer because it was unusual for a commoner to become a page in a princely household. Service in such a household provided an education not only in manners and martial arts but also in the literature of *chivalry. If St. Paul's School introduced Geoffrey to Ovid and Virgil, countess Elizabeth's household introduced him to *Roman de la Rose*, Machaut, Deschamps, and the courtly *romances.

Along with those to the page Geoffrey, Countess Elizabeth's accounts record donations to a damoiselle Philippa Pan. In 1366 a Philippa Chaucer was granted a life annuity of ten marks as domicella to Queen Philippa. This grant was made without reference to a husband and a year before Geoffrey was granted his annuity. It appears that Philippa Pan became Philippa Chaucer. There has been discussion as to whether this was a marriage of convenience. Philippa Chaucer was identified by the sixteenth-century herald Robert Glover as the sister of Katherine Swynford, mistress of Lionel's younger brother, *John of Gaunt, and mother of the Beaufort line from whom *Henry VII was eventually descended. It has been suggested that John of Gaunt was also the father of Philippa's son Thomas Chaucer. John of Gaunt was the most potent figure in government in the last years of Edward III and the first years of *Richard II. As duke of Lancaster (in the right of his wife Blanche) he created the "Lancastrian" political affinity that carried over into the usurpation of the throne by Gaunt's son by Blanche, Henry Bolingbroke (Henry IV). Gaunt was remarkably beneficent to both Philippa and Thomas Chaucer. The possibility that he was Thomas Chaucer's father is not popular with Chaucerophiles. The pros and cons are explored in *The Importance of Chaucer* (Fisher 19-24).

Geoffrey's service in Countess Elizabeth's household came to an end in September 1359 when he went to war in France in a company assembled by the countess's husband, Prince Lionel. This was in a campaign mounted by the Black Prince that ended with the Peace of Bretigny in May 1360. Chaucer was ransomed by the royal exchequer in March 1360, which indicates that he was actually in combat, and in October he was reimbursed by Prince Lionel for carrying letters from Calais to England.

This year of military service was the token required of all the affinity of an aristocracy whose business was war. After October 1360 Geoffrey disappears from the records for six years. These years he may have spent in an environment more compatible with his temperament, the Inns of Chancery and Inns of Court. The Inns of Chancery were preparatory institutions where clerks learned the Chancery script in which all records were kept, the legal French and Latin in which all business was transacted, and general office procedures. Acquiring these skills took about three years. After this basic education most students moved at once to clerkships in the national bureaucracy, guilds, or private households. Those with resources and influence to aspire to become attorneys sought membership in one of the Inns of Court, where they consorted with the lawyers, heard lectures, and read law until they were ready to be called to the bar.

Membership in an Inn of Court was a lifetime situation, like election to a fraternity. No records of any of the Inns of Court are extant before 1421, but those surviving subsequently show that esquires from noble families were frequently members. Like Addison's Mr. Spectator, many of these had no interest in practicing law. They were at the Inns of Court in order to learn to look after their own property and for the association membership provided. It would appear that Geoffrey lived at the Inner Temple for about three years before returning to service in the king's household. Speght's biography (1598) observed that "Master Buckley did see a record in the [Inner Temple] where Geffrey Chaucer was fined two shillingess for beatinge a Franciscane fryer in fletestreate." Other records show that this was a normal offense--fraternity life could be rowdy even then.

Philippa Chaucer had received her ten-mark annuity in 1366. On June 20, 1367, Geoffrey Chaucer was granted an annuity of twenty marks, and from this time until 1374 his name appears in the lists of royal esquires receiving grants of clothing and money. Evidently he lived in the palace and spent much of his time traveling abroad on diplomatic and financial missions--appropriate service for one skilled in composition and languages. He no doubt began reading his English poems to the court. His earliest important poem, *Book of the Duchess*, is an elegy on the death of Blanche, Duchess of Lancaster, wife of John of Gaunt and mother of the future King Henry IV. Blanche died in 1368. It must have taken some courage for Chaucer to compose this poem in English. English was still considered an inferior patois, unsuitable for laudatory poetry to a high-born lady. No doubt Chaucer was composing other songs and poems in English that demonstrated the capacity of the vernacular. He and the French poet Deschamps both said that he translated *Roman de la Rose*, but his translation has not come down to us (the version found in the Chaucer anthologies is not in Chaucer's dialect). This would have been a prime demonstration of the capacities of English since the *Roman* was the archetypal French court poem. But none of these poems, including the elegy on the death of Blanche, was considered significant enough to be copied for circulation. All come down in copies dated after Chaucer's death in 1400.

In 1374 Chaucer finally became independent. On April 23 he was granted a pitcher of wine daily (equivalent to perhaps ten pounds a year). On May 10 he was given a lifetime lease, rent free, of an apartment over Aldgate. On June 8 he was made controller of customs in the port of London (another ten pounds). And on June 13 Geoffrey and Philippa together were granted another ten-pound annuity by John of Gaunt. These grants, added to the previous annuities, made Geoffrey prosperous. The controllership of customs was a very important government position since the tax on the export of wool and the import of woolen cloth was the chief support of the Crown and national bureaucracy.

The language of the appointment specifies that Geoffrey was to keep the customs records in his own hand (evidence of his Chancery training) and remain constantly present in London, but there are frequent records of his being allowed to appoint a deputy controller to serve while he as absent on foreign missions of one kind or another. *Froissart said in his *Chroniques* that Chaucer was present in France at Montreuil-sur-Mer, during February-June 1377 in negotiations for the marriage of young King Richard II to Marie, daughter of the French king-- negotiations that broke off when the princess died. In Italy he could have met *Boccaccio and *Petrarch in 1372 and Boccaccio again in 1378. During his busy years at the wool quay he wrote two long poems to read to the royal court and the Inns of Court reflecting his bureaucratic and diplomatic experience, *Parliament of Fowls* and *House of Fame*, and he probably wrote versions of several short narrative poems, like "St. Cecelia" (the *"Second Nun's Tale"), "Palamon and Arcite" (the *"Knight's Tale"), and the Monk's tragedies that were later incorporated into the *Canterbury Tales* collection. This existence went on until John of Gaunt's government began unravelling in 1386.

For several years before his death in 1377 Edward III was in his dotage, and government was in the hands of his mistress, Alice Perrers, and his oldest surviving son, John of Gaunt. Gaunt and Alice ran a very corrupt administration; in 1376 Alice was impeached, but during the first years of Richard II (he was ten when he was crowned in 1377) Gaunt continued to run the government. By 1386 he and the young king had run it into the ground. Gaunt wisely decided to leave England to claim the throne of Spain in the right of his second wife, Costanza of Castile. Eleven barons were appointed to reform the government. In 1387 five barons, led by Gaunt's younger brother Thomas of Woodstock, stripped Richard of his rule and expelled and executed his friends. These were Lancastrian appointments made by Richard under the tuteledge of John of Gaunt. It reveals something about Geoffrey's political involvement that in the process of these reforms in 1386 he lost his controllership of customs and his house over Aldgate. He hed been provided for, however. In 1385 he had been appointed justice of the peace in Kent, and in 1386 he was elected a member of Parliament from Kent, so clearly he moved out to Kent and continued in the royal service. But in 1388 he transferred both of his exchequer annuities to one John Scalby.

Geoffrey evidently now had more time for writing than he had had before. *Troylus and Criseyde*, his most "finished" poem, dates from this period. Also, influenced perhaps by *Boccaccio's *Decameron*, he conceived the notion of a dramatic frame into which to collect the short narrative poems that he had been composing for many years. To set the stage, he wrote a prologue and a conclusion (the headlink to "The *Parson's Tale") that gave shape to the *Canterbury Tales*.

But Geoffrey's respite from administration did not last long. In 1389 Richard (now twenty-two years old) declared himself of age, dismissed Woodstock from the Council, and began to rule personally. One of his first actions was to appoint Geoffrey Chaucer clerk of the king's works. This was nearly as important as and much more strenuous than the controllership of customs. It involved riding around to oversee the upkeep of all the royal buildings, including the Tower of London, Westminster, Windsor, and other royal castles and manors. To pay workmen, he had to carry with him large sums of money. Twice in 1390 he was robbed, with injury, in Surrey at Hatcham and "Le Fowle Ok" on the way to oversee work on the royal manor at Eltham. Such activity did not encourage him to get on with his writing. Another clerk of the works was appointed in June 1391 and Geoffrey was given a sinecure appointment as subforester of North Petherton in Somerset that evidently continued until his death. In 1394 Richard renewed Geoffrey's exchequer annuity of twenty pounds. But Geoffrey held no further government posts--he was by this time over fifty years old. In 1399 he signed a fifty-three-year lease for an apartment in the garden of the Lady Chapel of Westminster Abbey. This amounted to buying the property, since in England most property is vested in long-term leases.

He turned back to the Canterbury collection, adding the rascals at the end of "The General Prologue" and composing or revising the *fabliaux, the "marriage group," and other tales, but never exerting himself to complete the plan he had long ago laid out in the prologue. He began to toy with astronomy, beginning work on *Treatise on the Astrolabe* and *Equatorie of the Planets.* But he had lost his drive. He had never considered himself a "writer" and felt no compulsion to finish any of his works. Immediately after the coronation of Henry IV, he addressed a *ballade of supplication for money, and Henry doubled his 1394 annuity. He wrote short poems to friends like Scogan and Bukton, but his poetic career was essentially finished. The last record is his quittance for the grant of a tun of wine is September 29, 1400. The date of his death on his tombstone in Westminster Abbey, erected in 1556, is October 25, 1400. He was buried in the Abbey because he was a parishoner, but by being buried there he inaugurated the "poets' corner" in the cathedral.

SELECTED BIBLIOGRAPHY

For text and bibliography to 1987, see *The Complete Poetry and Prose of Geoffrey Chaucer,* ed. John H. Fisher (New York: Holt, Rinehart, and Winston, 2nd ed., 1988). There is an annual annotated bibliography in *Studies in the Age of Chaucer.*

Allen, Mark. and John H. Fisher. *The Essential Chaucer: An Annotated Bibliography of Major Modern Studies.* Boston: Hall, 1987; Carlson, David R. "Chaucer, Humanism, and Printing: Conditions of Authorship in Fifteenth-Century England." *University of Toronto Quarterly* 64:2 (Spring 1995), 274-88; Chance, Jane. *The Mythographic Chaucer: The Fabulation of Sexual Politics.* Minneapolis: University of Minnesota Press, 1995; Crow, M. M., and C. C. Olson, eds. *Chaucer Life Records.* Oxford: Clarendon Press, 1966. Fisher, John H. *The Emergence of Standard English.* Lexington, KY: University of Kentucky Press, 1996; Fisher, John H. "Historical and Methodological Consideration for Adopting 'Best Text' or *'Usus Scribendi'* for Textual Criticism of Chaucer's Poems." *Text* 6 (1994), 165-80; Fisher, John H. *The Importance of Chaucer.* Carbondale: Southern Illinois University Press, 1992. Irwin, Bonnie D. "What's in a Frame? The Medieval Textualization of Traditional Storytelling." *Oral Tradition* 10:1 (Mar 1995), 27-53; Lambdin, Laura. and Robert T. Lambdin, eds. *Chaucer's Pilgrims: An Historical Guide to the Pilgrims of the Canterbury Tales.* Westport, CT: Greenwood Press, 1996; Rex, Richard. *'The Sins of Madame Eglentyne' and Other Essays on Chaucer.* Newark:University of Delaware Press, 1995; Taylor, Paul Beekman. "Time in the *Canterbury Tales.*" *Exemplaria* 7:2 (Fall 1995), 371-93

John H. Fisher

CHIVALRY. A term derived from *"chevalier,"* "horseman" or "knight," chivalry referes to customs connected with knighthood in the Middle Ages. Chivalry was originally associated with the recruiting of knights intending to go to war. This evolved to include the training of young knights to hunt, fight, and serve their lords. Finally, it reached the point that knights were thought to be not only courageous and adept in warfare, but also generous, courteous, and pious. To this was added the notion that knights should champion the weak.

With these changes, chivalry became an important part of a knight's life in peace as well as war. During this time tournaments abounded. A component was that of *courtly love, which redefined the knight's code. Courtly love required that a knight be dedicated to a lady of his choice, whether she loved him or not. Also, it required that he be some type of poet or musician.

SELECTED BIBLIOGRAPHY

Purdon, Liam O., and Julian N. Wasserman. "Chivalry and Feudal Obligation in Barbour's 'Bruce.'" *The Rusted Hauberk: Feudal Ideas of Order and Their Decline.* Gainesville: University Press of Florida, 1994, 77-95; Schwetman, John W. "Feudal Chivalry in Popular Medieval Battle Poems." *The Rusted Hauberk: Feudal Ideas of Order and Their Decline.* Gainesville: University Press of Florida, 1994. 229-44; Weiss, Victoria I. "The Play World and the Real World: Chivalry in *Sir Gawain and the Green Knight*" *Philological Quarterly* 72:4 (Fall 1993), 403-18.

Robert T. Lambdin

CHRÉTIEN DE TROYES (c. 1125-1191). French *romance writer Chrétien de Troyes elaborated upon earlier *Arthurian legends in such an intriguing way as to create, change, and record the highly stylized customs of *courtly love just beginning to flower in France at the time. Further, his works produced our current notions of the order of the Round Table by changing the basic course of the *Matter of Britain (as Arthurian legends are called). In Chrétien's hands King Arthur, Lancelot, and Tristran became elegant statesmen and lovers, quite a twist from earlier conceptions of the Camelot men that had focused upon their prowess in battle. Had Chrétien's renditions been less popular, it is unlikely that the stories of Camelot would have had such an impact upon Western thought, particularly upon the social consciousness of Victorian England which was filled with reformers.

Chrétien excelled in examining the problems of love versus duty and self versus society. The dates of Chrétien's life and death are uncertain, but it seems likely that he began writing around 1160 in Troyes, France, a time and place for encouraging chic, refined manners, and it seems that he stopped writing around 1190. Chrétien's audience was apparently quite receptive to the idea of a knight's adoration and exaltification of the lady, and his writing are much like the songs of the troubadours so popular at the time. Indeed, similarly thematic love songs have remained constant throughout recorded history.

The court of Champagne influenced Chrétien greatly, especially his relationship with the Countess Marie, daughter of *Eleanor of Aquitaine and Louis VII. It was the Countess Marie who encouraged the notion of courtly love. Among Chrétien's earliest work seems to have been a translation of Ovid's *Art of Love* that has been lost, along with his version of the Tristran legend. Surviving works include *Erec et Enid* (c. 1170), *Clige's* (c. 1175), *Lancelot or the Knight of the Cart* (c. 1179), *Yvain or the Knight with the Lion* (also c. 1179), and *Perceval or the History of the Grail* (written between 1180 and 1190); this final text was left unfinished; only one-third was written by Chrétien, and the rest was completed by others.

Translating Ovid's text seems to have influenced Chrétien's treatment of love as an all-important theme and of the perfect lover as an exceptional character. The elaborate code behind expressing any sentiment--especially those delivered to the beloved--is the topic of the four romances that Chrétien himself authored. All together, these texts present a fairly complete picture of the ideals of medieval French chivalry. They are composed in French and written in eight-syllable rhyming couplets.

SELECTED BIBLIOGRAPHY

Guerin, M. Victoria. *The Fall of Kings and Princes: Structure and Destruction in Arthurian Tragedy.* Stanford: Stanford University Press, 1995; Hunt, Tony. "Chrétien's Prologues Reconsidered." *Conjunctures: Medieval Studies in Honor of Douglas Kelly.* Keith Busby and Norris Lacy, eds. Amsterdam: Rodopi, 1994. 153-68; Lacy, Norris J. "Motivation and Method in the Burgundian 'Erec.'" *Conjunctures: Medieval Studies in Honor of Douglas Kelly.* Keith Busby and Norris Lacy, eds. Amsterdam: Rodopi, 1994. 271-80; Mickel, Emmanuel J., Jr. "The Conflict between Pitie and Largesse in the 'Chevalier de charrete.'" *Neuphilologische Mitteilungen* 95:1 (1994), 31-36; Uitti, Karl D. "Chrétien de Troyes's 'Clig9s.'" *Conjunctures: Medieval Studies in Honor of Douglas Kelly.* Keith Busby and Norris Lacy, eds. Amsterdam: Rodopi, 1994. 545-57; Wolfgang, Lenora D. "Chrétien's 'Lancelot': The Fragments in Manuscript 6138 of the Institut de France." *Conjunctures: Medieval Studies in Honor of Douglas Kelly.* Keith Busby and Norris Lacy, eds. Amsterdam: Rodopi, 1994. 559-74.

Laura Cooner Lambdin

CHRIST AND SATAN. Found in the *Junius manuscript and dated to the late eighth century, *Christ and Satan* belongs to the group of poems often referred to as "Cædmonian." This poem was originally credited to *Cædmon, due in part to its Anglican content. However, it is now attributed to a ninth century author who used the attributes of both Cædmon and *Cynewulf in his writing. The work contains three poems. The first is the "Laments of the Fallen Angels." The second poem, "Descent into Hell, Resurrection, and Ascension," is paralleled in other works such as *Beowulf, Daniel,* and *Andreas.* The final poem,

"Temptation of Christ by Satan," is incomplete, although it does display somewhat original work. Perhaps most interesting in *Christ and Satan* is the conception of Satan, who is portrayed as a pitiable character, a far cry from the contemptible fiend of other medieval works.

SELECTED BIBLIOGRAPHY

Finnegan, Robert Emmett. "Christ as Narrator in the Old English 'Christ and Satan.'" *English Studies* 75:1 (January 1994). 2-16; Harsh, Constance D. "'Christ and Satan': The Measured Power of Christ." *Neuphilologische Mitteilungen* 90:3-4 (1989), 243-53; Johnson, David F. "Old English Religious Poetry: 'Christ and Satan' and 'The Dream of the Rood.'" *Companion to Old English Poetry*. Henk Aertson and Rolf H.Bremmer, eds. Amsterdam: Vrije University Press, 1994. 159-87; Morey, James H. "Adam and Judas in the Old English 'Christ and Satan.'" *Studies in Philology* 87:4 (Fall 1990), 397-409; Portnoy, Phyllis. "'Remnant' and Ritual: The Place of 'Daniel' and 'Christ and Satan' in the 'Junius' Epic.'" *English Studies* 75:5 (September 1994), 408-22.

Robert T. Lambdin

CHRONICLES AND ANNALS. Medieval Chronicles and *Annals may very well have been the repository for medieval creative genius during some of literary history's darkest times. The historical drive preserved in such texts eventually developed into one of the cornerstones of medieval literature, the *romance.

The medieval terms "chronicle" and "annal" were often interchangeable, and the distinction is complicated further in their difference from earlier church and classical Roman chronicles and annals and our own use of such words. Generally, annals were the most simplistic form of historical record keeping during the medieval period. "Annal" could refer to a historical record that included short entries for years in succession, or it could refer to any one entry in an annal. Chronicles generally refer to more descriptive forms of annal keeping, but sometimes the term "chronicle" could be used to mean a text containing multiple years of annal entries. Although "chronicle" was often used to denote a text that included more description and exposition than an annal, chronicles were generally accepted to be straightforward, simple accounts of the events within the chronicler's area of coverage. More descriptive still than chronicles were *histories, which often elaborated on the historical entries of chronicles and annals and included lengthy speeches spoken by historical characters and exposition of their actions, often not based on specific evidence. The romance tradition can be seen to spring from the increasing popularity of histories. But chronicles (and annals, for that matter) could also contain the elaborative techniques more commonly attributed to histories and romances, so the distinction between the types of historical documents often requires some familiarity with the particular document in question, and often a document contains elements of annal, chronicle, and history.

The earliest historical records, and the most tenacious, surviving the decline in writing during the sixh and seventh centuries in England and on the continent, were no more than marginal or interlinear notations added to a monastery's Easter tables. Easter tables were used to determine the date of Easter (*see Festivals and Holidays*), a feast day for which the exact date varies from year to year, based in part on the phases of the moon. The annalist sometimes would include in the record a short notation, just one line or so, about the year. Major local or regional events were sometimes recorded, such as coronations of kings, the appointment of a new bishop, or the erection of a new building, and, even more commonly, astronomical or meteorological data were recorded--comets, eclipses, heavy storms, droughts, or floods. The events included invariably were of importance to the monastery and its locale, but often the recorded event is of little importance to later historians. Because the determination of the correct date of Easter was important, monasteries borrowed and shared their Easter tables. While copying the Easter dates the scribes included the marginal data from the tables as well. As numerous tables came in contact with each other through subsequent copying and recopying the chronicle was born.

But medieval historians were not working in a new genre when they ventured to record historical events; clerks and monks who could read were familiar with Roman and early Christian conceptions of history and chronicling. St. *Augustine had a powerful influence upon the medieval mind, especially with reference to how people viewed history or the progression thereof. Augustine, who helped solidify Christianity in England (one of the strongholds of chronicling), believed that there would be seven ages of history, the last of which would be in heaven. He assumed that medieval man was living at the end of the sixth age. Later church historians who relied on Augustine, particularly Orosius, a Spanish priest of the early fifth century, believed that the decline of the Roman Empire proved that Armageddon was near. Even though chroniclers often accepted that they were living at the end of history, they continued to see its preservation as important. *Isidore of Seville adopted Augustine's historical stages as well, but unlike Orosius, he believed that the Catholic Church continued the sixth age of history and that the end of the world was not necessarily imminent. In his *Etymologies* and his own historical writings he claimed that history was constituted by a true narration of events and that such a narration could serve a moral purpose and hence be beneficial to humankind. Chronicles that purport to recount the history of the entire world since Creation (such as those by Augustine, Orosius, and Isidore) are often referred to as universal chronicles or universal histories.

The medieval idea of historical truth probably differed greatly from our own. Fantastic events are quite regularly explained as being miracles, and legendary characters repeatedly come to life to perform marvels. In the prehistorical period, before the actual year-by-year accounting of events in a particular annal begins, there is usually a greater abundance of spectacular occurrences, but miracles are reported to the chronicler from his present day, often by "eyewitnesses." Along with fantastic events come fantastic attributions of believable historical events. Armies are repeatedly defeated because God seeks to punish their king, or, conversely, a battle turns in favor of a leader because of God's intervention. As mentioned earlier, chronicles recorded numerous astronomical events; frequently these occurrences were seen to have dire results in the historical world--comets and eclipses often foretold the death of kings. In general, any large-scale disaster that followed an astronomical occurrence was seen to have been foretold by the occurrence.

In addition to their easy acceptance of certain supernatural occurrences within history, medieval historians differed markedly from modern historians in both the perspective from which they wrote and their attitude toward causality and the interrelation of events. Medieval historians were often monks or clergy limited in their ability to travel, and even when the chronicler has experienced numerous cultures and locales, he often devoted himself to recording history as it was deemed important by his local audience. This often has the effect of making important local events (like a new building or a bishop's ordination) seem as important as or more so than historically important national events, such as faraway wars or major political changes. The distortion caused by the chronicler's perspective is easily rectified by modern historians, but they cannot recover the details of national events which the chronicler deemed inessential to his audience. Chroniclers also differed from modern historians in that generally they were not interested in the causes of a particular event, and as mentioned earlier they sometimes attributed events to supernatural causes. In general, the chronicler presented events and left his text at that, not offering his own insight into the reasons behind the events he narrated. As the interest in history grew, and grow it did, chronicles and histories were created with greater attention to detail and developing interest for the reading audience, but even the earliest historians included historical information that was popular with their hearers and often included amusing stories, legends, and anecdotes, not always directly relevant to their subject, for their audience's entertainment.

Some of the earliest historians to fall within the purview of medieval studies are the barbarian historians. The importance of these four early historians representing four different peoples is attested by numerous modern historians of the medieval period (Beryl Smalley and Walter Goffart both deal with this group ably, although to different degrees). *Jordanes's A. D. 554, history of the Goths; *Gregory of Tours's A. D. 594, *History of the Franks*; The Venerable *Bede's A. D. 735, *Ecclesiastical History*; and *Paul the Deacon's A. D. 799 *History of the Lombards* are accepted as the best extant early histories on their respective peoples. Although they differ markedly in their value to modern historians as factual documents, they reveal a great deal about the drive to record the events of a particular people, often for patriotic reasons.

The Venerable Bede is the most respected early historian and may be England's finest medieval historian. He avoided the temptation to find or create biblical or classical origins for the Britons, and his *History* to this day provides historians with the only reliable account they have of early British history. The work of the barbarian historians was well received within their own lands and often found its way to other countries. Each of these historians provided information and inspiration for later national historians, but none had as large an impact on historiography as Bede.

The English maintained interest in keeping at least rudimentary historical records through the ninth and tenth centuries, years when learning was on the decline. Beryl Smalley claimed that the historical drive all but died on the Continent during these "dark ages," but historical records were still maintained and created in England during this period. Bede included a chronological summary at the end of his *Ecclesiastical History* and probably added annals to it for the years 731-34, but additional annals by another writer(s) were added for the years 735-66. The English tradition of including annals in Easter tables was now apparently broadening to support the creation of annals for their own sake. Because annals were not particularly literarily demanding documents, they could be kept by anyone who was able to write; chronicles required only short entries for each year to keep up to date and could be continued by different people over time. During the early Middle Ages a number of chronicles or annals were created, and some still survive. Early *Anglo-Saxon chronicles originated in the eighth century, according to Gransden, and chronicles of differing levels of description and literary talent continued throughout the Middle Ages. In the late ninth century under the reign of King *Alfred the *Anglo-Saxon Chronicles* was begun. These early nonliterary productions kept alive the drive to record history and provided later, and more literary, chroniclers and historians with the raw material necessary to document their nation's history.

Although the study of history was not an accepted discipline in the medieval university, the interest in history or historical accounts--often of limited factual value--provided the impetus for numerous talented writers to try their hands at history or historical romances. Because these writers were often relying on older sources even for the most believable of the stories they recounted, it is often difficult to determine to what extent they believed fanciful historical accounts, such as tales of King Arthur or Brutus. In his study of how power exerted itself through discourse in fourteenth-century literature, Jesse Gellrich included two chapters on the importance of chronicles in creating and perpetuating political image and power.

As chronicles became more and more a literary device, the techniques employed became more and more rhetorical. Often the writer would give elaborate descriptions of places and people whom he could not possibly have seen and of which he probably had no such elaborate record. The writers gave life to their stories through including numerous details, many of which were created by the writer to fit his conception of the event. In addition to creating a setting for the event, writers would place speeches into the mouths of various characters, even though they often had no evidence that any such speech had been uttered. What these elaborative techniques do is to create a larger-than-life picture of the events. Although these techniques may first have been fully exploited by writers such as *Geoffrey of Monmouth, who recounted the history of Britain long before his time, they were refined by romance writers such as Wace or *Chrétien de Troyes, and were also used to write the biographical accounts of contemporary kings and nobles. The result of romance's influence on history writing was the creation of exaggerated accounts of recent events, written by poets, to honor or flatter a person of political power, oftentimes the poet's patron. These historical/literary accounts functioned to establish the individual lord's character and might be seen as political tools or propaganda for increasing the lord's popularity and reputation for chivalric deeds.

SELECTED BIBLIOGRAPHY

Brandsma, Frank. "The Eyewitness Narrator in Vernacular Prose Chronicles and Prose Romances." In *Text and Intertext in Medieval Arthurian Literature*. Norris J. Lacy, ed. New Yprk: Garland, 1996. 57-69. Brandt, William J. *The Shape of Medieval History*. New Haven: Yale University Press, 1966; Coleman, Joyce. "Talking of Chronicles: The Public Reading of History in Late Medieval England and France." *Cahiers de Littérature Orale* 36 (1994), 91-111; Eckhardt, Caroline D. "The Merlin Figure in Middle English Chronicles." *Studies of Merlin from the Vedas to C. G. Jung*. James Gollnick, ed. Lewiston, NY: Edwin Mellen Press, 1991. 21-39; Fines, John. *Who's Who in the Middle Ages*. New York: Barnes and Noble. 1970; Gellrich, Jesse M. *Discourse and Dominion in the Fourteenth Century*. Princeton: Princeton University Press, 1995. Goffart, Walter. *The Narrators of Barbarian History (A.D. 550-800)*. Princeton: Princeton University Press, 1988; Gransden, Antonia. *Historical Writing in England c. 550 to c. 1307*. Ithaca: Cornell University Press, 1974; Gransdan, Antonia. *Historical Writing in England II: c. 1307 to Early Sixteenth Century*. Ithaca: Cornell University Press, 1982; Hart, Cyril. "Some recent Studies of the *Anglo-Saxon Chronicles*." *Medium Aevum* 66:2 (1997), 293-301. Smalley, Beryl. *Historians in the Middle Ages*. New York: Scribner's, 1974; Sterns, Indrikis. *The Greater Medieval Historians: An Interpretation and a Bibliography*. Lanham, MD: University Press of America, 1980; Sterns, Indrikis. *The Greater Medieval Historians: A Reader*. Washington D.C.: University Press of America, 1982; Taylor, John. *English Historical Literature in the Fourteenth Century*. Oxford: Clarendon Press, 1987; Vollrath, Hanna. "Oral Models of Perception in Eleventh-Century Chronicles." In *Vox Intexta: Orality and Textuality in the Middle Ages*. Alger Nicholas Doane and Carol Braun Pasternack, eds. Madison: University of Wisconsin Press, 1991. 102-11.

Richard McDonald

CIMABUE, GIOVANNI (1240-1302). A Florentine, Giovanni Cimabue was a painter who pushed beyond the limits of the Byzantine style. He was influenced by the Gothic, and his style is very dramatic. He created *Madonna Enthroned with Angels and Prophets*, an altarpiece that is over twelve by seven feet with a three dimensional appearance of the Madonna's throne. Cimabue was very likely Giotto's teacher of painting as well as his older rival, which *Dante suggests in *Il Purgatorio* (XI, 94-96).

SELECTED BIBLIOGRAPHY

Gardner, Helen. *Gardner's Art through the Ages.* 6th ed. San Diego: Harcourt Brace Jovanovich, 1975; Sears, Elizabeth. *The Ages of Man: Medieval Interpretations of the Life Cycle.* Princeton: Princeton University Press, 1986.

Libby Bernardin

CITY OF GOD, THE. A treatise by St.* Augustine, *The City of God (De Civitate Dei)* is an apology for the accusation that the church was responsible for the fall of the Roman Empire. Composed from 413-426, Augustine defines human history as a conflict between the City of God and the Earthly City (*Civitas Terrena*). The City of God includes all of the Christians, while the Earthly City includes the pagans and heretics. Predictably, Augustine finds that the people in the City of God will achieve immortality because of their piety toward God. Conversely, the pagans and heretics are condemned to destruction.

SELECTED BIBLIOGRAPHY

Bright, Pamela. "Augustine and the Thousand Year Reign of Saints." *Augustine Presbyter Factus Sum.* Joseph Lienhard and Earl Muller, eds. New York: Peter Lang, 1993. 447-53; Burnell, Peter. "The Problem of Service to Unjust Regimes in Augustine's *City of God.*" *Journal of the History of Ideas.* 54:2 (April 1993), 177-88; Claussen, M. A. "'Peregrinatio' and 'Peregrini' in Augustine's 'City of God.'" *Traditio* 46 (1991), 33-75; Donnelly, Dorothy F., ed. *"The City of God": A Collection of Critical Essays.* New York: Peter Lang, 1995; Drabble, Margaret, ed. *The Oxford Companion to English Literature.* 5th ed. Oxford: Oxford University Press. 1985; Swanton, Michael. *English Literature before Chaucer.* New York: Longman, 1987.

Robert T. Lambdin

CLANVOWE, SIR JOHN (d. 1391). Sir John Clanvowe was a courtier and a contemporary as well as a friend of Geoffrey *Chaucer. Clanvowe distinguished himself as a diplomat and with his service to the king. He also composed several pieces of note, including *The Two Ways*, which recommended peace through godly existence.

It has been posited that Clanvowe was the author of *The Cuckoo and the Nightingale* and the *Boke of Cupide*, a short Middle English *debate poem wherein an earthy cuckoo loses his verbal battle with an amorous nightingale. The nightingale is so grateful to be awarded the victory that he demands that the birds assemble on Valentine's Day. Clanvowe is linked to this poem mainly because of its conclusion, which ends "Explicit Clanvowe". While this is intriguing, there is no direct evidence to link Sir John Clanvowe to any portion of this text.

SELECTED BIBLIOGRAPHY

Chamberlain, David. "Clanvowe's Cuckoo." *New Readings of Late Medieval Love Poems*. David Chamberlain, ed. Lanham, MD: University Press of America, 1993. 41-65; Garbáty, Thomas J. *Medieval English Literature*. Toronto: Heath, 1984; Patterson, Lee. "Court Politics and the Invention of Literature: The Case of Sir John Clanvowe." *Culture and History, 1350-1600: Essays on English Communities, Identities, and Writing*. David Aers, ed. Detroit:Wayne State University Press, 1992. 7-41.

Robert T. Lambdin

CLEANNESS. Named after its title word, *Cleanness* is also known as *Purity*. An alliterative, unrimed poem, *Cleanness* was composed in the second half of the fourteenth century. The only extant version of the poem is found in the renowned manuscript Cotton Nero A x in the British Library; this manuscript also contains *Sir Gawain and the Green Knight*, *Patience*, and *Pearl*. *Cleanness* is a verse homily that uses biblical allusions to push its point that the Divine presence accepts no one with an unclean body or soul.

Several scriptural subjects are examined in *Cleanness*; each is concerned with the worship of purity and the joys of lawful love. These subjects include the Parable of the Marriage Feast, the Fall of the Angels, the Deluge or Flood, the Destruction of Sodom and Gomorrah, Jerusalem's Plunder by Nebuchadnezzar, and the Fall of Belshazzar. The work does not stray far from the biblical versions of these stories; for example, the Fall of Belshazzar is presented in a rich descriptive narrative.

SELECTED BIBLIOGRAPHY

Blanch, Robert J. and Julian N. Wasserman. *From "Pearl" to "Gawain": "Forme" to "Fynisment."* Gainesville, FL: University Press of Florida, 1995; Drabble, Margaret, ed *The Oxford Companion to English Literature*. 5th ed. Oxford: Oxford University Press, 1985; Reichardt, Paul F. "Sir Israel Gollancz and the Editorial History of the *Pearl* Manuscript." *Papers on Language and Literature* 31:2 (Spring 1995), 145-63.

Robert T. Lambdin

"CLERIC'S TALE, THE." The story "The Cleric's Tale" in Geoffrey *Chaucer's *Canterbury Tales* (c. 1387-1400) is told by the cleric so it is fitting that its source is scholarly: *Petrarch's Latin translation of *Boccaccio's last story in the *Decameron*. Walter, the marquis of Saluzzo, is urged to marry so that he will have an heir. He marries Griselda, who is the most strikingly beautiful but also the poorest girl in town. Griselda is fully devoted to Walter, but he insists upon testing her loyalty. After each of their children are born, Walter takes them, saying that he must kill them because their mother is so lowborn.

Walter divorces Griselda and sends her home with nothing, but she is still devoted to him. He calls her back to his castle to plan his next wedding and to receive his new bride. Griselda never protests, so Walter rewards her by telling her that the supposed new bride and her brother are actually Griselda's own children whom she believed dead. They all live together happily ever after.

SELECTED BIBLIOGRAPHY

Bush, Douglas. *English Poetry*. New York: Oxford University Press, 1963; Garbáty, Thomas J. *Medieval English Literature*. Toronto: Heath, 1984; Lambdin, Laura C., and Robert T. Lambdin, eds. *Chaucer's Pilgrims: An Historical Guide to the Pilgrims in the "Canterbury Tales."* Westport, CT: Greenwood Press; Salter, Elizabeth. *Fourteenth-Century English Poetry*. Oxford: Clarendon Press, 1983.

Laura Cooner Lambdin

CLIGÉS.   A French *romance, written by *Chrétien de Troyes around 1175, *Cligés* mixes an early Byzantine tale with an Arthurian background and tells the story of the love of Alexander and Fernice, and further of their son Cligés's love for Soredamors.   In this story we see the generational development of *courtly love by the juxtaposition of two related couples. Cligés proves himself a superior lover to his father because he can easily describe the overwhelming sensations of love in extensive interior monologues. That Cligés's lady love is married to his uncle is reminiscent of the Tristan story in which Isode is wed to King Mark, Tristan's uncle. Fernice feigns death (parallel to the scene in *Romeo and Juliet*) so that she can be with her true love, Cligés.

SELECTED BIBLIOGRAPHY

Chase, Carol J. "Double Bound: Secret Sharers in 'Cligés' and the Lancelot 'Graal.'" *The Legacy of Chrétien de Troyes*. Norris Lacy, Douglas Kelly, and Keith Busby, eds. Amsterdam: Rodopi, 1988. 169-85; Guerin, M. Victoria. *The Falls of Kings and Princes: Structure and Destruction in Arthurian Tragedy*. Stanford: Stanford University Press, 1995; Mickel, Emmanuel J. Jr. "The Conflict between Pitie and Largesse in the 'Chevalier de charrete.'" *Neuphilologische Mitteilungen* 95:1 (1994), 31-36; Utti, Karl D. "Chrétien de Troyes's 'Cligés': Romance Translatio and History." *Conjunctures: Medieval Studies in Honor of Douglas Kelly*. Keith Busby and Norris Lacy, eds. Amsterdam: Rodopi, 1994. 545-57.

Laura Cooner Lambdin

CONRAD III (1093-1152) King of the Holy Roman Empire (1138-1152). Conrad was the first member of the Hohenstaufen dynasty, which accepted the full implication, historically, of the imperial tradition as well as the significance of Roman law. He and his successors were devoted to a policy of centralization and the increase of the *Imperium*, even in the face of a more and more powerful Papacy.

SELECTED BIBLIOGRAPHY

Dobozy, Maria. "The Theme of the Holy War in German Literature, 1152-1190: Symptom of Controversy between Empire and Papacy?" *Euphorion* 80:4 (1986), 341-62; Herzstein, Robert Edwin, ed. *The Holy Roman Empire in the Middle Ages: Universal State or German Catastrophe?* Boston: Heath, 1966; Zophy, Jonathan W. *The Holy Roman Empire: A Dictionary Handbook.* Westport: Greenwood Press, 1980.

R. Churchill Curtis

CONSOLATION OF PHILOSOPHY, THE. A philosophical work of *Boethius, *The Consolation of Philosophy* or *De Consolatione Philosopiae*, was composed around 524, while Boethius was in prison awaiting execution. The work, composed in alternating prose and verse, consists of a dialogue between Boethius and philosophy.

The author laments his sorrows and current position, while Philosophy, in the guise of a majestic woman, responds in a form of Neoplatonism and Stoicism. By doing so, she illustrates that earthly fortunes are unwholesome compared to the highest good and happiness, which can be found in God. She then demonstrates a reconciliation concerning the existence of evil, especially if God is all-good and all-powerful. She continues reconciling the paradox of man's free will in view of God's ability to have foreknowledge of everything. This work became extremely popular and was copied by many authors, including Geoffrey *Chaucer.

SELECTED BIBLIOGRAPHY

Drabble, Margaret, ed. *The Oxford Companion to English Literature.* 5th ed. Oxford: Oxford University Press, 1985; Frakes, Jerold C. *The Fate of Fortune in the Early Middle Ages: The Boethian Tradition.* New York: E. J. Brill, 1988; Heinrichs, Katherine. "'Lovers' Consolations of Philosophy' in Boccaccio, Machaut, and Chaucer." *Studies in the Age of Chaucer* 11 (1989), 93-115; Kaylor, Noel Harold, Jr. *The Medieval Consolation of Philosophy: An Annotated Bibliography.* New York: Garland, 1992.

Robert T. Lambdin

"COOK'S TALE, THE." Roger "Hogge" of Ware, the cook of Geoffrey *Chaucer's *Canterbury Tales* (c. 1387-1400), begins a bawdy tale to entertain the pilgrims traveling to the shrine of St. Thomas *Becket at Canterbury Cathedral. The story of Perkin, the apprentice who spends all his time chasing women and gambling, remains an unfinished fragment, apparently because the cook is far too drunk to speak further.

SELECTED BIBLIOGRAPHY

Bush, Douglas. *English Poetry.* New York: Oxford University Press, 1963; Garbáty, Thomas J. *Medieval English Literature.* Toronto: Heath, 1984; Lambdin, Laura C., and Robert T. Lambdin, eds. *Chaucer's Pilgrims: An Historical Guide to the Pilgrims in the "Canterbury Tales."* Westport, CT: Greenwood Press. 1996; Pearcy, Roy J. "Chaucer's Cook's Prologue, 1.4326." *Explicator* 45:3 (Spring 1987), 3-4; Salter, Elizabeth. *Fourteenth-Century English Poetry.* Oxford: Clarendon Press, 1983; Seymour, M. C. "'Of This Cokes Tale.'" *Chaucer Review* 24:3 (1990), 259-62.

Laura Cooner Lambdin

COPERNICUS, NICOLAUS (1473-1543). A Polish astronomer, Nicolaus Copernicus was a native of Torun who laid the foundation for modern astronomy. His *De Revolutionibus* (1543) upset the Ptolemaic system of astronomy, which had held since the second century. *Ptolemy had posited the geocentric theory which had been adapted by the church to produce the hierarchy of a man-centered universe. Copernicus found this to be untrue and his *De Revolutionibus* posited his theory that the earth and all the other planets revolved around the sun and spun on their axes. His work was not published until he lay dying.

Opposition to his findings was fierce. Copernicus had rejected thirteen hundred years of science and directly assaulted the teachings of the church; man was no longer the center of the universe. Copernicus's heliocentric theory was not accepted universally by the scholarly and scientific world for over one hundred years.

SELECTED BIBLIOGRAPHY

Chabran, Rafael. "Diego de Zuniga (1535-1600?), Job, and the Reception of Copernicus in Spain. *Ometeca* 1(2)-2(1) (1989-90), 61-68; Kelter, Irving A. "The Refusal to Accommodate: Jesuit Exegetes and the Copernican System." *Sixteenth Century Journal* 26:2 (Summer 1995), 273-84; Warren, Wini. "The Search for Copernicus in History and Fiction." *Soundings* 76:2-3. (Summer-Fall 1993), 388-406.

Robert T. Lambdin

CORPUS CHRISTI. Inspired by the visions of St. Juliana of Cornillion in the 1220s, the feast (*See* **Festivals and Holidays**) of Corpus Christi was established in 1264 by Pope Urban IV. It was only in the fourteenth century, however, that the feast was introduced throughout Europe. By the end of the Middle Ages it had become one of the most significant religious feasts of the Christian calendar. Corpus Christi celebrated the Eucharist--the consecrated Host transformed into Christ's body through the miracle of the Mass, a process known as transubstantiation. Since the doctrine of transubstantiation had only been fully defined in the twelfth century, this new festival was a way of calling attention to and celebrating it.

It was in urban areas that Corpus Christi became most important. The main mode of celebration came to be processions of the Eucharist in a silver vessel covered by a canopy and carried by priests or civic leaders. These processions became increasingly elaborate during the course of the later Middle Ages. Since the Eucharist represented the special status of the clergy, it was natural that the Corpus Christi processions also became a way of reflecting the hierarchy of medieval towns. While the order of the procession could vary over time and from place to place, it always reflected the hierarchy of the town, its civic organization, and especially its craft guilds. The procession was organized by guilds who competed with one another over questions of precedence and display in the Corpus Christi processions. Thus these processions became a form of display of power and authority in which craft guilds invested heavily. For example, a guild might commission a piece of art such as an altarpiece, a cross or a canopy for the festival. In England each guild produced a play performed in honor of the Corpus Christi celebrations.

SELECTED BIBLIOGRAPHY

King, Pamela M. "Corpus Christi, Valencia." *Medieval English Theatre* 15, (1993) 103-10; Parker, David A. "The Act of Supremacy and the *Corpus Christi* Carol." *English Language Notes* 30:2 (December 1992), 5-10; Rubin, Miri. "Corpus Christi: Inventing a Feast." *History Today* 40:7 (1990),15-21.

Miriam Davis

COURTLY LOVE. The concept of courtly love, the name of which is derived from Gaston Paris's term *amour courtois*, was first used to describe a specific set of mannerisms in an 1833 essay on *Chrétien de Troyes's *Lancelot*. It described love as it had been presented by the eleventh century troubadours of southern France. Courtly love symbolized a code of attitudes toward love, as well as the conduct considered suitable for lords and ladies. In courtly love the relation of a pining lover to his beloved was modeled on the interrelationship between the feudal follower and his lord. In this way courtly love exemplified the "look but don't touch" technique: a knight adores and respects a noblewoman, who is usually chaste and always unattainable. This love becomes more passionate, yet it is usually unrequited; the more the knight's love is denied, the hotter his passion becomes.

In courtly love the lover performed deeds and acts of courage for his beloved, but suffered because she remained indifferent. This usually meant that the love was either premarital or extramarital, thus preventing consummation or making it difficult and dangerous. Often the knight must keep the identity of his beloved secret, although he sometimes carried a token of her affection, such as a scarf, with him into battle. Obviously, a basic part of courtly love was the incompatibility of love with marriage. Yet the lover welcomed this suffering, for it inspired him to greatness.

It appears that courtly love was first popularized by the troubadours of southern France. Influenced by *Eleanor of Aquitaine's patronage, it quickly spread through France to England and Germany. Around 1185 Andreas Capellanus composed the *De Arte Honeste Amandi*, a primer for the practice of this art. This art also spread to the medieval authors. In the allegorical *Romaunt of the Rose* and the medieval *romances, the principles of courtly love were embodied. The cycles of Arthur (*See **Arthurian Legend***), Tristan and Iseult, and Troilus and Cressida all incorporate this tradition.

In the thirteenth century the elements of courtly love are found in Italian lyric poems of the *Stil novisti* of the *dolce stil nuovo*. Among the important artists of this genre were *Cavalcanti and *Dante in his *Vita Nuova*. This tradition further idealized the role of woman, spiritually elevated by the man who adores her. A variation of this tradition survived to the sixteenth century, evidenced by Sir Thomas Hoby's translation of Castiglione's *The Courtier*, a handbook for courtly behavior.

Ironically, medieval English literature did not produce a work in which courtly love was the central theme. This may be because the practice did not appear in England until after the mid-thirteenth century. Indeed, courtly love in England is almost satire, as evidenced by its depiction in *Sir Gawain and the Green Knight*.

SELECTED BIBLIOGRAPHY

Braekman, Martine. "A Chaucerian 'Courtly Love Aunter' by Henry Howard, Earl of Surrey." *Neophilologus* 79:4 (October 1995), 675-87; Kinoshita, Sharon. "The Politics of Courtly Love: La Prise d'Orange and the Conversion of the Saracen Queen." *Romanic Review* 86:2 (March 1995), 265-87; Mackey, Louis. "Eros in Logic: The Rhetoric of Courtly Love." *The Philosophy of (Erotic) Love*. Robert C. Solomon and Kathleen Higgins, eds. Lawrence: University Press of Kansas, 1991. 336-51.

Robert T. Lambdin

COURT OF LOVE, THE. Once erroneously attributed to Geoffrey *Chaucer, the early fifteenth-century allegorical poem *The Court of Love* is written in rime-royal and is obviously influenced by the *Roman de la Rose.* In the poem Philogenet loses his way in Admetus and Alcestis's palace in Cytherea. There Philabone informs Philogenet of the palace rules. She then leads him on a tour where she shows him persons who have both obeyed and broken the rules of love. Those who deliberately forsook these laws are now beset with regret. The poet then enters the service of the courtier Rosial. At first she treats him harshly, but she loosens up at the request of Pity. The poem ends with a choir of birds singing a hymn to the Church. While the authorship of this poem remains a mystery, the manuscript is signed as the work of a clerk, Philogenet of Cambridge.

SELECTED BIBLIOGRAPHY

Braekman, Martine. "A Chaucerian 'Courtly Love Aunter' by Henry Howard, Earl of Surrey." *Neophilologus* 79:4 (October 1995), 675-87; Kinoshita, Sharon. "The Politics of Courtly Love: La Prise d'Orange and the Conversion of the Saracen Queen." *Romanic Review* 86:2 (March 1995), 265-87; Mackey, Louis. "Eros in Logic: The Rhetoric of Courtly Love." in *The Philosophy of (Erotic) Love.* Robert C. Solomon and Kathleen Higgins, eds. Lawrence. University Press of Kansas, 1991. 336-51.

Robert T. Lambdin

CRUSADES, THE (1096-1270). The Crusades were a series of wars fought to free Jerusalem, the Holy City, from the Turks. The Turks had captured Jerusalem from the Saracens in 1071. Unlike the Saracens, the Turks had been hostile to the Christian pilgrims who were attempting to visit the Holy City, and there were instances of beatings and robberies. Pope Urban II of Rome roused the European soldiers to battle, and they went willingly, with cries of "God wills it!" Between the years 1096 and 1270, there were eight major crusades; only the first and third of these were successful.

The First Crusade lasted from 1096 to 1099. Unfortunately, some of the crusaders would not wait until the appointed time to begin the march; many of those who went ahead in the "people's crusade" were plagued with famine and ambushed by the Turks. In August 1096 the armies of knights and princes began the official march to Jerusalem, wearing the red cross on the front of their tunics. The troops marched across Asia Minor to Antioch and besieged the city for seven months. After the capture of Antioch the situation was reversed, and the Turks besieged the Crusaders from outside the city walls. Morale was low until Peter Barthelemy, a priest, told the Crusade leaders that he had dreamed of the head of a lance that would bring victory to the crusaders. Peter found the spear under the high altar of a church, and this event inspired the crusaders to defeat the Turks. Next the crusaders turned their attention to Jerusalem, and took the Holy City from the Turks on July 15, 1099. This victory was followed by a massacre of the Turks. Most of the crusaders subsequently returned home; the ones who stayed in Jerusalem chose Godfrey of Bouillon as their leader.

The Second Crusade (1147-49) was motivated by the restoration of widespread Muslim influence in Asia Minor. Led by *Conrad III of Germany and Louis VII of France, it ended in a decisive defeat of the Christian pilgrims. The Third Crusade (1189-91) was inspired by the Muslim ruler Saladin's seizure of Jerusalem. *Richard I the Lion-hearted and Philip II Augustus of France besieged Acre for twenty-three months, finally capturing it in July 1191. Philip then returned to France after a dispute with Richard; Richard was unable to take the Holy City but gained a three year truce from Saladin in 1192.

Unlike the other Crusades, the Fourth Crusade (1202-04) was not motivated by religious sentiment, but by political and commercial greed. It was organized to attack Egyptian Muslims. When the crusaders could not pay the Venetians for the boats they needed to cross the Mediterranean Sea, the Venetians suggested that they help capture Zara. The crusaders took this rival port in 1202 and then pushed on to Constantinople and captured it in July 1203. The power of the Byzantine Empire was greatly diminished by the defeat of Constantinople.

The Later Crusades were fought against the significantly weakened Egyptian power. The Fifth Crusade (1218-21) was fought in Egypt, and the Sixth Crusade (1228-29) was followed by the liberation of Jerusalem by peaceful negotiation. The Seventh Crusade (1249) was inspired by the recapture of the Holy City by the Turks in 1244. The leader, *Louis IX of France, was captured and forced to pay a king's ransom. Louis once again led the Eighth Crusade (1270), which failed after its leader died of plague.

Europeans' exposure to Eastern civilization as a result of the Crusades acquainted them with new products, knowledge, literature, and trade contacts. The Renaissance was a result of this exposure. Also, since the Europeans were thwarted by the Muslims from exploring the East, they turned to the West and discovered the New World.

SELECTED BIBLIOGRAPHY

Billings, Malcolm. *The Cross and the Crescent: A History of the Crusades*. New York: Sterling, 1990; Bisson, T.N. "Unheroed Pasts: History and Commemoration in South Frankland before the Albigensian Crusades." *Speculum* 65:2 (April 1990), 281-308; Dijkstra, Catherynke, and Martin Gasman. "Poetic Fiction and Poetic Reality: The Case of the Romance Crusade Lyrics." *Neophilologus* 79:1 (January 1995), 13-24; Lilie, Ralph-Johannes. *Byzantium and the Crusader States: 1096-1204*. Oxford: Oxford University Press, 1993; Sargent-Baur, Barbara N., ed. *Journeys towards God: Pilgrimage and Crusade*. Kalamazoo: Medieval Institute Publications, 1992.

Anna Shealy

CYNEWULF. Other than *Cædmon's "Hymn" the only Old English poet we can be sure of is Cynewulf, who signed his work by the *acrostic runes of his name. Four major poems can, with some degree of certainty, be ascribed to his pen: *The Christ, Juliana, Elene,* and *The Fates of the Apostles.* Internal evidence would lead scholars to believe he may have authored five other major medieval poems: *Andreas, The *Dream of the Rood, Guthlac, Judith, and The Phoenix.*

Attempts to discern autobiographic details have led to the suppositions that he was simply a priest who executed a decree in 803 or, more splendidly, bishop of Lindisfarne, who died about 781. *The Christ* begins with a "Hymn to Christ" in which he details descriptives from the Gospels that he skillfully conveys into *kennings: "wall-stone," "the flint unbroken," "Truth-fast," "the Craftsman." Thus the poet conveys a spiritual prophet into a kind of master mason who might have joined a medieval guild.

A section on Advent seems to have been inspired by the Roman breviary. A sermon by Pope *Gregory the Great provides material for "The Ascension" section, and an alphabetical Latin hymn on the Last Judgment, quoted by the Venerable *Bede, supplies the background for the final division of the Second Coming of Christ.

Individual poems include a little verse-drama of Joseph and Mary with the speaker's name inserted into the text like a modern prompt-book. The argument of the dialogue reveals the sinlessness of the Virgin, the Immaculate Conception of Jesus, and the submissivness of Mary to God's Will. The rune passage of the fourth poem identifies the poet as Courageous, Yearning, Need, Winsomeness, Used, Life-joys, Fortunes. The *Elene* tells of the appearance of the Cross to the Emperor Constantine and then, after long searching, the discovery of the True Cross and the site of Christ's Crucifixion by the Empress Helen (Elene), the mother of Constantine.

Generally the poems of Cynewulf are more narrative, more descriptive, and more revealing of the protagonist's motivation than the poetry of Cædmon. For example, an anonymous poem of the Cynewulfian School, *The Dream of the Rood* has been described as the "choicest blossom of the Old English Christian poetry." The intimate self-analysis and strict control of speaker and auditor relate *The Rood* to *The Elene* but there is no external evidence of authorship. It is interesting that a portion of *The Rood* is carved into the Ruthwell cross in Dumfrieshire. Also, like *Elene* and "Cædmon's Hymn," the basic structure is the *dream vision. As in The Bible, sleep-dream vision clearly relates the text to the self-revelation of the Divine rather than to the human knowledge of men, fitting into the medieval preference for the deductive argument of *scholastic logic, rather than the inductive process of later eras.

The dreamer is not identified, but the speaker is the tree from which the Cross was fashioned (showing the medieval fondness for relics), a Cross that alternates between "Fearful and grimy with gore" and "Gorgeous with gold; glorious gems." Thus in a brief poem the naturalistic story of the Crucifixion is narrated, and then the natural is transformed into the sacred cross of gold and gems that stands or hangs above the church altar. The poem skillfully moves from defeat to victory, from cruel death to Divine Grace, from secular history to Christian doctrine. Nevertheless, amid the metaphoric and allegorical sophistication of thought and diction, the kenning of *Anglo-Saxon survives: "victory-wood," "sorrowful tree," "wood-race," "Grim-visaged," "Limb-weary," and "Death-pangs." But even with these reminders of the primitive beginnings of medieval poetry, there breathes a new and confident affirmation of the afterlife:

> "I shall dwell in glory . . .with God's chosen ones
> In delights everlasting. May the Lord be my friend."

Whether or not *The Phoenix* is from the school of Cynewulf, it is certainly the borrowing of the Persian legend in order that it might be filled up with Christian allegory. If the whale is Satan, the Phoenix is clearly, by its rebirth, the Christ. The first ten stanzas express a charming picture of a perfect land, a New Eden, a true Utopia. No rain, snow, frost, fire, hail, or blazing sun blast this place. There is no mountain either, only a great fertile plain. The writer quotes learned sources that claim the plain to be "twelve cubits higher" than the landscape. Thus even in the biblical flood "the pleasant plain. . .stood all uninjured." Instead of being rain-beaten, it is watered by well-behaved rivers, clear springs, and obedient fountains. Only in the Last Judgment, says the clerical writer, will graves open and fire fall:

> "Nor ever comes change
> Till the Ruler Whose Wisdom. . .wrought its beginning
> His ancient creation . . .shall bring to its end."

The Phoenix is described as initially a "gray bird" singing more beautifully than any other bird, combining the accents of heavenly chorus, harp, and organ. But after a thousand years, "aged and old," he flies to an uninhabited land where he is exalted over the "race of birds" for a season (cf. *Chaucer, *Parliament of Fowles*), and then flies westward to Syria, where he builds a nest of "sweetest spices. . . and fragrant herbs."

The burning sun ignites the nest, the Phoenix is consumed, but his life is reborn. In this reincarnation the bird, gorgeously plumaged, carries ashes and bones back to his native dwelling. Then the allegory clicks in:

> So each blessed soul. . . through somber death
> After his life-days. . . of sore distress
> Gains life everlasting. . . knowing God's grace
> In bliss never-ending.

The recurring allegory of the phoenix attests to its literary perfection.

SELECTED BIBLIOGRAPHY

Cherniss, Michael D. "The Oral-Traditional Opening Theme in the Poems of Cynewulf." *De Gustibus: Essays for Alain Renoir*. John Miles Foley, J. Chris Womack, and Whitney A. Womack, eds. New York: Garland, 1992, 40-65;   Donohue, Daniel. "Postscript on Style in Old English Poetry." *Neuphilologische Mitteilungen* 92:4 (1991), 405-20; Wine, Joseph D. *Figurative Language in Cynewulf: Defining Aspects of a Poetic Style*. New York: Peter Lang, 1993; Wright, Charles D. "The Pledge of the Soul: A Judgement Theme in Old English Homiletic Literature and Cynewulf's 'Elene.'" *Neuphilologische Mitteilungen* 91:1 (1990), 23-30.

Elton E. Smith

D

DANCE OF DEATH. Believed to have originated in France in the thirteenth century, the Dance of Death is an allegorical representation of the predominance of death. The dance eventually developed into two forms. The first consisted of a dialogue between Death and his victims that ended with Death leading all off the stage to the grave. Earlier versions did not include personification of death; originally figures were taken away individually, each by its personal corpse. The other variation was the wilder *danse macabre*, in which the dead themselves, rather than the image of Death, led the dance. The dance seemed to become more and more popular, perhaps because of the recurring plagues. The name *danse macabre* may have been derived from the Dance of the Maccabees, which reenacted their slaughter at the hands of Antiochus.

The Dance of Death was a popular part of medieval art, occurring frequently in morality plays (*see* **Drama, Medieval**) and the works of artists. Located in the Cemetery of the Innocents in Paris, is the earliest known painting of the Dance of Death, painted in 1424. It is also found prominently in the woodcuts of the German Hans Holbein the Younger. Versions of the Dance of Death also appear in many Mystery Plays (*see* **Drama, Medieval**), especially those devoted to the Antichrist. An adaptation is also found in *Everyman*, in which the friends of the deceased fall away as the doomed man goes alone to the grave.

SELECTED BIBLIOGRAPHY

Taylor, Jane H. M. "The Dialogues of the Dance of Death and the Limits of Late Medieval Theatre." *Fifteenth Century Studies* 16 (1990), 215-32; Varty, Kenneth. "Villon's Three *Ballades du temps jadis and the danse macabre*." *Littera et Sensus: Essays on Form and Meaning in Medieval French Literature*. D. A. Trotter, ed. Exeter: Exeter University Press, 1989, 73-93.

Robert T. Lambdin

DANTE ALIGHIERI (1265-1321). Dante Alighieri was born in Florence sometime between May 14 and June 13, under the sign of Gemini, in the year

1265. Of the two dominant and constantly warring political parties in Tuscany at that time, Guelfs and Ghibellines, Dante's family supported the former, the party symbolized by square battlements on the architectural design of Florentine buildings. The Guelfs, whose slogan was "Civic Liberty," looked to the papacy against the Ghibelline "fishtails," who upheld the authority of the emperor. Dante's mother, Bella, died early in his childhood, sometime between 1270 and 1273. His father, who remarried and had three other children, died in 1283. In 1277 Dante was betrothed to Gemma Donati, whom he married in 1285 and with whom he had four children: three sons, Giovanni, Pietro, and Jacopo, names of the apostles who witnessed Jesus' transfiguration, and a daughter, Antonia, who became a nun in Ravenna with the name Sor Beatrice. When Dante was only nine years old he saw his beloved Beatrice Portinari for the first time and some nine years later he met her. For him it was love at first sight and she would become the artistic, intellectual, and spiritual inspiration of his entire life. The story of this love is recounted directly in Dante's *Vita nuova* and explored in its more philosophical, aesthetic, psychological, and spiritual dimensions in the *Convivio* and the *Commedia*. In 1289 he participated in two military expeditions, the campaign of Campaldino against the Aretines, in which the Ghibellines, the party of the emperor, were defeated, and he witnessed the surrender of Caprona near Pisa. On June 8, 1290 Beatrice died, an event that deeply affected his personal life and his artistic development, and that inspired his writing the *Vita nuova* during 1293-94. At this point in the spring of 1294 Dante met Charles Martel, the king of Hungary, in Florence, where Charles sojourned for three weeks awaiting his father Charles II's arrival from France. The younger Martel, born in 1271 and six years Dante's junior, was heir to the Kingdom of Naples and the country of Provence. In the eighth canto of the *Paradiso*, the sphere of Venus, Dante the Pilgrim meets the soul of his beloved friend, with whom he converses on the diversity of human talents and on the operations of Providence. Any hope that Charles Martel might become the redeeming emperor was destroyed when he died of cholera in 1295. In 1294 Pope Boniface VIII also inaugurated his plan of a theocratic papacy that would force the submission of all of Tuscany, including Florence, to papal control. In 1295 Dante entered public political life, which culminated between June 15 and August 15, 1300, when Dante was elected one of the seven priors of Florence for a term of two months. It is noteworthy that Easter 1300 is the fictional date of the journey he records in his magnum opus, *Commedia*. During the middle years of his life Dante regularly attended the philosophical-theological discussions held at the two prominent Florentine Dominican and Franciscan schools. He thus became one of the most widely read intellectuals and writers of his age. In 1301, when Charles of Valois, brother of the French King *Phillip IV, approached Florence to conquer it for Pope Boniface VIII, Dante was sent to Rome to negotiate with the pope. While he was away on this embassy, the Black Guelfs, who supported the pope, seized power in Florence and began systematic reprisals against the White Guelfs for whom Dante had shown sympathy. On January 27, 1302, Dante, in absentia, was sentenced to exile, falsely accused of barratry, and ordered to restore the supposedly stolen funds. Dante did not reply to the charges, and on March 10, 1302, he was permanently banished and condemned to death if he returned to Florence. Thus Dante went into exile for nineteen years until his death, and exile Dante referred to as "l'essilio che m'é dato, onor mi tegno" ("I am honored by the exile given to me"). This exile and his meeting with Beatrice are the two most decisive events of his life. During his exile Italy lost the papacy for seventy years to France, a period known as the Babylonian captivity. Also during these years *Petrarch was born in 1304, and *Boccaccio, Dante's first biographer, was born in 1313. In 1308 Henry VII of Luxemburg was elected emperor, in 1310 he descended into Italy, and in 1313 this "heaven-sent redeemer," as Dante referred to him, prematurely died, thus again dashing Dante's hopes for an empire.

For some years while in exile Dante had been working on the *Inferno,* which he completed in 1314, and the *Purgatorio,* which he completed soon after. Although Florence proposed in 1315 to repeal Dante's exile on the condition that he acknowledge his guilt, Dante proudly repudiated the offer for reasons he explained in a May 1315 "Letter to a Friend in Florence." He spent 1315-19 in Verona in the court of Can Grande della Scala, to whom he dedicated the *Paradiso.* Canto 17 of that cantica is a grateful celebration of his patron's generosity. In his famous letter to Can Grande Dante not only introduces the *Commedia* to his patron, but also presents an important discussion of the allegorical method. In 1319 he left Verona for Ravenna in acceptance of an invitation by the humanist Guido Novello da Polenta. Although he returned to Verona briefly on January 20, 1320, to read his lecture *Quaestio de aqua et terra,* he spent his remaining days in Ravenna, where he died on September 13 or 14, 1321. A handsome tomb holds his remains in Ravenna.

The Works

Vita nuova (1293-94). *Vita nuova* is a collection of thirty-one previously written poems to Beatrice introduced, connected, and interpreted with glosses in Italian prose that provide Dante's explanations of his poetic rationale and approach. Resembling *Boethius' *Consolation of Philosophy* and dedicated to Dante's friend Guido *Cavalcanti, the collection recounts the story of Dante's love for Beatrice, whom he considers a uniquely designated representative of divine goodness and beatitude on earth. This psychological autobiography of his love for Beatrice assumes a literary audience of readers who will recognize the experimental nature of the poems' structures and meanings. In this series of sonnets and canzoni that praise the "cor gentile" of his lady and show forth his "inward speech," Dante initiates a journey toward self-knowledge and his artistic exploration of the meaning of Beatrice in his life. In so doing he rejects the traditional formulas of *Provençal and *courtly conventions in search of both a new idea of love and a new poetic style that he calls the *dolce stil nuovo,* the new sweet style. The most memorable chapters of the *Vita nuova* are II, in which Dante is advised by the god of Love, who appears in a disguise as a pilgrim, to adopt a new defense; 11, in which he explains the meaning of the lady's greeting; XII, in which he is visited by the figure of love as a young man dressed in white; XIX19, in which he presents his canzone "Donne ch'avete intelletto d'amore (Ladies who have intelligence of love.); XXIII, in which Dante falls ill, and during the ninth day of his confinement the thought of mortality assails him and he writes the canzone "Donna pietosa e di novella etate" "A compassionate lady of tender years"; 31, in which the canzone Li occhi dolenti per pieta del core, (The eyes grieving out of pity for the heart), speaks of Beatrice's death; and 42, where Dante vows "to write of her that which has never been written of any other women," a promise culminating in the writing of the *Commedia*.

The *Vita nuova* displays not only Dante's technical mastery of the previous love traditions, Sicilian, ProvenHal, Guittone, *Guinizelli, Cavalcanti, but his transcendence of them to create a completely fresh and original artistic approach to love. Its historical importance also resides in the multiple voices that Dante assumes in this work, as lover, poet, and literary theorist and critic, voices enhanced by his unique portrayal of past, present, and future time frames. By a narrated revocation of his youthful experiences as a lover and a poet, Dante presents an *exemplum, a warning, that reenacts the amorous and artistic sins of his youth from the more mature perspective of literary critic and psychologist.

Convivio (1304-07). In his *Convivio, The Banquet*, Dante presents a feast of valuable knowledge and experience written for public benefit and service. The work was planned as a commentary on fourteen canzoni dealing with a broad range of topics including love and its intrinsic relationship to philosophy, reputation, nobility *(leggiadria)*, the need for unity, harmony, and world rule, friendship, the stages of human life and the practical virtues needed in each stage, overcoming the grief of death, and the preeminence of Italian over Latin as the language of learned discourse, among other topics. The work was to consist of fifteen treatises, the first being an introduction, and each of the others an analysis of the opening canzone. Only four books were completed; however, reference to the future books occurs in IV, xxvi, 8 where he announces his topic for the seventh book; in I, xii, 12, II, i, 4, and IV, xxxvii, 11 when he states that in book fourteen allegory and justice will be his topics; and in I, viii, 18 and III, xv, 14 in which he refers to the subjects to be discussed in book 15. While the incomplete nature of this work flaws its value and effectiveness, it is even more noteworthy that the work is marred by Dante's obvious motivation to impress his fellow Florentines as a philosopher during the early stages of his exile.

Dante acknowledges early, I, i, 16-19, that *The Banquet* is a continuation and extension of the subject matter of love and virtue treated in the *Vita nuova*; however, "in that earlier work my voice is that of someone just entering on his maturity; in this later one it is that of someone well advanced in that stage." Another major difference is that his explanations of the canzoni are primarily of their literal and allegorical or "mystical" significance. In Book I Dante surveys a series of topics related to literature and human behavior, particularly focusing on the nature of reputation and how it is formed in the human community; Book II he expounds on his theory of allegory and recounts how he attempted to surmount his grief over Beatrice's death by finding consolation in Lady Philosophy, a woman of great beauty and virtue; in Book III he explores the nature of philosophy, how "love is intrinsic to philosophizing" (III, xiii, 2), and how vice finds its root in lovelessness; Book IV is singularly notable for its perceptive analysis of the four phases of life, citing *Aristotle and Cicero, among others, to punctuate this most remarkable discussion of human physical and psychological development.

Dante's style and tone in *The Banquet* are those of a wise pedagogue, not only transmitting and mediating knowledge according to the medieval custom of allegorical explication, but also philosophizing on human experience and analyzing human motives, behaviors, and outcomes. His intention is to prepare and offer a banquet of learning for human intellectual, moral, and ethical consumption based on a menu of classical authors and his own observation and experience. His primary source is Aristotle, whom he calls "teacher and leader of human reason. . . philosopher most worthy of faith and obedience," a source he received through St. Thomas *Aquinas' commentaries on the Greek. Dante also draws on the *Summa contra Gentiles*, the Scriptures, Latin writers including Seneca, Cicero, Cato, Orosius, and Boethius, among others, the Arabian commentaries on Aristotle, St. *Augustine's *Confessions*, Albertus Magnus, Brunetto Latini, and Egidio Colonna, to name a few. Dante's goal here is to apply theoretical knowledge and direct experience to the actual contemporary problems of his age and to suggest feasible and pragmatic moral solutions, as, for instance, his discussion of the need for rulers of nations to acquire learning and wisdom themselves and to surround themselves with intelligent, learned, and wise counselors. Recognizing that people are often hindered and distracted by the demands and responsibilities of domestic and civic life from pursuing a study of philosophy, Dante prefers to reach this important audience by using the vernacular Italian to argue his case of how philosophy can enrich and ennoble human existence, how it can even be the source of practical solutions to seemingly mundane problems, and how reason ennobles man and draws him close to God. In IV, xx, 5 Dante discusses the nobility issue, the medieval equivalent of the twentieth-century "nature-versus-nurture" controversy, to conclude that it is the individual who ennobles the stock and not the other way around. In IV, v he expounds on his views about how ancient Rome had lived its preordained plan of divine providence for the redemption and welfare of humanity, again the medieval equivalent of manifest destiny. Discussing ideas to be taken up in more detail in the *De monarchia*, here Dante in an elevated and passionate tone laments the lack of a supreme ruler as a political exemplar and the usurpation of civil power by a corrupt church hierarchy and extols the need for the reestablishment of God's willed order that was evident in the divine election of the Roman Empire as the seat of Christianity and world political governance. In the *Convivio* Dante offers a taste of some of the significant topics to be explored in more depth in his masterwork the *Commedia* while giving a glimpse of his own personality as he struggled with the difficult intellectual, artistic, social, religious, and political issues of his day.

De vulgari eloquentia (1305). Dante's intention in writing *De vulgari eloquentia* was to establish order, stability, and acceptance for the changing vernacular language so that it would be elevated to the status of a literary language with conscious devices and standardized rules. Since the treatise was directed toward scholars and language specialists, Dante chose Latin to convey his idea that the native tongue is nobler and more natural than the artificial Latin. *De vulgari eloquentia* was to consist of at least four books, but left unfinished, like the *Convivio*, it has only book I and part of book II. Book I presents a remarkable overview of the linguistic geography of Italy, citing some seventeen dialects with specific examples and groupings. It discusses the origin of language and the cause of the diffusion of tongues and establishes Dante as a pioneer in the field of linguistic theory, history, and analysis. In this book he also identifies three main European linguistic families, Eastern, Northern, and Western. Within this latter Romance family he cites three variants: French or the language of *oui*, ProvenHal or the language of *oc*, and Italian, the language of *si*. In book 2 Dante focuses his discussion on the canzone, the noblest of poetic forms, and the various syntactical, metrical, and stylistic elements that contribute to the superiority of this form and indeed to the "illustrious vernacular" as a linguistic ideal.

De vulgari eloquentia is notable for Dante's historical consciousness and his awareness that the establishment of a single vernacular language would contribute to the political unity of peninsular Italy. By defending the vernacular, Dante was also defending Italian nationality, politics, law, poetry, and theology.

De monarchia (1316). In his Latin treatise *De Monarchia* Dante argues for the reestablishment of the proper relationship between church and empire by advocating an imperial authority that would protect civic integrity against violence, corruption, and disunity. Dante's ethical purpose and position on this issue emerge from his conviction that the purpose of secular government is to promote social harmony and individual intellectual growth through reason, justice, and peace, goals that could be advanced only by a politically powerful and independent monarch devoted to the secular welfare of the people. In Dante's view the whole scheme and purpose of human life and civilization as intended by God is to pursue the perfection of the mortal as well as the immortal dimensions of the human person. In this work, probably begun around the time of Henry VII's descent into Italy, Dante expands his focus of interest beyond provincial and peninsular concerns to deal with issues that relate to the earthly happiness and spiritual salvation of all humankind. The main points he argues in the three books of this completed treatise are that the pope and the emperor must be independent and coordinate, that a universal empire will promote the quest for human perfection in this life, and that the universal monarchy, as assumed by the Roman people, derives its providential legitimacy and authority directly from God and not through any human representatives of God's church on earth. Basing his statements on the observation and experience of actual historical conditions, Dante asserts that the ministers of the church had misdirected her from her appropriate role and mission as spiritual guide and moral exemplar to pursue instead the greed for earthly wealth, power, and territory. He relentlessly employs a wide range of argumentative methods, including biblical allusions, logical analysis, analogy, abstract reason, theological proofs and deductions, testimony of classical authors, miracles, and historical evidence, among other standard medieval methods, to instruct and persuade his audience regarding the necessity of temporal monarchy, the legitimacy of the Roman monarchy, and the direct providential claim of the Roman monarchy. The concluding chapter of the treatise is the most powerful statement of his condemnation of the church's failure to fulfill its institutional mission and his strongest advocacy of the universal monarchy as the guardian of earthly justice and peace.

Minor Works. Dante wrote a number of letters or epistles of which ten survive along with three notes written for the Countess of Battifolle. Included among the ten is one letter to Cardinal Nicholas of Ostia, papal legate to Tuscany, two to Cino da Pistoia and Moroello Malaspina, one to Oberto and Guido of Romena, one to the princes of Italy, one to the Florentine clergy, three composed during the descent of Emperor Henry VII into Italy, and one to Can Grande della Scala. The letters reflect Dante's classical education in the formal rhetoric of letter writing. The letters on Henry reveal the nature of his life in exile, record the development of his political thought between the *Convivio* and *De Monarchia*, and expound his ideas about the emperor also becoming the king of Rome. In addition to the epistles, Dante wrote two eclogues and a treatise entitled *Quaestio de aqua et terra* on the location of water in relationship to land, a topic of current dispute.

The Commedia (1314-1321). Dante's purpose for writing the *Commedia* reaches beyond the stated promise at the conclusion of *Vita nuova*, "to write of her that which has never been written of any other woman." In this work Dante's roles as teacher and reformer are expanded to include visionary and prophet. While fulfilling his promise to exalt Beatrice as no other woman has ever been exalted, to celebrate Beatrice and affirm her personal and artistic influence, Dante also sets forth a comprehensive aesthetic theology and cosmic view of providential history intended "to rescue those living in this life from a state of woe and to lead them into a state of blessedness." Moreover, the work synthesizes and brings to fruition the philosophical, linguistic, poetic, and political thought presented in his previous works, but it subsumes any polemical function within a carefully crafted poetic fiction. Although it begins as and is referred to by Dante himself as a "comedy" (*Inferno* XXI), a song of the people written in the vernacular of the people, it evolves into a "sacred poem," a divine comedy, the word "divine" being added in 1555 by an Italian editor after Boccaccio had referred to it in this manner in his *Life of Dante*. The story of the journey related in this work is not simply that of a unique pilgrim of the Middle Ages, who exposes through self-exegesis his own pain, but rather the journey of humankind as it moves in time and space on a cosmic stage from personal sin to grace, from self-imposed spiritual exile and psychological captivity to paradisal illumination, redemption, and transcendent freedom. Dante's perspective on this transcendent human drama is enhanced by virtue of his writing this magnificent work while in geographic exile from Florence, a perspective that allows for the first time the poet-pilgrim to emerge as the central persona and voice of this lyrical epic. In a work set forth as the simple story of a man lost in a dark wood who eventually finds his way through the help of some friends to recognize the vanity and futility of his previous life, Dante succeeds in poetically, psychologically, and spiritually elevating this personal account to assume the most sublime, complex, and encyclopedic vision of what it means to be human, and how the human and the divine are inextricably connected. Thus the *Commedia* is primarily a work of education intended to teach, to serve, and to transform its readers.

Dante's achievement in the *Commedia* is unparalleled; however, it rests on a foundation established by literary precedents and antecedents. The presence of Virgil as the pilgrim's guide attests to the special importance the Roman poet had in Dante's aesthetic scheme, and more will be said about his role and meaning later. Undoubtedly the Bible was one of Dante's primary sources and his knowledge, understanding, and interpretation of the holy book permeates Dante's epic as its essential subtext. Other significant sources are St. Augustine's *Confessions* and *City of God*, Ovid's *Metamorphoses*, St. Thomas Aquinas's *Summa Theologica* and his commentary on Aristotle's *Metaphysics*, *Isidore of Seville's *Etymologies*, and Brunetto Latini's *Tesoretto*. He was also influenced by the contemplative thought of Benedict, Peter Damian, and *Bernard of Clairvaux.

Reading a work that incorporates practically the sum total of the best thought in the western tradition presents difficulties for any reader, even the most sophisticated. We are struck by the encyclopedic and comprehensive scope, the profundity of meaning, the breadth of application and significance, the creative power and artistic craftsmanship, the depth of contemplativeness, and the extent of historical, providential, and classical knowledge. If any literary work can be called a "classic" in the Western tradition, then certainly the *Commedia* deserves that designation. In Jungian terms, it escapes the personal and the occasional, transmuting them into the universal and enduring. It reaches back into the sources of the tradition, bridges historical gaps and explicates events, transcends contingencies through the validity and durability of its insights and relevance, and provides a continuous and permanent fund for an understanding of who we are and what we mean as humans.

The innovation of the *Commedia* is based on how Dante revised and renewed the epic tradition as found in Homer's *Odyssey*, which he did not know directly but only through the Latin writers, and Virgil's *Aeneid*, and how he utilized biblical exegesis to authenticate his vision of God's love, order, and justice. While Dante was attracted to the vigor and persuasiveness of a Ulysses (*Inferno* XXVI), Aeneas and Paul function as his heroic models for his Christianized epic. Aeneas, Virgil's transcendent Roman hero and civic founder, was providentially destined to prepare for a universal Empire throughout which Paul would later be assigned the mission of spreading Christianity. Dante turns to Virgil, "the rich fountain of speech. . .the glory and light of other poets. . . his master and his author," as the guide through whom he will transform the secular themes and devices of the epic into a new Christian epic whose vision, purpose, and goal center on the glorification of God's love for humankind as exemplified through the Incarnation. The journeys of Aeneas and Paul are the classical and Christian human prototypes for the pilgrim's journey begun on Good Friday, 1300. An additional pattern and support for the pilgrim's visit to the realms of the afterlife is Christ's own suffering, death, and resurrection. Virgil represents the human rational capacity, which, while necessary, is inadequate alone to assure salvation. Moreover, Virgil embodies the wisdom and artistic craftsmanship of classical culture; however, while again significantly preparatory and prophetic, they are insufficient and limited.

Several issues are central to an understanding of the *Commedia*, including the role of Beatrice in Dante's poetic, spiritual, and intellectual evolution throughout his works, the impact his exile had on that development, the *Commedia*'s overall structure, numerological symbolism, the use of the allegorical method, the analysis of that allegory within an understanding of the cultural context, and finally the application of a variety of critical methodologies that will help to uncover its mysteries. Primarily the work exhibits the didactic medieval aesthetic whose goal is to educate the audience on moral, theological, ethical, political, and social issues using allegory both as a poetic vehicle and a pedagogical strategy. Dante sets forth his views on the purpose and use of allegory in the *Convivio* II. 1 and Epistola X to Can Grande della Scala. In the latter Dante acknowledges the polysemous nature of the *Commedia*, which is "of more senses than one," as he put it, one sense being literal and the second allegorical or mystic. In the former work he speaks of the "allegory of poets" as the "truth hidden under a beautiful lie," all of the rhetorical and poetic devices an artist uses to convey the meaning, and the "allegory of theologians" that emerges from the Bible and is a retrospective way of interpreting the text religiously or spiritually regardless of what the author may have intended. "Literal" for Dante means what the words actually say even though this meaning is stated as a fable or a fiction "Allegory" means what the fables or the fictions mean, the truthful lie submerged within the beautiful (*una belle menzogna*). Both kinds of allegory have a literal level; in poetry it is the fiction itself, and in theology it is the historical event recounted. The allegories in both senses seen in the meaning of such elements as the journey, Virgil, Beatrice, the dark wood, the beasts, the griffin, the chariot, the eagle, and so on, function as reformative teaching devices as well as revelations intended to refocus and redirect a misguided humanity toward salvation.

The overall structure of this work is tied to the numerological symbolism of the numbers 3, 4, 9, 10, and 100. There are 3 *cantiche* or canticles, with a perfect total of 100 cantos, 34 in the first cantica and 33 in each of the two following. The last canto of each cantica ends with the word "stars." The stanza form is hendecasyllabic *terza rima*, an interlocking rhymed tercet pattern carried throughout the work. Each cantica has about the same number of total lines. The geographic landscape of the realms of the afterlife, Hell, Purgatory, and Paradise, and the states of the spirits after death reflect as well the theological, moral, psychological, and socio-political dimensions Dante wished to address in the epic. Hell is an immense conical cavity beneath the Northern hemisphere with nine circles, numerous compartments within certain of these circles (Malebolges), and the frozen lake of Cocytus at the bottom. The areas of Hell beginning at the top are the Dark Wood where the Three Beasts, Lion, She-Wolf, and the Leopard, are encountered by the Pilgrim; the Gate and Vestibule of Hell, the Acheron River, and the Hill of Salvation, which are visible beyond the Dark Wood; Ante-Hell, where the "neutrals" or lukewarm, those who refused choice, reside; Limbo, the first circle, where the virtuous pagans, including Virgil, reside; the Upper Hell, consisting of circles for the sins of nature, self-indulgence, and incontinence: Lust, Gluttony, Avarice, and Wrath; and the Gate of Lower Hell, the City of Dis with the river Styx, consisting of the sins of Malice--Heresy, Violence with three concentric rings, Fraud with ten Malebolges, the pit of Cocytus, the river Phlegethon, Betrayal with four zones, Caina, Antenora, Ptolomaca, and Judecca, each exemplifying treachery to family, country, guests, and superiors, respectively. In Hell God is portrayed as a Judge, the atmosphere is noisy and dramatic in this black realm of despair, darkness, degradation, disorder, fire, and ice where the sinners' reason has been superseded by instinct, and the punishment is retributive and unmitigating. In rejecting their spirituality, the sinners in Hell have rejected God and have severed the interdependence of the human and divine nature of existence. The disobedient sinners repudiate punishment and are without a sense of other or community. The Pilgrim's reaction ranges from awestruck and childlike to terrified and vindictive, and his emotional reactions, such as fainting, fear, or anger, are individualized and personalized.

Dante's artistry in the *Inferno* reflects the classical, mythological, and Biblical traditions, as seen in such images as Minos, Charon, Cerberus, Plutus, Phlegyas, Geryon, the Furies, Medusa, the Minotaur, Centaurs, and Harpies, as well as Lucifer entrusted with the direct punishment of Judas, Brutus, and Cassius, the betrayer of Christ and the betrayers of Caesar and the Roman

Empire. Dante employs ancient and contemporary images to enliven the work with his interpretation of and perspective on memorable figures such as Paolo and Francesca, Ciacco, Farinata degli Uberti, Piero della Vigna, Brunetto Latini, Ugolino, Capaneus, Vanni Fucci, and Ulysses, among many others. The eternal punishments of the sinners are directly and metaphorically reflective of the sin that removed them from divine harmony, so that the uncommitted run after banners, the lustful are buffeted by storm winds, the heretics are in burning tombs, the evil counselors are concealed in flames, and so on. The *Inferno* represents the most popular and most widely read of the three *cantiche* due to the vivid, dramatic, and memorable portrayal of the eternal consequences of a life of sin. Readers have preferred its psychological drama, varied emotional appeal, and candid language, but have not always recognized how the artistic elements function in creating an overriding sense of the consequences of man's negated spirituality.

Purgatory is an immensely high mountain located at the antipodes of Jerusalem leading from earth to heaven. It is the kingdom of lyricism, forgiveness, hope, and harmony, a world of art and music as demonstrated by the numerous examples of artists and musicians: Casella, Belacqua, *Sordello, Oderisi, Statius, Bonagiunta, Guinizelli, and Arnaut Daniel, among others. In Purgatory the disposition to sin must be purged before the soul can assume its place of blessedness in Paradise. The guardian of Purgatory, the Roman Cato of Utica, represents the freedom from instinct and passion that the Pilgrim sought in his journey, the moderation and balance, the moral virtues of justice, prudence, temperance, and fortitude needed to harmonize the human with the divine will. Cato exemplified autonomous morality, a morality of choice, as opposed to the morality of constraint, a freedom to choose based on the responsibility of judgment. The first nine cantos of the *Purgatorio* present Ante-purgatory, where the souls of the tardily repentant are detained for various periods before the actual cleansing of Purgatory can begin and where the Pilgrim and Virgil encounter and have extensive discussions with Cato, Casella, Manfred, and Sordello, their guide through the Valley of Princes. At the Gate of Purgatory an angel engraves the seven p's, *peccatum*, on the pilgrim's forehead. The experience of the successive purgation of the seven cardinal sins will result in the removal of each of these p's and his eventual restoration to full rationality when he enters the Earthly Paradise at the top of the mountain. The mountain itself consists of seven terraces, each of which is occupied by sinners, beginning with the sins of misdirected or perverted love, Pride, its opposite being humility, and Envy, its opposite being fraternal love; the sins of love deficient or defective, Wrath, its opposite meekness, Sloth, its opposite diligence; and the final terraces exhibiting love defective, Avarice, its opposite being liberality, Gluttony, its opposite being temperance, and Lust, its opposite being charity. The order of the sins is reversed from that in Hell, with the most serious sins near the base of the mountain and the lesser sins placed accordingly up the slopes. At the top of the mountain is the Earthly Paradise where the pilgrim meets Beatrice and her handmaiden Matilda, the symbol of the active life. Here he witnesses a procession of the great spirits of the Old and New Testaments, a symbol of the living church of Christ as well as an allegorical reenactment of Dante's artistic, political, and philosophical ideas on the history of church-state relations. Matilda at this point in the Pilgrim's journey plunges him into the waters of the river Lethe, where all memory of sin is erased and then into the river Eunoe, where memory of virtue and good is renewed. With Beatrice's appearance Virgil leaves the Pilgrim to resume his place in Hell in the circle of the virtuous pagans.

Whereas in the *Inferno* Dante normally devotes each canto to a separate sin or sinner, in the *Purgatorio* he groups cantos in which he develops, alternates, or weaves together the stories of characters or topics over several cantos. In Purgatory God is portrayed as merciful in this realm of corrected reason, faith, poetry, and remedial purification. Colors, music, order, and imagination dominate the encounters and discussions. The sinners, unlike those in Hell, accept purgation and interact with each other and with their guest travelers with mutual goodwill. The Pilgrim emerges in the cantica as a fully developed protagonist, gracious, cheerful, and helpful. It should be remembered that Purgatory is a temporal realm, as Hell and Paradise are not. The elements of time and change in Purgatory suggest both mortality and hope, the decline and decay of the body as well as spiritual renewal and continuity. Memory is an important motif throughout, memory of an ancient time when the soul was pure and memory of what the soul has become due to sin. Dreams also announce the Pilgrim's spiritual readiness to access a new and more transcendent spiritual experience, as, for instance, the dream of the Eagle in canto IX, that of the Siren and her Song in canto XIX, and that of Leah and Rachel in canto XXVII. The struggle of purgation involves the imitation of the good example and the rejection of the negative example, enacting a spiritual program of contemplation and action. The procedure of purgation repeated on each terrace involves first the Whip, models from the life of Mary, the Bible, and pagan or mythological stories that demonstrate the proper exercise of the virtue that counters the sin being purged, and then the Bridle, examples from mythology and ancient history who succumbed to the sin.

While the *Purgatorio* portrays a lyrical mode, methods of exacting remedial punishment and issuing forgiveness are disciplined and systematic. Purgatory is a place where the sinners reconsider their lives, scrutinize their priorities and allegiances, and initiate the painful process of regeneration. The Pilgrim actively participates in this rigorous process of positive penitence. The Pilgrim is on a level of parity with the penitents sharing a common bond, a community of endeavor, suffering, and fellowship.

Following the "DXV" prophecy at the conclusion of the *Purgatorio*, Beatrice leads the Pilgrim up to the realm of blessedness, order, unity, and diversity. The *Paradiso* is the cantica in which Beatrice's shining eyes and smile dominate as she instructs and admonishes the Pilgrim like a saint, mother, or older sister. The structure of Paradise is patterned on the Ptolemaic plan of nine revolving concentric spheres in which the saints, who are signs or types of the Christ-vision the Pilgrim will see in the last canto, reside; Moon, for the Inconstant or Breakers of Vows, such as Piccarda Donati; Mercury, for the Active or Seekers of Fame such as Emperor Justinian; Venus, for the Amorous or Lovers, such as Charles Martel; Sun, for the Wise or the Religious Teachers, such as St. Thomas Aquinas and St. Bonaventure; Mars, for the Militant or Holy Warriors, such as Cacciaguida and *Charlemagne; Jupiter, for the Just or Righteous Rulers, such as King David and Constantine; Saturn, for the Contemplatives, such as Sts. Peter Damian and Benedict; the Fixed Constellations, for the Triumphant and Redeemed, such as Sts. Peter, James, and John, and Adam; the Primum Mobile for the Angels and Beatrice; and finally, the Empyrean occupied by the Blessed Virgin Mary and St. Bernard, who offers a beautiful prayer to the Queen of Heaven after which the Pilgrim experiences the immediate vision of the Incarnation and the vision of the heavenly hosts as the Celestial Rose.

The structure of Paradise reflects an inclusive, total cosmic vision of the universe based on all the known planetary knowledge during Dante's time. It is the realm where Dante explores in depth through allegory, logical analysis, examples, historical revocation, analogy, and many other devices the themes that interested him his whole life: the nature of the order in the universe, the providential role of the Roman and Holy Roman empires, the social and political structure of Italy, the concept of *schiatta* or family line, the contributions of monasticism, the tumultuous twelfth and thirteenth-century history of Florence, the ineffectuality of the Christian monarchs, the mystery of predestination, and the origin of languages, among many other topics. In the *Paradiso* God is portrayed as a loving, just, and merciful Father ruling an eternal kingdom of pure light, contemplation, spiritual freedom, and unmitigated joy. The perfection of silence and perpetual ecstasy prevails among these blessed souls, who each experience with complete satisfaction the fullness of capacity for beatitude. Paradise exemplifies the ideal, just state, the perfect community where factionalism and strife are unheard of under the divine governance of a rational, ordered cosmos. The Pilgrim's vision of the miraculous unity of the Trinity as a geometric figure, as a structure without content transcending the limitations of linguistic expression, epitomizes the climax of this grand, illuminating journey to the spiritual and psychological restoration of the human person to the divine likeness. He sees, as he was unable ever to see before, the second Person figured forth in pure light as *Nostra affige*, our likeness in Christ, a sight that transcends the insufficiency and inexpressibility of language. The Pilgrim suddenly understands the mysterious union of the human and divine nature. The mountain he had sought to climb in the dark wood of the *Inferno*, Ulysses' mountain in the foggy distance, has now been scaled. The vision of this central Christian belief is followed by instant understanding and love, a love that moves the sun and the other stars. This portion clearly demonstrates the differences between the three works.

SELECTED BIBLIOGRAPHY

Alighieri, Dante. *The Comedy of Dante Alighieri: Hell.* Dorothy L. Sayers, trans. New York: Penguin, 1949; Alighieri, Dante. *The Comedy of Dante Alighieri: Purgatory.* Dorothy L. Sayers, trans. New York: Penguin, 1955; Alighieri, Dante. *The Comedy of Dante Alighieri: Paradise.* Dorothy L. Sayers and Barbara Reynolds, trans. New York: Penguin, 1962; Barbi, Michele. *Life of Dante.* Paul G. Ruggiers, trans. and ed. Berkeley: University of California Press, 1954; Jacoff, Rachel, ed. *The Cambridge Companion to Dante.* Cambridge: Cambridge University Press, 1993; Musa, Mark. trans. *Dante's Vita Nuova.* Bloomington: Indiana University Press, 1973; Quinones, Ricardo J. *Dante Alighieri.* Boston: Twayne Publishers, 1979; Ryan, Christopher, trans. *Dante: The Banquet.* Saratoga,: ANMA Libri, 1989; Sapegno, Natalino, ed. *La Divina Commedia.* Vol. 1, *Inferno.* Florence: La Nuova Italia. 1955; Sapegno, Natalino, ed. *La Divina Commedia.*Vol. 2. *Purgatorio.* Florence: La Nuova Italia, 1956; Sapegno, Natalino, ed. *La Divina Commedia.* Vol. 3. *Paradiso.* Florence: La Nuova Italia, 1957; Wilkins, Ernest Hatch. *A History of Italian Literature.* Cambridge, MA.: Harvard University Press, 1974.

Silvia R. Fiore

DEATH AND LIFE: See **Debate Poetry, Medieval European.**

DEBATE POETRY, MEDIEVAL EUROPEAN. In the preface to his book entitled *Middle English Debate Poetry: A Critical Anthology,* John W. Conlee rightly pointed to the varied types of debate poetry that can be found in English dating from the medieval period; indeed, the same observation can be extended to apply more generally to all medieval debate poetry. As is true of many medieval genres, a situation that can perhaps point to fundamental problems with genre classification more generally (on this subject, see Hans Robert Jauss, *Toward an Aesthetic of Reception*) debate as a *lyric form defies neat categorization with respect to subject matter, formal considerations, or rhetorical approaches (didactic, satiric, and so on).

One can begin, for example, by asking what kinds of contentious verbal intercourse can be properly considered to be debate. We can understand dialogue as a subset of debate, yet it is necessary to distinguish dialogue in this context from, for example, dialogic discourse as it appears in dramatic strophic poetry. Similarly, disputation on religious subjects can often be understood as philosophical discussion that is a far remove from discourse between two lovers or satiric commentary on classical and medieval rhetorical education and/or practices. Works that present clear dichotomies established by the interaction of two interlocutors can also be clearly distinguished from poems in which there is a plurality of voices, the most common form of which is the so-called parliamentary debate in which there are several speakers, each representative of a larger group. *Chaucer's *Parliament of Fowls*, which falls into this latter category, exemplifies possibilities for polyvocality in the debate genre, while, on the other hand, Giovanni *Boccaccio's *Il* *Filostrato* is an example of a work that offers an extended narrative by a single voice that is merely framed by the literary context of the occasion of a courtly debate.

One must also consider the nature of the speakers, which can range in the medieval tradition from human beings to animals to seasons, to objects, and even to allegorical concepts. We find, for instance, numerous debates between or among lovers; or speakers of the same sex on the matter of love; or birds; or seasons; or objects (such as water and wine or various carpentry tools); or Christians and Jews; or even different occupations. Not only can the speakers be of diverse types, they can also stand in various relations to one another. Conlee limited his concept of debate literature to refer to "relatively evenly matched opponents" who are naturally in contention (x). While this relative equality perhaps alludes to and rightly reflects actual learned rhetorical practices, it excludes consideration of many poems, such as those that describe dialogues between Christ and man or between Christ and the Virgin, that might profitably be seen in the context of the debate.

The wide variety in the types of speakers suggests large generic questions that, especially for medieval literature with its notoriously blurry genre distinctions, can be quite thorny. When, for instance, does animal fable, itself a traditional poetic form, become debate literature? Similarly, how do we distinguish between allegorical conflict and debate (since, as Ernst Robert Curtius [206] noted, "allegory and polymathy bring poetry close to philosophy")? How do we structurally understand a debate that is incorporated into a *dream vision or otherwise embedded in a larger literary framework? Do we consider a lengthy didactic theological dialogue such as the *Dives and Pauper* on the subject of the Ten Commandments as part of the debate tradition or separate from it?

While many of these finer distinctions can be left to and are perhaps only truly useful for the practiced eyes of medievalists, the questions themselves point to the richness of sources, formal, thematic, and philosophical influences and intertextualities, and poetic practices themselves that make debate poetry so fascinating. The variety within debate literature (and this is true of other medieval genres as well) also points to the conceptual and structural fluidity that informs much of medieval literature and accounts in part for its remarkable vitality and continued appeal. Twentieth-century readers, accustomed to quite modern notions of divisions of thought into categories designed to distinguish between aesthetic, ethical, theological, and philosophical modes of perception and consequent discourse, have the opportunity of seeing, through the extant debate literature of the Middle Ages, how much more fully integrated thought and rhetoric were assumed to be, grounded, of course, on the presumption of Catholic ideology.

The possibilities for structural and thematic borrowing, revision, and variation that are in evidence in the extant body of debate poetry are particularly interesting for the light they shed on the sociohistorical climate in which the literature was produced. In *Oppositions in Chaucer* Peter Elbow

(14-15) pointed to the basic tendency of the human mind to work with polarity, with ideas of opposition or contrast (cited in Conlee, *Middle English Debate Poetry*, xi). This is certainly true, but one cannot underestimate the effect of Catholic theological oppositions (represented, for example, in distinctions between the human and the divine; the body and the soul; God and Satan; vice and virtue, and so on) that undoubtedly permeated medieval culture. One must also consider as a fundamental backdrop to virtually all notions of dialogic exchange the unequal (Conlee's term is "vertical" [xv]) verbal interaction between penitent and confessor during performance of the sacrament of confession. Catholic assumptions about the efficacy and truthful uses of language that are implicit in the relationship between sinner and confessing clergyman necessarily informed actual linguistic practice (even as they conversely reflected it), and this use of language would have had to directly influence poetic practice and political claims for poetry.

The complexities of the variations of debate that can be found in the literature and the usefulness of the niceties of literary classification notwithstanding, there is among medievalists a received notion of what constitutes debate poetry. Moreover, important connections among works conventionally understood as belonging to the corpus of debate literature can be ascertained across temporal, geographical, and linguistic variations as well as across conceptual classifications such as those referred to earlier. What follows, then, is a brief overview of some of the influences on and most important examples of the body of texts that is generally recognized by scholars as medieval debate poetry, with an emphasis on the English tradition.

The subject of classical influence on medieval literature is a complicated one that involves influences within classical literature itself, medieval acquaintance, either direct or indirect, with classical sources, and, quite another matter, medieval understanding of the received classical authors. For example, during the Middle Ages both Ovid and Virgil were extremely popular, but knowledge of the place of either poet within the context of ancient literary tradition would not have been fully available. Thus the modern reader of medieval texts can see a wider perspective than would have been available to the medieval writer himself, and while it is useful to see this larger picture, it is important to remember that such a view is in some respects anachronistic. There are, however, discernible lines of transmission dating from ancient texts with respect to different kinds of poetic and philosophical discourse that converge in debate poetry of the Middle Ages.

One can perhaps be justified in tracing the poetic roots of the debate genre as far back as classical eclogue or idyll beginning with Theocritus, a third-century b.c. poet from Alexandria; his eclogues contain dialogue that is probably modeled on ancient Greek song contests. In terms of direct influence on the Middle Ages, however, we should logically turn first to the work of Roman poets, especially to Virgil's *Eclogues* and parts of Ovid's corpus (on Ovidian influence, see Conlee, *Middle English Debate Poetry*, xiv). The later Roman poets Nemesianus and Calpurnius Siculus also wrote eclogues that would have been known by learned authors of medieval Latin debate poetry. Another influential eclogue was that by Theodulus, which was actually, according to Charles Homer Haskins, a Carolingian work that was understood during the Middle Ages to be classical (132).

The strictly literary influences are complemented by the inheritance of classical theories and practices of rhetoric and grammar that were known and modified during the Middle Ages. How rhetoric and grammar were understood and related to poetic practice is again a large subject in its own right about which much has been written, but the twelfth-century debate literature is certainly in part a reflection of the central position that was accorded to these arts in a proper medieval education; indeed, scholastic debate was an important component of the experience of a schoolboy, and it seems clear that many debate lyrics drew upon and parodied this pedagogical practice (see Haskins, chapters 4-6).

From another angle, it is surely important to consider the influence of the classical philosophical dialogue beginning with Plato on the more serious religious and philosophical didactic debate poetry of the Middle Ages. Only the *Timaeus* had been translated into Latin by the twelfth century (there was a fourth-century translation by Chalcidius), but the *Meno* and the *Phaedo* were known in Greek (see Haskins, 70, 299, 343-45; Curtius, 544-46). There was additional indirect knowledge of Plato through writers like Cicero, *Boethius, and *Augustine and through Arabic sources, but of immediate concern here is not so much the role of Platonic thought as the medieval awareness of the dialogue form of philosophical argumentation.

More relevant to the flowering of debate literature is the renewed interest in dialectic as seen through the reintroduction of *Aristotle's corpus (Haskins, chapters 4, 11). Maria Rosa Menocal pointed to the twelfth-century reintroduction of Aristotelian thought via Arabic sources and commentaries as participating in the intellectual renaissance of that century in Europe (see *The Arabic Role in Medieval Literary History: A Forgotten Heritage*). While it was Aristotle's thought that found favor in this period, Platonism was indeed alive, and its most active period during the Middle Ages was the twelfth century (Haskins 343). As will be discussed later, that climate fostered an efflorescence of debate literature that both celebrated and challenged contemporary rhetorical practices and their philosophical underpinnings. Especially through the Sicilian courts of Roger, William I, and Frederick II, much classical Greek and Roman literature--including important philosophical texts--that had been preserved in the Middle East began to find its way back to Western Europe (see Menocal; Haskins, chapters 9-11).

The classical influences on medieval European debate literature are complemented by Arabic and Hebrew influences, most of which found their way into European literature through cultural intermingling in Andalusian Spain and Sicily. Arabic influences on European *courtly love in particular are being increasingly recognized by Western scholars; additionally, there is evidence of direct transmission of Spanish Arabic sources to England (Chaucer, for instance, may have had direct knowledge of literature from Spain). The interface between classical Arabic and European literary traditions is a subject that continues to provide fertile ground for literary exploration.

For the purposes of understanding medieval debate poetry, it is useful to examine one specific type of love poem that evolved in Andalusia, the *muwashshaha*, because it contains a dramatic shift in voice and style that is not found in classical Arabic poetry (see James T. Monroe, *Hispano-Arabic Poetry*, 6-7; Menocal, chapter 4; Alice E. Lasater, *Spain to England: A Comparative Study of Arabic, European, and English Literature of the Middle Ages*, chapter 3). Maria Rosa Menocal provides a useful description of the form:

> The final strophe, the *kharja*, is indeed strikingly different from the rest of the poem. . . . The purely linguistic distinction between the strophes is classical Arabic and the *kharja* in the Mozarabic vernacular is coterminous with a difference in the poetic voice or speaker involved. . . . The different parts of the poem are thus composed in different languages, not only from the strictly linguistic point of view but also in the sense that the parts are spoken by quite different poetic voices, with different tones and styles. . . . In fact these texts lend themselves particularly well to a reading in which we understand that the poem is talking about itself and about literature and language at least as much as it is about its external subject. It is not difficult to perceive that in their structure the poems set up a series of overlapping oppositions, creating a dialectic between the two kinds of poetry involved. (*Arabic Role*, 99-100)

What is germane here is the existence of a literary source for a binary dialectical structure that is distinct from the classical aesthetic or philosophical ones that influence the debate genre. Since a genre like the *pastourelle* demonstrates at least one link between the courtly love tradition as developed in both Provence and Sicily and the Western debate tradition, we can fairly safely imagine larger kinds of connections--both formal and conceptual--between debate poetry and Arabic influence that have yet to be excavated (see Conlee, *Middle English Debate Poetry*, xxxiv-vi). These links would, of course, include philosophical ones, to some of which Menocal referred to in her discussions of Arabic influences on *Dante and Boccaccio (115-32, 138-42; see also Monroe, 6 ff.).

Another Arabic influence that bears directly upon debate literature is the use of avian interlocutors. The twelfth-century Persian Khaqani Shevani wrote a poem entitled "The Language of the Birds" that is apparently related to the better-known work of his Persian contemporary Farid Ud-Din Attar, the *Conference of the Birds* (the *Manteq at-Tair*; c. 1177). There is another poem that Attar could have known, slightly earlier, by Sana'i (died c. 1150) that employs birds as well. Additionally, Attar may have been influenced by the use of birds in the Indian *Kalila and Dimna*, which the tenth-century Rudaki had translated into Persian verse (see Farid ud-Din Attar, *The Conference of the Birds*, 15-16). Also important is the fact that Avicenna wrote a short narrative treatise, "The Bird," in which the bird represents the human soul; this would undoubtedly have found its way into European culture through the avenues referred to earlier and would thus have added another significant philosophical dimension to the formal literary use of the speaking-bird tradition.

Any discussion of Andalusian influence on Western European literary forms must, of course, take into account the Jewish component of the world of Al-Andalus. The work of Maimonides, who wrote in Arabic because it was more prestigious than his native tongue, is a case in point whose influence is recognized as a matter of course. There are many other philosophical and literary figures from the Jewish tradition whose contributions have yet to be fully explored and whose cultural inheritances are at least partially obscured from modern view by their associations with and fusion with the Arabic influences on Europe. Medieval Spain is a critical region for the intermingling of Hebrew poetic tradition and the poetic forms that developed in the European vernacular, especially during the period from 1000 to 1200 A. D. (see David Goldstein, trans. *Hebrew Poems from Spain*.) While any unraveling of these complex interrelationships is well beyond the scope of this brief survey, it is critical that they be acknowledged for their indirect influence on European literary theory and practice.

Latin Medieval Debate Literature. Although it cannot properly be considered an example of the debate genre, one is almost compelled to begin any discussion of debate literature by mentioning the fourth-century Spanish Catholic Prudentius's *Psychomachia*. The work, modeled upon ancient epic, describes a contest between various virtues and vices for a human soul. Although most of the poem involves description of the actual battle being waged, there is some verbal exchange, generally in the form of taunts, among the contestants. Prudentius is generally credited with having invented Christian *allegory, and his personification of the vices and virtues (itself derived from Roman literary sources) was extremely popular and much emulated during the Middle Ages. *De Nuptiis Philologiae et Mercurii* (The Marriage of Philology and Mercury) by *Martianus Capella is another fifth-century allegory that enjoyed great popularity and influence. As W. T. H. Jackson states, "Almost all allegories adopt a 'frame' within which they work--the dream, the battle, the journey, the hunt"; in this respect they are related to the development of the debate tradition (*Medieval Literature: A History and a Guide*, 101).

Jackson's reference to the dream brings to mind another type of literature derived from the Latin tradition to which the medieval debate is indebted: the dream vision. Macrobius's commentary on Cicero's *Dream of Scipio* (*Somnium Scipionis*), for example, was among the Latin texts that were known in the twelfth century. In this work Homer, Virgil, Cicero, and Plato are established as the principal ancient thinkers, which fact itself has a bearing on the conceptual foundations of debate poetry. In addition to having an important effect on the direction of medieval literary commentary and philosophical thought, Macrobius's commentary stood as an important classical influence on medieval dream poetry, which, in turn, is especially closely related to the vernacular debate literature of the period, as will be demonstrated below. John Conlee distinguished between what he saw as debate poems that simply borrow from the dream tradition a framework that explains otherwise implausible events and those poems, which he referred to as "dream debates," in which the dream itself becomes thematically and formally important to the debate presented in the poem (*Middle English Debate Poetry*, xxx). However one ultimately decides to classify the debate, it remains clear that Latin dream literature was a critical source for a great flowering of medieval dream literature, which, in turn, has a direct bearing on the present subject (see Lasater, 79-88, on the dream vision).

Moving a bit closer to the Middle Ages, we find *Gregory the Great, who in the sixth century wrote a work in four chapters, the *Dialogues*, on the subject of the lives of the Italian fathers. Among the poetic works of the eighth-century Alcuin is the famous *Conflictus Veris et Hiemis*, a short debate between Spring and Winter. The *De Divisione Naturae* of the ninth-century Johannes Scotus is a philosophical work on the universe arranged in the form of a dialogue between a *magister* and his *discipulus*. Also from the 9th century is the *Contest between the Lily and the Rose* (*Rosae Liliique Certamen*) of Sedulius Scottus.

The so-called twelfth-century renaissance provided a climate of intellectual inquiry conducive to debate literature. One of the most influential texts of the Middle Ages, *Andreas Capellanus's *De Arte Honeste Amandi* (usually known by the English title *The Art of Courtly Love*), contains a series of dialogues between lovers (for the benefit of a friend named Walter) that can be considered, if not properly debate, certainly closely related to the debate genre (here, too, we can see connections with earlier texts).

Another work that can more clearly be classified as debate is the *Debate of Phyllis and Flora* (*Altercatio Phyllidis et Florae*), which can be found in the *Carmina Burana*. The two eponymous interlocutors are engaged in praising their lovers, one a knight and one a cleric, and a final decision in favor of the latter is eventually made by the god of love. This work spawned many imitations, among them the famous *Florence et Blancheflor*, which appears in variant forms. Also on the subject of relative merits of knightly and clerical lovers is the satiric *Council of Remiremont*, in which the discussants are nuns. As W.T.H. Jackson pointed out, poems on this subject "may reflect an actual rivalry between the clerics and knights for influence with ladies at court" (64). The satiric or parodic use of female speakers in debates about the worth of (male) lovers became a subject of sustained popularity during the Middle Ages through the fifteenth century.

Among other poems written in Latin from the period are the *Dialogue between Water and Wine* and the *Dialogue between the Body and the Soul* by Walter *Map, who lived in England but was probably from Wales. Also influential was the learned satire *De Planctu Naturae* of Alain de Lille, partly in verse and partly in prose, in which the narrator encounters Nature, who, along with some companions, recites her complaints against mankind. Of special interest regarding the debate tradition is Alain's passage about birds, which seems to have influenced Geoffrey Chaucer and other poets who composed avian debates. Alain's *Anticlaudianus* is another allegory in which Nature complains about the corrupt state of mankind. In the late twelfth or early thirteenth century Caesarius of Heisterbach, a Cistercian monk who was probably born at Cologne, composed the lengthy twelve book *Dialogus Miraculorum*, which takes the form of a dialogue beween a monk, who provides instructive exampla, and a novice who responds to the monk's tales. The books, each of which treats a broad subject (e.g., conversion, confession, the Virgin, demons, temptation), taken together, provide a practical guide to the Christian life.

Medieval Debate Literature in Italy and France. The lyric poetry of medieval Italy was largely influenced by *Provençal poetry, which was especially embraced in the Sicilian court of Frederick II, and it was principally through this avenue that the debate genre reached the peninsula. Much has been written on medieval Italian lyrical forms and the influence of the troubadours on the *stil novisti*. The reader is referred to the volumes dealing with the *duecento* (Bentoni) and the *trecento* (Sapegno) in the *Storia letteraria d'Italia* for an overview of the period (for a good beginning in English-language texts, see also the works of Peter Dronke).

Among the Latin works of Dante that should be touched upon briefly here are the *Quaestio de aqua et terra* (the attribution to Dante is not fully certain because the work did not appear until 1508) and the *Eclogae*. The Italian works that might be germane to the debate form include the *Convivio* (*The Banquet*), in which the influence of several major philosophical works, among them the works of Aristotle and Boethius' (sixth century) *Consolation of Philosophy* (*De Consolatione Philosophiae*), is evident (see Albert Russell Ascoli, "The Unfinished Author," 47-51). It was Dante's plan that the *Convivio* was to have dealt significantly with allegory; as the unfinished work stands, it involves an extended, complexly constructed conversation with important thinkers on the subject of philosophical and poetic authority and can thus be loosely categorized as a debate.

One should consider several of Giovanni Boccaccio's works in connection with debate literature. The *Filostrato* (composed in 1335?) establishes a courtly setting of debate as the frame within which the story of Troilus and Criseyde is narrated by the lover/speaker. The *Filocolo* (1336-38) also includes an aristocratic occasion for discussion about love (in book 4); indeed the so-called question of love or *demande d'amour* was an extremely popular medieval subject that often found expression in narratives assuming frameworks of actual debate even if they did not actually contain all the positions to which such frames alluded. Boccaccio's *Comedia delle ninfe*, more commonly known as the *Ameto* (1341-42) is tangentially related to the debate genre in that it describes a bucolic setting (and here Boccaccio is indebted to the classical eclogue and its descendants) in which various tales are related through the voices of seven nymphs. The *Amorosa Visione* (1342) is also worth mentioning here for its use of the dream vision and allegory. The *Corbaccio* (1365), it should be noted, also uses the occasion of a dream for a discussion of love, and some have seen it as an influence on Chaucer's *House of Fame*, which will be mentioned later. Among the Latin works composed later in Boccaccio's career are sixteen eclogues, the *Buccolicum Carmen*, which reflect Dantean and Petrarchan as well as classical influences.

The debate has a long-standing history in French literature, and its influence on both the English and Italian traditions is fundamental; indeed, many English poems are little more than translations (sometimes fairly inept) of French sources. There was a long-standing history of allegorical writing in France that is connected to the allegories mentioned earlier, but the most outstanding French work was certainly the thirteenth-century *Roman de la rose*. More germane to this discussion is the *tenson*, a *Provençal lyric form of debate between two or more people, often on the subject of love. From the thirteenth century the allegorical works of Thiebaut de Champagne and those of Rutebeuf should be mentioned. From the fourteenth century are the works of Guillaume de Machaut, whose corpus also includes allegorical poems and debate poems dealing with love. In the fifteenth century François *Villon's *Grand Testament* (1461) contains a debate between body and soul. Noteworthy in terms of the English works that will be discussed later is a group of poems on the subject of the Three Living and the Three Dead (itself a subject widely treated in medieval literature and visual arts) that can be seen as analogues to the alliterative *The Parlement of the Thre Ages*. Finally, there is a body of didactic literature in French that uses allegorical methods and/or treats themes that appear in debate poetry (for a brief initial catalog, the reader is referred to Jackson, 118-21).

In Germany lyric forms that are analogous to those that have been treated here did not appear until the twelfth century, at which point they were clearly directly influenced by French models, but they did not participate in the debate tradition being examined here except obliquely (see Jackson, 123-62). What is clearly relevant to this discussion, however, is the early-fifteenth-century *Ackermann aus Bohmen* by Johann von Tepl, which is a dialogue between Death and the plowman/author.

English Medieval Debate Literature. Debate poetry in English appeared as early as the Carolingian revival and grew in popularity through the twelfth century, changing during that period from principally Latin religious works to secular works in the vernacular (Conlee, *Middle English Debate Poetry* xiv-xv, xx-xxii). As an example of the earliest debate literature in English, Conlee includes in his anthology a fragment of an alliterative poem he called "The Grave," which from a linguistic standpoint falls between Old English and

Middle English and which is surely connected to the later highly developed tradition of body-and-soul debates (largely thirteenth-century). Among these poems, "Als I lay in a winteris nyt" is perhaps the most finely crafted. It survives in seven manuscripts, evidence of its popularity, the earliest of which can be dated from the end of the thirteenth century (see Conlee, 18-21).

The *Owl and the Nightingale*, which was probably composed during the late twelfth or early thirteenth century, has long been recognized as one of the masterpieces of English literature. This anonymous work written in octosyllabic couplets is itself testimony to the importance of the debate genre in that it is as much a parody of that literary form as it is a commentary on human behavior and a serious demonstration of the effectiveness of rhetorical persuasion. The narrative voice tells us that while walking one summer day he overhears the two disputing birds that, we learn, are arguing before an audience of songbirds. In the description of their *conflictus* that follows, he makes clear his own knowledge of and interest in the rhetorical strategies employed by the avian contestants. The author of the poem is clearly well versed in the rules of classical rhetoric, and he uses the vehicle of the poem to both expose and appreciate the manipulative capabilities of language. The Owl and the Nightingale both inadvertently reveal themselves to be relatively unskilled speakers whose arguments are impelled by ignorance and bias rather than by careful reasoning. The narrator himself, on the other hand, becomes increasingly visible as a highly trained rhetorician (whom some associate with the figure to whom the birds appeal at the end of the poem) whose skilled observation of the *conflictus* should serve as a model to the reader. The structure of the poem participates in the parody presented since the birds appeal to a decision by an outsider, Master Nicholas, whose verdict is outstanding as the work closes; this lack of logical closure is itself a strong satiric statement of the uses to which debate can be put and to the relations between truth and rhetoric that the entirety of the poem calls into question.

In the introduction to his modern translation of the poem, Brian Stone offered a brief but useful synopsis of the philosophical and literary-historical environment from which this poem was generated. He also offered a partial, though not fully satisfactory, way of reading the allegorical positions suggested by the arguments posited by the two birds. Stone did recognize, however, the interactions of diverse systems of values that are brought to bear on the dispute when he noted that the "perorations, taken together bind three main things: Latin recognition of the interaction of the spiritual and sensual in love; the ecstatic sense of being which is equally the attribute of courtly love and the medieval Church; and a common-sense, wise morality" (180).

Another important (although much simpler and less poetically successful) avian debate from the Middle English period is the stanzaic *Thrush and the Nightingale*, composed in the second half of the thirteenth century (possibly as a translation of an Old French work). Here the subject is the worth of women, with the Nightingale serving as their proponent (there is, of course, a long history of association between the nightingale and lovers going back to classical literature) and the Thrush as their detractor. The work opens conventionally with a springtime pastoral setting, and the debate begins almost immediately, with the Thrush asserting his own male experience with women as a determining factor in his position. The two interlocutors exchange arguments stanza by stanza until, in the end, the Nightingale cites the example of the Virgin Mary: "Thoru wam wes al this world i-wend? / Of a maide meke and milde; / Of hire sprong that holi bern / That boren wes in Bedlehem" (170-73), and the Thrush concedes his position: "I suge that ich am ouercome / Thoru hire that bar that holi sone / That soffrede woundes fiue" (184-86). The poem lacks philosophical, literary, and rhetorical sophistication, yet it is of historical importance since it conjoins the debate tradition and the popular subject of the worth of women (rendered, in this case, in fully predictable terms).

The subgenre of bird debate continues through the Middle English period, with other notable examples involving nightingales being *The Cuckoo and the Nightingale*, a late fourteenth-century work about the value of love long attributed to Chaucer, but now thought to have been written by either Sir John *Clanvowe or Thomas Clanvowe (John's son?); *The Clerk and the Nightingale*, written in rhyming quatrains, which again considers the worth of women; and *The Merle and the Nightingale*, a late fifteenth-century poem usually ascribed to William *Dunbar on the comparison between romantic love and love of God. There are, of course, other avian disputes that do not involve nightingales, such as the "Ballad of the Crow and the Pie" which has connections to the *pastourelle*, and, of course, the bird parliaments of the fourteenth century that will be discussed later.

When we turn to the so-called *alliterative revival, we find one of the most important poems of the period, popularly known as *Wynnere and Wastour* (the title reads "Here Begynnes A Tretys and god Schorte refreyte by-twixe Wynnere And Wastoure"), which was probably composed near the middle of the fourteenth century. There is one extant manuscript dating from the fifteenth century that contains an incomplete version of the text; the ending is missing, which fact obviates the possibility of assessing with complete confidence what the anonymous poet's ultimate intentions might have been concerning the sociopolitical satire presented in the poem.

The work opens with a short prologue that denounces the corruption of contemporary English life, after which the narrative voice describes the contents of a dream he has had while resting during a journey into a "green world" setting that is curiously disturbing and unconducive to rest:

> So ruyde were the roughe stremys and raughten so heghe,
> That it was neghande nyghte or I nappe myghte,
> For dyn of the depe watir and dadillyng of fewllys.
> Bot as I laye at the laste, than lowked myn eghne,
> And I was swythe in a sweuen sweped be-lyue.
>   (quoted from Conlee, *Middle English Debate Poetry*, 69)

As the dream vision is described, we see two opposing armies; the first, more elaborately described, belongs to Winner and consists of merchants, clergymen, and lawyers, while Waster's army is comprised of the higher-ranking aristocracy, landowners, and military classes. Representatives of each army are brought before the king to argue their respective positions, and what ensues is the actual debate between Winner, who prides himself and his fellows on temperance and frugality ("Aye when I gadir my gudes, than glades myn hert" [227]), and Waster, who accuses Winner of neglect of the poor and undermining of the economy through miserliness ("See, Wynner," quod Wastoure, "Thi wordes are vayne./ With oure festes and oure fare we feden the pore" [294-5]). The argument raises serious questions about the relations among the classes in fourteenth-century England that are sometimes introduced directly (as, for example, with references to specific orders of friars) and are sometimes dealt with in more abstract, even philosophical, terms.

The reaction of the king to the arguments presented is to separate the two contestants by sending Winner to the papacy established in Avignon and Waster to the Cheapside district of London. This is perhaps an evasion of the problem of trying to reconcile the differences between the two forces, or it might perhaps be an admission of the impossibility of the two positions being brought to amicable conclusion by the king. Conlee even suggested that this separation could be considered the first step in the king's attempt "to bring these contradictory forces under control" (65). Whatever the poet's eventual sociopolitical statement may have been, the work stands as an eloquent commentary on the complex social relations in England during a period when the middle class was expanding and that expansion was redefining relations between and among not only the classes but the inherited aristocratic political structure on which England had come to rely politically.

Death and Life, also a fourteenth-century alliterative poem, is a distinctly Christian poem that presents two disputants, Lady Life and Lady Death, whose debate occupies the second fit of the text. The first section opens with the narrator's invocation to Christ, which is followed by a conventional description of his springtime wandering and falling into a dream state. In his dream the speaker encounters Lady Life and her company, whose nurturing activities are interrupted by the arrival of Lady Death and her companion. Death's work is temporarily halted by Sir Countenance, sent by God at the request of Lady Life, and this hiatus provides the opportunity for the debate itself, which is essentially an assertion by each figure of her power over the other. The resolution comes with Lady Life recounting Christ's victory over death and leading her creatures toward eternal life, whereupon the dreamer awakens and the poem closes.

This is a work that presents a relatively straightforward message about Christian concepts of salvation and the eternal life of the soul, but it is particularly interesting in its use of the two personified figures. Their connections to earlier allegorical figures like Boethius's Lady Philosophy and characters in *Piers the Plowman*, *De Planctu Naturae*, and the *Roman de la* characters in *Piers the Plowman*, *De Planctu Naturae*, and the *Roman de la Rose* call up a wide range of literary associations that the anonymous poet clearly had in mind. These, combined with other literary allusions liberally interspersed throughout the text, point to an erudite poet whose project involved couching an unambiguous assertion of Christian truth in a complex chain of literary associations designed to widen and complicate the theological implications of the situation presented in the text.

Another important debate poem of the alliterative period, *The Parliament of the Three Ages* (*The Parlement of the Thre Ages*), is exemplary of the popularity of the polyvocal debate form in fourteenth-century England. This work, which is based in part on the earlier fourteenth-century French *Les Voeux du Paon* (see Thorlac Turville-Petre, *Alliterative Poetry of the Later Middle Ages*, 67), presents personifications of three periods in the life of man, Youthe, Medill(e) Elde (Middle Age), and Elde (Old Age). The poem has notable stylistic affinities with other fourteenth-century poetry, and its subject, a popular one in medieval literature, has a long literary history that can be traced back as far as the lyric poem on the ten ages of man written by Solon, the famous Greek politician and social reformer.

In the *Parliament* the narrator is a hunter whose springtime wanderings lead first to his pursuit and killing of a deer and then to his sleeping and having a dream whose subject becomes the central subject of the poem. The three allegorical figures are described in wonderful detail, after which follows a brief debate between Youthe and Medill Elde. After their discussion Elde advises both figures to heed his advice ("Makes youre mirrours bi me, men, bi youre trouthe; / This schadowe in my schewere schunte ye no while. / And now es dethe at my dore that I drede moste" (290-92; quoted in Conlee, 118; spelling modernized here). He then cites the examples of the Nine Worthies (Caesar, Alexander, Hector; David, Joshua, Judas Maccabeus; *Charlemagne, Godfrey, and Arthur), four wise men (Aristotle, Virgil, Solomon, and Merlin), and famous lovers to demonstrate that all of man's greatness is fleeting and to announce, in both Latin and Middle English, his basic philosophy: "*Vanitas vanitatum et omnia vanitas*, / That all is vayne and vanytes and vanyte es alle" (639-40). He essentially dismisses the debate between Youthe and Medill Elde by reminding them that "Elde es sire of Medill Elde and Medill Elde of Youthe" (652). On that note the dreamer is suddenly awakened, and the poem comes to a rapid conclusion.

Among its many connections, both formal and thematic, to other poetry of the alliterative period, *The Parliament of the Three Ages* calls to mind other parliament poems, including "A Parliament of Birds," a relatively short stanzaic poem on romantic love that is part of the Chaucer Apocrypha, and Chaucer's *Parliament of Fowls* (*Parlement of Foules*; 1370s?), one of the greatest of the Middle English debate poems. The *Book of the Duchess* (1369-70) and the *House of Fame* (c. 1379-80) are also relevant parts of the Chaucerian corpus. Chaucer's use of the debate has received considerable critical attention; the reader need only consult either the Robinson or the

(Benson) Riverside editions of Chaucer's works to find a wealth of material with which to begin his or her own examination of the texts, their sources, and the occasions of their composition. While it is not within the scope of this entry to analyze either the Chaucerian debate poems themselves or the artistic and critical work they have generated, it is important to point to some of the ways in which these poems are connected to the other texts that have been discussed thus far.

The *Book of the Duchess*, the *House of Fame*, and the *Parliament of Fowls* all involve love visions, and, as Robinson noted, Chaucer makes extensive use of French sources in particular. The *Parliament* also makes direct use of Macrobius's *Dream of Scipio*, which the narrative voice is reading as he falls asleep. Further, the *Book of the Duchess* finds the dreamer listening to the songs of birds as his vision begins, and the dreamer in the *House of Fame* encounters an eagle who transports him to Fame's palace. The *Book of the Duchess* is largely indebted to French sources, among them the *Roman de la Rose* and the works of Machaut, and it is clear that Chaucer knew both the *Dream of Scipio* and the *Marriage of Philology and Mercury* (for good source information, see Robinson's explanatory notes on all three poems in question; see especially the introductory notes for the *Parliament* in which Robinson discussed Chaucer's knowledge of earlier bird debates; also see Benson's notes in *The Riverside Chaucer*). The poet was clearly building upon various literary commonplaces and traditions that have been mentioned earlier thereby creating a sophisticated poetic discourse in which these ingredients could be interwoven.

The *Parliament* opens with the narrator reading the *Dream of Scipio*, the subject of which he briefly relates. The narrator falls asleep and, in the dream vision that follows, he encounters the "forseyde Affrican" (120), who escorts him first to a garden in which he encounters allegorical figures and then to a temple in which he meets various gods and literary figures from ancient mythology. Finally, the narrator informs us that he comes upon Nature herself, who is surrounded by birds: "Ne there nas foul that cometh of engendrure / That they ne were prest in here presence, / To take hire dom and yeve hire audyence" (306-08).

We learn that it is Valentine's Day, the day on which the birds convene annually before Nature, and there follows a brief catalog of the attending fowls, after which the narrator begins to recount the contest he hears among the birds regarding which best loves the "gentil formel" (535). The discussion, as might be expected, touches on the nature of love itself, and finally Nature decides that she will leave the choice of a mate to the formel herself to make. The bird then declares that she will take a year to consider her choice, the rest of the birds are matched with their mates, and the convocation sings a song in praise of the passing of winter. The poem concludes rapidly with the narrator awaking and intending to turn his attention to other reading.

This brief survey concludes with the fifteenth century, during which debate continued to be popular. The Scot William Dunbar, who is among the so-called Chaucerian imitators, was the author of a satire on courtly love called the "Tretis of the Twa Mariit Wemen and the Wedo." Roots of this debate can be traced, through other debates by female interlocutors on the subject of men, as far back as the *Council of Remiremont*, demonstrating the continued vitality of the debate genre through the Middle Ages. *The Merle and the Nightingale*, mentioned earlier, is another of Dunbar's debate poems. Robert *Henryson, another Scot, also composed debate and pastoral, and his fables include the talking birds familiar from the debate as well as the fable and *fabliau traditions. One should also consider the work of John Gower, given his borrowing from diverse inherited literary traditions that were available to him (on this and Chaucerian borrowing from Arabic sources, see Lasater, 125-38). John Lydgate's corpus is perhaps a fitting place to end, for it is in his work that we can see extended didactic allegory and also borrowings from avian debate literature ("The Churl and the Bird") that combine to reassert the continued popularity of debate poetry and its close formal, thematic, and philosophical ties to other literature of the Middle Ages.

As even this brief overview demonstrates, debate literature has a place within Western European literary history that is at once important and difficult to define and delimit. How the idea of debate as a dialectical method of inquiry was understood at different historical moments can suggest much to modern readers about basic philosophical perspectives either actively employed or implicitly relied upon by writers. Medieval assumptions about the suitability of particular subjects for debate--and, indeed, the sustained use of some of these-- can also reveal useful information about the social, philosophical, and aesthetic interests and concerns of various authors' milieux. Furthermore, formal and thematic literary connections among debate poems across geographic, linguistic, and temporal distances can help us to ascertain patterns of cultural transmission during the Middle Ages. Above all, a sustained look at a related body of work--in this case seen loosely as debate poetry--can afford the modern reader an opportunity to appreciate both the cultural continuities that were so highly valued during the Middle Ages and the ruptures, sometimes deliberate and sometimes not, that make clear how diverse were the many individual voices that are all too often and too simplistically grouped together as "medieval." The debate poetry of the Middle Ages speaks to a wide range of practical and theoretical issues and reflects the ways in which medieval authors were able to avail themselves of a vast and complex literary heritage and to extract from it ideas, styles, formal frameworks, and points of view that could be renovated and reinterpreted through their own distinct voices.

SELECTED BIBLIOGRAPHY

Allen, Philip Schuyler. *Medieval Latin Lyrics*. Chicago: University of Chicago Press, 1931; Andreas Capellanus. John Jay Parry, Trans. *The Art of Courtly Love*. New York and London: Norton, 1969; Ascoli, Albert Russell. "The Unfinished Author." In *The Cambridge Companion to Dante*. Richard Jacoff, ed. Cambridge: Cambridge University Press, 1993; Attar, Farid ud-Din. *The Conference of the Birds*. Afkham Darbandi and

Dick Davis, trans. Harmondsworth: Penguin, 1984; Barnum, Priscilla Heath. *Dives and Pauper*. EETS 280. Oxford: Oxford University Press, 1980; Bertoni, Giulio. *Il Duecento*. In *Storia letteraria d'Italia*. Milan: Francesco Vallardi, 1910, reprinted 1964; Branca, Vittore. *Boccaccio: The Man and his Works*. Richard Monges, trans. New York: New York University Press, 1976; Brook, G. L., ed. *The Harley Lyrics: The Middle English Lyrics of Ms. Harley 2253. Old and Middle English Texts*. G. L. Brook, gen. ed. Manchester: Manchester University Press, 1948, reprinted 1964; Brown, Carleton, ed. *English Lyrics of the XIIIth Century*. Oxford: Clarendon Press, 1932, reprinted 1962; Caesarius of Heisterbach. *The Dialogue of Miracles*. H. Von E. Scott and C. C. Swinton Bland, trans. Broadway Medieval Library. London: Routledge and Sons, 1929; Chaucer, Geoffrey. *The Riverside Chaucer*. Larry D. Benson, ed. 3rd ed. Boston: Houghton Mifflin, 1987; Chaucer, Geoffrey. *The Works of Geoffrey Chaucer*. F. N. Robinson, ed. 2nd ed. Boston: Houghton Mifflin, 1957; Conlee, John W., ed. *Middle English Debate Poetry: A Critical Anthology*. East Lansing, MI: Colleagues Press, 1991; Conlee, John. "*The Owl and the Nightingale* and Latin Debate Tradition," *Comparatist* 4 (1980); Curtius, Ernst Robert. *European Literature and the Latin Middle Ages*. W. R. Trask, trans. New York: Bollingen, 1953; Dante. *A Translation of the Latin Works of Dante Alighieri*. Temple Classics. London: Dent, 1904; Dronke, Peter. *Dante and Medieval Latin Traditions*. Cambridge: Cambridge University Press, 1986; Dronke, Peter. *Medieval Latin and the Rise of European Love-Lyric*. Oxford: Clarendon Press, 1965; Dronke, Peter. *The Medieval Lyric*. New York: Harper and Row, 1968; Dudley, D. R. and D. M. Lang, eds. *The Penguin Companion to Literature 4: Classical and Byzantine, Oriental, and African Literature*. Harmondsworth: Penguin, 1969; Dunn, Charles W. and Edward T. Byrnes. *Middle English Literature*. New York: Harcourt Brace Jovanovich, 1973; Elbow, Peter. *Oppositions in Chaucer*. Middletown, CT: Wesleyan University Press, 1975; Goldin, Frederick, ed and trans. *German and Italian Lyrics of the Middle Ages*. Garden City: Anchor/Doubleday, 1973; Goldin, Frederick, ed. and trans. *Lyrics of the Troubadours and Trouveres*. Garden City, NY: Anchor/Doubleday, 1973; Goldstein, David, ed. and trans. *Hebrew Poems from Spain*. New York: Schocken, 1965; Gower, John. *Confessio Amantis*. Reinhold Pauli, ed. 3 vols. London: Bell and Daldy, 1857; Gragg, Florence Alden. *Latin Writings of the Italian Humanists*. College Classical Series. New Rochelle, NY: Caratzas Brothers, 1981; Grattan, J. H. G. and G. F. H. Sykes, eds. *The Owl and the Nightingale*. EETS 119. London: Oxford University Press, 1935, reprinted 1959; Harrington, K. P. *Medieval Latin*. Chicago and London: University of Chicago Press, 1962; Haskins, Charles Homer. *The Renaissance of the Twelfth Century*. Cambridge, MA: Harvard University Press, 1927, reprinted 1982; Jackson, W. T. H. *Medieval Literature: A History and a Guide*. London and New York: Collier Macmillan and Collier, 1966; Jacoff, Rachel, ed. *The Cambrige Companion to Dante*. Cambridge: Cambridge University Press, 1993; Jauss, Hans Robert. *Toward an Aesthetic of Reception*. Timothy Bahti, trans. Minneapolis: University of Minnesota Press, 1982; Lasater, Alice E. *Spain to England: A Comparative Study of Arabic, European, and English Literature of the Middle Ages*. Jackson: University Press of Mississippi, 1974; Menocal, Maria Rosa. *The Arabic Role in Medieval Literary History: A Forgotten Heritage*. Philadelphia: University of Pennsylvania Press, 1987; Monroe, James T. *Hispano-Arabic Poetry: A Student Anthology*. Berkeley: University of California Press, 1974; Murphy, James J., ed. *Medieval Eloquence: Studies in the Theory and Practice of Medieval Rhetoric*. Berkeley: University of California Press, 1978; Prudentius. *The Poems of Prudentius*. H. J. Thomson, trans. 2 vols. Loeb Classical Library. London and

Cambridge, MA: William Heinemann and Harvard University Press, 1949; reprinted 1969; Rumi. *Mystical Poems of Rumi*. A. J. Arberry, trans. Chicago: University of Chicago Press, 1968; Rumi. *Mystical Poems of Rumi 2*. A. J. Arberry, trans. Chicago: University of Chicago Press, 1979; Sapegno, Natalino. *Il Trecento*. In *Storia letteraria d'Italia*. Milan: Francesco Vallardi, 1933, reprinted 1973; Scaglione, Aldo. "The Mediterranean's Three Spiritual Shores: Images of the Self between Christianity and Islam in the Later Middle Ages." In *The Craft of Fiction*. Leigh A. Arrathoon, ed. Rochester, MI: Solaris Press, 1984; Stanley, Eric Gerald, ed. *The Owl and the Nightingale*. London: Thomas Nelson and Sons, 1960; Star, Jonathan, and Shahram Shiva, trans. *A Garden beyond Paradise: The Mystical Poetry of Rumi*. New York: Bantam, 1992; Stone, Brian, trans. *The Owl and the Nightingale, Cleanness, St. Erkenwald*. Harmondsworth: Penguin, 1971, reprinted 1977; Tuetey, Charles Greville, trans. *Classical Arabic Poetry*. London: KPI, 1985; Turville-Petre, Thorlac. *Alliterative Poetry of the Later Middle Ages*. Washington, DC: Catholic University of America Press, 1989; Wilson, Peter Lamborn, and Nasrollah Pourjavady, trans. *The Drunken Universe: An Anthology of Persian Sufi Poetry*. Grand Rapids, MI: Phanes Press, 1987.

Nancy M. Reale

DECAMERON, THE (IL DECAMERONE) (1349?-1351) Arguably the most famous prose narrative of the fourteenth century, *Decameron* was written as a partial response to the Black Death that devastated Florence in 1348 and 1349, and also as the natural continuation of a larger aesthetic literary agenda that spanned some fifteen years, Giovanni *Boccaccio's masterpiece continues to fascinate readers and draw the attention of scholars. The work itself, a frame narrative that encloses the storytelling adventures of its brigata of narrators-- comprised of seven young women and three young men--exploits the occasion of plague to flee from the city to a picturesque spot outside of Florence, complete with all the conventional trappings of the *locus amoenus*. The title, derived like many of his other works from the Greek, means "Ten Days." The young aristocratic narrators plan to fill up some of the time of their sojourn with storytelling, each day appointing a king or queen to select a theme for the day, and then relating appropriate tales to illustrate the topic, a technique foreshadowed in *Il *Filocolo*, under the deeply philosophical *questione d'amore* rubric.

The dissemination of the *Decameron* to its reading public was gradual; the first three days were circulated first, with other days to follow at various intervals. From the start, controversy surrounded the radical departure from convention that these stories represented. Therefore, included in the text of the *Decameron* are several intrusions by the author that attempt to explicate or clarify the purpose of the text. Nevertheless, the critics quickly reacted to the work; this criticism consisted predominantly of outrage about the explicitly sexual themes, action, and imagery contained in many of the tales. This reaction, very narrow and limited in its understanding of the text, was caused mainly by the fact that the narrative design or structural unity that is an integral part of the *Decameron* did not emerge until the entire text was revised and published toward the end of the 1360s. Even then, scholars disputed the value of such texts, trivial in topic and lacking in the high seriousness that was expected from intellectual figures.

The *Decameron* represents Boccaccio's theory and practice of vernacular literature as he understood it. As Giuseppe Mazzotta suggested, the *Decameron*, like the *Divine Comedy* before it, is an encyclopedic vernacular text, containing all relevant themes, genres, and metaphors that were central to humanist culture. It is a profound work, a culmination of Boccaccio's humanist imagination. Its impact on Western literary culture is immeasurable Castiglione, de Mezières, Cervantes, Tasso, Ariosto, Bembo, and countless others were inspired to explore the possibilities of vernacular culture after its publication.

At the heart of Boccaccio's agenda in the *Decameron* is an exposition of the fundamental playfulness and ambivalence of the human condition, coupled with a sense of anxiety about the ability of human language to account adequately or even partially for the power of divine revelation. This agenda engages the polemics that surrounded the debates about the value of poetry that created such conflicts during the development of humanism in the late Middle Ages and early Renaissance. The central difficulty in acquiring a firm grasp of the unity of the *Decameron* lies in its celebration of the fragmentary and ephemeral nature of transitory human experience, which Boccaccio evidently viewed as the only appropriate metaphor to contrast with divine stability. Logically, then, the central theme of the *Decameron* is that of the human imagination in all of its manifestations, from the base to the transcendent. Perhaps even more striking, the style is filled with joy and humor, exploiting the topos of laughter and the notion that literature, like love, has an intrinsic therapeutic value in human life.

A secondary theme of the *Decameron* is that of aesthetics, which Boccaccio privileged, according to Mazzotta, as "the source of knowledge for the play of illusion flowering in the imagination of his storytellers." To Boccaccio and other humanists, aesthetics and literature were one and the same thing: the only mode that allowed for the encyclopedic vision that permitted the human imagination to escape the boundaries of other classic and liberal forms of learning. In the *Decameron*, then, Boccaccio explored the possibilities for unity within chaos, speculation within orthodoxy, and insisted that literature is the only vehicle that can cater to all of human need simultaneously. Using the occasion of plague, a metaphor for chaos, the stories of the *Decameron* engage in rhetorical and aesthetic solutions to human suffering and locate these solutions in love and compassion.

Further, scholars appreciate the *Decameron* for its pioneering exploration of what Branca called the mercantile epic. This is the first vernacular work to successfully meld the values of aristocratic and bourgeois classes, while simultaneously developing an appropriate prose style to accommodate the figures, metaphors, and tropes that gave Latin its literary power. The structure of the prose has been exhaustively studied by Branca; that scholar also forcefully acknowledged the power of Boccaccian style as influential on the development of modern fiction. Following his early experiments in *Filostrato* and *Teseida*, Boccaccio exploited the juxtaposition between historical allusion and idealized *exempla in order to create his elaborate imaginary universe. As Branca pointed out: "Symbol and chronicle, example and legend thus can meet at last, can reconcile and illumine their different dimensions, previously opposed or rather alien to one another, in this new descriptive, figurative dimension; a dimension in which descriptions without losing any of their exemplary and eternal value are on the contrary set down with power and identified precisely within time and space." It was a formidable accomplishment and exemplary model for the beginnings of modern fiction.

SELECTED BIBLIOGRAPHY

Allen, Judson. *The Ethical Poetic of the Later Middle Ages.* Toronto: University of Toronto Press, 1982; Bergin, Thomas. *Boccaccio.* New York: Viking Press, 1981; Branca, Vittore. *Boccaccio: The Man and His Works.* R. Monges, trans.and Dennis McAuliffe, ed. New York: New York University Press, 1976; Kirkham, Victoria. *The Sign of Reason in Boccaccio's Fiction.* Florence: Olschki, 1993; Mazzotta, Giuseppe F. *The World at Play in Boccaccio's "Decameron."* Princeton: Princeton University Press, 1986; Potter, Joy. *Five Frames of the "Decameron."* Princeton: Princeton University Press, 1982; Suzuki, Mihoko. "Gender, Power, and the Female Reader: Boccaccio's *Decameron* and Marguerite de Navarre's *Heptameron.*" *Comparative Literature Studies* 30:3 (1993), 231-52.

Theresa Kennedy

DEOR'S LAMENT. The division of the *Old English poem *Deor's Lament* into six strophes with recurrent refrain, uncharacteristic of *Anglo-Saxon verse, but often used by Scandinavian writers--makes it difficult to give a definite date or to know whether we are dealing with the translation or an Old Norse original. Good arguments can be produced to support either supposition.

Nithhad, a crafty king, fetters (or hamstrings) Weland, the Vulcan of Norse myth, in order to steal the magic ring that gives him the power to fly. But the king's daughter Beadohild, along with her brothers, visits Weland so that he may mend their rings. In the mending the goldsmith recovers his own magic ring with its power of flight, kills the brothers, and after stupefying Beadohild with liquor, rapes her. Although ultimately victorious, Weland is described by the minstrel with dark imagery: His companions ". . . were pain and sorrow." The "gracious God" may give rich honors to many earls, but only woes to Nithhad.

Even the *minstrel Deor finds himself passed over by a skillful singer Heorrenda and the earldom promised to him given instead to his rival. For

Weland, Nithhad, and Deor, the only consolation is the consolation of Time offered six times in the refrain: "That has passed over: . . . so this may depart." The thought of the minstrel bears a striking similarity to the biblical book of Ecclesiasties (9:11). I returned, and saw under the sun, that the race is not to the swift, nor the battle to the strong, neither yet bread to the wise, nor yet riches to men of understanding, nor yet favor to men of skill; but time and chance happeneth to them all.

SELECTED BIBLIOGRAPHY

Banjeree, Jacqueline. "'Deor': The Refrain." *Explicator* 42:4 (Summer 1984), 4-7; Fjalldal, Magnus. "Was His Name Deor?" *NOWELE* 17 (March 1991), 53-62; Risden, E. L. "Deor and the Old English Ode and Gnomic Compassion." *In Geardagum* 11 (1990), 57-70.

Elton E. Smith

DE SOTO, HERNANDO (1499?-1542). In 1539 de Soto was granted a patent by Phillip II of Spain to colonize the gulf coast of what today is the state of Florida. His expedition wandered the southeastern United States, eventually turning westward, and discovered the Mississippi River in 1541. De Soto and his men crossed the great river into territory now encompassing Arkansas and Oklahoma. In 1542, while exploring further down the Mississippi toward the Gulf of Mexico, de Soto died, and it was left to others to carry on his efforts. Explorers who came after de Soto were unsuccessful in their attempts to colonize this part of the New World, and colonization efforts were abandoned in 1561. However, new expeditions were later launched to protect the Bahamas Strait between the coast of Florida and the Bahamas.

SELECTED BIBLIOGRAPHY

Clayton, Lawrence A. *et al*, eds. *The De Soto Chronicles: The Expedition of Hernando de Soto to North America in 1539-1543*. Tuscaloosa: University of Alabama Press, 993; Duncan, David Ewing. *Hernando de Soto: A Savage Quest in the Americas*. New York: Crown, 1995.

R. Churchill Curtis

DIAS, BARTHOLOMEU (1450?-1500). In 1487 Bartholomeu Dias, on a mission for his government, was sailing known, earlier demonstrated routes southward, down the west coast of Africa. He met violent storms south of the Bight of Africa and was blown south of the tip of the continent. The shore that he next laid eyes upon was to the northeast, indicating that he had rounded the

Cape of Good Hope. Dias continued northward but was forced to put about by his rebellious crew. He returned to Portugal in December 1488.

Dias was not yet done with the explorer's life, commanding one of the vessels that accompanied Pedro Cabral in 1500. This group of thirteen vessels touched Brazil, which Cabral named Tierra de Vera Cruz. Dias also voyaged to India in 1500, returning the following year.

SELECTED BIBLIOGRAPHY

Axelson, Eric. *Congo to Cape: Early Portuguese Explorers.* New York: Barnes & Noble, 1973; Faber, Harold. *The Discoverers of America.* New York: Scribner, 1992.

R. Churchill Curtis

DICETO, RALPH (c. 1120s-1202). Ralph Diceto (Ralph of Diss) was closely allied to court circles. Born in the 1120s, he became a canon of St. Paul's and visited Paris sometime in the 1140s, perhaps to study at the university. By 1153 he was the archdeacon of Middlesex, and in 1180 he was made dean of St. Paul's. His friends in court kept him up to date on current history, and his *Ymagines Historiarum* is a detailed Latin chronicle of life in the English court, containing excerpts from letters and other information he received from the court.

He is also remembered for his epitome of world history from the creation to 1148 called the *Abbreviationes Chronicorum.* Gransden called his work the most ambitious attempt at world history written up to his time. His survey of sources included forty-seven separate influences. His one major weakness was his uncritical acceptance of earlier historical sources, including *Geoffrey of Monmouth's *Historia Regum Brittaniae*.

SELECTED BIBLIOGRAPHY

Gellrich, Jesse M. *Discourse and Dominion in the Fourteenth Century.* Princeton: Princeton University Press, 1995; Goffart, Walter. *The Narrators of Barbarian History (A.D. 550-800).* Princeton: Princeton University Press, 1988; Sterns, Indrikis. *The Greater Medieval Historians: An Interpretation and a Bibliography.* Lanham, MD: University Press of America, 1980; Sterns, Indikis. *The Greater Medieval Historians: A Reader.* Washington D.C.: University Press of America, 1982; Taylor, John. *English Historical Literature in the Fourteenth Century.* Oxford: Clarendon Press, 1987.

Richard McDonald

DIVINE COMEDY, THE. See **Dante Alighieri**.

DOMESDAY BOOK. The *Domesday Book* is a later record of the 1088 survey and census of most of England that was compiled by order of *William the Conqueror. It is also referred to as the Book of the Day of Assessment. In this book all property is described and evaluated in terms of ownership, domain, and worth of farm animals and other possessions. Using these attributes, the work also served as a tally of the populace and their livestock.

The book's surveys are broken into three parts. The first lists the inhabitants at the time of Edward the Confessor (1042-1066). The second is from the time of William's transfer of the estates to their new owners (1086). The third is from the time of the survey (1086) and includes an estimate about an estate's future potential. This record book was important because it became the final authority on property litigation (dome means judgment). It served as the basis for assessing taxes until 1527. The manuscript is in London's Public Record Office.

SELECTED BIBLIOGRAPHY

Kapelle, William E. "*Domesday Book*: F. W. Maitland and His Successors." *Speculum* 64:3 (July 1989), 620-40; Roffe, David. "Place Naming in *Domesday Book*: Settlements, Estates, and Communities." *Nomina* 14 (1990-1991), 47-60; Stafford, Pauline. "Women in *Domesday*." *Reading Medieval Studies* 15 (1989), 75-94.

Robert T. Lambdin

DONATELLO (1386-1466). Donatello created a realism based on man and nature and, early in his career, recognized the principle of weightshift, or depiction of motion. This principle of the Greeks revived by Donatello presented figures of a flexible structure that move by shifting weight from one supporting leg to the other. Accepted by his peers as authoritative, he was at ease with the real, the ideal, and the spiritual. One critic suggested that his human forms were diverse and that he took as his province the whole terrain of naturalistic and humanistic art. His *St. George* (1415-17) presents an image of proud youth, with torso twisted slightly, suggesting power, intelligence, and resolution. His depiction of the prophet Zuccone shows the sculptor's ability to characterize according to his own insight, departing from conventional interpretation. This statue, the most striking of five figures produced between 1416 and 1435, also demonstrates the sculptor's grasp of psychological realism.

SELECTED BIBLIOGRAPHY

Gardner, Helen. *Gardner's Art Through The Ages.* 6th ed. San Diego: Harcourt Brace Jovanovich, 1975.

Libby Bernardin

DRAMA, MEDIEVAL. One of the remarkable ironies of European drama's second genesis is that it emerged from the same institution that had been instrumental in suppressing its first manifestation. The early Church objected to Roman dramatic productions because they frequently included mortal combat and other activities viewed as pagan immoralities. Roman dramatic spectacles were banned in the fifth century by the recently Christianized Roman emperors, and the once-popular entertainment was virtually wiped out. The break with the past was so complete that those instrumental in developing medieval drama over four hundred years later had very little knowledge of their predecessors and literally had to reinvent dramatic practice.

Medieval drama developed over the course of three centuries, from the tenth to the thirteenth, and its origin is commonly traced back to the Christian Mass of the ninth century.

The Roman Catholic liturgy was inherently dramatic even before the advent of any practices that could be construed as early plays. The Mass involved highly ceremonial and meticulously arranged gesturing and posturing by the clergy. The service included a dramatic sense of presence and place. After all, the host was considered to be literally present upon the altar, and the altar itself was the platform upon which the ceremony and spectacle of the Catholic Mass was performed. The reading of the gospel had long involved dramatic qualities--a ceremonial movement of the book to the appropriate position within the sanctuary and a ritualized censing. Moreover, much of the formalized service was thought to mimic Christ's life and death. For example, the Mass itself and particularly Holy Communion were reenactments of the Last Supper, and the singing of *Gloria in Excelsis* symbolized Christ's triumph over death. Other practices such as the procession of palms on Palm Sunday involved many dramatic elements.

That part of the liturgy considered by most scholars of the period to be the direct ancestor of modern and early modern drama is antiphonal singing, which involved musical texts sung responsively. They were predramatic since they involved the representation and reproduction of varying voices, a practice that constituted a precursor to dialogue, and yet, these compositions initially involved no action and few lines. The earliest of the pre-dramatic songs were developed as a part of the Easter Mass in an effort to make the Resurrection (the most pivotal moment in Christian theological history) more tangible and, therefore, more meaningful for the congregation. These compositions are referred to as *Quem Quaeritis* because they reproduce the dialogue associated with the two Marys' visit to Jesus' tomb on Easter morning. *Quem Quaeritis* is an abbreviation of the angel's question for the Marys: "Whom do ye seek in the tomb?" The composition was sung in Latin, and its earliest forms were usually only three sentences, involving question, reply, and rebuttal.

Eventually, the dramatizations of the Easter Mass became more deliberate and self-conscious. They grew from the merely dramatic into actual plays. The similarity between the liturgy and drama was no longer incidental, but intentional. At the same time, the subject matter to be dramatized became more diverse, although it still remained within the scope of the Easter liturgy. These embellishments included the portrayal of Christ resurrected, his appearance before the disciples, his ascension, and the Pentecost. The first conflict was probably the re-enactment of the race to the tomb by Peter and John. Not only did the subject matter of these liturgical elaborations begin to vary more widely, but the compositions themselves became increasingly more complex, and although it is a controversial practice to assume that the more simplistic compositions always predate the more complex, one must reasonably assume an indirect evolution of the primitive praxis into the intricate.

By the eleventh century, dramatic customs were firmly ensconced in the Roman liturgy and were now associated with other celebrations within the Church's yearly cycle. The Christmas liturgical season was the next to be embellished with dramatic spectacle, and these compositions, originally modeled on the *Quem Quaeritis*, evolved much more rapidly than their Easter predecessors. The Christmas celebrations began rather quickly to include events peripheral to the Nativity scene: the encounter between Herod and the Magi, the slaughter of the innocents, and the stories of the prophets. Oddly, the first reenactment of the Passion did not appear until the thirteenth century, and its subject matter revolved around Mary's lamentation at the cross. Perhaps the medieval church regarded the Crucifixion as too solemn and grievous to be vulgarized by dramatization. The process of expanding the subject matter for dramatic display continued in the twelfth century. The works composed during this period were intended for other seasonal observations of the church, such as the Feast of the Conversion of Saint Paul.

Liturgical drama was neither a subtle nor a professional art form. All of the roles were played by clergymen, and there was no effort at psychological complexity in the character development. The scripts had very few stage directions. Although there were a variety of symbolic settings for the action of the plays, there was little effort at realism in staging. Occasionally a few props may have been used. The expansion of the plays into fully developed dramas was accomplished in part by including additional dialogue both before and after the central event, but mostly by combining the plays of a single seasonal celebration.

Early medieval drama's break from the church occurred in the thirteenth century. It was not accomplished by incremental steps but by edict. It was banned because it had begun to compete with the services. However, this break with the Church did not involve a significant transformation in subject matter. The content of drama still consisted entirely of sacred material. There was perhaps a broadening of artistic license achieved by the separation. As long as plays were a part of the liturgy, they were confined in their scope; they had to show appropriate reverence for sacred events. The secularization of drama permitted the inclusion of humor and substantial, not always textual, elaborations. It also permitted the inclusion of vernacular languages, a change that made the productions accessible to a much wider audience.

The next phase in the development of modern European drama is perhaps the most well known of the medieval forms--the mystery plays.   One of the events that facilitated the generation of the mystery or cycle plays was the establishment of the Feast of *Corpus Christi, created by the Council of Vienne and known to be widely practiced in England by 1318.   The holiday was unusual among the major religious celebrations because it had no scriptural narrative as its antecedent.   On the first day of the celebration the Host was ritualistically carried through the streets to the door of the church, followed by a procession of sacred and secular authorities.   The feast was established in early June (the fourth through the sixth), probably because the weather was hospitable and the days were long.   The activities included in the celebration-- sporting, dancing, and singing--seem to emphasize outdoor, physical exercise; thus long warm days would be requisite. (*See* **Festivals and Holidays**.) By the end of the fourteenth century the holiday included as much as three full days of drama, enacted outside on makeshift stages.

Each town had its own complete cycle of plays, and the local trade guilds were responsible for their production. "Myster" meant trade; thus the term "mystery play."   Trade guilds were collectives that included the local members of a single profession, such as grocers, cooks, carters, and dyers, to name only a few.   Their objectives as a professional society consisted of various activities: the regulation of commerce, the training of apprentices, and the moderation of goods.   The guilds' involvement in the Corpus Christi plays was a public service.   The organizations had recently become a significant force in medieval society, and Corpus Christi permitted them to reveal their affluence and to commit some of their wealth to civic improvement. The Church was only too happy to allow the guilds to sponsor the event since the plays could be quite expensive and could attract large crowds.   The dramatic productions of the guilds appear to have evolved from less complicated activities. In the early years of the celebration the tradesmen began by carrying biblical posters in the parade of the Host.   They later produced floats with biblical themes and eventually started to enact brief plays, no doubt modeled on liturgical drama. Since the guilds were rich, they would try to exceed each other with their extravagant productions, hoping to impress civic and ecclesiastical authorities, and would even compete for the right to produce the plays.

The subject matter of the mystery plays is the biblical history of the world from the Creation to the Apocalypse, with special emphasis on the pivotal events in the life of Jesus Christ.   Each guild would enact a single significant episode in the lengthy scriptural narrative.   The plays are often referred to as "cycles" because the subject matter is cyclic in form, moving from the Fall to Redemption and judgment. The purpose of the plays was didactic, seldom literary, although the plays do seem to have a coherent and aesthetically pleasing, typological organization based upon echoing, foreshadowing, and culmination.   The varying characters and dramatic situations within the cycles are unified by their resemblances to each other.   For example, before the appearance of Christ in the series, several characters display Christlike qualities. In the story of Abraham and Isaac, a father is compelled to sacrifice his son to redeem sin. Yet at the last moment he is permitted to replace the child with a lamb. In addition, the intended offering, Isaac, is forced to carry on his back the wood that will burn his body; this, of course, is a foreshadowing of the cross. Another typological parallel includes the respective transgressions of Satan, Adam, and Eve; falling becomes a motif within the cycles. The plays are structured climactically through the theme of redemption: Christ replaces Adam; Mary redeems Eve; the cross replaces the tree of prohibition; and the great conflagration of the judgment day succeeds the flood.

There was often a curious logic in the assignment of particular plays to particular guilds. The grocers often enacted the Fall because they had access to apples. Of course, the story of Noah was produced by the shipwrights' guild. Goldsmiths frequently portrayed the Magi since the play involved the presentation of rich gifts to the Christ child. The breaking of bread in the Last Supper qualified the bakers' guild for the production. The cooks often presented the Harrowing of Hell since they were in a position to produce the requisite smoke.

The logistics of producing the cycles has been a point of controversy. It is widely accepted belief that the plays were enacted on mobile pageant wagons; whether or not these wagons were actually moved in the course of the celebration is a sticking point among scholars of medieval drama. The pageant wagons were wide platforms on wheels, often pulled by horses. They were quite expensive to maintain, and as a consequence, they would frequently be shared by more than one guild. The traditional view is that the various wagons were rolled around the city to predesignated locations and waiting crowds. Eventually, the entire cycle would be enacted at each of numerous locations, thus facilitating the enjoyment of a large number of celebrants. The stage directions of the Towneley cycle suggest that the plays were produced in the round, since the action moves rapidly from one platform to another. This organization may have involved a large space enclosed by the circled wagons. With such an arrangement, the audience would have been able to move rapidly from one platform to the next perhaps simply by turning around. The stage directions for the *Ludus Coventriae* were so complicated that the cycle must have been produced in a single location. Some of the stage directions for the plays suggest the simultaneous use of platforms at varying elevations. How this was accomplished is not entirely clear. It is possible that the wagons were pulled alongside makeshift platforms.

The timing of the productions must have been another logistical problem. Some of the cycles had almost fifty plays. It would be difficult to present them even over the course of three days, yet the York cycle (one of the longest) was produced in only one day. The York plays would begin at dawn--the players were ordered to assemble at 4:30 in the morning and extend beyond dusk. In another arrangement the plays were spread out over the three days of the festival. The first day's presentations would include the principal events of the Old Testament: the Creation, the fall of Lucifer and Adam, the murder of

Abel by his brother, the story of Noah and the flood, Abraham's sacrifice of Isaac, and so on. The second day would involve episodes from the life of Jesus Christ, the Annunciation to the Crucifixion. On the third, the resurrection to the Last Judgment would be represented; these latter plays included portrayals of the lives of the saints.

One of the great mysteries of the mystery plays surrounds recruitment of the necessary number of actors for the productions. In some areas of the country there was probably no difficulty finding a sufficient number of willing participants; however, in other locations the entire population of the town was not sufficient to fill the number of parts in the local cycle. The York cycle required no less than twenty-seven Christs. It is probable that individuals were playing multiple parts. The towns may even have recruited from the members of traveling acting companies. Yet the events remained amateur productions. The acting was notoriously poor, a fact immortalized in the sylvan production of the mechanicals at the end of Shakespeare's *A Midsummer Night's Dream* and in Hamlet's association of overacting with the bluster and rage of the cycle's Herod.

Records reveal that the production of Corpus Christi plays was widespread among the English towns. Documentation exists to verify cycles in "Aberdeen, Bath, Beverley, Bristol, Canterbury, Dublin, Ipswich, Leicester, Worcester, and possibly Lincoln and London." However, there are only four extant cycles in manuscripts: the York cycle, the Towneley cycle, the Chester cycle, and the *Ludus Conventriae*. The York production included forty-eight plays and was probably written between 1430 and 1440. The Chester plays, of which there are twenty-five, are believed to be the oldest existing cycle, originally staged around 1375. The Towneley cycle of thirty-two plays has been associated with Wakefield. Scholars have estimated that these plays were written around 1450; however, the only records of their performance are for 1554 and 1556. The *Ludus Coventriae*, also known as the Hegge plays and composed approximately 1392, include forty-two individual episodes. One location suggested for the production of these latter plays is Lincoln, but the evidence is not strong. Possessing a cycle series contributed to a town's prestige.

One complicated issue is the authorship of the mystery plays. The people who penned the plays were no doubt clerics, but complete cycles cannot be associated with single writers. The plays were revised and edited for two hundred years. The common practice in the growth of the cycles was to solicit writers either to add new plays or to rewrite the old ones. The guilds were not stable institutions, and often when a guild was disbanded, the cycle play was taken up by another that would have changes made in the manuscript to suit its own interests and emphases. Even those few writers who can be identified and who are considered accomplished from a literary standpoint are associated with only a select number of works within the given cycle. The so-called *Wakefield Master is credited with only six of the plays in the Towneley cycle. His authorship is identifiable through his novel use of nine-line stanzas and his appreciation of comedy. Even his work is considered revisionary. However, among his credits is that play regarded as the acme of Medieval drama--*The *Second Shepherd's Play,* commonly anthologized and taught even to underclassmen. Another particularly accomplished writer revised the York Crucifixion sequence, creating a painful realism and pathos. There is some evidence that the various participating towns would share individual plays and sometimes whole sequences. There are six plays in the Towneley dramas that are virtually identical to plays in the York sequence. Perhaps some towns lacked the financial or artistic resources to produce their own set of plays. In this case there may have been collaboration between towns, either by pooling resources or by simply buying and borrowing. They may also have solicited the work of common writers who were not tied to any particular region. Of course, the most substantial revisions occurred after the Reformation, when much of the subject matter of the plays became unacceptable.

Although it did not happen immediately, the Reformation brought about the end of the mystery plays. The suppression began in the middle of the sixteenth Century (1560s through 1570s) when church authorities forbade the production of plays celebrating the Virgin Mary because they smacked of Catholicism. Later prohibitions included the representation of Christ or God on stage. Such portrayals were considered blasphemies. There are sixteenth century alterations in the York cycle evidently intended to conform to the doctrine of the new church. This process of censorship and alteration continued into the last decades of the sixteenth century, when it even plagued the rapidly evolving Renaissance drama. Censors eventually banned any mention of the Christian God on stage, resulting in references to the "gods" in the obviously Christian dramas of the late sixteenth and early seventeenth centuries. The Feast of Corpus Christi and its various celebratory activities were eventually ruled pagan and idolatrous by the reformed church. The last recorded enactment of the mystery plays was in Chester in 1581.

The medieval saints' plays, which developed alongside the mysteries and which were occasionally included within the cycles, met the same fate as the latter at the Reformation. In all likelihood, the saints' plays were subject to even more zealous efforts at suppression than were the mysteries since their focus on the lives and miracles of the saints made them vulnerable to the accusation of idolatry. In the fine arts, the church had found the iconography of the saints to be explicitly Catholic and, therefore, only worthy of elimination. Perhaps the dearth of surviving texts of saints' plays can be attributed to the same process. Before the Reformation, for instance, there were numerous plays about Thomas *Becket; however, the anti-Catholic zeal of the reformers was specifically directed toward the cult of the saint because *Henry VIII regarded him as a traitor to his king and demanded that pictures of him be destroyed. It is likely that plays about Becket met the same fate.

Although there are only three extant Saint plays, it is believed that at one time most religious institutions possessed a drama honoring their patron. This practice extended also to trade guilds. For example, St. Crispin, the patron saint of shoemakers, was honored with a play by the shoemakers' guild. In addition to its devotional objective, this practice was, at least partially, intended to generate enthusiasm and public awareness for the particular craft. However, there are records indicating that the plays were occasionally enacted by the guilds to generate money for church restoration and repair.

The three surviving saint plays include *St. Paul, Mary Magdalene*, and the somewhat atypical *Play of the Sacrament*. The predominant theme in these compositions is conversion, whether it be the conversion of the saint himself or herself, as in *St. Paul,* or the work of the saint in converting others, as in the *Play of the Sacrament. Mary Magdalene* includes both the scriptural and the apocryphal. It tells of the travels and miracles of Mary. Other Saints once honored in this way include St. Nicholas, St. Katherine, St. Eustace, St. Laurence, St. George, and many others.

The staging of these dramas was in many ways similar to that of the cycle plays. They were often performed outside on pageant wagons. However, on occasion, they were enacted within the church, depending upon the season. Like the mystery cycles, saint plays may have been enacted in the round in order to facilitate a more efficient production of numerous episodes. Most of the time, these plays were not gathered to form lengthy cycles portraying multiple saints. There were, however, collections of plays detailing the lives of individual saints, collections of scenes that might have taken several days to produce. The surviving *Mary Magdalene* includes as many as fifty separate episodes.

The medieval drama that is perhaps the most well known, probably because of its influence on Renaissance playwrights, is the morality play. The earliest moralities are attributed to the late fourteenth and early fifteenth centuries. The *Play of the Lord's Prayer* is dated 1384, and the *Creed Play,* 1408. These dates make moralities contemporary with the great mystery cycles. However, the two art forms differed substantially. The morality play did not borrow biblical narratives for its subject matter; instead, its objective was to illustrate a moral or ethical principle, and whereas the cycle and saint plays were celebratory, the moralities were didactic.

The morality is allegorical, illustrating the struggle between the forces of good and evil for the soul of a representative human figure. Thus the central character is generally a symbolic representation of the entirety of humanity-- Everyman or Mankind--torn between good and bad influences. In the play *Everyman the titular character prepares for death and, in his fear of damnation, requests that the various aspects of his earthly existence accompany him into the afterlife to facilitate his salvation, so he interrogates Kindred, Fellowship, and Goods, all of whom abandon him in his hour of need. In the end, only his Good Deeds will accompany him on his journey into death. Similarly, in the morality *Mankind* the principal character, Mankind, appeals to Mercy to rectify his life and guarantee his salvation. Practicing his newfound virtue, he chases away the villains Mischief, Nought, Nowadays, and New-guise, who, angered over being thwarted, renew their efforts to destroy

Mankind. After a brief lapse in which he commits himself to drinking and wenching, Mankind   is once again saved by Mercy.   *The *Castle of Perseverance* is perhaps the most complicated morality. Here vices and virtues fight for the soul of Humanum Genus, who, walled up in the castle, is subjected to assaults by varying manifestations of wickedness.   Humanum Genus ultimately prevails against his enemies through the intercession of virtues such as Humility, Patience, Love, Abstinence, Chastity, Generosity, and Industry.

The three aforementioned dramas, which constitute the best known of the medieval morality plays, illustrate the common themes of the genre. Morality plays are commonly based upon any of three metaphors: the representation of life as a pilgrimage, the pattern of fall and repentance, or the battle between the forces of good and   evil (psychomachia). The plays invariably illustrate the pathway to repentance and salvation, acting as a paradigm for moral behavior. The central figure's soul is in jeopardy, and he or she must employ all of his or her resources to avoid perdition. The forces of evil are committed to thwarting humanity's efforts at virtue. Interestingly, the morality always teaches its lesson through positive example. The plays end happily with humanity either admitted into heaven or committed to the path of virtue.

One of the more interesting attributes of the morality play is its inclusion of comedy. While the cycle plays occasionally contain comic elements, the moralities frequently do. Often the comedic elements center around a representation of vice, whose cunning machinations are a source of amusement. He exploits Mankind's weaknesses, and he may lie or disguise himself in order to deceive the central figure. In *Mankind* Titivillus, dressed as a devil and carrying a net, tempts Mankind, while Mischief tells Mankind that Mercy has been hanged for stealing a horse. Generally the *Vice announces his intentions to the audience, expecting to evoke   admiration for his cleverness. One cannot help but recognize the potential for comedy in the representation of the various and vulgar human evils striving mightily and yet unsuccessfully for the destruction of humanity, particularly when they are all routed from the stage either by Mankind himself or by heavenly virtues. Perhaps the playwrights' motivation for representing vice as humorous was to trivialize evil, to make it seem less threatening. It is easy to see the influence of this tradition on such notorious Shakespearean villains as Iago and Richard III.

The production of the morality plays included some unusual characteristics. At least one scholar has suggested that all morality plays involved a castle setting, and although such a broad generalization may be indefensible, *The Castle of Perseverance* certainly had just such a set since one is described in the stage directions. The staging area contains a central castle surrounded by numerous scaffolds and a moat. The productions of moralities usually took place either in churches or guildhalls, although it is difficult to imagine how the aforementioned set could have been erected anywhere but outdoors. The dramatic troupes were not composed primarily of tradesmen as with the mystery and saint plays. The moralities were sponsored by the schools and the court and were acted by traveling companies of four men and a boy. These traveling troupes of actors eventually made their way to London, where, in 1576, they formed the first permanent playhouse in England.

The morality plays are generally regarded as the link between medieval and Renaissance drama, and one of the unique attributes of the moralities seems to confirm this thesis. The morality plays were a vehicle for social and political satire and even for political instruction. John *Skelton's *Magnyfycence* was intended to instruct Prince Henry (later Henry VIII) in the kingly virtues. Moreover, the play is regarded as a direct attack on Cardinal Wolsey for his refusal to support Henry's efforts at reforming the church. John Bale's *King Johan* was one of England's first history plays. It also had political objectives insofar as it explored the parallel between King *John and Henry. Indeed, the parallel between the Renaissance history play and the moralities is very clear. While the morality play depicts the struggle for the soul of Mankind by vice and virtue, the history play addresses the salvation of the kingdom by focusing on the monarch's vacillation between good and bad counselors.

The morality play seems to have fared much better than other forms of medieval drama after the Reformation, perhaps because it was not explicitly scriptural. Its influence on the great age of English drama was considerable. One need only examine Christopher Marlowe's *Dr. Faustus* in order to recognize the profound impact the antecedent dramatic tradition had. Faustus, a representative Mankind figure, is torn between the good and bad angels, between the minions of hell and those of heaven. He is confronted by allegorical vices through the pageant of the *seven deadly sins, and falling into sin for a lengthy period, he nevertheless attempts repentance at the end of his life. In what is perhaps the most telling difference between the morality and high Renaissance drama, Faustus is not saved at the end of the play; he is torn apart and dragged off to hell.

SELECTED BIBLIOGRAPHY

Beadle, Richard ed. *The Cambridge Companion to Medieval English Theatre.* Cambridge:Cambridge University Press, 1994; Bevington, David. "Castles in the Air: The Morality Plays." In *The Theatre of Medieval Europe.* Eckehard Simon, ed. Cambridge: Cambridge University Press, 1990. 97-116; Bevington, David. *Medieval Drama.* Boston: Houghton Mifflin, 1975; Briscoe, Marianne G., and John C. Caldwell, eds. *Contexts for Early English Drama.* Bloomington: Indiana University Press, 1989; Davidson, Clifford, ed. *The Saint Play in Medieval Europe.* Kalamazoo, MI: Medieval Institution Publications, 1986; Davidson, Clifford, and John H. Stroupe, eds. *Drama in the Middle Ages: Comparative and Critical Essays.* 2nd ed. New York: AMS Press, 1990; Diller, Hans Jurgen. *The Middle English Mystery Play: A Study in Dramatic Speech and Form.* Frances Wessels, trans. Cambridge: Cambridge University Press, 1992; Emerson, Richard K. ed. *Approaches to Teaching Medieval Drama.* New York: Modern Language Association, 1990; Happé, Peter. *English Mystery Plays: A Selection.* London: Penguin, 1975; Happé, Peter. *Four Morality Plays.* New York: Penguin, 1987; Hardison, O. B. *Christian Rite and Christian Drama in the Middle*

Ages. Westport, CT: Greenwood Press, 1965; Neuss, Paula, ed. *Aspects of Early English Drama.* Totowa, NJ: Barnes and Noble, 1983; Ricks, Christopher, ed. *English Drama to 1710.* New York: Peter Bedrick, 1987; Rose, Martial, ed. *The Wakefield Mystery Plays.* New York: Norton, 1969; Simon, Echehard, ed. *The Theatre of Medieval Europe.* Cambridge: Cambridge University Press, 1993; Taylor, Jerome and Alan H. Nelson, eds. *Medieval English Drama: Essays Critical and Contextual.* Chicago: University of Chicago Press, 1972; Tricomi, Albert H., ed. *Early Drama to 1600.* Binghamton, NY: Center for Medieval and Renaissance Studies, SUNY, 1987; Young, Karl. *The Drama of the Medieval Church.* 2 Vols. Oxford: Clarendon Press, 1933.

James Keller

DREAM ALLEGORY (VISION). In the Middle Ages the dream was a conventional narrative frame that became widely used. In the dream allegory the narrator usually falls asleep and while sleeping has a miraculous dream. It is this dream that becomes the actual story. During the Middle Ages these works were usually allegorical. The sheer volume of extant manuscripts demonstrates the popularity of this convention, and even today many of the works remain popular. The major medieval dream allegories include the *Romance of the Rose,* *Dante's *Divine Comedy,* Geoffrey *Chaucer's *Book of the Duchess* and *House of Fame,* the anonymous *Pearl,* and William *Langland's *Piers the Plowman.*

SELECTED BIBLIOGRAPHY

Cherniss, Michael D. "Two New Approaches to (Some) Medieval Vision Poems." *Modern Language Quarterly* 49:3 (September 1988), 285-91; Holman, C. Hugh, and William Harmon. *A Handbook to Literature.* 5th ed. New York: Macmillan, 1986; Lynch, Kathryn C. "The Logic of the Dream Vision in Chaucer's *House of Fame.*" in *Literary Nominalism and the Theory of Rereading Late Medieval Texts: A New Research Paradigm.* Richard J. Utz, ed. Lewiston, NY: Edwin Mellen Press, 1995. 179-203; Ryan, Marcella. "Chaucer's Dream Vision Poems and the Theory of Spatial Form." *Parergon* 11:1 (June 1993), 79-90.

Robert T. Lambdin

"DREAM OF THE ROOD, THE." An *Old English poem found in the *Vercelli Book, "The Dream of the Rood" was written in the second half of the 10th century. A variant of a part of the poem is found carved in runes on a late seventh or early eighth century stone cross in Ruthwell, Scotland. The relation between the manuscript and runic versions of the poem is not certain. It is usually assumed that both derive from an Anglian original written around A. D. 700. It is also possible, however, that the manuscript version merely quotes strategically from traditional verses and is in large part a later composition.

The poem belongs to the popular medieval genre of the *dream vision. The narrator reports a dream in which the cross, or rood, upon which Jesus was crucified appears to him and relates its history, from its beginnings as a tree in the forest, through the Crucifixion and its own metaphorical death, burial and resurrection (the invention of the cross by Juliana). The rood ends by exhorting the narrator to report the dream to other people as a token of the promise of salvation. The poem then concludes with the narrator's own testimony of the rood's spiritual comfort and his hope for eternal life, themes so common during this period.

"The Dream of the Rood" draws on a variety of traditional themes of Germanic poetry. The rood's description of its making invokes the vocabulary of the *riddles. The crucifixion is related not in terms of suffering as was popular in the later Middle Ages but as a voluntary heroism, as if Christ were a Germanic warrior in the mold of *Beowulf. The rood portrays itself as one of Christ's retainers, a member of the *comitatus*, anguished at being forced to serve as the instrument for its lord's death, unable to avenge itself upon those who caused Christ to be crucified. These Germanic elements are no pagan survivals, however. They reflect a thorough assimilation of *Anglo-Saxon culture with the religious ideas of Latin Christianity.

SELECTED BIBLIOGRAPHY

Clemoes, Peter. "King and Creation at the Crucifixion: The Contribution of Native Tradition to the 'Dream of the Rood' 50-6a." In *Heroes and Heroines in Medieval English Literature*. Leo Carruthers, ed. Cambridge, Brewer, 1994. 31-43; Hill, Thomas D. "The Cross as a Symbolic Body: An Anglo-Latin Liturgical Analogue to 'The Dream of the Rood.'" *Neophilologus* 77:2 (April 1993), 297-301; Johnson, David F. "Old English Religious Poetry: 'Christ and Satan' and 'The Dream of the Rood.'" In *Companion to Old English Poetry*. Henk Aerston and Rolf Bremmer, eds. Amsterdam: Vrije University Press, 1994. 159-87; Pigg, Daniel. "'The Dream of the Rood' in Its Discursive Context: Apocalypticism as Determinant of Form and Treatment." *English Language Notes* 29:2 (June 1992). 13-22.

Karl Hagen

DUNBAR, WILLIAM (1465?-1530). William Dunbar was a Scottish poet. He began his career as a Franciscan friar and later served as a diplomat for King James IV of Scotland. Dunbar's best works include the political allegory "The Thrissel and the Rois" (The Thistle and the Rose), composed in 1503. He wrote from 1503 to 1508 the religious dream vision "The Dance of the Sevin Deidly Sinnis" (The Dance of the Seven Deadly Sins) and the allegory "The Golden Targe," a work styled after *The Romaunt of the Rose*. He also wrote the "Lament of the Makirs" in 1508, a work that compares favorably with those of François *Villon.

SELECTED BIBLIOGRAPHY

Blanchot, Jean-Jacques. "Heroes and Anti-heroes in Dunbar's Poetry." In *Heroes and Heroines in Medieval English Literature*. Leo Carruthers, ed. Cambridge: Brewer, 1994. 125-36; Lucas, Stuart. "Foreign Influences in the Vocabulary of William Dunbar." *Scottish Language* 9 (Winter 1990), 52-65; Norman, Joanne S. "William Dunbar: Scottish Goliard." In *Selected Essays on Scottish Language and Literature*. Steven R. McKenna, ed. Lewiston, NY: Edwin Mellen Press, 1992. 41-54.

Robert T. Lambdin

DUNS SCOTUS, JOHN (c.1265-1308). John Duns Scotus was a great British medieval philosopher. who entered the Franciscan order at Dumfries in 1278. Around 1300 he presented a celebrated commentary on Peter Lombard's *Sententiae* at Oxford; he later repeated his discussion at Paris. Duns Scotus opposed the antipapal policy of Philip the Fair (*Philip IV) and was included with those expelled from Paris in 1305. He died three years later in Cologne.

The main contributions of Duns Scotus to the corpus of literature are two commentaries on the *Sententiae*: the *Reportata Parisiensia* (c. 1306) and the *Opus Oxoniense* (c. 1297). During his short life he wrote many other works, but he is considered important in terms of the *Scholastic movement because he spearheaded the wedge between philosophy and theology. Duns Scotus was a Thomist who believed that one needed to be detached from God to truly understand his grandeur. He was considered a realist in philosophy, his main belief was that the supreme function of the mind is the will; he also was a firm proponent of the doctrine of the Immaculate Conception. It seems that his beliefs were based in part on the thoughts of Ibn Gabirol, also known as Avicebron (c. 1020-c. 1070).

His thoughts concerning the Immaculate Conception, coupled with his belief in the tenet of faith and will (as opposed to reason), moved him away from the more straightforward *Aquinas. Further, Duns Scotus incorporated paganistic *Aristotelian philosophy into his ideas. In this way, Duns Scotus serves as a crossing point from the thirteenth century system construction to the fourteenth century cynicism.

His decision to urge philosophy's greater dependence on divine revelation, a thought based in part on his belief in the limitations of human reason, caused a great rift within the Scholastic community. Oddly, this led to a reaction quite the opposite of what Duns Scotus wished, for the philosophy became less concerned with theology. Duns Scotus also opposed the teaching of classical studies, which is noteworthy for a less impressive reason. The philosophers of the Renaissance used his name (or derivations of it) in a derogatory way. The term "dunce" (also "Duns" or "Dunse") became a reference for someone incapable of real learning; from this the term "dunce" has evolved to mean a dull-witted or stupid person.

SELECTED BIBLIOGRAPHY

Alanen, Lilli. "Descartes, Duns Scotus, and Ockham on Omnipotence and Possibility." *Franciscan Studies* 45 (1985), 157-88; Boler, John. "The Moral Psychology of Duns Scotus: Some Preliminary Questions." *Franciscan Studies* 50 (1990), 31-56; Ward, Bernardette Waterman. "Philosophy and Inscape: Hopkins and the *Formalitas* of Duns Scotus." *Texas Studies in Language and Literature* 32:2 (Summer 1990), 214-39.

Robert T. Lambdin

DUNSTAN, ST. (c. 910-98). Dunstan was one of the leaders of the tenth-century monastic revival in England. Raised near Glastonbury, he was familiar with the traditional monastic elements. Thus Dunstan, who also spent several years on the Continent, was well equipped to meld into the British monasteries the components of both the traditional and the continental ways. He gained the support of King Æthelstan, but later fell from grace and withdrew to Winchester; in 934, Ælfreah convinced Dunstan to take monastic vows. King Edmund restored Dunstan, appointing him in 939 to be abbot of Glastonbury. Dunstan retained Edmund's favor and remained in his place after the ascension of Eadred in 946.

Allegedly, Dunstan angered Eadred's successor, Eadwig, when he commented upon the king's attention to two "loose women" at his coronation. Dunstan left for Flanders in 956, but returned and was archbishop under Edgar. Dunstan was able to juggle this tenuous position because he combined the spiritual aspects mandated by his office with the political statesmanship he had to master to work with Edgar. Even so his duties as counsel to the king often clashed with his spiritual ideals. Dunstan believed strongly that church and state were inseparable; in exchange for the sanctity of the church, the king was God's choice to control the government. It was this close connection between Dunstan and the king that made the British church special.

In 963 Dunstan set in motion the great monastic revival, along with *Æthelwold. In less than a century more than sixty monasteries and nunneries were revived or established, with the orders changed so that they mixed the traditional elements with the new-found learnings of the Continent. Around 970 Edgar, Dunstan, and the other bishops met and adopted the *Regularis Concordia*, a monastic agreement that established norms for the way religious life would be carried out in the English monasteries. This agreement assured that while the monasteries would become communities unto themselves, they would never lose touch with the outside world. Dunstan's movement continued after his death; by the Norman Conquest some one thousand religious houses existed.

Because of his input, the monasteries grew to be a reflection of Dunstan's ideologies. They mirrored his wide range of interests, including art and philosophy, and their open nature prevented both the clerics and England from becoming isolated from knowledge. The monasteries grew to be havens for art, the composition of sacred texts, and the transcribing of all types of texts and translations. Indeed, the English church of Dunstan was noted for its artistic creativity.

SELECTED BIBLIOGRAPHY

Barker-Benfield, B. C. "Not St. Dunstan's Book?" *Notes and Queries* 40(238):4 (December 1993), 431-33; O'Hare, Colman. "Dunstanus Saga: England and the Old Norse Church." *American Benedictine* Review 33:4 (Dec 1982), 394-422.

Robert T. Lambdin

E

EARTHLY PARADISE. Earthly Paradise was an idyllic place of perfection--in terms of beauty, peace, and immortality--widely believed to exist on earth during the Middle Ages. This almost heavenly site was often identified with the garden of Eden. It was hypothesized that the earthly paradise was located somewhere in the Near East; theologians pointed to the book of Genesis for proof of its existence. This book clearly presents the idea that Eden was not destroyed after Adam and Eve were expelled from it; man was forbidden entrance to the garden by an angel with a flaming sword.

Others placed the Earthly Paradise in the Far East. John the Presbyter alleged that the garden was within three day's journey of his kingdom, a legendary land located somewhere in the heart of Asia. Others placed it in maps and reports as in the Atlantic, Pacific, or Indian oceans.

SELECTED BIBLIOGRAPHY

Masciandaro, Franco. *Dante as Dramatist: The Myth of the Earthly Paradise and Tragic Vision in the "Divine Comedy."* Philadelphia: University of Pennsylvania Press, 1991. Wright, Dorena Allen. "The Meeting at the Brook-side: Beatrice, the Pearl-Maiden, and Pearl Prynne." *ESQ: A Journal of the American Renaissance.* 28:2 (107) (1982), 112-20.

Robert T. Lambdin

EDDA. The term "edda" reflects the Old-Norse name for two Icelandic collections of early Scandinavian mythology. The *Poetic Edda* manuscripts, which were composed somewhere between the ninth and twelfth centuries, were discovered by Bishop Brynjolt Sveinsson in the seventeenth century. Sveinsson erroneously attributed this volume to Sæmund Sigjussen (1056-1133) calling the work *The Edda of Sæmund.* This *Poetic Edda* was compiled in the thirteenth century, but several of the thirty-four lays that tell the heroic mythological stories of the old Norse gods were composed centuries earlier. The heroic lays usually glorify German heroes such as Sigurðr and Helgi, while the mythological lays are concerned with the Voluspá, a history of the Norse from their creation until the apocalypse. Additionally, these manuscripts include the Hávamál and the words of Odin.

The *Prose Edda*, also known as the *Snorra Edda*, is a kind of "how to" book about making poems. It is composed in four sections, including a prologue and three parts. Written by *Snorri Sturluson, the work tells a series of mythological stories. The Prologue describes the creation of the world and catalogs the old pagan gods. Following the Prologue are three parts that are presented in the form of dialogues between Gylfi and the Norse gods.The first section, the *Gylfaginning*, introduces the young to the ancient myths; indeed, this portion of the *Edda* is one of the main sources of information about Norse mythology. The *Skáldskaparmál* (poetic diction) is where Snorri presents the origin of *Skaldic verse. This section tells the story of early Scandanavian mythology; the technical elements of the *kenning and *heiti* are also explicated. The final section is the *Háttatal* (List of meters) is a long poem which provides a technical analysis of meters. Each strophe presents a different type of poetic form. Because of the instructions, mythological elements, and technical elements, the *Prose Edda* is an invaluable text to scholars of this period.

SELECTED BIBLIOGRAPHY

Bagge, Svere. *Society and Politics in Snorri Sturluson's "Heimslringla."* Berkeley: University of California Press, 1991; Motz, Lotte. *The Beauty and the Hag: Female Figures in Germanic Faith and Myth.* Vienna: Fassbaender, 1993; Quinn, Judy. "The Naming of Eddic Mythological Poems in Medieval Manuscripts." *Parergon* 8:2 (Dec 1990), 97-115.

Robert T. Lambdin

EDWARD I (1239-1307), king of England (1272-1307). Edward was an able leader and great legislator. He followed the family motto *Pactum Serva* (keep troth), but tempered it with realism. He was the first true English king, surrounding himself with able ministers and lawyers. Edward's reign was marked by frequent consultation with the knights and townspeople, not always in Parliament. The institutions of the English state began to take shape.

Edward conquered Wales in 1283 and asserted the full dominion of the English Crown. Since his second son was born during this expedition, Edward titled him Prince of Wales, and thus began the customary bestowal of this title upon the heir to the throne. It was from the Welsh that Edward gained great confidence in the longbow and made it England's own.

Edward was originally successful against the Scots as well. He took advantage of divided Scottish allegiance (three claimants) to seize the land. He began subjugation by carrying away the Stone of Scone, a slab marking Scotland's traditional place of coronation. Oppressive administration by Edward's nobles brought rapid rebellion, led by William *Wallace who early on was supported by the gentry and commoners but not by the Scottish nobles. In 1305 Edward succeeded first in driving Wallace into exile and then in capturing and executing him. Scotland was then incorporated under the British Crown. Scottish law was retained, and Scottish nobles sat in Parliament, but the nobles were forced to give up their fortresses. An English lieutenant was sent to Scotland and given power to rule. Scottish nationalism found a leader in *Robert the Bruce. Edward was on an expedition against him when he died in 1307.

In domestic affairs Edward continued to follow his predecessors' path in strengthening the throne. Up to the late 1200s Jews, because they were a source for loans, were protected by the rulers of England, but by 1290, public opinion had turned strongly against them, and Italian banking houses, such as the Bardi and Peruzzi, were ready to replace Jews as ready sources of royal loans. Foreign trade, like banking, was in the hands of foreigners, and there were few native merchants, except in the wool export trade. The English staple, wool manufacturing, was established in Antwerp under Edward.

Edward was also finally able to gain victory over the clergy and the papacy. He was able to meet the rising cost of governing by gaining the right, from the Parliament of 1275, to an increase in export duties on wool. Leather trade was granted to Edward as a monopoly, the first such monopoly for the throne. The king was able to demand of Parliament the furthering of the rules concerning an extension of knighthood, and, by doing so, a considerable increase in revenue. Called the Distraint of Knighthood, the act ensured a militia under control of the king. Other legislative successes followed. Edward established the free transfer of land. Any new vassal could hold lands only directly from the king or one of his tenants-in-chief.

In 1295 Edward established the Model Parliament. He included in its rules the extraordinarily important phrase *Quod omnes tangit ab omnibus approbetur* ("Let that which touches all be approved by all"). Bishops, abbots, earls, barons, knights, burgesses, and representatives of the charters and parishes were summoned.

In 1297 Edward confirmed all charters in a document, almost as historically important as the Magna Carta, called the Confirmatio cartarum, a document extorted from the Crown by a coalition of barons and the middle classes. This Confirmatio cartarum granted to the merchants full freedom of trade and safe conduct, in return for a new schedule of customs dues.

Edward's reign is remarkable for his frequent consultation with the middle class. The nation became educated not only in the elements of self-government but also in new ideas and closer contact between the people and the Crown.

SELECTED BIBLIOGRAPHY

Brault, Gerard J. "Styles of Verbal Blazon in the Reign of Edward I." In *Medieval French and Occitan Literature and Romance Linguistics*. Rupert T. Pickins, ed.

Kalamazoo: Medieval Institute Publications, 1993. 489-505; Knutson, Roslyn. "Play Identifications: The Wise Man of West Chester and John a Cumber; Longshanks and Edward I. *Huntington Library Quarterly* 47:1 (Winter 1984), 1-11.

R. Churchill Curtis

EDWARD III (1327-1377), king of England (1327-1377). Edward III spent the first three years of his reign under regency. During that time *Robert the Bruce of Scotland invaded England and forced recognition of Scottish independence in 1328, not a very auspicious beginning. His personal rule began two years later and is notable for great accomplishments, both militarily and domestically. Edward III's reign brought England increased landholdings in France. At Crécy and Poitiers Edward claimed victory, positioning dismounted horsemen behind hedges of stakes, an innovative tactical maneuver. The English longbow was used to terrible effect against the crossbowmen and undisciplined cavalry of the French, and use of the longbow decided the battle in favor of the English. The battles also marked the full cooperation of the yeomanry and the aristocracy, giving the English a unique military power as well as a new social orientation.

Edward was an affable and majestic individual who opened his reign with generous concessions to the baronage and a welcoming attitude toward the complaints of the middle class. He grew steadily in popularity, in the main, because his wars were popular. But war is an expensive endeavor, and its expenses played into the hands of Parliament. It also allowed his barons and burgesses to establish a privileged position. Without immediate redress when the king broke promises of reform, they were able to apply financial pressure. The king could still legislate outside the Parliament by ordinances, but Parliament was gaining the initiative. Non-feudal levies and changes in levies required parliamentary sanction, and all ministers of the king were appointed with parliamentary approval. Parliament demanded that a grant be spent as directed; a specific grant was even voted for use against Scotland. Appointment of parliamentary treasurers and collectors also was instituted. These measures were all accomplished by 1377.

Parliament continued to sit as a single body, but deliberated in sections. The knights and burgesses met separately until 1339, and this marked the beginning of Commons and was followed by the designation of an individual, the Speaker, who was empowered to speak for all. The prelates and magnates sat by almost hereditary right. The framework of what was to become the House of Lords had begun to be established.

During Henry III's reign, conservators of the peace had been established. They had no judicial power. In 1332 their jurisdiction, which already included inquests, was increased to include indictments for felonies and trespass. By 1360 they were established as police judges, and by 1485, they had absorbed the functions of the sheriffs. Chosen from the local gentry and under royal commission, they constituted an amateur body of administrators. As a recognizable force, the conservators of the peace are today seen in many parts of the world touched by British colonialism.

Edward accomplished much despite the many difficulties confronting his rule; during 1348-49 an estimated one-half of the population died as a result of the Black Death. This precipitous drop in the population, coupled with war prosperity, dislocated the wage and price structure of the country. The Statute of Laborers fixed wages and compelled all able-bodied unemployed to work. The labor shortage accelerated the transition from servile to free tenures and fluid labor.

War prosperity affected everyone and led to a general surge of luxury. Landowners, confronted with a labor shortage, began to consolidate landholdings, enclosing acreage for sheep-raising. The accumulation of capital and landholdings became the foundation for great fortunes. The yeomanry, exhilarated by its joint military achievement with the aristocracy, lost its traditional passivity. New ferment began in the lower levels of society as they saw their potential for growth. It is this change that is evidenced in *Geoffrey Chaucer's *Canterbury Tales.

By 1362 a considerable amount of social unrest became more visible. For example, this era saw the publication of William *Langland's Piers the Plowman, a vernacular indictment of corrupt government and ecclesiastical life. Langland was the voice of the old-fashioned, godly England, bewildered and angered by the new situation. This period also saw the flourishing of the great itinerant preachers, with their theological emphasis on scriptural egalitarianism.

As if these economic and social difficulties were not enough, John *Wycliffe, Edward's chaplain, published his Civil Dominion. He called for a propertyless church. He also argued that Christians hold all things of God under contract and sin destroys this contract, thus removing title to all lands and assets. Wycliffe wrote a philosophical and theological treatise, not a practical application, but extremists ignored this point. Wycliffe was a remarkable precursor to the Reformation. He, along with others, was responsible for the first vernacular Bible. He wrote widely circulated pamphlets in both Latin and English.

It was Wycliffe's doctrine, called Lollardy (see Lollards), was extremely popular, emphasizing a return to a clergy that would renounce ownership of secular assets. After Edward's death this ferment exploded in 1381 in the *Peasants' Revolt. In the end, the charters of some towns were annulled, and the gentry and other classes were brought to heel under heavy repression. Notwithstanding these efforts to return to the past, serfdom continued to decline. After a lengthy period of dreary civil war called the *Wars of the Roses, control of the English throne passed to the house of Tudor in the person of *Henry VII (1485-1509). It was Henry, whose line lasted until 1603.

SELECTED BIBLIOGRAPHY

Omrod, W. M. *The Reign of Edward III: A Crown and Political Society in England, 1327-1377.* New Haven: Yale University Press, 1990; Sams, Eric, ed. *Shakespeare's Edward III.* New Haven: Yale University Press, 1996.

R. Churchill Curtis

EDWARD, EDWARD. Perhaps the best known of the medieval domestic *ballads, *Edward, Edward* was first recorded in Percy's mid-eighteenth-century *Reliques of Ancient English Poetry.* It is nonetheless universally recognized as a product of the Middle Ages, based on internal evidence. The song relates a conversation between a young man, Edward, and his mother, following a question-and-answer pattern in alternating stanzas.

Edward has come home with his sword dripping blood, and his mother inquires as to the source. At first, Edward claims to have killed his hawk, and then his horse, but his mother knows that neither is true and forces him to admit it. Edward then confesses to having killed his father. Not at all suspicious or surprised, the mother simply asks what his fate will be for the crime, and is equally willing to accept without argument that Edward will go to sea in a "bottomless boat" (i.e., he will be set adrift in a scuttled craft), an ancient punishment for the murder of kin. Again showing no remorse, the mother asks what Edward will do with his possessions and what he will bequeath to his family. His response is surly: since he must die, no one will get the benefit of his wealth. Most telling, however, is the "curse of hell" he leaves to his mother for her evil "counsel." In this way he implicates her in the crime, imbuing the song with a particularly dark view of human nature.

Edward, Edward leaves no mystery for the reader once the implicit accusation of the mother is recognized. However, it exemplifies the value system of medieval balladry in the pragmatic monetary concern of the mother and the generally selfish attitude of the son. Moreover, given balladry's penchant for subverting symbols and motifs of aristocratic literature, the song invites analysis of Edward's initial claims to have killed his hawk and horse, both symbols of the ideal knight of the chivalric tradition. All in all, the song inverts every behavioral norm expected of a young noble according to the courtly ideology. Finally, both the question-and-answer format of the ballad and the materialistic concern of the mother invite comparison with *Lord Randal.*

SELECTED BIBLIOGRAPHY

Lanier, Parks. "Dialogue and Detection in 'Edward' (Child 13B)." *Tennessee Folklore Society Bulletin* 48:4 (Winter 1982), 98-104; Morgan, Gwendolyn. *Medieval Balladry and the Courtly Tradition.* New York: Peter Lang, 1993; Morgan, Gwendolyn. *Medieval Ballads: Chivalry, Romance, and Everyday Life.* New York: Peter Lang, 1996; Oates, Joyce Carol. "The English and Scottish Traditional Ballads." *Southern Review* 15

(1979), 560-66. Pearsall, Derek. *Old and Middle English Poetry.* London: Routledge and Kegan Paul, 1977.

Gwendolyn Morgan

ELEANOR OF AQUITAINE (c. 1122-1204). Eleanor of Aquitaine's roots in medieval literature can be traced to her grandfather, Guilhemtt, the earliest known troubadour. She, however, gained fame as Queen to Louis VII of France, who married her for her large dowry. They did have two children before they were divorced in 1152. St. *Bernard of Clairvaux encouraged this divorce because he believed Eleanor to be too worldly.

Immediately upon her divorce from Louis, Eleanor married Henry Plantagenet, soon to be *Henry II, with whom she had eight additional children including two, *Richard (1151) and *John (1167) who would become kings of England. Since Eleanor was the heiress of Aquitaine in the south of France, Henry claimed this portion for his empire, an action that reinitiated wars against France. These disputes between the two medieval powers would continue for four hundred years.

Eleanor's allegiance shifted to her sons in their rebellion against Henry in 1173. This led to her being imprisoned for some fifteen years. When Henry died in 1189, Richard took power and released his mother. In turn, she protected him while he was away fighting the *Crusades as during his absence John frequently attempted to usurp the throne. When Richard died in 1199, John ascended to the throne; these events occurred after the siblings' reconciliation, a feat brought about by Eleanor. Eleanor continued to play a role in the politics of John's reign. Of seminal import to her were the arts, to which she was an influential patron. Records show that Eleanor was particularly kind to the *Provençal troubadours, and that she also backed the development of *courtly poetry. This tradition was continued by her daughter, Marie de Champagne.

SELECTED BIBLIOGRAPHY

Ailes, Marianne. "French Studies: Early Medieval." *Year's Work in Modern Language Studies* 54 (1992), 49-67, Benton, John F. *Culture, Power and Personality in Medieval France.* London: Hambledon Press, 1991; Carney, Elizabeth. "Fact and Fiction in 'Queen Eleanor's Confession.'" *Folklore* 95:2 (1984), 167-70; Goodrich, Norma Lorre, ed. *The Ways of Love: Eleven Romances of Medieval France.* Boston: Beacon Press, 1964; Mason, Germaine. *A Concise Survey of French Literature.* New York: Greenwood Press, 1969; Monestier, Jean. "'Halianor, reina, maire nostre, . . .'" *Barnat* 3 (December 1988), 1318-22; Speer, Mary B. "Old French Literature." in *Scholarly Editing: A Guide to Research.* D. C. Greetham, ed. New York: Modern Language Association of America, 1995; Spivack, Charlotte Staples. *The Company of Camelot: Arthurian Characters in Romance and Fantasy.* Westport, CT: Greenwood Press, 1994.

Robert T. Lambdin

ELEGIAC POETRY. Since the pagan philosophy of the afterlife is dim, at best, and so much of the Old and Middle English period celebrates the heroic deaths of warriors in battle, the *elegy form is of great importance in adding humanistic value to otherwise senseless savagery. The obvious biblical pattern for the elegiac form is David's lament for King Saul and Prince Jonathan in II Samuel 1:19-27, around 840 B. C. Like many of the later classic elegies, David's Lament for the Defeat of Gilboa begins with the parenthetical boast that it is recorded in the Book of Jasher that Jonathan taught the use of the bow to the "children of Judah." The formal elegy begins with a chorus, thrice repeated, with minor variations:

> "The beauty of Israel is slain upon thy high places;
>   How are the mighty fallen!"

There follows the injunction not to mention this defeat in the Philistine cities of Gath and Askelon because the bitter news would make the women of the Philistine's rejoice. Then comes the convention of cursing the geographical site (Mt. Gilboa) for permitting this catastrophe. In terms of conventional warrior tribute, the bow of Jonathan and the sword of Saul are praised. The customary elegiac "lie" is uttered:

> "Saul and Jonathan were lovely and pleasant in their lives;
>   And in their death they were not divided."

(Herein lies the special problem of the double-elegy: David considers the son "lovely and pleasant in life," but not the father. Further, since they got along so badly, the claim that "in their death they were not divided" is only true physically.)

The daughters of Israel are enjoined to weep for all who will never again bring them the spoils of battle. The chorus is half repeated, and then David jettisons his attempt at a single elegy for both father and son for one that concentrates upon the one he really mourns, Jonathan, claiming what would not seem strange in the ninth century before Christ, in the Classical Era of Greece and Rome, or in the Old English period: "Thy love to me was wonderful, passing the love of women."

The elegy closes with the second half of the chorus, "How are the mighty fallen," and then climaxes in an astonishing antiwar curse, "and the weapons of war perished!" Like many *Anglo-Saxon verses, parallel construction is dominant, and the most conventional of rubrics are applied to the heroes: "the shield of the mighty," "anointed with oil," "swifter than eagles," and "stronger than lions."

In this biblical elegiac tradition, "The *Wanderer is a particularly rich and complex work. Often appearing in the same text as "The *Seafarer," a poem similar in theme, the protagonist of "The Wanderer" of longs for honors, although his loneliness stems from fate, misfortune in battle, and the decimation of his kin. He laments, "often alone . . . at early dawn / I make my moan." Yet he knows that a manly man would silence his own complaints, "keep his own counsel," and recognize that *Wyrd (the Germanic Fate) is his ultimate foe and no man can help. Dreams of glory produce only bitterness.

In exile in a foreign land, sick at heart, "I long ago laid . . . . my loyal patron / In sorrow under the sod." Since then he has become a wanderer, gadding about, recalling lost comrades. In sleep he dreams of his deceased lord, and kisses and clasps him just as in happier past days. But when he wakes, the dream is gone. Viewing the the variety of mischances that fall upon lords, earls, and princes, he devises a picture of a truly wise man. Patient, not hot-hearted, nor hasty-tongued, nor rash, he also abstains from the related vices of boasting, eager aggressiveness,and arrogance so prevalent in other works from this period. Everywhere he sees the marks of death, the fall of heroes and all the waste in the world. He is finally driven to pen the most hopeless verdict: "All is on earth is . . . irksome to man." Treasure is fleeting, true friends are fleeting, kinsmen are fleeting so that "all idle and empty . . . the earth has become." The quest of honor is "a noble pursuit," but ultimately all Glory belongs to God, "Who grants us our salvation." If the ultimate structure of the elegy is reminiscent of David's lament, the sentiment is similar to the words of the Preacher, the son of David, king in Jerusalem: "Vanity of vanities . all is vanity" (Ecclesiastes 1:1, 2).

SELECTED BIBLIOGRAPHY

Alexander, Michael, Trans. *The Earliest English Poems: A Bilingual Edition*. Berkeley and Los Angeles: University of California Press, 1970; Campbell, Jackson J. Ed. *The Advent Lyrics of the Exeter Book*.: Princeton University Press, 1959; Conybeare, John Josias. *Illustrations of Anglo-Saxon Poetry*. William Daniel Conybeare, Ed. New York: Haskell House, 1964; Hamer, Richard. *A Choice of Anglo-Saxon Verse, Selected, with an Introduction and Parallel Verse Translation*. London: Faber and Faber, 1970; Hanning, Robert, and Joan Ferrante. Trans. *The Lais of Marie de France*. New York: E. P. Dutton, 1978; Kaiser, Rolf. *Medieval English: An Old English and Middle English Anthology*. West Berlin: Markobrunner Str. 21, 1961; Kennedy, Charles. *An Anthology of Old English Poetry: Translated into Alliterative Verse*. New York: Oxford University Press, 1960; Kennedy, Charles. *Old English Elegies: Translated into Alliterative Verse with a Critical Introduction*. Princeton: Princeton University Press, 1936; Lehnert, Martin. *Poetry and Prose of the Anglo-Saxons*. Vol. 1: *Texts*. Halle: Veb Max Nicmayer Verlag, 1960; Mora, Maria Jose. "The Invention of the Old English Elegy." *English Studies* 76:2 (March 1995), 129-39; Spaeth, J. Duncan. *Old English Poetry: Translations into Alliterative Verse with Introduction and Notes*. New York: Gordian Press, 1967.

Elton E. Smith

ELEGY. The elegy is a formal poem describing the poet's meditations on a solemn theme, usually death of a particular person. It is a classical form that is common to both Latin and Greek literatures. The elegy originally signified almost any type of serious meditation on the part of the poet, whether this reflective element covered death, love, or war. In classic writing the elegy was more distinguishable by its use of elegiac meter than by its subject matter. Up to and continuing through the seventeenth century, the elegy could be both a love poem and a poem of mourning. Thereafter, the poem of mourning became virtually the only meaning of elegy. Notable English elegies include the *Old English poem "The *Wanderer," the medieval *Pearl*, Geoffrey *Chaucer's *Book of the Duchess*, and Donne's "Elegies." These poems indicate the variety of method and mood. A specialized form of elegy, popular with English poets, is the pastoral elegy, of which Milton's "Lycidas" is an example.

SELECTED BIBLIOGRAPHY

Mora, Maria Jose. "The Invention of the Old English Elegy." *English Studies* 76:2 (March 1995), 129-39; Shaw, David. "Elegy and Theory: Is Historical and Critical Knowledge Possible?" *Modern Language Quarterly* 55:1 (March 1994), 1-16.

Rebecca Chalmers

EL LIBRO DE BUEN AMOR. A mid-fourteenth century miscellany of poems *El Libro de Buen Amor* is the first in Spanish literature to include its author's name. Juan Ruiz, the archbishop of Hito, is thus the first celebrated Spanish poet. Although the collection features what seem to be autobiographical passages, no correspondence has been made between the recounted events and the life of the author.

The work includes a number of cuaderno via verses, as well as sermons, street ballads, and *exempla, or moral fables. It opens with a prayer to the Virgin Mary and a plea for help with the poet's troubles. The next selection is a sermon addressed to clerics, devoid of the exempla included in sermons for the public, which distinguishes between *loco amor*, or sinful, worldly love of the flesh, and *buen amor*, the love of God. The intention of the book is also stated here: to inculcate the superiority of *buen amor*.

In the less edifying sections of the book, however, the reader can find colorful accounts of amorous adventures and other worldly indulgences. Some scholars especially emphasize the tongue-in-cheek tone of the didactic portions and the stark contrast between the moral purpose and the literary indulgence in accounts of *loco amor*. Irony is apparent in the mock epic that stages a battle between Carnival and Lent. Beneath the humor in the book is a serious commentary on such religious practices as confession and such social ills as poverty and the plight of the poor. Also intended as a form of instruction for aspiring poets, the book experiments with a wide range of verse forms.

SELECTED BIBLIOGRAPHY

Deyermond, Alan. *A Literary History of Spain: The Middle Ages*. London, Ernest Benn Limited, 1971; Deyermond, Alan, W. F. Hunter and Joseph T. Snow, eds. *Medieval and*

Renaissance Spanish Literature: Selected Essays by Keith Whinnom. Exeter, UK: University of Exeter Press, 1994; Deyermond, Alan, and Jeremy Lawrance. *Letters and Society in Fifteenth-Century Spain: Studies Presented to P. E. Russel on his Eightieth Birthday.* London: The Dolphin Book Co., 1993; Gerli, E. Michael, and Harvey L. Sharrer, eds. *Hispanic Medieval Studies in Honor of Samuel G. Armistead.* Madison, WI: Hispanic Seminary of Medieval Studies, 1992; Green, Otis H. *The Literary Mind of Medieval and Renassance Spain.* Lexington: University of Kentucky Press, 1970; Green, Otis H. *Spain and the Western Tradition: The Castilian Mind in Literature from El Cid to Calderon.* Vol. 1. Madison, WI: University of Wisconsin Press, 1963.

Rebecca Stephens

EMARÉ. *Emaré* is a mid-fourteenth century English verse *romance. It is a Breton *lai in the "Constance" tradition. In the lay an emperor, Sir Artyus, marries Dame Erayne, a beautiful woman "full of love and goodnesse" (35), who dies soon after giving birth to Emaré. The child is sent to a lady named Abro, who teaches her the manners and courtesies necessary for her position. The king of Sicily (Sir Tergaunte) presents the emperor with a richly embroidered and bejeweled cloth that was woven by the daughter of a heathen emir; in the four corners of the cloth are scenes depicting famous pairs of lovers. The emperor sends to Abro to have his daughter return to him; when she arrives, he is so impressed with her poise and beauty that he decides to make her his wife. While he is waiting for dispensation from the pope to marry his daughter, the emperor has the cloth made into a robe for Emaré. She, however, refuses her father's plan to wed her, so he sets her adrift wrapped in her cloak, without food, water, or oar, to float out to sea. Immediately after she leaves, the Emperor rues his hasty decision.

The wind and rain drive the boat across the sea to Galys (or Galicia). Sir Kadore, the king's steward who lives in a castle by the shore, happens to be down at the beach when her boat floats ashore. Identifying herself only as "Egaré" (the feminine version of "Degaré"--"the lost one"), she swoons, and he takes her back to his castle to recuperate. When she has recovered, Kadore hosts a feast for the king of Galys, who sees Emaré, falls in love with her, and decides to make her his queen despite the objections of his mother, who insists that Emaré is a creature of the other-world. While the king is away at a war helping the king of France against the Saracens, Emaré gives birth to a son (christened Segramour) who has the birthmark of royalty; however, the king's mother intercepts Emaré's letter with the news, substituting her own letter claiming that Emaré gave birth to a devil. Another exchange of letters results in Emaré and the baby being set adrift with only her robe on the wild water. After a terrifying seven nights, the boat arrives in Rome, where a merchant named Jurdan discovers them, takes them home, and acts as a foster-father until the boy is seven. Meanwhile, back in Galys the king has returned home and is distressed to discover his mother's treachery; as punishment, she is exiled bereft of her property. Finally, the king sails to Rome to seek penance from the pope and finds his son and wife. The emperor in his old age also comes to Rome for penance and discovers Emaré; he acknowledges his daughter, confirming her royal blood, and the story ends.

This variation of the tale of Constance, which Geoffrey *Chaucer and John Gower also treated separately in other formats, blends oriental imagery into the tale of a fairy princess lost and found. The reaction of several characters to Emaré's demeanor, commenting on her other-worldly qualities, indicates that she might be the daughter of a fairy liaison, which would classify the lay as one of G. V. Smithers's type II story-patterns; however, nothing in the actual story indicates that her mother was a fairy.

SELECTED BIBLIOGRAPHY

Arthur, Ross G. "'Emaré's Cloak and Audience Response." In *Sign, Sentence, Discourse: Language in Medieval Thought and Literature.* Julian Wasserman and Lois Roney, eds. Syracuse: Syracuse University Press, 1989. 80-92; Bolton, W. F. *The Penguin History of Literature: The Middle Ages.* London: Penguin, 1993; Finlayson, John. "The Form of the Middle English Lay." *The Chaucer Review* 19 (1985): 352-368; Smithers, G. V. "Story-Patterns in Some Breton Lays." *Medium Ævum* 22.2 (1953), 61-92.

Peggy Huey

ENVOY (ENVOI). Particularly associated with French *ballade forms, the envoy is a conventional stanza that appears at the conclusion of certain poems. Envoys are usually addressed to prominent people, such as princes or judges. Also, they repeat a refrain line found throughout the ballade. The envoy is usually four lines long, employing the *bcbc* rhyme scheme. It usually served as a conventional summary and conclusion, as exemplified by *L'envoy de Chaucer.*

SELECTED BIBLIOGRAPHY

Chickering, Howell. "Form and Interpretation in the Envoy to the 'Clerk's Tale.'" *Chaucer Review* 29:4 (1995), 352-72; Farrell, Thomas J. "The 'Envoy de Chaucer' and the 'Clerk's Tale.'" *Chaucer Review* 24:4 (1990), 329-36; Holman, C. Hugh, and William Harmon. *A Handbook to Literature.* 5th ed. New York: Macmillan, 1986; Robinson, Fred C. "Bede's 'Envoi' to the Old English History: An Experiment in Editing." *Studies in Philology* 78:5 (Early Winter 1981), 4-20.

Robert T. Lambdin

EREC ET ENIDE. Written by *Chrétien de Troyes (c. 1170), a French *romance writer, *Erec et Enide* is the story of a knight of Arthur's court who adores his bride inordinately, so much so that he neglects his social responsibilities in order to stay by her side. The charming Enide is a good and faithful wife, but Erec's obsession leads him to suspect her fidelity. Through a series of misadventures the lovers are taught to temper their relationship into one more befitting a feudal lord and lady who have obligations to those whom they rule. By the conclusion Erec and Enide have proven their abilities to fulfill the duties of their station and so are crowned as heirs to his father's kingdom. The source of the story is the patient Griselda theme of folklore.

SELECTED BIBLIOGRAPHY

Dembowski, Peter F. "Textual and Other Problems of the 'Epilogue' of *Erec et Enide*: Medieval Studies in Honor of Douglas Kelly." In *Conjectures*. Keith Busby and Norris Lacy, eds. Amsterdam: Rodopi, 1994, 113-27; Gaudet, Minnette. "The Denial of Feminine Subjectivity in Chrétien's *Enide.*" *Romance Languages Annual* 5 (1993), 40-46; Rollo, David. "From Apuleius's 'Psyche' to Chrétien's *Erec and Enide*." In *The Search for the Ancient Novel*. John Tatum, ed. Baltimore: Johns Hopkins University Press, 1994. 347-69.

Laura Cooner Lambdin

ERL OF TOULOUS, THE. *The Erl of Toulous* is a Breton *lay in which the mighty emperor (Sir Dyaclysyon) from Almayn (Germany) usurps land belonging to Sir Barnard, the earl of Toulous. Because of the injustice of the emperor's actions, the earl attacks. The emperor has a beautiful spouse, Dame Beulybon, who begs him to return the stolen property to the earl, but the emperor, of course, refuses, so they go to battle, the emperor's seven battalions against the earl's more than forty thousand men (the earl is not the only person the emperor has treated this way). While many people are killed on both sides (over sixty thousand on the emperor's side alone), the earl finally wins the field, and the emperor flees to a nearby castle. When the emperor cries to his wife about the injustice of his loss, she informs him that he lost because he was in the wrong.

The scene then shifts over to the earl, who has captured many of the emperor's men for ransom. One of them is Sir Trylabas, a favorite of the emperor, who describes in detail the emperor's wife. The description so enamors the earl that he promises Trylabas his freedom in exchange for a night of the woman. The knight agrees to the conditions; though he does consider betraying the Earl, instead he forthrightly explains the situation to the lady, who insists that he live up to the terms of his promise and agrees to meet the earl in her chapel. She gives him a ring, and he returns home vowing to love her forever.

Meanwhile, giving in to his traitorous impulses, Trylabas arranges to have the earl waylaid on his way home. After slaying the knight and his accomplices, the earl flees into the forest, eventually making his way home after much peril, only to pine for love of Beulybon. Finally, he slips back into the emperor's castle to tell the lady of his love; she, however, can only remind him that she is already married. In their efforts to avert all suspicion from the earl, several knights who help him sneak into the castle conspire to place and discover a young innocent knight in the empress's bedchamber, whom they kill. For the appearance of wrongdoing, the empress is thrown in the castle's dungeon. The emperor, who has been away in hiding after his defeat, dreams that two bears attack his wife, tearing her asunder; he hurries home to find his wife charged with infidelity, the punishment for which is burning. During her trial an old knight points out that the charges may have been brought out of jealousy; Sir Antore certainly was given no opportunity to defend himself before he was slain.   Acknowledging the possible justness of the old knight's comments, the tribunal decides that a trial by combat will decide the empress's fate; they advertise far and wide for a champion for her. The earl of Toulous comes to her rescue disguised as a monk, clears her name, burns the traitorous knights, and disappears. When the emperor discovers who saved his wife, he offers the earl a hand of friendship and returns the stolen lands that started the events of the story. Three years later the emperor dies, and the lords elect Bernard to replace him. Bernard also marries the empress, and they have many children to continue the line.

This poem, which begins like a *chanson-de-geste*, a typical chivalric love story in which the poet basically outlines the story, first appears in the Thornton manuscript, which is usually dated 1422-40. In contrast with *Sir Orfeo*, which offers the paradigm of the lay, this poem has the fewest qualities associating it with the genre; according to John Finlayson, it really is more of a short *romance (362).

SELECTED BIBLIOGRAPHY

Bolton, W. F. *The Penguin History of Literature: The Middle Ages.* London: Penguin, 1993; Finlayson, John. "The Form of the Middle English *Lai*." *Chaucer Review* 19 (1985), 352-68; Furnish, Shearle. "The Modernity of 'The Erle of Tolous' and the Decay of the Breton Lai." *Medieval Perspectives* 8 (1993), 69-77; Hulsmann, Friedrich. "The Watermarks of Four Late Medieval Manuscripts Containing 'The Erle of Tolous.'" *Notes and Queries* 32(230):1 (March 1985), 11-12; Rumble, Thomas. *The Breton Lays in Middle English.* Detroit: Wayne State University Press, 1965.

Peggy Huey

EVERYMAN. The anonymous *allegory *Everyman* is certainly the most widely known and often anthologized of all Medieval Morality plays (*see* **Drama, Medieval**).   It was composed around 1495, consists of 921 lines, and is preserved in four separate manuscripts.   There is no record of its having ever been staged for its contemporary audience. The sources that have been identified for the play are numerous. *Everyman* may actually be a translation of a Dutch play entitled *Elckerlijc*; however, there is no certainty as to which play scrved as a source for the other. The probable source for both the English and the Dutch versions is a poem entitled *Barlaam and Josaphat*, composed by St. John of Damascus in the eighth century. Yet the narrative has an even earlier antecedent in Asian tradition. A Buddhist story of a man and his four wives has been identified as a source for *Barlaam and Josaphat*. The Buddhist tale tells of a man who, setting forth on a journey, asks his four wives--body, wealth, relations, and deeds--to accompany him. All of the wives, with the exception of deeds, refuse to attend him.

The Buddhist parable bears a remarkable resemblance to *Everyman*, in which the titular character is summoned by death to undertake a journey into the grave. Everyman first tries to bribe death, but when he realizes that the effort is fruitless, he attempts to persuade others to accompany him. Fellowship, Kinsmen, and Goods refuse to follow him into the grave, and although Good Deeds is devoted to Everyman, the virtue is too weak and weighed down by sin to get up. He does, however, offer the assistance of Knowledge, who takes Everyman through the appropriate penitential steps as prescribed by Catholic doctrine: Confession, Contrition, Absolution, and Satisfaction. At the end of the process, Good Deeds is liberated from the heavy weight of sin and is able to accompany Everyman into the grave. Everyman is subsequently welcomed into paradise by an Angel.

Despite its renown as the most accessible morality play, *Everyman* is actually atypical within the genre. It includes only a portion of the morality structure, which generally begins with a struggle for the soul (psychomachia) of the central character and leads to the figure's eventual salvation. *Everyman*, instead, focuses exclusively on the final phase of the morality narrative--the coming of death. The play thus eliminates the usual struggle between good and evil for the soul of the protagonist. As an allegorical representation of all of humanity, *Everyman*, by example, teaches the audience of death's inevitability as well as the proper path to salvation, one of the most common themes of medieval literature.

SELECTED BIBLIOGRAPHY

King, Pamela M. "Morality Plays." In *The Cambridge Companion to Medieval English Theatre*. Richard Beadle, ed. Cambridge: Cambridge University Press, 1994. 240-64; Kolve, V. A. "*Everyman* and the Parable of the Talents." In *Medieval English Drama: Essays Critical and Contextual*. Jerome Taylor and Alan H. Nelson, eds. Chicago: University of Chicago Press, 1972. 316-40.

James Keller

EXEMPLUM.   An exemplum (plural, exempla) is a moralized tale predominant in the Middle Ages when authors made use of tales, anecdotes, and incidents, both fictitious and real, to present morals or to illustrate doctrines.

These works appealed to medieval audiences because of their concreteness, narrative, and human interest, in addition to their moral applications.

For the use of preachers in the Middle Ages, collections of exempla, classified according to subject, were prepared. Among the best examples of these collections is Jacques de Vitny's *Exempla*, which dates to the early thirteenth century. This genre degenerated into a series of anecdotes that became merely humorous satire. This appealed to many, so the exempla were protested by *Dante in the thirteenth century and *Wycliffe in the fourteenth century. Wycliffe went so far as to omit exempla from his sermons in his reform program.

The exempla's influence on medieval literature was great and widespread. *Chaucer used this form freely; in the *"Nun's Priest's Tale" Chanticleer tells Pertelote an anecdote to demonstrate that dreams do have meaning. The *"Pardoner's Tale" itself is an exemplum that demonstrates the evils of avarice.

SELECTED BIBLIOGRAPHY

Brawer, Robert A. "St. Augustine's Two Cities as Medieval Dramatic *Exempla*." in *"The City of God": A Collection of Critical Essays*. Dorothy F. Donnelly, ed. New York: Peter Lang, 1995. 183-98; Holman, C. Hugh, and William Harmon. *A Handbook to Literature*. 5th ed. New York, Macmillan, 1986; Von Moos, Peter. "The Use of Exempla in the *Policraticus* of John of Salisbury." In *The World of John of Salisbury*. Michael Wilks, ed. Oxford: Blackwell For Ecclesiastical History Society, 1984. 207-61.

Robert T. Lambdin

EXETER BOOK, THE.   Copied around 940, the Exeter Book contains some of the most important works of *Old English poetry. Bishop Leofric donated the volume to Exeter Cathedral where it remains. Among the poems in the volume are "The *Wanderer," "The *Seafarer," *Deor's Lament*, *Widsith*, "The Wife's Lament," "The Husband's Message," and "Resignation." These works are a portion of the Exeter Book's *elegies and run the gamut from being blatantly pagan ("The Wanderer") to the shadowy ("The Seafarer"). Additionally, the volume contains almost a hundred *riddles, demonstrating that they were an extremely popular form at this time. The riddles in the Exeter book are composed in both Latin and *Anglo-Saxon. The volume also contains longer religious poems, such as *Cynewulf's *Juliana* as well as a *Physiologus* and the *Maxims*.

SELECTED BIBLIOGRAPHY

Conner, Patrick W. "The Structure of the Exeter Codex (Exeter, Cathedral Library, MS 3501)." In *Anglo-Saxon Manuscripts: Basic Readings*. Mary P. Richards, ed. New York: Garland, 1994, 301-15; Irving, Edward B., Jr. "Heroic Experience in Old English

Riddles." In *Old English Shorter Poems: Basic Readings* Katherine O'Brien O'Keefe, ed. New York: Garland, 1994. 199-212; Lapidge, Michael. "Stoic Cosmology and the Source of the First Old English Riddle." *Anglia* 112:1-2 (1994), 1-25; Zimmerman, Gunhild. *The Four Old English Poetic Manuscripts: Texts, Contexts, and Historical Background*. Heidelberg: C. Winter, 1995.

Robert T. Lambdin

F

FABLIAUX.   The popularity of fabliaux lasted 150 years, and they also influenced the later literature of Western Europe. The fabliau is related to the fable, taking its etymological root from the word. Writers of the Old French period coined the term "fabliau." In comparison with the older form of the fable, the fabliau differs in four areas: First, instead of using animal characters, the fabliau uses everyday people. Furthermore, the fabliau is light and usually humorous, while the fable is serious in nature. Building on the former precept, the fabliau is the only genre of Western literature that contains no moral or instructive purpose; the fable resembles a biblical parable in that it is written to teach a lesson.   Lastly, fabliaux are always in verse (octosyllabic rhymed complets with the exception of one). Fables are written in either verse or prose.

There are 160 fabliaux from extant manuscripts between the last years of the twelfth century and 1346. These tales vary in length and subject matter and are from the regions of northern France, particularly Paris and the provinces of Picardy, Flanders, and Normandy. Most fabliaux are parodies of traditional situations in courtly *romances in a mock-heroic imitation of the romance style. This trend indicates that the fabliaux audience must have had some familiarity with the courtly romances; therefore, they must have belonged to the literate middle to upper classes of society. The authors of the fabliaux belonged to the same range of social class; most of them earned their living as entertainers. One of the personages who receives regular sympathetic treatment in the fabliaux is the poor student or cleric, indicating that many of the authors belonged to this class. Most exchanged a recitation of the tale in a private household for a night's room and board; due to their wandering nature and interchange of stories, these authors are largely anonymous today. Fabliaux were also recited at many different public occasions, such as in courts or in taverns. They were popularly told as part of the entertainment on pilgrimages. For example, the *Canterbury Tales* is comprised of many fabliaux, the most famous of which may be "The *Miller's Tale."

Fabliaux are usually written in the "low style," with the tale sometimes in the form of a dirty joke using crude and vulgar words and observations. As mentioned earlier, the fabliau is written in verse, which is usually not skillful and merely serves to achieve the denouement. The tales are filled with lively and witty dialogue. Indeed, the fabliaux are the first genre to employ extensive dialogue. The story, however, is tightly woven to achieve the humorous conclusion. This jocularity is sometimes superficial and sometimes more bawdy, mocking the traditional mores. Scorn for contemporary attitudes toward priests, women, peasants, and cuckolded husbands abounds. Priests and monks especially are treated in a hostile manner, and women are portrayed as unscrupulous and promiscuous. "The Wife of Orleans" provides an example of this degradation of the female character. Many of the stock male characters are merchants and lusty bachelors. Most of the fabliau's action revolves around the bedroom and the unfaithful sexual escapades of the women, although there are no elements of the sensual in the tales. The characters are not usually well developed, with the exception of those in the fabliaux of Geoffrey *Chaucer and Giovanni *Boccaccio.

The genre of the fabliaux influenced later literature; in France the fabliaux were adapted in farces and also in more scholarly works such as *Le Livre du Chevalier de la Tour Landry* (1371). In the seventeenth century Jean La Fontaine reworked the fabliau form of Boccaccio in his *Contes et Nouvelles*.

SELECTED BIBLIOGRAPHY

Burns, E. Jane. "This Prick Which Is Not One: How Women Talk Back in Old French Fabliaux." In *Feminist Approaches to the Body in Medieval Literature*. Linda Lamperis and Sarah Stanbury, eds. Philadelphia: University of Pennsylvania Press, 1993. 188-212; Fisher, John Hurt. "City and Country in Fabliaux." *Medieval Perspectives* 1:1 (Spring 1986), 1-15; Hellman, Robert, and Richard O'Gorman, trans. *Fabliaux: Ribald Tales from the Old French*. New York: Thomas Y. Crowell, 1965; Neville, Grace. "Medieval French Fabliaux and Modern Urban Legends: The Attraction of Opposites." *Bealoideas* 57 (1989), 133-49; Watson, Michael G. "Variations on a Theme: Secrecy in Chaucer's Fabliaux." *In Geardagum* 10 (August 1989), 29-43.

Anna Shealy

FANTOSME, JORDAN (c. 1100-c. 1170s). Jordan Fantosme's work *Chronique de la guerre entre les Anglois et les Ecossois* (Chronicle of the war between the English and the Scots) is a good example of chronicle writing in the French or *Anglo-Norman style, more detailed and literary than English chronicling (*see* **Chronicles and Annals**). Although Fantosme used personal experience and the accounts of eye witnesses as the basis for much of his account of the war, his Anglo-Norman verse history strongly resembles a *Chanson de geste* or a *romance. Because the English king, *Henry II was away in France and hence not present to serve as a hero of the work, Fantosme spread the hero roles around among his numerous loyal nobles. Fantosme created an epic-like story in which a number of heroes take part in numerous battles. Both sides, the Scots and the English, are shown to have some justification for their actions in the war. The work ends with Henry II's forces winning, but primarily because Henry has repented for his execution of Thomas *Becket, and God has shifted his support to Henry's troops. Fantosme was able to combine the interest his audience had in chivalric stories with a relatively factual account of the events occurring between King Henry II's supporters and his rebellious son, Prince Henry, and the Scottish lords King William and Earl David.

SELECTED BIBLIOGRAPHY

Brandt, William J. *The Shape of Medieval History.* New Haven: Yale University Press, 1966; Lodge, Anthony. "Literature and History in the *Chronicle* of Jordan Fantosme." *French Studies* 44:3 (July 1990), 257-70; Smalley, Beryl. *Historians in the Middle Ages.* New York: Scribner's, 1974; Sterns, Indrikis. *The Greater Medieval Historians: An Interpretation and a Bibliography.* Lanham, MD: University Press of America, 1980.

Richard McDonald

FEAST OF FOOLS. The Feast of Fools was a celebration of status inversion, in which the inferior clergy in cathedrals and collegiate churches the inferior clergy mockingly usurped the roles of their superiors. Centered mainly in France (although it was also celebrated in other parts of Europe), this ritual dates from at least the twelfth century and could be celebrated on the Feast of the Circumcision (January 1), the Feast of the Holy Innocents (December 28), or other dates. It began as a festival of subdeacons, low ranking clergymen, who took over the church services for a day and developed into a riotous celebration of mockery.

The inferior clergy would choose a "bishop" or "pope" of fools who led cathedral services and often led the celebrants in a procession through the streets. Sometimes a boy bishop was chosen. While laymen would dress as monks or priests, the clergy dressed as women or *minstrels or wore masks while they danced and sang improper songs in the cathedral. The Feast of Fools was sometimes associated with the Feast of Asses, in which an ass was brought into the church and braying was included in the service. Popular with the inferior clergy and townspeople, the Feast of Fools was frequently condemned by church officials for leading to unseemly and indecent behavior. Its origin is uncertain, although some scholars argue that it derived from the Kalends, a celebration of the Roman god Janus.

SELECTED BIBLIOGRAPHY

Cosman, Madeleine Pelner. *Medieval Holidays and Festivals: A Calendar of Celebrations.* New York: Scribner, 1981; Schmidt, Paul Gerhard. "The Quotation in Goliardic Poetry: The Feast of Fools and the Goliardic *Strophe cum Auctoritate.*" In *Latin Poetry and the Classical Tradition: Essays in Medieval and Renaissance*

Literature. Peter Gooman and Oswyn Murray, eds. Oxford: Clarendon Press, 1990. 39-55.

                                                                    Miriam Davis

FERDINAND II OF ARAGON (1452-1516), and **ISABELLA OF CASTILE** (1451-1504). Successful at ejecting the Moors from the Iberian peninsula (1492), Ferdinand and Isabella were also successful in suppressing the aristocracy of Castile as well as in controlling the Church within their lands. Ferdinand was greatly interested in trade. His administration had much to do with setting up the structure undergirding most of the commercial expansion in the sixteenth century.

Ferdinand was greatly ambitious and greedy concerning Italy. He thus became embroiled in a series of alliances from 1496 to 1516 that resulted in Spain's financial difficulties, difficulties unsolved until the reign of Charles I (1516-1556), the founder of the Spanish Hapsburgs. Without going into details of Ferdinand and Isabella's support for the voyages of Columbus and others, it should be noted that they did make these voyages possible.

In 1504 Isabella died, and Ferdinand continued to rule alone until 1516. With this final unification of the throne in the person of Ferdinand began the use of the term "Spain" in the Iberian peninsula.

SELECTED BIBLIOGRAPHY

Liss, Peggy K. *Isabel the Queen: Life and Times*. Oxford: Oxford University Press, 1992; Rubin, Nancy. *Isabella of Castile: The First Renaissance Queen*. New York: St. Martin's, 1991; Stevens, Paul. *Ferdinand and Isabella*. New York: Chelsea House, 1988.

                                                              R. Churchill Curtis

FESTIVALS AND HOLIDAYS. The medieval calendar was rich in festivals and holidays that not only marked the seasons of the year, but also offered amusement and distractions from the ordinary course of life and work. Such distractions played no small part in the lives of medieval people since, in addition to the weekly Sunday observance and abstention from work, the medieval church also recognized at least forty saints' days and other major holidays such as Christmas and Easter. Local religious feasts, which varied from place to place, also contributed to the cycle of festivities. Finally, in addition to religious holidays, those "of the folk" or those dating from the pagan past continued to be celebrated. So frequent were festivals and holidays in the Middle Ages that it has been estimated that such celebrations accounted for fully a third of the calendar year.

Some of these feasts served to mark the stages of the agricultural year with reminders of the importance of the planting, growing, and harvesting seasons. Other holidays taught or reminded medieval Christians of aspects of their faith. In not a few cases festivals that in the Middle Ages were Christian in nature had been pagan in origin and, thus, did both. Following the advice that

Pope *Gregory the Great had given to Augustine, the sixth century missionary to the Angles and Saxons, and the first Archbishop of Canterbury, the Church successfully fused celebrations that had originated in the distant pagan past with Christian religious rites so that native peoples were permitted to continue, under Christian colors, their traditional customs. Thus many medieval holidays that were ostensibly Christian in character in fact commemorated ancient fertility rites as well as Christian tradition. For example, the feasts of All Saints (November 1), Candlemas (February 2), May Day (May 1), and Lammas (August 1) were part of an ancient cycle of agricultural feasts, yet in the Middle Ages three of the four (All Saints, Candlemas, and Lammas) were celebrated with church feasts.

The medieval year was divided into four seasons based on the agricultural year and marked by holidays. Winter lasted from Michaelmas, the Feast of St. Michael and All Angels, on September 29, until Christmas and was the time when wheat and rye were sown. Oats, barley, peas, and beans were planted from Easter to Lammas, on August 1, and harvest, or autumn, stretched from Lammas to Michaelmas. Because of their pagan background, many medieval festivals reflected this agricultural year. Many feasts, for example, fell between the major phases of the farming calendar, between sowing seasons or at the end of the harvest. Some medieval holidays, such as Christmas and *Halloween, were celebrated on fixed dates. Others, most notably Easter, depended on the liturgical year and were movable. Despite the religious character of many of these holidays, they usually involved not just church attendance but also merrymaking--eating and drinking, song and dance, drama and general revelry--so much so that they sometimes provoked the criticism of church officials.

The longest holiday of the year, the Christmas holiday, lasted from Christmas Eve on December 24 to Epiphany on January 6. Twelfth Night, the Eve of Epiphany on January 5, was the culmination of the Christmas festival. Falling in the middle of winter after winter crops had been planted but before the sowing of spring crops, the Christmas holiday had its origins in the pagan celebrations of winter solstice, but by the Middle Ages was celebrated as the birth of Christ. It was a time of extended holiday, feasting, and merrymaking for all social ranks. In many instances, for example, the normal services owed to lords by their tenants were suspended. While tenants might owe special rents such as ale or fowl, lords traditionally reciprocated by providing Christmas dinner out of these rents.

Because the Christmas holiday lasted twelve days, it was also known as the Time of the Twelves, with the number twelve as a common motif for Christmas feasts. At such a feast, for instance, each table might be set for twelve, twelve holiday foods might be served, and each guest receive and give twelve gifts. Decorations would include branches of holly, laurel, and mistletoe, sometimes grouped in clusters of twelve. One twelfth-century observer noted of Christmas in London that "every man's house, as also their parish churches, was decked with holme [holly], ivy, bay, and whatsoever the season of the year afforded to be green." A Christmas kissing bush made of evergreen branches and mistletoe decorated with ribbons, fruit, and nuts hung from the ceiling, and a person passing underneath it was expected to kiss his nearest neighbor.

Singing and acting played important roles in Christmas festivals, as they did in many medieval celebrations. The Christmas feast could only begin when a character called "Lucky Bird" or "First Foot" had crossed a green line marked on the floor called the Christmas threshold and had collected a coin from each guest for luck. The Yule candle or Yule log also had to be lit. Wassailings, or songs wishing for a successful coming year, were part of the traditional Christmas celebrations, including those aimed at trees, a direct holdover from the fertility rituals of the pagan past. Wassailings, for example, would circle a tree, their songs reflecting a wish for an abundant yield from the tree. Finally, the singers would toast the tree with cider and then pour the cider around the tree's roots. Other Christmas traditions, such as refusing to eat until the animals were fed, or giving an animal the first piece of the Christmas feast, also reflected thanks for the fecundity of the natural world that played so important a role in fertility rites. Later, of course, such practices were explained in terms of the Christian tradition and the birth of the baby Jesus among the animals.

Other parts of the Twelfth Night celebrations were also clearly descended from ancient pagan fertility rites. For example, in the oxhorn dance, six people wearing horned headdresses danced around a wassail tree. The original purpose of such a dance was to reawaken the spirits of the earth in order to assure the coming of spring. The oxhorn cake, which was placed on the head of one of the dancers, was a gift for the spirits of the animals upon whom humans also depended for survival.

Merrymaking during the Christmas holidays included playacting and games of various sorts. "The Bee in the Middle," for example, in which the Bee (a player wearing a mask) attempts to sting the players seated around him, while they try to avoid being stung, was a ritual game that seems to have combined ancient notions of animal sacrifice with Christian notions of God's sweetness and light. As part of Twelfth Night festivities, a King and Queen of the Bean were chosen. In two special "Twelfth Cakes" were baked a bean and a pea (or small jewels in wealthier households), and the man who got the bean was the King and the woman who got the pea was the Queen. The King and Queen were seated at the high table for the feast.

Most notable, however, were performances by mummers, or traditional holiday performers. Sometimes these masked actors would act out pantomimes and perform dances in the guise of such traditional characters as the Hobby

Horse. Mummers also performed plays, and while those extant date only from the sixteenth century, they no doubt had medieval antecedents. A common theme in these plays was death and resurrection, also reflecting, no doubt, the hope for the return of spring after the death of winter and the Christian notion of triumph over death. In the play of St. George, for example, St. George was killed and brought back to life again. On the final day of the Christmas celebrations, Twelfth Night fires were lighted--either twelve small fires and one large fire out of doors or twelve smaller candles and one large candle or candelabrum indoors. While these fires probably were originally part of a pagan ritual, intended to ensure fertility for the coming year, in the Middle Ages they were said to represent the twelve days of Christmas and Christ or the Twelve Apostles and either Jesus or the Virgin Mary.

Winter festivities did not end with Twelfth Night and the end of the Christmas holidays. Plough Monday, or Rock Monday, was the first Monday after Epiphany and seems to have originated in another festival celebrating the fertility of the soil. Dating in England back to the *Anglo-Saxon period, it was originally part of the ritual associated with the plowing of the first furrow of the year and offering a sacrifice of some sort to the soil. In the Middle Ages it marked the return to work after the Christmas holidays, although probably not much was actually accomplished until the next day. Festivities that most likely date back further than the Middle Ages included a plow race in the common pasture among the men of the village. It was also customary for young men to decorate themselves and a fool" plow with ribbons and decorations and take the plow through the village asking for money. Anyone refusing them ran the risk of having the ground in front of his door plowed up. The money they collected was traditionally used to pay for the Plough Light, a light kept burning year-round in the parish church.

The box in which this money was collected was called "Bessy's (or Betsy's) Box" and was carried by a traditional character, a man made up as a woman. Other characters such as the fool and the fox would join Bessy in performing traditional mummers' plays on Plough Monday. These plays usually involved a ritual murder or execution and, like much of the Christmas festivities, derived from ancient fertility rites, suggesting a sacrifice in order to assure a bountiful harvest.

Candlemas, which fell on February 2 and marked the real beginning of spring plowing, also seems to have had its origin in an ancient festival, but in the Middle Ages it was celebrated as the feast of the Purification of the Virgin. This religious feast originated with the Christian church as an answer to the pagan festival of Lupercalia and was celebrated by processing through the town or village carrying candles.

February 14 was St. Valentine's Day. Although tradition includes legends of several St. Valentines who lived and perhaps were martyred in the early Christian period, it is not known how this name came to be linked with the pagan goddess of love, Venus. Nevertheless, St. Valentine's Day was a time of celebrating love, with love lanterns, love-knot jewelry, and special "love foods" such as pheasant and quail eggs, geese, or apples and pears. At St. Valentine's Day feasts each guest was expected to wear a love token which might be a love-knot, a pin in the shape of a sideways 8 representing love without end, or a capital A, representing the Latin saying *amor vincit omnia* (love conquers all)!

Easter took its name from Oestre, or Eostra, a pagan dawn and spring goddess, but the pagan celebration of the triumph of the sun and spring over winter was assimilated to the Christian belief in Christ's triumph over death. A movable feast, dependent on the spring equinox, it could fall anywhere from March 22 to April 25. Lent--or Quadragesima--was the period of spiritual preparation before Easter, a forty-day period of fasting and abstinence. Shrove Tuesday, the last day before the beginning of Lent, and the day on which one made confession and received penance, became a time of sport and entertainment, a period of frivolity before the seriousness of Lent.

During Lent it was traditional for the cross and images in the church to be veiled, except for Sundays, and for the Sanctuary also to be screened off. At some point in the Holy Week services the veil to the Sanctuary would be removed with the reading of the words "And the veil of the Temple was rent in twain." On Palm Sunday, the week before Easter, the cross and the Host were carried in procession, followed by the congregation carrying branches of wood. On Good Friday the cross was set up and the congregation kneeled before it and kissed it. From Friday to Easter morning the cross and the Host, surrounded by candles, were symbolically "buried" in a special part of the church. On the night before Easter all the lights were put out and a new light ceremonially lit. On Easter morning the cross and the Host were carried, with great ritual and drama, to the altar.

However, Easter was celebrated not just in church ceremonies, but also with plays and dances which were part of the traditional medieval feasts and holidays. In addition to the mummers who might perform plays such as St. George and the Dragon, Morris (a corruption of "Moorish") dancers also performed. These Morris dancers performed traditional dances, stamping and jumping in the air, accompanied by drums, cymbals, and pipes that had originated as part of pagan practices to reawaken spring. Mystery plays (*see* **Drama, Medieval**) were also performed. These plays might deal with the story of Christ's death and resurrection or tell other traditional Bible tales, such as that of Noah and the Flood, which also symbolized renewal and rebirth.

Eggs played a prominent and symbolic role in Easter celebrations. Beautifully decorated pace (or Passover) eggs were frequently given as gifts for the mummers who performed during these celebrations. Eggs were part of special rents paid at Easter or could be given as gifts to the lord of a manor who, as at Christmas, provided a meal. They were also sometimes given to priests by their parishioners. Eggs had symbolized the constant regeneration of the earth, but they were adapted by Christian tradition to represent the regeneration of the Resurrection.

The second Monday and Tuesday after Easter was Hocktide, which seems to have evolved from the reminder regarding the payment of dues or rents. In some places it was a time where men either beat, bound, or hoisted up in the air one woman a day, and the women reciprocated on the next day. While in some places Hocktide provided a pretext for collecting money for charitable purposes, it had become so rowdy by the end of the Middle Ages that some church officials attempted to ban it.

Some scholars argue that the great festivals of the Middle Ages, the Christmas and Easter celebrations, reflect a shared structure. The holiday began with a religious feast, followed by a period of holiday from normal work, and ended finally with another festival that was a "feast of the folk." Christmas began with the Christmas feast, which was followed by twelve days of holiday. Plough Monday marked the end of the Christmas holidays and the return to work. Likewise, the Easter festival began with Easter itself and was followed by a week of holiday whose end was marked by Hocktide.

The origins of All Fools' Day are unclear, but the first of April was a time for turning the normal order of the world on its head. At an April Fools' feast, everything happened in the reverse from the normal order: the high table was served last, servers bowed in the wrong direction and the seat of honor was reserved for a jester, the Lord of Misrule. All Fools' Day could sometimes be associated with a mock church holiday called the *Feast of Fools, which could be held in January. This feast, too, centered around the inversion of status, and its celebrations included not only services that were conducted in a burlesque manner, but the appointment of boy bishops, a Pope of Fools, or a Lord of Misrule. In France a variation of this theme was the Feast of Asses, in which an ass was brought into the church, and services were conducted by someone braying in the voice of an ass. The revelry and buffoonery of these feasts became so great that occasionally church officials attempted to forbid them. Scholars disagree about whether these celebrations of inversion derived from the pagan festival of Kalends that also celebrated the inversion of status and license, but such celebrations as All Fools' and the Feast of Fools no doubt served the purpose of affirming the need for order and hierarchy.

May Day celebrations, like Easter, originated with pagan rituals assuring the return of spring, but remained a celebration of the laity, having little to do with Christianity. In the Middle Ages the first of May marked the beginning of the summer and was traditionally a time of romance. Sometimes young people would spend the night before May Day in the woods, returning only in the morning with flowers and greenery. Maypoles were decorated with flowers and ribbons, and, at least by the thirteenth century, a king and queen of May were selected.

Games played an especially important role in May Day celebrations. Originating from the ancient belief that the gods listened to those who were the best, contests were held to determine who was the fastest, who could jump or throw the furthest, who was the best archer, and so on. Backgammon, chess, and billiards were also May Day games. By the later Middle Ages the *Robin

Hood legends were featured preeminently in May Day celebrations, with the playing of Robin Hood games and performances by Morris dancers representing many of the traditional characters of the Robin Hood stories such as Robin Hood, Maid Marian, and the Friar.

According to church tradition, Ascension Day, the fortieth day after Easter, originated in the fifth century when the bishop of Vienne instituted a custom of ritual procession and supplication, asking for divine protection. The Rogation Days were the Monday, Tuesday, and Wednesday before Ascension and were days to petition for divine protection and forgiveness. This festival was celebrated in the countryside as Gangdays and served as a means of delineating and enforcing village boundaries. The priest led the village with the cross, banners, and bells in procession around the boundaries of the village and paused at traditional spots to pray and bless the harvest.

Whitsunday was the feast of the Pentecost, held seven weeks after Easter, and was another extended holiday from ordinary labors after an important church feast. This feast commemorated the coming of the Holy Spirit upon the earliest Apostles and was, of course, celebrated in the church with a special mass. But it was also celebrated as the third of the Maytime feasts, with feasting, entertainment, and a week's holiday from work.

Midsummer Eve in June marked the summer solstice, the longest day of the year. Dating from pagan times, it celebrated the arrival of summer after the sleep of winter. The key feature of Midsummer Eve was the open bonfire held out of doors. The original name for this fire was "bone fire," from the animal bones that once fueled it. Although its origins were purely pagan, in the Middle Ages it was associated with the Feast of the Nativity of St. John the Baptist. But the pagan roots of this festival remain clear. A thirteenth-century monk's description of the festivals held on St. John's Eve recounted that bones were collected and burned, and fires were carried through the fields in order to drive away evil dragons. A wheel, which was rolled, symbolized the arrival of the sun at its highest point--solstice.

The feast of *Corpus Christi was an unusual holiday because it did not have its origins either in pagan or early Christian tradition, but was a feast established in the later Middle Ages. Although it was established by the papacy as a movable feast (which could be celebrated between May 21 and June 24) in 1264, it did not become widely celebrated until the fourteenth century. Yet it became one of the most important festivals, especially in urban centers.

Corpus Christi was instituted by the papacy to celebrate the doctrine of transubstantiation, a doctrine of increasing importance in the late Middle Ages. The central figure of this festival came to be the ceremonial procession of the Host through the streets, with ceremonies attended by all the major dignitaries of the town. Led by lighted torches, the Host was carried by priests in a silver receptacle under a canopy in procession, attended by various municipal officials.

Lammas, held on August 1, was a feast celebrating the harvest and was held during the period between the hay and corn harvests. As usual in the

Middle Ages, this essentially agricultural celebration was associated with a Christian festival, St. Peter ad Vincula. Lammas comes from the Anglo-Saxon loaf mass or *hlaf-mass*, and on this day bread was blessed and God was thanked for the harvest. All of the festivities of Lammas centered around the harvest. Bread, for example, formed a centerpiece of the celebrations: in addition to numerous muffins and buns, a bread castle might be created and eaten along with shortbread, gingerbread, and plum bread.

Halloween and All Souls' Day are excellent examples of the merging of Christian and pagan traditions. All Hallows was the ancient feast of the dead, held on November 1, at the end of the ancient year, when the evil spirits were believed to be active. While the church attempted to Christianize this festival by turning it into the feast of All Saints, its origin could not be forgotten and the next day, November 2, was celebrated as All Souls, a day of prayer for the souls of the dead. As with many other formerly pagan feasts, fire played a significant role in All Hallows Eve--or Halloween--celebrations. Bonfires were lit to frighten away evil spirits, and children in masks begged for soul cakes.

While these holidays, while the major ones of the medieval year, they represent only a fraction of the many days of feasting in the calendar. Local holidays frequently represented local interests. For example, a saint whose relics were in a nearby cathedral might have his or her own local feast day. Thus the feast days of Edward the Confessor, *Dunstan, and Thomas *Becket were celebrated near Canterbury, those of Wenceslas, Procopius, and Ludmilla at Prague, and those of Florianus, Proculus, and Petronius at Bologna. Some feasts might be particular to certain groups. St. Catherine's Day (November 25), for example, honored a female martyr of the fourth century who was considered the special protectress of women, and so it was often celebrated as a woman's feast. Of course, during the Middle Ages the number of holy and feast days was increased with the addition to the calendar of saints such as *Francis of Assisi, Thomas *Aquinas, and Catherine of Siena.

While the full calendar of feasts and festivals, holy days and saints days, was no doubt welcome to much of the population who enjoyed the respite from work they entailed, such numerous holidays could also cause problems. The ordinary demands of commerce and agriculture were sometimes incompatible with frequent holidays, and at certain times and in certain places compromises had to be made. On occasion, people complained that the number of obligatory feast days on which they had to abstain from work was interfering with their livelihood. In fact, the strictness of the observation of particular feasts depended to a large extent on local custom. While the church attempted to enforce church attendance and the cessation of labor on the most important feasts of the year, work that was considered necessary or unavoidable seems to have been permitted. The complaints of church officials certainly seem to indicate that labor was performed on holidays, sometimes by choice of the worker and sometimes by that of his employer. Nevertheless, it is clear that the variety of festivals and celebrations, with the accompanying feasts, sport, playacting, games, and general merrymaking, provided the medieval populace with frequent respite from the hardships and monotony of life.

SELECTED BIBLIOGRAPHY

Chambers, E. K. *The Medieval Stage.* vol.1. Oxford: Clarendon Press, 1903; Cosman, Madeleine Pelner. *Medieval Holidays and Festivals: A Calendar of Celebrations.* New York: Academy of Sciences, 1981; Homans, George C. *English Villagers of the Thirteenth Century* . New York: Russell & Russell, 1941; Kellner, K. A. Heinrich. *Heortology: A History of the Christian Festivals From Their Origin to the Present Day.* London: Oxford University Press, 1908; Rodgers, Edith Cooperrider *Discussion of Holidays in the Later Middle Ages.* New York: Columbia University Press, 1940; Rubin, Miri. "Corpus Christi: Inventing a Feast," *History Today* 40:7 (1990): 15-21; Whistler, Laurence. *The English Festivals.* London: Curtain, 1947; Wright, A. R. *British Calendar Customs.* 2 vols. London: Publications for the Folk-lore Society, 1936-1940.

Miriam Davis

FIGHT AT FINNSBURGH, THE.   The *Fight at Finnsburgh* is a fragment of an Old English epic heroic poem. Although this may be the oldest English epic, the original manuscript has been lost, and the only extant reference appears in George Hickes's *Thesaurus* in 1705 from a single page "singulare folium, in codice MS. Homiliarium Semi-Saxonicarum qui extat in Bibliotheca Lambethana." This fragment belongs to the epic song of Finn alluded to in lines 1068-1159 of *Beowulf* mentioning two fights, of which the fragment probably refers to the first fight in which Hnaef is killed.

In the narrative line Finn, king of Frisia, abducted Hildeburh, but probably with her consent. Hoc, her father, pursued the abductor and was slain in battle. Twenty years later, the sons of Hoc are old enough to avenge their father's death. Perhaps the existence of such epic fragments kept alive the anger that would otherwise have subsided.

In the revenge invasion of Frisia, Hnaef and a son of Finn are killed, an uneasy peace is concluded, and the slain warriors are burnt. But since the fierce winter is too far advanced, oddly enough, Hengest and the surviving Frisian warriors stay with Finn.

But the behavior of Hengest makes it obvious that he is still not to avenge his father. Thus the Frisians decide to attack Hengest and his men while they lie asleep in the great hall. This is presumably the night attack described in the Finnsburg fragment. Although Hengest is slain by Hunlafing, Guthlaf and Oslaf escape. Returning with fresh troops, they kill Finn and carry off his queen Hildeburh. Unlike the more developed epics, the fragment tells only a single narrative, makes almost no moralistic commentary, and thus can easily be woven by *scops into longer, more complex epics.

More characteristically, Hengest is referred to in *kennings as the "battle-young king," and the metaphoric "birds-of-slaughter" are evoked. References to "moon" and "waking" suggest that this fragment refers only to the night raid. The catalog of heroes (by birth or courage) includes Sifeferth and Eaha, Ordlaf and Guthlaf, Hengest, Guthere, and Garulf, giving particularity to what would otherwise be an anonymous night raid. The list concludes with the hyperbolic praise to the fallen combatants: "Never heard I of heroes . . . more hardy in war, / Of sixty who strove . . . more strongly or bravely," and the rather unlikely claim that the battle waged and waned for five days.

SELECTED BIBLIOGRAPHY

Breeze, Andrew. "'Finnsburgh' and 'Maldon': Celaes Bard, Cellod Bard." *Notes and Queries* 39 (237):3 (September 1992), 267-69; Dane, Joseph A. "'Finnsburgh' and *Iliad* IX: A Greek Survival of the Medieval Germanic Oral-Formulaic Theme, the Hero on the Beach." *Neophilologus* 66:3 (July 1982), 443-49; Jacobs, Nicolas. "The Old English Heroic Tradition in the Light of Welsh Evidence." *Cambridge Medieval Celtic Studies* 2 (Winter 1981), 9-20; Ostman, Jan Ola. "'The Fight at Finnsburgh': Pragmatic Aspects of a Narrative Fragment." *Neophilologische Mitteilungen* 95:2 (1994), 207-27.

Elton E. Smith

FILOCOLO, IL (1336-38?). An early epic prose narrative written by Giovanni *Boccaccio during his Neapolitan period, *Il Filocolo* is among the first of his major works. It records the long and involved adventures of a pair of lovers, Florio and Biancifiore, tracing their lives from their childhood infatuation to their painful separation, joyous reunion, marriage, and triumphant return to their home. This is the first of the poems written under the direction of the mythical "Fiammetta," the fictional beloved who inspired Boccaccio in his conventionalized approach to aristocratic poetry. It draws on predominantly French sources (*see French Literature*) for its plot structure and depends on allusions from Ovid, Valerius Flaccus, Lucan, *Dante, Statius, and Virgil to round out its intertextual virtuosity. It is divided into five books, which in turn are divided into 459 chapters and is episodic in its structure. Boccaccio uses many chapters of *Filocolo* for long digressions that emphasize a variety of classical and medival motifs, including exploratory discussions about the nature of love framed in the traditional genre of the *questione*. Thirteen questions are included, all subjected to close scrutiny by a variety of interlocutors. In this sense, then, the *Filocolo* is an important precursor to the loose and often antithetical structure of the *Decameron*.

The plot is extremely complex, and critics tend to be impatient with and critical of the poem. As Bergin noted, "Its failings are all too apparent: the digressions are annoying, the lengthy speeches and the self-conscious parading of classical erudition, the want of discipline, are aesthetic blemishes." Most scholars cull the *Filocolo* for insights about the life of the young Boccaccio, since knowledge about his intellectual experiences in Naples is limited. Unfortunately, most of the biographical allusions are invented and are therefore unreliable; nevertheless, the introductory material provides significant insight into the cultural milieu that generated and expanded the conventional treatments of *courtly love embraced by the cosmopolitan Angevin court at Naples under the rule of Robert. Moreover, other scholars have argued that *Filocolo* represents the first attempt at a modern novel. Indeed, its influence on the development of the picaresque *novelle* appears clear.

The *Filocolo* is also of interest to scholars who study the transmission of literary texts across Europe during the period and note that its creative and innovative approach to genre influenced writers of later generations, including Sannazaro, Tasso, and possibly Milton, who may have drawn his imagery for his infernal council in book II of *Paradise Lost* from *Filocolo*, Book I, chapter 9. Of greater importance to medievalists, perhaps, is the occasional borrowing of material in *Filocolo* by Geoffrey *Chaucer. Chaucer used parts of the discussion from Question 13 in his *"Franklin's Tale"; *Troylus and Criseyde*, the *Legend of Good Women* and the *"General Prologue" to the *Canterbury Tales* all borrow from *Filocolo*. Thus its influence on contemporary and later authors marks this work as an important beginning to a long and illustrious literary career.

SELECTED BIBLIOGRAPHY

Bergin, Thomas. *Boccaccio.* New York: Viking Press, 1981; Branca, Vittore. *Boccaccio: The Man and His Works.* Richard Monges, trans. and Dennis McAuliffe, ed. New York: New York University Press, 1976; Downing, Christine. *The Goddess, Mythological Images of the Feminine.* New York: Crossroad Press, 1981.Kirkham, Victoria. "Reckoning with Boccaccio's 'Questioni d'Amore.'" *Modern Language Notes* 89 (1974), 47-59; Kirkham. Victoria. "Two New Traditions: The Early Boccaccio of English Dress." *Italica* 70:1 (Spring 1993), 79-88; McGregor, James. *The Image of Antiquity in Boccaccio's "Filocolo," "Filostrato," and "Teseida."* New York: Peter Lang, 1991; Olson, Glending. *Literature as Recreation in the Middle Ages.* Ithaca: Cornell University Press, 1982; Smarr, Janet M. *Boccaccio and Fiammetta: The Narrator as Lover.* Urbana: University of Illinois Press, 1986.

Theresa Kennedy

FILOSTRATO, IL (1335?) After the *Decameron, Il Filostrato* is the most famous of Giovanni *Boccaccio's vernacular poems. An epic poem in twelve books of *ottava rima,* the work is notable for its evidence of growth and maturity in the poet. The poem relates the story of Troilo, son of Priam, and his hopeless love for the faithless Cressida, who betrays him with the Greek hero Diomedes. The affecting pathos of the tale inspired many imitations, the most important of which include Geoffrey *Chaucer's *Troylus and Crisyde, and Shakespeare's Troilus and Cressida. The poem draws on a variety of sources, including the second book of Virgil's Aeneid, for the character of Troilus, and, more important, from Benoît's Roman de Troie and Colonna's Historia Troiana. Boccaccio incorporates into the poem what he has learned during his poetic apprenticeship in Naples about the "dolce stil nuovo," or sweet new style that so inspired the vernacular poets of the thirteenth and fourteenth centuries in Europe.

Scholars tend to be impatient with the explicit sexual imagery present in Filostrato, and generally regard the poem as cynical, immature, or underdeveloped. However, most of the important themes of a typical *courtly love narrative are present, and Boccaccio explores questions about the relationship of love to fortune in Boethian terms here, a topic to which he would return with the *Teseida. At the heart of the Filostrato is the notion that historical circumstance must always overcome transitory emotions like love, and to misunderstand this truth of lived experience will result in tragedy, death, and despair. Boccaccio structures his story by juxtaposing the conventional wisdom that surrounds the manner in which a stylized love affair is conducted and subsequently ended with the pragmatic realities and harshness of fortune, metaphorically the Trojan setting.

The end result is to provide a stark contrast between the pleasure of poetic words and their incompatibility with historical reality. Boccaccio does this predominantly by exposing the characters' different philosophical positions with reference to this conventional questione d'amore: Cressida and Pandaro reflect on the pragmatic side of the debate, while Troilo laments his experiences in hyperbolic rhetoric. This internal structure, in turn, has been reinforced by the prologue, where Boccaccio explains that the purpose of his book is to convince his beloved, possibly Fiammetta--his mythic addressee during his Neapolitan period--to return to him. By providing a narrative example of his sufferings, Boccaccio indicates his hope that the style of the text will overcome the substance of her resistance.

Il Filostrato, then, is a work about the relationship between the exaltation of love and the pressures of history. Its allegorical and didactic moments may have been intended to appeal to the middle-class taste of a new and growing reading public, creating a coalescence between mercantile and aristocratic literary traditions. His portrait of the golden Cressida, as an objectification of desire, is perhaps his most successful poetic portrait in the text, and this characterization will return later in his Decameron.

SELECTED BIBLIOGRAPHY

Bergin, Thomas. Boccaccio. New York: Viking Press, 1981; Branca, Vittore. Boccaccio: The Man and His Works. Richard Monges, trans. and Dennis McAuliffe, ed. New York: New York University Press, 1976; Downing, Christine. The Goddess: Mythological Images of the Feminine. New York: Crossroad Press, 1981; Havely, Nigel.

Chaucer's Boccaccio. Rochester, NY: D. S. Brewer, 1980; Kirkham, Victoria. "Reckoning with Boccaccio's 'Questioni d'Amore.'" *Modern Language Notes* 89 (1974), 47-59; McGregor, James H. *The Image of Antiquity in Boccaccio's "Filocolo," "Filostrata," and "Tesseida."* New York: Peter Lang, 1991; Olson, Glending. *Literature as Recreation in the Middle Ages.* Ithaca: Cornell University Press, 1982; Reale, Nancy. "'Bitwixen Game and Ernest': *Troilus and Criseyde* as a Post-Boccaccian Response to the *Commedia.*" *Philological Quarterly* 71:2 (Spring 1992), 155-71; Smarr, Janet M. *Boccaccio and Fiammetta: The Narrator as Lover.* Urbana: University of Illinois Press, 1986; Stillinger, Thomas C. *The Song of Troilus: Lyric Authority in the Medieval Book.* Philadelphia: University of Pennsylvania Press, 1992.

Theresa Kennedy

FIONN CYCLE, THE. See Celtic Literature.

FLORIS AND BLANCHEFLOUR. Floris and Blancheflour is the name of a medieval metrical *romance that appears in both French and English literature. The work is also called *Floire et Blancheflor*, and it dates from the first part of the thirteenth century. While the work appears in four later manuscripts, each of which oddly does not have an opening line, the tale is based upon a French original.

In the romance, Floris, the son of an evil Saracen king, falls in love with Blancheflour, the daughter of a Christian lady. Blancheflour's mother had been captured by the Saracens, so she and Floris grew up together. As is typical in a romance, the young couple fall in love with each other. This leads to Blancheflour's banishment; yet before she leaves, she gives Floris a ring that will alarm him should she fall into trouble. Floris cannot simply allow his love to go, so he sets off to find her. He does not get far when the ring warns him that she is in danger. This sets in motion a series of trials and events in Floris's search for his lady. Eventually he traces her to an oriental emir's harem, which Floris enters concealed in a basket of roses.

They are discovered and are sentenced to death. Ultimately they convince the emir to commute their sentence. He later pardons them and is so enthralled by their love for each other that he marries them himself, and the couple leave the harem for a life of bliss. *Floris and Blancheflour* has its roots in the *Tales of the Arabian Nights*. It was one of the most popular Middle English romances and also becomes the subject of Giovanni *Boccaccio's *Filocolo*.

SELECTED BIBLIOGRAPHY

Lindahl, Carl. "The Oral Undertones of Late Medieval Romance." In *Oral Tradition in the Middle Ages.* W.F.H. Nicolaisen, ed. Binghamton, NY: Medieval and Renaissance

Texts and Studies, 1995. 59-75; Wentersdorf, Karl P. "Iconographic Elements in 'Floris and Blancheflour.'" *Annuale Mediaevale* 20 (1981), 76-96.

Robert T. Lambdin

FLOURE AND THE LEAFE, THE. *The Floure and the Leafe* is a *dream allegory of about six hundred lines composed in *rime-royal. Critics originally believed the work to be one of Geoffrey *Chaucer's, but this theory was later debunked, and now many believe that the poem was composed by a unknown woman.

In Middle English poetry the flower and the leaf signify the two parties in the mannered courtly *debates of the French, especially the work of Deschamps. In this poem the subjects concern the green flower, which signifies either a merry life or love, and the white leaf, symbolic of the gravity of life or honor. The English version begins with the narrator wandering in a grove. He sees the white band of knights and their ladies, emblematic of the leaf, which is also representative of Diana, the goddess of chastity. Nearby the narrator also espies the green agents of the flower, symbolic of Flora, or those who delight in the excesses of life. The narrator weighs the implications of both parties before awaking from his sleep.

SELECTED BIBLIOGRAPHY

Pearsall, Derek, ed. *"The Floure and the Leaf," "The Assembly of Ladies," "The Isle of Ladies."* Kalamazoo: Medieval Institution Publications. 1990; Snyder, Cynthia Lockard. "'The Flour and the Leaf': An Alternative Approach." In *New Readings of Late Medieval Love Poems*. David Chamberlain, ed. Lanham, MD: University ress of America. 1993; Zesmer, David M. *Guide to English Literature: From "Beowulf" through Chaucer and Medieval Drama*. New York: Barnes & Noble, 1965.

Robert T. Lambdin

FLYTYNGE. A flytynge, or invective, is a mock poetic duel or war of wit and words for the pleasure of the participants and its audience. The form as genre has multiple origins, as invectives are found in most literatures, including Greek, Latin, Italian, French, Norse, and Celtic. Although similar forms are found in the *jeux-partis* of French literature, the flytynges of the Scots were probably rooted in ancient Celtic tradition and in the songs of the Gaelic *bards.

The outrageous verbal abuse was strengthened by the outrageous Gaelic belief that the words could cause actual physical harm or blisters on the face. The earliest Scottish example of the genre is *The Flyting of Dunbar and Kennedy*

(1492-93), followed by *Polwart and Montgomerie Flyting*. *James V even participated in a flyting with Sir David Lindsay.

   The Flyting of Dunbar and Kennedy is an example of a real flytynge. Dunbar and Kennedy's insults include, among other things, that the other was a beggar, had poisoned a king, is fit only to be a hangman's assistant, is no real poet, and had swallowed frog sperm.

   Some debate whether or not the participants of a flytynge had any true ill-will toward each other, but it is likely that they had as much fun piling up their insults as the audience did in hearing them. The wide vocabulary and harsh *alliterative verse make the genre an interesting study in middle Scots language, and the wit and outrageous exaggeration of the participants' verbal arrows make the flyting, at the very least, entertaining.

SELECTED BIBLIOGRAPHY

Bold, Alan Norman. *Scotland: A Literary Guide*. London: Routledge, 1989; Zesmer, David M. *Guide to English Literature: From "Beowulf" through Chaucer and Medieval Drama*. New York: Barnes & Noble, 1965.

J. Scott Plaster

"FOWLES IN THE FRITH." One of the most fascinating Middle English lyrics, this five-line poem uses imagery to create a kind of ambiguity between religious and secular meanings:

> Fowles in the frith,
> The fisshes in the flood,
> And I mon waxe wood.
> Much sorwe I walke with
> For beste of boon and blood.

The lines contain three or four stresses and end with a rhyme scheme of *abbab*. Each line contains a unified sound through the use of alliteration: "Fowles" and "frith"; "waxe" and "wood, " and so on. The final line uses the synecdoche of bone and blood to create a vivid image of humanity.

   The poem begins with the speaker's observations of the birds and fish in their environments, but he adds that he "mon [might] waxe wood [grow mad]." The ambiguous explanation for this madness is given in the last two lines where he states that he walks with much sorrow for "beste" of bone and blood.

   The ambiguity of this poem lends itself to critical controversy. While some scholars feel that it is a secular love lyric, others see it as a religious declaration. Raymond Oliver's observation that there is a "contrast between the birds and fish, who are in their proper places with the speaker, who is at odds with his world and himself," is appropriate for either interpretation. The diction of the poem contributes to its different levels of meaning. For example, the word "frith" means "woods" but also "divine law, " and the word "beste" may mean best or beast. Lewis and Nancy Owen noted that line 5 may shift the source of the madness from a cold woman to a "suffering Christ, " resulting in a tension between secular and spiritual love.

SELECTED BIBLIOGRAPHY

Oliver, Raymond. *Poems without Names: The English Lyric, 1200-1500*. Berkeley: University of California Press, 1970; Owen, Lewis, and Nancy Owen, eds. *Middle English Poetry: An Anthology*. Indianapolis: Bobbs-Merrill, 1971; Reiss, Edmund. "The Middle English Lyric." In *Old and Middle English Literature*. Dictionary of Literary Biography. Eds. Jeffrey Helterman and Jerome Mitchell. Detroit: Gale, 1994. 392-399; Sigal, Gale; *Erotic Dawn-Songs of the Middle Ages: Voicing the Lyric Lady*. Gainesville: University Press of Florida, 1996; Stevick, Robert D., Ed. *One Hundred Middle English Lyrics*. Rev. Urbana: University of Illinois Press, 1994.

Sigrid King

FRANCIS OF ASSISI, ST. (1181-1226). A cleric and a scholar, Francis was the founder of the Franciscan order. He was born at Assisi in Umbria in 1181. His father, Pietro, was a wealthy Assisian cloth merchant, and his mother, Pica, belonged to a noble family of Provence. Francis was educated by the priests of St. George's at Assisi for elementary instruction and later learned from the school of the Troubadours. His early years of education were unremarkable, for he cared little for his father's lifestyle.

Francis's youthful carefree character was nothing like the strict morality of his later life. He was uninterested in becoming a merchant like his father, and not knowing what career to pursue at the age of twenty he went out with some townspeople of Assisi to fight the Perugians. The Assisians were defeated, and the Perugians held Francis captive for more than a year in Perugia. While in captivity or soon after returning home from captivity, he resolved to pursue a military career. He left to take up arms in the Neapolitan States against the emperor, but an illness interrupted his route at Spoleto. Here he had a dream in which a voice told him to return to Assisi. He did so immediately in 1205.

He began to seek with prayer the answer to his calling; he gave up his extravagant attire and wasteful ways. Not long after he had returned to Assisi while praying at the chapel of St. Damian's, he heard a voice saying, "Go, Francis, and repair my house, which as you see, is falling to ruins." Francis took this literally to refer to St. Damian's. He immediately sold his horse for the money needed to restore the chapel. His father was outraged at this behavior. Fearing his father, Francis hid himself in a cave near St. Damian's for about a month. He returned home, was beaten by his father, and returned to

St. Damian's, where he found shelter with the officiating priest, but was cited before the city consuls by his father. His father forced his son to forego his inheritance, which Francis was glad to do.

Francis began wandering the hills behind Assisi, improvising hymns of praise. He begged for stones in Assisi for the restoration of St. Damian's. He carried these to the old chapel and began rebuilding it himself. Afterwards Francis restored two other chapels: St. Peter's and St. Mary of the Angels. Meanwhile, he was zealous in works of charity, especially in nursing the lepers.

After hearing in the Gospels that the disciples of Christ were not to possess material goods, Francis removed his shoes, cloak, staff, and wallet. He obtained a coarse woolen tunic, the dress worn by poor Umbrian peasants, and tied it around him with a knotted rope. He went forth urging people to penance, brotherly love, and peace. His example began to draw others to him; Bernard of Quintavalle, a magnate of the town, was the first to join and was followed by Peter of Cattaneo. Francis led his new followers to the public square, and they gave away all of their belongings to the poor. They wore similar woolen tunics and built themselves small huts near Francis's at Porziuncola. Before long, several others became followers.

When the number of followers had increased to eleven, Francis drew up a written rule for them. The First Rule, as it is called by the Friars Minor, is short and simple, and seems to be a mere adaptation of the gospel already selected by Francis for the guidance of his first companions. The Friars Minor were named either after the minores, lower classes, or with reference to Matthew 25: 40-45 as a perpetual reminder of humility. When the rule was written, Francis and his followers went to Rome to seek the approval of Pope *Innocent III. Innocent, moved by a dream about Francis, gave verbal sanction to the rule submitted by Francis and granted the Friars Minor permission to preach everywhere. About 1211 they obtained a permanent place of residency near Assisi, the chapel of St. Mary of the Angels. The Friars Minor built small huts adjoining the sanctuary, and from this settlement they went forth two by two exhorting people.

In 1212 Clare, a young heiress of Assisi, sought Francis out and begged to be allowed to join in the manner of life he had founded. Francis cut off her hair, clothed her in the habit of the minors and received her into a life of poverty. Francis provided a suitable residence for her and for the other pious women who had joined her at St. Damian's in a dwelling adjoining the chapel. They were the monastery of the Second Franciscan Order of Poor Ladies, now known as Poor Clares.

The first general chapter of the Friars Minor was held in May 1217, at Porziuncola. The order divided the Christian world and themselves. Francis reserved France for himself and preached also in Rome. On one occasion in 1221, while Francis was preaching at Camara, a small village near Assisi, the members of the congregation were so moved that they presented themselves to him and begged to be admitted into his order. This was the first of the Third Order, as it is now called, of the Brothers and Sisters of Penance, which Francis intended as a middle state between the world and the cloister for those who could not leave their home.

Around 1220 it had become apparent that the simple, familiar, and unceremonious ways that had marked the Franciscan movement at its beginning were disappearing. Cardinal Ugolino, who would later become Pope Gregory IX, tried to reestablish the doctrines of the Franciscan movement. At the Chapter of Mats in 1220 or 1221 Francis relinquished his position as general of the order in favor of Peter of Cattaneo. Peter died less than a year later and was succeeded by Brother Elias, who continued in that office until the death of Francis.

Francis's influence on medieval literature was important. He taught people to use their own voice through spontaneous hymns. Francis's introduction of celebrating the Nativity by reproducing the *presepio*, which is considered the first mystery-play in Italy, may have helped to revive drama in the Middle Ages (*see Drama, Medieval*). Francis's own writings include the poems "The Canticle of the Sun" and "Laudes Creaturarum," his documents on the Gospel, which are simple and informal, the rules of the Friars Minor, and letters.

Few medieval lives have been more thoroughly documented than Francis's, and in addition to his writings, we have early papal bulls and other diplomatic documents, biography by Thomas of Celano, one of Francis's first followers, a joint-narrative by Leo, Rufinus, and Angelus, and the legend of St. Bonaventure. Later important works about Francis and the Franciscan order include Paule Sabafier's "Vie de St. Francois."

SELECTED BIBLIOGRAPHY

Brooke, Rosalind B. "Recent Work on St. Francis of Assisi." *Analecta Bollandiana* 100 (1982), 653-76; Gelber, Hester Goodenough. "A Theater of Virtue: The Exemplary World of St. Francis of Assisi." In *Saints and Virtues*. John Stratton, ed. Berkeley: University of California Press, 1987. 15-35; Nugent, Dorothy Louise. "Chesterton's 'St. Francis of Assisi.'" *Chesterton Review* 9:4 (1983), 348-58, Trapp, Jacob. "Saint Francis of Assisi: After Eight Hundred Years." *Studia Mystica* 5:4 (Winter 1982), 3-6.

Rebecca Chalmers

"FRANKLIN'S TALE, THE." This Breton *lai (lay), found in Geoffrey *Chaucer's *Canterbury Tales*, is set in Brittany, where a knight named Arveragus of Kayrrud lives. He loves Dorigen, the fairest lady under the sun. When he takes her for his wife, he swears to do nothing against her will, but to always bow to her sovereignty. After they have been married a little more than a year, he travels to England to seek his honor in arms. Dorigen remains at home and mourns his absence, haunting the cliffs from which he sailed away from her.

One May morning she and her friends are out in the garden, which is blooming like Paradise. After dinner they begin to dance; Dorigen watches a young squire, Aurelius, a lusty "servant to Venus" (215) who is in love with Dorigen. However, Aurelius dares not say anything directly to her; he relies instead upon the lays and songs that he creates to tell of his love. When he finally confesses his love for her, she agrees to love him the "best of any man" (275) if he removes all the rocks from the coast. Then she admits that she knows that this is an impossible task, given him because he should not love another man's spouse. Sorrowfully, Aurelius confines himself to his house and begins to waste away. In despair he prays to Lord Phoebus and his sister Lucina for a miracle; then he falls into a trance.

Finally, Arveragus returns home. While the happy couple is reunited, Aurelius remains languishing in torment for two years and more, with only his brother to comfort him. This brother is a clerk who had been at Orleans for several years, where he discovered a book of natural magic dealing with the phases of the moon. He travels to Orleans to find someone who can accomplish (at least magically) the task given his brother so that Dorigen will have to keep her promise to love Aurelius, thereby saving his life. The magician finally arrives to attempt this feat during December, beginning his calculations to make the rocks disappear for a week or two. When he succeeds, Aurelius hurries to Dorigen, reminding her of her vow to love him if he has accomplished this task.

Totally alone now (Arveragus has gone away again), Dorigen ponders what to do, since she never expected Aurelius to succeed. She even considers suicide to maintain her honor, which would put her into noble company with other women who have chosen the same fate. When Arveragus returns three days later, she explains the situation to him; he agrees that she must keep her word and sends her forth with a squire and a maid. Aurelius follows her to the garden where they first met, where she informs him that she is there at the behest of her husband. Realizing the nobility of the love between Dorigen and her husband, Aurelius graciously takes himself out of the picture, releasing Dorigen from her promise. Dorigen returns to her husband, and they live happily together for a long time. Aurelius now regrets having squandered his inheritance on the magician and goes to pay that debt. However, when he explains the entire situation to the magician, he is released from his promise to pay as the story ends.

In the beginning this tale clearly echoes the sentiments Chaucer has the Wife of Bath express in her tale--the idea that women desire to be treated as equals, not as property. However, by the end of the tale the emphasis seems to have shifted to the power of true love to overcome all obstacles it faces (if we consider Aurelius's love as more lust than anything else). This tale fits into the genre as a symbolic representation of the problems associated with *courtly love, providing the supernatural elements with the actions of the magician, who responds courteously himself at the end when he releases Aurelius from his debt. The reader is left to ponder which of the characters shows the greatest nobility with his or her actions. The story is also unique in that it is set in Roman times, using Roman names and reference to Roman gods, overtly eschewing all indications of Christianity.

SELECTED BIBLIOGRAPHY

Cook, Robert. "Chaucer's 'Franklin's Tale' and 'Sir Orfeo.'" *Neophilologische Mitteilungen* 95:3 (1994), 333-36; Scott, Anne. "'Considerynge the Beste on Every Syde': Ethics, Empathy, and Epistlemology in the 'Franklin's Tale.'" *Chaucer Review* 29 (1995), 390-415; Van Dyck, Carolynn. "The Clerk's and Franklin's Related Subjects." *Studies in the Age of Chaucer* 17 (1995), 45-68; Wheeler, Bonnie. "'Trouthe' without Consequences: Rhetoric and Gender in Chaucer's 'Franklin's Tale.'" In *Representations of the Feminine in the Middle Ages*. Bonnie Wheeler, ed. Dallas: Academia, 1993. 91-116.

Peggy Huey

FRENCH LITERATURE. While the poems of the great medieval French author François *Villon remain the most familiar of all the medieval French works, there was a great literary tradition that preceded him by centuries. The first six hundred years or so of French literature have long been neglected by readers and scholars who care more for the aesthetics that evolved in the seventeenth-century France of Molière and Rabelais. Yet the medieval French compositions played a huge role not only in France, but also throughout Western civilization.

From the ninth through the eleventh centuries, unfortunately, we have few extant French works. While it can be assumed that there were many other texts composed during this period, no one can be sure exactly how prominent French literature was during this time. It was not until the twelfth century that French literature, especially poetry, emerged in the elaborately rich forms that are readily available today. This initial movement of compositions would not only affect France and the mainland of Europe, but would also have a great impact upon the literature of Britain. During this time France was among the leaders in culture and intellect. This scholarly aptitude sowed the seeds of literature that were to become the Arthurian *romances (*see **Arthurian Legend**); the attitudes French compositions portrayed became the basis for works dealing with *courtly love and *chivalry.

England, especially, was closely tied to the literature of medieval France. Due largely to the Norman Conquest of 1066, French was the language of the English court. Therefore, most of the nobles spoke French, while English was the language of peasants. It should not be surprising that many of the extant medieval French works were either composed in England or were copies of continental French works produced for these wealthy English readers. Thus the literature of medieval France is in many ways indistinguishable from the literature of England.

Italy was gradually becoming the cultural leader of Western civilization by the fourteenth century. However, while the center of the arts shifted, this does not mean that France became a literary wasteland. Indeed, the literature of France continued. While these works were not as novel as the traditions established in the previous three centuries, the continuation of creative thought and literary compositions produced a lasting corpus of literature that again flourished with Villon's works of the fifteenth century.

To gain a proper understanding of the evolution of French literature, one must concentrate upon some six hundred years of literary tradition. The importance of religion is a continuous theme during this period, primarily because most of the educated men belonged to the Church. The works were initially composed of *hagiography, prayers, sermons, and verse. Indeed, the clerics of this age were some of the best poets. These canons, monks, and bishops were handed some fodder for composition themes. This was the time of the great *Crusades; the emotions elicited by these enormous campaigns appeared again and again in songs and poetry over a two hundred year period. Throughout medieval French literature the themes of deep religious feelings are prominent.

Many of these older compositions also reflect the ideas found in a civilization dominated so much by the Church and the all encompassing feudal society. In fact, it was feudalism that provided some of the broadest themes in the secular poetry of medieval France. The oldest types of poems of this genre to come down to us are the *chansons de gestes. These heroic poems date to about 1100, and nearly one hundred of them survive in their entirety, including the most famous work of this genre, La *Chanson de Roland. While many of the authors of the chansons are concerned basically with military themes and abilities, the more noted of these works are concerned with moral dilemmas such as the hero's loyalty to his lord, to his family, or, most importantly, to God. The majority of these heroes are subjects from French history; however, the works are not steeped in French history.

Nowhere is this clearer than in La Chanson de Roland, perhaps the greatest and the most famous of the chansons de gestes. The story is based upon incidents that occurred in 778: *Charlemagne's rear guard is defeated by Basque mountaineers. Roland, the leader of the rear guard, is the nephew of Charlemagne. His troops are attacked by the Saracens, who have been tipped off to the troops' whereabouts by Ganelon, Roland's father-in-law. This event has been totally transformed; the poem occurs in the imagination of someone living some three hundred years later, incorporating the anachronism of his own feudal society and the problems so incurred into the poem. Several of the better writers of the chansons present their protagonists with significant psychological insight and understanding. The poets characteristically have great narrative skill and are graphically intense.

However, not all of the poems are as tragic as *La Chanson de Roland*. Many of the *chansons* incorporate a tasteful olio of humor and drama. An example of this is the *Moniage Guillaume*, a work in which the author presents both the pathos and the inconsistency of the mores involved when a warrior becomes a monk in his later years.

In the middle of the twelfth century the first of the great French romances was composed. This genre differs greatly from the *chanson* because, for the first time in French literature, love becomes an important factor in the work, and heroines take their places beside the heroes. This addition throws a wrench into the themes considered in the *chansons*: incorporated into the themes of loyalty to lord, friends, and God is the question of self-indulgence. The romances begin to explore new perspectives of love in terms of its symptoms, the conduct of the lover, and the place in life for *amour*. These works, called *les romans courtois*, quickly replaced the *chansons* in popularity, especially among the French upper class of the late twelfth century. This group seemed to have an endless fascination with the questions of love.

*Chrétien de Troyes is perhaps the foremost of the authors of the French *romans courtois*. He set up the models for this genre by elevating the role that romantic love plays in the conflict of the work, especially in terms of the psychological insights that are connected with love. This psychological perspective is treated in a subtle manner, according to the laws of *courtoisie*, especially as it applies to courtly love. Thus it is in the *romans courtois* that the dialectics concerning the errant knight are first examined, an approach that delivers new ideals of conduct and, inevitably, a new way of looking at life. The protagonist, especially in Chrétien's Arthurian literature, is considerably more secular than the epic warriors of the *chansons*. Incorporated into the *romans courtois'* texts were classical elements, including those of Ovid and Virgil, that, although unknown to the protagonists, shape and influence their thoughts and deeds.

The *romans courtois* remained popular, especially among the ruling elite, for many years, although the absurdly hyperbolic movements that resulted in the folly of the court of love were short, as will be evidenced later in the courtly movement. However, this genre quickly spread throughout the Continent, and the romance became an integral part of many cultures; it was especially prevalent in English literature, and there is even a similar type found in *Islamic literature.

With the evolution of this genre came new stylistics. In the *chansons de geste*, the authors had frequently used assonanced groups of ten-syllable lines or *laisses*. The final words of each line did not rhyme, but the final vowel of each line in each *laisse* was similar. Each line then had a slight pause, a trait that resulted in a sort of stilted verse, a technique necessary in the portrayal of the *chanson's* noble subjects. In the romances the verses were not as rigid; indeed, they were much more flexible and ornate. The medieval French authors originally composed their *romans courtois* in rhymed octosyllabic couplets. The rules for composing the *romans* became less stringent, and soon the poets were manipulating their texts into any forms that suited their desires.

At the same time that the *romans courtois* were becoming so popular, the *Provençal (referring to the language of southern France) poets were refining a new type of *lyric poetry. It was in the first half of the twelfth century that these poems first appeared. Again, this genre gave rise to a new way of developing ideas. The Provençal lyricists, more popularly known as the troubadours, created another genre steeped in technique and literary conventions. The theme of the troubadours was love, not secular or allegiance to a lord, but raw, emotional passion. The troubadours adhered to a strict manner in the composition of their poems. The theme of their works was always love. For each and every new composition they created a different stanza form; the poems were then five to seven stanzas long, highlighted by each section being metrically identical. These works were then put to music in novel forms created by the troubadours.

This Provençal language differed so greatly from the Old French that it is often omitted from many Old French texts. However, the impact Provençal had upon the literature of France cannot be denied. Soon these conventions spread from their home in southern France to all of northern France. By the end of the twelfth century the impact of this tradition was found in the works of Châtelain de Coucy and Conon de Béthune. These poets are renowned for their passionate metrical skill. The topics of their works were much the same as those of the troubadours: devotion to the theme of love and the idealization of women.

It is this period in medieval French literature that is most often described as a revolution, for it was at this time that the conventions of courtly love came into vogue. This was a movement of such magnitude that it had a profound effect upon the upper classes of Europe. Thus this was not just a literary but a cultural movement. The volumes of courtly literature, when incorporated into the upper classes, produced a mode of elegance and opulence that had been previously unknown in the royal courts. The whims and fancies of the ruling elite were demonstrated by more emphasis being given to a higher standard of living. It became chic to travel more, and leisure time increased. This was the seed of the excessive opulence that would some four hundred years later result in a bloody revolution.

During this period women were given new and important roles in the literature. Men grovel and strive for glory and greatness at their behest. Great deeds are attempted by these nobles in the pursuit of honor--and of a token from the object of their adoration. Marie de France went so far as to establish "rules" for courtly love. The magnified roles of women led to a bulk of literature that moved away from the notion of loyalty to king and country and became more romantic.

It was this preoccupation with romantic love that would occupy not only the literature of France but also that of much of the European continent. It was at this time that many great themes were developed that continued to frequent literature for hundreds of years. Certainly this was a time of grand literary shaping. Benoît de Sainte-Maure composed his *Romance of Troy*. This work drew much of its historical material from classical literature, but Benoît expanded the tales into more majestic episodes. By amplifying the works in such a way, Benoôt was able to incorporate and apply a more weighty analysis of love. This reliance upon old stories and myths gave way to the invention of new characters that resulted in the creation of novel works that were only set in history. This resulted in the first compositions about *Troilus and Cressida, two characters who are very important in English literature. Drawing upon Celtic legends (*see* **Celtic Literature**). Early French romance writers developed and presented the story of Trisram and Iseult, a couple who would influence English literature for centuries in the writings of Thomas *Malory, Alfred Lord Tennyson, and Matthew Arnold. Still other French romanticists further developed the field of Arthurian legend, which became very popular at this time. With its roots in the Celtic literature of Wales, this literature boomerangs from Britain to France and then back again to Britain.

It was Chrétien de Troyes who first brought to Western Europe the scandalous stories of Arthur, Lancelot, and the search for the Holy Grail. While there is no debate that these stories existed long before Chrétien manipulated them, he was the first author to present them with such narrative skill that they became instantly successful--not only in France, but throughout Europe. Chrétien was a master at incorporating a realistic treatment of the characters into the magical and mysterious dark side of ancient Britain. The obvious popularity of this genre is seen in the vast numbers of authors and texts concerning Arthur even today.

The realism and popular acceptance of Chrétien's works may have led to the plethora of Arthurian-legend authors who followed. Among the most noted here is Jean Renart, one of the best of a number of poets who followed Chrétien's lead in giving the romances more realism in their construction. Renart's tales differ from the stark realism of Chrétien's; they center more upon lively wit, often dealing with amusing observations of Renart's peers. Today some sixty to seventy medieval French romances survive.

It cannot be overstressed that the literature of this time was not all courtly related. While stories of courtly love did make up a great part of the literature of the ruling elite, other genres that strayed from the courtly tone flourished. At about the same time that the courtly romances prevailed, the underside, a wealth of satirical compositions, was developed. This included works like the *Roman de Renart* and genres such as the *fabliaux, both of which would play large roles in the coloring of French lyrical poetry. The *Roman de Renart* is a *beast epic, but it is not a unified work. It is a collection of animal stories that consists of twenty-seven episodes. The poem, developed in the late thirteenth century in northeastern France, takes place in an animal world that is organized on a feudal basis. The dominating figure in the work is Renart, a fox, whose masterful quality is his shrewdness. It is this very trait that allows him to overcome his nemesis, Isengrim the wolf. Ironically, while Renart usually outwits the stronger animals, when he attempts to deceive his weaker foes, such as Chanticleer (*see* **"Nun's Priest's Tale"**) the cock, he is usually defeated. Thus many believe that Renart is a metaphor for the bourgeoise.

Renart is the first and, arguably, the most famous in a series of rogue heroes in French literature. Because of the sharpness of his wit, readers tend to forget (or at least overlook) that he is a rascal. The *Roman de Renart* is a parody of medieval feudalism and chivalric idealism. Thus it is among the best examples of the new-found spirit of mockery of the established institutions that the French would label *l'esprit gaulois*.

These differences were abetted by the growth of towns, which created a new series of social changes that threatened the courtly ideals, for suddenly the middle class found itself in a position through which it could compete with the wealthy. This is exemplified in the town of Arras, which flourished in the thirteenth century. Here there was great literary activity that persisted for hundreds of years. The most important poet of Arras, Adam de la Halle, still composed poems in the courtly tradition; indeed his works are among the best extant examples of this genre. But in Paris Rutebeuf, who wrote for aristocratic patrons, often bemoaned his own poverty in a direct, realistic style that lamented his personal ill fortune. Simultaneously in Lorraine Colin Muset, in his poems, celebrated the splendor of the easy life and the pleasures of good food. Clearly the social differences that would later tear France asunder were being established.

Perhaps this change is nowhere better indicated than in the thirteenth-century *Roman de la Rose*, arguably the most famous work of all medieval French literature. The work was started around 1240 by Guillaume de Lorris. Its goal was to examine and scrutinize the course of a love affair. De Lorris presented the story in a kind of *dream vision, one narrated by the lover. In the *Roman de la Rose* the heroine is never presented as a woman. Instead, she is presented as a rosebud. She is found by her lover in the enchanted garden of the God of Love. The lover's efforts to reach and pick the flower are metaphors representing the course of his love. His efforts are both abetted and deterred by a cast of allegorical heroes, including Chastity, Shame, Pity, and Fear. Clearly these characters who both help and hinder the lover are representative of some of the moods of his lady. Other characters, such as Hope and Sweet Thought, represent more his predicament. Still other characters are emblematic of the lovers' society, including Riches and Reason. The subject of the *Roman de la Rose* clearly falls into the vein of elevated love and seemingly was directed to the courtly public. But where the *Roman de la Rose* establishes its special place in French literary history is in its allegorical treatment of the emotions of love. This would quickly become a literary trend all over Europe. It did not hurt that Guillaume de Lorris was also a brilliant writer, so the poem was destined to success. Unfortunately, the poem was never completed, perhaps due to the author's death. Nevertheless, the fragment would be a beacon for later literature.

Some forty years after the *Roman de la Rose* was left unfinished, it was picked up by Jean du Meun. He was also a dazzling writer, but he had other ideas for the poem. Before the lover was allowed to finally grasp the object of his affection, de Meun added some eighteen thousand lines to the poem. These additions strayed from Guillaume's initial narrow focus of the course of a love affair; de Meun incorporated his ideas on seemingly every conceivable topic of interest to him, including social relations, morals, religion, and philosophy. His conception of the love scene was the polar opposite of Guillaume's, as de Meun completely rejected the notion of courtly love and its jaded tradition, choosing instead to deal with love as Nature's means to continue the species. This idea is clearly more dogmatic in its approach than was Guillaume's. Further, de Meun made women the object of some of his most vicious satire. The advice that is provided to the lover is deeply rooted in the possible implications of a sexual war.

Yet de Meun's additions are not only scathing attacks on women. They are full of sardonically humorous comments that are at times blanketed in a kind of sympathetic understanding. These additions furnished later writers a lode of information and tools for their compositions. Much of the foundation of Geoffrey *Chaucer's Wife of Bath is found in the *Roman de la Rose*. François Villon also modeled most of his *La Belle Hëaulmière* on this text. The complete *Roman de la Rose*, in spite of the discrepancies of its two authors, had a huge following. Its timelessness is probably more attributable to the ambitious works of de Meun than to the engaging fancies of Guillaume. It was perhaps the most widely read of all the medieval French poems, for hundreds of manuscripts survive even today.

By the fourteenth and fifteenth centuries the literature of medieval France was beginning to take on a more modern look. Prose fiction found a niche in popularity, so narrative poetry began to fall by the wayside. Lyrics became more popular, forming quite a vast portion of the total compositions. It had also become somewhat stylish for authors to attach their names to their works; thus there is a great decline in the amount of anonymous works and a sharper recognition of literary quality. The greatest authors of this period were somewhat shady; they led uproarious, if not scandalous, lives. Much is known about their lives, and their works are preserved largely the way that these authors wished them to be. In a sense, this was one of the first times that authors reached celebrity status. Among the most noted of these poets are Guillaume de Machaut, Eustace Deschamps, Christine de Pisan, Charles d'Orléans, and François Villon. Also at this time, the *ballade and *rondeaux* became popular.

By this late point in medieval French literature, originality was pretty much passé; the literature had become formulaic. Most writers rode the crest of popularity of the *Roman de la Rose*. They opted to select one or more allegorical characters, much like those in the *Roman de la Rose*. To this they added some of the remnant attributes of the courtly love fad; items here include the hyperbolic lover dying because of his unrequited love for his beloved or the cliché of the inaccessible lady. These conventions were then formulaically placed into ballades or *rondeaux*, two forms that were easily molded to accept these contrived configurations. While many of these authors reflected great skill in adapting their works into these forms, today many of the texts appear stilted--unless the poet chose to be daring and add some originality to the genre.

This is evident in the works of Machaut, whose polished texts contain a suave approach to technical perfection. Machaut was in the service of the king of Bohemia until 1346, when he was allowed to enter the royal house of France. He was responsible for establishing the rigid form of the ballades, chants royals, *rondeaux*, and the lay. By integrating matter from his personal life into his poems, he was among the first poets to begin the transition from the impersonal works of the troubadours to the introspective works that would be mastered by François Villon. Among his finer narrative poems is the *Jugement du roy de Navarre* (c. 1349). His poem *Le Livre du voir-dit* is supposedly a true account of the love he inspired in a young girl who found this emotion simply by reading his poetry. Geoffrey Chaucer borrowed heavily from Machaut's *Livre de la fontaine amoureuse* in his composition of *The *Book of the Duchess*, and was very much influenced by the work of this great French poet.

Machaut also composed a great deal of secular and religious music, including what may be the earliest polyphonic setting of the Mass ordinary by one composer, the *Mass for Four Voices*. However, perhaps his greatest musical accomplishment was his establishment of a tradition for the arrangement of both vocal and instrumental parts in secular songs, which became the standard mode of setting *rondeaux* and ballades for nearly a century after his death in 1377.

Just as Machaut carved out his own niche in lyrical poetry, so too did many others. Charles d'Orléans, in his poetry, was eminently successful in applying the allegorical inheritance from the *Roman de la Rose*. In his work he personified moods, sentiments, and even seasons; by doing so, he created a unique world with a festive atmosphere and enchantment. Christine de Pisan attempts to revive the courtly spirit, perhaps as a means of establishing a reaction to a growing tide of anti-feminism. Her work is delicately sincere in its presentation of the emotion of love from the perspective of a woman. Eustache Deschamps's poetry is exhaustively realistic and covers a wide range of diverse topics. While the poetry may have become contrived, it was far from static.

The works of these great authors paved the way for François Villon, perhaps the greatest, but definitely the last of the renowned medieval French authors. His reputation as a scoundrel is overshadowed only by his corpus of compositions. He was originally named François de Montcorbier or François de Loges, but he adopted the name of his patron, the chaplain of a university church who adopted him around 1438. After he received his master of arts degree from the Sorbonne in 1452, all that is known about his life is that it was filled with turmoil. He was apparently a brilliant man, having graduated with his master's degree before he was twenty-one. He was imprisoned on more than one occasion for various violent crimes and theft. He was involved in a series of brawls, including one in 1455 where he killed a priest. Henceforth he was repeatedly under arrest. His *Petit Testament* (1456) is a series of *lais* parodying the style of legal volition, which explains that Villon is leaving Paris because of a broken heart, bequeathing a number of worthless things to his friends and enemies.

A poem of some two thousand lines, the *Grand Testament* is his most renowned. This work runs the gamut of emotions, from pathetic behests to biting humor. The work is somewhat autobiographical as it reviews his life as a beggar and a thief. Interspersed with both ballades and *rondeaux*, this work contains the famous "Ballade des dames du temps jadis" which would later be translated by Dante Gabriel Rossetti as "The Ballad of Dead Ladies. " In 1462 he was involved in another brawl that resulted in a second death; Villon was sentenced to death by hanging. This verdict inspired him to write his "Ballade des pendus" (The ballad of the hanged men). This work denounced human justice and appealed for divine intervention. Ironically, after he composed this work, his colleagues succeeded in having his sentence commuted to a banishment of ten years. Villon then disappeared, and there is no further reference to him. His works remained popular; a collection of them was collated and published in 1489.

But it was not until the ninteenth century that Villon's popularity peaked. He became a favorite because of his status as a kind of rogue-hero, a man who thumbed his nose at the ruling elite. In this way he was idealized much the same as the British *Robin Hood--he was only a colorful and a sympathetic outlaw. Episodes of his life became the fodder for other authors, especially the English; these incidents are mostly legendary and can be found in works such as Robert Lewis Stevenson's "Lodging for the Night. " Rossetti and Algernon Charles Swinburne translated his ballades. Thus Villon the writer is paid the ultimate compliment by being transformed into the literary hero.

It is obvious that the literature of France played a vital role in the history of medieval literature. It offers a bounty of work that clearly shows the shifts from the feudal estates to the ruling elite and is a parallel of the culture that would so bloodily erupt in civil war in 1789. The roots are all here, from the chivalry of the early French works, the connection of man with his Church and his master, the king or the feudal lord. This introspection gave way to a more universal examination, the uplifting quality of the epic hero found in the *chansons*. These works, while glorious in their composition, became the natural victuals for vicious counters that are seen in the fabliaux, the entertainment of the lower class. As poets focused more on the emotion of love, new genres were developed. These psychological works reflected a changing society that was questioning its true religious and political foundations. Naturally the dialectic initiated by these perspectives begged for more introspection and development. When the *Roman de la Rose* presented examinations of the notions of science and social relations, it was clear that the literature had moved from a means of entertaining and, therefore, teaching to one that questioned the learnings of the past. Thus the good life of the romantic hero was usurped by the scandals of those such as François Villon, a criminal who was glorified. While it may tend to be overlooked, the truth is that French literature played an integral role in the development of medieval society. It is of capital interest to historians of civilization because of its rich contextual ideals that demonstrate their worldwide influences. At the same time, these works provide an intense type of pleasure, one that demands to be recognized alongside the later and better-known literature of France. Indeed, the works of the troubadours, Machaut, Christine de Pisan, and Villon belong with those of Molière, Rabelais, and Hugo.

SELECTED BIBLIOGRAPHY

Ailes, Marianne. "French Studies: Early Medieval." *Year's Work in Modern Language Studies* 54 (1992), 49-67; Benton, John F. *Culture, Power, and Personality in Medieval France*. London: Hambledon Press, 1991; Brook, Leslie C. "The Anonymous Conclusion Attached to Guillaume de Lorris's *Roman de la Rose*." *Neophilologus* 79:3 (July 1995), 389-95; Goodrich, Norma Lorre, ed. *The Ways of Love: Eleven Romances of Medieval France*. Boston: Beacon Press, 1964; Mason, Germaine. *A Concise Survey of French Literature*. New York: Greenwood Press, 1969; Speer, Mary B. "Old French Literature." In *Scholarly Editing: A Guide to Research*. D. C. Greetham, ed. New York: Modern Language Association of America, 1995; Spivack, Charlotte, and Roberta Staples. *The Company of Camelot: Arthurian Characters in Romance and Fantasy*. Westport, CT: Greenwood Press, 1994.

Laura Cooner Lambdin

"FRIAR'S TALE, THE." "The Friar's Tale" in Geoffrey *Chaucer's *Canterbury Tales* (c. 1387-1400) is Friar Huberd's expression of his dislike for the Summoner, a fellow pilgrim journeying to the shrine of Saint Thomas *Becket at Canterbury Cathedral. In the tale, which is phrased as a sermon against greed, a Summoner is in league with the Devil to extort funds. As the Summoner and the Devil travel together exchanging information about their best fraudulent methods, they pass a man cursing his horse, cart, and hay to eternal damnation; however, because the man does not truly mean what he says, the Devil is unable to take action. Later the Summoner tries to con an innocent woman by claiming that she has committed adultery, which must be reported to the archdeacon. The woman says that she wishes the Summoner was in hell, and because she means what she says, the Devil happily sends the Summoner to eternal damnation.

SELECTED BIBLIOGRAPHY

Bush, Douglas. *English Poetry.* New York: Oxford University Press, 1963; Garbáty, Thomas J. *Medieval English Literature.* Toronto: Heath, 1984; Kamowski, William. "The Sinner against the Scoundrels: The Ills of Doctrine and 'Shrift' in the Wife of Bath's, Friar's, and Summoner's Narratives." *Religion and Literature* 25:1 (Spring 1993), 1-18; Lambdin, Laura C. and Robert T. Lambdin, eds. *Chaucer's Pilgrims: An Historical Guide to the Pilgrims in the "Canterbury Tales".* Westport, CT: Greenwood Press, 1996; Miller, Clarence H. "The Devil's Bow and Arrows: Another Clue to the Identity of the Yeoman in Chaucer's 'Friar's Tale.'" *Chaucer Review* 30:2 (1995), 211-14; Salter, Elizabeth. *Fourteenth Century English Poetry.* Oxford: Clarendon Press, 1983; Thiel, Gayle. "Chaucer's Friar and Saint Hubert: What's in a Name?" *Parergon* 10:1 (June 1992), 95-101.

Laura Cooner Lambdin

FROISSART, JEAN (c. 1337-c. 1404). Jean Froissart was born in Valenciennes in Hainault in the 1330s and established connections with the English court early in his life; he may have been schooled at the court. He was one of a growing number of secular clerks, in the service of courts or patrons, who began writing *chronicles during the fourteenth century. He had at least four patrons during his life. He served at an early age as a clerk in the court of Queen Philippa of England and wrote the first version of his *Chroniques* for her. His *Chroniques* deals primarily with the reign of *Edward III and the events of the *Hundred Years' War up until 1400. Froissart was well-traveled, especially in England, and used his experiences with the different geographics and peoples to enhance the liveliness of his history. His *Chroniques* is not always accurate and often strives more to capture the ideal chivalric episode than a factual recounting of events. He rewrote and rededicated his work to different patrons and his attitude toward the English and the French changed over time--from favoring the English to favoring the French. His switch from patrons of British sympathies to ones of French sympathies may account for some of his alterations. He relied heavily on Jean Le Bels' *Chroniques* for the years it covers (1329-61), but at times he also relied on what he heard, sometimes from firsthand observers, or what he observed for himself to complete the years 1361-1400. In addition to history, Froissart wrote poetry and *Meliador*, a chivalric *romance set in Scotland.

SELECTED BIBLIOGRAPHY

Bennett, Philip E. "The Mirage of Fiction: Narration, Narrator, and the Narratee in Froissart's Lyrica-Narrative *Dits*." *Modern Language Review* 86:2 (April 1991), 285-97; Brandt, William J. *The Shape of Medieval History.* New Haven: Yale University Press, 1966; Figg, Kristen Mossler. "Critiquing Courtly Convention: Jean Froissart's Playful Lyric Persona." *French Studies* 48:2 (April 1994), 129-42; Gransden, Antonia.

Historical Writing in England II: c. 1307 to Early Sixteenth Century. Ithaca: Cornell University Press, 1982; Palmer, J. J. N., ed. *Froissart: Historian.* Totowa, NJ: Rowman and Littlefield, 1981; Smalley, Beryl. *Historians in the Middle Ages.* New York: Scribner's, 1974.

Richard McDonald

G

GAMELYN, TALE OF, THE. A metrical *romance, *The Tale of Gamelyn* is also referred to as *The Cook's Tale of Gamelyn* because the work was erroneously attributed to Geoffrey *Chaucer and is found in a number of manuscripts of the *Canterbury Tales. In *The Tale of Gamelyn* Gamelyn is the youngest of three brothers and is abused by his siblings. Their father leaves his heirs his property in equal shares, but the eldest robs Gamelyn of his share. After a series of reversals, Gamelyn proves his tenacity by defeating the court wrestler and fleeing to the forest. Thus Gamelyn is perhaps the ultimate source for Orlando and Oliver in William Shakespeare's *As You Like It.* In the forest Gamelyn becomes the head of a band of outlaws. The second brother tries to help him, but is imprisoned by the eldest. Gamelyn returns to ultimately overthrow the wicked brother, who is now sheriff, along with his cohorts, a dishonest judge and jury.

SELECTED BIBLIOGRAPHY

Hoffman, Dean A. "'After Bale Cometh Boote': Narrative Symmetry in the *Tale of Gamelyn.*" *Studia Neophilologica* 60:2 (1988), 159-66; Kauper, Richard W. "A Historian's Reading of *The Tale of Gamelyn.*" *Medium Ævum* 52:1 (1983), 51-62; Lynch, Andrew. "'Now, Fye on Youre Wepynge!': Tears in Medieval English Romances." *Parergon* 9:1 (June 1991), 43-62; Swanton, Michael. "'A Ram and a Ring': Gamelyn 172 et Seq." *English Language Notes* 20:3-4 (March-June 1983), 8-10.

Robert T. Lambdin

GAWAIN (PEARL) POET, THE (fl. 1360-1400). Four alliterative poems, all found in a single manuscript in the Cotton collection of the British Museum are ascribed to the West Midlands writer known as the *Gawain (Pearl)* Poet. They have been named *Pearl, Purity* (or *Cleanness*), *Patience,* and *Sir Gawain and the Green Knight.* This poet has also been accredited with a fifth poem, *St. Erkenwald,* which is not found in the Cotton collection.

The greatest works in the manuscript, *Sir Gawain* and *Pearl,* are remarkable as metrical achievements. Each stanza of *Sir Gawain and the Green Knight* consists of two parts. The first part has an irregular number of four-stress, unrhymed, alliterative long lines; the second part has five short lines, cross-rhyming *ababa* in the bob and wheel meter. *Pearl* is even more intricate metrically. The poem contains 101 stanzas in 20 groups; 19 groups contain 5 stanzas and one group contains 6. The 5 stanzas in a particular group all end with the same word. This word also appears in the first half-line of each stanza in the group, linking the 5 stanzas together. This word is also a rhyme word.

Purity, a verse homily, draws upon a wealth of biblical allusions to make its point that no one can approach the Divine Presence with an unclean body or soul. *Patience* retells the story of impatient Jonah and shows how one should not react to changes in human fortune. *St. Erkenwald* recounts the legend of the bishop of the East Saxons who secured salvation for a righteous heathen judge (who was dead) by weeping over his corpse. Although scholars have made numerous attempts to identify the artist and to reconstruct his or her personality or background, the results remain inconclusive.

SELECTED BIBLIOGRAPHY

Barron, W.R.J. "Chrétien and the 'Gawain' Poet: Master and Pupil or Twin Temperaments?" In *The Legacy of Chrétien de Troyes*. Norris Lacy, ed. Amsterdam: Rodopi, 1988. 255-84; Blanch, Robert J. "Supplement to the 'Gawain' Poet: An Annotated Bibliography, 1978-1985." *Chaucer Review* 25:4 (1991), 363-86; Faley, Michael. "The 'Gawain' Poet: An Annotated Bibliography, 1978-85." *Chaucer Review* 23:3 (1989), 251-82; Kowalik, Barbara. "Traces of Romance: Textual Poetics in the Non-Romance Work Ascribed to the 'Gawain' Poet." In *From Medieval to Medievalism*. John Simons, ed. New York: St. Martins Press, 1992. 41-53; Stanbury, Sarah. *Seeing the "Gawain" Poet: Description and the Act of Perception*. Philadelphia: University of Pennsylvania Press, 1991.

Rebecca Chalmers

GENEALOGY OF THE GENTILE GODS, THE (1360?-1371). A massive work by Giovanni *Boccaccio, *The Genealogy of the Gentile Gods* celebrates the pagan and classical heritage so treasured by the humanists of fourteenth-century Europe. Written over many years, this text spans Boccaccio's lifetime and was perhaps already begun by the time Boccaccio returned to Florence in 1341. As the Florentine writer's interest in humanism expanded under the influence of *Petrarch, the *Genealogy* came to represent a kind of literary *summa* of materials available for literary invention during the period. This Latin text may also represent a recursive shift in seriousness by Boccaccio from the secular and erotic pleasures he celebrated in his vernacular poetry to the moral and religious concerns of a literary philosopher. The work remains, though, in Boccaccio's view at least, the most important of his literary accomplishments.

The *Genealogy* is encyclopedic in its scope and ambition. It is comprised of fifteen books, each treating a family of important gods and goddesses, framed by a genealogical tree. Also included here, according to Romano's catalog, are no fewer than 175 authors ranging from classical figures such as Homer, Virgil, and Ovid to contemporary ones, including Petrarch and *Dante. Boccaccio's great love of reading, his experiences at libraries in both Florence and Naples, his studies of Greek with Leontius Pilatus, and his interest in vernacular culture all converge in this handbook to literature and literary theory. Central to the compositional inspiration for this text is Boccaccio's avid desire to share with a growing reading public the sources and materials that would allow for the understanding of the complex allegorical and mythographical tradition that informs medieval Europe's literary culture. His exegetical explanations, perhaps inspired by his auto-exegesis in the *Teseida*, are rich and varied. Boccaccio, moreover, does not limit his allegorical interpretation to the purely religious, but includes a keen sense of the importance of history in his explications.

The final two books of the *Genealogy* have received the greatest attention from scholars, although a complete English translation is now under way. Book 14 is an elaborate defense of poetry that engages directly and energetically the polemical debates raging in Florence and elsewhere during this period. Briefly, that polemic centered on the notion that poetry was a distraction, a waste of time and energy that seduced learned men from religious study. Following Petrarch and perhaps departing from an earlier position, Boccaccio argues that poetry is a noble and important endeavor, requiring great knowledge, moral authority, and skill.

Specifically, it is lawyers and hypocrites who come under fire; Boccaccio characterizes them as ignorant, either, in the case of the former, because the writing of poetry does not lead to wealth, or, in the case of the latter, because they can only understand narrative in a prurient or lewd way. Ultimately, like Petrarch, and Dante before him, Boccaccio argues that poetry has its inventive roots in divine inspiration and therefore must be accounted as a great good. Underscored throughout his argument in defense of poetry is his definition of the veil of metaphor, or the integumentum, which crystallizes in the notion that the presence of the divine can only be discerned by understanding how spiritual truth is concealed within the literal.

Book 15 is notable in that it contains some more reliable biography than Boccaccio had allowed us to consider in some of his earlier works, including *Filocolo*, *Filostrato*, and *Teseida*. In chapter 6 of Book 15, Boccaccio acknowledges his own poetic and literary inspirations. In addition to Leontius Pilatus, his teacher of Greek, he notes the importance of Dante, Petrarch, and Paolo of Perugia. Many scholars have noted that the final chapter of this work exploits a more intimate and personal style than any of Boccaccio's other works. The compendium, which Boccaccio allegedly continued to revise until his death in 1374, represents an extremely profound accomplishment that allows its readers a glimpse not only of the wide erudition of this often maligned poet, but an insight into his great love and devotion for his subject.

SELECTED BIBLIOGRAPHY

Bergin, Thomas. *Boccaccio*. New York: Viking Press, 1981; Branca, Vittore. *Boccaccio: The Man and His Works*. Richard Monges, trans. and Dennis McAuliffe, ed. New York: New York University Press, 1976; Hill, Alan G. "Wordsworth, Boccaccio, and the Pagan Gods of Antiquity." *Review of English Studies* 45:177 (February 1994), 26-41; Hyde, Thomas. "Boccaccio: The Genealogies of Myth." *Publications of the Modern Language Association* 100:5 (October 1985), 737-45; Osgood, Charles, trans. *Boccaccio on Poetry*. Princeton: Princeton University Press, 1930; Roman, Vincenzo, ed. *Genealogie deorum gentilium libri*. 2 vols. Bari: Laterza, 1951; Wilkins, Ernest H. *A History of Italian Literature*. Rev. ed. Cambridge: Harvard University Press, 1974.

Theresa Kennedy

"GENERAL PROLOGUE, THE." Geoffrey *Chaucer began his *Canterbury Tales* (c. 1387-1400) with an extremely helpful poetic description of each of the pilgrims traveling together on horseback to the shrine of Thomas *Becket at Canterbury Cathedral, a popular springtime pilgrimage during this period. It is this catalog of characters that is referred to as "The General Prologue." This section of the text contains most of the physical descriptions that we have of many of the pilgrims. We are told that it is April and the narrator joins twenty-nine other pilgrims, each representing a different class or vocation so as to present a microcosm of medieval England. It is also in "The General Prologue" that the host of the Tabard Inn from whence the pilgrims depart, Harry Bailley, determines that each pilgrim will tell his companions two tales along the journey to Canterbury and two more on the return trip. After they return to the Inn, the best storyteller will receive a free dinner. The *Canterbury Tales* is an unfinished masterpiece with Chaucer completing only twenty-four of the tales.

SELECTED BIBLIOGRAPHY

Andrew, Malcolm. "Context and Judgement in the 'General Prologue.'" *Chaucer Review* 23:4 (1989), 316-337; Andrew, Malcolm, ed., *et al*. *The Canterbury Tales: 'The General Prologue.'* Norman: University of Oklahoma Press, 1993; Berry, Craig A. "Borrowed Armor/Free Grace: The Quest for Authority in *The Faerie Queen* and Chaucer's 'Tale of Sir Thopas.'" *Studies in Philology* 91:2 (Spring 1994), 136-66; Bush, Douglas. *English Poetry*. New York: Oxford University Press, 1963; Garbáty, Thomas J. *Medieval English Literature*. Toronto: Heath, 1984; Salter, Elizabeth. *Fourteenth Century English Poetry*. Oxford: Clarendon Press, 1983.

Laura Cooner Lambdin

GENESIS. Found in the *Junius manuscript, *Genesis* is an Old English poem of nearly three thousand lines that was originally erroneously attributed to *Cædmon. The poem contains an interpolated section, often referred to as "Genesis B," that encompasses lines 235-851. These lines derive from a Saxon original.

Written vividly, this section concerns the Fall of the Angels. Their battle with God is highly detailed and graphic. Henry Sweet, in his *Anglo-Saxon Reader,* entitled this excerpt that some believe is the source for Milton's *Paradise Lost.*

SELECTED BIBLIOGRAPHY

Derolez, R. "'Genesis': Old Saxon and Old English." *English Studies* 76:5 (September 1995), 409-23; Orchard, Andy. "Conspicuous Heroism: Abraham, Prudentius, and the Old English Verse 'Genesis.'" In *Heroes and Heroines in Medieval English Literature.* Leo Carruthers, ed. Cambridge: Brewer, 1994. 45-58; Sweet, Henry, ed. *Anglo-Saxon Reader.* Oxford: Oxford University Press, 1988.

Robert T. Lambdin

GENESIS AND EXODUS. A mid-thirteenth-century poem, the Middle English *Genesis and Exodus* is based upon Petrus Comestor's *Historica Scholastica.* It compares unfavorably with works from the time of *Cædmon. The themes in the poem are concerned not only with the books from the Bible named in the title, but also with Numbers and Deuteronomy. The poem relates scriptural history from the Creation to the Garden of Eden and Fall from Paradise to the life and death of Moses. However, the text includes only the parts of the Scriptures that are directed toward a plan of salvation.

SELECTED BIBLIOGRAPHY

Iyeiri, Yoko "The Middle English 'Genesis and Exodus', Line 3324." *Notes and Queries* 39(237):3 (September 1992), 275-76; Lindstrom, Bengt. "Notes on the Middle English 'Genesis and Exodus.'" *Neuphilologische Mitteilungen* 96:1 (1995), 67-79; Minkova, Donka. "Verse Structure in the Middle English 'Genesis and Exodus.'" *Journal of English and Germanic Philology* 91:2 (Apr 1992), 157-78.

Robert T. Lambdin

GENGHIS KHAN (1162-1227), Mongol emperor. Convinced that it was heaven's will that he unite the world by force, Genghis Khan, the first great leader of the Mongols almost single-handedly launched an empire. Forging a powerful army from the nomad tribes of his region, Genghis first led it against the urban societies south of the Gobi Desert. After a protracted campaign against the Empire of the Jins, he turned his attention to the west. Ghengis was noted for his brutality; the worst of his terrible wrath was spent against the Khwarizm Moslems of central Asia. A string of their great cities was left in ruins, their inhabitants were slaughtered, their wealth was plundered, and their artisans were transported across Asia to serve the empire. When Genghis turned southward toward India, his generals Jebe and Subedei undertook an expedition unrivaled since the days of Alexander the Great. Circling the Caspian Sea, they left a trail of dead Georgians, Russians, Turks, and others. Far to the rear of this campaign, in Tangut, there was an uprising against the empire. Genghis returned east to Xi Xia, where he died near the capital in 1227, but not before ordering his generals to take no prisoners!

SELECTED BIBLIOGRAPHY

Kitagawa, Swiichi. "Middle Eastern Literature on the Divine Kingship of Chingis Khan." *Bulletin of the Institute for the Study of North Eurasian Cultures* 16 (1984), 43-67; Moses, Larry. "Triplicated Triplets: The Number Nine in the Secret History of the Mongols." *Asian Folklore Studies* 45:2 (1986), 287-94; Ratchnevsky, Paul. *Genghis Khan: His Life and Legacy*. Oxford: Blackwell, 1992.

R. Churchill Curtis

GEOFFREY DE VINSAUF (fl. c. 1200). Perhaps the most celebrated prose writer of his day, Geoffrey of Vinsauf was an expert on rhetoric, as evidenced by his *Nova Poetria* and *Summa de Coloribus Rhetoricis*. Geoffrey *Chaucer, in "The *Nun's Priest's Tale," laments his lack of Geoffrey de Vinsauf's skill to address Chaunticleer's dilemma. He specifically cites de Vinsauf's *Nova Poetria*, a work concerned with the Friday in 1199 when *Richard I died. As important as de Vinsauf's works were in the Middle Ages, today he is gaining some favor, and his works are becoming important in the study of medieval poetic aesthetics.

SELECTED BIBLIOGRAPHY

Burnley, J. D. "Chaucer, Usk, and Geoffrey of Vinsauf." *Neophilologus* 69:2 (Apr 1985), 284-93; Drabble, Margaret. *The Oxford Companion to English Literature*. 5th ed. Oxford: Oxford University Press, 1985; Jordan, Robert M. "Todorov, Vinsauf, and Chaucerian Textuality." *Studies in the Age of Chaucer* 2 (1986), 51-57.

Robert T. Lambdin

GEOFFREY OF MONMOUTH (1084-1154). Geoffrey of Monmouth was born in 1084 to a Welsh or Briton family living in Monmouth. There is relatively little known for sure about Monmouth's life, but he probably taught in Oxford--before the founding of the university--and served as bishop of St Asaphs in 1152. Geoffrey shares the twelfth century with three other well-known historians, all of whom are respected for their more factual contributions to British history: *Orderic Vitalis, *William of Malmesbury and *Henry of Huntingdon. Geoffrey's *Historia Regum Brittaniae (History of the Kings of Britain) is a lively story of the heroes and rulers of England from the twelfth century B. C. to the seventh century a.d., written in Latin. Indrikis Sterns found that although Geoffrey's History contains few historically useful facts, it does show the growing nationalism of the British people in its unparalleled popularity with its contemporary audience.

Geoffrey seems to seek out fantastical stories, legends, and events from numerous sources, including sources that have real historical value--*Bede, William of Malmesbury and Henry of Huntingdon. He claims to be working from a very old *Anglo-Saxon book that was lent to him, but many historians doubt the existence of such a book and see Geoffrey's work as one of a creative imagination bringing together the fantastical elements of numerous sources with a level of elaboration they had not yet received. Geoffrey offers the first known story of King Lear, and he treats the Brutus, Arthur and Grail stories (see **Arthurian Legend**) with a level of description surpassing what had come before. He undoubtedly used oral tradition to generate some of his stories or to add additional details to existing stories. Although he sometimes refers to his sources, often he does not. When he does, in some instances, he has been shown to be misreading his source or merely using the source's name to add weight to a story of his own construction.

Around two hundred manuscripts of The History of the Kings of Britain exist and some fifty of them date from the twelfth century. Although he may merely be an early *romance writer masquerading as a historian, as Antonia Gransden contended, Geoffrey's work captured the imagination and budding patriotism of his public and promised that the people of Britain were special. His History inspired numerous romance writers including Wace who wrote the Roman de Brut around 1155. Wace's poetic, free translation of Geoffrey's work into *Anglo-Norman elaborates on many parts of the Arthur story which Geoffrey merely mentions. Wace's work then influenced *Layamon to write an extended translation in his 1190 Brut in Middle English *alliterative verse. *Chrétien de Troyes, the premiere twelfth-century romance writer, was also influenced by Geoffrey's History.

SELECTED BIBLIOGRAPHY

Brandt, William J. The Shape of Medieval History. New Haven: Yale University Press, 1966; Curley, Michael J. Geoffrey of Monmouth. New York: Twayne, 1994; Geoffrey of Monmouth. The History of the Kings of Britain. Lewis Thorpe, Trans. Baltimore: Penguin, 1966; Gransden, Antonia. Historical Writing in England c. 550 to c. 1307. Ithaca: Cornell University Press, 1974; Smalley, Beryl. Historians in the Middle Ages.

New York: Scribner's, 1974; Sterns, Indrikis. *The Greater Medieval Historians: An Interpretation and a Bibliography.* Lanham, MD: University Press of America, 1980.

Richard McDonald

GEOFFREY OF VILLEHARDOUIN (c. 1150-c. 1213). The writer Geoffrey of Villehardouin was one of the leading officers of the Fourth *Crusade and so his *chronicle provides a unique insight into the decision making and discrepancies that arose over the crusade's deviation from its intended purpose and target. His work *La Conquete de Constantinople* (The Conquest of Constantinople) is both Geoffrey's memoirs and an explanation of the diverting of the crusade from Jerusalem to Constantinople.

Villehardouin was born in the early 1150s and was the son of a French nobleman of Champaign. In 1185 Geoffrey was able to secure--through his family ties, the position of marshal of Champagne--a job in which he served as his lord's deputy in war and administrative affairs. In addition to detailed descriptions of the battles of the Fourth Crusade, Villehardouin shares eyewitness information and factual accounts of the decision process that led to the diverting of the crusade from the Holy Land.

Geoffrey is generally accepted as a trustworthy narrator with regard to the information he describes, but his biases are apparent in what he chooses not to include. He generally tries to present the crusade and the crusaders in a favorable light. He is merciless in his criticism of any who deserted the crusade after its diversion, but he is also willing to let the events speak for themselves-- regardless of his own interests. After the death of the crusade leader, Marquis Boniface II, in 1207, Villehardouin ends his chronicle.

Villehardouin's chronicle provided audiences with exciting action and tales of distant places and peoples. Crusade stories of all kinds fascinated Western audiences because they presented the mostly forbidden world of pagan ideas and customs.

SELECTED BIBLIOGRAPHY

Brandt, William J. *The Shape of Medieval History.* New Haven: Yale University Press, 1966; Shaw, M.R.B. *Chronicles of the Crusades: Joinville and Villehardouin.* Baltimore: Penguin, 1963; Smalley, Beryl. *Historians in the Middle Ages.* New York: Scribner's, 1974; Sterns, Indrikis. *The Greater Medieval Historians: An Interpretation and a Bibliography.* Lanham, MD: University Press of America, 1980.

Richard McDonald

GERMAN LITERATURE. It can be asserted that German literature started around 750 when the formation of a continuous writing in a German language began. As with the literature of many other European countries, the seeds of German writing lie in the introduction of Christianity. In Germany, this meant the Roman paganistic culture was supplanted by Christian writing that created a literary period around 850 known as "Old High German. " From the war chants and battle cries of the pagan culture evolved the beginnings of German writings that are closely associated with the introduction of the monasteries because it was clerics who copied oral histories into manuscripts.

The poems of this early period are primarily alliterative songs of praise and glory. The first known example is the *Wessobrunn Prayer*, a work from Bavaria that was written down in the ninth century. The majority of the prayer is in prose, but the beginning of the work is preceded by a few lines of *alliterative verse concerning the Creation. Oddly, these lines are very similar to a poetic *edda. This shows that the literature of the Germans begins as an olio, influenced by the Norse sources of the North and the Latin of the South. It is assumed that the Christian elements were added to the pagan Norse poem in an attempt to make the new teaching more understandable and acceptable by cloaking it in a traditional poetic form. This same technique is found in several other Old High German poems, most notably the *Muspilli* (which deals with the Last Judgment) and the *Hêliand* (also known as the "Savior").

The first German poet known by name was a northern monk, Otfid of Weissenburg. His works are dogmatic, resembling in theme previous works such as the *Hêliand.* Otfid also translated the Gospels into the uncultivated and barbarous language of German. His works are divided into short sections meant to be read aloud. Very selective in his themes, Otfid abandoned the alliterative style of the early German poets in favor of end-rhyming verses. Indeed, his compositions led to the end of alliterative verse in German; after his time no more alliterative poems are found in the literature of his country.

This "Otfidian Revolution" of the ninth century encouraged the development of German prose and also a growing canon of Latin literature. As was typical of the literatures of other countries in the medieval times, most of the work initially was religious in theme. Oddly, German religious literature did not flourish as a result of the success of Otfid's work, but there are numerous extant examples that demonstrate his influence. These anonymous works include a short Bavarian poem on St. Peter, some prayers, and an odd poem on *Christ and the Woman of Samaria*, which seems to be an adaptation of one of Otfid's works. At the end of the ninth century the panegyric *Ludwigslied* was composed, possibly by a cleric interested in war and history. This work concerns Louis III, the West Frankish king who defeated the Normans at Saucourt in 881. The poem is easy to date, for Louis died exactly one year after this great victory, and he is referred to as living in the poem. The work shows the power of the Carolingian empire during this time. It is believed that this was an attempt by the French to spread their fame to Germany; also, its homiletic tones make this work distinctly Christian. Thus it could be that the

Ludwigslied, much like the English *Beowulf*, is an olio of techniques. It links the old German panegyric poems to a warrior prince with Christian concerns.

The literature of Germany then became almost only prose. One of the most popular works of the tenth century was a rendering of the texts of *Isidore of Seville, whose writings were frequently translated throughout Europe from the Latin in which he originally composed them. Here Latin is nicely translated into the vernacular with few mistakes. This translation established the foundation for a wide range of religious prose tracts that were extremely popular in Germany from the tenth century to the times of the *Crusades (1096-1270). While composition seems to have declined in the tenth century, the monasteries at least maintained the writing tradition.

Perhaps the greatest work to come from the Old High German period is the *Walterious Manufortis*, a German heroic tale composed in Latin around 930. The work is based upon oral sources and retells the story of Walter of Aquitaine and his lover, Hildegund, who are reared as hostages at the court of Atli the Hun. They devise a plan to escape to Walter's homeland. After a series of traumatic adventures the couple make their way to Aquitaine, where they live and rule together for thirty years.

Also, around the tenth century, *beast fables become very popular, such as the *Ecbasis cuiusdam captivi per tropologian*. In the *Ecbasis* a young calf who has escaped from its stall is lured into a wolf's den. The wolf plans to eat it the next day. In the interim the wolf tells his friends the otter and the hedgehog a story. Because the wolf has waited, a search party has time to find and rescue the calf. The moral of the story is the danger of trying to escape from the strict discipline of monastic life into a worldly atmosphere.

In drama, early writers such as Terence became favorites of the people. The stricter members of the clergy wanted to eliminate the worldly literature and replace it with works that were more dogmatic. They felt that the growing obsession with classical writing was detrimental to Christian morality, so these religious writers began composing plays based upon those of ancient writers but replacing the ancient ideas with Christian themes including the praise and defense of virginity. *Hrotsvitha of Gandersheim (c.1100) composed at least six Latin comedies based upon Terence. While these plays were not meant to be performed, they do contain clear plots, rapid movement, and stichomythic dialogue. It is Hrotsvitha whose adaptations of Latin legends become the basis for the development of the Faust legend.

At the close of the Old High German period Notker III, or Teutonicus (d. 1022), produced his translations of the *trivium and the *quadrivium, the *liberal arts that made up the core of the medieval school curriculum. Notker also translated the *Consolation of Philosophy* of *Boethius, as well as *Aristotle's *Categories* and *Hermeneutics*. His translations are clear and idiomatic, for Notker was very interested in the problems of language and developed a system of orthography through which he could translate even the most subtle of linguistic differences. Through his efforts the seven liberal arts became very valuable because of the bearing that they had on theology.

With the onset of the eleventh century great political stirrings rumbled throughout Europe. The First *Crusade was launched in 1096. This growing unquiet led to a small movement of German ascetic poets. Among the best of these was Heinrich von Melk, who was responsible for the first satire in German literature. His *Von des tôdes gehugede* or *Memento Mori* was probably composed around 1150-60. In it he attacked the growing knightly class, which was beginning to play a leading role in society. He bluntly accused all classes of society of leading sinful lives. Even priests were guilty of the sin of "simony" or performing sacred rituals only for riches. His grim perspective of the society powerfully favored the old monastic system over the growing militaristic and courtly regimes.

Again, New Testament themes were also prevalent. Frau Ava, the first known female author of German poetry, composed *Leben Jesu*. At this remarkable work's conclusion, Frau Ava offered that she had two sons. Both became priests and while one had died young, they both had taught her the "sense" of their theology. It appears that Ava took their teachings to heart, for she became a pious recluse who died in 1127. Her style was simple and warm, contrasting directly with the stark learned expositions of her day. It seems as though her writing widely encouraged somewhat kinder poems among her countrymen. Also growing at this time was the cult of Mary, which espoused the Blessed Mother's virtues as a loving and protective figure to whom anyone could apply for intercession in times of need. This movement led to the softening emotional development reflected in works of the twelfth century.

Around 1150 German literature underwent another change. The homiletic and hagiographic continued, as evidenced by the *Kaiserchronik* (c. 1135), a 17,000-line account of secular history. However, this work differed from the biblical tales of instruction that had flourished; indeed, it established the basis for the German *chronicles. This was an important time because the chroniclers did not condemn the growing *chivalric movement. Authors were more prone to be members of the aristocracy than the church. Thus scorn for the peasants became a common theme. Even *courtly love made a brief appearance with no signs of condemnation. Indeed, the anonymous *Kaiserchronik* contains the episode of Tarquin and Lucretia, which posits the same theme found in Geoffrey *Chaucer's Patient Griselda in "The *Clerk's Tale." The source seems to have been a Latin chronicle that systematically expanded to include anecdotes from varied sources. While the work is elegant, which ensured that the chronicle would have a lasting popularity, there is still no evidence of original compositions.

Even the other most popular work from this time, the *Alexanderlied*, composed by Konrad, a priest, was derived from a French source, the work of a Trier priest named Lamprecht. This is the first extant translation of a French work into German; the theme is a testimony of the Crusades. The heroes of the poem are French; they are Christian warriors. But what is important here is that they do not exemplify French patriotism. Instead, the author has integrated into the text the crusading spirit, and it is this that appealed to lay readers of Germany. For example, in the work Charles, perhaps the brother of Pope Leo, becomes a symbol of God on Earth. His job is to extend the boundaries of Christendom by either converting or exterminating the unbelievers. Thus the work becomes an allegory of the ongoing duel between the kingdoms of God and the devil.

To this picture of Charles the author added other intriguing traits. He is grim to his enemies and kind to the poor. His faith in God makes him merciful to evil, for he is a just man. Thus he is the ideal ruler. When Charles prays to God to free Spain from the heathen Saracens, an angel appears to him and tells Charles that he has been assigned the task of freeing Spain. Charles calls for his twelve paladins and assures them that they will receive the heavenly crown of martyrdom if they join him. Konrad's work contains no psychological development or individualism. He cuts much of the French original's excesses, such as protracted battle scenes, striving instead for a type of harmonious balance. It is this brazen type of spiritual conqueror who will give way to the overt social class heroes of the Middle High German period.

The literature of the Middle High German age (c. 1175-1300) is almost solely a reflection of the class-crazed order of chivalry. The works of this era peak around 1200 when chivalry was at its apex throughout Europe. Its rapid decline parallels the actual decline of knights themselves. While not all of the great authors of this period were actually knights, their works are soaked in the ideals of the chivalric code and were composed for an audience of people who obviously idealized these sorts of themes.

This change from secular to courtly is a reflection of what was occurring politically throughout Germany. The Holy Roman Empire was at its peak under Frederick I, whose reign lasted from 1152 to 1190. The power Frederick gained was maintained by his barbarous son, Henry VI, whose short reign ended in 1197. The next fifty years were tumultuous as varying factions fought for the power of the throne.

Yet during this time the literature grew into what many consider the Classical Age of medieval German literature. This period is usually designated by two words: courtly and chivalric. The literary production had become centered around the courts; thus the content was usually chivalric, reflecting the deeds of the knights. In Frederick's court of Hohenstaufen the knights formed a special class of their own. For over a century they dominated the society. By doing so, they created a closed society that included the establishment of new canons of taste and behavior. The chivalric ideal was perfect for this group. Its requirements, including a combination of elegance, warrior skills, and fitness, helped to create some fascinating literature.

The order of chivalry rose from the military needs of a feudal society. For centuries the army had been marked by its elite, the heavy cavalry. This was a special group because such a corps was expensive to equip; its members were usually drawn from the upper classes. Therefore, the corps was made up mainly of landed gentry and richer peasants. Given the socio-economic stature of these individuals, it is only natural that they quickly banded together. To be selected for such elite training became an honor, and intricate rites and initiations followed a due course of training.

The order of chivalry developed during the wars of Frederick I, perhaps beginning in 1184 when he knighted his two sons in an elaborate ceremony that attracted visitors from all over Europe. Too, other continental influences, such as the works from France and the Crusades, served to internationalize chivalry. This was particularly true during the Second Crusade (1147-49), in which the Germans played a leading role. In addition to the glory gained from this great religious endeavor, knights' statures were elevated because tournaments and festivals became popular forms of recreation. As a result, knights were perceived as almost supernatural in the eyes of the general populace. Thus the knights of Germany had more in common with their French counterparts than they did with the majority of their own countrymen.

This new culture developed its own set of values, which were the perfect tools for authors to use when writing of these glamorous figures. The ideas of chivalry became more and more in line with Christianity, due in part to the influence of the Crusades. However, this still left the knight with the problem of having to deal with *got und der welt gevalen*--literally, having to reconcile the pleasing of God with the pleasing of the world. The essence of courtly behavior became *zuht*, or good breeding and manners, traits that were outwardly expressed by *mâze*, or self-restraint. Honor, or *êre* was the sum of all the knightly virtues. Thus the most honorable of the knights were those who were held in high public opinion. However, the honor and all else worth having could be achieved only by strenuous striving for the unreachable. Thus the ideal became those knights who led an active life for a cause without shunning any types of danger. This led to a type of discipline that became harder and harder to achieve.

This striving for a measured and an ordered way of life provided knights with an excellent means of self-education; it became a mixture of a kind of Christian ideal with stoic thoughts. Therefore, the church could hardly argue with such a philosophy. But this knightly group became more arrogant and pompous, a natural progression given the basis of the philosophy. With the advent and inclusion of courtly love, the stricter members of the church found this movement to be growing closer to the same type of *superbia* through which Lucifer fell from grace. Thus the church leaders began to raise objections, the same kind of disapproval that inevitably led to the dissolution of the courtly movement throughout the Continent.

But clerics could do little to stem the popularity of this genre, so the literature of this period belongs for the most part to the courts. Court epics concerning knights and their deeds were immensely popular. Among the most widely found works were those concerned with the *Arthurian legend. In 1214 Ulrich von Zatzikhoven composed *Lanzelot*, which gains its fame not because of its construction, but because it is the first extant German poem of this genre. It contains some elements found in *Chrétien de Troyes's *Lancelot*, but *Lanzelot* simply is not a very good poem.

The court epic found its niche in the compositions of Gottfried von Strassburg, whose *Tristan* displays a good knowledge of theology and an uncanny grasp of French. His rendition of *Tristan* is derived from many versions of the story, although he relied heavily on Thomas de Bretagne, a Norman. The success of this work resulted in a widespread appreciation of this topic, and the resulting Tristan romances are placed into two groups: the *minstrel version and the courtly version. Gottfried's version is a very didactic work. The author interweaves a great deal about medieval pedagogy and the medieval courtly code into his work. The ultimate conclusion, that of the theme of *got und der welt gevalen*, demonstrates that the act of pleasing the world must be in tandem with the ideals of Christianity. Thus the tragedy of *Tristan* lies in the incompatibility of honor with love--in both Christian and chivalric terms.

Perhaps because courtly love themes had been exhausted, during the thirteenth century there was a return to the production of a considerable body of literature that served religious and didactic purposes. As a result, two distinct kinds of writing flourished during this period: religious epics and compendiums of secular ethics and morals. Perhaps the best religious epic is the *Kindheit Jesu* (c. 1345), composed by Konrad von Fussesbrunnen, an Austrian knight. Konrad's work is a simple narration of the marriage of Mary and Joseph, the birth of Christ, and the flight to Egypt. The work continues to describe the childhood of Jesus. The poem is a religious work in the style of the courtly romance; the work served as an act of penance for Konrad's all-too-worldly life. As noted, poems dealing with the Virgin Mary were quite popular in Germany, and so the thirteenth and fourteenth centuries produced quite a few of these. Pleasant poems about Mary abound, including the *Marienleben of Wehrner*, composed around 1400. Also during this period *hagiography remained popular, particularly as a moralistic reaction to the growing number of courtly romances.

Perhaps the greatest known work from this period is the *Nibelungenlied*, an epic poem in four-line stanzas. It was composed sometime in the late twelfth or early thirteenth century, but the author and the dates remain unknown. While the influences of the poetic edda and *sagas are obvious, this is novel, for it is one of the first works to draw upon German legend, eliminating much of the Scandinavian myths and superstitions. For example, Siegfried, the hero, is the king of the Netherlands, a far cry from his role as a descendant of the god Odin in northern literature. This downsizing of his character makes him into a much more typical medieval romantic hero.

Siegfried sets out to woo the beautiful Kriemhild. Her three brothers, Burgundian kings, learn that Siegfried was the man who killed the Nibelung kings, taking their name, their treasure, and the famous "cape of darkness" that cloaks the wearer in invisibility. The kings also learn about Siegfried's strength. Reminiscent of the Achilles myth, Siegfried's skin is almost entirely invulnerable, except for a spot that was covered by a fallen leaf while he bathed in the blood of a dragon he had slain.

Siegfried and the three kings unite to fight the Saxons. He then agrees to help one of them, Gunther, as he woos Queen Brunhild of Iceland. Siegfried does this on the condition that he be allowed to marry Kriemhild. Brunhild has sworn that she will only marry the man who can best her in three competitions: tossing a spear, throwing a stone, and jumping. With Siegfried cloaked in invisibility and by his side, Gunther bests the woman, and a double marriage is performed. However, Brunhild is not convinced that Gunther could beat her; on their wedding night she ties him in a knot and hangs him on the wall. Siegfried is again forced to save the unfortunate Gunther. He cloaks himself and wrestles with Brunhild, taking from her a girdle and a ring that he gives to Kriemhild. The two women later meet and have a fierce argument outside a cathedral. Here Kriemhild proves, by displaying the ring and the girdle, that Brunhild had been duped.

At this point the *Nibelungenlied* again strays from its Scandinavian ancestor. Brunhild's role diminishes, and the role of Hagen becomes dominant. Perhaps made jealous by Siegfried's glory, Hagen tricks Kriemhild into revealing Siegfried's one vulnerable spot. He then arranges for a great hunting trip where he murders Siegfried. Hagen, in collusion with Kriemhild's brothers, then seizes the treasure hoard, one of Siegfried's wedding gifts to Kriemhild, and sinks the barge in the Rhine River. The widow, still grieving Siegfried's death, is proposed to by Atli, the king of the Huns, and she accepts on the condition that he take a role in her plan for vengeance. After the wedding they invite her brothers for a visit; with the help of Hildebrand and Dietrich of Bern, they attack the disloyal brothers. When Hagen, the last living Burgundian refuses to disclose the treasure's locale, Kriemhild kills him. Hildebrand is horrified that one woman could be so vengeful. He kills Kriemhild, leaving only Atli and Dietrich to lament the dead.

After the *Nibelungenlied*, one heroic epic of note is the *Kudrun*. This work is atypical of much of the literature of the time because it is a romantic and sentimental work; it can perhaps be considered more of a psychological novel than a heroic epic. The unknown author of this poem used many sources to create his work. In the *Kuduan* we find Oriental griffins, Scandinavian Valkyries, and many components of the *Nibelungenlied*. Yet this extravagant work seems to have been as immensely unpopular as the *Nibelungenlied* was popular. After this work came many other heroic epics, but by the fourteenth century literature of a markedly different character would prevail. The Classical period of German literature posited themes that would remain popular for some three centuries. The works progressed from the short courtly *lyric to the huge epic poems like the *Nibelungenlied* in a few short centuries. However, this age of idealism was to be replaced by an age of realism. The truth was that the world was rapidly leaving the glorified image of the knight behind. Thought as opposed to romance and battle was becoming more important to a civilized society.

The end of what can be described as medieval German literature again parallels a culture that was quickly growing out of a nebula shell. The thirteenth century had its knights, gentlemen in pursuit of courtly ideals and love. The fourteenth century was a time of citizens. With this shift came the impression of decline, perhaps an offshoot of the seeming loss of knightly values. It appears that this division occurred around 1350, a time that was marked by several events. In 1346 Charles IV ascended to the throne; by 1348 he established the university in Prague. Learning was at the forefront. However, it was the uncontrollable that brought about perhaps the most change. From 1348 to 1349 Germany, like most of Europe, was ravaged by the Black Plague. These developments led to a dismantling of the courtly tradition. With the demise of the chivalric ideals, the growth of citizenry became important. It was these changes that carried the Middle Ages into the Renaissance. In the fourteenth century this movement was extremely strong in Bohemia. Here, where the center of the empire was located for several years in Luxemburg, the court was bilingual. Gunpowder was invented, paper was much less expensive, and by the fifteenth century Gutenberg had invented the printing press.

The growing academic movement was highlighted by *Scholasticism, wherein the *schoolmen struggled to reconcile the relation between faith and knowledge. The works of Aristotle were translated from Greek to Arabic to Latin to German; scholars questioned the Christian elements found in this pagan writing. St. Thomas *Aquinas wrote most of his unfinished *Summa Theologica* which represents the apex of the Scholastic movement. Indeed, these mystics created quite a corpus of literature.

Yet the foundations of this movement were laid not by Aquinas but by his teacher, Albertus Magnus, who is considered the founder of the German professional tradition. Magnus taught for some fifty years; his principal accomplishment was translating the entire works of Aristotle known to Western scholars, thus making him one of the fathers of modern science. While he did not do much in the way of scientific experimentation, his keen sense of observation enabled him to make many original discoveries. This dialectic led to the problem of philosophy as it relates to religion. Natural science here at its roots was destined to grow so quickly that it would become its own discipline, completely different from theology.

Yet the importance of Albertus Magnus transcends his achievement; in a sense he becomes the personification of the shift from the medieval feudal society that glorifies the virtues of knights and lords to the more democratic culture that considers the rights of individuals to question their rulers and the hierarchy of the church. The old symbolic thinking gave way to a new consideration of phenomena. Instead of looking for the homiletic lessons of animals' traits, scientists began to discover how they function in order to understand and explain animals as living entities. Thus, under the tutelage of Albertus Magnus and his students, Germany was led out of the Middle Ages and into the Renaissance, both literarily and scientifically.

The literature of medieval Germany parallels much of the growth and development found in the compositions from other European countries. It is remarkable in as many ways as it is forgettable. The examination of the Germanic texts as they progress from the simplest of poems to the hagiographies and dogmatic writings of the clerics reveals a remarkable similarity to the growth of literature in the other countries of the Continent, such as Spain and France, as well as to the writing of England. It is only natural that these initial works were incorporated into the paganistic compositions that predate the growth of Christianity. As the feudal society grew, so too did the legends of the deeds of the valiant. The image of the damsel in distress is not the private property of the British and the French; it also belongs to the Germans and the Bavarians. Just as the rest of Europe outgrew the closed societies of the feudal lords and the Church, the writers of Germany demonstrated that they too had unanswerable questions about their place in the universe--and God's role in their lives. Ironically, the same horrible disease that obliterated much of the populace was responsible for the growth of thought and literature. After the Black Plague of the mid-fourteenth century, peasants became a more important part of civilization and realized that they could demand good wages for their crafts and skills. In this regard Germany, and the world, would never be the same again.

SELECTED BIBLIOGRAPHY

Campbell, Ian R. "Hagen's Shield Request--*Das Nibelungenlied*, 37th Aventiure." *Germanic Review* 71:1 (Winter 1996), 23-34; Claussen, Albrecht. "Love, Sex, and Marriage in Late Medieval German Verse Narratives, Lyric Poetry, and Prose Literature." *Orbis Litterarum* 49:2 (1994), 63-83; McConnell, Winder. "Repression and Denial in the *Nibelungenlied*." *Amsterdamer Beiträge zur Älteren Germanistik* 43-44 (1995), 363-74; Palmer, Craig B. "A Question of Manhood: Overcoming the Paternal Homocrotic in Gottfried's 'Tristan.'" *Monatshefte* 88:1 (Spring 1996), 17-30; Robertson, John George. *A History of German Literature*. 6th ed. Elmsford, NY: London House and Maxwell, 1970; Rushing, James A., Jr. "Matriarchy in the *Nibelungenlied*." *Germanic Notes and Reviews* 26:1 (Spring 1995), 8-12; Thomas, J. W. trans. "Tristan as a Monk." *Tristania* 16 (1995), 104-44; Westphal, Sarah. "Camilla: The Amazon Body in Medieval German Literature." *Exemplaria* 18:1 (Spring 1996), 231-58; Willaert, Frank. "'Havendas': Fourteenth Century Dancing Sons in the Rhine and Meuse Area." In *Medieval Dutch Literature in Its European Context*. Erik Kooper, ed. Cambridge: Cambridge University Press, 1994. 168-87.

Robert T. Lambdin and Laura Cooner Lambdin

GEST. The word "gest, " usually found only in the literary titles of medieval English works, meant that the tale was going to be one of war or adventure. This is seen in the fourteenth-century example, the *Gest Historiale of the Destruction of Troy*. "Gest" was probably borrowed from the Old French "geste" (see *Chanson de Geste*). Similarly, a Latin version of the word appears in the famous collection from about 1250, the **Gesta Romanorum* or *Deeds of the Romans*.

SELECTED BIBLIOGRAPHY

Anderson, Eric R. "Game and Reality in Medieval and Renaissance Outlaw Narratives." *Aethlon* 8:2 (Spring 1991), 73-88; Holman, C. Hugh, and William Harmon. *A Handbook to Literature*. 5th ed. New York: Macmillan, 1986; Ikegami, Masa. "The Language and the Date of 'A Geste of Robyn Hode.'" *Neophilolische Mitteilungen* 96:3 (1995), 271-81.

Robert T. Lambdin

GESTA ROMANORUM. The *Gesta Romanorum,* also known as the *Deeds of the Romans,* is an odd text that supplies simply a collection of miscellaneous works without any apparent order or framework. The edition was presumably arranged in England in the late thirteenth century; it was first printed in 1473. Due to its popularity, it was frequently reprinted, often in different versions that include anywhere from one hundred to two hundred different tales.

In the 165 or so extant manuscripts the episodes are loosely assigned to the reign of a Roman emperor. The work contains little real history. Instead, the stories, like the *allegories and *bestiaries, attach morals or "applications." These were primarily used by preachers or clergymen for sermon fodder, but the *Gesta* is not a religious work. The episodes come from a variety of sources.

The *Gesta Romanorum* was originally composed in Latin and then translated into French and English, as well as many other European languages. Authors such as Giovanni *Boccaccio, Geoffrey *Chaucer, Thomas *Hoccleve, and William Shakespeare frequently drew upon the *Gesta* for plot material.

SELECTED BIBLIOGRAPHY

Drabble, Margaret, ed. *The Oxford Companion to English Literature*. 5th ed. Oxford: Oxford University Press, 1985; McJannet, Linda. "*Gesta Romanorum:* Heroic Action and Stage Imagery in *Antony and Cleopatra*." *Shakespeare Bulletin* 11:1 (Winter 1993), 5-9.

Robert T. Lambdin

GEST OF ROBIN HOOD, A. Dating from at least the fifteenth century, whence comes the earliest extant manuscript of the *ballad, *A Gest of Robin Hood* was once thought to have been an amalgamation of several songs "stitched together." However, despite its remarkable length of over 1,800 lines, the ballad clearly possesses a cohesive story line, sufficient forward and backward references, and certain recurring motifs, all of which indicate otherwise. The *Gest* is typical of the yeoman songs in plot, characterization, and theme.

There are several stories interwoven in the *Gest*. The main plot deals with a knight who has been unfairly dispossessed by an unscrupulous abbot. The knight meets *Robin Hood, tells his tale of woe, and wins his sympathy. Robin not only lends him the money to recover his land, but also sees the knight attired and horsed according to his station and sends members of his own outlaw band with him to maintain an appearance befitting his social status. The knight recovers his patrimony and later repays Robin, rescuing a yeoman in distress along the way. He finally offers Robin sanctuary in his castle when the latter is pursued by the treacherous sheriff of Nottingham. This dogged pursuit glorifies the highwayman.

The second tale recalls Little John's deception of the sheriff (who has "borrowed" him for a year from the knight, who in turn has him on loan from Robin Hood). John makes off with the sheriff's gold and, to add insult to injury, converts his cook to Robin's band. Another subplot addresses the sheriff of Nottingham's treachery and Robin's skill at arms. Attending an archery contest in disguise--and, of course, winning the prize--Robin is recognized by the sheriff, who attacks him and his band. This is particularly ignoble since Robin had previously released the sheriff unharmed upon a promise that he would never harm the merry outlaws. Little John is seriously injured in the ensuing melee, and the outlaws seek refuge in the castle of the knight they have befriended in the main plot. Word is sent to the king, who subsequently dispossesses the knight and seeks to capture Robin and his band in the forest. In disguise, the king is quickly convinced of Robin's loyalty and nobility and so makes him a member of his own household and pardons the knight. After dwelling at court for some years, Robin pines for the outlaw life and returns to lead his forest band once more. Eventually he is murdered by an abbess and her lover.

Robin Hood represents the yeoman hero in that he embraces the chivalric code, living up to it much better than the aristocrats and religious leaders in the ballad, and yet retains his canniness and adeptness at survival. He is, of course, outlawed for poaching venison, and as we might expect in a yeoman ballad, he embraces the feudal hierarchy, observing it even in his own band. Also notable in *A Gest of Robin Hood* is its borrowing from the Arthurian tradition the custom of the leader insisting upon some adventure before eating dinner. For a full discussion of the characteristics of the yeoman ballads, see the entry for **Ballad.**

SELECTED BIBLIOGRAPHY

Anderson, Eric R. "Game and Reality in Medieval and Renaissance English Outlaw Narratives." *Aethlon* 8:2 (Spring 1991), 73-88; Bellamy, John. *Robin Hood: An Historical Enquiry.* Bloomington: Indiana University Press, 1985; Ikegami, Masa. "The Language and the Date of 'A Geste of Robyn Hode.'" *Neuphilologische Mitteilungen* 96:3 (1995), 271-81.

Gwendolyn Morgan

GHIBERTI, LORENZO (1378-1455). Winner of the lively competition for a design for the Baptistry of Florence, Lorenzo Ghiberti was trained as both a goldsmith and a painter. His training developed his skills in harmonizing the effects of both sculpture and painting, creating fluent surfaces.

The *Gates of Paradise* of ten square panels depicting Old Testament stories were later praised by Michelangelo. Some panels, such as the *Meeting of Solomon and the Queen of Sheba* are painterly, while others include figures that appear almost in the full round, with sculptured heads. One great achievement was a sense of depth not seen until his reliefs.

SELECTED BIBLIOGRAPHY

Gardner, Helen. *Gardner's Art Through the Ages.* 9th ed. San Diego: Harcourt, Brace, Jovanovich, 1975; Paolucci, Antonio. *The Origins of Renaissance Art: The Baptistry Doors, Florence.* New York: Braziller, 1996.

Libby Bernardin

GILDAS (c. 516-570). Gildas's *De Excidio et Conquestu Britanniae* (*On the Destruction and Conquest of Britain*) is the earliest extant history of Britain by an inhabitant of the Island. His exact date of birth is unknown, and he was probably of Welsh descent.

He was most likely a monk who fled to Brittany during the invasions of the Angles and Saxons. His history details some of the geography of the island and then discusses history from the Roman occupation to the coming of the Anglo-Saxons.

Gildas relied heavily on folklore and mixed historical stories with more fanciful accounts. He was a highly religious writer and saw the Britons' defeat by Rome as divine justice for their faithlessness. His is the only contemporary account we have of the Anglo-Saxon migration; all later accounts are based on his imaginative retelling of the Roman victory that forever changed his peoples' destiny.

SELECTED BIBLIOGRAPHY

Brandt, William J. *The Shape of Medieval History*. New Haven: Yale University Press, 1966; Higham, Nicolas John. "Gildas, Roman Walls, and British Dykes." *Cambridge Medieval Celtic Studies* 22 (Winter 1991), 1-14; Smalley, Beryl. *Historians in the Middle Ages*. New York: Scribner's, 1974; Sterns, Indrikis. *The Greater Medieval Historians: An Interpretation and a Bibliography*. Lanham, MD: University Press of America, 1980; Wheeler, Bonnie. "The Masculinity of King Arthur: From Gildas to the Nuclear Age." *Quondam et Futurus* 2:4 (Winter 1992), 1-26; *Works of Gildas and Nennius, The*. J.A. Giles, trans. London: J. Bohn, 1841.

Richard McDonald

GIOTTO DI BONDONE (1266-1337). Giotto was an Italian painter from Florence influenced by Pietro Cavallini, Giovanni *Cimabue, and the ancient art of Rome. Giotto inaugurated a method of pictorial experiment through observation and, in the spirit of experimenting Franciscans, opened an age that could be called "early scientific." He believed that the visual world must be observed before it can be understood.

His most famous paintings include *Madonna Enthroned, Lamentation, St. Francis Preaching to the Birds,* and *The Meeting of Joachim and Anna.* He also designed the cathedral of Florence in 1334, which stands apart from the cathedral of the Italian tradition. Giotto's tower is the whole of its clearly distinguished parts and is reminiscent of the Romanesque, but it also anticipates the ideal of Renaissance architecture: to express itself in logical relationships and to aim for works that are self-sufficient and can exist in complete independence.

Madonna Enthroned is a large painting (tempera on wood) about ten by seven feet in dimension and can be seen at the Galleria Degli Uffizi in Florence. The painting portrays the Madonna as a stable goddess. *Lamentation* is part of his fresco cycle in the Arena Chapel at Padua. The theme is the mourning of Christ's mother, his disciples, and the holy women over the dead body of Christ before its entombment. The figures in *Lamentation* are sculpturesque, simple, weighty forms that are unrestrained by their mass from appropriate action. The mourners around the body of Christ express a broad spectrum of grief. The landscape is one of jagged rocks, which links this scene with the adjoining one of Giotto's *Resurrection* and *Noli me tangere*. Giotto provides such linkages of framed scenes throughout his works. These works continue to impress audiences.

The Meeting of Joachim and Anna in the Arena Chapel has a simple and compact style, like his other paintings; the figures are carefully related to the single passage of architecture, the Golden Gate. The story, related in the Apocrypha, is managed with Giotto's usual clarity and dramatic compactness.

Giotto painted frescoes of the life and death of St. *Francis of Assisi for the Franciscan church of Santa Croce in Florence, including *The Death of St. Francis. St. Francis Preaching to the Birds* is another of the St. Francis paintings; it illustrates the simplicity of Giotto's statement and his reduction of the number of figures to the minimum required for the story. A serious controversy revolves around the great cycle of frescoes depicting the life of St. Francis in the upper church at Assisi; these are traditionally attributed to Giotto and dated about 1300. Current scholarship suggests that the St. Francis cycle was painted in the 1290s, and while the influence of Giotto's style is not denied, it is felt that it is better exemplified in other works. Some scholars believe that the Assisi frescoes were most likely done by Florentine artists influenced by Giotto.

Giotto's murals in the Bardi and Peruzzi chapels of Santa Croce served as textbooks for generations of Renaissance painters from *Masaccio to Michelangelo and others later. These later artists were able to understand the greatness of Giotto's art better than his immediate followers.

SELECTED BIBLIOGRAPHY

Gardner, Helen. *Gardner's Art through the Ages.* 6th ed. San Diego: Harcourt Brace Jovanovich, 1975; Salvini, Roberto. *Giotto: Bibliografia.* Rome: Istituto Nazionale d'Archeologia e Storia dell'Arte, 1970.

Libby Bernardin

GIRALDUS CAMBRENSIS (GERALD DE BARRI) (c. 1146-1220). Giraldus was a Welshman who chronicled the conquest of Ireland by *Henry II. He was educated in Paris and had a distinguished career as a churchman. He became the archdeacon of Brecon, but then his nationality halted his promotions. Because he was Welsh, Giraldus was rejected for the see of St. David's, first by Henry II and again by Archbishop Hubert. In a bizarre twist, he appealed this to Rome; to further his cause, he solicited the support of the Welsh. This infuriated his superiors so much that he was named an outlaw. He fled to the continent but was captured and imprisoned at Châtillon. Giraldus later reconciled with the king and the archbishop. In 1184 he went with Prince *John to Ireland. Giraldus also returned to school to teach in Lincoln from 1196 to 1198.

Giraldus's literary contributions include *Topographia Hibernica* (Topography of Ireland) and *Description of Wales*. Both chronicle his own experiences. The *Topographia* was composed shortly after the conquest of Ireland, while his *Description* was the result of his visit to Wales with Ranulf de *Glanville to preach the Third *Crusade. He was devoted enough to his clerical studies to compose the *Gemma Ecclesiastica*, a book of instructions for Welsh priests.

SELECTED BIBLIOGRAPHY

Breeze, Andrew. "Giraldus Cambrensis and Poland." *BBCS* 34 (1987), 111-12; Griffiths, J. Gwyn. "Giraldus Cambrensis *Descriptio Kambriae*, 1 16." *BBCS* 31 (1984), 1-16; Nichols, Stephen G. "Fission and Fusion: Meditations of Power in Medieval History and Literature." *Yale French Studies* 70 (1986), 21-41; Rollo, David. "Gerald of Wales *Topographia Hibernica*: Sex and the Irish Nation." *Romanic Review* 86:2 (March 1995), 169-90.

Robert T. Lambdin

GLANVILLE, RANULF DE (c. 1150). Ranulf de Glanville, a justice, was erroneously credited as penning the first great treatise on the laws of England, *Tractatus de Legibus et Consuetudinibus Angliae*. He was a companion of *Giraldus Cambrensis when the latter traveled to Wales to preach about the Third *Crusade.

SELECTED BIBLIOGRAPHY

Drabble, Margaret. *The Oxford Companion to English Literature*. 5th ed. Oxford: Oxford University Press, 1985; Turner, Ralph V. "Who Was the Author of 'Glanvill'? Reflections on the Education of Henry II's Common Lawyers." *Law and History Review* 8:1 (Spring 1990), 97-127.

Robert T. Lambdin

GLASGERION. *Glasgerion* is an Old English *ballad that relates the activities of Prince Glasgerion, whose musical talents win for him the hand of the daughter of the king of Normandy. Before the nuptials can take place, he is duped by the court page who replaces Glasgerion at the ceremony. When the princess discovers this ruse, she becomes so tormented that she kills herself. An enraged Glasgerion discovers the truth, slays the page, and turns his sword upon himself.

SELECTED BIBLIOGRAPHY

Morgan, Gwendolyn. *Medieval Balladry and the Courtly Tradition*. New York: Peter Lang, 1993; Morgan, Gwendolyn. *Medieval Ballads: Chivalry, Romance, and Everyday Life*. New York: Peter Lang, 1996; Richmond, Edson W. *Ballad Scholarship: An Annotated Bibliography*. New York: Garland, 1989.

Rebecca Chalmers

GLEEMAN. *Anglo-Saxon musical entertainers, gleemen were usually professionals who traveled the countryside, reciting poetry for a living. These works were usually composed by others, although some gleemen did compose their own music.

Gleemen were sometimes attached to kings' courts, but they were less dignified in position than the *scop. Usually the scop composed, while the gleeman recited or sang the scop's works, accompanied by a harp or other instrument. Through the years the term "gleemen" has come to be loosely associated with any kind of medieval composer or reciter.

SELECTED BIBLIOGRAPHY

Holman, C. Hugh, and William Harmon. *A Handbook to Literature.* 5th ed. New York, Macmillan, 1986.

Robert T. Lambdin

GNOMIC POETRY. Like the biblical Book of Proverbs, gnomic poetry consists of wise sayings of folk origin. Group II, from the *Exeter Book collection, properly celebrates (cf. Proverbs 31: 10-31) the value of a good woman, in this case, a Frisian wife.

The Father Almighty sends the weather, for good or for ill; the victorious king gratefully adorns his worthy queen; but the wives of Frisian sailors are a special blessing. They will not shame their husbands with wickedness, nor "love a stranger . . . while their lord is afar." Firm in their faith and resolute in their marriage vows, they eagerly await their mates' return; they wash their soiled garments and provide fresh, new supplies. In short, "It is pleasant on land . . . when the loved one awaits you."

SELECTED BIBLIOGRAPHY

Deskis, Susan E. "The Gnomic Woman in Old English Poetry." *Philological Quarterly* 73:2 (Spring 1994), 133-49; Karkov, Catherine and Robert Farrell. "The Gnomic Passages of *Beowulf.*" *Neuphilologische Mitteilungan* 91:3 (1990), 295-310; Risden, E. L. "'Deor': The Old English Ode and Gnomic Compassion." *In Geardagum* 11 (1990), 57-70.

Elton E. Smith

GREGORY THE GREAT (540-604), pope (590-604). Gregory came from a rich senatorial house and rose steadily, becoming prefect of Rome in 573. The following year he founded six monasteries in Sicily and one (St. Andrews) in Rome, immediately afterward retiring to the monastic life. He was named to the papal embassy, serving from 579 to the year 586, when he was named abbot of St. Andrews. Gregory was viewed as a very severe leader, yet, against his will, he was elected Pope in 590 and began an immediate and vigorous administration.

He stressed clerical celibacy and, to ensure that elections were carried out fairly, demanded exclusive clerical jurisdiction over ecclesiastical office holders. Church revenue was divided into four shares: for the bishop, the poor, the clergy, and church buildings. The revenue was thus produced and expanded to meet the tremendous demands on Rome for charity. His administration of the wide estates of the church was honest and brilliant. He continued the corn doles, regular allotments of corn to the poor in Rome and elsewhere. In addition to his outreach to the poor, aqueducts were repaired and urban administration, especially in Rome, was reformed.

Gregory expanded the influence of the papacy, maintaining that the pope was, by divine designation, head of all churches. Appeals to Rome were heard, even against the patriarch of Constantinople, whose claim to the title of universal pope was denied. Gregory boldly assumed the role of emperor in the West along with the powers of a temporal prince, counterbalancing the prestige of Constantinople. From his administration date the foundations of later claims of papal abolutism.

As the first monk to become pope, Gregory developed a close alliance between the Benedictines and the papacy at the expense of the bishops. The monks were given charters and were protected from the bishops. The Benedictine rule was imposed. A great missionary campaign began with the aid of the monks. Gregory was the last of the great Latin fathers and is considered the first of the medieval prelates, a link between the classical Greco-Roman tradition and the medieval Romano-German period.

SELECTED BIBLIOGRAPHY

Gildea, Joseph, trans. *Source Book of Self-Discipline: A Synthesis of "Moralia in Job" by Gregory the Great: A Translation of Peter Waltham's "Remediarium Conversarum"*" New York: Peter Lang, 1991; McReady, William B. *Miracles and the Venerable Beda.* Toronto: Pontifical Institute of Mediaeval Studies, 1994; McReady, William B. *Signs of Sanctity: Miracles in the Thought of Gregory the Great.* Toronto: Pontifical Institute of Mediaeval Studies, 1989.

R. Churchill Curtis

GREGORY VII (1015-1085), pope (1073-1085). Educated at Rome, Gregory was of peasant stock. He was strongly influenced by the Cluniac movement. Neither an original thinker nor a scholar, Gregory was an intensely practical man who was also of lofty moral stature. After a brilliant career in the church Curia, Gregory was elected pope, with strong Roman support; however, German bishops had opposed his election, and his consecration was postponed.

His sin (or mistake) was to attempt the compromise of that which was not compromisable, uniting the Holy Roman Empire and the Roman Church, Constantinople and Rome.

His differences with The Holy Roman Emperor *Henry IV became even more schismatic when Gregory informally announced his position in *Dictatus*. In this he claimed that the Roman Church had never erred and could never err; that the pope is supreme judge, that he may be judged by none, and that there is no appeal from him. Gregory's series of claims precipitated the Investiture Controversy, which caused the Church and the empire many difficulties from 1075 to 1122. The controversy was finally settled with the Concordat of Worms, which recognized papal decrees against simony, clerical marriage, and lay investiture. The concordat also continued the excommunication of Henry IV and Henry V, emperors of the Holy Roman Empire.

SELECTED BIBLIOGRAPHY

Bennett, Helen T. "Pope Gregory's *Liber Regulae Pastoralis* and Chaucer's *Canterbury Tales*. *Medieval Perspectives* 9 (1994), 24-40; Hall, Thomas N. "A Gregorian Model for Eve's 'Biter Drync' in Guthlac B." *Review of English Studies* 44:174 (May 1993), 157-75; Williams, Schafer, ed. *The Gregorian Epoch: Reformation, Revolution, Reaction?* Boston: Heath, 1964.

R. Churchill Curtis

GREGORY OF TOURS (538-594). Gregory of Tours is considered one of the barbarian historians and helped establish the idea of a national history for his people. Gregory was a Frank (ancestors of the modern French) who was born in Clermont in Auvergne and was chosen bishop of Tours in 573. He came from a wealthy family and seemingly chose to enter the clergy at a young age. He had numerous relatives who held offices within the church. He was the first bishop to be a historian and also was one of the first bishops to become a prodigious writer. On his death he left behind a considerable amount of writing: eight books of *hagiography (stories of saints' lives and miracles) and his ten- volume *Historiae*, later renamed *Historia Francorum* (*The History of the Franks*). The *Historiae* is a chronological narrative of the Frankish people tracing the origins of the Franks back to Noah's son Japhet and making them ancestors to the Trojans, who eventually settled in Gaul. The ten-volume history spans the time from Creation to the early 590s, when Gregory completed it. The first four volumes deal with the years from Creation to 575 and the last six contain Gregory's contemporary history of the Merovingian age.

Gregory believed that people could learn important lessons (moral lessons) from history and saw himself as fulfilling that need. His portrayal of Merovingian royalty is sometimes unflattering, and he frequently digressed into discussions more relevant to the clergy of Clermont and Tours. Although some of his historical assertions are mere fabrications and even his contemporary historical facts are sometimes questionable, he is the first French historian and was relied on by many later historians of the medieval and subsequent periods.

SELECTED BIBLIOGRAPHY

Brandt, William J. *The Shape of Medieval History*. New Haven: Yale University Press, 1966; Carozzi, Claude. "*Le Clovis de Gregoire de Tours*." *Le Moyen Age* 98:2 (1992), 169-85; Goffart, Walter. *The Narrators of Barbarian History (A.D. 550-800)*. Princeton: Princeton University Press, 1988; Smalley, Beryl. *Historians in the Middle Ages*. New York: Scribner's, 1974; Sterns, Indrikis. *The Greater Medieval Historians: An Interpretation and a Bibliography*. Lanham, MD: University Press of America, 1980.

Richard McDonald

GROSSETESTE, ROBERT (1170?-1253). Nearly every facet of Robert Grosseteste's life and work is debated by other scholars, from his own time to the present. While two contemporaries, Matthew *Paris and Roger *Bacon, praised his great intellectual insights and his courageous opposition to ecclesiastical abuses, another, Thomas Gascoigne, emphasized his urbanity, hospitality, and orthodoxy. His followers in the Lincoln Diocese and elsewhere, especially John *Wycliffe and the *Lollards, considered him a saint, but the Curia refused to canonize him because he supported the Magna Carta and consistently fought papal taxation and misuse of benefices. Schools everywhere knew him as Lincolniensis, yet his fame was not established until a century and a half after his death.

Although he was born into a lowly family, he became a respected member of the household of the bishop of Hereford, William de Vere. Some time after the death of de Vere, in 1198, he became a teacher of the arts at Oxford. From there he went to study and lecture in Paris. Before 1230 he returned to Oxford and eventually became its first chancellor. In 1235 he became bishop of Lincoln, the largest diocese in England. More interested in ethics than in dialectics, he administered his office with a strictness that made him many enemies.

His concern for the spiritual welfare of the common people made him a forceful preacher, in Latin to the clergy but in English to the laity. It also made him friendly to the work of the preaching friars, both Dominican and Franciscan. While the multitude of studies of his life frequently begin with deletion of spurious items from his bibliography, most commentators recognize the extraordinary scope and volume of his writing: more than 200 sermons, a collection of 147 short discourses, more than 60 longer treatises, translations from Greek, Latin, and French, and many letters, some of considerable length, dealing with theology, ecclesiastical administration, and all branches of the physical sciences.

In all his intellectual endeavors he emphasized the study of original sources rather than translations or abridgements, asserting that the study of Greek and Hebrew was essential to good scholarship. He understood mathematics and the physical sciences as intrinsic in understanding Creation and its spiritual values. His *Computus* and *Computus Ecclesiasticus* anticipated Roger Bacon's views of the errors in the unreformed Julian calendar. His *Compendium Scientiarum* attempts to classify all departments of knowledge: divisions of philosophy, a compendium of natural philosophy, mathematics, metaphysics, grammar, rhetoric, logic, medicine, arithmetic, music, geometry, astronomy, optics, astrology, politics, economics, and ethics. An example of his comprehensive view of spiritual and physical phenomena is presented in his short work *De Luce*. Light is here described as the *prima forma corporalis* of Creation; it diffused itself in all directions to the extreme limits of the universe in the moment of time; it is inseparable from all matter; it is the perfection of all things. In similar fashion he sought to expound Genesis 1:26, which places humanity at the center of creation, by giving symbolic values to all other physical things. In his comments on the Psalms he found many useful symbols: trees, rivers, animals, mountains, and so on. In his *Hexaemeron* he asserted that God is all in all, the life of all living things, the perfection of everything, and he saw God as most clearly revealed in shafts of light.

Of more interest to less philosophical readers are the 147 short memorable sayings in *Dicta Theologica*, in which he defined such common terms of church doctrine as faith, grace, justification, prayer, humility, the mercy and justice of God, and true and false prophets. The effectiveness of his definitions and illustrations helps to explain his popularity as a preacher and lecturer. Even more specific are the 45 articles of the *Constitution* he addressed to the rectors, vicars, and parish priests of his diocese following the great Council of the English Church held at St. Paul's, London, in 1237. In the first of the articles he charged his clergy to be able to instruct their parishoners--in English--on avoidance of the *seven deadly sins, the meaning of the sacraments, and the general principles of the Christian faith. Beyond these doctrinal matters he urged reverent demeanor during the celebration of the Eucharist and gave detailed rules for ministering to the sick, conducting funerals, instructing children and adults, visiting nuns, and many other routine situations in their work. The need to insist that the clergy not engage in trade or usury nor marry indicates that these rules were not universally observed throughout the Western Church at this time. His translations and commentaries on several of *Aristotle's works, such as the *Sophistici Elenchi, Predicaments, Prior Analytics*, and *Posterior Analytics*, were of interest to scholars; his translation of *Testament of the Twelve Patriarchs*, an account of Jacob and his sons, was popular with a wider audience.

It is apparent from this brief review of Grosseteste's voluminous works that he is of greater significance to students of political, scientific, and religious history than to the students of English literature. However, he did encourage the use of English in preaching, and while somewhat mythologized by the Lollards, he contributed to the eventual triumph of English in both science and religion. He was perceptively conversant with the learning of his time and believed in the unity of all knowledge, as discovered not only in the study of all available written sources but also from observation. His courage in resisting laxity and corruption in ecclesiastical affairs as well as his innovative use of language strengthened these characteristics in post-medieval English.

SELECTED BIBLIOGRAPHY

Goering, Joseph. "The Early Penitential Writings of Robert Grosseteste." *Recherches de Theologie Ancienne et Médiévale* 54 (1987), 52-112; Goering, Joseph, and F.A.C. Mantello. "Two Opuscula of Robert Grosseteste: *De Universi Complecione* and *Exposicio Canonis Misse.*" *Mediaeval Studies* 53 (1991), 89-123; Lewis, Neil. "The First Recension of Robert Grosseteste's *De Libero Arbitrio.*" *Mediaeval Studies* 53 (1991) 89-123; McEvoy, James. *The Philosophy of Robert Grosseteste.*Oxford: Clarendon Press, 1982; McEvoy, James. "Robert Grosseteste on the Ten Commandments." *Recherches de Theologie Ancienne et Médiévale.* 58 (January-December 1991), 167-205; Southern, R.W *Robert Grosseteste. The Growth of an English Mind in Medieval Europe.* Oxford: Clarendon Press, 1986; Stevenson, Francis Seymour. *Robert Grosseteste, Bishop of Lincoln.* London: Macmillan and Company; New York: Macmillan Company, 1899.

Esther Smith

GUINIZELLI, GUIDO (1235-1276).

"I am Guido Guinizelli--here so soon,
    for I repented long before I died. "
And King Lycurgus raged with grief, two sons
        Discovered their lost mother and rejoiced--
        I felt the same (though more restrained) to hear
That spirit name himself--father to me
        And father of my betters, all who wrote
        A sweet and graceful poetry of love.
I heard no more, I did not speak, I walked
        Deep in my thoughts, my eyes fixed on his shade,
The flames kept me from coming close to him.
At last my eyes were satisfied. And then
        I spoke, convincing him of my deep wish
to serve him in whatever way I could.

(Musa, *Dante's Purgatory,* 282)

It is on the Seventh Cornice of Purgatory (canto XXVI) among the penitents of natural and unnatural Lust that *Dante encounters Guido Guinizelli, to whom he refers to as "il padre mio e delli altri miei miglior" (father of me and father of my betters). In this canto Dante not only vividly demonstrates how love is the root of both virtue and vice, but also establishes the significance and the relevance of Italian poetic tradition, and particularly of Guinizelli's influence, to his own artisitc practice and achievement. In this way, Guinizelli is one of Dante's most noted characters.

Little is known of Guinizelli's life, and what is known is frequently contested. He was born in Bologna, a member of the Ghibelline Principi family, aristocrats who upheld the authority of the emperor in opposition to the ever-growing territorial encroachment of the papacy. His family background and political involvement as a jurist resulted in his banishment from Bologna along with the other Ghibellines in 1274. He died sometime before November 1276. Initially he was a follower of Guittone d'Arezzo's ornate and rhetorical poetical style, but he soon broke away to lead his own school of Bolognese poets, including Lapo Giani, Cino da Pistoia, Guido *Cavalcanti, and later Dante himself. As the founder of the *dolce stil nuovo*, a new and uniquely national literature of the Italians, Guinizelli emerges as the most illustrious of the Italian poets to precede Dante, despite the existence of only twenty-two extant *canzoni and sonnets.

In developing the *dolce stil nuovo* in the culturally rich Tuscan environment, Guinizelli succeeded in nationalizing the spirit and elevating the style of the Sicilian poets by incorporating a scientific and philosophical dimension that rendered his love poems more logical, allegorical, and mystical. Guinizelli's analogies, metaphors, poetic language, and concept of love reflect his effort to write not from the heart but from the head, to analyze love and its effects, and to reject the Italian dependence on foreign and other traditions by a Tuscanization of the style and thought of his approach to the love poems. His most beautiful and most well-known canzone, "Alcor gentil ripara sempre amore" (Love always seeks the gently virtuous heart) summarizes the major ideas on love found in the *courtly love tradition, but does so in his philosophical, analytical, and even boldly scientific manner. The poem uses vivid images, similes, and metaphors ("bright flame of a candle" "diamond in iron ore") to describe the *cor gentil* (noble heart) and to present his debate on the nature of true nobility, concluding that it is a reflection of inner excellence and worth rather than external status or inheritance. The speaker goes on to assert that the lady in whose noble heart love dwells inherently and exclusively should share her nobility (*gentillessa*) with a faithful lover, likening this generous act to God's brilliant bestowal of Himself upon the angels. The final stanza offers a dramatic paradisal scene with the speaker standing at the judgment seat rebuked by God for boldly employing a divine relationship in a poetic simile on secular love.

This canzone provided Dante with the poetic program of angelic praise (*laudere*) of the noble, beautiful lady that became a prototype for is *Vita nuova*, as he acknowledged in his most memorable sonnet, "Amore e'l cor gentil sono una cosa, si come il saggio in suo dittare pone" ("Love and the gracious heart are a single thing, as the wise one tells us in his poem"). In Guinizelli Dante found not only a source for poetic idiom and philosophical metaphors, but also the metaphysical idea of portraying the lady as literally an angelic conductor to the divine that became the core for his *Commedia*. Guinizelli for Dante thus indeed played the role of both poetic father and prophet in establishing the *dolce stil nuovo* manifesto as the poetic vehicle for articulating philosophic truth through love. Guinizelli's originality and influence are also explicitly acknowledged in Dantes *De vulgari eloquentia* and are likewise reflected in the philosophical code of the *Convivio* and the apocalyptic vision of divine love in the *Paradiso*.

It is noteworthy that Dante Gabriel Rosseti chose to translate Guinizelli's poems and that T. S. Eliot mentioned Guinizelli, along with Cavalcanti, Cino, and Dante, as one of those who possessed the same "mechanism of sensibility which could devour any kind of experience" that Eliot identified as the basis for his praise of John Donne ("The Metaphysical Poets"). But, of course, John Dryden and Samuel Johnson would not have approved of Guinizelli's perplexing "the minds of the fair sex with nice speculations of philosophy" ("A Discourse Concerning the Original and Progress of Satire").

SELECTED BIBLIOGRAPHY

Edwards, Robert R. "Guinizelli's Readers and the Strategies of Historicism." *Philological Quarterly* 71:4 (Fall 1992), 419-36; Musa, Mark, trans. *Dante's Purgatory*. Bloomington: Indiana University Pres, 1981; Sapegno, Natalino, ed. *La Divina Commedia. Vol. II: Purgatorio*. Florence: La Nuova Italia, 1973; Tambling, Jeremy. "'Nostro peccato fu ermafrodito: Dante and the Moderns." *Exemplaria* 6:2 (Fall 1994), 405-27.

Silvia R Fiorc

GUY OF WARWICK (c. 1300). The Middle English *romance *Guy of Warwick* is rooted in an *Anglo-Norman original. The stunts and adventures of Guy are quite characteristic of heroes of the non-Arthurian romances such as *King Horn* and *Havelok the Dane*. In the romance Guy is socially inferior to his beloved Fenice, the earl of Warwick's daughter, so he must prove his worth in order to win her hand. In the second portion Guy, in typical romance form, turns to religion. He becomes a pilgrim, abandoning his love, and journeys to fight the evil Saracens. In the third portion Guy returns to England, where he engages in combat with the Danish giant Colbrand; he also butchers the powerful Dun Cow of Dunsmore and subdues a winged dragon. Returning as the typical romance hero, Guy settles near Warwick as a hermit. Daily he goes to his castle and begs for bread from Fenice, who fails to recognize him. The ruse continues until Guy, on his deathbed, conveys to her his ring. In a touching reconciliation she returns to him and closes his dying eyes.

The romance was extremely popular, although by today's standards it may seem somewhat typical or dull. *Guy of Warwick* had several reincarnations, including a sequel, *Reinbrun, Gy Sone of Warwike*. This romance concern's Guy's warrior son. Even in the Renaissance Guy remained popular, and several short ballad-like pieces were composed about him. Indeed, one may find novel literature concerning Guy as late as 1630.

SELECTED BIBLIOGRAPHY

Burton, Julie. "Narrative Patterning and 'Guy of Warwick.'" *Yearbook of English Studies* 22 (1992), 105-16; Dannenbaum, Susan Crane. "'Guy of Warwick' and the Question of Exemplary Romance." *Genre* 17:4 (Winter 1984), 351-74; Drabble, Margaret, ed. *The Oxford Companion to English Literature*. 5th ed. Oxford: Oxford University Press, 1985; Mills, Maldwyn. "Structure and Meaning in 'Guy of Warwick.'" In *From Medieval to Medievalism*. John Simons, ed. New York: St. Martin's, 1992. 54-68.

Robert T. Lambdin

H

HAGIOGRAPHY. Hagiography, or the writing of saints' lives, was one of the most popular forms of biography in the early Middle Ages. These accounts often contained miraculous events and were not especially historically accurate. Accounts of the lives of kings often show the influence of hagiography, and the elaborative techniques used in this genre are closely related to the development of medieval *histories. (*See Chronicles and Annals*.)

SELECTED BIBLIOGRAPHY

Binchy, D.A. "Pre-Christian Survival in Medieval Irish Hagiography." In *Ireland in Early Medieval Europa: Studies in Memory of Kathleen Hughes*. Dorothy Whitlock, Rosamond McKitterick, and David Dumville, eds. Cambridge: Cambridge University Press, 1982. 165-78; Boyer, Regis. "An Attempt to Define the Typology of Medieval Hagiography." In *Hagiography and Medieval Literature: A Symposium*. Hans Nielson Bekker, *et al*, eds. Odense: Odense University Press, 1981, 27-36; Head, Thomas F. *Hagiography and the Cult of Saints: The Diocese of Orleans, 800-1200*. Cambridge: Cambridge University Press, 1990; Rollason, D. W. *The Mildrith Legend: A Study in Early Medieval Hagiography in England*. Leicester: Leicester University Press, 1982.

Richard McDonald

HALLOWEEN. Celebrated on October 31, Halloween is an example of the way in which traditional pagan practices continued to be celebrated in the Christian Middle Ages. The ancient Celts (*see Celtic Literature, Early*) celebrated the conclusion of the year at the end of October, which was called Samhain, or Summer's End. A feast held on November 1 was one of the four major agricultural feasts of the ancient cycle of feasts. It was the time, according to ancient custom, when supernatural beings, including the spirits of the dead, were believed to be active and had to be propitiated. These traditional celebrations were merged with the Christian feasts of All Saints on November 1, which, dating from the ninth century, had grown out of commemoration of the martyrs, and All Souls on November 2, which dated from the tenth century and was dedicated to prayers for the souls of the dead.

The festival of November 1, All Saints, was known as All Hallows, and the night before as All Hallows Eve, or Hallow E'en. The bonfires lit that night were relics of the pagan past, as were those on Midsummer Eve, and it was traditional for masked children to go "souling," that is, begging for soul cakes--a shortbread cookie--for the supernatural beings and threatening reprisals if they did not receive any.

SELECTED BIBLIOGRAPHY

Cosman, Madeleine Pelner. *Medieval Holidays and Festivals: A Calendar of Celebrations.* New York: Academy of Science, 1981; Homans, George C. *English Villages of the Thirteenth Century.* New York: Russell & Russell, 1941; Santino, Jack, ed. *Halloween and Other Festivals of Death and Life.* Knoxville: University of Tennessee Press, 1994. Whistler, Laurence. *The English Festivals.* London: Curtain, 1947.

Miriam Davis

HARDYNG, JOHN (1378-1465). John Hardyng is the author of a set of *chronicles written in verse form. These works, which Hardyng wrote sometime between 1440 and 1457, delve deeply into the historically significant events that occurred in England from its founding by Brutus until 1437. A major concern of Hardyng's *The Chronicla of John Hardyng* is the argument in favor of the English kings dominion over Scotland. Because of this point, it is believed that the *Chroniclas* was composed in the interests of Henry V and Henry VI.

The original work remained popular and was revised in a second edition that leans toward the Yorkist perspective. The major change in this edition is that a eulogy for Henry V has been deleted from the text. Also, Henry VI is declared to be somewhat stupid. It was this observation that became the prevailing view of Henry VI; thus *The Chronicla of John Hardyng* is seen to be the major authority on the subject of royalty.

SELECTED BIBLIOGRAPHY

Drabble, Margaret, ed. *The Oxford Companion to English Literature.* 5th ed.Oxford: Oxford University Press, 1985; Edwards, A. S. G. "*Troilus and Criseyde* and the First Version of Hardyng's *Chronicle.*" *Notes and Queries* 35(233):1 (March 1988), 12-13; Kennedy, Edward Donald. "John Hardyng and the Holy Grail." In *Arthurian Literature VIII.* Richard Barber, ed. Woodbridge: Brewer, 1989. 185-206; West, Gilian. "Hardyng's *Chronicle* and Shakespeare's 'Hotspur.'" *Shakespeare Quarterly* 41:3 (Fall 1990), 348-51.

Robert T. Lambdin

HARLEIAN MANUSCRIPTS, THE. The Harleian manuscripts are a collection of Old and Middle English literature that is now housed in the British Library. Robert Harley, the earl of Oxford, began assembling this collection, which now numbers some 50,000 books, 350,000 pamphlets, and 7,000 volumes of manuscripts. It also contains some early biblical texts composed in Hebrew, Latin, and Greek, as well as historical records. Perhaps the greatest collection of Old and Middle English literature, the manuscripts provide readers with an impressive glimpse of medieval life.

SELECTED BIBLIOGRAPHY

Backhouse, Janet. "The Making of the Harley Psalter." *British Library Journal* 10:2 (Autumn 1984), 97-113; Green, Richard Firth. "An Epitaph for Richard, Duke of York." *Studies in Bibliography* 41 (1988), 218-24; Hunt, Tony. "The 'Novele cirurgerie' in MS London, British Library Harley 2558." *Zeitschrift fπr Romanische Philologie* 103:3 (1987), 271-99.

Robert T. Lambdin

HARLEY LYRICS. The Harley *lyrics are located in Harley 2253, and are perhaps the most famous of all of the *Harleian manuscripts. This collection contains thirty-two lyrics copied in the early fourteenth century, but it is believed that they all date to a much earlier time. The lyrics contained here are thought to be among the best composed in England during this period. Among the most renowned are *Alysoun, "Lenten is Come with Love to Toune," and "Blow Northern Wynd." The works in this manuscript are invaluable in their clear presentation of medieval ideologies.

SELECTED BIBLIOGRAPHY

Fulton, Helen. "The Theory of Celtic Influence on the Harley Lyrics," *Modern Philology* 82:3 (1985), 239-54; Matonis, A.T.E. "The Harley Lyrics: English and Welsh Convergences." *Modern Philology* 86:1 (August 1988), 1-21; Stemmler, Thomas. "Miscellany or Anthology? The Structure of Medieval Manuscripts: MS. Harley 2253, for Example." *Zeitschrift für Anglistik* 39:3 (1991), 231-37.

Robert T. Lambdin

HARROWING OF HELL. *Harrowing of Hell* is a Middle English poem of some 250 lines written around 1250 that recounts the story of Christ's three days in Hell. The medieval version alleges that while there, he freed the souls of all of the good people who had been condemned simply because the gates of Heaven were closed after Adam's original sin. The gospel of Nicodemus (c. 200) accounts for much of the source material in this poem. The tale must have been extremely popular, for versions of it are found in other Old and Middle English prose, as well as in major literary works such as William Langland's *Piers the Plowman*. The *Harrowing of Hell* also became a prevalent theme in the mystery plays (*see Drama, Medieval*).

The poem begins with a narrative introduction. This, in turn, is followed by individual speeches assigned to major figures, including Christ, Satan, Adam, Eve, and Moses. After Christ arrives at the gates of Hell, he enters and claims Adam. Satan is enraged and promises that he will claim one soul on Earth for every soul Christ releases. Christ is not moved by Satan, whom he overpowers and binds. Christ is then free to release all of those who will serve him. Given the construction of this poem with its individual parts, it is easy to see why the producers of plays found the work accessible.

SELECTED BIBLIOGRAPHY

Brzezinski, Monica. "The 'Harrowing of Hell,' the 'Last Judgement,' and 'The Dream of the Rood.'" *Neuphilologische Mitteilungen* 89:3 (1988), 252-65; McCarey, Peter, and Mariarosaria Cardines. "The 'Harrowing of Hell' and Resurrection: Dante's *Inferno* and Blok's *Dvenadtsat.*" *Slavic and East European Review* 63:3 (July 1985), 337-48.

Robert T. Lambdin

HAVELOK THE DANE. *Havelok the Dane* is both the name and the hero of a thirteenth century Middle English *romance that was written in Lincolnshire. Havelok is the orphaned son of the great Danish king Birkabegn and is exposed at sea because of his deceitful guardian, Godard. Havelok's raft finds its way to Lincolnshire, where the orphan is found by the fisherman, Grim. Havelok is assigned kitchen duty at the Godrich estate, where he meets and falls in love with Goldborough, the disinherited princess and daughter of King Ethelwold of England. She has fallen out of favor with her father because she stands in the way of some ambitious nobles. Grim and Goldborough note Havelok's nobility, made obvious by a mystical light that shines over his head. Havelok learns the truth of his nobility and weds Goldborough, and the three return to Denmark. They have Godard hanged and reclaim the throne. Then, with an army of Danes, Havelok returns to recover his wife's possessions. He then ascends the throne of Denmark.

This romance parallels several documented events in history. Havelok has been recognized as Anlaf Cuaran, the son of Sihtric, the Viking king of Northumberland. Sihtric himself gained fame as the king defeated at *The *Battle of Brunnanburgh* in 937. Regardless of these historical points, most of the romance's other events are fictional. This work remains one of the most popular Middle English romances due in part to its historical connection to the past of England and its sustained energy.

SELECTED BIBLIOGRAPHY

Aerston, Henk. *"Havelok the Dane:* A Non-courtly Romance." in *Companion to Middle English Literature.* N.H.G.E. Veldhoen and H. Aerston, eds. Amsterdam: VU University Press, 1995. 29-50; Bradbury, Nancy Mason. "The Traditional Origins of *Havelok the Dane.*" *Studies in Philology* 90:2 (Spring 1993), 115-42; Lidstrom, Bengt. "A Further Note on *Havelok.*" *Notes and Queries* 42 (240):1 (March 1995), 22-23; Liuzza, Roy Michael. "Representation and Readership in the Middle English *Havelok.*" *Journal of English and Germanic Philology* 93:4 (October 1994), 504-19; Purdon, Liam O. "The Rite of Vassalage in *Havelok the Dane.*" *Medievalia et Humanistica* 20 (1994) 25-39.

Robert T. Lambdin

HEIMSKRINGLA, THE. The *Heimskringla* collection of short *sagas recounts the histories of the kings of Norway to 1177. It was composed by *Snorri Sturluson, who took some liberties in transcribing these histories. Thus the work is noted as a literary piece rather than as a history. Yet Sturluson's work does contain some factual information about the politics of the time. It is also important because the *Heimskringla* includes a section devoted to Knðtr (*Canute), the Danish king. Sturluson's work provides graphic details of Viking invasions and the sacking of England. The work's title is gleaned from its opening two words, "Kringla leimsin," which mean "orb of the world." Perhaps the most important story contained here tells of Saint Olafur Haraldsson, the king of Norway from 1015 to 1030. Also located in the *Heimskringla* are references to the *Hryggjarstykki,* an Old Norse text now lost. From the information provided here, it can be determined that the *Hryggjarstykki* was also a collection of stories about kings.

SELECTED BIBLIOGRAPHY

Bagge, Sverre. "From Sagas to Society: The Case of *Heimskringla.*" In *From Sagas to Society: Comparative Approaches to Early Iceland.* Gisli Palson, ed. Enfield Lock, Eng: Hisarlik, 1992. 61-75; Bermann, Melissa A. "Egils Saga and *Heimskringla.*" *Scandinavian Studies* 54:1 (1982), 21-50; Jesch, Judith. "The Praise of Astridr Olafsdottir." *Saga Book* 24:1 (1994), 1-18.

Robert T. Lambdin

HENRY I (c. 1008-1060) Capetian, king of France (1031-1060). Henry was an active and brave ruler whose reign, although he attempted reforms, marked the absolute nadir of the capetian rule. His brother Robert led a rebellion against him. Henry was forced because of this alliance to seek assustance from the duke of Normandy. His brother was pacified when he was granted the Duchy of

Burgundy. Henry then led a coalition against the duke of Normandy, but was defeated; thus Normandy became more important than the Capetian line for decades.

SELECTED BIBLIOGRAPHY

Belloc, Hilaire. *Miniatures of French History*. Peru, IL: Sherwood Sugden, 1990; Poly, Jean-Pierre. *The Feudal Transformation*. New York: Holmes Meyer, 1990.

R. Churchill Curtis

HENRY II (1133-89) king of England (1154-1189) first master of the House of Plantagenet. Henry of Angevin's realm contained England, Normandy, Anjou, Maine, an Touraine by inheritance; Poitou, Aquitaine, and Gascony by marriage with *Eleanor of Aquitaine; Brittany; and Wales, Ireland, and Scotland. These disparate parts were bound together only by the person of the ruler. Henry restored the good order of England by dismissing the mercenaries, tearing down unlicensed castles, reconquering Northumberland and Cumberland, reassuming the Crown's land lost earlier. He also restored the Exchequer and the Great Council. Feeling secure that England was now a strong entity, Henry spent more than half of his reign elsewhere.

Thomas *Becket became archbishop of Canterbury in 1162 and almost immediately became embroiled in conflict with Henry II over the authority of the ecclesiastical courts and their clerks. "Should clerics be tried in the courts for crimes? Should the Crown control episcopal elections?" Becket was forced to yield, but fled to France. Finally reconciled with Henry, Becket returned to England in 1170. Once again Henry and Becket began to argue when Becket excommunicated bishops friendly to Henry. Becket was martyred in the Cathedral of Canterbury when he was killed by four of Henry's knights. This incident removed all choice on the part of Henry, and clerical power became resurgent until the reign of Henry VII.

Henry also spent much of the time of his rule dealing with reorganization of the armed forces, called Assizes of Arms. Every free man was made responsible for defense of the realm, the king thus assuring a national militia for defense. Henry's military organization was to be put to the task many times in defense of his homeland. It was during this time that Henry showed his leadership skills. Many times Henry's people stopped invading hordes.

Henry established a number of innovations in government. His judicial reforms included increased concentration of judicial business; designation of a permanent central court; and an extension of the transfer of judicial business. Henry established the great source of common law (a law universal in the realm). One of his itinerant judges, Glanvill, wrote a *Treatise on the Law and Customs of the Kingdom of England*, the first serious book on the common law.

Additional major accomplishments occurred in the reorganization of the Exchequer, in the many innovations in the raising of revenue, in the extension of trade with the German states, and in the establishment of primogeniture to control the break-up of large estates.

SELECTED BIBLIOGRAPHY

Amt, Emilie. *The Ascension of Henry II in England: Royal Government Restored, 1149-1159.* Rochester, NY: Boydell Press, 1993; Martin, Janet Marion. "Cicero's Jokes at the Court of Henry II of England: Roman Humor and the Princely Ideal." *Modern Language Quarterly* 51:2 (1990), 144-66; Sieman, James R. "Landlord not King: Agrarian Change and Inarticulation." In *Enclosure Acts: Sexuality, Property, and Culture in Early Modern England.* Richard Burt and John Michael Archer, eds. Ithaca: Cornell University Press, 1994. 17-33.

R. Churchill Curtis

HENRY III Salian, king of the Holy Roman Empire (1039-1056). Due to the rise of trade and towns, Henry's reign was marked by great prosperity. Both he and his wife, Agnes of Poitou, were ardent Cluniacs, but retained control of the church. He was in firm control of all German churches except Saxony, which retained a modicum of independence.

SELECTED BIBLIOGRAPHY

Bernhardt, John Williams. *Itinerant Kingship and Royal Monasteries in Early Medieval Germany, ca. 936-1075.* Cambridge: Cambridge University Press, 1993; Hill, Boyd H. *Medieval Monarchy in Action: The German Empire from Henry I to Henry IV.* London: Allen & Unwin, 1972.

R. Churchill Curtis

HENRY IV Salian, king of the Holy Roman Empire (1056-1106). Henry was an intelligent and resolute, but undisciplined, individual. On a personal level, he and his wife were to argue, separate, and reconcile numerous times, but once he had reconciled with her, he re-established the Ottonian habit of using the church as a source of income. He also began the recapture of royal lands and revenue and planned the consolidation of the monarchy in the manner of the French throne. Henry, in the midst of suppression of the Saxon rebellion, sanctioned the reforms of *Gregory VII. Difficulties associated with disagreement between Henry, his German bishops, and Gregory had precipitated a long struggle, called the Inverture Controversy, and had disturbed relationships. This uneasy state of affairs lasted until the reign of Emperor Henry V and the Synod of Worms in 1122. At that time agreement was finally reached that in Germany elections were to be conducted in the presence of the emperor or his representative;

simony and violence were prohibited, or if disagreement occurred, the emperor was to decide; the emperor also was to be invested with the outward symbols of office. In Italy and Burgundy consecration followed, ending the public argument, but this did not stem the ongoing rivalry between the papacy and the emperor.

SELECTED BIBLIOGRAPHY

Bernhardt, John Williams. *Itinerant Kingship and Royal Monasteries in Early Medieval Germany, ca. 936-1075.* Cambridge: Cambridge University Press, 1993; Hill, Boyd H. *Medieval Monarchy in Action: The German Empire from Henry I to Henry IV.* London: Allen & Unwin, 1972.

R. Churchill Curtis

HENRY OF HUNTINGDON (c.1084-c.1157). Henry of Huntingdon, although creating fewer separate works than *William of Malmesbury and showing less discrimination in his overall use of sources, may very well have been the most ambitious historian of his time, creating a history that spanned from about 100 B. C. to his present day, the *Historia Anglorum*. Hebegan writing what became a ten-volume collection in 1133 and wrote and rewrote the work up until 1157. He had been commissioned by Alexander of Blois to write, in Latin, a history of the English people from the earliest time to the present. He relied heavily on *Bede for his earliest information and on the *Anglo-Saxon Chronicles* for the period after the *Ecclesiastical History* ended until his own time.

Eight of Henry's ten volumes comprise the history of Britain, while one other volume contains the miraculous deeds of some of Britain's saints and another three letters Henry had written for publication. Henry, who was little influenced by historians of his own time, shared some of *Geoffrey of Monmouth's interest in legendary sources--including accounts of King Arthur (*see Arthurian Legend*) into his text and relying on *Nennius for much of his content. Although overall he was a more factual historian than Geoffrey he had a tendency to moralize or sermonize about historical events. For example, he saw the Normans--whom he thought brutal--as an affliction that the English deserved, especially because of their weak leadership under reign of King Stephen.

Although it appears that Henry never achieved the popularity of Geoffrey, his work reached beyond England during his lifetime, as attested by extant manuscripts on the Continent. There are strong similarities between the content of *Orderic Vitalis, William of Malmesbury, and Henry which could mean that they all had access to a source unknown to us, but there is no evidence that Henry used the work of any of his contemporaries. Nevertheless, Henry of Huntingdon made a huge contribution to the medieval histories. (*See Chronicles and Annals.*)

SELECTED BIBLIOGRAPHY

Gransden, Antonia. *Historical Writing in England c. 550 to c. 1307.* Ithaca: Cornell University Press, 1974; Greenway, Diana. "Henry of Huntingdon and the Manuscripts of His *Historia Anglorum.*" In *Anglo-Norman Studies.* R. Brown, ed. Woodbridge, Eng.: Boydell, 1987, 103-26; Huntingdon, Henry. *The Chronicle of Henry of Huntingdon.* Thomas Forester, trans. 1853. New York: AMS Press, 1968; Smalley, Beryl. *Historians in the Middle Ages.* New York: Scribner's, 1974; Sterns, Indrikis. *The Greater Medieval Historians: An Interpretation and a Bibliography.* Lanham, MD: University Press of America, 1980; Stirneman, Patricia. "Two Twelfth Century Bibliophiles and Henry of Huntingdon's *Historia Anglorum.*" *Viator* 24 (1993), 121-42.

Richard McDonald

HENRYSON, ROBERT (1420? - 1505?). Robert Henryson was one of the Scottish Chaucerians (*see Scottish Literature*). Not much is known about this fifteenth-century poet's life, apart from his work. From the title page of one of his poems we learn that he was a schoolmaster in Dunfermline, although we find little of the expected stern tone in his poems. He probably received his master of arts at a European university and could have been the Robertus Hendisone who was a teacher of law at the University of Glasgow in 1462. Some of his poems make reference to and show his knowledge of legal vocabulary. He was probably the most learned of the Scottish Makars and achieved popularity as a poet during his lifetime. In 1508 fellow poet William *Dunbar wrote of Henryson as already dead.

Although his poems are written almost exclusively in the Chaucerian stanza, Henryson acknowledges a debt to Geoffrey *Chaucer, but never is a mere imitator. He achieves an artistic level of his own that rivals his model in such works as *The Moral Fables* and *The Testament of Cresseid*, a sequel to Chaucer's *Troylus and Criseyde*. Henryson's poem is written in the rhyme-royal of Chaucer's work, with a rhyme scheme of *ababbcc*, and with alliteration to help vary his expression and make his effect more pronounced. Though not as complex as Chaucer's *Troylus*, Henryson's *Testament* achieves the tragiclike intensity of a *ballad, and his verse carries a sense of harmony and melody. Henryson establishes the bleak mood befitting a tragedy and recounts the classical tale of Cresseid, who, when she loses her beauty to leprosy, blames it on the gods and not the natural forces to which she and all humans are bound. Henryson's tragic tale of "fickle" Fortune is just as stirring today, as he offers no Christian comfort, just the power of the inflexible gods over human free will.

Henryson also explored another popular form, the *beast fable, a genre in the tradition of Aesop in Greek and one that had been used in the study of grammar and rhetoric. *The Moral Fables*, probably a product of the 1480s (but left uncompleted), presented tales of talking animals to illustrate human character and shortcomings and integrated expansive *moralitates*, or morals that presented various readings of the tales and events. Like the cock and fox tale in Chaucer's "The *Nun's Priest's Tale," Henryson's fables warned readers of the dangers of flattery and vainglory while propounding the virtues of prudence and moderation. His tales are known for his depictions of animal life and nature, and the form also allowed for comic and mock-heroic effect. His fables are sometimes twofold, with sociological and humanitarian themes implicit in the tale itself, and with conventional *moralitates* at the end.

At a time when the communal vision of national life was slowly disintegrating, Henryson captured the changing climate and issues of his period in an accessible form. In "The Taill of the Uponlandis Mous and the Burges Mous" he contrasted the lives of the rural and mercantile mice and the effects of their environment in the Scottish age of the rise of the city. Henryson also included a tale in the Reynardian tradition, which exposed conniving and hypocritical social climbers, monks, and friars, in his "The Fox and the Wolf." The interpretations laid on by his concluding *moralitates* are sometimes disjunctive, which illustrates that the same tale can have more than one interpretation. Henryson's tales sometimes present the darkest aspects of human nature and always are effective in illustrating the disastrous consequences of human shortcomings and evil.

Henryson's other works include longer narratives such as the classical *Orpheus and Euridice*, also written in Chaucer's rhyme-royal, and a number of shorter works. His total contribution comprises examples of most medieval genres and forms, including the *romance, the testament, the *debate poem, the beast fable, ballad-like works, and pastoral narrative. Perhaps the most talented of the Scottish Makars, Henryson illustrated his prowess not in virtuosity but variety, and employed a rich palette of medieval forms to depict the humanity and atmosphere of his evolving Scotland.

SELECTED BIBLIOGRAPHY

Barrow, J.A. "Henryson: The Preaching of the Swallow." *Essays in Criticism* 25 (January 1975): 25-37; Craun, Edwin. "Blaspheming Her Awin God: Cresseid's Lamentation in Henryson's *Testament*." *Studies in Philology* 82 (Winter 1985): 25-41; McKenna, Steven R. *Robert Henryson's Tragic Vision*. New York: Peter Lang, 1994; McDiarmid, Mathew P. *Robert Henryson*. Edinburgh: Scottish Academic Press, 1981; Powell, Marianne. *Fabula Docet: Studies in the Background and Interpretation of Henryson's Fables*. Odense: Odense University Press, 1982; Storm, Melvin. "The Intertextual Cresseida: Chaucer's Henryson or Henryson's Chaucer." *Studies in Scottish Literature* 28 (1993), 105-22.

Richard McDonald

HENRY THE MINSTREL. Henry the Minstrel (Blind Harry) is perhaps the best known of the Scottish poets. Little is known about the man; it is hypothesized that he was a Lothian, but there is no documentation to prove this. In 1460 Henry composed *The Wallace*, a poem based upon the life of

William *Wallace that is one of the most famous of the Scottish poems. The work pays homage to this Scottish patriot in some 12,000 lines of heroic couplets that recall the great feats of Wallace. The author claims that the work is based upon the writings of John Blair, a man documented as Wallace's chaplain. The earliest version of Henry the Minstrel's version appears in a 1488 compilation by John Ramsey, who was also the scribe of John *Barbour's *The Bruce*.

SELECTED BIBLIOGRAPHY

MacDonald, Alasdair A. "William Dunbar, Andro and Walter Kennedy, and Hary's *Wallace*." *Neophilologus* 68:3 (July 1984), 471-77; Walsh, Elizabeth. "Hary's Wallace: The Evolution of a Hero." *Scottish Literary Journal* 11:1 (May 1984), 5-19; Wilson, Grace G. "Barbour's *Bruce* and Hary's *Wallace*: Complements, Compensations and Conventions." *Studies in Scottish Literature* 25(1990), 189-201.

Robert T. Lambdin

HIGDEN, RANULF (c. 1280s-c.1364). Ranulf Higden was probably born in the 1280s and was a Benedictine monk at St. Werburgh's Abbey in Chester in 1299. His main historical work, the *Polychronicon*, was popular during his day and throughout the rest of the Middle Ages. Higden began this universal history in 1327 and rewrote it numerous times until his death around 1360. The work consists of seven books that include an anthropological and geographical history of the world from Creation to Higden's day. He brought together information from numerous different sources and creates an encyclopedic history that surpassed in popularity all medieval historical works except *The History of the Kings of Britain* and *Bede's *Ecclesiastical History*. Higden used a wide variety of classical and Christian authorities and often identified his sources. He frequently checks his sources against one another and questions the veracity of historical facts that differ between sources. He questioned many of the more outlandish statements in his sources, for example, the fantastic achievements of Arthur (*see **Arthurian Legend***) as presented by *Geoffrey of Monmouth. He still adopted many historical facts that are discredited today, but his use of reason and comparison between sources presages some of the techniques of modern historians.

SELECTED BIBLIOGRAPHY

Clopper, Lawrence M. "Arnewaye, Higden, and the Origin of the Chester Plays." *Records of Early English Drama Newsletter* 8:2 (1983), 4-11; Dekeyser, Xavier. "Romance Loans in Late Middle English: A Study." *Cahiers de l'Institut de Linguistique de Louvain* 17:1-3 (1991), 153-62.

Richard McDonald

HISPANIC MEDIEVAL LITERATURE. The Iberian peninsula, which today includes the nations of Spain and Portugal, struggled throughout the medieval period to achieve political sovereignty. Three waves of invaders, beginning with the Romans in 206 B. C., followed by the Germanic tribes in the fifth century and then the Moors (Moslems, Arabs, and Mussulmans) in 711, delayed the level of national or cultural unity enjoyed by Italy, France, and other European countries. Between the eighth century and 1492, when Ferdinand and Isabella led the final defeat of the Moors, the region remained culturally and linguistically diverse, united primarily by intermittent efforts of regional groups to resist and repel the invaders. Even this common cause suffered at the hands of regional monarchs seeking to expand their influence and geographical boundaries. As a result, the literary history of the region began relatively late; the earliest surviving works, the *lyric poems known as the kharjas, date back to around 1100. Yet in spite of its late beginnings, a clear Hispanic medieval literary tradition can be found to echo many of the practices, themes, and concerns that appear in the literatures of other European countries. These include refinement and development of the language, movement between an oral and a written tradition, a fascination with *chivalry, and fundamental questions regarding man's relationship with God.

The Spanish language as it is spoken and written today emerged as a form of Vulgar Latin that grew alongside the classical Latin brought to the peninsula by the Romans. The Germanic Visigoths continued the official use of classical Latin, while each of the provinces developed a distinct dialect, more or less derived from Vulgar Latin. Elements of a distinct early Spanish language can be traced to the sixth century Etymologiae of *Isidore of Seville. A Spanish language independent of the mother tongue emerged toward the end of the eighth century; it is known as romance. Spanish in the twentieth century includes three dialects: Leonese-Asturian, Navarro-Aragonese, and the most widely used, Castilian. In general, Spanish is one of the most stable languages in the world; it has undergone very few changes since it first emerged.

Both Hebrew and Arabic cultures and languages have left evidence of their presence on the peninsula as well. The twelfth-century kharjas, for example, consist of poetic fragments in an early Spanish tongue embedded in Hebrew poems. The influence of Arabic appears more in vocabulary than in syntax. An example is the Arabic word "cid," meaning lord, the title given to the hero of Spain's earliest and most famous epic poem. Also spoken on the Peninsula are Portuguese, Catalan and Basque.

Spanish literature of the Renaissance and the Golden Age owes an important debt to a widespread oral and popular tradition established in the Middle Ages. Professional singers known as "juglares" entertained Spaniards of all social and economic classes with their ballads, short epico-lyric poems about the exploits of national heroes. Although the transcription of oral poetry and song did not begin until the sixteenth century, the themes, subject matter, and occasionally the language and syntax date many of these works as products of the Middle Ages. Some of the ballads enjoyed by the general population in the fourteenth century and later may have been extracted from longer medieval epic and narrative poems.

In a striking parallel with the literary history of England, Hispanic medieval literature embraces both the chivalric tradition and a number of seemingly contradictory Christian values and themes. Otis H. Green addressed these contradictions in his seminal article "The Medieval Tradition: *Sic et Non*." He identified three kinds of chivalry: that of the knights fighting for glory and honor, that of the ladies who set the knights upon a supreme trial in the pursuit of *courtly love, and that of the priests. The priests' battles, exemplified in the fourteenth century prose work *The Book of the Knight of God Whose Name Was Zifar, Who Because of His Exercise of Virtue and Heroic Deeds Became King of Menton*, involve the protection of the good and weak, defense of the church and clergy, and a constant war against enemies of the Faith (Green 8). Green pointed out the excesses of vengeance, dueling, and warring in pursuit of the paradoxical aims of honor and faith, suggesting finally a subtle logic that would allow for such contradictions in medieval life and literature. Such a logic displaces the literal sense of the Ten Commandments ("Thou shalt not kill," for instance) onto a more figurative and ultimately more spiritual space of justice and faith.

The courtly love tradition, expressed both in lyric poetry and in prose fiction, is similar to that of English literature. The man and the woman are of noble descent; the man generally proclaims himself inferior to the woman and unworthy of her love, but he seeks redemption through the reward of that love. There is often a transfer of religious emotion and religious imagery to sexual love. The woman may or may not reciprocate the man's passion, and their relationship is often kept secret. Little mention is made of marriage, and some encounters are implicitly adulterous. Finally, courtly love results in frustration, either because it remains unconsummated or because disaster befalls the lovers upon consummation. The legends of King Arthur (*see* **Arthurian Legend**) were well known on the peninsula, possibly imported from France.

Religious themes, most notably as they appear in hagiographical tales of the saints' lives, echo throughout the medieval literary history of the peninsula. Considering the strength of the Roman Catholic Church throughout Spain and Portugal and the locus of writing in the monasteries, this is neither surprising nor inconsistent with other strands of Hispanic medieval literature. The late Hispanic medievalist John Walsh devoted a great deal of attention to the collection and preservation of religious literature of the period. Alan Deyermond has produced a catalog of lost hagiographic works. With these general foundations, all common to the medieval literatures of Europe, Spain forged a cultural identity and a strong literary tradition. This tradition can best be traced through a study of the genres of verse, both epic and lyric, drama, and prose, both fictional and nonfictional, and drama.

Verse: Richard E. Chandler suggested that the traditions of lyric and epic/narrative poetry in medieval Spain and Portugal were not always clearly separated. Although the *Cantar de Mío Cid belongs with certainty to the epic genre, these formal lines were crossed by other poets, including Gonzalo de Berceo of the twelfth century.

The discovery of the lyric kharjas in 1948 refocused the scholarly attention given to lyric poetry of medieval Spain and Portugal. Kharjos are brief lyrical fragments written in the archaic Spanish dialect known as Mozarabic and appended to longer poems written in Hebrew or Arabic. One such fragment dates from approximately 1042. The longer poems, generally panegyric, are called muwassaha. In contrast to the subject matter of the muwassaha, the kharjas address a young woman's love and longing for her absent love or a homosexual love. The fragments are not addressed to the speaker's beloved, but seem rather to reflect figuratively the relationship between poet and patron. Deyermond has suggested the latter reading, rather than a literal sense of sexual love.

Several of the kharjas incorporate the dawn song, a form found in a number of European medieval traditions. The dawn song tells of lovers who have spent the night together and must part at dawn; in another variation this song represents a joyful reunion of lovers at the dawn. Like the songs of young women's love, however, the dawn is sometimes used as a metaphor for the lover.

The greater significance of the kharjas is the light they shed on the evolution of lyric poetry through channels of popular song and literature. Lyric poetry continued to flourish throughout the medieval period, both as a popular entertainment provided by the juglares and as a polished literary art practiced by learned and cultured poets, including Spanish and Portuguese royalty and respected clergy. The fusion of the kharjas with the more cultured language of the muwassaha indicates a mingling of the popular and the cultured lyric traditions. It is likely that the learned poets transcribed popular verse as they prepared to incorporate its rhythms and themes into more polished forms.

There were, however, preferred dialects for lyric poetry: Galician-Portuguese and the French-based Catalonian. The Catalonian poets may have gained an interest in the genre through their contacts with Provence in southern France, where a certain strain of lyrical lament developed into technical excellence. This troubadouresque verse reflected a sterile, highly formalized game of love practiced by courtiers. In Galicia, with its simple rustic way of life and lively peasant culture, the *Provençal poetry inspired not only cultured imitations but also a popular strain that celebrated its native customs. Galician lyric poetry remained strongest between the twelfth and fourteenth centuries. Poets from other provinces often wrote in the Galician dialect; among these was *Alfonso X, el sabio, a Castilian monarch who ruled between 1252 and 1284. The Castilian dialect was considered too primitive to capture the linguistic finesse needed to express the intricacies of lyrical subject matter.

A substantial body of Galician-Portuguese poetry survives in collections known as cancioneiros. These collections, among which are Cancioneiro da Vaticana, Cancioneiro da Ajuda, and Cancioneiro Colocci-

Brancuti, have assisted scholars in identifying three general types of lyric poetry written in the thirteenth and fourteenth centuries. First are the cantigas de escarnio, satirical and often obscene songs; second, the cantigas de amor, laments spoken by a male lover; and third, the cantigas de amigo, love songs of lonesome women. The cantigas de amigo take their name from their frequent repetition of the word "amigo. "

Although scorned as a dialect for cultured lyrical verse, Castilian served as the principal tongue for the serranillas, a genre of occasional and ceremonial songs and unrecorded poetry. Later poets, particularly those of the Spanish Golden Age, admired the rustic charm and energy of these songs and drew upon them widely. Another Castilian form is the villancico, a poem consisting of a glosa, which develops the theme, and an estribillo, several lines that open and close each stanza. These poems remained part of the oral tradition until the beginning of the fifteenth century. Spoken by a woman, these poems address not only romantic longings, but also such issues as a woman's resistance to becoming a nun and another's concern over the possibility of having Moorish blood (Deyermond 23).

Until the discovery of the lyric kharjas, scholars of Hispanic medieval literature generally focused their attention on the epic and/or narrative poem in their histories of the development of verse forms. The heroic subject matter of the epic suited the embattled political state of the peninsula. Deyermond suggested that the epic helps to unify a people in times of political turmoil and war. This seems likely in the medieval regions of Spain and Portugal, whose (often anonymous) poets celebrated internal and external military exploits through highly realistic epic verse.

The earliest extant example is *Cantar de Mio Cid*, dated around 1140, an epic account of the life of the hero, Rodrigo DPaz de Vivar, who was born in 1043 in an area north of Burgos. The Cid and a number of other epic heroes suffer routinely at the hands of their own kings, a sign of the internal strife that kept the region divided for most of the medieval period. Well known subjects include Rodrigo el Ultimo Godo, the last of the Gothic kings, who legend states allowed Spain to fall to the Moors; Los Infantes de Lara, seven brothers betrayed in battle by an uncle and later avenged by a half brother; and Rey don Sancho II, a Castilian king and contemporary of the Cid. The only epic hero for whom a historical counterpart has not been found is Bernardo del Carpio, a warrior instrumental in the defeat of Roland at Roncesvalles. Further, this poetry is the most realistic of European medieval epic, with little of the fantastic or supernatural characteristic of its French or German counterparts. In many cases place names and dates can be verified. In fact, historical documents routinely cited and drew upon epic verse as source material, and a good deal of the history of the genre is derived from such references.

For the most part, Hispanic epic poetry shows no regularity of meter or versification. In *Cantar de Mio Cid* lines range in length from ten to twenty syllables, with a dominant pattern of fourteen. Some of this irregularity may be attributed to the copyists. The rhyme scheme in this and other epics is assonance.

Epic poetry declined in the fourteenth century; some scholars speculate that this decline occurred as the genre moved away from the realm of the popular poets into the hands of more learned ones whose accurate but dull creations failed to stir the popular imagination. As the epic waned, the popular ballad began to grow as a form of popular expression; versions of medieval ballads are still being recorded and adapted today by Spanish and Portuguese poets. Medieval epic poetry enjoyed a revival in Spain's sixteenth-century Golden Age, to some degree in form, but principally as a rich source of subject matter for fictional prose.

For a more consistent and uniquely Spanish medieval verse, scholars point to the narrative cuaderna via, a shorter narrative form. These poems have fourteen-syllable lines broken in the middle by a caesura. The rhyme scheme is *aaaa, bbbb*; a full rather than an assonant rhyme predominates. Cuaderna via was written in the thirteenth century by learned poets who distinguished themselves from the juglares by their ability to "count syllables." The subject matter generally focused upon saints' lives and miracles of the Virgin.

Like the epic and lyric peninsular verse, cuaderna via seems to combine oral and written traditions in a way that encouraged its growth. Deyermond noted a number of references to speech in phrases such as "I shall tell you," (69). To account for these references as well as the comparative complexity of these poems, Deyermond suggested that they were read to small, homogenous audiences in semi-private settings, perhaps on occasion to groups of pilgrims. From these audiences, the genre's form and content spread to the mouths of the juglares and ultimately to a more general and public audience. Among the creators of cuaderna via is the first known Spanish poet, Gonzalo de Berceo. His hagiographic works reflect both his clerical education and vocation and his rhetorical and cultural connection with the common people.

Other verse traditions that emerged in the thirteenth and fourteenth centuries include moral, satirical, and debate poems. Moral and satirical poetry exalted moral virtue while attacking vice in society. The Jewish poet Sem Tob wrote the *Proverbios morales* in this mode. Following a widely practiced European form, the twelve-syllable octave verse known as versos de art mayor also appeared in the anonymous poem *Danza de la muerte*. In this poem Death summons before his court thirty-three victims, each becoming the object of satire on behalf of his social station. Political satires known as coplas first appeared in the fifteenth century; these poems aimed their invective at the nobililty, often for their cowardice. The anonymous *Coplas del Provincial*, in the view of Chandler, exemplifies an "inexcusable" and "libelous slander" (59). In a more temperate vein are the *Coplas de Mingo Revulgo*, an allegorical shepherd's lament.

A Hispanic version of the debate poem can be found in Arabic and Hebrew as early as the ninth century and in Latin around the beginning of the tenth. Following the European tradition, this genre appealed to educated and uneducated audiences alike. Rhetorical contexts and devices varied among poets and audiences; topics ranged from the theological to the erotic to the economic. The thirteenth-century debate poem *Razon de amor con los denuestos del agua y el vino* puzzles scholars with its combination of a romantic narrative/lyric and a terse debate between water and wine.

Nearly all of the traditions and innovations associated with medieval Hispanic poetry can be found in *El *Libro de Buen Amor,* the collected works of Juan Ruiz, arcipreste de Hita. A lyricist, satirist, and practitioner of cuaderna via, Ruiz elevated Spanish poetry by experimenting with form and diction.

In a pattern typical of Western Europe, medieval *drama in the Hispanic peninsula emerged from its solely liturgical, didactic origin to a more popular form of entertainment. A scarcity of evidence once again forces scholars to conjecture based on a single example of twelfth-century liturgical drama, archival records of a *Corpus Christi cycle drama in the late fifteenth century, and allusions to drama in other historical documents.

Drawing upon these scanty resources, scholars suggest that liturgical drama grew out of the dramatic potential of the Mass. Its earliest forms included dialogues based on Scripture and dialectical chants. Natural subjects for this drama were the Christmas and Easter stories; later expansions corresponded with cycles and festivals of the Church: Epiphany, Day of the Innocents, Palm Sunday, Good Friday, and Corpus Christi. These plays were performed in Latin in the churches with clerics serving as the actors.

Although it is likely that Spain experienced liturgical drama with other European nations as early as 900, the earliest and only existing manuscript is thought to date from the mid-twelfth century, within a few years of *Cantar de Mio Cid.* This play, *El Auto de los reyes magos,* enacts the Epiphany cycle. The presence of a large number of French Cluny monks gives credence to the suggestion that this play derives from a Latin language original written in Orleans. *El Auto* enacts the meeting of the three shepherds (or perhaps the magi) as they travel to Bethlehem. A sudden shift places them before Herod for an antagonistic encounter The fragment breaks off with the solitary Herod brooding over the encounter and calling in his astrologer It is assumed that the play actually ended with an adoration scene at the manger.

This early play, not only the second-oldest surviving literary work of Spain, but also the second oldest liturgical drama to be discovered in Europe, shows a clear delineation of character as the shepherds (magi) muse over the Star of Bethlehem, and later as Herod reveals his doubt over the advice he receives. Chandler pointed out the realistic characterization and "the beginning of the polymetric tendency in the Spanish theater" (69), both of which find counterparts in early epic poetry.

Gradually the liturgical drama absorbed secular speech and themes that were inappropriate for its home in the sanctuary. Lay actors began to perform their art in marketplaces for wider audiences. The presence of uneducated shepherds in the religious plays provided an opportunity to exploit a more secular dialect, attitude, and sense of humor.

Historical documents also indicate a tradition of purely secular drama, or teatro profano, although no traces of these plays remain. The seminal legal and historical document *Siete Partidas, prepared under the sponsorship of Alfonso X, el Sabio, mentions such a tradition, including plays of mockery (juegos de escarnio). The Siete Partidas clearly stated the church's disapproval of such plays, whose satire of church matters most likely bordered upon sacrilege.

Another gap in evidence between the thirteenth and sixteenth centuries leaves scholars with the singular tool of speculation. With the oral, performance-based tradition inherent in the poetry of the Middle Ages, it is possible that drama developed slowly. At the same time, the contributions of Spanish drama to European Renaissance literature suggest a gradual development in complexity and artistry over the course of these three centuries. As the medieval period was coming to an end, Juan del Encina, known as the father of Spanish theater, was coming of age.

La *Celestina, a prose drama consisting of twenty-one acts, is associated with the history of drama in Spain. Because it clearly was written to be read and not performed, it is more often considered a dramatic prose work. It was produced during the end of the fifteenth century by Fernando de Rojas, a converted Jewish lawyer.

Nonfictional Prose: Access to the medieval legacy of poetry and drama in the Hispanic peninsula relies heavily upon another genre, that of nonfictional and historical prose (see History). Fact and fiction in the medieval period often combined to inform historical records. This practice proved to be an advantage for scholars seeking to reconstruct the history of specific works and genres that could not be located in manuscript form.

The earliest nonfictional prose works were *chronicles of events written in Latin and compiled by the monasteries. Although these rough works were often inaccurate and incomplete, the writings of two clerics stand out for their literary and historical value. Lucas de Tuy, known as "el Tudense," lived in the mid-twelfth century and wrote the Chronicon mundi in 1236. This work was translated into Spanish under the title Cronica de Spana por Luchas de Tui. Don Rodrigo Jimenez de Rada, Archbishop of Toledo, is known for his Historia Gothica, written in Latin in the thirteenth century and translated into Spanish as Estoria de los godos.

Because Spain served as the geographical channel through which ideas and their literary expressions made their way from the Orient and the Middle East to Western Europe, translation became a thriving occupation, particularly in the culturally rich city of Toledo in the twelfth century. Scholars traveled to this city from all of Europe to be enlightened in such diverse subjects as astronomy, medicine, mathematics, and philosophy.

The most significant development of nonfictional prose, however, occurred during the reign of Alfonso X, "el Sabio," or the "Learned King" (1221-1284). An accomplished lyric poet, this king compensated for his military and political mediocrity with an outstanding commitment to arts and letters. Under his sponsorship Spanish (particularly the Castilian dialect) became the language of official documents. While the nation continued to bristle under Moorish rule, with little progress toward reconquest, Alfonso El Sabio launched a more formidable campaign to explore and document history, the law, and a number of scientific and technical disciplines.

The best known historical document commissioned by Alfonso X was the *Cronica general*, referred to today as *La primera cronica general* after the 1906 edition compiled by Menendez Pidal. This work begins with the sons of Noah and traces the history of humanity through the death of Fernando III, father of Alfonso X. A nationalistic strain characterizes the work, even in portions addressing the ancient world and topics remote from Spanish history. A section detailing the reconquest during the reign of Ferdinand III includes fragments of epic poems that are of particular interest to literary scholars. Accurate and artfully written, the *Cronica* remains an unparalleled achievement in the cultural history of the nation. Equally ambitious was the world history entitled the *General estoria*, which remained unfinished at Alfonso's death.

Prior to Alfonso X's reign the peninsula lived under an unorganized and inconsistent code of laws. Elements of Gothic and Roman law overlapped to create a porous and less-than-stable alliance among noblemen and the reigning monarch. In the *Siete Partidas* Alfonso set out to create a single legal standard for the citizens of Castile, partly to stabilize the monarchy and prevent insurrections. Although this legal code was implemented fully only a century later, the work was immediately recognized as a legislative innovation. For the literary scholar, the *Siete Partidas* also serves as a colorful and detailed account of life, manners, customs, dress, and entertainments of thirteenth-century Spain.

Alfonso X also commissioned scientific and technical works in areas of interest to him. His *Lapidario* investigates the magical properties of precious stones. The *Libros del saber de astronomio* and the *Tablas Alfonsies* consist mostly of translations of Arabic works on astronomical science.

Under the shadow of his father's ambitious research and documentation efforts, Sancho IV directed the conclusion of the *Primera cronica general*. Although the interest in history and letters sparked by Alfonso X remained strong throughout the fourteenth and fifteenth centuries, output was less distinguished. Juan Manuel (1282-1349), a nobleman, warrior, and chronicler, lived a dangerous life of political and military intrigue against reigning Spanish monarchs and Moors alike. His historical writings, however, tend toward the didactic.

Fictional Prose: Spain's Golden Age of literature, which spanned roughly from 1500 to the closing years of the seventeenth century, often obscures the literary accomplishments of the medieval period. This is certainly the case with fictional prose. Yet without denying the merit and lasting appeal of Cervantes's *Don Quixote* and other innovations in the picaresque novel, one can demonstrate that medieval peninsular literature offered a rich foundation for these later masterpieces. More suited for the cadences of prose than for poetry, the Castilian dialect gained respect among the learned as its subtleties developed through fictional narrative. Catalan, Portuguese, and Leonese dialects are also represented in early versions of the genre.

Early fictional prose drew upon a number of sources for subject matter and form, including the Bible, the Greek adventure novels, the Roman fictional social discourses, and the parables, fables, and apologues of the Orient. The latter influence reached Spain first, then later made its way north through the other European countries. Oriental tales of these kinds probably originated in India, then spread through North Africa and the Arabic countries. The Moorish invaders then brought them to the peninsula, where they were joined into loose frameworks similar to the *Arabian Nights*. These highly moral tales were fictional only in the structural device of the frame. However, as Chandler argued, they served as the most powerful influence on Spanish narrative prose in the Middle Ages. The collections were known as *exempla, and they thrived in Spain between the thirteenth and fifteenth centuries.

A number of exempla survive to document the success of this literary form. The *Disciplina clericalis* is the earliest example to appear in Spain. This collection of Oriental stories was written in Arabic and translated into Latin by Pedro Alfonso in the early twelfth century. The frame device in these stories involves a father giving advice to his son; the tales each dramatize a particular moral or ethical principle. The first collection of this kind made available to Spanish readers, it was translated into the Spanish language in the fifteenth century. It was widely read and freely plagiarized by later writers.

The oldest known fictional work in the Spanish language is the *Libro de Calila e Dimna*. Translated from Arabic under the sponsorship of Alfonso el Sabio in 1251, this group of tales can be traced to Sanskrit originals. Calila and Dimna are wolves who battle with a lion and an ox in a number of struggles that allegorize both political and universal human conflict. The wolves engage in philosophical and satirical dialogue on the faults and failings of human nature. In addition to its influence upon later Hispanic and European writers, *Calila e Dimna* also remains an important artifact documenting the early history of the Spanish language.

Other exempla include the *Libro de los engannos e assayamientos de las mugeres* (Book of the Deceits and Wiles of Women), and *Barlaam y Josaphat*. The former, translated from the Arabic in 1253, illustrates the low social status of women in Medieval Spain through the trial and punishment of a queen for licentiousness. The latter adapts the Buddha legend, replacing many of the fantastic sequences with discourses on Christian theology. Themes and incidents from the exempla echo throughout the later fiction and drama of Spain.

Among the cultural imports from France to Spain are the seeds of another type of narrative prose, the medieval novel of chivalry. The medieval versions of these novels, mostly translations and adaptations from the French or the Italian, helped to move the genre toward its Renaissance culmination in works such as the *Amadis*, the *Tirant*, and the two *Palmerines*. Spanish novels of chivalry fall into four categories or cycles: the Carolingian, the cycle of antiquity, the Arthurian, and the cycle of the *Crusades.

The Carolingian cycle addresses the life of Emperor *Charlemagne, including the famous story of Roncesvalles. Spanish versions of these works include *Maynette* and *Historia de Carlo Magno y de los doce pares*. The best known Spanish adaptation of the cycles of antiquity is the *Historia troyana*, a dramatization of the siege and destruction of Troy.

The Arthurian cycle, the best known of all European chivalric novels or romances, relates the stories of the British King Arthur and the Knights of the Round Table, with certain magical elements represented by the character of Merlin. Although the subject matter of the Arthurian cycle is British, medieval French writers are credited with expanding the early Celtic verse versions into narrative tales. Spanish interpretations include the *Demanda del Santo Grial*, *Tristan*, and the *Baladro del sablo Merlin*.

It is believed that early versions of the famous romance *Amadis de Gaula* circulated through the peninsula in the fourteenth century. This Arthurian adaptation may have been commissioned by Alfonso XI at the beginning of the thirteenth century, although others have suggested a Portuguese origin. The Renaissance version of this romance, dated 1508 and produced by Garci Rodríguez de Montalvo, was widely read and adapted by French, English, Italian, and German writers. Its elucidation of the knight's code of honor and virtuous manners was translated into English and French.

The cycle of the Crusades, while dealing with these historical events in a blend of fact and fiction, is best represented by *La ran conquista de ultramar*, written in the late thirteenth century. This work offers historical and fictional accounts of the Crusades, including the conquest of Jerusalem by Godfrey de Bouillon and a number of episodes from French romances.

All of the early fictional and prose traditions described previously combine in *El Caballero Zifar*, the anonymous first full-length novel in Spain. This work combines a rambling account of the life of Saint Eustace with a chivalric tale of the adventures of the heroic knight Zifar. This knight-errant experiences the courtly love rituals associated with the inaccessible lady. Echoing the circular structure of Greek adventure novels, Zifar is separated from and then reunited with his first wife, Grima. Woven throughout the work are apologues and other moralistic, didactic passages. *Zifar* is the first Spanish work to use popular language, the first to use proverbs and jokes, and most likely the first to present a forerunner of Don Quixote's Sancho Panza character.

The first known writer of Spanish fiction is Juan Manuel, grandson of Fernando III and nephew of Alfonso X, el Sabio. In addition to his reputation as a historian, Manuel is also celebrated as the first Spanish prose stylist. He brought to life the Spanish language in his novel *Libro del Conde Lucanor*, written between 1323 and 1335, with multi-layered meanings and resonant words. Of the work's four parts, only the first is famous; it refigures the Oriental moral tales as the Count Lucanor seeks advice from his counselor, Patronio.

Closely related to the novel of chivalry is the sentimental novel, a semi-autobiographical love story featuring a knight-errant engaged in episodes of tragic or ill-fated love. Often epistolary in form, these novels occasionally featured discourses asserting the rights of women. The earliest known sentimental novel, *El siervo libre de amor*, was written approximately 1440 by Juan Rodriguez de la Camara, a champion of women's rights. This work was highly influenced by *Boccaccio's *La Fiammetta*. The best known of the sentimental novels is *Carcel de amor*, first published in 1492 by Diego de San Pedro. Circulated in numerous Spanish and foreign language editions, this novel influenced the major Spanish works, the *Celestina* and *Don Quixote*.

As the fifteenth century ended, the prose traditions of the period were helping to shape several other forms that were to blossom in Spain's sixteenth-century Golden Age and later. The pastoral novel, a combination of prose and poetry portraying a highly idealized and artificial landscape, emerged in the 1504 work *Arcadia* by Jacopo Sannazaro. The Moorish occupiers of medieval Spain provided the subject matter of the historical novels, exemplified by the anonymous *Historia del Abencerraje y de la hermosa Jarifa*, circa 1565. This and other works idealized the "nobility" of the Moors at a time when the newly independent Spaniards actually held little respect for their former occupiers. The most famous of the Hispanic prose genres is the picaresque novel, the episodic, highly satirical tale epitomized by *Don Quixote de la Mancha*. Although this form appeared well after the close of the medieval period, its beginnings can be seen in such works as the fourteenth century *Cabellero Zifar*.

SELECTED BIBLIOGRAPHY

Primary Works in English Translation: Webber, Ruth H., ed. *The Hispanic Ballad Today*. New York: Garland, 1989; Wilhelm, James J. *Lyrics of the Middle Ages: An Anthology*. New York: Garland, 1990.

Secondary works: Bell, Aubrey F.G. *Castilian Literature*. 1938. New York: Russell and Russell, 1968; Cantavella, Rosanna. "Medieval Mary Magdalen Narratives." In *Saints and Their Authors: Studies in Medieval Hispanic Hagiography in Honor of John K. Walsh*. Jane E, Connolly, Alan Deyermond and Brian Dutton, eds. Madison, WI: Hispanic Seminary of Medieval Studies, 1990; Chandler, Richard E., and Kessel Schwartz. *A New History of Spanish Literature*. Baton Rouge: Louisiana State University Press, 1961; Connolly, Jane E., Alan Deyermond and Brian Dutton, eds. *Saints and their Authors: Studies in Medieval Hispanic Hagiography in Honor of John*

K. Walsh. Madison, WI: Hispanic Seminary of Medieval Studies, 1990; Deyermond, A.D., *A Literary History of Spain: The Middle Ages.* London: Ernest Benn Limited, 1971; Deyermond, Alan, W.F. Hunter, and Joseph T. Snow, eds. *Medieval and Renaissance Spanish Literature: Selected Essays by Keith Whinnom.* Exeter, UK: University of Exeter Press, 1994; Deyermond, Alan, and Jeremy Lawrance. *Letters and Society in Fifteenth-Century Spain: Studies Presented to P.E. Russel on his Eightieth Birthday.* London: The Dolphin Book Co., 1993; Gerli, E. Michael, and Harvey L. Sharrer, eds. *Hispanic Medieval Studies in Honor of Samuel G. Armistead.* Madison, WI: Hispanic Seminary of Medieval Studies, 1992; Green, Otis H. *Spain and the Western Tradition: The Castilian Mind in Literature from El Cid to Calder.:n.* Vol. 1. Madison, WI: University of Wisconsin Press, 1963; Green, Otis H. *The Literary Mind of Medieval and Renaissance Spain.* Lexington: University Press of Kentucky, 1970; Harney, Michael. "Economy and Utopia in the Medieval Hispanic Chivalric Romance."*Hispanic Review* 62:3 (Summer 1994), 381-403. Lloyd, Paul M. "On Conducting Sociolinguistic Research in the Middle Ages." In *Hispanic Medieval Studies in Honor of Samuel G. Armistead.* E. Michael Gerli and Harvey L. Sharrer, eds. Madison, WI: Hispanic Seminary of Medieval Studies, 1992; Northup, George Tyler. *An Introduction to Spanish Literature.* Chicago: University of Chicago Press, 1965; Ticknor, George. *History of Spanish Literature.* Vol. 1. New York: Gordian Press, 1965; Whinnom, Keith. "Spanish Literary Historiography: Three Forms of Distortion." In *Medieval and Renaissance Spanish Literature: Selected Essays by Keith Whinnom.* A.D. Deyermond, W. F. Hunter, and Joseph T. Snow, eds. Exeter, UK: University of Exeter Press, 1994, 96 113.

Rebecca Stephens

HISTORIA BRITTONUM (c. 800). A ninth century chronicle apparently written by a Welsh historian, the *Historia Brittonum* seems intended to reflect a revival of Welsh nationalism. Arthur (*see Arthurian Legend*) is a great warlord, rather than a king, who pushes the British force to victory in twelve great battles; in one, the Battle of Badon Hill, Arthur kills 960 of the enemy by his own hand. This work may be a fictional creation of a character to be admired, but it became the basis for many Arthurian legends. The *Historia Brittonum* is little more than an outline of "newspaper headlines." Yet from this seed was sprung the character of Arthur who plays such a prominent role in later literature, myths, and legends.

SELECTED BIBLIOGRAPHY

Barber, Richard, ed. *The Arthurian Legend.* London: Dorset, 1979. Bryden, Inga. "Arthur as Artefact: Concretizing the Fictions of the Past." *Angloki* 1:2 (Winter 1993-94), 149-57; Garbáty, Thomas J. *Medieval English Literature.*Toronto: Heath, 1984; Jones, W. Lewis. *King Arthur in History and Legend.* Cambridge: Cambridge University Press, 1911; Lacy, Norris J.,ed. *The Arthurian Encyclopedia.* New York: Bedrick, 1986.

Laura Cooner Lambdin

HISTORIA REGUM BRITTANIAE (1136). The *Historia Regum Brittaniae* is a fictional account of the history of England that was believed to be fact by many later generations, well into the Renaissance. The text helped solidify the *Arthurian Legends and claim for King Arthur a legitimate place in history. *Geoffrey of Monmouth claimed to have translated an ancient book written in the English language, which had been given to him by Walter, archdeacon of Oxford. Few scholars believe in this source, inasmuch as citing such authorities was a standard ploy of medieval writers, although it is possible that the author may have had a written copy of ancient oral folklore.

The history of England is traced from the fall of Troy until Brutus flees to Britain. Geoffrey was the first to record Arthur's conception as the product of Merlin's disguising Uther Pendragon as the Duke of Cornwall, the husband of Igerna. This echoes a similar tale in the *romances of Alexander the Great. Geoffrey's Arthur is challenged in his court and urged by counselors to cross the channel and sweep through northern France. He fights in a great battle and is hailed as king, but dies before he can be crowned.

The work seems a patriotic history that gives the *Anglo-Norman aristocracy a British hero/ruler as noble as *Charlemagne. For the first time we see contemporary politics involved in the English *chronicle: the Norman interest in bringing Brittany into their sphere of influence is reflected in the large part that the Bretons play. There is also the possibility that Geoffrey intended Arthur's Roman expedition to reflect Henry's conquest of France. Largely owing to the tradition of Geoffrey, Arthur becomes a symbol of British national spirit and a practical model for medieval and Renaissance kings.

SELECTED BIBLIOGRAPHY

Coates, Richard. "A Gloss on 'A Nefando Ambrane' in the *History of the Kings of Britain.*" *ANQ* 2:4 (October 1989), 123-24; Neuendorf, Fiona Tolhurst. "Negotiating Feminist and Historicist Concerns: Guinevere in Geoffrey of Monmouth's *Historia Regum Brittaniae. Quondam et Futurus* 3:2 (Summer 1993), 26-44.

Laura Cooner Lambdin

HISTORIES. The literary history that developed from medieval *chronicles and *annals is closely related to the medieval *romance. As the listening and reading public became more interested in historical occurrences, historical documents were written with a greater attention to detail and creating drama. Writers of increasing literary talent began to devote themselves to recounting the events of the distant and recent past, and their public expected them to include speeches and specifics of action that would not necessarily be based on historical truth, but would generate an entertaining story. The many extant histories attest to this genre's popularity.

SELECTED BIBLIOGRAPHY

Brandt, William J. *The Shape of Medieval History*. New Haven: Yale University Press, 1966; Fines, John. *Who's Who in the Middle Ages*. New York: Barnes, 1970; Gellrich, Jesse M. *Discourse and Dominion in the Fourteenth Century*. Princeton: Princeton University Press, 1995; Goffart, Walter. *The Narrators of Barbarian History (A.D. 550-800)*. Princeton: Princeton University Press, 1988; Gransden, Antonia. *Historical Writing in England c.550 to c.1307*. Ithaca: Cornell University Press, 1974; Smalley, Beryl. *Historians in the Middle Ages*. New York: Scribner's, 1974; Taylor, John. *English Historical Literature in the Fourteenth Century*. Oxford: Clarendon, 1987.

Richard McDonald

HOCCLEVE (OR OCCLEVE), THOMAS (c. 1369-1426). Thomas Hoccleve is considered among the best poets of fifteenth century England. While only a small portion of his canon of works remains, he was known as a vociferous composer. Many of his extant works are moral, but another portion describes events of his life. He is considered to be among the first "English Chaucerians." In this regard Hoccleve was one of the few authors of this time who successfully wrote works that followed the tradition set forth by Geoffrey *Chaucer in his *Canterbury Tales*.

One of his major works is *Le Male Règle de Thomas Hoccleve*, a biographical poem of penitence. In this work Hoccleve confesses various youthful follies, including twenty years of excessive drinking and reckless actions in which he tried to take liberties with the women at the Paul's Head Tavern. His other works include other "series poems" based upon his life, such as "The Complaint" and "The Dialogue with a Friend," a discussion of poetry written as an exchange between two friends. So personal is Hoccleve's work that many of his poems concern his mental breakdown.

SELECTED BIBLIOGRAPHY

Edmond, Mary. "Thomas Hoccleve: Some Redatings." *Review of English Studies* 46:183 (August 1995), 366-72; Stokes, Charity Scott. "Thomas Hoccleve's 'Mother of God' and 'Balade to the Virgin and Christ:'" Latin and Anglo Norman Sources." *Medium Evum* 64:1 (1995), 74-84.

Robert T. Lambdin

HOLCOT, ROBERT (died c. 1349). Robert Holcot was a Dominican who was influenced by the philosopy of William *Ockham. Holcot was especially inspired to preach that humans had free wills and were therefore responsible for their actions and the paths that their lives take. This theological thought was the polar opposite to that of his peer Thomas Bradwardine, who often sermonized on the concept of predestination. The teachings of Holcot so offended Bradwardine that he considered Holcot to be a "New *Pelagian"; this derogatory term implied that Holcot denied the doctrine of original sin. This was not true, but it did lead to a kind of philosophical skirmish between the two.

Holcot's *Moralitates Historiarum*, a series of metaphorical works that may be sources for the *Gesta Romanorum* is considered to be among his most noted works. He composed vast amounts of works for he was a prolific writer. His enduring legacy may be that his compositions rely upon metaphorical expressions of abstract ideals as a means of instructing his audience.

SELECTED BIBLIOGRAPHY

O'Mara, Philip F. "Holcot and the Pearl Poet." *Chaucer Review* 27:1 (1992), 97-106; Tachau, Katherine H. "Looking Gravely at Dominican Puns: The 'Sermons' of Robert Holcot and Ralph Friseby." *Traditio* 46 (1991), 337-45.

Robert T. Lambdin

HORN CHILDE. The northern *romance *Horn Childe* was composed sometime after 1290. The plot resembles that of *King Horn*, another great romance, but it does contain some great differences. *Horn Child* is a kind of male Cinderella story that keeps the main form of *King Horn* but loses much of the vigor of its source. In *Horn Childe* Horn is a prince who is forced to flee to southern England, where he finds safety. There Horn also falls in love with the king's daughter, Rimnild. Horn's friends betray his love to the king, and he is forced to flee. His journeys take him first to Wales and then to Ireland.

Before he left, Rimnild gave him her magic ring, a typical act of the romances, so Horn is assured to return and claim her. Before this occurs, Horn cleanses Ireland of its pagans and establishes a code of Christianity. He then goes back to England where he gains requital against the two friends who betrayed him. These actions pave the way for his marriage to Rimnild.

As a romance, *Horn Childe* was extremely popular. It inspired the *ballad "Hind Horn." Also, it is believed that this romance is the one referred to in Geoffrey *Chaucer's "Tale of *Sir Thopas" in his *Canterbury Tales*.

SELECTED BIBLIOGRAPHY

Frakes, Jerold C. "Metaphysical Structure as Narrative Structure in the Medieval Romance." *Neophilologus* 69:4 (1985), 481-89; 238-49; Lindahl, Carl. "The Oral Undertones of Late Medieval Romance." In *Oral Tradition in the Middle Ages*. W.F.H. Nicolaisen, ed. Binghamton, NY: Medieval and Renaissance Texts and Studies, 1995. 59-75.

Robert T. Lambdin

HOUSE OF FAME, THE. Composed between 1379 and 1384, *The House of Fame* is an unfinished poem by Geoffrey *Chaucer. It is believed that this love-vision symbolized the union of Richard II and Anne of Bohemia, although others see it as an attack on *John of Gaunt for appearing in public with his mistress, Catherine Swynford. *The House of Fame* is structured like a French allegorical vision in 2,158 lines of octosyllabic couplets.

While the poem begins as a French love-vision, it draws upon many major sources, including Ovid, *Boethius, *Dante, and *Petrarch; however, the major source is *Boccaccio's *Il *Filostrato.* In the first section of the work the poet re-creates his *dream vision and describes his visit to the Temple of Venus. There he happens upon an inscribed version of Virgil's woeful tale of Aeneas and Dido. In the second book a great eagle converses with the narrator before delivering the narrator to the House of Fame, a place that the eagle has determined will instruct the narrator more about the art of love. The third book centers upon Lady Fame doling out both fame and slander to her applicants. To others she denies renown. The narrator is puzzled, as this all seems to be done arbitrarily. The narrator is then whisked away to the House of Rumor, where the lower folks, such as the gossips and courtiers, reside. The poem then abruptly ends, unfinished.

SELECTED BIBLIOGRAPHY

Garbáty, Thomas J. *Medieval English Literature.* Toronto: Heath, 1984; Lynch, Kathryn C. "The Logic of the Dream Vision in Chaucer's *House of Fame.*" In *Literary Nominalism and the Theory of Rereading Late Medieval Texts: A New Research Paradigm.* Richard Utz, ed. Lewiston, NY: Mellen, 1995. 179-203; Vankeerbergen, Bernadette C. "Chaucer's *House of Fame*: A Journey into Skepticism." *Medieval Perspectives* 1994 (9), 158-69.

Robert T. Lambdin

HROTSVITHA (ROSWITHA) (c.1100). Hrotsvitha was the Benedictine abbess of Gandersheim in Saxony. By adapting Terrence's classical comedies for use as teaching tools, she saved the plays from being destroyed. This demonstrates the happenstance occurrences that preserved some classical texts while others were obliterated.

SELECTED BIBLIOGRAPHY

McEnerney, John I. "Proverbs in Hrotsvitha." *Mittellateinisches Jahrbuch* 21 (1986), 106-13; McNaughton, Howard. "Hrotsvitha and the Dramaturgy of Liminality." *Journal of the Australian Universities Language and Literature Association* 80(1993), 1-16.

Robert T. Lambdin

HUCHOWN (c.1400). The name Huchown refers to a mysterious figure who may or may not have even existed. A "Huchown of the Awle Ryale" is mentioned by the Scottish chronicler Andrew of *Wyntoun to be the author of the alliterative *Morte Arthure*, *Awntyrs of Arture*, and the *Pistyll of Susan*. Lack of documentation and credible evidence concerning Huchown's existence have led some to name Hew of Eglinton as Huchown. This would be important because William *Dunbar refers to Hew in his "Lament for Maharis." Yet because all of these claims are inferences, nothing can be ascertained as true. The speculation is debunked even more when it is noted that these three poems were most likely composed by three totally different authors, but this does not explain why Andrew would create a contemporary poet. At one time other works, including the four poems of the *Pearl* manuscript, were erroneously attributed to Huchown.

SELECTED BIBLIOGRAPHY

Drabble, Margaret, ed. *The Oxford Companion to English Literature.* 1932. 5th ed. Oxford: Oxford University Press, 1985; Swanton, Michael. *English Literature before Chaucer.* New York: Longman, 1987.

Robert T. Lambdin

HUGH OF LINCOLN, ST. (1246-1255). Hugh of Lincoln was a young boy allegedly crucified in Lincoln by the Jew Copin. Hugh's starved and tortured body was allegedly discovered in a well and buried in the cathedral near the body of Robert *Grosseteste. Many miracles then were said to have occurrred there. Additionally, it was believed that he spoke to his mother after his death and identified his murderer. As a consequence of this hideous act, many Jews were hanged. Geoffrey *Chaucer's *"Prioress's Tale" concludes with a reference to Hugh. Also, a number of *ballads were composed in his name, including "Sir Hugh," "Hugh of Lincoln," and "The Jew's Daughter."

SELECTED BIBLIOGRAPHY

Drabble, Margaret, ed. *The Oxford Companion to English Literature.* 5th ed. Oxford: Oxford University Press, 1985; Mayr-Harting, Henry, ed. *St. Hugh of Lincoln: Lectures Delivered at Oxford and Lincoln to Celebrate the Eighth Centenary of St. Hugh's Consecration as Bishop of Lincoln.* Oxford: Clarendon Press, 1987.

Laura Cooner Lambdin

HUMFREY, DUKE OF GLOUCESTER (1391-1447). The youngest son of Henry IV of England was remembered as the "good Duke Humfrey." He was named duke of Gloucester in 1414 and served with credit in the French wars of Henry V. On Henry's death in 1422 Humfrey claimed to be regent of England for his infant nephew, Henry VI, but Parliament allowed him only the title of protector. In 1422 he made a doubtfully legal marriage with Jacqueline, heiress of Holland and Hainault, and undertook on her behalf a campaign in the Low Countries against Philip, Duke of Burgundy, on whose alliance the English position in France depended.

By 1425 Humfrey abandoned the war and Jacqueline; their marriage was annulled. He then married one of Jacqueline's ladies, Eleanor Cobham, in 1428. Humfrey quarreled with the king's great-uncle, Bishop Beaufort, and the quarrels became so bitter that the duke of Bedford had to hurry home from France to avert open warfare. Humfrey's power lessened as Henry VI grew toward manhood and gave his confidence more and more to the Beaufort party.

Humfrey's wife was condemned to public penance and imprisonment for sorcery in 1441. In 1447 Humfrey was also arrested as he arrived at the Parliament in Suffolk. He died four days later, on February 23, 1447. The cause of his death is unknown, but was probably due to shock and cold weather. The public believed that he had been murdered at the instigation of the Beaufort faction and Queen Margaret, wife of Henry VI.

SELECTED BIBLIOGRAPHY

De la Mare, A.C. "Documents Given to the University of Oxford by Humfrey, Duke of Gloucester." *Bodleian Library Record* 13:1 (October 1988), 30-51; De la Mare, A. C. "Documents Given to the University of Oxford by Humfrey, Duke of Gloucester." *Bodleian Library Record* 13:2 (April 1989), 112-21; Gillam, Stanley. *The Divinity School and Duke Humfrey's Library at Oxford.* Oxford: Clarendon Press, 1988.

Rebecca Chalmers

HUNDRED YEARS' WAR, THE (1337-1453). The Hundred Years' War between France and England is the longest war in recorded history. The dispute began when *Edward III, the English king, declared that he was the rightful king of France because he had inherited the crown through his mother. Philip VI of France resented Edward's claim, and in retaliation he arrested some English sheep growers who were selling their wool in Flanders. The Flemish people allied with England, beginning the Hundred Years' War.

The English attained a great victory at Crécy, defeating the French with their new weapon, the longbow. They then took the town of Calais, which opened the door into France for the English. For the next ten years the fighting lagged as Europe was preoccupied with the destruction caused by the Black Death. In 1355 fighting resumed, and the English went to battle in southern France. The battle at Poitiers was characterized by recurring circumstances: the superior numbers of the French forces were defeated because they were weighed down with heavy armor and could not defend themselves against the English longbow. A treaty with England was signed at Bretigny in 1360, but Charles V of France soon broke the treaty, thereby resuming the war. He was more successful than his predecessors. At the time of his death only Calais and Bordeaux were still in English hands. Agincourt was the site of the next large battle, which was the third great English victory stemming from the English longbow and lighter armor. This victory led to the Treaty of Troyes (1420), which mandated that Henry V would marry the daughter of Charles VI of France and that Henry would act as regent until Charles's death, when Henry would become king of both England and France. The deaths of both these monarchs within a short period of time threw the treaty into heated dispute. Joan of Arc appeared to lead the French to successive victories over the English; she led the dauphin into Reims to be crowned as Charles VII. At the end of the war in 1453 only Calais remained under English control.

SELECTED BIBLIOGRAPHY

Ainsworth, Peter F. *Jean Froissart and the Fabric of History: Truth, Myth, and Fiction in the Chroniques.* Oxford: Oxford University Press, 1990; Curry, Ann. and Michael Hughes, eds. *Arms, Armies and Fortifications in the Hundred Years' War.* Rochester: Boydell, 1994; Curry, Ann. *The Hundred Years' War.* New York: St. Martin's, 1993.

Anna Shealy

I

ILLUMINATED MANUSCRIPTS. Many illustrations found in catacombs and painted on early church walls came from a long tradition of artistic manuscripts dating as far back as the pharaohs of Egypt and the Hellenistic Greeks of Alexandria. The intellectual center of Constantinople provided opportunity for the study of these manuscripts depicting Hebrew, Greek, and Christian themes. This accessability resulted in copying and recopying of the subject matter down through the centuries. The invention in the early imperial period of the *codex* (creating a book with pages), *vellum* (veal skin), and *parchment* (lamb skin) improved the quality of the manuscripts and made it possible for records of ancient civilizations to survive.

The oldest painted manuscript known is the Vatican Vergil from the early fifth century and is pagan in content, representing a scene from pastoral life. The Vienna Genesis is the earliest well-preserved manuscript that contains a biblical scene. The representation of the figure of Rebecca at the well is intended to be iconic or narrative, the page painted on purple ground and lettered in silver. The oldest illuminated book containing illustrations of the New Testament is the Rossana Gospels.

SELECTED BIBLIOGRAPHY

Peterson, Erik. "The Bible as Subject and Object of Illustration: The Making of a Medieval Manuscript: Hamburg 1255." In *The Early Medieval Bible: Its Production, Decoration, and Use.* Cambridge: Cambridge University Press, 1994; Ross, Leslie. *Text, Image, Message: Saints in Medieval Manuscript Illustrations.* Westport, CT: Greenwood Press, 1994; Stevick, Robert D. *The Earliest Irish and English Bookarts: Visual and Poetic Forms before A.D. 1000.* Philadelphia: University of Pennsylvania Press, 1994.

Libby Bernardin

INNOCENT III (1161?-1216) pope (1198-1216). Innocent was chosen by the Roman Curia to restore the political power of the papacy. His family was to produce eight other elected popes. A believer that the papacy should be the center of a macrocosmic world-state, Innocent envisioned this to be a single ecclesiastical/religious community with secular control. He believed it to be his responsibility as pontiff to ensure justice, maintain peace, prevent and punish sin, and aid the unfortunate. He had a clear grasp of essentials, but he was frequently opportunistic and lost moral position as a result. He claimed the right of the papacy to intervene in the elections of Holy Roman emperors. He was a brilliant administrator and provided for the first full collecting and proper treatment of papal documents and decrees. Clearly, his pontificate was the zenith of the medieval papacy.

Under Innocent, papal political claims were finally vindicated. By 1213 he had gained suzerainty (at least over affairs of the church) in England, Aragon, Bulgaria, Denmark, Portugal, and Hungary, coming close to the dream of a universal Christian commonwealth.

Innocent fought urban and other forms of heresy by his recognition and continuous support for the Friars Minor, the brotherhood of the Franciscans under the leadership of *Francis of Assisi, and the Dominicans, a preaching order. Each of these orders was urban, devoted to preaching and charity.

By 1215 Innocent's leadership had reached its highest point when he called the Fourth Lateran Council. This council issued decrees that established church beliefs of tremendous significance. These decreed sacraments to be the channel of grace and the chief sacrament to be the Eucharist.

SELECTED BIBLIOGRAPHY

Dor, Juliette. "*Humilis Exaltetur*: Constance, or Humility Rewarded." In *Heroes and Heroines in Medieval English Literature*. Leo Carruthers, ed. Cambridge: Brewer, 1994. 71-80; Freedman, Paul. "A Letter of Pope Innocent III Concerning a Dispute between Vic and Tarragona." *Römische Historische Mitteilungen* 30 (1988), 87-91; Powell, James M., ed. *Innocent III: Vicar of Christ or Lord of the World?* Washington, DC: Catholic University of America Press, 1994.

R. Churchill Curtis

INTERLUDE. The interlude was a type of dramatic entertainment that originated during the reign of *Henry VIII. While these plays were performed throughout England in halls, inns, and colleges, they were especially popular at the Tudor Court. Interludes were mostly performed by troupes of professionals, and the short plays usually had limited episodes and few characters.

Interludes probably originated as short skits between meal courses. The popularity of this genre grew very quickly, and they eventually succeeded in supplanting morality plays (*see* **Drama, Medieval**) as the dramas of choice. The allegorical characters often used comedy to posit their lessons. Because the interludes were performed during meals, they tended to be shorter than the other types of plays.

The root of the name "interlude" is uncertain. While it may refer to the idea that the short dramas were performed during breaks in feasts, the name may also refer to the notion that it was a "ludus" ("to play") performed by several actors. As the genre grew, the interlude left the dining hall, and interludes were performed between acts in longer plays. Additionally, there were educational interludes, used to teach moral lessons, generally written in Latin, utilizing stock characters. These plays were performed at schools. Whether the interludes were staged in the the school or the court, they signify the transition from the medieval mysteries to the more developed Elizabethan dramas.

SELECTED BIBLIOGRAPHY

Davis, Nick. "Allusions to Medieval Drama in Britain, IV: Interludes." *Medieval English Theatre* 6:1 (July 1984), 61-91; Edgecomb, Rodney. "The Nature of Literary Interludes." *Durham University Journal* 52:2 (July 1991), 253-57; Happe, Peter. *Song in Morality Plays and Interludes.* Lancaster, England: Medieval English Theatre. 1991; King, Pamela M. "Minority Plays: Two Interludes for Edward VI." *Medieval English Theatre* 15 (1993), 87-102.

Robert T. Lambdin

IPOMADON. The Middle English *romance *Ipomadon* is derived from a French original. There are three extant copies of *Ipomadon* in English: one, which dates to the early fourteenth century, is composed in prose. The second, perhaps a fourteenth century work, is perhaps the most well-known. It consists of nearly nmine thousand lines of twelve-line tail rhyme stanzas. The third is a shorter version composed in rhyming couplets, that dates to the fifteenth century. While copies of the manuscript appear scarce, the very idea that the story survives in some form over two hundred years demonstrates that it must have been somewhat popular.

In the romance, based upon Hugh of Rutland's tale (c. 1190), Ipomadon, the prince of Apulia, falls in love with La Fiere, the duchess of Calabria. He is able to win her affection only by performing great deeds while disguised from her. While this romance is typical of many in the Middle Ages, it was obviously not one of the most popular. Given the limited number of extent manuscripts, it can be inferred that this English version was not as successful as its French source.

SELECTED BIBLIOGRAPHY

Diensburg, Bernhard. "The Middle English Romance *Ipomadon* and Its Anglo-Norman Source." in *Anglistentag*. Rudiger Ahrens, ed. Tubingen: Niemeyer.1990. 289-97.

Robert T. Lambdin

IRISH ANNALS. Irish annals from the medieval period are numerous, but the earliest extant *annals, the *Annals of Inisfallen,* date from the late eleventh century. Most specialists in Irish history agree that the *Inisfallen* text and a number of later and similar annals all probably rely on an earlier source, which is now lost. Other early Irish annals include the *Annals of Ulster,* the *Annals of Tigernach,* the *Annals of Roscrea,* the *Annals of Loch Ce,* and the *Chronicum Scotorum.* Many of the manuscripts of these texts are imperfect, missing in some cases a few leaves and in others whole sections, but they attest to a drive to chronicle in Ireland that could date back as far as the *Anglo-Saxon Chronicle.* The annals are sometimes written in Irish, sometimes in Latin, and sometimes in a hybrid of the two. The annals from Ireland, like their English and continental counterparts they often include believable historical accounts; among the most renowned are the Viking invasions and the deaths of kings-- alongside entries mentioning the names of legendary Irish heroes. (*See* **Chronicles and Annals.**)

SELECTED BIBLIOGRAPHY

Drumville, David. "On Editing and Translating Medieval Irish Chronicles: The 'Annals of Ulster.'" *Cambridge Medieval Celtic Studies* 10 (Winter 1985), 67-86; Grabowski, Kathryn and David Dumville. *Chronicles and Annals of Medieval Ireland and Wales.* Suffolk: Boydell Press, 1984; Killion, Steven B. "Bedan Historiography in the Irish Annals." *Medieval Perspectives* 6 (1991), 20-36; McCarthy, Daniel. "The Chronological Apparatus of the 'Annals of Ulster' AD 431-1131." *Peritia* 8 (1994), 47-79; O'Croinin, Daibhi. "Early Irish Annals from Easter-Tables: A Case Restated." *Peritia* 2 (1983), 74-86.

Richard McDonald

IRISH LITERATURE. Scholars divide the early prose narratives of Ireland into four main groups or cycles: (1) the Mythological Cycle, which concerns Ireland's earliest inhabitants and the people of the *síde* (the Celtic Otherworld); (2) the Ulster Cycle, which depicts the exploits of the Ulaid, the heroic warrior-elite of Ulster, and in particular the exploits of Cú Chulainn; (3) the Kings Cycle, which treats the activities of allegedly historical Irish kings; and (4) the Fionn Cycle, which chronicles the adventures of the swashbuckling Fionn mac Cumhall and his companions in a group known as the Fian. These divisions are not absolute, however, and characters from one cycle may appear in the tales of another. A large amount of these various literatures do exist, demonstrating their popularity.

The Mythological Cycle. A key work in the Mythological cycle is *The Book of Invasions,* which was begun by sixth-century monks who wanted to preserve a record of the origins of the Irish people. Their work was finally written down in the twelfth century as the *Leabhar Gabhála Éireann* (The book of the conquest of Ireland), generally known as *The Book of Invasions*. According to this work, Ireland's first invaders arrived before the time of Noah's Flood. All of them perished in the Flood--all except a man named Fintan, who lived on through the later invasions of Ireland in the form of a salmon, an eagle, and finally a hawk. Ireland's second invaders were the Partholonians. They engaged in the first battle ever fought on Irish soil, against a mysterious, demonic race known as the Fomorians. Before being decimated by a great plague, the Partholonians established Ireland's first guesting-house and brewed Ireland's first ale. Ireland's third invaders originated in Greece. Led by Nemed, they established Ireland's two great royal forts and carved out the twelve great plains of Ireland. They were constantly at war with the Fomorians, and after Nemed's death the Fomorians conquered them and forced them to pay an annual tribute of two-thirds of their corn, their milk, and their children. The Children of Nemed rebelled against the Fomorians and attacked their island stronghold, only to be soundly defeated. Most of them were killed, and those who survived divided into two small factions; from these factions came two of the most important groups of Irish invaders.

One surviving group of the Children of Nemed sailed to Greece, where they became known as the Fir Bolg. When conflicts arose between them and their Greek hosts, the Fir Bolg built curraghs (boats made from skins) and set out for the land of their ancestors. After returning to Ireland, the Fir Bolg established the five great provinces of Ulster, Leinster, Munster, and Connacht, with Meath in the center. They instituted a concept of kingship in which the king was believed to be semi-divine, and they established Ireland's ancient system of social classes in which the lower classes were ruled by a warrior elite.

The fifth group of invaders of Ireland were the Tuatha Dé Danann, "the People of the Goddess Danu, " whom scholars believe to be the old gods of Celtic mythology. The Tuatha Dé descended from the other group that survived the ill-fated attack on the island of the Fomorians. After leaving Ireland, they had settled in northern Greece, where they became skilled in the druidic arts. Eventually they too sailed west in search of their ancient homeland, taking with them four sacred objects: the stone of Fál, which shrieked at the inauguration of a rightful king; the invincible spear of Lugh; the sword of Nuada, from which none could escape; and the never-depleted cauldron of the Dagda.

After sheltering briefly in Scotland, the Tuatha Dé landed in Ireland, immediately setting fire to their boats so none could flee from the Fir Bolg. They fought many battles against the Fir Bolg before defeating them, and in one of these battles, the First Battle of Magh Tuiredh, Nuada, their king, lost an arm. Because it was not appropriate for their king to be impaired, Nuada was forced to abdicate; later, after being fitted with a silver arm, he was able to resume his kingship. Once they defeated the Fir Bolg, the Tuatha Dé Danann turned their attention to the Fomorians, the age-old enemy of Ireland's peoples. Their great conflict with the Fomorians is described in the Second Battle of Magh Tuiredh, which survives as an independent epic and is one of the most important sources of early Irish mythology. This work depicts the exploits of Lugh, who succeeded Nuada of the Silver Arm. Lugh led the Tuatha Dé to victory by casting a stone into the eye of Balor of "the baleful eye," causing Balor's venomous gaze to be directed against his own people. After the Second Battle of the Magh Tuiredh, the Fomorians were expelled from Ireland once and for all. The Tuatha Dé established their royal court at the Hill of Tara, which provides the setting for several tales in the Mythological Cycle.

The preceding invasions set the stage for the coming of Ireland's final group of invaders, the Sons of Míl, whose descendants--the Gaels--reigned thereafter as the dominant people of Ireland. Originating in Spain, the Sons of Míl arrived in Ireland, only to be confronted by the powerful magic of the Tuatha Dé Danann. By heeding the advice of their own druid-poet Amergin, the Sons of Míl were able to defeat the Tuatha Dé. A truce was established between these last two groups of Ireland's people, and the Tuatha Dé agreed to occupy the territory beneath the ground, while the Sons of Míl retained the land above ground. Thus the Tuatha Dé Danann moved to the *síde*, the fairy mounds of Ireland, and became Ireland's immortal fairy folk.

Many of the tales from the Mythological Cycle are set in the Boyne River Valley near the great complex of Neolithic remains surrounding Newgrange. One of these tales is "The Wooing of Étaín, " which contains three separate episodes in which pairs of men vie for possession of the beautiful Étaín. In the first one Oengus attempts to win Étaín away from her possessive father, and in the next two rival lovers compete to possess her. At one point in the middle tale, Étaín is magically transformed into a large scarlet fly, and she is blown about Ireland for seven years. Eventually she lands in a golden vessel and is swallowed by a nobleman's wife, who soon becomes pregnant. The child she gives birth to is Étaín, returned once more to human form.

The Ulster Cycle. The tales comprising the Ulster Cycle may reflect events that occurred in Ireland between the years 100 B. C. and A. D. 100. They are set in Ulster during the reign of Conchobar mac Nessa, and their chief figure is the Irish hero Cú Chulainn. At the heart of the Ulster cycle is the *Táin Bó Culaigne*; this is an extended narrative sequence describing a great conflict between Ulster and Connacht. Supplementing the *Táin* in the Ulster Cycle are several additional tales that provide essential background information to the main narrative. One of the most important of these "foretales" is "The Labor Pains of the Ulaid and the Twins of Macha, " which explains why the men of Ulster have been overcome by a strange physical incapacitation (their "labor pains") and why Cú Chulainn must face the army of Connacht all by himself. "The Exile of the Sons of Uisliu" is also important, explaining why a large group of Ulstermen, including the great hero Fergus mac Roich, have defected to Connacht. Their defection stems from the tragic story of the Deirdre, a woman of incomparable beauty who was fated to bring suffering to Ulster. At one point in this story, after Fergus has offered a pledge to ensure the safe return of the exiled sons of Uisliu, Conchobar ignores Fergus's pledge and has the men executed; that great breach of honor causes Fergus and three thousand of his followers to abandon Ulster and join the court of Medb and Ailill in Connacht.

The action in the *Táin* is initiated by Queen Medb's desire to steal the great bull known as Donn of Cooley away from Ulster. The army of Connacht advances against Ulster with that intention, and the warriors of Ulster, due to Macha's curse, are unable to fight because of their bodily pains. Only the boy Cú Chulainn is available to protect Ulster, which he does by challenging the greatest heroes of Connacht to fight him in a series of single combats. Cú Chulainn performs brilliantly in these encounters, though his secret intention is merely to delay the enemy's advance until his fellow Ulstermen are released from their pains. When the people of Connacht finally realize what Cú Chulainn has been doing, it is too late. The Ulstermen's pains have disappeared; entering the battle, they quickly rout the forces of Connacht.

Cú Chulainn, the central figure of the Ulster Cycle, is an invincible hero who has chosen to have a short but glorious life rather than a long but inglorious one. He is the son of a human mother and a divine father (Lugh) and thus, like many an early hero, is a demi-god. At one point in the *Táin* after Cú Chulainn has grown weary from his many individual combats, Lugh comes to him from the *side*, tends his wounds, and fights in his place, allowing his son to get some much needed sleep. The story of Cú Chulainn's boyhood is related as a flashback in the *Táin* by Fergus, who describes the impressive fashion in which Cú Chulainn first arrived at Conchobar's court. He also relates how the boy--whose birth name was Sétantae--came to be called Cú Chulainn, which means "the hound of Culann." After Cú Chulainn had slain the watchdog of Culann the smith, the boy agreed to atone for his deed by serving for a time in the dog's place, thus earning him his new name.

One of Cú Chulainn's most important characteristics is his *ríastarthae* or "warp spasm," a kind of battle fury that comes upon him in the midst of conflict. When Cú Chulainn is seized by this, his body is drastically transformed: "You would have thought that every hair was being driven into his head. You would have thought that a spark of fire was on every hair. He closed one eye until it was no wider than the eye of a needle; he opened the other until it was as big as a wooden bowl. He bared his teeth from jaw to ear, and he opened his mouth until the gullet was visible. The warrior moon rose from his head" (Gantz 136). When Cú Chulainn's battle fury is on him, he must be plunged into three huge vats of water, one after the other, before he can cool down again.

"The Boyhood Deeds of Cú Chulainn" provides an account of the youth's early training. His first mentor is Cathub the druid, and later he is trained by the warrior-woman Scáthach. Under her tutelage Cú Chulainn masters a great number of "hero's feats, " including the use of the *gáe bolga,* a kind of underwater spear thrust. Only Cú Chulainn knows how to use this terrible weapon, which he employs against the men of Connacht in the *Táin*, and which he also uses against his own son Condlae in the poignant story "The

Death of Aífe's Only Son," a tale in which father and son engage in mortal combat.

One of the most important tales in the Ulster Cycle is the story known as "Bricriu's Feast." As one scholar has observed, this tale contains "just about everything: a mythic subtext, a heroic competition, visits to and from the otherworld, humour and parody and a rambling, patchwork structure" (Gantz, 219). At issue in the tale is which of the three heroes--Lóegure Búadach, Conall Cernach, or Cú Chulainn--is most deserving of "the champion's portion, " the best and biggest serving at the feast to which Bricriu has invited the greatest heroes of Ulster. The three claimants engage in a series of competitive feats, the last of which involves an exchange of head-chopping blows with a huge churl. "I will cut off your head tonight," the churl tells them, "and you will avenge that by cutting off my head tomorrow night." When the time comes for them to receive their appointed blows, Cú Chulainn's rivals fail to appear. But Cú Chulainn, true to his word, keeps his rendezvous with the fearsome axeman, and when the churl brings the axe down upon his neck, the blade turns up and Cú Chulainn is struck by the blunt side. By his courage and honor Cú Chulainn has proven that he is deserving of the champion's portion. "Bricriu's Feast" is one of the earliest narratives to contain the beheading game, a motif that lies at the heart of the Middle English *romance *Sir Gawain & the Green Knight.

The Fionn Cycle. The stories contained in the Fionn Cycle differ considerably from those in the Ulster Cycle, for these narratives celebrate the exploits of a group of roving warriors known as the Fian--or Fenians--men who are hunters, fighters, and wanderers and who are not tied to any specific societal context. Chief among these heroes of early Irish folklore is Fionn mac Cumhall, about whom legends circulated in Ireland and parts of Scotland for hundreds of years and continue to do so even to the present day. Whereas scholars previously believed that the Fionn legends stemmed from the exploits of a real person, that they now believe they reflect the mythic deeds of one of the old gods of the Gaels, making these tales more akin to the Mythological Cycle than to the Ulster Cycle.

Perhaps the most distinctive feature of the Fionn Cycle is its nostalgic tone and mood of retrospection. Typifying this is the twelfth-century frame-tale "The Colloquy of the Old Men, " one of the most important works in the cycle. In this work Oisín (Fionn's son) and Caoilte mac Rónán (one of Fionn's closest companions), who are now old men, meet St. Patrick and travel through Ireland with him. As they travel, they tell him a series of tales, recounting their many great adventures and reliving their past glories as they are brought to mind by the features of the Irish landscape through which they pass.

Like Cú Chulainn in the Ulster Cycle and Percival in the *Arthurian legends, Fionn was a precocious and prodigious youth. While he was still in his mother's womb, his father died at the battle of Cnucha. Fearing that her son Demne (Fionn's birth name) would be murdered by his father's enemies, his mother sent him away to be brought up in the quiet inland forests of Ireland by the druidess Bodball and the warrior-woman Fiacal. Thus at an early age Fionn became expert in the arts of war and magic. Growing restless, the boy set off on his own, and after various adventures, including one in which his name was changed from Demne to Fionn (meaning "The Fair One"), he became the pupil of an old poet named Finneces who lived on the River Boyne near a pool containing the salmon of knowledge. Fulfilling an ancient prophecy, Fionn caught the salmon and ate it, thereby gaining the knowledge of all things, including the art of healing. From then on, whenever Fionn placed his thumb in his mouth, he could read the future. (Fionn became unbeatable at chess; by chewing on his thumb he always knew the best move to make.) Using his many skills in arms, magic, and prophetic knowledge, Fionn defeated his enemies and rose to the kingship of the Fenians--at the ripe old age of eight.

Most of the tales about Fionn portray him as a wise and generous leader, but one of the most famous stories from the Fionn Cycle offers something of a contrast. This is the tragic love story of "Diarmuid and Gráinne, " a tale that was popular in Gaelic Scotland as well as in Ireland and that was one of the sources for the medieval love story of Tristan and Isolde. In this story King Fionn, now advanced in years, desires to marry the beautiful young daughter of the King of Ireland. When Fionn arrives at the king's court in Tara, among his entourage is the handsome youth Diarmuid, the grandson of Duibhne (from whom the Campbells of Scotland claim descent). Diarmuid has a dark love spot on his forehead, and any woman who sees it falls hopelessly in love with him; as a result, he has learned to wear his helmet low on his brow when he is around women. One hot day Diarmuid raises his helmet to wipe his face and forehead, and Gráinne, already infatuated with him, sees the love spot and is hopelessly smitten.

The youthful lovers flee into the wilderness, pursued by Fionn and his men. Several times they are nearly captured, but each time they escape. Eventually sympathizers within Fionn's court persuade him to forgive Gráinne and Diarmuid and accept them back at court. Fionn agrees to this, but in his heart he can never forgive Diarmuid. After Diarmuid kills a magic boar that no one else can kill, he inadvertently steps on the boar's poisonous quills with his bare feet. Diarmuid begs Fionn to heal him by allowing him to drink water from his hands. Three times Fionn brings water for him from a nearby well; the first two times he remembers his old hatred and allows the water to trickle through his fingers, the third time his conscience gets the better of him and he tries to heal Diarmuid, but by then he has delayed too long and Diarmuid dies. Gráinne marries Fionn and eventually forgives him for Diarmuid's death; yet Diarmuid remains her one great love.

The story depicting the death of Fionn, who is now more than 230 years old, involves treachery, a breach of hospitality, and a terrible battle in which Fionn and a band of his most trusted Fenians are defeated. It appears that they have been killed in this battle, but in fact they have not, for the people of the Otherworld take them away to the *síde* and heal them. As in some versions of the Arthurian legend, it is said that Fionn and his companions lie sleeping beneath the *síde*; when their country needs them, they will emerge from the earth and come to Ireland's aid.

It is probable that there was once a rich tradition of *lyric poetry in medieval Irish literature, but very little of it has survived. Some of the finest examples of Irish lyric poetry may be seen in passages that occur within the prose narratives. In the *Táin*, for example, passages of lyric poetry sometimes appear in the narrative at key points, providing brief interludes in the action. Some of the most impressive poetry occurs in the tale from the Ulster Cycle known as "The Wasting Sickness of Cú Chulainn," in which the hero becomes enamoured of a beautiful woman from the Otherworld.

Many themes, characters, and narrative situations were passed from early Celtic literature into the other vernacular literatures of medieval Europe. Nowhere is this more apparent than in the genre of medieval *romance; indeed, works in the Arthurian tradition probably preserve more elements stemming from Celtic literature than from any other. The Celtic Otherworld (fairyland, or the Land of Faerie) also came to occupy a prominent place in many works of literature, especially romances, Breton *lays, and *ballads. In some instances the Otherworld is largely tangential to the mortal realm and barely impinges upon it, as in Marie de France's lay of Sir Lanval. In other instances it is a place into which mortals are forced to journey, usually at great peril. Sir Orfeo, the hero of the Middle English lay, braves the dangers of fairyland in order to rescue his wife and lady-love Heurodis, who was stolen away by the king of the Otherworld. In the Middle English poem "Thomas of Erceldoun, " Thomas goes willingly to the Otherworld in the company of his Otherworldly lover; eventually, though, he must return to the mortal realm to avoid experiencing a terrible fate. A less willing visitor to the Otherworld is Tam Lin in the Scottish ballad "Tam Lin," who has been abducted by the Queen of Faerie. It is only by the courageous actions of the pregnant Janet, who boldly appears at Miles Cross at the hour of midnight on Halloween, that Tam Lin can be saved from his Otherworldly abductress.

SELECTED BIBLIOGRAPHY

Translations: Cross, T. P. and C. H. Slover, eds. *Ancient Irish Tales*. New York: Henry Holt, 1936; reprinted New York: Barnes and Noble, 1969; Gantz, Jeffrey, trans. *Early Irish Myths and Sagas*. New York: Penguin, 1981; Jackson, Kenneth H. trans. *A Celtic Miscellany*. New York: Penguin, 1971; Kinsella, Thomas, trans. *The Táin*. Oxford: Oxford University Press, 1969; Macalister, R. A. S., ed. and trans. *Lebor Gabála Érenn (The Book of the Taking of Ireland)*. 5 Vols. Dublin:Irish Text Society, 1938-54; O'Rahilly, Cecille, ed. and trans. *Táin Bó Cúalnge from the Book of the Dun Cow*. Dublin: Dublin Institute for Advanced Studies, 1978. O'Rahilly, Cecille, ed. and trans. *Táin Bó Cúalngne from the Book of Leinster*. Dublin: Dublin Institute for Advanced Studies, 1967.

Background: Beach, Sarah. "Breaking the Pattern: Alan Garner's 'The Owl Service' and the *Mabinogion.*" *Mythlore* 20:1(75) (Winter 1994), 10-14; Carney, James. *Studies in Irish Literature and History.* Dublin: Dublin Institute for Advanced Studies, 1955; Chadwick, Nora. *The Celts.* New York: Penguin, 1970; Cunliffe, Barry. *The Celtic World.* New York: McGraw-Hill, 1979; Dillon, Myles. *Early Irish Literature.* Chicago: University of Chicago Press, 1948; Flower, Robin. *The Irish Tradition.* Oxford: Clarendon Press, 1947; Jones, Gwyn, and Thomas Gwyn, trans. *The Mabinogion* London: Dent, 1989; MacCana, Proinias. *Celtic Mythology.* 2nd ed., New York: Bedrick, 1985; Murphy, Gerard. *Saga and Myth in Ancient Ireland.* Dublin: Dublin Institute for Advanced Studies, 1961; O'Rahilly, T. F. *Early Irish History and Mythology.* Dublin, Dublin Institute for Advanced Studies, 1946; Rees, Alwyn and Brinley Rees. *Celtic Heritage.* London: Thomas and Hudson, 1961; Ward, Charlotte. "A Formulaic Consideration of the *Mabinogion,* Branch I, 'Pwyll Pendeuic Dyuet.'" *Etudes Celtiques* 29 (1992), 423-39.

John Conlee

ISIDORE OF SEVILLE (c.560-636). Isidore of Seville was born to a noble family in southern Spain. He entered the church at a young age and eventually became bishop of Seville after 600. His main literary contribution was his *Etymologiae* (Etymologien) a twenty-volume encyclopedia that included a comprehensive summary of classical knowledge of geography, art, and science. His historical work was less acclaimed, although he is remembered as being influential in fostering a positive attitude toward historical record keeping; his *Etymologiae* contains passages stressing the importance of historical knowledge. He is the author of a universal chronicle of world history, and his *Historia Gothorum, Vandalorum, et Sueborum* (History of the Goths, Vandals, and Suevi) is in some ways reminiscent of *Jordanes' *De Origine Actibusque Getarum.* (*See Chronicles and Annals.*)

SELECTED BIBLIOGRAPHY

Brandt, William J. *The Shape of Medieval History.* New Haven: Yale University Press, 1966; Gransden, Antonia. *Historical Writing in England c. 550 to c. 1307.* Ithaca: Cornell University Press, 1974; Smalley, Beryl. *Historians in the Middle Ages.* New York: Scribner's, 1974; Sterns, Indrikis. *The Greater Medieval Historians: An Interpretation and a Bibliography.* Lanham, MD: University Press of America, 1980; Swiggers, P. "Theorie et pratique de la grammaire chez Isidore de Seville." *Orbis* 33:1-2 (1989), 57-69. Wigginton, Waller B., and Trent D. Stephens. "The Monsters and Theology of Isidore of Seville, Ulisse Aldovandi, and Modern Science." *Rendesvous* 25:1 (Fall 1989), 67-82.

Richard McDonald

ISLAMIC LITERATURE. The Islamic culture of the Middle Ages is widely known for its efforts to preserve the writings of other ancient cultures, such as that of the Greek. However, not much attention was given to the examination of native works of Islam. This is ironic given the many benefits Middle Ages Europe received from Islamic treatises about the sciences, such as medicine, geography, mathematics, astronomy, and philosophy. Also, the Islamic culture provided a rich heritage of literary works; westerners are familiar with some, such as the *Koran*, the *Thousand and One Nights*, and the *Rubáiyát of Omar Khayyám*, but most are relatively unknown. Of course, language problems aided this continental ignorance. These works were written in an alphabet of Semitic script, so translation and conceptualization problems were unavoidable.

During the medieval period the Muslim or Islamic empire was so large that it included a great diversity of peoples. Naturally, many of these groups had preserved their ancient cultures and languages. This is important because even though Arabic became the literary language for many of these regions, over time, local influences again became infused into the culture so that certain native languages and literatures again came into use. For example, this was particularly true in Persia, where the Arabic alphabet became a part of the Persian language. By the eleventh century a portion of northwestern India, now known as Pakistan, had become one of the major centers of Islamic literature of Persian descent. Persian remained the prevalent language here until the 1830s, when Urdu succeeded it. Urdu also borrowed heavily from Persian sources of the seventeenth century.

Around 711 central Asia became a part of the Muslim empire. This area became a mainstay of Islamic literature and scholarship, especially in the areas of Samarkand, Bukhara, and Fergana. Much of the literature from this region was composed in Turkish; when the area was overrun by the Ottoman Turks and others, the invaders' languages displaced Arabic in some sections. This accounts for the fourteenth century Turkish literature, which was elaborate, yet heavily influenced by Persian techniques and vocabulary.

Three distinct caliphates ruled the medieval Islamic empire. The rules of the Patriarchal (632-61), the Umayyad (661-750), and the `Abbasid (750-1258) caliphates were ended by the Ottoman Turks, who invaded and sacked Baghdad in 1258. The Turks murdered the caliph and ended Muslim rule in the eastern section of the empire. To this point, the early religious zeal found in these caliphates inspired the beginnings of two distinct works that would not be completed for centuries. These works initially came about because of the death of Muhammad, the spiritual and political leader of Islam. The first is the *Hadith*, which is the record of the sayings and deeds of Muhammad. Because the Islamic community had been taken by surprise by his sudden death, it was deemed necessary that all of Muhammed's words and actions be preserved. This was especially important because it was believed that every aspect of his life was inspired by God. Within several centuries, this corpus of work had been solidified into a body of work that was considered complete; today the

Hadith is cherished as a major source of Islamic law and moral guidance, second only to the Koran in importance.

The other important early Islamic text is a compilation of the sayings of Ali, Muhammad's son-in-law, who was the fourth caliph. Ali's followers later established a major division of Islam, Shi'ah. This work, too, took several centuries to complete; it was not until the tenth century that it was finished. Called *The Road to Eloquence*, this work is one of the first inspirational texts composed in prose; it has provoked numerous commentaries and imitations in other languages and cultures.

The reign of the Umayyad caliphate was pocked with civil wars and the rise of internal rivalries. This unrest contributed to the emergence of a type of poetry that would become a favorite vehicle for expression of these sects' divergent perspectives. This period produced three great poets, Al-Akhtal, Jarir, and Tamman ibn Ghalib Abu Firas (al-Farazdaq), each of whom wrote in support of his own political faction.

Al-Akhtal was an ardent supporter of the policies of Mu'awiyah I, the first Umayyad. Jarir and al-Farazdaq were bitter enemies who were active in the courts of the caliphs and their governors, fervently supporting their regimes. They delighted the tribesmen with their biting satires against each other. Ironically, this rivalry provides us with a rich corpus of material about the social and political climate of eighth-century Islam. These two composed in the *qasida* form, and their works display an affluence of vocabulary and imagination. The *qasida* was developed by pre-Islamic Arabs and is still found in Arabic literature today. It is constructed as an elaborate ode of twenty to one hundred verses, maintaining a single end rhyme through the entire piece. *Qasidas* usually open with a short prelude, often a love poem; the object here is to gain the reader's attention. The prelude is followed by an account of the narrator's journey, often embellished with descriptions of his mode of transport (horse or camel) and with desert scenes or events. The main theme, at the conclusion of the *qasida*, is a tribute to the author's patron, his tribe, or, at times, himself. After the Islamic takeover, this genre served as a means to praise God. Additionally, *qasidas* were used to eulogize Muhammad or to give songs of commendation or lamentation for the saints. The *qasida* was a great vehicle for the poet to display his own knowledge.

'Umar ibn Abi Rabi'ah, a poet from Mecca, was one of the foremost developers of the *ghazel* as a love poem. These were love lyrics of five to twelve verses that probably derived from the *qasida*'s opening section; their content was usually religious or secular. The majority of his poems concern amorous adventures with women who came to Mecca on pilgrimage. The poet al-Wilad ibn Yazid, also notorious for his use of the *ghazel*, gained more notoriety as a poet than as a warrior, even though he was one of the last Umayyads. He is noted for his poems that excelled in frivolous love verses and his odes that praise the virtue of wine. Conversely, in Medina highly idealized poetry much like the chivalric *romances of medieval continental Europe became fashionable. This genre, attributed to the author Jamil, glorifies lovers who become martyrs by dying, surrendering to the power of true love.

Compared to the brief ninety-year period of the Umayyads, the Abbasid caliphate was much more enduring, lasting for more than five centuries. During this period the golden age of Islamic literature occurred. The capital of the Islamic world during this time was Baghdad. Here, works from all over the empire came together, and the writers of this culture began to adapt and rework elements from these other cultures. Major poets of this period include Abu Nuwas, Ibn al-Mu'tazz, Ibn Da'ud, al-Mutanabbi, and al-Ma'arri. Perhaps the most renowned of this group was Abu Nuwas, who stood alone with his command of language and imagery. His works are noted for their verses that are witty, yet cynical. He also composed clever drinking songs that attacked the orthodox Muslims. His motto is purported to have been "Accumulate as many sins as you can. "

One of the first literary critics was al-Mu'tazz who in his *Book of the Novel and the Strange* composed literary rules concerning the use of metaphors, similes, and puns. He felt that poetry should involve the richest embellishment of verses by all kinds of literary conventions. Indeed, his works were often overpowered by his stylistics and verbiage.

This period also continued the romantic idealized works that were in vogue at the end of the Umayyad caliphate. In *ghazel* poetry one of the central themes was often that of the lover who would rather die than achieve union with his beloved. The author Da'ud in his *Book of the Flower* relied heavily upon this notion. This idea was originally used in a secular manner; later it was usurped as a major concept of religious mystic poetry. Works with this theme were found throughout the Islamic empire, and it can also be discovered in Persian, Turkish, and Urdu poetry. The influence of this genre even made its way to Spain, where Ibn Hazm, a theologian, composed his *Ring of the Dove*, a prose work interspersed with poetry that concerns pure love and is based upon his personal experiences.

One of the mainstream of the classical Islamic *qasida* poets is Al-Mutanabbi, whose compositions were noted for their exaggeration, onomatopoeia, and formal perfection. Yet it is the verses of the Syrian al-Ma'arri, a blind poet, that are perhaps the most enduring, so much so that he is still popular today, despite the idea that his verses were so complex in their double end rhymes that even his contemporaries needed help interpreting them. His works are extremely dark and pessimistic; the skeptical nature of his poems is a polar opposite of the heroic romanticism of his time. Al-Ma'arri expressed disdain for the upper classes of his day and displayed an obvious contempt for their hypocritical ways. Yet his anger was not directed solely at the elite. His *Paragraphs and Periods* offended pious Muslims, who believed that the work was a parody of the Koran. His sarcastic attack on Arabic literature is also seen in the "Epistle of Pardon," in which he describes a visit to the world of the afterlife.

During the reign of the Abbasid caliphate the first real movement in literary prose is found. Writers expounded their seemingly unquenchable curiosity for all kinds of knowledge. It was this movement that led them to accumulate and translate scholarly and philosophical treatises from other cultures, including the ancient Greeks. Ibn al-Muqaffa translated the fables of the Indian sage Bidpai into Arabic. This massive body of work provided the Muslims with a seemingly endless supply of beast tales and parables, somewhat similar to those of Aesop. He also translated from Persian into Arabic the *Book of Kings*; this work, a collection of pre-Islamic mythology, was readily preferred by the sophisticated Muslims to the meager accounts of the Arabs' heathen past. Al-Muqaffa also translated many works on ethics and the conduct of governments. These became the models for the literature of the late Middle Ages in both the Islamic empire and continental Europe. Such texts were known as "Mirrors for Princes"; an example is Machiavelli's *The Prince*.

Similarly, al-Jahiz of Bosra wrote treatises on many subjects as a response to the growing interest in life beyond the Islamic empire. Literary style and effective use of language were the subjects of his *Elegance of Expression and Clarity of Exposition*; also, his *Book of Misers* is an anthology of stories concerning cupidity. Al-Jahiz, even though he was renowned as a free spirit, also saw the need to support government policy. This resulted in his composing *Exploits of the Turks*, a work that glorified the military prowess of the Turkish soldiers who provided his government with strength. Finally, his *Book of Animals* is a compilation of Arab traditions, proverbs, and superstitions.

Following the new prose tradition, Abu Hayyan at-Tawhidi wrote a book that denounced the weaknesses of two of the caliph's governors. His prose is vigorous yet eloquent. This era ended with the growth of the *maqamah*, a genre that was basically used to tell entertaining stories in a very complicated style. These works frequently were used to display the author's grasp of wit and learning, and they often became so enwrapped in the author's convoluted terminology and word structure that they were very difficult to understand in their native language--much less translate into another. Among the best authors of this form are al-Hamadhani, who is credited with inventing the genre, and al-Hariri of Basra, who is considered the master of the form. His fifty extant *maqamahs* resemble more the short stories of the later Western tradition than any other genre that was contemporary to him.

Very far from the center of Islamic culture in Baghdad during the Abbasid caliphate, the literature of Spain (*see Hispanic Medieval Literature*) prospered during its Muslim occupation. Indeed, it was here that some of the greatest authors and traditions of Islamic literature evolved. Avicenna and Averroës were prominent in the field of philosophy. Averroës particularly, was the Arab commentator on *Aristotle; his attention to this subject made Aristotelian philosophy the basis of much of the Christian theology in Europe. Averroës's renown also came from his attack on the Islamic mystic al-Ghazali. Al-Ghazali had composed the *Incoherence of the Philosophers*, which elicited from Averroës *The Incoherence of the Incoherence*. However, al-Ghazali earned repute as one of the masters of mystic writing for his *Revival of the Religious Sciences*.

Another outstanding mystic, Ibn al-'Arabi, was educated in the Spanish tradition. Yet he is renowned for his poetry and prose which would play a major role in the shaping of Islamic thought. His most famous work is *The Meccan Revelations*, but he is also noted for his volume of love poetry, *The Interpreter of Desires*. In this work wisdom is the point of the narrator's quest.

In North Africa Arab scholars also made great contributions to geography after the ninth century. Al-Idrisi produced a spectacular map of the world. With this he enclosed a detailed description called *The Delight of Him Who Wishes to Traverse the Regions of the World*. However, Ibn Battutah was perhaps peerless as a world traveler. A native of North Africa, Ibn Battutah traversed Asia to the Far East, including India, and Africa as far south as the Niger region. It is estimated that he covered some 75,000 miles in his journeys and visited almost every Islamic country. In 1353 he composed the *Rihlah*, which is priceless for its commentary on the state of Islamic society during this time.

Also during the Abbasid period Persia produced a great body of Islamic literature. Among the most prominent authors to emerge from this area were Firdawsi, Awhad ad-Din (or Anvari), al-Biruni, Omar Khayyám, Jalal ad-Din ar-Rumi, Sa'di, and Amir Khosrow. Firdawsi, or Abu ol-Qasem Mansur, is known as the greatest poet of Persia. He wrote the national epic *Book of Kings*, yet the only true account of his life comes to us from the twelfth century poet Nezami-ye Aruzi, who visited Firdawsi's home of Tus and collated stories about him.

Firdawsi was born about 935 to wealthy parents. He began composing *Book of Kings* (*Shah-nameh* in Persian) to earn money for his daughter's dowry. Nearly 120,000 lines long, this epic is based upon a prose work of a similar name that was itself a translation of the history of Persian kings from the ancient times to the seventh century. He completed the poem in 1010 and presented it to the sultan of Ghanza, Mahmud. Firdawsi hoped that the sultan would pay him well for it, yet he was shocked to find that the sultan's offer was so trifling that Firdawsi gave it away.

This angered Mahmud, forcing Firdawsi to flee to Herat and then to Mazanderan. Later Mahmud tried to atone for his folly by sending Firdawsi a great amount of indigo, quite a valuable commodity at that time. As luck would have it, the gift arrived the very day Firdawsi was being buried; Firdawsi's daughter refused the offer. Over time the *Book of Kings* remained one of the most popular works in the Persian language because it is easily translated into modern Arabic.

Formal eulogies called "panegyrics" were also popular types of writing during this time. Anvari was among the most accomplished writers of this genre, which used the *qasida* form of poetry. Among his most noted efforts is the *Tears of Khorasan*, which mourns the passing glory of the Seljuk Turks.

Anvari's knowledge was not limited to literary types; he was skilled in many of the sciences, including astronomy, music, and philosophy.

Al-Biruni was one of the most highly educated men of his time. He was fluent in many languages, including Hebrew, Turkish, Sanskrit, and Syriac. His most noted compositions include *Chronology of Ancient Nations*, *Elements of Astrology*, and a work on astronomy, *The Mas'udi Canon*.

Omar Khayyám was another famous mathematician who became more noted for his compositions. His *Rubáiyát* is a volume of quatrains that was translated into English by Edward FitzGerald and published in 1859. Each quatrain by itself is an individual poem. However, all of the quatrains are related by Khayyám's brilliant interweaving of recurring common themes. While he is among the most famous of the Persian authors, there is some question as to the validity of his authorship of the entire work because his contemporaries paid him little or no attention.

Jalal wrote mystical poetry in the *masnavi* style (described later). His most famous work is entitled simply *Masnavi* and is an encyclopedia-like work of some 26,000 verses. The subject of the *Masnavi* is mystic thought of the thirteenth century. Many Islamic mystics believe that this text is second in importance in Islamic literature, falling behind only the Koran. Jalal also wrote many beautiful love lyrics that some say are even better than the *Masnavi*.

Sa'di was also one of the greatest figures of medieval Persian poetry. His *Orchard* is composed entirely in verse and is dedicated to the local caliph. It consists of stories that demonstrate the virtues expected of all Muslims. His other famous work, *The Rose Garden*, is almost the opposite of *Orchard*. *The Rose Garden* is composed almost entirely in prose, although several short poems are included in it. This work contains advice, proverbs, and humorous reflections.

Amir Khosrow was among the greatest and the last of the Persian-language authors of medieval Islam. He composed panegyrics for seven consecutive rulers of Delhi. He is noted for his *Pentology*, which emulated the work of another Persian author; composed in the *masnavi* technique, it contains five long idylls about general Islamic literary themes. By Khosrow's death in 1325 the Abbasid caliphate had long since ended. With his passing went the golden age of Islamic literature, ironically usurped by the regional literature it had originally displaced in such places as Persia, Asia, and North Africa.

Today medieval Islamic literature is becoming more mainstream as the difficult, traditionally rigid and distinct styles are more readily translated. Classical Arabic poetry was composed with the principle of monorhyme employed. This means that a single rhyme echoed throughout the entire poem, regardless of its length. Within this rhyming pattern there were sixteen basic meters in five groupings; the author was not allowed to stray from any of these meters. As mentioned, some of the prominent forms in medieval Islamic literature were the *qasida*, the *ghazel*, and the *maqamah*. Islamic literature was also composed in *qitahs*, which were used for less serious topics, mainly in satires, jokes, and word games. The *masnavi* was native to Persia. It means "the doubled one" and was simply a work composed in rhyming couplets. This genre became very popular because it allowed the author to tell a long story uniting literally thousands of verses. This is as close as the medieval Islamic literature came to producing epics, which the Arabs frowned upon because epics were based in fiction. Finally, the *roba'i* was also derived from pre-Islamic Persian poetry. The *roba'i* was composed in quatrains that rhymed in the first, second, and fourth lines. The most famous work in this style is the *Rubáiyát of Omar Khayyám*.

SELECTED BIBLIOGRAPHY

Bulliet, Richard W. "Orientalism and Medieval Isalmaic Studies." In *The Past and the Present of Medieval Studies*. John Van Engen, ed. Notre Dame: University of Notre Dame Press, 1994, 94-104; Bulliet, Richard W. "Printing in the Medieval Islamic Underworld." *Columbia Library Columns* 36:3 (May 1987), 13-20; Burton, John. *An Introduction to the "Hadith."* Edinburgh: Edinburgh University Press, 1994; *Compton's Encyclopedia and Fact Finder*. Chicago: Compton's Learning Co., 1991; Hamarnah, Walid. "The Reception of Aristotle's Theory of Poetry in the Arab-Islamic Mediaeval Thought." In *Poetics East and West*. Milena Dolezelova-Velingerora, ed. Toronto: Toronto Semiotic Circle, 1988-89. 183-201; Renard, John. *Islam and the Heroic Image: Themes in Literature and the Visual Arts*. Columbia: University of South Carolina Press, 1993; Stetkevych, Suzanne Pinckney. *The Mute Immortals Speak: Pre-Islamic Poetry and the Poetics of Ritual*. Ithaca: Cornell University Press, 1993; Street, Tony. "Medieval Islamic Doctrine on the Angels: The Writings of Fakhr al-Din al-Razi." *Parergon* 9:2 (Dec 1991), 111-27; Sundaresa Iyer, K. V. *Dust and Soul of Fitzgerald's "Omar Khayyám."* Madras: Kalakshetra Publications, 1977.

Laura Cooner Lambdin and Robert T. Lambdin

I SYNG OF A MYDEN. *I Syng of a Myden* is a short, *lyric poem composed of five quatrains with incremental repetition of the first and third lines in the three central stanzas. The lines contain two or three stresses, and the stanzas rhyme either *abcb* or *abab*. This lyric is an excellent example of an allegorical poem that combines elements of the secular with the sacred.

The first stanza begins with the voice of the poet singing of a "myden" who is "makeles," a woman who chose as her son the "Kyng of alle kynges." The second stanza describes how the son came "also stylle" to his mother like dew that falls on the grass in April. The third stanza repeats the image but changes it slightly by describing the son coming to his mother in her "bowr" like dew that falls on a flower. The fourth stanza reiterates the central image, but this time the son comes to where his "moder lay" like dew that falls on "the spray." The final stanza explains the mysterious imagery by stating that there never has been another mother and maiden like this woman, for this lady is God's mother.

Edmund Reiss has noted that this lyric is both a reverdie and a poem of adoration, thus it combines the secular with the sacred genre. The language of the poem reflects this overlap with courtly nouns, like "king" and "lady/mayden." The double meaning of "makeles" as both mateless and matchless reflects the complex nature of Mary and presents the paradox of virgin birth. Rather than following the courtly tradition, in which a matchless woman chooses a suitor, here Mary is choosing a son. The poem's paradoxical nature is made more complex, as Reiss pointed out, by the depiction of Christ, who was both chosen by Mary and came to her (in the form of the Holy Spirit). "Stylle/still" makes Christ gentle and reflects the night of his birth. The symbolism in the poem is related to its religious *allegory. The garden, bower, and spray are all symbols of new life, the dew is a symbol of the Holy Ghost and of fertility, and April is a time of procreation. Nancy and Lewis Owen saw even the number of stanzas as symbolic of the five joys of Mary, and the three interior stanzas as a kind of Holy Trinity or a representation of the annunciation, conception, and birth. Thus the movement from grass to flower to spray suggests a growing fruitfulness.

SELECTED BIBLIOGRAPHY

Barratt, Alexandra, ed. *Women's Writing in Middle English*. London and New York: Longman, 1992 ; McClellan, William. "Radical Theology or Parody in a Marian Lyric of Ms Harley 2253. " In *Voices in Translation: The Authority of "Olde Bookes" in Medieval Literature*. Deborah M. Sinnreich-Levi and Gale Sigal, eds. New York: AMS Press, 1992. 157-68; Pickering, O. S. "Newly Discovered Secular Lyrics from Later Thirteenth-Century Cheshire. " *Review of English Studies* 43 (1992): 157-80; Reiss, Edmund. *The Art of the Middle English Lyric: Essays in Criticism*. Athens: University of Georgia Press, 1972; Reiss, Edmund. "The Middle English Lyric. " *Old and Middle English Literature*. Dictionary of Literary Biography. Vol. 146. Jeffrey Helterman and Jerome Mitchell, eds. Detroit: Gale, 1994. 392-399; Sigal, Gale. *Erotic Dawn-Songs of the Middle Ages: Voicing the Lyric Lady*. Gainesville: University Press of Florida, 1996; Stevick, Robert D., Ed. *One Hundred Middle English Lyrics*. Rev. Urbana: University of Illinois Press, 1994

Sigrid King

ITALIAN LITERATURE. Most of the earliest literature of medieval Italy, whether it was folk songs, minstrel verse, or didactic narrative, was composed in verse. It was not until several hundred years later that the beautiful *lyric forms were joined by a passionate, typically Italian prose form. While there are plenty of religious texts, the literature of medieval Italy differed slightly from that of other early European countries because it was predominantly composed of love poems. At a time when the medieval Catholic Church dominated all facets of life, the norm in Europe was for authors to produce mostly works glorifying God or the saints.

The literature of Italy in the Middle Ages reflected three different cultural levels. The first was folk literature, which consisted mainly of folk songs and tales. The second was the literature of popular entertainers, like the *minstrels, who wrote songs and works in either verse or prose intended to attract both sophisticated and unsophisticated audiences, depending upon the performance setting. The third type of literature was that of the "ordinary sense," compositions of all sorts (poetry, prose, songs) written by authors both to interest and to provide pleasure to an audience with some education.

The peasantry and humble city dwellers comprised much of the audience of the "folk" literature, which was composed in both verse and prose, usually in the vernacular of the region concerned. The songs were of two types: lyric and narrative. In Sicily in the early thirteenth century existed the *strambotto*, a single-stanza octave with eleven-syllable lines. This genre found its way to Tuscany by the end of the thirteenth century, where adaptations of the *strambotto* called the *rispetto* flourished. These works were mostly love songs anonymously composed, learned by the traveling performers, and spread throughout the land. Additionally, songs included dance tunes called *ballata* that consisted of a two-line refrain and several stanzas. The leader of the song would sing the first refrain, which was then echoed by the members of a chorus. The leader would then sing a stanza, and the chorus would follow with the refrain; the leader then sang the second stanza, and the chorus repeated the refrain, and so on. Other popular folk music included serenades, lullabies, religious songs, and May songs.

The narrative lyrics of the minstrels varied in form and length. These works were more dramatic in structure; the narrators were often speaking for themselves. While many of these works were secular, the majority of them, particularly the latter works, seem to have been religious. Among the most popular themes of the thirteenth century were the gospel stories and *hagiography. These works were often sung on pilgrimages or at religious festivals (*see* **Festivals and Holidays**). The secular narratives were more of a romantic sort; most were tragic. Irregardless of theme, these were usually sung by a single voice, although a second voice could have joined in for harmony. The *ballata*, however, was sung by many voices.

During the papacy of *Innocent III (1198-1216), the church attained its apex of power, and the literature of the "ordinary sense" came into prominence. Two new monastic orders developed during this period, the Franciscan and the Dominican. The teachings of these groups played a vital role in the development of the literature and philosophy of medieval Italy. St. *Francis of Assisi (1181-1226) led a movement that preached humility. This was a stark contrast to the world of greed where most, including the clerics, were interested more in personal possessions than in personal salvation. St. Francis wrote the first piece of true literature composed in Italian, a psalm that is often referred to as *Laudes creaturarum* (The Praises of God's Creatures). It is composed in free verse, and the lines are linked by assonance.

During this same time some north Italians were writing works in their own dialects. Two Lombards, Uguccione da Lodi and Gerardo Patecchio, wrote some brilliant works. Da Lodi's works were usually didactic, but realistic. Patecchio wrote *Le noi* (Annoyances), a poem that was probably meant for entertainment. Additionally, Tommasino di Cerclaria, a cleric of northeastern Italy, composed a poem in German, *Der Wälsche Gast* (The Italian Guest). This work is over 15,000 lines long and discusses many topics, from table manners to moderation.

The second quarter of the thirteenth century in Italy centered around the reign of Frederick II (1194-1250). Frederick was intelligent and curious; he mastered many languages, including Greek, Latin, and Arabic. In addition to his duties with the government, he was also keenly interested in architecture and writing. He was a generous patron of the arts and founded the University of Naples. He himself was responsible for the composition of an elaborate Latin treatise on falconry, complete with several hundred illustrations. During his reign a group of some thirty poets were assembled and patronized his court. These "Frederician poets" were representative of much of Italy, coming from such diverse regions as Sicily, southern Italy, and Tuscany. Several of these poets were even trained in law. Their works were eclectic, showing much continental influence, including that of the French *Provençal poets and the German *minnisingers.

About 125 poems of the Fredericians are extant. There are about 85 *canzoni, while the rest are sonnets. The Frederician sonnets consist of fourteen eleven-syllable lines; their rhyme structure creates both an octet and a sestet. While the rhyme scheme of the octet was always *ababababab*, the sestet could rhyme either *cdecde* or *cdcdcd*. Perhaps the most prominent composer of Frederician sonnets was Giacomo da Lentino, whom some believe is the true inventor of the sonnet.

At the same time in northern Italy, Provençal poets of lyric verse thrived. Among the best-known of these is *Sordello of Mantua, who became a troubadour, taking his songs from court to court. His travels took him to Spain, Portugal, and France. Of his works, the most important may be a *sirvente*, a type of political poem, which led *Dante to choose him for some advice in the *Purgatorio*. The first composition in Italian prose also occurred during this time. The work is a meager one; it is a collection of fifteen sentence-length notions called the *Gemma purpurea*. This was a guide to writing letters by Guido Faba, a rhetoric teacher at the University of Bologna. He probably also composed a work called *Parlamenta et epistole* (c. 1242), which contains nearly one hundred models for all types of writing, including letters and public addresses. Each of these Italian versions is accompanied by another in Latin.

The second half of the thirteenth century in Italy was a time of great social and political upheaval; conversely, it was also a time of artistic glory. When Frederick II died in 1250, the Italian medieval empire began to fragment. Frederick's son Conrad IV held power for a time in southern Italy, but the pope offered this kingdom to Charles of Anjou, who defeated Manfred in 1266. Factional strife echoed throughout Italy; the Tuscan cities of the North battled each other for power. Yet during this unrest art and architecture became prominent. Majestic cathedrals were erected in Santo Spirito in 1269 and Santa Maria Novella in 1278. Pisa flourished as an artistic city. Nicola Pisano created magnificent sculptures that adorned the great churches. Painters flocked to places such as Florence, Siena, and Rome and, in a religious fervor, painted intricate, dignified iconographic depictions of holy persons.

Three leading poets of this time were Guittone d'Arezzo, Guido *Guinizelli, and Guido *Cavalcanti. Guittone is considered the first prolific Italian poet; some three hundred of his poems are extant. He was born near Arezzo around 1225. While he was young, he honed his craft by composing love poems; some were canzoni, others were sonnets. Additionally, he was among the first poets to integrate the folk form of the ballata into poetry. Around 1260 Guittone was converted and joined the order of the Knights of the Blessed Virgin Mary. He remained a member until his death around 1293. The canzoni and sonnets of his later life were starkly different from the seductive love poems of his youth. These later works contain a driving sense of morality and earnestness. In perhaps the most impressive of his later canzoni, Guittone comments here upon the nature of nobility, finding that it is one's heart, not ancestral background, that creates true nobility.

Guido Guinizelli hailed from around Bologna. In 1274 he was banished from Bologna with two others, and he died two years later. He was one of Guittone's most ardent admirers; Guinizelli once sent Guittone a canzone and a sonnet, asking him to correct the faults in the works. There are some twenty extant poems composed by Guinizelli, mostly written as canzoni or sonnets. In his canzone "Al cor gentil ripara sempre amore" Guinizelli fuses the idea of both beauty and angelic service in describing his lady. This may be the first union of these ideas, which became a vital poetic conceit. This would especially influence *Dante, who referred to Guinizelli as "father" (of his inspiration).

Guido Cavalcanti, born between 1250 and 1255, was a friend of Dante's, although Cavalcanti was a good deal older. Cavalcanti was born into one of the elite families of Florence; he was a man of some intellect, pride, and education, for he was well versed in philosophy. Cavalcanti's fifty or so extant poems are mostly sonnets, *ballate*, or canzoni, but there are also some works that glorify and praise, similar to those of Guinizelli. However, the majority of his works are psychological investigations of the qualities of love. His viewpoint was that love existed continuously in the mind in the image of a cherished ideal, such as Beauty. It was this ideal, to Cavalcanti, that became active emotionally when a man beheld a woman who was the essence of this impression. Thus the real and the imagined images coincided in the lover's mind. His work was very influential on several younger Florentine poets, but precious few were ever able to master Cavalcanti's idea of harmonics in their works.

The influence of these three spread quickly throughout Italy. In Tuscany and Bologna Guittone seems to have been the poet of choice, for many other writers tried to emulate his works. Perhaps the most successful of these imitators was Rustico di Filippo, who transformed the sonnet from a genre of serious love poetry into humorous works bent on eliciting guffaws. Also, one of the first women composers known to have written Italian verse emerged in the late thirteenth century. She was a Florentine woman known only as Compiuta Donzella (the accomplished damsel). At least three sonnets have been attributed to her.

In the latter portion of the thirteenth century academics stepped to the forefront in a new surge of intellectualism. Writers deliberately turned away from the composition of works in Italian, turning instead to Latin. These were the first scholars to be linked with the humanistic movement. Members of this movement tended to be more individualistic, so there was no proliferation of one single type of literature composed. This activity was first seen in Padua in the writings of Judge Lovato Lovati (1241-1309); therefore, he is deemed to be the first Italian humanist. Lovati's writings were all in Latin, and they display a good knowledge of the familiar classical writers. Among Lovati's favorites were Livy and Seneca. Lovati's renown as a poet was great, for even *Petrarch commented favorably upon his works. However, only six lines out of two long poems known to be composed by him are extant. One poem was about Tristram and Iseult, and the other concerned the strife of the Guelphs and the Ghibellines.

After 1250 the use of prose in Italian works became voluminous. While it was mostly used for translation of French and Latin classics, this newfound interest did result in the development of collections of novelle called novellino. The novellino varied in length; some of the novelles were very short. So, too, was the content different. This form contains action stories, brief anecdotes, and collections of clever sayings. The heroes found in the novelles include religious figures such as Jesus and his disciples,   kings such as *Charlemagne and Arthur (see **Arthurian Legend**), and various sundry knights, magicians, ladies, scamps, minstrels, and teachers. It seems as though all were fair game for inclusion in novelles. The general tone of these works was chivalric, although humor was often a core element. The novelles concentrate upon the stories themselves and proceed from start to finish without embellishment. Naturally, this form is derived from many sources, including Oriental, biblical, classical Greek, Latin, and French works.

Arthurian legends and stories, long favorites in Italy, became much more popular at this time. Minstrels originally brought these tales from France. By the latter part of the thirteenth century the French Arthurian *romances were brought to Italy and translated into Italian prose. Some artists even tried creating their own Arthurian stories. The first known Italian composer of Arthurian works is Rustichello of Pisa; his Meliadus, written around 1275, is a compilation of material derived from French sources. Rustichello chose to write in French rather than Italian prose. The first Arthurian romance composed in Italian was completed around the end of the thirteenth century.

The *Tristano riccardiano* follows the traditional Tristan story, but adds some variations to the episodes and details of the work.

The return of Marco *Polo from China introduced a new type of writing, the *chronicle. Many of the first works of this genre are concerned with Polo, but a movement toward more hagiographic chronicles soon followed. Salimbene of Parma wrote the *Chronica* in 1287, which covers history from 1167 to 1287. While it is especially concerned with the history of Parma, it incorporates much from throughout Europe. This work is somewhat crude, but it is important because it is so inclusive of world history.

· These elements all interwove to create what must be the golden age of medieval Italian literature. During this period three of the greatest Italian writers created and perfected their works. First and foremost in this regard is Dante Alighieri (1265-1321), the first major author to write in Italian. He was born in Florence and was well educated in both classical and religious literature. While he was young, he became active politically and fought in the war between the Guelfs and the Ghibellines. Dante himself was a Guelf, belonging to the Bianchi faction. Unfortunately for Dante, the Bianchis' rivals, the Neri, came to power in 1301. Dante and many of his peers were sentenced to perpetual banishment in 1302, with the penalty of death by burning if they were ever found again in Florence. The Bianchi then allied themselves with the Ghibelline party and several times unsuccessfully attacked Florence. In 1313 Emperor Henry VII died, ending all hopes of the reunification of Germany and Italy. After this, Dante spent most of his time writing the *Divine Comedy* under the patronage of Ghibelline leaders. He may have begun this work by 1300, but the majority of it was composed after 1315. The final part was not completed until just before his death in 1321.

In 1274 Dante first met Beatrice, the woman who became his muse and frequent subject. Nine years later they met again and he was deeply smitten. In 1290, after her death, he composed his *La vita nuova*, which reveals how greatly he had loved her. This work is the first to disclose that she was the inspiration for many of his works. Around 1292 Dante married Gemma Donati, with whom he had two sons and two daughters. For whatever reason, she chose not to accompany him into exile in 1302.

Dante's other works include a number of lyrics and canzoni. Many of his sonnets appear in *La vita nuova*. From 1304 to 1306 he wrote *De vulgari eloquentia*, which was a Latin treatise about the use of the vernacular. Dante felt that Italian, and not Latin, should be used in composition so that the language would be recognized as a serious literary language. This, in turn, would unite the separate Italian cultures behind a sense of national pride. His work also analyzes several Italian dialects, predating the science of linguistics by hundreds of years. Because he so well understood the construction of language, Dante was able to use his native Tuscan in the composition of his *Divine Comedy* and *La vita nuova* so convincingly that this dialect was established as the precursor to modern Italian.

His Latin treatise *De monarchian* (On the Monarchy), composed around 1313, established Dante's political perspective that would become a key theme in his *Divine Comedy*. In this work he posited his belief that a central authority, in this case the Holy Roman Empire, was necessary. At the same time he deplored the major infighting between the political rulers and the papacy. His writings concluded that true peace would be achieved solely when the monarchy was established for the universal good; this would occur only when the rulers understood their dependence on God, thus allowing reverence and spirituality into the church and state. This, to Dante, would allow for church and state to function as allies rather than adversaries.

Several of Dante's contemporaries, such as Cino da Pistoia, never reached the heights of popularity that Dante or Cavalcanti attained, but they should be recognized for some of their accomplishments. Many in Dante's inner circle wrote canzoni and sonnets that are extant. Of particular note is the canzone da Pistoia wrote to Dante after the death of Beatrice. Others like Cecco Angiolieri found their niche in composing humorous and realistic verse. Folgere da San Gemignano, a minstrel, preserved many of the lyrics and sonnets he presented to his audience. This was a great time for the minstrels, who were welcomed throughout the land by audiences hungry for their romances and stories. The works were transformed from their native French into Italian. Both epics and *cuntari*, the poems of the minstrels, were put to music and sung, accompanied by stringed instruments. If the poem was too long to be sung totally in one session, it was performed over the course of many nights.

This era also fostered humanistic thought. Albertino Mussato (1261-1329) composed the *Ecerinis*, one of the first humanistic tragedies. It concerned the thirteenth-century tyrant Ezzelino da Romano and is essentially a written indictment of his tyranny. Modeled upon the works of Seneca, the *Ecerinis* is more of an oration than an action piece. The work was so well received in Padua in 1315 that Mussato was honored in a grand civic ceremony. This humanistic movement began to spread, making its way to Bologna, Tuscany, and Florence. The seed of the great Italian Renaissance was strewn.

However, this movement was temporarily interrupted by the Black Death which swept over Western Europe in 1348. This was just the latest in a time of hardships for Italy, which was suffering from internal strife and religious ambiguity, for there still were two papacies, one in Rome, the other in Avignon. Yet the development of culture did not cease with these intrusions. A major force in the ongoing outgrowth of this shift was Petrarch.

*Petrarch, or Francesco Petrarca (1304-1374), was born in Arezzo, but he spent much of his youth in Avignon and Carpentras. He studied law at Bologna, but his interests fell mainly into both Latin and Greek literature and writing. His renown as a scholar and poet was such that he was crowned at Rome in 1341 with the laurel, a ceremony that had not been performed since ancient times. He spent the latter part of his life wandering from city to city. He was friends with Giovanni *Boccaccio and was very interested in the revival of classical learning. It was his dedication to this resolve that made him the founder of Renaissance humanism. He earned his designation as the first "modern man" because of his many attributes that set him apart from his contemporaries. He loved nature dearly, as is evidenced by his descriptions and feats of mountain climbing. He also was frank in his resorting to meditation over psychological conflicts. Unlike many of his peers, he preferred Plato to *Aristotle, but he is most renowned for his humanistic writing concerning his love, Laura. His adoration of his beloved transcended the hyperbolic conventions of the courtly tradition.

Petrarch was a prolific correspondent, and many of his letters survive. Additionally, he composed works in Latin, such as *De viris illustribus* (On illustrious men), and epic poems, such as his *Africa*, which features Scipio Africanus as its hero. He also wrote the dialogue *Secretum*, which takes the form of a debate. In the *Secretum*, Petrarch reveals his love of Laura and the laurel (fame), which conflict with his spiritual feelings. His writings also include many treatises, some eclogues, and even a guide book to the Holy Land.

But his most important works are his Italian poems, collected in a *canzione*, or songbook. This folio, often called the *Rime* or *Rime sparse* (Scattered lyrics), includes sonnets, canzoni, *sestine, ballate* and *madrigals. Editors later broke this work into two sections, *In vita di Madonna Laura* (During the life of my lady Laura) and *In morte di Madonna Laura* (After the death of my lady Laura). It is not believed that Laura was a real woman, yet Petrarch presents her image in a way much more realistic than the conventional ladies of the Provençal troubadours or in the literature of *courtly love. Indeed, she is even more ethereal than the *donna angelica* (angelic ladies) found throughout the poems of this time, seen especially in Dante's Beatrice.

Some of Petrarch's poems were addressed to friends while others were penned for contemporary patrons and concerned current affairs. Other works are even religious; however, the most dominant theme in Petrarch's work is Laura. He created in her a woman whose beauty and actions captivated the poet, causing him both joy and remorse, for a relationship with her was unworkable. Petrarch achieved this conflict by recording in the works explicit psychological details formalized in figurative language and other literary devices. When Laura died, the poet found no relief in the grief that replaced his previous despair. This resulted in a more spiritual tone that borders on consolation. This collection of works became the source and the inspiration for an entire movement called European Petrarchism that dominated poetry for centuries.

Petrarch's other vernacular work is the *Trionfi*, which was inspired by Dante and composed in *terza rima*. This composition allegorically describes the procession of Love, Chastity, Death, Fame, Time, and Eternity and contains both historical and literary persons as examples. Included in this work again is Laura. Petrarch was still revising this piece when he died in 1374.

Petrarch's influence became nearly universal. Geoffrey *Chaucer used Petrarch's translation of the Latin Griselda story, found also in the Boccaccio's *Decameron, as an inspiration for his *"Cleric's Tale" in the *Canterbury Tales. Chaucer also derived a portion of *Troylus and Criseyde from a piece of Petrarch's Rime. English Petrarchism became extremely strong, as seen in the works of Sir Thomas Wyatt and Henry Howard Surrey in the sixteenth century. Petrarch's influence continued until the nineteenth century. In the English Renaissance the Trionfi was also an important source for authors such as Henry Parker and Percy Bysshe Shelley.

The humanistic ideas of Petrarch, carried forth by his younger devotees, far outweighed all other influences as humanism developed in Italy. His lyric poetry's effect on later lyrics has been even greater. Although Chaucer's use of Petrarchism was the beginning of the Italian's influence in foreign lands, it continued into Spain and Dalmatia in the fifteenth century and moved to France and heavily into England by the sixteenth. Many of the poems were set to music by Italians, French, and Germans. Among the great composers to use Petrarchan themes were Dufay and Liszt.

While Petrarch was spinning his craft, another Italian author rose to prominence. Giovanni Boccaccio (1313-1375) was born near Certaldo, but he spent at least a part of his life in Naples. He was a member of the Neapolitan high society, but he chose to shun his father's merchant business for a career in law. From 1341 until his death, he lived mainly in Florence, where he opted for a career as a man of letters. This allowed him to write prolifically; included in his canon are many types and styles of prose and poetry that were novel to Italian and even European literature. Thus he rightfully claims a place next to Petrarch as one of the founders of the Italian Renaissance. Toward the end of his life he composed some scholarly works in Latin; their themes, reflecting an interest in classical antiquity, became seminal texts in the growing humanistic movement. Of similar regard is his attempt to have Homer translated from Greek to the vernacular to ensure accessibility at a time when few knew Greek. Petrarch recommended that he become a patron to a Greek scholar until the work was completed. Unfortunately, the scholar was incompetent and the result was a poor translation.

Boccaccio's works run the gamut of style and genre. He composed the first Italian hunting poem in terza rima, Caccia di Diana (Diana's hunt) from 1334-36. His *Filocolo contains the "Thirteen Questions of Love," while the *Filostrato was the first romance in ottava rima composed by a man of letters. The *Teseida is the first Tuscan epic composed in octaves. From 1341 to 1342 he wrote the Ameto, which is astounding in that it is a prose romance in a pastoral setting. His ability to accommodate various styles is obvious in the Amorosa visione (1342-43), an allegorical poem in terzine, and also in his Fiammetta, a psychological romance with a character comparable to Laura or Beatrice. Perhaps his most overlooked work is the Ninfale Fiesolano, the first Italian idyll. This was followed by the Decameron, which is his most famous work. Additionally, he composed some Latin treatises as well as a commentary on the *Divine Comedy*.

The incursion of these great Italian authors signals the end of the Italian medieval period, some 150 years before the English Renaissance. There are several contemporaries of Boccaccio and Petrarch who are worth noting, including Fazio degli Uberti, who composed lyrics. Many of his works exposed an obvious understanding of deep suffering, and his political canzoni vehemently support the Ghibellines. Antonio Pucci from Florence was a prolific poet of humorous sonnets, especially in the form of the *sonetto caudato* or "tailed sonnet" in which the fourteenth line is followed by a short line that rhymes with it. The poem then ends with a closing couplet that introduces a new rhyme. Pucci also composed several *cantari* that were obviously for public consumption. Since his job was town crier, he was always privy to an audience, and he seemed to take great pleasure in telling adventurous stories.

In Venice, Niccolò da Verona composed works intended for minstrels in which he invented plots and delineated characters. His *Prise de Pampleune* (The capture of Pamplona) reverts to a setting in Moorish Spain while his *Pharsale* is Roman in its theme. Also, in Umbria the *lauda gave way to religious drama. Religious tracts also were featured at this time, especially in the compositions of the Florentine Dominican Iacopo Passavantri (c. 1302-1357). Perhaps his best work is the *Speccio della vera penitenza* (The mirror of true penitence) which is a treatise based upon a series of sermons he delivered in 1354. The piece is impressive for its moral dignity and sense of religious urgency. Interspersed with *exempla, the *Speccio* clearly drives home its concerns of the danger of sin and its consequences.

The literature of medieval Italy acts eerily as a precursor to similar writings throughout Europe. From its early mimetic tracts of German and French texts, the works of Italy flowered at a pace unparalleled in medieval literature. The religious and hagiographic works that progressed quickly were usurped just as abruptly by the elevated rhetoric of the romances. However, for some reason the quest for intelligence infected the writers of Italy at a time when the rest of the world seemed content to follow the efforts of the knights in their quests for utter spirituality. What occurred next, in the scathing political commentaries of Dante and the growing humanism of Petrarch and Boccaccio, germinated the growth of ideas never before seen in the idylls of man. The very idea that thought and scholarship could produce tracts that elicited even more of the same is phenomenal, and this triad did more for the expansion of thought than perhaps any other trio in history. Not only were they responsible for the growing ideology of their country, they were the beginnings of a growth of original Western thought which soon altered the philosophy of this era. Italian writers wrote not only in Italian but also in Latin, French, and English, so this was truly a culture of inclusion, which makes it unique: its literature cannot be separated from the works of other countries. From the lower comedy of the folk literature to the deeply personal love lyric, the literature of medieval Italy is truly impressive.

SELECTED BIBLIOGRAPHY

Axelrod, Mark. "Dante's Foil: Death and the Divine Afflatus." *La Fusta* 9 (Fall 1993), 97-100; Fiore, Silvia R. "The Silent Scholars of Italian Humanism: Feminism in the Renaissance." In *Interpreting the Italian Renaissance: Literary Perspectives*. Antonio Toscano, ed. Stony Brook, NY: Forum Italicum, 1991. 15-27; Franke, William. *Dante's Interpretive Journey*. Chicago: University of Chicago Press, 1996; Hawkins, Peter S. "Divide and Conquer: Augustine in the *Divine Comedy*." In *"The City of God": A Collection of Critical Essays*. Dorothy F. Donnelly, ed. New York: Peter Lang, 1995. 213-31; Hyde, John Kenneth. *Literacy and Its Uses: Studies on Late Medieval Italy*. Manchester: Manchester University Press, 1993; Irwin, Bonnie D. "What's in a Frame? The Medieval Textualization of Traditional Storytelling." *Oral Tradition* 10:1 (March 1995), 27-53; McGlaughlin, M. L. *Literary Imitation in the Italian Renaissance: The Theory and Practice in Literary Imitation in Italy from Dante to Bembo*. Oxford: Clarendon Press, 1995; Russell, Rinalinda, ed. *Italian Women Writers: A Bio-Bibliographical Sourcebook*. Westport, CT: Greenwood Press, 1994; Vittorini, Domenico. *The Age of Dante: A Concise History of Italian Culture in the Years of the Early Renaissance*. 1957. Westport, CT: Greenwood Press, 1975; Whitfield, John Humphreys. *A Short History of Italian Literature*. 1960. Westport, CT: Greenwood Press, 1976.

Robert T. Lambdin and Laura Cooner Lambdin

IVAN III (1440-1505) Romanov, tsar of Russia (1462-1505). Ivan III is considered the first national sovereign of Russia. Cautious and persistent, he was, with great effort, able to annex most of the rival principalities. After a series of wars he subjugated Novgorod, and in 1471 Novgorod was forced to renounce its close alliance with Lithuania and pay a tribute to Ivan. After 1478 a second war was successfully concluded, with Novgorod forced to give up its independence; its troublesome upper classes were deported to central Russia. In 1485 Ivan annexed Tver, putting an end to Russia's most dangerous rivals. In 1494 Ivan drove out the German merchants, ending the Hanseatic presence. Ivan's lands thus encompassed a huge territory extending all the way east to the Urals. By 1503 he had also annexed the White Russian and Little Russian territories.   These accomplishments led to Russia's place in the diplomatic intercourse of Europe and active relations with the West.

Ivan married Zoë, last female relative of the Greek Emperor Constantine, thus establishing the claim of Russian rulers as successors of the Greek emperors and as protectors of Orthodox Christianity. The marriage also introduced the concepts of autocracy and the ceremonial court to Moscow.

SELECTED BIBLIOGRAPHY

Duffy, James P. *Czars: Russia's Rulers for More Than One Thousand Years*. New York: Facts on File, 1995; Raleigh, Donald J., ed. and A. A. Iskenderov, comp. *The*

Emperors and Empresses of Russia: Rediscovering the Romanovs. Armonk, NY: Sharpe, 1996.

                                                                    R. Churchill Curtis

IVAN IV (1530-1584) Romanov, tsar of Russia (1533-1584). Although he ascended the throne at age three, Ivan IV did not assume power until much later. He had himself proclaimed tsar in 1547. In the same period he established a council of personally appointed advisors to counterbalance the Duma—the Council of Boyars. This was followed in 1549 by the calling of the Zemski Sobar, the national assembly, to broaden public support for the crown.

From 1552 to 1556 Ivan struggled to wrest Kazan and Estrakhan from the Tartars. This conquest gave Russia complete control of the Volga and opened the way for further expansion to the southeast.

SELECTED BIBLIOGRAPHY

Duffy, James P. *Czars: Russia's Rulers for More Than One Thousand Years.* New York: Facts on File, 1995; Hunt, Priscilla. "Ivan IV's Personal Mythology of Kingship." *Slavic Review* 52:4 (Winter 1993), 769-809; Perrie, Maureen. *The Image of Ivan the Terrible in Russian Folklore.* Cambridge: Cambridge University Press, 1987; Raleigh, Donald J., ed. and A. A. Iskenderov, comp. *The Emperors and Empresses of Russia: Rediscovering the Romanovs.* Armonk, NY: Sharpe, 1996.

                                                                    R. Churchill Curtis

J

JAPANESE LITERATURE. The medieval period in Japanese history is the Kamakura period, which lasted from 1186 to 1336. Just prior to this period, beginning in 1086, the system of government in Japan had been the insei or cloistered emperors system of government in which emperors gave up their thrones in order to rule from behind the scenes.

An emperor on the throne had too many other duties at court to devote enough attention to the power plays that were necessary to keep Japan protected from threats like invading hordes of Mongols, and internal strife as well, as far as many of the rulers were concerned. They felt that true power could only be exercised from behind the scenes instead of from upon the throne; thus the manorial system with the Fujiwara family as the greatest manor holders prevailed until 1192. In this year Minamoto Yoritomo founded the shogunate at Kamakura, and the Kamakura period began.

Unfortunately, the establishment of a ruling class whose power lay not in their intellect but in their ability to make war necessarily and unsurprisingly led to a decline in the intellectual climate of Japan, as is true of any society in which the ruling bodies have to protect their kingdoms from being ripped apart at every turn, rather than having to worry about more manageable problems with trade policy and the like. Just as in Europe during the Middle Ages monks and priests were mainly the keepers of the flame of intellect, so in medieval Japan the Buddhist monks and priests were largely responsible for keeping learning alive.

In both places, of course, some members of the royal court and the ruling bodies managed to find time to develop themselves intellectually, and some even artistically. In fact, one of the images from this era is of the court intellectual or poet who renounces public life and retreats either to the monastery or to a solitary hermitage. There, free from the turmoil surrounding life in the court, they could clear their minds, simplify their lives, and seek the enlightenment that would make their work sublime. Not everyone migrated immediately to the hills to live in huts, however, so much great literature was written in and around the court.

One of the major court-supported literary endeavors was the twenty-one royal collections of waka. These poetry collections varied according to the ruler collecting them, the poet or poets who were tasked with responsibility for compiling them, and the philosophy of whichever school of poetry was in ascendance when the compilation was made.   Although waka was being replaced by renga (linked stanzas) and haikai (poetical epigrams) in the Kamakura era, the waka was the poetic form of choice for the royal collections. The Kamakura era saw a rejuvenation of older poetic forms linked with the development of new forms, and a growing awareness of the significance of the events of the present day to literature.

The royal collections were frequently preceded by an utaawase, which was a poetry competition in which at least two poets were given topics on which to write a set number of verses, which were ranked according to the decision of a qualified judge or judges, generally either well-respected poets or critics, or both. At first, the poets were given the topics only at the competition, but later the rules were changed so that they could receive the topics before coming to the match. Later the jikaawase arose out of the utaawase; this was a competition with oneself that the poet individually submitted to the same sort of judge who would officiate an utaawase.

Such competitions began as mere mental exercises, but over time became serious affairs within the intellectual community. They were the means of establishing a poet's reputation, of winning favor with patrons at court, and of gaining commissions to put together collections of their own poetry or invitations to contribute poetry to royal collections, as well as setting up an atmosphere in which the poet's talents could be exercised through the spur of competition with another of equal talent.

The royal figures who held such competitions were generally not only patrons of the arts monetarily, but also occasionally contributed their own expertise in writing and evaluating poetry, sometimes even qualifying themselves as knowledgeable critics. Gotoba, for instance, who in 1201 held the 1,500 round poetry match, the Sengohyakuban, created a climate for poets during the early part of the Kamakura period that was more than friendly. He held the massive competition in order to gain quality material for his planned royal compilation, and as such, had ten judges for the utaawase, over whom he acted as ultimate judge.

The *Shinkokinshu*, which is considered one of the finest of the royal collections, not only was ordered by Gotoba, but he also participated actively in the collection of material for the compilation. In addition to holding the Sengohyakuban, Gotoba supervised the poets he had compiling the work, and he had frequent disagreements with Fujiwara Teika, who acted as the head compiler, over philosophical differences they had with the conception of the *Shinkokinshu* and how all the poems should balance out.

Gotoba's vision for the *Shinkokinshu* was that it should encompass examples of the finest poetry from the *Man'yoshu*, which is the earliest and most valued collection of Japanese poetry, through the finest modern poetry he could collect. Ultimately, Gotoba so much wanted control over the collection that he wound up taking the unfinished manuscript of the *Shinkokinshu* with him when he was exiled to Oki. Poets like Teika and the others who were fortunate enough to be working at or with the court during Gotoba's period of power, though they may have had periodic clashes with him, benefitted greatly from Gotoba's patronage.

The monogatari were another major form of literature in Kamakura-era Japan. These narrative pieces combined history, the oral tradition, and literature in prose or poetry. Much like the heroic epics sung by the *scops of medieval Europe, monogatari were meant to be performed orally to the accompaniment of a four-stringed lute, or biwa. Although they were written down during this period, the monogatari were frequently culled from the traditional myths and stories of the Japanese and thus were sometimes the product of centuries of retelling. Some, however, were the products of more recent histories and related important military engagements both within Japan and against outside invaders. The *Heike Monogatari* is the most popular of this genre and details the struggle for power between the Taira and Minamoto clans from 1131 to 1191.

The nikki is another of the major literary forms and, like the monogatari, is mostly prose but sometimes mixed with poetry. Nikki is generally translated as simply "diary," but a nikki is not necessarily a day-to-day journal of the author's life. A nikki is any chronicle that tells the story of a period of the author's life, any work that is autobiographical rather than biographical or narrative. This form of literature was popular with female authors, from empresses to court servants. Abutsu Ni's *Isayoi Nikki* is one of the most popular nikki from the Kamakura era.

The Kamakura period saw great influence on the world of literature built up by dynasties of literary families. For instance, Fujiwara Shunzei, one of the greatest of the early Kamakura-era poets, and the son of a poet, spawned a line of writers. Fujiwara Shunzei no Musume was his granddaughter and a fine waka poet. Fujiwara Tameie was the grandson of Shunzei and the first of the Nijo poets--a conservative movement within Japanese poetry that wanted to ape the traditional poets rather than learning what they could from their ancestors and adapting it to modern poetry. The Nijo school split off at Tameie's death under the supervision of his eldest son, Tameuji. Tamenori, Tameuji's younger brother, took control of the Kyogoku school, which joined the Reizei school against the Nijo. The Reizei, led by Tamesuke, Tameie's eldest son by Abutsu Ni (who was also a writer), were a liberal faction like the Kyogoku, and together both schools produced what scholars consider some of the best poetry of their era.

Hogen Monogatari, *The Tale of the Hogen War*, was written near the beginning of the Kamakura period, but the exact date and author of the piece are unknown. The first of the three volumes of this history concerns the gathering of the armies by Sutoku, who wished to take power, and the reigning sovereign Goshirakawa, who assumed power after the death of Toba in 1156. The second volume details the battle, climaxing with the appearance of the seven-foot-tall warrior Chinzei Hachiro Tametomo. Despite all his best efforts, Sutoku is beaten by the army of Goshirakawa, and he is forced to submit. The final volume is filled with tragedies: the wife of one of Sutoku's main allies, Minamoto Tameyoshi, commits suicide, and Sutoku himself is exiled.

Uji Shui Monogatari is a collection of early Kamakura setsuwa, a short story that is part of a larger collection, but does not necessarily have a main theme that is repeated in all the stories in the collection. The stories in this collection were written between 1190 and 1242. The themes, though they vary widely, generally concern some aspect of human nature, and the stories are believed to have been collected for a readership of average intellect to teach them moral lessons about the motives and limitations of men.

The author of the *Heiji Monogatari*, the story of the Heiji War, is unknown, as is the exact date of the piece, but it is placed at the beginning of the Kamakura period. It is comprised of sections of prose intermixed with sections of poetry and is in three parts. The first part is used to set the stage for the climax, which occurs in the second part, and the final part relates the aftermath of events. Fujiwara Nobuyori tries to overthrow the dictatorship of Taira Kiyomori, fails, and is ultimately executed.

Sumioshi Monogatari, another early Kamakura-period story, bears a striking resemblance to *Cinderella*. A middle councillor has a daughter by his first wife, who dies when the girl is seven. The woman he marries after her is as mean to the girl as Cinderella's stepmother is to her. Shosho, the son of a grand councillor, hears that the girl is mistreated by her stepmother, so he goes to her house to marry her and take her away. The evil stepmother tricks him into believing that her youngest daughter is the girl he seeks, so he marries her. Later he rescues the stepdaughter from Sumioshi, where she has fled for refuge, and marries her.

Fujimara Shunzei (1114-1204) was one of the poets and critics of the early Kamakura period. Son of the poet Toshitada, Shunzei began composing poetry at an early age and was able both to work within the traditional styles and to be innovative. His ability to work within and appreciate different poetic forms made him popular as a judge of poetry as well. It was this reputation that led to his being commissioned in 1187 to compile the seventh royal collection of poetry, the *Senzaishu*.

The *Senzaishu* boasts poems from several opposing schools and styles because of Shunzei's efforts to balance the collection. Shunzei's opinion counted for a great deal. His approbation helped encourage many young poets to continue developing their talent and even advanced the career of several older poets by pulling pieces from their personal collections that showed a different side to their talents.

In the two-part *Korai Futeisho*, which he compiled in 1197, Shunzei created a sort of canon of poetry by his inclusion of copious examples to illustrate his points about modern poetic theory. Earlier in his career Shunzei was honored by Shokushi Naishinno, the wife of the former sovereign and later a great poet in her own right, by her request to compile a collection of his own poems for her. This was the *Choshu Eiso*, put together in 1178.

Shunzei's granddaughter, Fujiwara Shunzei No Musume, was also a poet and is considered one of the greatest female Japanese waka poets of all time, though second to Shokushi Naishinno. Shokushi Naishinno is considered one of the finest poets of her day and is remembered for her facility with descriptive poetry and the passionate feeling reflected in all her poetry.

Saigyo, one of the best-loved poets in Japanese history, was a poet-priest in the early part of the Kamakura period. *Mimosusogawa Utaawase* and *Miyagawa Utaawase* are two of his better-known collections of poetic matches against himself. Poets used to frequently write sets of competing poems, the poet trying to outdo his own effort, and they would then send these jikaawase or utaawase to a respected critic to judge their merits.

The *Sankashu* is Saigyo's main collection of poems, with the first part being comprised of seasonal poems, the second of love poems, and the third of a set on various topics. Saigyo is unusual in that although he was a monk who rejected the world, his poetry very accurately reflects the everyday struggles, mental and emotional, of mankind.

The Roppyakuban Utaawase was a poetry match convened by Fujiwara Yoshitsune consisting of six hundred rounds and involving six poets. Each of the poets wrote a sequence of a hundred poems on set topics for Fujiwara Shunzei to judge.

Kamo No Chomei, though he began his career at court, moved increasingly farther away from that life over the years and devoted himself ever more fully to the arts. Chomei's stance, being slightly apart from the opposing factions within the art world at the time, presents us with a clearer picture of the scene than a partisan account could.

The *Mumyosho* (1209-10) is one of his most famous works, a seemingly loosely flowing commentary on a conglomerate of topics related to the poetry of his age, including not only theory and technical information, but stories of the poets themselves. *Hojoki* (1212) is considered by most scholars to be his finest work and contains an account of the great fire of Kyoto in 1177, the famine of 1181, and the earthquake of 1185, all of which Chomei witnessed before his retreat to his mountain hut. Chomei's *Hojoki* is of great importance not only as an individual piece of literature, but also because it reflects one of the key movements within the literati in Kamakura-era Japan. With so much strife within the court itself and with war threatening from the outside, artists did not have the proper climate in which to create works of beauty. Many artists left the court for lives of solitary contemplation either in the monastery or in secluded hermitages.

Gotoba arranged one of the most spectacular poetry utaawase in 1201 at his palace in order to obtain good modern poetry for the compilation *Shinkokinshu*. The Sengohyakuban Utaawase was a match between thirty poets who each had to write a hundred-poem sequence. The match was officiated by ten judges, with Gotoba acting as final judge.

Also produced by order of Gotoba in 1201, the *Shinkokinshu* was a twenty-book collection of 1,978 ancient and modern poems collected by

Fujiwara Teika, Fujiwara Ariie, Fujiwara Ietaka, Jaturen, Minamoto Michitomo, and Fujiwara Matsune. Gotoba took a great deal of interest in the compilation of the poems and assumed a great deal of editorial responsibility in the selection of which poems to include. However, the prefaces, unusual because they were written in both Chinese and Japanese, though they read as though Gotoba had written them, were written by Fujiwara Yoshitsune and Hino Chikatsune.

Fujiwara Teika (1162-1241), Kamakura poet and critic, was one of the main compilers of the *Shinkokinshu*. Son of the poet Fujiwara Shunzei, Fujiwara Teika was a well-known poet by the time he competed in his first major poetry contest, the Futamigaura Hyakushu in 1186. In 1193 he participated in the six hundred round Roppyakuban Utaawase contest held by Fujiwara Yoshitsune, and his success in setting himself apart in that contest seemed to portend a successful career. When the house of Kujo fell in 1196, Teika saw himself falling into poverty, so he produced the *Shoji Ninen in Shodo Onhyakushu* sequence of waka poems in 1200 to impress Gotoba. This compilation sparked an association that was both productive and frustrating for Gotoba and Teika.

Teika participated in the 1201 Sengohyakuban Utaawase as both competitor and judge, which led to his work on the compilation of the *Shinkokinshu*. Teika and Gotoba had many battles over the philosophy behind the compilation, and therefore numerous disagreements over criteria for inclusion of poems. Teika assembled a collection of his own poems, *Shui Guso*, in 1216, but by 1220 he was again in trouble, this time because of strife between Gotoba and himself. Gotoba's banishment in 1221 by the Kamakura regime saved Teika's career and kept him financially comfortable into old age.

To keep himself occupied after leg ailments kept him from participating actively in life at court, Teika began working on the copying out of classical works, some by his own hand and some under his supervision. He continued to write poetry and was commissioned by Gohorikawa (1221-32) to compile the *Shinchokusenshu*, another official collection of poetry. The fact that several critical and biographical works were written about Teika after his death attests to the high level of regard his contemporaries had for his thinking and his work.

The *Heike Monogatari* is the tale of the battle between the Heike and the Genji houses, which represent the Teika and the Minamoto houses, who fought between 1131 and 1191. The tale was a familiar one to the Japanese of the Kamakura period, part of their recent national history, and so many different versions exist. The theme of this tale is the hopelessness of the doomed Heike house, the romantic tragedy of a glorious family destined to fall because of the winds of fate. The characters are larger than life, loving more deeply, dying more horribly, and behaving more heroically than reality could support. The rewriting over years of oral performances served to refine this work into one of the greatest monogatari in Japanese literature.

Daughter of Fujiwara Shunzei and sister of Fujiwara Teika, Kenshun Mon'in Chunagon was one of the early Kamakura diarists. She took a position at court serving the daughter of Goshirakawa, who ruled from 1156 to 1158. Her name and the first half of her diary derives from her service with the Kenshun Mon'in during the upheavals at court spawned by the Gempei wars. Her nikki's only real worth is that it contains a great deal of useful historical information and details of life at court.

Minamoto Sanetomo became the third shogun of the Kamakura era in 1203 upon the death of his brother, Yoriie. Sanetomo inherited the unrest caused by the rival Hojo house in the time of his father's rule, and he was assassinated for political reasons at twenty-three. Sanetomo's efforts at composing waka were extravagantly praised. Later critics have been less effusive, but admit that his poetry showed promise of ripening into something very fine. The *Kinkai Wakashu* was his personal collection of his works, which total somewhere near 753.

Priest and poet, Jien was the product of a noble family and eventually became archbishop of Tendai Buddhism. His connections allowed him to enter the literary circles surrounding Fujiwara Shunzei and Fujiwara Teika, the venerable father-and-son poetry dynasty. Between 1219 and 1220 he wrote the *Gukansho*, a six-part treatise on the principles of true government, which runs from the legendary first sovereign through the Kamakura era. This is the work he is best remembered for, but he also wrote many poems that were highly acclaimed and had the second highest number of poems in the *Shinkokinshu* of Gotoba.

The *Kaidoki*, written by an unknown author, is a travel narrative written by a man travelling from Kyoto to Kamakura. The author had taken orders in Kyoto and lived as a recluse until 1223, when he set out on his journey. Along the way he stopped to visit famous spots, but began to worry about his elderly mother and so returned home. Once he was at home, reflection on his journey led him to a deepening of his religious faith.

Kenrei Mon'in Ukyo No Daibu derived part of her name from her service with Kenrei Mon'in, consort of Takakura, who reigned from 1168 to 1180. She also served at the court of Gotoba twice. Her *Kenrei Mon'in Ukyo no Daibu Shu* was written well after her service with Kenrei Mon'in ended and is part diary, part collection of poetry, and part prose narrative. The balance exhibited in the weaving together of the three genres in this work, and the twenty-two poems she had placed in official collections, attest to her skill as a writer.

The travel narrative *Tokan Kiko* is from the middle of the Kamakura period, and authorship has never been authoritatively assigned, although several likely candidates have been eliminated. Although it is considered of little literary merit, the *Tokan Kiko* is one of the major narratives of a journey down the Tokaido road and is believed to have influenced the *Heike Monogatari* and the *Gempei Josuiki*. The author narrates his trip from Kyoto to Kamakura in 1242, and it is believed that the same author wrote of the same trip taken twenty years earlier in the *Kaidoki*.

Son of Gotoba and sovereign from 1210 to 1221, Juntoku was a waka poet from the age of fourteen. He competed in poetry matches from 1215 onward and also involved himself in his father's political activities against the bakufu, which got him exiled to Sado. He wrote the *Kimpisho*, which was a treatise on court matters, and the *Yakumo Misho*, which was a six-part treatise on poetic theories of his age, written as a sort of reference book for poets.

Gosaga, who ruled between 1242 and 1246, ordered the *Shokugosenshu*, a collection of waka, compiled. Fujiwara Tameie, compiler and poet of the conservative Nijo school, completed the work in 1251. It consists of twenty books and has a total of 1,368 poems. The *Shokukokinshu* was also a collection of waka Gosaga ordered compiled. Fujiwara Tameie also worked on this one, along with Fujiwara Motoie, Fujiwara Ieyoshi, Fujiwara Yukie, and Fujiwara Mitsutoshi, all of whom were members of the Nijo school. This compilation, completed in 1265, also had twenty books and was 1,925 poems in length. Both of these compilations are considered by modern scholars to be mediocre in comparison to the earlier royal collections of the Kamakura period.

Nichiren (1222-1282) was a religious reformer from the middle part of the Kamakura period, who founded the Nichiren sect. He criticized bakufu policy in his *Rissho Ankokuron*, which was presented to Hojo Tokiyori in 1260. He was exiled to Ito and later to Sado for his intolerance, but was eventually pardoned. His magnetic personality and ability to adapt his style to the recipient while still projecting himself into his letters have made his personal correspondence among his most popular literary leavings.

The *Gempei Josuiki* or *Seisuiki* is a late Kamakura monogatari that scholars believe to have been written by a succession of priests. Its forty-eight parts provide a foil for the version of the Gempei wars presented in the *Heike Monogatari*, containing many incidents that do not appear in the earlier work. It is less coherent in style than the *Heike Monogatari* and is considered to have been less widely disseminated, but it is generally agreed that the *Gempei Josuiki* influenced the *Taiheiki*, at least in style.

Senkaku was an early Kamakura scholar who devoted his expertise to the azamauta of the *Man'yoshu*, the earliest collection of Japanese poetry, which was compiled sometime in the late Nara or early Heian periods. His treatise, the *Man'yoshu Chusaka*, completed in 1269, was one of his best-known scholarly works and the result of a lifetime of painstaking work with various manuscripts.

The *Fugashu* was the seventeenth royal waka collection, and was ordered compiled in 1343-49 by Kogon, ruler of the northern line between 1332 and 1333, and by Hanazono, who ruled from 1308 to 1318. This collection is unusual in that it is the only royal collection actually compiled by a sovereign, and in that Hanazono actually contributed the Japanese and Chinese prefaces himself. This collection has the standard twenty books, but at 2,211 poems, it is the third-largest of the royal collections. Scholars consider this compilation the last of the important royal waka collections.

The *Shokushuishu* was another royal collection of poems and, like the *Shokugosenshu* and the *Shokukokinshu*, was a lackluster compilation made under the auspices of Nijo school poets. It was ordered in 1276 by Kameyama and completed in 1279 by Fujiwara Tameuji, the compiler. It has the standard twenty books and contains 1,461 poems.

Abutsu Ni, mid-Kamakura waka poet and diarist, was one of the wives of Fujiwara Tamaeie. Her major role was as advocate for her family, particularly for her son, Reizei Tamesuke, for whom she traveled to Kamakura in 1280 to aid him in a legal battle for the incomes from the farms Tamesuke received as part of his inheritance. Her *Isayoi (Izayoi) Nikki* contains the account of her journey, along with many poems. She also wrote the *Niwa no Oshie*, an instruction book to court ladies-in-waiting, and the *Yoru no Tsuru*, a collection of her husband's lessons on poetry.

Asukia Gayu, a member of the government in the mid-Kamakura period, is best known for his travel writings, all of which display taste and sensibility. His personal collection of poetry in *Rinjo Wakashu* and his entries in the *Shokukokinshu* and other royal compilations, are considered lackluster at best. His knowledge of classical Japanese literature also served to enhance his reputation as a learned man, but the *Mumyo no Ki*, the *Mogami no Kawaji*, the *Saga no Kayoi*, the *Miyakoji no Wakare*, and the *Haru no Miyamaji*--his travel writings--are considered the best use of his talents.

Kyogoku Tamekane (1254-1332) was a late Kamakura poet whose interest in poetry was equalled by his taste for politics. Considered to have been the leader in his time in criticism as well as in poetry, Tamekane was commissioned by Fushimi, who ruled from 1308 to 1318, to compile the *Gyokuyoshu*, the longest of the royal collections of poetry. Hanazano, who ruled with Fushimi, later had Tamekane compile another anthology, the *Fugashu*. *Tamekane Kyo Wakasho* was his major poetical treatise, which explained elements of the Kyogoku-Reizi school of poetry and the influence of Buddhism on modern poetry. Nijo Tameyo (1320-1388), member of the Nijo school of poetry and rival of Kyogoku Tamekane, compiled the *Shingosenshu* and the *Shokusenzaishu*.

A servant to Gofukakusaand later to the consort of Fushimi, Gofukakusa In Nijo was a late Kamakura diarist and poet. Her diary, *Towazugatari*, is unusual in that she sets it out to be her confessions, and it begins with her being set up as concubine to Gofukakusa. The first three sections detail her life at court, whereas in the last two she has become a nun. This work is considered one of the most readable of the court diaries.

Shokusenzaishu was the fifteenth of the royal collections of waka. In 1318 Gouda, who ruled from 1274 to 1287, ordered Fujiwara Tamyo to compile the work, and it is basically composed of poems from the Nijo school. It has the standard twenty books and contains 2,159 poems. Its follower is the *Shokugoshuishu*, which was ordered compiled by Godaigo, who ruled from

1318 to 1339. Compilation was begun by Fujiwara Tamefuji and completed in 1325 by Fujiwara Tameseda, both members of the Nijo school. It also has the standard twenty books and contains 1,347 poems.

SELECTED BIBLIOGRAPHY

Aston, W.G. *A History of Japanese Literature*. New York: D. Appleton and Company, 1989; Brower, Robert H., and Earl Miner. *Japanese Court Poetry*. Stanford: Stanford University Press, 1961; Ikeda, Daisaku. *On the Japanese Classics: Conversations and Appreciations*. Burton Watson, trans. New York: Weatherhill, 1979; Miner, Earl, Hiroko Odagiri, and Robert E. Morrell. *The Princeton Companion to Classical Japanese Literature*. Princeton: Princeton University Press, 1985.

Sara Parker

JEAN SIRE DE JOINVILLE (1224-1317). Jean Sire de Joinville (John of Joinville) is one of the most famous and successful writers of *chronicles of the *Crusades. His *Life of St. Louis* is representative of the zenith of French historical production, according to Indrikis Sterns. Joinville was born in 1224 to a French noble family. Both Jean's father and uncle had participated in earlier crusades. Jean served as King *Louis IX's seneschal and accompanied Louis on two separate crusades, in 1248 and later in 1270. Louis had been captured during his first crusade and died during the second.

    Joinville recounts the events surrounding the crusades and especially their impact on Louis and the nobles around him. He includes much information on the habits and clothing of the foreigners they meet. His text sometimes reads like memoirs and other times like a saint's life or the eulogy for a good friend. Joinville's interest in telling the deeds of Louis for the moral edification of his audience is probably his primary goal, but his work was warmly received both for the portrait of a saint it provided and for its descriptions of faraway mysterious lands, their peoples, and their customs.

SELECTED BIBLIOGRAPHY

Perret, Michele. "Histoire, nomination, reference." *LINX* 32(1995), 173-88; Shaw, M.R.B. *Chronicles of the Crusades: Joinville and Villehardouin*. Baltimore: Penguin, 1963; Slattery, Maureen. *Myth, Man, and Sovereign Saint: King Louis IX in Jean de Joinville's Sources*. New York: Lang, 1985; Smalley, Beryl. *Historians in the Middle Ages*. New York: Scribner's, 1974; Sterns, Indrikis. *The Greater Medieval Historians: An Interpretation and a Bibliography*. Lanham, MD: University Press of America, 1980.

Robert T. Lambdin

JEROME, ST. (c. 340-420). Born in Strido, Jerome is remembered as one of the four "Doctors of the Church." After his baptism Jerome wandered about; after a period of debauchery he turned to life as a recluse. Some years later he returned to Rome, where he became the religious advisor to a group of Roman women. He tired of this and, in 386, ventured to Bethlehem, where he resided until his death.

Jerome is generally represented as an aged man in the garb of a cardinal who is either writing or studying; beside him is a lion. This image was derived from the legend wherein Jerome was lecturing to his class when a lion entered the schoolroom. The animal lifted its paw, showing a thorn embedded in it. While the other students and teachers fled, Jerome pulled the thorn and dressed the wound. Thus the lion became his constant companion.

In literature, Jerome is mainly recalled for his contribution to the *Chronicles* of Eusebius (*See Chronicles and Annals*). More important, though, is his translation of the Bible, the *Vulgate, which was the standard version during the medieval period. Jerome's *Epistle against Jovinian* later became a major influence on the works of Walter *Map.

SELECTED BIBLIOGRAPHY

Olin, John C. "Erasmus and St. Jerome: An Appraisal of the Bond." In *Erasmus of Rotterdam: The Man and the Scholar*. J. Sperna Weiland and W. T. M. Frijoff, eds. Leiden: Brill, 1988. 182-86; Oppel, John. "St. Jerome and the History of Sex." *Viator* 24 (1993), 1-22; Vadakkekara, Cletus Matthew. "Ascetical Fasting According to St. Jerome." *American Benedictine Review* 39:1 (Mar 1988), 1-14.

Robert T. Lambdin

JOHN (1167?-1216) king of England (1199-1216). With the support of Norman barons against the claims of his own nephew Arthur, John was crowned, but was almost immediately confronted by rebellion and, far worse, the invasion of some of his French possessions by *Philip II. In the end, John was saved on the Continent by his vassals in southern France, who clearly preferred an absent Angevin to an encroaching Capetian. Resisting south of the Loire, John, whose loss of the lands north of the Loire reduced the prestige and power of the English throne, severed the Norman baronage in England from their English connections and turned their interests back to the island, with decisive constitutional and social consequences.

John also became entangled in an eight-year struggle with the papacy over control of Canterbury. When the throne was unable to control an election to that seat, Pope *Innocent III intervened and appointed Stephen *Langton. John refused to recognize Langton as archbishop and deposed him, confiscated the lands of the see, and expelled the monks from Canterbury. In return, Innocent laid an interdict upon England. John, without raising great public outcry, confiscated the property of all English clergy who followed Innocent's order. He weathered the storm, but, aware of rising opposition and treason in the realm, settled the issues by promising indemnity to the clergy and paying homage to the pope for all.

The first political-constitutional struggle in English history led to the Magna Carta and resulted from an effort of the feudal barons, supported by Archbishop Langton and public opinion, to enforce their rights under their feudal contract with the king. This move did not attempt to destroy the monarchy or the royal administration. Preliminary demands of the barons were made in 1213, during the same period in which John also had to deal with concessions to the papacy and nascent civil war. Further, the city of London opposed John. All of these factors led to John's acceptance of the Great Charter at Runnymede.

The Magna Carta was essentially a feudal document detailing reforms extracted by feudal barons from their lord, but with national implications in its reforms. Concessions to the barons included reform in the extraction of scutage, aid, and reliefs; in the administration of wardships and in the demands for feudal service, among other issues. Concessions to the agricultural and commercial classes included those to mesne tenants who were granted a number of rights, including uniform weights and measures; affirmation of the ancient liberties of London and other towns.

The most significant provision of the Magna Carta, chapter 39, stated that "no freeman shall be arrested and imprisoned or disposed or outlawed or banished or in any way molested; nor will we set forth against him, unless by the lawful judgment of his peers and the law of the land." Even these clauses were feudal and specific in background, but centuries of experience transformed them into a generalized formula of constitutional procedure, making them the basis of the modern English constitution.

SELECTED BIBLIOGRAPHY

Boyd, Brian. "King John and the 'Troublesome Raigne': Sources, Structure, Sequence." *Philological Quarterly* 74:1 (Winter 1995), 37-56; Cousin, Geraldine. *King John.* Manchester: Manchester University Press, 1994; Evans, Max. "King John: A memoir from the Heart." *South Dakota Review* 33:3-4 (Fall-Winter 1994), 388-401.

R. Churchill Curtis

JOHN OF GAUNT, duke of Lancaster (1340-1399). The fourth son of *Edward III, John of Gaunt was the father of Henry Bolingbroke, who would become Henry IV. As the founder of the house of Lancaster, John became one of the most powerful political figures in England. Initially, during *Richard II's reign, John effectively served as the acting regent of Britain. Upon Richard's return from the *Crusades, John became his enemy. Renowned as a tyrant, for years John was often at odds with his detractors, including his brother, the Black Prince.

As a patron of the arts, John associated closely with both John *Wycliffe, who worked for him, and Geoffrey *Chaucer, to whom Gaunt was a patron. It is commonly asserted that Chaucer's *Book of the Duchess* was composed as an *elegy for Blanche, John's wife, who died in 1369. This is indicative of the seemingly close relationship that the two had. Gaunt's patronage, coupled with Chaucer's role as a courtier, accounts for much of the chivalric and aristocratic overtones to the poet's works.

SELECTED BIBLIOGRAPHY

Hardman, Phillipa. "*The Book of the Duchess* as a Memorial Monument." *Chaucer Review* 28:3 (1994), 205-15; Kelly, H. Ansgar. "Shades of Incest and Cuckoldry: Pandarus and John of Gaunt." *Studies in the Age of Chaucer* 13 (1991), 121-40.

Robert T. Lambdin

JOHN OF SALISBURY (c. 1120-1180). A scholar, philosopher, theologian, and historian, John of Salisbury was born in relatively modest circumstances. He studied under Peter *Abelard at Paris and later at Chartres, where he was also a teacher. He became an administrator under Theobald, the archbishop of Canterbury, a job that continued under Thomas *Becket, with whom John often ventured abroad. When Becket's conflict with *Henry II occurred, John went with Becket to Rheims and there Salisbury wrote the *Historia Pontificalis*. John witnessed Becket's martyrdom at Canterbury in 1170, and later composed biographies of Becket as well as St. *Anselm; in these works he reasoned for their canonization.

Toward the end of his career John returned to Chartres as bishop in 1176, where he continued to earn a reputation as one of the most learned and cultured men of his age. Because of this hunger for knowledge, John inspired many in the twelfth century Renaissance of the continent. Included in his canon of works is the *Policraticus* or "Statesman's Guide," an eight-volume piece that studies political theory. The *Policraticus* is known as an encyclopedia of miscellanies, a method that illustrates the eclectic nature of the Middle Ages. Additionally, he composed the *Metalogicon*, a four book treatise that defended the *trivium, especially *Aristotle's view of it; and his *Letters*, of which some three hundred remain and serve as historical sources.

SELECTED BIBLIOGRAPHY

Hicks, Eric. "A Mirror for Misogynists: John of Salisbury's *Polycraticus* (8.11.) in the Translation of Denis Foulechat." In *Reinterpreting Christine de Pizan*. Earl Jeffrey Richards, ed. Athens: University of Georgia Press, 1992. 77-107; Nederman, Cary J., and Catherine Campbell. "Priests, Kings, and Tyrants: Spiritual and Political Power in John of Salisbury's *Polycraticus*." *Speculum* 66:3 (July 1991), 572-90; Pepin, Reginald, trans. "John of Salisbury's *Entheticus.*" *Allegorica* 9 (Winter-Summer 1987-88), 7-133; Pepin, Reginald, trans. "'On the Conspiracy of the Members,' Attributed to John of Salisbury." *Allegorica* 12 (1991), 29-41.

Robert T. Lambdin

JONGLEUR. Jongleur is the French term for a professional musical entertainer from the Middle Ages. Jongleurs were similar to the *Anglo-Saxon *gleemen and also the later *minstrels. While jongleurs primarily sang or recited *lyrics, *ballads, and stories, they also composed original works. Also included in their act were nonmusical types of entertainment such as juggling and tumbling. Jongleurs are important because they, as well as the minstrels, traveled from nation to nation, taking with them an olio of literary forms of entertainment.

SELECTED BIBLIOGRAPHY

Harvey, Ruth E. "Joglars and the Professional Status of the Early Troubadours." *Medium Evum* 62:2 (1993), 221-41; Quinn, William A. "Chaucer's 'Janglerye.'" *Viator* 18 (1987), 309-20; Sayers, William. "The Jongleur Taillefer at Hastings: Antecedents and Literary Fate." *Viator* 14 (1983), 79-88.

Rebecca Chalmers

JORDANES (fl. mid-6th century). Jordanes's *De Origine Actibusque Getarum (On the Descent and Exploits of the Getae)* is a history of the Goths written in the mid-sixth century and is most likely an adaptation of Cassiodorus's now-lost, more extensive Gothic history. Jordanes was himself a Goth and probably a Catholic monk or cleric. His three-part work actually includes two earlier sections on Roman and Christian history, but he is most remembered for his national history of the Goths, a people who migrated into the Roman territories from the northern German and Scandinavian regions. His history attempts to establish a classical and biblical origin for the Goths and traces their history in a less-than-rigorous chronology (*see Chronicles and Annals*) up until 551 A. D. Many of the songs and stories that Jordanes included in his history are also found in German and Scandinavian ancient folklore, although numerous critics, including Walter Goffart, are willing to admit that much of Jordanes's material could have been taken directly from the twelve-volume history of the Goths by Cassiodorus.

SELECTED BIBLIOGRAPHY

Barnish, S.J.B. "The Genesis and Completion of Cassiodorus' Gothic History." *Latomus* 43:2 (April-June 1984), 336-61; Brandt, William J. *The Shape of Medieval History.* New Haven: Yale University Press, 1966; Goffart, Walter. *The Narrators of Barbarian History A. D. 550-800.* Princeton: Princeton University Press, 1988; Smalley, Beryl. *Historians in the Middle Ages.* New York: Scribner's, 1974; Sterns, Indrikis. *The*

Greater Medieval Historians: An Interpretation and a Bibliography Lanham, MD: University Press of America, 1980.

Richard McDonald

JUDAS. The earliest *ballad recorded in manuscript form, *Judas* dates from the thirteenth century. One of only four ballads on religious themes surviving the Middle Ages, it is, in fact, not a true folk ballad at all, but a clerical literary imitation, the result of an attempt on the part of the clergy to "rehabilitate" the established folk-song tradition by writing alternate lyrics to already popular tunes.

As the dearth of surviving specimens indicates, the endeavor was not a success. Like the fifteenth-century *Saint Stephen and Herod*, another clerical revision, *Judas* draws its tale from biblical and apocryphal tradition, in contrast to the one surviving religious folk ballad, *The Bitter Withy*. (For a full discussion of medieval religious ballads, see the entry for **Ballad**.)

Judas relates how Jesus entrusts the title character with thirty pieces of silver to buy supper for the apostles. On his way to town Judas meets with his sister, who curses him for believing in "that false prophet." He then falls asleep and is robbed of the money. Pilate approaches him, asking if he will sell his lord for gold; Judas responds that he will do so only for the thirty pieces of silver he has lost.

The ballad closes with fragments of conversations at the Last Supper, in which Judas denies that he has betrayed Jesus, Peter asserts that he will protect his lord against Pilate's "knights," and Jesus assures Peter that the latter will betray him three times before the cock crows. Of course, despite Peter's denial, this action will come to fruition.

Surprisingly for a literary ballad of the period, *Judas* exhibits the folk tradition's typical practice of passing judgment through ridicule, for the title character is simply too stupid to see that he will come off better if he accepts gold instead of silver for his betrayal. Moreover, it does not occur to him that his motive for treachery--to regain the thirty pieces of silver so that Jesus will not be angry with him--is at odds with the inevitable result.

His loss of the money while napping and his sister's belittling of him are also comic. Nonetheless, the mainstream Christian message of the ballad comes through loud and clear. For the difference between this and the commoners' perception of spiritual consolation, *Judas* should be compared with *The Bitter Withy* and the popular fifteenth-century folk lyric, *A Bitter Lullaby*.

SELECTED BIBLIOGRAPHY

Cantor, Norman. *The Medieval Reader*. New York: Harper Collins, 1994; Edson, Richmond. *Ballad Scholarship: An Annotated Bibliography*. New York: Garland, 1989; Fowler, David C. *A Literary History of the Popular Ballad*. Durham: Duke University

Press, 1968; Morgan, Gwendolyn. *Medieval Balladry and the Courtly Tradition.* New York: Peter Lang, 1993; Morgan, Gwendolyn. *Medieval Ballads: Chivalry, Romance, and Everyday Life.* New York: Peter Lang, 1996; Pearsall, Derek. *Old and Middle English Poetry.* London: Routledge and Kegan Paul, 1977.

Gwendolyn Morgan

JUDITH. *Judith* is an Old English poem found in the **Beowulf* manuscript. Some of its first portion is fragmented, and it dates from anywhere between the eighth and tenth centuries. The poem itself is a paraphrase of the apocryphal story of Judith, was composed in honor of Æthelflaed, the Lady of the Mercians, and describes the Assyrian banquet during the siege of Bethulia. There, Judith, a Jewish maiden, is brought before a belligerently drunk Holofernes. After an evening of debauchery Holofernes staggers back to his tent. He makes garrulous advances toward the woman, who takes offense, beheads him, and escapes. She carries the head to her people and provides them with the inspiration to defeat the Assyrians, who are then forced to flee.

This dramatic epic fragment provides a very graphic portrayal of the events. It contains a sense of excitement, for there are few passages that seem strained or incongruous. Most criticism usually concerns the fragmented construction of the work, which allows only speculation about the rest of the manuscript.

SELECTED BIBLIOGRAPHY

Clayton, Mary. "Ælfric's *Judith*: Manipulative or Manipulated?" *Anglo-Saxon England* 23 (1994), 215-27; Lucas, Peter J. "*Judith* and the Woman Symbol." *Yearbook of English Studies* 22 (1992), 17-27; Magennis, Hugh. "Contrasting Narrative Emphases in the Old English Poem *Judith* and Ælfric's Paraphrase of the *Book of Judith.*" *Neuphilologische Mitteilungen* 96:1 (1995), 61-66.

Robert T. Lambdin

JULIAN OF NORWICH (c. 1342-1413?). Julian of Norwich was an English mystic of the fourteenth century and author of the vision contained in the book known as the *Sixteen Revelations of Divine Love*, which was not written before 1393. She was probably a Benedictine nun, living as a recluse in a moor, of which traces still remain in the east part of the churchyard of St. Julian in Norwich, which belonged to Carrow Priory. According to Julian's book, the revelation was shown to her on May 8 or May 14, 1373, when she was thirty years old. Attempts have been made to identify her with Lady Julian Lappet, the anchoress of Carrow, references concerning legacies to whom occur in documents from 1426 to 1478, but this is manifestly impossible. Only three manuscripts of the full text are known to exist. The earliest dates from the sixteenth century and can be found in the Bibliothèque Nationale in Paris. The other two are both in the British Museum and are not independent of each other; they belong to the seventeenth century.

These revelations are an example of the later medieval mysticism in England. Julian describes herself as a simple, unlettered woman when she received the visions, but she evidently acquired some knowledge of theological phraseology in the years between the vision and the composition of the book. Her work shows the influence of Walter Hilton as well as neoplatonic analogies.

The record found in *Sixteen Revelations of Divine Love* reflects twenty years of meditation upon that one experience, and more than fifteen years later she received the explanation, the key to her religious experience and to all religious experiences. The key for Julian was love. With this illumination the whole mystery of Redemption and the purpose of human life became clear to her, and even the possibility of sin and the existence of evil did not trouble her, but was made "a bliss by love."

SELECTED BIBLIOGRAPHY

Baker, Denise Nowakowski. *Julian of Norwich's "Showings": From Vision to Book.* Princeton: Princeton University Press, 1994; Johnson, Lynn Staley. "The Trope of the Scribe and the Question of Literary Authority in the Works of Julian of Norwich and Margery Kempe." *Speculum* 66:4 (October 1991), 820-38; Sprung, Andrew. "'We Nevyr Shall Come out of Hymn': Enclosure and Immanence in Julian of Norwich's *Book of Showings.*" *Mystics Quarterly* 19:2 (June 1993), 47-59.

Rebecca Chalmers

JUNIUS MANUSCRIPT, THE. Along with the Cotton Manuscripts, The Exeter Manuscript, and the *Vercelli Book, the Junius Manuscript is one of the major manuscripts that contains Old English poetry. The document is named after Francis Junius, who first printed the collection in 1655. The works were originally erroneously attributed to *Cædmon; Junius originally named the manuscript "Cædmon the monk's political paraphrase of Genesis, etc." Included in the collection are such seminal works of Old English poetry as *Genesis*, *Exodus*, and *Christ and Satan*.

SELECTED BIBLIOGRAPHY

Hauer, Stanley R. "The Patriarchal Digression of the Old English 'Exodus,' Lines 362-446." *Studies in Philology* 78:5 (Early Winter 1981), 77-90; Raw, Barbara C. "The Construction of Oxford, Bodleian, Junius 11." *Anglo-Saxon England* 13 (1984), 187-207.

Robert T. Lambdin

K

KATHERINE GROUP, THE. The Katherine Group contains five Middle English poems, all of which are devotional and date from 1190 to 1225. These poems are *Seinte Marherete, Seinte Iuliene, Seinte Katerine, *Sawles Warde*, and *Hali Meiyhad*. The works are composed in a dialect similar to that found in the *Ancrenne Wisse*, and they compare favorably with *Elfric's works as alliterative, rhythmic compositions.

In this grouping the three *hagiographies are all about heroic virgins. These three, St. Katherine of Alexandria, St. Juliana of Nicomedia, and St. Margaret of Antioch, are frequent subjects in medieval hagiography. For example, Katherine was stripped, beaten, imprisoned, and then torn apart by spike-covered wheels that turned simultaneously in different directions. Nothing seemed to harm her body or weaken her resolution to resist the heathens who tortured her. By the time that she was finally beheaded, she had converted many heathens through her unfailing faith. The grouping here may be intentional, for each may have been persecuted by Diocletian in the early fourth century. An example of the popularity of these saints can be seen in the hagiographic poem *Juliana* by *Cynewulf.

SELECTED BIBLIOGRAPHY

Bately, Janet. "On Some Aspects of the Vocabulary of the West Midlands in the Early Middle Ages: The Language of the 'Katherine Group.'" In *Medieval Studies Presented to George Kane*. Edward Donald Kennedy, Ronald Waldron, and Joseph Wittig, eds. Woodbridge: Brewer, 1988. 55–77; Laing, Margaret. and Angus McIntosh. "The Language of the *Ancrenne Riwle*, the 'Katherine Group' Texts, and 'The Wohunge of Ure Lauerd' in BL. Cotton Titus D XVII." *Neuphilologische Mitteilungen* 96:3 (1995), 235-63; Margherita, Gayle. "Desiring Narrative: Ideology and Semiotics of the Gaze in the Middle English 'Juliana.'" *Exemplaria* 2:2 (Fall 1990), 355-74; Millett, Bella. "The Saints' Lives of the 'Katherine Group' and the Alliterative Tradition." *Journal of English and Germanic Philology* 87 (January 1988), 16-34.

Robert T. Lambdin

KELLS, BOOK OF. The Book of Kells is an eighth-century illustrated vellum manuscript written in Irish majuscule and belonging to a group of works called "Hiberno-Saxon." The Book of Kells contains the Gospels of Matthew, Mark, Luke, and John. It is believed that the book originated after Iona was sacked and was completed at the monastery of Kells. It is now held at Trinity College's library in Dublin.

The book is large and was probably meant as an altar book, and it is composed in Irish majuscule. It is held to be one of the greatest examples of Christian Celtic art. Some of the common traits found in the book are the inclusion of decorated initials of letters that are fitted into the shapes of animals such as a lion, calf, eagle, or snake. Besides the Gospels, the book also contains canon tables, summaries of the Gospels (the *breves causae*), argumenta, and lists of Hebrew names and interpretations. The Gospel of Matthew includes a genealogy.

Included in this ornate text are strange designs of animals, plants, mazes and swirls; 31 of the pages are full-length illustrations, including one for the particular symbol of each of the Gospels. Also included are pictures of Jesus, Mary, and other evangelists. Oddly, the book also incorporates into its design Celtic symbols that predate Christianity. The book was not collated until 1621, when James Ussher put the piece together.

SELECTED BIBLIOGRAPHY

Harbison, Peter. "Three Miniatures in the Book of Kells." *Proceedings of the Royal Irish Academy* 85 C:7 (1985), 181-94; Henderson, Isabel. "Pictish Art and the Book of Kells." In *Ireland in Early Mediaeval Europe: Studies in Memory of Kathleen Hughes.*, Dorothy Whitlock, *et al.*, eds.1982. 79-105; O'Mahoney, Felicity, ed. *The Book of Kells: Proceedings of a Conference at Trinity College Dublin 6-9 September 1992*. Dublin: Scholar Press, 1994.

Rebecca Chalmers

KEMPE, MARGERY (c. 1373-1439). Margery Kempe was a noted mystic. She married John Kempe of Lynn when she was twenty. After the birth of her first child, Kempe began to have visions of Christ on the Cross. The relationship between Kempe and her husband ended when Margery abandoned John after giving birth to some fourteen children. She felt that she must dedicate her life to her God because her visions had increased and she was given to incidents of "cryings" in which she would have uncontrollable outbursts of sobbing fits.

After leaving John, Margery traversed the continents, venturing to such exotic locales as Jerusalem and Rome. She later detailed accounts of her travels in *The Book of Margery Kempe*. This text, which was probably transcribed by another as Margery dictated, vividly recounts other parts of her life, including an indictment for heresy conducted by the archbishop of York.

The Book of Margery Kempe is deeply rooted in mysticism, but it stands on its own merit for several other reasons. First, it presents a female perspective, a rare point of view in medieval literature. Additionally, her work is one of the first fully autobiographical compositions. Her work therefore has universal appeal.

SELECTED BIBLIOGRAPHY

Hoppenwasser, Nanda. "The Human Burden of the Prophet: St. Birgitta's Revelations and *The Book of Margery Kempe.*" *Medieval Perspectives* 8 (1993), 153-62; Shklar, Ruth. "Cobham's Daughter: *The Book of Margery Kempe* and the Power of Heterodox Thinking." *Modern Language Quarterly* 56:3 (1995), 277-304; Wright, Michael J. "What They Said to Margery Kempe: Narrative Reality in Her Book." *Neophilologus* 79:3 (July 1995), 497-508.

Laura Cooner Lambdin

KENNING. Kenning is a figure of speech using a descriptive or figurative circumlocution, a technique found in *Anglo-Saxon and Norse poetry. *Beowulf* contains many kennings; for example, "sea" becomes "whale road" or "gannet's bath." Also, a spear is "ash-wood," while a battle is a "storm of swords."

SELECTED BIBLIOGRAPHY

Marold, Edith. "Nygerving and Nykrat." *North Western European Language Evolution* 21-22 (April 1993), 283-302; McManus, Damian. "Irish Letter-Names and Their Kennings." *Eriu* 39 (1988), 127-68; Weber, Gerd Wolfgang. "Of Trees and Men: Some Stray Thoughts on Kennings as Metaphors--and on Ludvig Holberg's Arboresque Anthropology." *North-Western European Language Evolution* 21-22 (Apr 1993), 419-46.

R. Churchill Curtis

KING HORN (dated c.1225). *King Horn* is the earliest extant English verse *romance. It is derived from an earlier work by an *Anglo-Norman poet known as Thomas. It tells the story of Horn, the son of the king of Suddene (Isle of Mann). He is set adrift by Saracen pirates, who murder his parents. This is odd because these "Saracens" are from Scandinavia. Perhaps this is evidence that it was impossible to keep overtones of the *Crusades out of the romances. Eventually Horn and twelve friends are cast away in a rudderless boat; chance takes them to Westernesse, where he raised by the king. He falls in love with Rymenhild, the king's daughter, but duty calls Horn away to fight knightly adventures. While he is away, Fikenhild, a colleague of Horn, betrays the lovers, causing Horn's banishment. Fikenhild later marries Rymenhild.

The banishment turns out to be good for the hero, for it gives him an excuse for military action. In Ireland Horn performs many exceptional deeds and has great adventures. Disguised as an adventurer, he saves Ireland from the Saracens but declines the reward offered to him by the king: his daughter's hand in marriage. A disguised, cloaked Horn journeys to Westernesse and finds Rymenhild. He proves to her his identity by showing her a magic ring she had given him. Horn kills Fikenhild and then journeys to recapture Suddene from the Saracens. After his successful conquest Horn returns to find Rymenhild in a second marriage. He vanquishes the husband, and the couple then return to Suddene as king and queen. *King Horn* is one of the best examples of a medieval romance because it so clearly contains the traditional elements of the genre.

SELECTED BIBLIOGRAPHY

Hearn, Matthew. "Twins of Infidelity: The Double Antagonists of 'King Horn.'" *Medieval Perspectives* 8 (1993), 78-86; Jamison, Carol Parrish. "A Description of the Medieval Romance Based upon 'King Horn.'" *Quondam et Futurus* 1:2 (Summer 1991), 44-58; McGillvray, Murray. *Memorization in the Transmission of Middle English Romances*. New York: Garland, 1990; Speed, Diane. "The Saracens of 'King Horn.'" *Speculum* 65:3 (July 1990), 564-95.

Robert T. Lambdin

KINGIS QUAIR. The *Kingis Quair*, or King's Book, composed around 1423, was first published in 1783 by William Tyler after it was discovered in a manuscript collection of poems by Geoffrey *Chaucer and other poets, now housed in the Bodleian Library at Oxford. Obviously composed by two separate scribes, the manuscript's colophon in Latin ascribes the poem to James the First, the illustrious King of Scots. Whether James I is the actual author has been debated feverishly and still cannot be certainly concluded. Skeptics point out that the *Kingis Quair* misrepresents historical facts, and by relating it to other works, they attempt to place it at a time incompatible with James. It has also been argued that the poem belongs to a body of anonymous poems of the fifteenth century. It is likely, though not certain, that the author and subject of the work are the same personage.

James I, the heir to the throne of Scotland, was confined for nineteen years at the English court. Young James had been captured while en route to France, where his father Robert III had hoped that his heir would remain in safety. Robert III died in 1406, shortly after learning that his son was being held for ransom. Henry IV was considering releasing James in 1412, but when he died, his son Henry V recommitted James as claimant to the throne but under English capture. While in the court, James fell in love with Joan, daughter of John Beaufort, earl of Somerset.

The speaker of the *Kingis Quair* has fallen in love with a beautiful maiden. Iin a moving dream sequence, the poet ascends and appears first to Venus, goddess of love, and then to Minerva, goddess of wisdom, asking for guidance to try to freely win his love. The poem glorifies matrimonial love that struggles against Fortune with Good Hope.

The *Kingis Quair* reflects the philosophical concepts of *Boethius (c. 480-524), whose work was widely translated at the time; it also contains a structural similarity to dream sequence writing of the fifth-century author Ambrosius Theodosius Macrobius and some literary influence from John Lydgate's *Temple of Glass* and Geoffrey *Chaucer's "The *Knight's Tale", and *Troylus and Criseyde*. The poem's rhyme royal stanza is handled skillfully in a language mixing Scots and Chaucerian English that was probably never spoken. Of the so-called Scottish Chaucerians (*see* **Scottish Literature**), the work attributed to James I is probably the most imitative, although with probably more originality than Chaucer's English protégés Lydgate and Thomas *Hoccleve. James I is also credited with two other poems, "Christis Kirk" and "Peblis to the Play." If John Majors's assertions in his Latin *History of Great Britain* are correct, then James I not only helped make Scotland a nation, but contributed to its literature as well.

SELECTED BIBLIOGRAPHY

Carretta, Vincent. "The *Kingis Quair* and *The Consolation of Philosophy*." *Studies in Scottish Literature* 16 (1981), 14-28; James, Claire F. "The *Kingis Quair*: The Plight of the Courtly Lover." In *New Readings of Late Medieval Love Poems*. David Chamberlain, ed. Lanham, MD: University Press of America, 1993. 95-118; Quinn, William. "Memory and the Matrix of Unity in the *Kingis Quair*." *Chaucer Review* 15:4 (Spring 1981), 332-55; Spiller, Michael R. G. "The *Donna Angelicata* in The *Kingis Quair*." *Scottish Studies* 4 (1984), 217-27.

J. Scott Plaster

KNIGHTLY TALE OF GOLOGRAS AND GAWAIN, THE. An impressive *romance of arms and battle that survives from late medieval Britain, *The Knightly Tale of Gologras and Gawain* offers a celebration of violence encompassed by rules. Only one copy of the original edition remains; it can be found in the National Library of Scotland. *Gologras and Gawain* consists of two distinct episodes, the second almost four times the first in length. The two parts work together to produce a unified meaning, though not through a contrastive structure. The larger structure both repeats and supports the smaller unit. The two episodes are drawn from a French romance, the *First Continuation* of *Chrétien de Troyes's *Perceval*. *Gologras and Gawain* seems to have been written not long before the Scots printers Andrew Chapman and David Myllar, published the poem at Edinburgh in 1508. It is written in a

Middle Scots dialect that has much in common with the vocabulary of *Awntyrs off Arthur*, *Sir Gawain and the Green Knight* and other northern Middle English alliterative poems.

It consists of thirteen-line stanzas, identical to the *Awntyrs*. The first nine lines of each stanza are alliterative long lines; the last four lines are short, two-stress lines forming a separate quatrain (a "wheel"), which is linked by final rhyme to the ninth line. The rhyme scheme is *abababababcdddc*.

In *Gologras and Gawain*, Arthur (*see* **Arthurian Legend**) and his knights undertake an expedition to Italy on a pilgrimage, and the destination is the Holy Land. On the way to Jerusalem Arthur notes an opulent castle. Sir Spynagros, who serves as commentator through the second episode, explains that the castle belongs to Gologras, who owes allegiance to no lord. This angers Arthur, and he vows to gain lordship over Gologras. After completing their pilgrimage to the Holy Land, Arthur and his knights besiege Gologras, and the combats end in a one-to-one encounter between Sir Gawain and Sir Gologras. In the end Gawain triumphs. Gologras demands to die honorably at Gawain's hand, but Gawain insists that Gologras keep his life. Gologras agrees to keep his own life on one condition: Gawain must give the appearance of defeat. Gawain agrees, but the poem ends with Gologras pledging his loyalty to King Arthur.

SELECTED BIBLIOGRAPHY

Blanch, Robert J. and Julian Wasserman. *From* "Pearl" *to* "Gawain": "*Forme*" *to* "*Fynyshment*." Gainesville: University of Florida Press, 1995; Mann, Jill. "Gawain and the Romantic Hero." In *Heroes and Heroines in Medieval English Literature*. Leo Carruthers, ed. Cambridge: Brewer, 1994, 105-17; Moffat, Douglas. "Fearful Villainy." *Essays in Medieval Studies* 11 (1994), 119-36.

Rebecca Chalmers

"KNIGHT'S TALE, THE." "The Knight's Tale" is a story told by the Knight pilgrim of *Chaucer's *Canterbury Tales* (c. 1387-1400). The Knight tells the first story, and he is the first Pilgrim described in the *"General Prologue." It is only fitting that the Knight begins the storytelling as he is the most gentile and highborn of the group.

The tale is a *romance about the battles of Theseus of ancient Athens, a typical story to be told by a fighting man (the Knight has just returned from work himself). It also involves a love triangle that is based upon *Boccaccio's *Teseida*: two knights, Palamon and Arcite, see Emily walking in a garden from the window of a tower where they are imprisoned, and they both fall in love with her.

Theseus challenges Palamon and Arcite to return in a year with a hundred knights to fight for Emily's hand. Emily prays to Diana, Palamon prays to Venus, and Arcite prays to Mars. Arcite wins the joust but is thrown from his horse as he rides toward the prize and suffers mortal injuries. This allows Palamon to happily marry Emily.

SELECTED BIBLIOGRAPHY

Amtower, Laurel. "Mimetic Desire and the Misappropriation of the Ideal in 'The Knight's Tale.'" *Exemplaria* 8:1 (Spring 1996), 125-44; Bush, Douglas. *English Poetry.* New York: Oxford University Press, 1963; Clogan, Paul M. "'The Knight's Tale' and the Ideology of the Roman Antique." *Medievalia* 18 (1992), 129-55; Crane, Susan. "Medieval Romance and the Feminine Difference in 'The Knight's Tale.'" *Studies in the Age of Chaucer* 12 (1990), 47-63; Garbáty, Thomas J. *Medieval English Literature.* Toronto: Heath, 1984; Lambdin, Laura C., and Robert T. Lambdin, eds. *Chaucer's Pilgrims: An Historical Guide to the Pilgrims in the "Canterbury Tales."* Westport, CT: Greenwood Press. 1996; Salter, Elizabeth. *Fourteenth Century English Poetry.* Oxford: Clarendon Press, 1983.

Laura Cooner Lambdin

KOREAN LITERATURE. The Koryo period, which lasted from 918 to 1392, is the dynasty that encompasses the medieval period in Korea's history. At the beginning of this period Korean society was just beginning to restructure itself to become a modern society. Koreans adopted many of the social, political, and ideological aspects of the T'ang dynasty in China, though they wished at the same time to retain their individuality as a society. Although the historical records kept by the Koreans in the Koryo dynasty are no longer extant, later sources and contemporary foreign sources reveal a great deal about the Koryo society.

One of the most striking changes in this dynasty was the rise of bureaucratization. Civil service examinations were instituted in 958 under the reign of King Kwangjong, who ruled from 949 to 975, and were necessary to join the higher levels of officialdom. As a result, one's ancestors were no longer the only avenue for attaining prestige within the upper levels of society. Even the military was partially restructured based on the results of these civil service exams. The highest-ranking officers in the military were no longer those who demonstrated the highest level of military prowess, but under King Songjong, who ruled from 981 to 997, civilians who performed exceptionally on the exams were awarded command positions.

The classes in Korean society at this period were very stringently divided, and being born into the right family had previously been the only way for one to be part of the upper echelons. However, with the rise of what can be termed the bureaucratic aristocracy, the higher levels of society were now open to those with the intellectual ability to pass the exam, as long as it was combined with a suitably illustrious set of ancestors. A requirement for the civil service examination was proof that one came of a decent family. As early as 1055 one would not be permitted to take the examination unless proof were provided that one's genealogy was acceptable. Thus, the examinations did not provide a mechanism for the lower classes to invade the upper classes by sheer force of intellectual merit. What they did allow was for members of the upper class who did not occupy high positions within the upper class to improve their positions within their strata. In fact, society was so strictly divided that as late as 1308 King Ch'ungson issued a list of families that were acceptable for members of the royal house to marry.

One's ancestry was defined both matrilineally and patrilineally, so one could claim prestige based not only on one's own blood relatives, but also on the basis of the prestige of the family into which one married. The male, once he married, had the option of choosing to reside in a sort of family compound with either his own family or his wife's family. Such a decision was generally made on the basis of which situation would be most advantageous economically. Upon the death of a parent, inheritances were divided up equally between the siblings, regardless of gender. In addition, in proving an ancestral basis for qualification for an official position, one could use either the matrilineal or patrilineal line as well.

Koryo society was also affected by the introduction of Confucianism. The mark of a true gentleman was that he recited Chinese poetry and adhered to Confucian principles of morality. However, the largest influence on everyday life in Korea during this period was still Buddhism.

The faith in the protection of Buddha is epitomized by the Koryo Tripitaka, a series of woodblocks on which the entire Buddhist canon is carved. Both personal and state-supported rituals were still Buddhist, and Buddhist monks were still considered invaluable for the performance of such rituals. In fact, the temples and monasteries were supported not only by the general populace, but also by the royal house and the aristocrats.

Although the Mongols domination of Korea lasted about one hundred years, their occupation did not leave much of a mark on Korean society. Even though the Mongols were admired for their military prowess, the Mongolian social and political customs never influenced the Koryo society noticeably. The Mongols were never very interested in making an imprint on the countries they overran. Their main concern was in obtaining control of the economic resources inherent in whatever land they conquered, and they were more disposed to learn from the peoples they conquered.

Korean medieval literature consists mainly of folk literature, literature written in Chinese, and literature in the vernacular. Within these three divisions, the normal genres of poetry, prose, drama, epic, and the rest appear, but because Korean scholars used Chinese as their language for formal writings like European scholars used Latin for formal compositions, the distinction must be made between the two.

Until the fifteenth century Chinese remained the primary written language in Tibet. The Silla Buddhists constructed a system to transcribe Korean into Chinese logographs. The distinction between formal writings and folk literature is also important because the court society was very different from the society of the general population, just as the pastoral poetry of European shepherds was very distinct from the mannered works of the court composers. Korean literature from early periods is relatively accessible to modern scholars due to the efforts of learned monks like Iryon who acted to preserve the native culture.

Most of the literature that has come down to us from the Koryo period is in the form of poetry. Although some few prose pieces have been preserved, the bulk of what we have are sijo and Koryo *lyrics, both of which were meant to be sung to a musical accompaniment. Kasa, which were discursive or narrative verses, were also meant to be sung, were not divided into stanzas, and were of varying lengths. The hwarang were an indigenous institution that recruited men of ability for national service, educated them as soldiers, statesmen, and poets, and taught them to sing such poetry, much as the *scops sang epics in Europe. Koryo lyrics, which were a product of the indigenous Korean culture, combined folk songs and art songs into a composition that was sung to a musical accompaniment. The use of onomatopoeia and nonsense syllables within the refrains was designed to enhance the slightly hypnotic effect of the interplay between the verbal and musical rhythms, evoking certain feelings in the listener. The majority of Koryo lyrics are about love in some form, whether it be sexual or spiritual, the love of a person or the love of one's lord.

The *Song of P'yongyang* expresses the fear that a lover who is journeying away from home will find another love in distant lands and never return. *Winter Night* is the anguished cry of someone begging her "false love" to say what she can do to prove herself worthy of his love and make him stay. The gentle lyric *Song of the Gong* praises the virtuous king and promises fidelity to the lord and faithfulness to the speaker's lover. In contrast, *Will You Go?* is almost hysterical; the words tumble over themselves and the rhythm rushes the reader headlong as the speaker begs his lover to come back as quickly and easily as she has left him. *Ode on the Seasons* is a pledge of undying love to one who does not return the sentiment. *The Turkish Bakery* is about earthly love, the song of a servant girl who is accosted by men at the bakery, the tavern, the well, and the temple, and who goes with each one to lie in "his bower."

Sijo, which is believed to have originated in the beginning of the Koryo dynasty, was a predominantly oral form of vernacular poetry in which the rhythm both of the language and of the musical accompaniment blended with the meaning to evoke responses from the listener. Scholar Jaihiun Kim explained this by noting the main spirit of the sijo is expressed in the simplicity of naked emotion. Each line consists of four rhythmic groups with a minor pause at the end of the second and a major pause at the end of the fourth. The three lengths of sijo are the p'yong sijo, or plain sijo, the ossijo, the medium sijo, and the long version, which is the sasol sijo.

Ch'oe Ch'ung (984-1068) was a respected scholar in the field of neo-Confucianism. Only two of his poems survive. Both are untitled and were originally written in Chinese. One is a meditation on the inevitability of death and the mutability of all things, no matter how great. The other is a lament for the more peaceful times in the period of a legendary king, Fu-Hsi. The poet expresses regret that he did not live in the period when life was simple and peaceful.

Yi Kyu-Bo (1168-1241), an important scholar in Korea's Koryo dynasty, wrote *The White Cloud Tales*. One of his finest sijo embodies the peace of a mind and spirit at rest. The speaker of the poem lies in a yard on a carpet of petals on a warm day and just enjoys the feeling of serenity and comfort. Another of his poems, *The Cock*, depicts the musings of an old man who shoos the cocks away from where they are scratching for worms. He says that he does so because he cannot stand to see the worms eaten. He further justifies his actions by stating that he does not need to get up and work and likes to sleep late, so he has no need or desire to hear the cock crow at dawn.

Yi Kyu-Bo also wrote prose tales. His story *On Demolishing the Earthen Chamber* is about unswerving loyalty to the gods rather than loyalty to the state, as one might expect from a statesman. In his tale a father discovers his sons digging an earthen chamber that will stay warm in winter so that the women of the household can knit without their fingers freezing and so flowers can be grown out of season. The father tells his sons that it is an affront to Heaven to construct anything that will tamper with the normal course of life in accordance with the seasons, because to change what the gods have created in their infinite wisdom is to question their creation, their wisdom, and their authority. He threatens to beat them all if they do not destroy what they have started and repent heartily.

A Dialogue with the Creator is the story of a man who questions the Creator about the nature of the universe and of divine love. He points out that Heaven has both provided for man's care and put things on the earth to harm him, and he considers this a contradiction. The Creator replies that everything is the result of fate and as such is both uncontrollable and inexplicable, so only those who accept Tao and understand this can function comfortably and well.

Then the man asks if since Heaven, Earth, and Man were created out of one original force, and since there are bad things in man and earth, are there also bad things in heaven? The Creator assures him there are not, since just as any man who holds Tao and so is in perfect harmony does not hold anything bad, so Heaven, which is in perfect harmony, also does not harbor anything bad. The questioner's final query is how the Creator can not know anything about creation. The Creator's reply is that he did not even know that men called him the Creator.

U T'ak (1263-1343), like Ch'oe Ch'ung, was an important early neo-Confucian scholar. The first of his two poems that survive is about a man who attempts unsuccessfully to fight old age by blocking the road with thorns and using a stick to beat it off. The second is about an older man who laments that he did not enjoy the spring breeze while he could, because he sees that it has melted the snow off the mountains. He wishes he had let it blow through his hair and melt some of the hoar from his head.

Yi Chonyon (1269-1343) served at court for almost four decades as scholar to four different kings. Only one poem exists that has been definitively attributed to him. It presents a moonlit night just on the cusp of spring in which the speaker, noticing a nightingale perched in the branches of a peach tree, wonders if the bird can see the promise of new life just beginning to bud. He laments that he cannot sleep for the ache this beauty creates within him.

Yi Saek (1328-1396) was also a respected neo-Confucian scholar at the end of the Koryo dynasty, and despite his loyalty to the last days of that dynasty, he suffered after being sent into exile. In one of his sijo the speaker stands in a valley where snow remains, and wonders where the plum blossoms bloom. His hopelessness is reflected in his lament that he does not know in which direction to journey to get out of the cold valley.

Yi Chono (1341-1371) was a historian late in the Koryo era. Of the three poems he has left modern scholars, one of his cleverest is about clouds. The speaker asks how we can think that clouds have no mind when we see them chasing about the sky attempting to blot out the light of the sun.

Ch'oe Yong (1316-1388) was more a soldier than a poet. Though he left us two sijo, he is better known as a chief military commander. The first of his poems is about a young man's desire to prepare himself for battle and prove his love of country. The second concerns the enduring nature of the pine. The tree tells the listener not to laugh because he has to carry a load of snow, because the frivolous flowers and snowflakes that look so pretty are very transient, while he endures for ages.

Chong Monju (1337-1392) acted as an ambassador to Ming China and Japan in an attempt to improve relations with the two neighboring countries. He was assassinated soon after writing *The Fidelity Song*, which glows with fealty for his lord. The speaker asserts that though he may die numerous deaths, nothing could make him disloyal to his lord.

Cho Chun (1346-1405) served in the court of the last two kings of the Koryo dynasty. Two of his poems survive, both of which are the words of a man who has fallen asleep after drinking too much and is gently awakened by a slight shower of rain and then by a fisherman's pipe.

Chong Tonjon (?-1398) was also a scholar in the late part of the Koryo dynasty. His only poem that has come down to us is about the fall of the dynasty. The speaker notes that the old dynasty has passed like the flowing of an imaginary stream, and he surmises that they cannot gain anything by questioning it, but must accept that life flows onward.

Kil Chae (1353-1419) acted as Minister of Annals for a time during the Koryo dynasty and retired to write poetry when the dynasty fell. One of the two poems of his that survive is about how the five hundred years of the past dynasty seem like a dream now that the heroes of that age are gone.

Medieval Korean prose is generally classified according to its rhetorical function, whether it be factual, discursive, narrative, or what have you. A great deal of the prose of the Koryo dynasty is religious in nature even though not all of the educated men were monks. Yi Kyu-Bo (1168-1241) was a statesman who worked his way up to first privy councilor. Monk Sigyongam (1270-1350), was the teacher of the National Preceptor Pogak (1329-1392) and was a disciple of Zen (in Korean, Son) Buddhism. In 1314 Yi Che-Hyon (1287-1367) traveled to Peking, the Mongol capital, to join the Korean king who was in residence there. Monk Sigyongam penned *A Record of the Bamboo in the Bamboo Arbor of the Woltung Monastery*, a Zen story of monks discussing the virtues of bamboo. In answer to the master's query about why each one likes bamboo, the first four monks eloquently praise its flavor, its utility, its beauty, and its endurance. Sigyongam tells them that they have missed the essence of the bamboo and have only spoken of its externals. He tells the master that the bamboo led him to understand how man becomes stronger as he grows, and how nature is hollow, and the roots remind him of man becoming a Buddha. Yi Che-Hyon, who passed the state examination in 1302 and embarked on a career in service of the state at the age of seventeen, left service at twenty-eight to serve the exiled king Ch'ungson. At fifty-four he left service and retired to devote himself to his writing. His *Descriptions of the Cloud Brocade Tower* is a descriptive piece about a tower that stands in the middle of the crowded capital city. It was erected by Lord Hyonbok, Kwon Yom, because the site on which it sits affords the visitor a view of all the lotuses in the lake, in addition to glimpses of the peaks of Dragon Mountain. Yi Che-hyon exhorts the reader to realize that there are scenes of great natural beauty everywhere if one only takes the time to pay attention to them.

Yi Che-Hyon also wrote poetry in Chinese. *Ancient Airs (Four Poems)* is a short four-part work that deals with different aspects of loneliness. The first part is about a young girl who is left pining away in a jade tower when her lover rides off and she is unable to follow. The next is about a man who sends all visitors away and strums a lute, meditating and trying to convince himself that he is strong enough to handle the tribulations of the world. The third section treats the advice of a friend to one who has chosen to become an ascetic. He suggests that one needs to experience life in its contradictions and extremes, not lock oneself away because the world seems like a mere "grass hut." The final part concerns a scholar who works nine days out of ten cooped up with his scrolls. On the tenth day he ventures out into the world to find out what people are doing. His trip shows him that their lives are insipid and that he is better off with his scrolls.

National Preceptor Chin'Gak (1178-1234) wrote Zen poetry in Chinese, which was another major genre of Korean literature. *Night Rain* is the musing of a man who is listening to the rain and hearing "whispers of reality." The rain sings to him as he listens to it with an empty mind, letting it pour into him. He realizes as he listens that he has allowed himself to absorb the feeling that the rain has created, and he therefore no longer needs the sound of the rain to connect himself to the all.

National Preceptor T'aego (1301-1382) also wrote these types of riddling explanatory poems. *Nothingness* advocates the Zen quietness of mind necessary to be receptive to observation and enlightenment. When one is unmoving, mentally more so than physically, everything that is around to input into the brain may enter because there is nothing already there to block the flow. When one is moving, one is unable to receive enlightenment. Enlightenment comes from this inaction, this nothingness, just like chrysanthemums blooming in frost.

Iryon is perhaps one of the most important figures in Korean literature because he acted as the preserver for posterity of the some of the earliest examples of it. A Zen master of the thirteenth century, he put together a collection in 1285 of the foundation myths and other stories in order to preserve the literary heritage of Korea. It contains such stories as *Husband Yono and Wife Seo* and *King Suro, Founder of Karak*. The *Samguk Yusa*, as the collection was named, also preserved the biographies of major religious figures like Master Uisang and Master Wonhyo.

SELECTED BIBLIOGRAPHY

Chung, Chon-wha, ed. *Korean Classical Literature: An Anthology*. London: Kegan Paul International, 1989; Deuchler, Martina. *The Confucian Transformation of Korea: A Study of Society and Ideology*. Cambridge, MA: Harvard University Press, 1992; Hyun, Peter, trans. *Voices of the Dawn: A Selection of Korean Poetry from the Sixteenth Century to the Present Day*. London: John Murray, 1960; Kim, Jaihiun, trans. *Classical Korean Poetry: More Than 600 Verses since the 12th Century*. Freemont, CA: Asian Humanities Press, 1994; Lee, Peter H., ed. *Anthology of Korean Literature: From Early Times to the Nineteenth Century*. Honolulu: University Press of Hawaii, 1981; Uchang, Kim, trans. "Essays by the Great Scholars of the Past (I): Yi Kyubo, Yi Che Hyon, Kim Sisup, and Yi Ik." *Korea Journal*. 18 (1978): 39-44.

Sara Parker

KULHWCH AND OLWEN (c.1100). One of the tales of the Welsh *Mabinogion*, *Kulhwch and Olwen* is an important prose narrative. It is perhaps the earliest true *romance of *Arthurian Legend. In the work Kulhwch is the hero who enlists the aid of Arthur and his followers to help him accomplish the difficult tasks set up for him by Ysaddadin, a giant. The reason for these trials is Kulhwch's desire to marry the giant's daughter, Olwen.

SELECTED BIBLIOGRAPHY

Bromwich, Rachel, and D. Simon Evans, eds. *Culhwch ac Olwen*. Cardiff: Gwasg Prifysgol Cymru, 1980; Diverres, Armel. "Arthur in 'Culhwch and Olwen' and in the Romances of Chrétien de Troyes." In *Culture and the King: The Social Implications of the Arthurian Legend*. Martin B. Shictman and James P. Carley, eds. Albany: State University of New York Press, 1994. 54-69; Edel, Doris. "The Arthur of 'Culhwch and

Olwen' as a Figure of Epic-Heroic Tradition." *Reading Medieval Studies* 9 (1983), 3-15. Miller, D. A. "The Twinning of Arthur and Cei: An Arthurian 'Tessera.'" *Journal of Indo-European Studies* 17:1-2 (Spring-Summer 1989), 47-76; Radner, Joan N. "Interpreting Irony in Medieval Celtic Narrative: The Case of 'Culhwch ac Olwen.'" *Cambridge Medieval Celtic Studies* 16 (Winter 1988), 41-59; Roberts, Brynley F. "'Culhwch ac Olwen', the Triads, Saints Lives." In *The Arthur of the Welsh: The Arthurian Legend in Medieval Welsh Literature*. Rachel Bromwich, *et al*, eds. Cardiff: University of Wales, 1991. 73-95.

J. Scott Plaster

L

LA CELESTINA. The novel *La Celestina*, written in 21 acts, is attributed to Fernando de Rojas, an attorney and converted Jew who lived in Talavera, Spain, at the turn of the sixteenth century. Rojas may have written all or part of this very popular work, which exists in several editions.

Heavily influenced by *Petrarch, *La Celestina* dramatizes the story of the young aristocrat Calisto as he wanders into the garden of Melibea and falls instantly in love with her. When Melibea responds coolly to his pursuits, Calisto engages the help of Celestina, the ultimate evil figure. Through merciless intelligence and guile Celestina gains access to Melibea and convinces her to return Calisto's affections. These *courtly lovers, as well as the satanic Celestina, meet the just end that morality dictates under the circumstances.

Like Shakespeare, Rojas created in this work a realistic portrait of the vulgar world of the underclasses. Even the minor characters are presented in a convincing relief; their bawdiness and the crude, coarse language and behavior recounted in the work have been celebrated and condemned. The explicit moralizing balances somewhat this tendency, but this feature of the work contradicts the natural, everyday language of the lower-class drama.

SELECTED BIBLIOGRAPHY

Gerli, E. Michael. "Complicitous Laughter: Hilarity and Seduction in *Celestina*." *Hispanic Review* 63:1 (Winter 1995), 19-38; McGrady, Donald. "'Entrado Calista una huerta' . . . and Other textual Problems in the *Celestina*." *Hispanic Review* 63:3 (Summer 1995), 433-40; Northup, George Tyler. *An Introduction to Spanish Literature.* Chicago: University of Chicago Press, 1960.

Rebecca Stephens

LALLANS. Lallans is the poetic name given to the historic speech of Lowland Scotland and now the word for the poetic language of the Scottish Renaissance movement. Robert Burns used the term to describe his poetry in his *Epistle to William Simpson of Ochiltree.* The language is somewhat a literary creation, to the extent that it was no longer spoken and, when written, consisted of archaic words found only in dictionaries. Lewis Spence and Hugh McDiarmid began a Lallans movement in 1946 to recreate the Scots language and to incorporate the newly rediscovered vocabulary into literary usage. Spence was a journalist for the *Scotsman* and the *British Weekly*, and was one of the founders of the Scottish National Party. He began experimenting with the ancient language, reviving the middle Scots dialect and vocabulary in works such as "Portrait of Mary Stuart" and "Holyrood." Hugh MacDiarmid, born C. M. Grieve, had more poetic talent and later joined the movement by at first contributing lyrics anonymously to the *Scottish Chapbook* and later *Sangschaw* and *Pennywheep*. The word "lallans" was the topic of an extended debate in the *Glasgow Herald* in 1948 and the title of the magazine of the Scot's literary society.

SELECTED BIBLIOGRAPHY

Barrow, G. W. S. *Bruce and the Community of the Realm of Scotland*. Berkeley: University of California Press, 1965; Mainster, Phoebe A. "How to Make a Hero: Barbour's Recipe: Reshaping History as Romance." *Michigan Academician* 20 (Spring 1988), 225-238; Trace, Jacqueline. "The Supernatural Element in Barbour's *Bruce*." *Massachusetts Studies in English* 1 (Spring 1968), 55-65.

J. Scott Plaster

LANCELOT or **THE KNIGHT OF THE CART.** *Lancelot* was written by *Chrétien de Troyes, a French *romance writer. In *Lancelot* we find the most memorable parts of Chrétien's work and the scenes that have had the most lasting impact upon literary thought. This text fully describes true sustained *courtly love, a passionate, yet elaborately spiritual and removed adoration of a knight for his lady, Lancelot for Queen Guinevere. The hero is made to look foolish several times for love, but is consistently willing to risk his reputation for his lady's pleasure.

Guinevere is locked in a prison, so Lancelot survives a series of trials while attempting her rescue (such as crawling across the naked blade of a long, sharp sword that forms a bridge), but is rebuffed by Guinevere upon her release for hesitating to enter a cart used to transport criminals. Ultimately, Lancelot's devotion and courteous words win over the queen, but she was furious with his momentary reluctance to accept humiliation on her behalf. The poem *Lancelot* demonstrates how popular and important *Arthurian legend was to this literary period.

SELECTED BIBLIOGRAPHY

Guerin, M. Victoria. *The Falls of Kings and Princes: Structure and Destruction in Arthurian Tragedy*. Stanford: Stanford University Press, 1995; Hunt, Tony. "Chrétien's Prologues Reconsidered." In *Conjunctures*. Keith Busby and Norris Lacy, eds. Amsterdam: Radopi, 1994. 153-68; Wolfgang, Lenora D. "Chrétien's 'Lancelot': The Fragments in

Manuscript 6138 of the Institut de France" In *Conjunctures*. Keith Busby and Norris Lacy, eds. Amsterdam: Rudopi, 1994. 559-74.

Laura Cooner Lambdin

LANFRANC (c. 1015-89). Lanfranc was a master of dialectic and theology who became the archbishop of Canterbury in 1070. Prior to this promotion, Lanfranc had established one of the foremost schools north of the Alps at Bec. His life paralleled the growth of the church in the eleventh century. Lanfranc was well educated; he was especially proficient in the writings of the classical authors, particularly as they related to learning. He saw the growth of ideas and was a contributor to papal reform. When he went to England, he reformed the calendar, paying little respect to the English saints. He reformed the *Regularis Concordia* to more reflect his French background, although he did not enforce these changes outside of Canterbury.

SELECTED BIBLIOGRAPHY

Clover, V. Helen, and Margaret T. Gibson, eds. and trans. *The Letters of Lanfranc, Archbishop of Canterbury*. New York: Oxford University Press, 1979; Gibson, Margaret T. *Lanfranc of Bec*. New York: Clarendon Press, 1978.

Robert T. Lambdin

LANGLAND, WILLIAM (c. 1330-1386). It is believed that William Langland is the author of **Piers the Plowman*; however, everything about his life, including his very identity, is questionable. Evidence indicates that Langland lived sometime in London; the dialect of *Piers the Plowman* presents evidence that its author had acquired some of the characteristics of the West Midlands dialect. Some believe that Langland was born to Stacy de Rokayle from Oxfordshire, but even this is unclear. In any case, *Piers the Plowman*, perhaps the greatest work from the Middle English **alliterative revival, is attributed to him.

Piers the Plowman* was obviously a popular work, for about fifty different manuscripts remain. Curiously, there are three vastly different versions. The A-text, of some 2,500 lines, was composed between 1367 and 1370. The B-text dates from 1377-79. It emends the A-text and adds almost 5,000 lines. The C-text is about the same length as the B-text, but the work appears to have been greatly revised; it was composed about 1385-86. The poet himself could have made all these emendations to the texts, but this seems unrealistic. While *Piers the Plowman* dates from the same time as the works of Geoffrey **Chaucer, its composition resembles that of **Old English poetry because it was deliberately written in an archaic dialect.

Piers the Plowman is an allegorical moral and social satire, composed in a variation of the popular *dream-vision format. The work is actually a sequence of vision poems. The narrator relates what he sees in a series of dreams. The works are provocative in that the narrator often infers that he sees more than he relates. His first vision gives an account of his vision of a field full of people, a metaphor for the World. The field lies between the Tower of Truth (God) and the dungeon of evil (Hell). A wide cross-section of society wanders in the fields, including plowmen, clerics, and merchants.

The narrator espies a beautiful lady who tells him that the tower is God's house; the dungeon, called the Castle of Care, is the home of Satan. She then reveals herself as the Holy Church. He questions his ability to distinguish between good and evil and is shown another beautiful lady who is to be married to Satan. What ensues is a metaphorical allegory in which Reason finally dispenses advice on how justice should be served.

In the second vision Reason has become the royal favorite. This vision exposes the *seven deadly sins, which are allowed to confess and repent for their actions. They search for truth, but their journey is halted until Piers, a plowman, appears to lead them to absolution. Before he can lead the pilgrims, Piers explains that he must plow his half-acre; he urges those who would follow him to do the same. Eventually Piers is pardoned by Truth (God). This pardon is questioned by a priest, and the dreamer awakens. He then reflects upon the true insignificance of the papal pardon when it is compared with the satisfaction gleaned from simply leading a good life and not giving in to indulgences.

While much of *Piers the Plowman* is confusing and uncertain, it is this lack of literal cohesiveness that makes the poem so wonderful. The text demands imagination and the power of metaphorical interpretation. Thus the work does not simply teach a blatant homily; it elicits thought.

SELECTED BIBLIOGRAPHY

Cole, Andrew. "Trifunctionality and the Tree of Clarity: Literary and Social Practice in *Piers Plowman*." *ELH* 62:1 (Spring 1995), 1-27; Dolan, D.P. "The Plowman as Hero." in *Heroes and Heroines in the Middle English Literature.* Leo Carruthers, ed. Cambridge: Brewer, 1994. 97-103; Dyer, Christopher. "*Piers Plowman* and Plowmen: A Historical Perspective." *Yearbook of Langland Studies.* 8 (1995), 155-76; Fisher, John. *The Emergence of Standard English.* Lexington: University Press of Kentucky, 1996; Smith, D. Vance. "The Labors of Reward: Meed, Mercede, and the Beginning of Salvation." *Yearbook of Langland Studies* 8 (1995), 127-54.

Rebecca Chalmers

LANGTON, STEPHEN (c. 1155-1226). Stephen Langton's sermons, lectures, and writings are unpublished and are found only in widely scattered manuscripts; however, he and they played a significant role in the turbulent years of the reign of the crafty and unpopular King *John (1199-1216). Langton was born in Lincolnshire, England, studied and taught in Paris, was made a cardinal, in Rome, in 1206, and archbishop of Canterbury in 1207. However, since John and Pope *Innocent III (1198-1216) were fighting for dominance, John refused to permit Langton to enter England until 1213. When in 1215 the king and the pope were reconciled, Langton was unjustly suspended from Canterbury and exiled in France, in part for his pivotal role in winning the Magna Charta (1215). After John's death in 1216 Langton became for the next ten years a chief advisor to young Henry III. He served in this capacity for a number of years.

Langton's lectures were *questiones* or rhetorical questions followed by expository answers using both Scripture and everyday illustrations. For example, if a man is unjustly treated by his monarch, should another subject help him to escape? The answer depends upon the kind of community involved, a kingdom ruled by one man or a commonwealth, and although one should assist sufferers whenever possible, allegiance to authority defines considerations. Several times Langton dealt with the power of the pope. He maintained that while the pontiff was the mouthpiece of God, he could not use his authority to permit or promote anything contrary to the law of nature, which Langton equated with the fundamental law expounded in Scripture. He conceded that problems of interpretation were bound to arise. For example, while tithing was biblically mandated for laymen, the pope could justifiably grant exemption to religious orders, for their property was held for Mother Church and exempt from the rule for laymen.

While these lectures were popular for the next two centuries, they have less pertinence for today. As a preacher and biblical commentator Langton has a wider reputation, in part because he reorganized the books of the Paris Bible and divided the context into chapters that greatly aided teaching, changes largely continued in today's Bibles. His commentaries may be found in most European manuscript libraries. In Dominican circles he is remembered for such studies as that on the twelve Minor Prophets. In the church at large he made more of an impression with his preaching. One of his best-known sermons is "The Penitence of the Magdalene." The sacraments of penance and confession were a favorite theme for Langton, especially during his exile at Pontigny. During the comparative leisure of this period he also wrote historical accounts of the life of King *Richard I and of Muhammad, works now lost, and some poetry, chiefly hymns.

In all his work Langton's style combines the simple and direct with the subtle and allusive, including conceits and hair-splitting refinements. His orthodoxy was colored by his perceptive observations and sympathetic acquaintance with all types of individuals and groups. Because he consistently ordered his actions by holy principles applied to practical realities, he often suffered abuse at the hands of both the church and the state, and was tempted to become a hermit or a monk. But his principles demanded active service and his resulting scholarship has lasting value.

SELECTED BIBLIOGRAPHY

Duggan, Anne. "The Cult of St. Thomas in the Thirteenth Century." In *St. Thomas Cantilupe, Bishop of Hereford: Essays in His Honour*. Meryl Jancey, ed. Hereford, Eng: Friends of Hereford Cathedral, 1982. 21-44; Powicke, Frederick Maurice. *Stephen Langton*. Being the Ford Lectures Delivered in the University of Oxford in Hilary Term 1927. New York. Barnes & Noble, 1965; Roberts, Phyllis B. "Archbishop Stephen Langton and His Preaching on Thomas Becket in 1220." In *De Ore Domini: Preacher and the Word in the Middle Ages*. Thomas Amos, Eugene A. Green, and Beverly Mayne Kienzle, eds. Kalamazoo: Medieval Institute Publications, 1989. 75-92; Roberts, Phyllis B. "Stephen Langton's *Serma de Virginibus*. In *Women of the Medieval World: Essays in Honor of John H. Mundy*. Julius Kirschner and Suzanne Wemple, eds. Oxford: Blackwell, 1985. 103-18.

Esther Smith

LAUDA. The lauda was a form of religious song popular in Italy during the medieval and early Renaissance periods. These works used the *ballata* form: a stanza of varying length followed by a two line refrain. They were usually composed for lay confraternities. Jacopene da Todi (1230-1306) is probably the earliest noted composer of the lauda. He initiated the form, and his successors perfected the style as it became increasingly dramatic; also, dialogue, action, and setting became important.

Thus the lauda became the Italian equivalent of the English mystery play (*see **Drama, Medieval***), or the sacra rappresentazione (sacred representation). With the onset of the Renaissance, these plays lost their popularity, yet their influence remained, especially on the secular and neoclassical dramas that replaced them. During the Renaissance several lauda were written, but not by religious originators. They became texts for musical settings and were performed by individual artists.

SELECTED BIBLIOGRAPHY

Barr, Cyrilla. *The Monophonic Lauda and the Lay Religious Confraternities of Tuscany and Umbria in the Late Middle Ages*. Kalamazoo: Medieval Intitute Publications, 1988; Macey, Patrick. "The Lauda and the Cult of Savonarola." *Renaissance Quarterly* 45:3 (Autumn 1992), 439-83.

Robert T. Lambdin

LAXDALE SAGA. From the early Middle Ages, the *Laxdale Saga* is an Icelandic *saga that deals with Gudran, who falls in love with Kjarten. Gudran is selfish and willful, characteristics explored in the saga. Kjarten goes to the court of King Olaf; while he is there, his cousin, Bolli, tells Gudran that Kjarten and Olaf's sister, Ingebjorg, have become friendly. Gudran becomes irate and marries Bolli. When Kjarten returns to Iceland and hears of the marriage, he marries Hrefna to spite Gudran. He gives an ornate headpiece to Hrefna, a piece that Ingebjorg had given to Kjarten as a gift for Gudran. This so exasperates Gudran that she creates a feud between the two families by having the headpiece stolen. A series of raids and battles ensues; Kjarten is killed because of the bad judgment of the woman he loved.

SELECTED BIBLIOGRAPHY

Bylock, Jesse. "Egill Skalla-Grimsson: The Dark Figure as Survivor in an Icelandic Saga." In *The Dark Figure in Medieval German and Germanic Literature*. Edward R. Haymes and Stephanie Cain D'Elden, eds. Coppingen: Kummerle, 1986. 151-63; McTurk, R. W. "'Cynewulf and Cyneheard' and the Icelandic Sagas." *Leeds Studies in English* 12 (1981), 81-127; Puhvel, Martin. "The Mighty She-Trolls of Icelandic Saga and Folklore." *Folklore* 98:2 (1987), 175-79.

Robert T. Lambdin

LAY (LAI), BRETON. Critics generally consider the Middle English lay as a sub-genre of the *romance, one in which *courtly love, the world of fairies, and the age of *chivalry predominate. The lay, however, has definitive characteristics that differentiate it from the romance. Like the romance, the lay involves a search or a quest; "the hero acts as an individual, not a representative of his [or her] society"; and the action occurs "in an exotic setting . . . distinct from the everyday world" (Gibbs 4). The difference is basic, according to Edith Rickert: the lay "is always short (usually under a thousand lines), generally episodic, and is clearly intended to be sung to musical accompaniment" (xxiii). The adventures depicted in the lay tend to be quite dramatic, making them easily recited in one sitting, because they leave any psychological development of the characters for the longer romances; in fact, most of the characters in the lays are mere caricatures. To some extent, the relationship between the lay and the romance is comparable to the relationship today between the short story and the novel, although occasionally the connection appears closer: for example, the subject matter in the lay could be expanded into a romance, or a romance would be shortened into a lay. The lay almost certainly traces its derivation to Celtic (*see* **Celtic Literature, Early**) sources (whether Welsh, Irish, or a blend thereof), frequently even claiming early in the poem to be a translation of lost Celtic tales of love and the supernatural; however, as the form became popular, the poets worked from any source, classical or otherwise, adding information appropriate to their theme. After the *Crusades poets began introducing Oriental matter into the poems, adding an additional element of mystique to the works.

The prologue to *Lay Le Freine* (lines 1-18), which in some manuscripts also appears appended to *Sir Orfeo*, offers the only evidence regarding the characteristics associated with the lay during the time of its construction: to a harp's accompaniment, the lay tells of war and woe, joy and mirth, treachery and guile, adventures that happened long ago; many introduce fairies, while most deal with love. Apparently, the original Breton *lais* (of which no specimens survive) were songs in the Breton language accompanied by a harp, then followed by a *conte* or narrative that explicated the lyrical *lai*. These *contes* provided the basis for Marie de France's twelfth century poems that became the source of many of the Middle English versions. Twentieth-century analyses of the Middle English form, however, find that beyond the commonality of being "a short narrative poem, characterized by a concentration on simplicity of action," there is a more general division of the form into two basic types: "the principal type of *lay* is essentially a short romance which usually involves some supernatural element," most often as a liaison with a fairy; "the other an ordeal tale which generally involves improbable coincidences" (Finlayson 367).

By asking what he perceivds as "the right questions," G. V. Smithers has discovered three basic "story-patterns" in the major Old French and Middle English works usually classified as lays. His patterns offer refinements on the guidelines offered by John Finlayson (Smithers 61). The first, which is illustrated in the *Lanval/*Sir Launfal* poems, has four main stages: an "obstructive circumstance" that creates some difficulty for the hero, "the amorous liaison with a fairy, the breach of the taboo" regarding the limitations the fairy lover places upon their relationship, "and the resolution of the crisis" (Smithers 62). The second pattern, which has *Emaré* as its example, adds a child as a result of the liaison between the fairy and the mortal (Smithers 66). The third pattern is distinctive in that the lovers are mortal, and the resulting child reunites the parents after engaging in combat with the father, who was previously unknown to him (Smithers 75). The delineations Smithers saw are clearer in the Old French works; by the time the stories appear in Middle English, the lines start to blur--for example, *Sir Degaré* is actually a blend of type II (the child as a product of fairy liaison) and III (the child doing battle with the father).

Eight Middle English works are generally classified as lays: *Emaré*, *Lay Le Freine*, *Sir Degaré*, *Sir Gowther*, *Sir Launfal*, *Sir Orfeo*, and *The *Erl of Toulous*, which are recorded in miscellanies with romances, and "The *Franklin's Tale" from Geoffrey *Chaucer's *Canterbury Tales*. All of these works except *Sir Degaré* claim to be lays in the opening lines of the poem (typically, within the first twenty lines); critics usually classify *Sir Degaré* with this group because of its length, its Breton setting, and the connection with fairies. While two of them (*Sir Launfal* and *Lay Le Freine*) are clearly derived from *lais* written by Marie de France, only *Orfeo* and *Emaré* claim to have a relationship with the Breton lay (though their sources as lays have not been found). Marie de France is credited with creating an interest in preserving the tales she had heard (of which no example exists today) of the various adventures depicted in the lays, recording them in her native French, and styling them to be enjoyed at court. She composed twelve *lais* in the twelfth century before 1189, when *Henry II died. The Middle English variation of the form came about as later poets translated her tales into the language of the common people or created new tales of their own.

The term "Breton" itself is ambiguous when used in conjunction with the lay; it can refer to the area in northwest France known as Brittany or to the parts of the island now referred to as Great Britain that the Celts continued to hold after the *Anglo-Saxon conquest. Chaucer's *"Man of Law's Tale" provides support for the latter being what poets really meant when they claimed a kinship with the Bretons. In lines 541-46 the Man of Law describes the "olde gentil Britouns" as the Christian folk who fled to Wales to avoid the pagan (Germanic) conquerors who came across the sea from the North (quoted in Yoder 75). Another advantage of this Welsh connection is the explanation it provides for the many Celtic influences (the supernatural characters and the fairies or *fées*, as in Morgan la Fée) found in the principal type of the lay.

The Breton or Middle English lay was popular during two distinct periods of time in English history. The first period was during the first half of the fourteenth century, when the form migrated from the French aristocracy down to the common English-speaking audiences of the wandering *minstrels. The tastes of the populace influenced the evolution of the Middle English form to the point where the hopes, aspirations, and perceptions of the lower classes appear as they do nowhere else in English literature. Chaucer's imitation of the form in "The Franklin's Tale" revived general interest in the genre during the late fourteenth and early fifteenth centuries.

SELECTED BIBLIOGRAPHY

Bliss, A. J., ed. "Introduction." *Sir Launfal*. New York: Barnes and Noble, 1960. 1-52; Bliss, A. J., ed "Introduction." *Sir Orfeo*. London: Oxford UP, 1954. ix-li; Bolton, W.F. *The Penguin History of Literature: The Middle Ages*. London: Penguin, 1993; Bromwich, Rachel. "A Note on the Breton Lays." *Medium Ævum* 26 (1957), 36-38; Bullock-Davies, Constance. "The Form of the Breton Lay." *Medium Ævum* 42 (1973), 19-31; Donovan, Mortimer J. *The Breton Lays: A Guide to Varieties*. Notre Dame: University of Notre Dame Press, 1969; Finlayson, John. "The Form of the Middle English *Lay*." *Chaucer Review* 19 (1985), 352-368; Furnish, Shearle. "The Modernity of 'The Erle of Tolous' and the Decay of the Breton Lai." *Medieval Perspectives* 8 (1993), 69-77; Gibbs, A. C., ed. "Introduction." *Middle English Romances*. Evanston: Northwestern University Press, 1966. 1-25; Guillaume, Gabrielle. "The Prologues of the *Lay le Freine* and *Sir Orfeo*." *Modern Language Notes* 36 (1921), 458-64; Ker, W. P. *Epic and Romance*. 1908. New York: Dover, 1957; Loomis, Laura Hibbard. *Medieval Romance in England*. 2nd ed. New York: B. Franklin, 1960; Rickert, Edith. *Early English Romances in Verse: Done into Modern English by Edith Rickert: Romances of Love*. New York: Cooper Square, 1966; Rumble, Thomas C. *The Breton Lays in Middle English*. Detroit: Wayne State University Press, 1965; Schmidt, A.V.C., and Nicolas Jacobs, eds. "The Breton Lays and Sir Orfeo." In *Medieval English Romances: Part One*. New York: Holmes and Meier, 1980. 21-33; Severs, J. Burke. "The Antecedents of Sir Orfeo." In *Studies in Medieval Literature: In Honor of Professor Albert Croll Baugh*. MacEdward Leach, ed. Philadelphia: University of Pennsylvania Press, 1961.

187-207; Smithers, G.V. "Story-Patterns in Some Breton Lays." *Medium Ævum* 22.2 (1953), 61-92; Yoder, Emily K. "Chaucer and the 'Breton' Lay." *Chaucer Review* 12 (1977) 74-77.

Peggy Huey

LAY LE FREINE (LAY OF THE ASH). In the *lay *Lay Le Freine*, when the spouse of a neighboring knight gives birth to twins, the ruler's wife accuses the woman of infidelity (only by sleeping with two men could a woman have twins). One year later, however, her words come home to haunt her when she bears twin girls. To save her reputation, she sends one of the girls away. Since the baby is left with an elaborate coverlet under an ash tree, the people who find her call her Le Freine (the Ash). After growing up in a convent, she becomes the mistress of the local knight, who loves her and would marry her except for her status as a foundling. This lay, so typical of the genre, demonstrates many of the conventions that made this genre so popular.

Instead, he agrees to marry the daughter of a neighboring knight for political reasons. On her love's wedding night, being the good and pure person she is, Le Freine offers her new mistress the only thing she has of any value--she spreads upon the wedding bed the elaborate coverlet she has kept with her all these years. When the bride's mother enters the room, she recognizes the coverlet--it is the one she used to protect the daughter she had to spirit away so many years ago. Confessing the truth, she reclaims her lost daughter; the knight's marriage to the sister is annulled, and he marries Le Freine, his true love. Once again the convetntions of the lays demands that the tale would end in this manner.

This fairly faithful translation of Marie de France's *lai* emphasizes Christian providence--the good and pure characters win in the end. This poem differs from most of the lays in that the incidents occurring in the poem do not involve fairies; instead, jealousy provides the cause. There is also no real adventure in the poem; the focus here is merely on separation and coincidental reconciliation.

The appearance of this poem in the same manuscript as *Sir Orfeo*, as well as the similarity of a number of phrases in the two poems, suggests that a single author or translator produced them. *Sir Degaré*, which also appears in this manuscript, shares with this poem many motifs such as incest and religious people (hermits and nuns) raising a lost child of a nobleman who has some token that supplies identification of the child's heritage, enabling the child to be reunited with the parents. The common motifs, plus some similarities in certain passages, suggest that a relationship also exists between the author or translator of *Lay Le Freine* and *Sir Degaré*, although they may simply mean that the lay poets relied heavily on formulaic motif and verbal metric patterns for their compositions.

SELECTED BIBLIOGRAPHY

Bolton, W. F. *The Penguin History of Literature: The Middle Ages.* London: Penguin, 1993; Bullock-Davies, Constance. "The Form of the Breton Lay." *Medium Ævum* 42 (1973): 19-31; Donovan, Mortimer J. *The Breton Lays: a Guide to Varieties.* Notre Dame: University of Notre Dame Press, 1969; Gibbs, A. C., ed. "Introduction." *Middle English Romances.* Evanston: Northwestern University Press, 1-25; Guillaume, Gabrielle. "The Prologues of the *Lay le Freine* and *Sir Orfeo.*" *Modern Language Notes* 36 (1921): 458-464; Jacobs, Nicolas. "'Sir Degare', 'Lay le Freine,' 'Beves of Hamtoun,' and the 'Auchinleck Bookshop.'" *Notes and Queries* 29 (277): 4 (August 1982), 294-301; Loomis, Laura Hibbard. *Medieval Romance in England.* 2nd ed. New York: B. Franklin, 1960; Rickert, Edith. *Early English Romances in Verse: Done into Modern English by Edith Rickert: Romances of Love.* New York: Cooper Square, 1966; Rumble, Thomas C. *The Breton Lays in Middle English.* Detroit: Wayne State University Press, 1965; Smithers, G.V. "Story-Patterns in Some Breton Lays." *Medium Ævum* 22.2 (1953): 61-92.

Peggy Huey

LAYAMON. An *Anglo-Saxon priest of Worcestershire, Layamon is the author of *Brut* (c. 1190), the first English copy of Wace's *Roman de Brut* (c.1154). Layamon substituted the native alliterative meter for Wace's continental poetic form of octosyllabic couplets. The theme is the glory of Celtic Britain (see **Celtic Literature, Early**) rather than Saxon England.

The *Brut* begins with Aeneas's departure from Troy and ends with Cadwalader's departure to Rome. Most emphasized is King Arthur (*see* **Arthurian Legend**), who is revered as a great warrior leader and national hero who was given special abilities at birth by elves.

While Wace wrote of Arthur as a chivalric figure full of pretty words about *courtly love, Layamon made Arthur a fighting man involved in battles that are a series of bloodbaths. Layamon also expanded particularly well upon Arthur's birth with attendant elves and Arthur's death barge, as well as upon Wace's accounts of the Round Table. Layamon's Arthur is an Englishman, brave, lusty, honest, and enduring--unafraid of the blood and gore of battle. This Arthur boasts of his warlike deeds ferociously in ways that make the reader feel his exuberance even today.

SELECTED BIBLIOGRAPHY

Alamichel, Marie Francoise. "King Arthur's Dual Personality in Layaman's 'Brut.'" *Neophilologus* 77:2 (April 1993), 303-19; Bryan, Elizabeth J. "Truth and the Round Table in Lawman's 'Brut.'" *Quondam et Futurus* 2:4 (Winter 1992), 27-35; Cable, Thomas. "Lawman's 'Brut' and the Misreading of Old English Meter." In *Language and Civilization: A Concerted Profusion of Essays and Studies in Honor of Otto Hietsch, I & II.* Claudia Blank, ed. Frankfurt: Peter Lang, 1992. 173-82; Le Saux, Francoise.

"Narrative Rhythm and Narrative Content in Layamon's 'Brut.'" *Parergon* 10:1 (June 1992), 45-70.

Laura Cooner Lambdin

LEGEND OF GOOD WOMEN, THE. *The Legend of Good Women* is another of Geoffrey *Chaucer's unfinished poems; it is over 2,700 lines long and is composed in decasyllabic couplets. Perhaps the best portion of this work is in the prologue, where the poet gleefully describes his delight at wandering through the meadows on a lovely May morning. He seems especially fond of the daisies.

The narrator falls asleep, and the rest of the work occurs in a *dream vision. He dreams that the god of Love, along with Queen Alceste, appears and expresses his displeasure that the poet has translated the *Romaunt of the Rose* and composed *Troylus and Criseyde*. These works, explains the god of Love, discourage men from following the credo of *courtly love. At this point Alceste intervenes, pointing out that Chaucer has composed other works in which love is exalted. She then asks that Chaucer be allowed to redeem himself by composing a collection of sketches about twenty women who have served Love well. This is followed by short illustrations of women who suffered or died because they were faithful in love or because their men were treacherous. The examples provided, based upon stories of Virgil and Ovid, include Cleopatra, Thisbe, Dido, Hypsipyle, Medea, Lucrece, Ariadne, Philomela, Phyllis, and Hypermnestra. The poem ends unfinished.

The *Legend of Good Women* is important because it contains the earliest extant use of the heroic couplet (iambic pentameter lines rhymed in pairs) in written English. Alfred Lord Tennyson refers to this in his "A Dream of Fair Women."

SELECTED BIBLIOGRAPHY

Bush, Douglas. *English Poetry*. New York: Oxford University Press, 1963; Delany, Sheila. *The Naked Text and Chaucer's "Legend of Good Women."* Berkeley: University of California Press, 1994; Garbáty, Thomas J. *Medieval English Literature*. Toronto: Heath, 1984; Hanrahan, Michael. "Seduction and Betrayal: Treason in the 'Prologue' to the *Legend of Good Women*." *Chaucer Review* 30:3 (1996), 229-40; Minnis, Alastair J. "Repainting the Lion: Chaucer's Profeminist Narratives." In *Contexts of Pre-Novel Narrative: The European Tradition*. Roy Eriksen, ed. Berlin: Mouton de Gruyter, 1994. 153-83; Quinn, William A. *Chaucer's "Rehersynges": The Performability of "The Legend of Good Women."* Washington, D. C.: Catholic University of America Press, 1994; Salter, Elizabeth. *Fourteenth-Century English Poetry*. Oxford: Clarendon Press, 1983.

Robert T. Lambdin

"LENTEN IS COME WITH LOVE TO TOWN" (c. 1314). "Lenten Is Come with Love to Town," a short poem, is probably the most famous of the Middle English *lyrics. The tone is one of simple joy, a naive adoration of the plants and animals at their most alive and full blossoming. In three stanzas the speaker moves from noticing the bleakness of winter to animals coupling in spring and, finally, to his own sexual frustration because women are so proud or disdainful of his advances. Ending on a rather bleak note, the speaker exclaims that if he cannot find love, he will go mad and run wild in the forest. That this spring lyric was meant to be sung seems likely.

SELECTED BIBLIOGRAPHY

Breeze, Andrew. "Welsh Mil 'Animal' and the Harley Lyric 'Lenten Ys Come.'" *Notes and Queries* 40(238):1 (March 1993), 14-15; Bush, Douglas. *English Poetry.* New York: Oxford University Press, 1963; Garbáty, Thomas J. *Medieval English Literature.* Toronto: Heath, 1984; Swanton, Michael. *English Literature before Chaucer.* New York: Longman, 1987.

Laura Cooner Lambdin

LIBEAUS DESCONSUS. *Libeaus Desconsus*, a late fourteenth-century *romance, is attributed to Thomas Chestre; the title is a corruption of *le bel inconnu* (the fair unknown). In the romance Gingelein, the illegitimate son of Gawain asks Arthur (*see* **Arthurian Legend**) to make him a knight. Since his name is unknown (i.e., because he is a bastard), Arthur knights him Libeaus Desconsus. After his knighting, the work tells of Gingelein's rescuing the imprisoned Lady of Sinadoune.

      Critics of *Libeaus Desconsus* find that portions of the work are referred to in Geoffrey *Chaucer's *"Sir Thopas" in the *Canterbury Tales*. In Chaucer's work he is "Sir Lybeux." Also, the narrative style of "Thopas" is similar to the form of *Libeaus Desconsus*. This is yet another example of the popularity of the Arthurian legends.

SELECTED BIBLIOGRAPHY

Knight, Stephen. "The Social Function of the Middle English Romances." In *Medieval Literature: Criticism, Ideology, and History.* New York: St. Martin's, 1986. 99-122; Lindahl, Carl. "The Oral Undertones of Late Medieval Romance." In *Oral Tradition in the Middle Ages.* W.F.H. Nicolaisen, ed. Binghamton, NY: Medieval and Renaissance Texts and Studies, 1995. 59-75.

Robert T. Lambdin

LIBERAL ARTS. In the Middle Ages the liberal arts refers to the seven branches of learning: grammar, logic, rhetoric, arithmetic, geometry, music, and astronomy. The fixing of the fields at seven was rooted in the Bible's Proverbs 9:1, which notes that wisdom's house had seven pillars hewn by her. Law and medicine were excluded from the liberal arts because they were concerned with practical matters. Today the liberal arts include subjects related to and including languages, sciences, philosophy, and history. The term comes from the Latin *artes liberales*. Because the freemen (or liberals) were the only ones privileged enough to pursue a scholarly lifestyle.

SELECTED BIBLIOGRAPHY

Leader, Damian Riehl. "John Argentein and Learning in Medieval Cambridge." *Humanistica Lovaniensia* 33 (1984), 71-85; Mooney, Linne R. "A Middle English Text on the Seven Liberal Arts." *Speculum* 68:4 (1993), 107-52; Stahl, William Harris, Richard Johnson, and E. L. Burge, trans. *Martianus Capella and the Seven Liberal Arts.* New York: Columbia University Press, 1977.

Robert T. Lambdin

LINDSAY, SIR DAVID (1490-1555). A Scottish poet and the earliest Scottish dramatist, Sir David Lindsay of the Mount was more popular than poetic, some critics argue, for despite the fact of his tremendous following for years after his death and numerous reprintings of his work, some find very little to like in his poetry. His career covered the last of the middle ages of Scottish literature, and despite some modern appraisals, his popularity extended for at least two hundred years.

It was said that every Scottish cottage had two books, the Bible and David Lindsay. Very little is known of his youth. He was raised either in Cupar in Fife or near Haddington in East Lothian and was probably educated at the University of St. Andrews. He was in the Scottish royal court in the service of James IV and was appointed usher to the newborn prince James in 1512. After James IV's death the Douglas faction controlled of the heir James, and Lindsay was dismissed, but he returned to the court he so loved after the faction was overthrown.

Lindsay became very involved in royal affairs, being appointed as Scottish ambassador to Flanders and later accompanying royal envoys to France to negotiate a marriage for the new king. In court his stories entertained the young prince, and as a sort of King's Poet his work *Ane Plesant Satyre of the Thrie Estaitis* was performed for the royal party on Twelfth Night in 1540. His relationship with the court lasted into Queen Mary's reign. It was this familiarity with the political pulse of the nation and his ability to charm the winning political side that earned Lindsay public approval as well as success as a satirist and reformist.

Aiming at corruptness in the church and in legal affairs, Lindsay's satire preached and moralized, playing into popular sentiment with his use of ribald language and straightforward style. *The Dreme* (1528), Lindsay's first major work, is a *dream allegory in which the poet is led by Dame Remembrance through Hell, Purgatory, the Stars, Heaven (reminiscent of the one in *Dante's *Paradiso*), Earth, Paradise, and Scotland. He realizes and bemoans the ruin to which his Scotland has fallen. In a note that would recur in Lindsay's later work, the poem concludes by giving some instructive advice to the king.

The work that would have to be called Lindsay's most important text is the earliest surviving drama written in Middle Scots, *Ane Plesant Satyre of the Thrie Estaitis in Commendatioun of Vertew and Vituperatioun of Vyce*, but it has been suggested that this drama was probably not his first or only play. Though it took some eight hours to perform, *The Thrie Estaites* was a note or two lighter than its related morality play (*see* **Drama, Medieval**), and includes some of the usual cast, Flatterie, Falset, and Dissait, disguised as Devotioun, Sapience, and Discretioun in hoods of monks and friars. Satirizing political and church corruption, Lindsay shows his broadest poetic range in this work, from the aereate Chaucerian (*See* **Chaucer, Geoffrey**) stanzas of Sensualitie to the colloquial tail-rhyme of John the Common Weill. Lindsay incorporated not only these forms of Chaucer and his followers, but also the more popular bob-and-wheel and tail-rhymes to great effect.

Lindsay also explored the animal tale in *The Testament and Complaynt of Our Soverane Lordis Papyngo*. The testament, a parody of a religious form, was probably written in 1530. The poet has been training the king's Papyngo (parrot) to speak and whistle. The parrot, ignoring wise advice, climbs to the top of a tree and falls. As an assortment of figurative clerics (the Pie, the Raven, and the Kite) assemble to administer the last rites, the bird recites her last wishes, an early example of such dying animal testimony oddly popular in the eighteenth-century revival period.

The timbre of Lindsay's poetry effectively embodies the early Scottish democratic attitude, a resolute resistance to authority and unquenchable spirit of independence. In *The Thrie Estaitis*, and again in *Papyngo*, themes of social justice and democracy are clear in his biting satire against the Old Church. Instead of the implicit allegorical satire of others before and after him, he preferred the common idiom as the medium to carry his bite. Giving poetic voice to popular sentiment, Sir David Lindsay, champion of the common weal, was accepted and applauded in the reform movement of sixteenth-century Scotland and after.

SELECTED BIBLIOGRAPHY

Smith, Janet M. *The French Background of Middle Scots Literature*. Edinburgh: Oliver and Boyd, 1934; Speirs, John. *The Scots Literary Tradition, An Essay in Criticism*. London: Faber, 1962; Williams, Janet. "David Lindsay's 'Antique' and 'Plesand' Stories." In *A Day Estivall: Essays on the Music, Poetry, and History of Scotland and England and Poems Previously Unpublished*. Aberdeen: Aberdeen University Press, 1990. 155-66; Wittig, Kurt. *The Scottish Tradition in Literature*. Edinburgh: Oliver and Boyd, 1958.

J. Scott Plaster

LOLLARDS. John *Wycliffe led the fourteenth century English movement of the Lollards that demanded ecclesiastical reform. The Lollards felt that the church in England had become so corrupt that it was virtually unredeemable. They believed that the only true way of life was biblical. The wealth and the power wielded by the clergy especially disturbed the Lollards. They pushed hard for reform based upon the poverty of Christ that was explicated by the Gospels.

The Lollards' rise to power in the fourteenth century coincided with a historical flux. At a time when the majority of believers were being decimated by warfare, disease, and poverty, the English clergy were living comfortably because they had amassed great wealth and even more power. After Wycliffe's death in 1384 the Lollards strengthened, and by 1395 almost one-half the populace of England was considered Lollard. The House of Lancaster repressed the Lollards in the fifteenth century. This caused their numbers to wane, but it also produced a small group of zealots. Since this sect had no real leadership, the movement fractured, and by the sixteenth century, they were essentially extinct.

While the Lollard movement did not directly lead to the Reformation, it did have a lasting legacy. The general populace placed the clergy under great scrutiny, which led to a lessening of the clerical abuses. The Church's ecclesiastical holdings and possessions were greatly reduced. The Lollards also insisted and saw to it that the Bible was translated into the vernacular and made available to the common folk.

SELECTED BIBLIOGRAPHY

Fletcher, Alan J. "John Mirk and the Lollards." *Medium Ævum* 56:2 (1987), 216-24; Hann, Ralph, III. "The Difficulty of Ricardian Prose Translation: The Case of the Lollards." *Modern Language Quarterly* 51:3 (1990), 319-40; Powell, Susan. "Lollards and Lombards: Late Medieval Bogeymen?" *Medium Ævum* 59:1 (1990), 133-39.

Robert T. Lambdin

LOPEZ DE AYALA, PEDRO (1332-1407). Pedro Lopez de Ayala wrote the often horrifying story *Crónica de Rey don Pedro* (A Spanish chronicle of Pedro the Cruel) in the mid-fourteenth century. Within it he narrates the events of Pedro's administration including his fights with his wife, mistress, friends, and enemies. The *Crónica* exposes the events that led to King Pedro's downfall and is important for its almost psychological analysis of how the actions of the participants affect each other. The story, although it is in many ways factual, dramatizes how an evil king is dealt with by divine justice. Lopez de Ayala used letters and dialogue to bring to life the harsh treatment felt by those around Pedro. He drew heavily on oral tradition surrounding the king and used the conventions of *romance and *history to elaborate on his sources. (*See* ***Chronicles and Annals.***)

SELECTED BIBLIOGRAPHY

Lopez de Ayala, Pedro. *Las Muertas del Rey Don Pedro.* Madrid: Alianza, 1971; Mirrer, Louise. *The Language of Evaluation: A Sociolinguistic Approach to the Story of Pedro el Cruel in Ballad and Chronicle.* Amsterdam: J. Benjamins, 1986.

Rebecca Stephens

LORD RANDAL. *Lord Randal* is one of the tragic domestic *ballads. Its earliest extant transcriptions date from the eighteenth century, although analogues in Italian existed in the early seventeenth. However, the song being originally English, it obviously predates these, and a number of scholars believe that it commemorates the fate of Ranulf of Chester, who lived in the fourteenth century. Others, following Garbáty and Entwistle, assign a fifteenth-century date. Regardless, the ballad follows the same question-and-answer format evident in *Edward, Edward, Riddles Wisely Expounded,* and others, and like *Edward, Edward* it delineates the stanzas on the pattern.

Lord Randal tells of a young man returning from hunting who is feeling ill. His mother questions him about the events during his absence and finds that he has met his "true love," eaten the fried eels she prepared for him, and seen his hawks and hounds die after consuming the leftovers. Not surprisingly, she concludes that he has been poisoned, with which he concurs. At this point the mother, rather than sparing any sympathy for her doomed son, asks him about his bequests of land and wealth to his various family members, which he then makes. To the evil beloved, however, in spite he leaves merely "hell and fire."

This ballad begs close comparison with *Edward, Edward,* with which it shares its format, the imminent death of the hero, and the materialistic mother concerned with inheritance rights. In concert with the anti-courtly sentiments of medieval balladry, this song also credits indulgence in the gentler emotions, a foolish choice in the untrustworthy ballad universe, with the demise of honor and nobility (symbolized by Randal's hawks and hounds). Thus *Lord Randal* demonstrates many of the conventions seminal in the study of the medieval ballads.

SELECTED BIBLIOGRAPHY

Bird, S. Elizabeth. "'Lord Randal' in Kent: The Meaning and Context of a Ballad Variant." *Folklore* 96:2 (1985), 248-52; McCarthy, Terence. "Robert Graves and 'Lord Randal.'" *Tennessee Folklore Society Bulletin* 48:2 (Summer 1982), 48-52; Paquin Robert. "'Le Testament du Garcon': Acadie." *Folklore* 91:2 (1980), 157-72.

Gwendolyn Morgan

LOUIS VI (1081-1137) Capetian, king of France (1108-1137). Louis VI was an extraordinarily brave soldier—intelligent, affable, avaricious, and widely admired by the peasantry, the commercial classes, and the clergy. The first popular Capetian, he was able to consolidate his Norman frontier in a series of conflicts with Henry I of England and steadily reduce the number and importance of his lesser vassals as far as the Loire. He granted charters to anyone willing to establish colonies in what were considered wastelands. He frequently supported the communes as well as his barons in their greed toward church lands. The Charter of Lorris that he issued was widely copied in town charters. Louis began the long alliance of the Capetian line with bourgeois interests.

As a protector of the church, Louis gained an access to the lands of his vassals. He opened careers at court to talented clergy and the bourgeois. When forced to compromise with the church over feudal patronage and investiture, Louis accomplished this with such grace that France's king became, in effect, the eldest son of the church. The first Capetian to intervene successfully outside his own lands, Louis defeated an alliance of Henry I of England and the Emperor Henry V, repelling a German invasion.

SELECTED BIBLIOGRAPHY

Belloc, Hilaire. *Miniatures of French History*. Peru, IL: Sherwood Sugden, 1990; Poly, Jean-Pierre. *The Feudal Transformation: 900-1200*. New York: Holmes & Meyer, 1990.

R. Churchill Curtis

LOUIS IX (1214-1270) Capetian, king of France (1226-1270). Louis IX's reign was during the golden age of medieval France. Considered the most chivalrous man of his age, Louis was looked upon as the ideal medieval king, believing that France must always be ethical in its dealings with its citizens as well as other nations. His promotion of justice brought him national support and made him the conciliator of Europe.

Louis was successful in adding territories to France; in 1242 he accomplished the final subjugation of Aquitaine and Toulouse by defeating a rebellion of southern barons in league with Henry III of England. In 1259 he was able to trade parcels of land with England, yielding Perigord and Limousin to England and gaining renunciation of all English claims to Normandy, Maine, and Poitou.

Louis was distinctly unsuccessful in taking up the Cross twice, once in an ill-conceived *crusade against Egypt in which he lost his entire army and had to be ransomed himself. Later he set out for Tunis and died there of pestilence, having accomplished nothing. The country was quite prosperous during his reign; it had to be in order to afford these two unsuccessful crusades. In this way

Louis demonstrates all of the follies that went into the crusades, and the effects that they had on his subjects.

SELECTED BIBLIOGRAPHY

Belloc, Hilaire. *Miniatures of French History*. Peru, IL: Sherwood Sugden, 1990.

R. Churchill Curtis

LOUIS XI (1423-1483) Capetian, king of France (1461-1483). Louis XI was a brilliant diplomat, well educated but feeble of body. He was the architect of royal absolutism and reconstruction. Louis perfected the governmental system begun under *Charles V, establishing the shape of the constitution, which lasted until 1789. He gained a good revenue source in the final recognition by the king of the *taille*, the *aides*, and the *gabelle*. The standing army was improved, especially in the emphasis placed upon artillery. Most important, Louis avoided many threatening situations by employing diplomacy and seldom raged war. Feudal anarchy and brigandage were stopped, and eventually a wise economic policy restored national prosperity despite grinding taxation. Anjou, Maine, and Provence were added to the Crown's land and ended Louis's concern about France's eastern frontier.

SELECTED BIBLIOGRAPHY

Belloc, Hilaire. *Miniatures of French History*. Peru, IL: Sherwood Sugden, 1990.

R. Churchill Curtis

LYRIC. In 1951 Arthur K. Moore lamented the difficulty of defining the lyric, noting that "To describe it in terms of length, content, point of view, form, origin, or manner of presentation is to invite a multitude of vitiating exceptions." Knowing this, perhaps it is best to approach the lyric through its etymological roots in the Greek word *lyra*, a stringed musical instrument, so that on its most basic level we know that the lyric must have songlike qualities that help distinguish lyric poetry from narrative and dramatic poetry. In fact, Middle English poets do not appear to have used the term "lyrics"; instead, they sometimes called their works "songs." The word "lyric" did not appear in this context until it was used by sixteenth-century Elizabethan literary critics. Like a song, the Middle English lyric poem is usually short and tends to express strong feeling, although not necessarily the emotion of the lyricist. Some longer lyrics have narrative cores, and critics have differed over their inclusion in the lyric genre. In general, though, the Middle English lyric can be distinguished from the Middle English narrative poem in that its central concern is not to narrate an event so much as to express an emotion or idea.

The Middle English lyric occurred between the twelfth and the early sixteenth centuries, although the lyrics do not flourish until the thirteenth through the fifteenth centuries. The earliest lyrics were shorter and frequently accompanied by musical notations, indicating that they were intended to be sung or danced. These early lyrics are usually anonymous and based on oral culture that is not part of the courtly tradition. It was not until the latter part of the fourteenth century, when the more complex French lyric modes, such as the *ballade, were introduced, that lyrics began to move more toward a written tradition. In the last decades of the fourteenth century the lyrics changed in style and content, becoming more complex in nature and more easily attributable to a specific poet. Today there are several hundred Middle English lyrics remaining. There are at least four important sources for the Middle English lyric: *Anglo-Saxon verse, Latin Christian and secular traditions, French verse, and the European *minstrel tradition.

Anglo-Saxon verse consisted of the *scop, accompanying himself on a musical instrument, singing heroic narrative poetry with a four-beat line, frequent alliteration, and a *caesura. Other Anglo-Saxon antecedents are the occasional use of stanzaic form, meter (the two stressed syllables in the short line), and rhyme technique. These elements begin to appear in Middle English poetry as early as the twelfth century. The Anglo-Saxon elegies "The *Wanderer" and "The *Ruin" contain some metrical similarities to Middle English lyrics.

Another source for the Middle English lyric is the Latin Christian tradition, particularly the devotional writings, sermons, Scriptures, liturgy, Psalms, commentaries, and hymns. Many of these writings, although prose, had an important impact on the content, imagery, and language of Middle English lyrics. Rosemary Woolf traced the English religious lyric directly back to the Latin devotional movement, as practiced by St. *Anselm, archbishop of Canterbury (1033-1109), St. *Bernard of Clairvaux (1090-1153), and St. *Francis of Assisi (1181-1226). The devotional movement emphasized the meditation on Christ's passion and the Virgin's joys and sorrows. Many of the Latin hymns fall under the category of the *planctus Mariae*, or the complaint of Mary at the site of Christ's crucifixion, a theme that appears in the Middle English lyric. In addition to the influential content, Latin hymns contain regular meter, rhyme, and stanza form as far back as the fourth century, and several Middle English stanza forms resemble Latin stanzas. In the latter half of the medieval period the lyric, while still influenced by the Latin hymn in terms of content and expression, became more based on the poet's original designs for meter and form.

In addition to the Latin Christian tradition, there are Latin secular traditions that occasionally appear in the Middle English lyric. Latin secular lyrics cover a wide range of topics, from the profane to the topical and satirical. Two of these traditions particularly stand out. The first is the satire on women, which first appears in Middle English around the twelfth century. While based initially on religious doctrine, the debate about women became incorporated into courtly literature. The second element from the Latin secular tradition is the drinking song, sung by wandering scholars, which can be found in the Latin of the anonymous *Carmina Burana*, a thirteenth-century manuscript from the Bavarian Benediktbeuren monastery, for example.

A third major source for the Middle English lyric is the French lyric, which began to appear in England after the Norman Conquest in 1066. The French lyric tradition developed from yearly May dances during which dancers moved in a circle and responded to a singer's verses with jointly sung refrains. These early French lyrics were called *caroles*, dances accompanied by singing. The syllabics and end rhyme of French poetry were an important influence on the Middle English lyric. French genres frequently found in Middle English poetry include the *chanson d'aventure* and the *pastourelle*, and French forms include the ballade, the *rondel, the carol, the burden, and the *envoy. For more detailed descriptions of these elements, see the discussion of form later in this entry. Another important element of French lyric influence was the *courtly love idea, in which a man serves a distant or unattainable woman and suffers mental and physical anguish until his desire to win her is fulfilled. The French poet Jean *Froissart, who came to England and enjoyed the patronage of Queen Philippa from 1361 to 1369, is a recognized influence on the lyrics of Geoffrey *Chaucer. Froissart's 199 lyrics include *pastourelles, chansons royales*, ballades, and *rondeaux*, many of which express the courtly love ideas that clearly influenced lyrics like Chaucer's *Complaint to His Lady*. In some Middle English lyrics the secular worship of the courtly lady is transformed into the worship of the Virgin Mary.

A fourth important source for the Middle English lyric was the music of the wandering minstrels, variously called the *troubadours (from Provence), the *trouvéres (from northern France), or the *minnesinger (from Germany), who traveled through Europe from the ninth to the thirteenth centuries. The second half of the twelfth century was the golden age of the troubadours. The music of the troubadours and trouvéres developed from the French May dances described earlier. These singers would either accompany themselves with an instrument, sing unaccompanied, or be accompanied by an assistant, or juglar. The lyrics of the troubadours were written for entertainment of the aristocracy (*chanson courtoise*), but they contained elements of the seasonal folk dances, particularly in their frequent allusions to spring. Troubadour poetry emphasized technique, utilizing over eight hundred different meters. Forms created by the troubadours include the ballade (dance song) and the *pastourelle*. There are over four hundred identified Italian, French, Spanish, and Portuguese troubadours, but none who wrote in English. Their poetry was intended for the aristocracy, and the aristocracy in England up through the thirteenth century, when the troubadours disappeared, still spoke French. Their influence in England was facilitated by the marriage of Eleanor of Guienne (daughter of William of Poitou, "the father of the troubadours") to the English *Henry II.

During her reign from 1154 to 1206, French troubadours came to perform at the English court. Troubadour lyrics frequently focused on the difficulties of love and contrasted the speaker's sadness with the promise of new life inherent in spring, a subject that is echoed in Middle English lyrics.

These four sources for the Middle English lyric combined to provide it with certain identifiable characteristics: lyrics were more public than private, they frequently contained a nature motif, they demonstrated certain elements of style and sound, and they frequently appeared in recognizable forms. Scholars of Middle English poetry generally agree that the lyric's purpose was more public than private. Lewis and Nancy Owen argued that in most poems, "we do not feel that we are being introduced to a uniquely personal perception of experience, but rather being reminded of a commonly shared experience whose nature and value are already established and familiar." In many ways the lyrics are more conventional than individual. While the lyrics generally are not expressions of individual "selves," Rosemary Woolf argued that the poets were aware of their public role, of "being watched," as she put it. The persona speaking in most Middle English lyrics is usually a well-recognized biblical or social figure, rather than the poet. The majority of the lyrics are anonymous, a situation that results from a sense during this period that it was not important to know who wrote them. Although most Middle English lyrics are public in nature, in the latter half of the period some poets occasionally wrote poems that are more self-expressive, particularly Chaucer, Thomas *Hoccleve, William *Dunbar, John Lydgate, and Robert *Henryson.

Another characteristic of Middle English lyrics is that many of them begin with or contain some specific reference to nature, an influence from the troubadour songs. At times these lyrics are just a joyous celebration of the changing of the seasons, such as *Sumer Is Icumen In, but other times nature is an important part of an overall symbolic motif. The famous secular lyric *Alysoun begins with the setting "Bitweene Merch and Averil, / When spray biginneth to springe," but the same imagery of spring may be used in a religious lyric celebrating the Virgin Mary.

The Middle English lyric demonstrates certain elements of style, such as aureation, *allegory, word play, and vibrant language, and certain elements of sound, such as repetition, rhyme, and alliteration. In terms of style, the medieval lyric is sometimes marked by "aureation," extreme stylistic ornamentation, particularly by Latin phrases used in praise of the Virgin Mary. Aureate verse particularly makes use of alliteration and assonance and coins new words. An example of aureate verse is Dunbar's *Hale! Sterne Superne*, which juxtaposes the line "*Ave! Maria, gracia plena*" with "Haile! freshe floure feminine," containing both the Latin ornamentation and alliteration.

Another characteristic of the lyric style of this period is allegory, appearing at times in the form of a *riddle, as in *I Syng of a Myden, or as a joke, as in the poem in which the speaker lay all night by a rose, which he dared not steal, and yet he bore the "flour" away (i.e., he deflowered the "rose"). This allegory is made more ambiguous by the frequent association of the rose image with the Virgin Mary. Symbolism and metaphor are related elements that frequently occur in Middle English poems. For example, April frequently appears in poems as a symbol of new life or regeneration. The many levels of meaning may lead to the use of irony and paradox, both of which are at work in the devotional *Now Gooth Sunne under Wode, in which the wood represents both the cross of Christ and a forest. Lyrics also frequently employ puns, such as the word "makeles" in *I Syng of a Myden*, where it means both matchless and mate-less.

Vibrant language is another interesting aspect of style in the Middle English lyric. The language varies from colloquial and occasionally crude to courtly and polished. In a boisterous Christmas carol by James Ryman, for example, the speaker complains about the food and drink, noting the "stinking fishe not worthe a louse." The words of a lyric may be shockingly realistic or gently euphemistic, as is much of the courtly language introduced into the love lyric around the end of the fourteenth century. Macaronic verse (verse combining two or more languages) clearly demonstrates the comingling of French, Latin, and English and the variety of sources for the Middle English lyric. The combination of Latin with English for religious poems adds a dignity and seriousness to a lyric like Ryman's fifteenth-century nativity poem *Angelus inquit pastoribus* in lines 3 and 4: "Upon a night an aungell bright / *Pastoribus apparuit*" (appeared to the shepherds). In comic verse, the combination of languages can create a nonsense effect for satire.

Middle English lyrics also utilized certain elements of sound. One very important element of sound is repetition, which may occur in single words, in lines, as a verse for a song, or as incremental repetition. As a type of repetition, parallelism (or anaphora) is a common technique, as demonstrated in the poem "Wanne mine eyhnen misten," where the speaker describes what happens when he dies in a series of "when . . . then" statements detailing the body's decay. Alliteration is another important sound element, as in the first line of the complaint against blacksmiths, describing them as "Swarte-smekyd smethes, smateryd wyth smoke." Assonance is also used for emphasis, as in the line from *Alysoun* describing "hire browe brounc." End rhyme is also very common in Middle English lyrics, and a kind of slant rhyme sometimes appears.

In addition to displaying certain characteristics of style and sound, the Middle English lyric also appears in recognizable forms. In early Middle English lyrics meter, which varies widely, seems to be determined by counting the number of stressed accents rather than the number of syllables. This is a holdover from *Old English poetry. Another holdover is the caesura, or pause, that sometimes appears. Many early Middle English verse lines contain four stressed accents, regardless of the number of syllables present. The emphasis on counting stresses only was eventually replaced by the conventional "foot" measure, based on the model of classical prosody. Line breaks in poems tend to occur at the point where the speaker would pause.

Stanza forms vary from the simple pairs of rhyming couplets (*aabb*) or quatrains of alternating rhymes (*abab*) to the more complex stanza forms of the rhyme-royal and ballade. In longer lyrics stanza breaks may be marked by a change in speaker or a repetition of a line.

Some very frequent poetic forms were the ballade, the rondel, the carol, and the rhyme-royal. The ballade should not be confused with the *ballad, which is most frequently a narrative poem. The traditional form of the ballade is three octave stanzas, rhyming *ababbcbc*, with an optional envoy rhymed *bcbc*. The envoy (from the French *envoi*) is a conventional address to a patron or person of importance that repeats the refrain line and consists of four lines usually rhyming *bcbc*. Ballade stanza length can vary from seven to ten lines, and the line length may vary. Another element of the ballade is the refrain, which contains the motif of the poem and occurs after each stanza. An example of the ballade is Chaucer's "Balade de bon conseyl."

Another frequent form, the rondel, which is a variant of the *rondeau*, may have been introduced as a stanza form by Chaucer from the French. While fourteen lines are most common, the length of the poem can vary from seven to fourteen lines. A two-line refrain occurs throughout the poem and frequently appears at the very end. The most common rhyme scheme is *ABbaab ABabba AB*, containing only two rhymes with the capitalized rhymes as repeated words. An example is Chaucer's Saint Valentine roundel in *The Parliament of Fowls*, which begins "Now welcome somer, with thy sonne softe."

The carol, which appeared in the late fourteenth century, is now thought of as a religious lyric, but it was originally defined primarily by its form rather than by its content, so it may also be secular. The carol includes a regular stanza form and a burden after each stanza, which functions as a refrain but is also found at the beginning of the poem. The most common rhyme scheme for the stanza is *aaab*, with the last line rhyming with the burden's *bb* scheme. Originally, carols were not associated with Christmas and only came to have that connection later in the medieval period. Christmas religious carols focus on the Nativity, while secular carols focus more frequently on the festivals of the season. An example of a Christmas carol is *Lullay, Lullay, Litel Child*, which has a four-line stanza rhyming *aaab* and a burden rhyming *ab*. In this carol the speaker is mankind and the lyric is addressed to Christ. Some five hundred or so Middle English carols remain, less than one hundred of which are secular. In Middle English the word "carol" is used to mean "ring-dance." It is intended to be sung as an accompaniment to dancing, and probably comes from the French *carole*, a ring-dance that can be traced back several centuries earlier in France.

The rhyme-royal is a fourth popular form during this period. Rhyme-royal consists of a seven-line iambic pentameter stanza with the rhyme *ababbcc*. Chaucer, William Dunbar, Thomas Hoccleve, and John Lydgate all used rhyme royal.

The imagery of nature, the public purpose, and the elements of style, sound and form all appear in the two most frequently cited types of Middle English lyric: the secular and sacred. While these are the traditional divisions into which lyrics are assigned, some contemporary critics point out that this distinction is artificial and reductive because most lyrics contain elements of both. Ironically, the Franciscans occasionally used the secular lyric in sermons and noted down favorite secular lyrics in the margins of sacred texts. Priests also used preexisting secular lyrics and wrote religious words for them so that their congregations would remember their message. Many of the early secular lyrics seem to have been recorded in fragments, especially the popular lyrics (the *chansons populaires*). There are also courtly lyrics (*chansons courtois*), which appear in complete form later in the period. In general, the purposes of the secular and sacred lyrics may be described as Raymond Oliver classified them: to celebrate (an occasion or season), to persuade (for religious or courtship purposes), or to define (a widely accepted position or doctrine, or a state of being).

Most medieval lyrics are religious, rather than secular, at a ratio of four to one. The reasons for this are obvious, since most copying of manuscripts was done by religious orders and, in most cases, secular lyrics served no practical purpose for the religious orders and thus were less likely to be preserved. In fact, many of the religious lyrics exist in multiple manuscripts, but secular lyrics are usually found only in one. In some cases, such as the songs that celebrate ancient holidays, the nature of the lyric was one of pagan influences and thus was inappropriate for monastic copying. David L. Jeffrey described the Middle English religious lyric as "more often physical than metaphysical," "immediate than reflective," "characterized by emotion rather than thought," and intended to evoke an "identification of the subject with the object of the poem." Many of the religious lyrics are practical in nature and were composed in English as a way of instructing the illiterate populace in religious belief. The lyric may have been used as part of religious ceremony, outside the Latin liturgy, as part of religious drama, as part of church festivals, or in private devotional practices. Approximately 10 percent of Middle English lyrics are translations, including poems by William Herebert, James Ryman, and John Lydgate. In the church service itself, poems used in preaching can be found in collections of Latin sermons (such as the Franciscan preaching book *Fasciculus Morum*, which is written in Latin but includes English lyrics). Some of these use mnemonic devices to help the congregation remember a point of religious doctrine. Religious lyrics were also used in hymns during the services.

Because sacred lyrics use a wide variety of forms, they can best be described by content rather than form. Rosemary Woolf designated four popular categories: poems on Christ's Passion, poems on death, poems on the Virgin and her joys, and poems on the compassion of the Blessed Virgin.

Poems on Christ's Passion are designed to create in the mind of the layperson a visual image of Christ suffering in his human form and to evoke through that image strong feelings of compassion and love. The earliest important collection of these poems was found in John of Grimestone's preaching book. The speaking voice in the poems on the Passion can be that of a mediator exhorting the reader to see Christ crucified or of Christ himself urging the reader to "Loke man to my back hou yt ys ybeten, / Loke to my sydyn wat blod it havyn iletyn." These passion poems have a connection with the secular complaint tradition, in which the speaker complains of his treatment by his beloved or laments the state of the world or his own particular state. In some of the Passion poems, Christ is analogous to a lover-knight, with whom the speaker is in love. Couched in the terms of the love poem, these lyrics express the idea that the love of Christ is the ultimate love, for which one speaker says, "I sygh and sob both day and nyght for one so fayre of hew"--that "one" being Christ.

A second type of sacred poem is the poem on death. These poems attempt to create an image in the mind of the reader of the appearance of a dying person and the reality of physical decay in order to provoke a response of fear. The fear caused by these "signs of death," or *Proprietates Mortis,* is intended to bring the reader/listener to salvation. These poems are related to the penitential movement, which emphasized the fear of death to move Christians to repentance and a more religious life. A good example is the fifteenth-century poem in which the speaker explains that he now must "leeve liif that lyvest in welthe." In the persona of a wealthy man who has now died, the speaker says, "I was ful fair, now am I foul." His fair flesh "bigynneth forto stynke," and "wormis" find him as their "mete" and their "drinke."

Other less graphic poems appeal to the reader through well-known imagery of the wheel of Fortuna or the *Dance of Death, in which people of all social ranks eventually join the dance. Other death poems take the form of apostrophes to death, as in James Ryman's *O Cruell Deth Paynfull and Smert*, in which the speaker asks, "Why art thou so cruell to man / Of hym no man grisly to make?" Also in this category may be included the poem of contempt of the world or the *contemptus mundi* tradition, which expresses the Middle English anxiety about the transitory nature of this world. This type of complaint frequently uses the *Ubi sunt* topos, which sets up a series of parallel "where are" clauses that demonstrate how all material things pass away. An example of this tradition is the late thirteenth-century "Where beth they, beforen us weren, / Houndes ladden and havekes beren, / And hadden feld and wode?" which conjures up images of the lords and ladies enjoying the material pleasures during life but suffering the pangs of hell for their enjoyment of comforts. Poems on death also frequently use natural images of winter and sunset to emphasize change.

The third type of religious poetry, poems on the Virgin and her joys, includes poems that praise the Virgin (frequently using secular traditions), poems that celebrate the Virgin's five joys (the Annunciation, the Nativity, the Epiphany, Easter, her Death, her Assumption), and poems that, like lullabies, picture the Virgin with the Christ child. Poems that praise the Virgin frequently focus on her beauty in ways that are evocative of French love lyrics, using traditional metaphors, such as the rose and lily, as in the fifteenth-century carol that has as its burden "Ther is no rose of swych vertu / As is the rose that bare Jesu."

Poems on the compassion of the Blessed Virgin frequently place Mary at the site of the cross: "They leyde hym dede me before, / Me thouth for sorw my lyfe was lore." The *Planctus Mariae*, the complaint of Mary, shows how her own suffering has brought her to an understanding and compassion for others. At other times she is described weeping over the Christ child as she foresees his death. A well-known example is the poem written around 1400 that begins with the speaker's description of Mary's appearance to him "In a tabernacle of a toure / As I stode musing on the mone." Mary proceeds to describe her role as mother both of Christ and of mankind.

Although there are fewer secular lyrics, they demonstrate the same interesting variety seen in the sacred poems. Most of the secular lyrics occur after the 1370s, when English was more frequently used at court, but there are some scattered early secular lyrics. The earlier lyrics focus more on daily celebrations or activities, such as drinking songs. These early secular lyrics are usually shorter and more straight-forward than the later secular lyrics, which are sometimes called "art lyrics" for their intricate artistry. There are approximately three hundred of the later courtly love lyrics, which celebrate (or satirize) the beauty of a woman, plead a lover's case, or complain against a beloved's hard-heartedness or fickleness. Chaucer is the first great Middle English court poet, and he and those who followed in his footsteps used the conventional rhetoric of the aristocratic tradition. Most of these court poems were written for entertainment purposes, as opposed to the sacred poems, which were written for more practical purposes. Chaucer's *Parliament of Fowls* is an example of this genre. Most critics agree that the remaining secular lyrics must be a very small percentage of what once existed. Among the earlier secular lyrics are political poems and poems of social commentary. Many other secular poems are also taken from French genres, such as the *reverdie*, the *pastourelle*, the *chanson d'aventure*, and the *alba*.

The political poems were written primarily between 1250 and 1350. One of the first political lyrics was the satiric "Richard, thah thou be ever trichard [deceiver]," written about 1265, which celebrates Simon de Montfort's defeat and capture of Richard, earl of Cornwall, in 1264. Another interesting political lyric serves as a warning to "be ware and be no fool" and to "Thenke apon the ax, and of the stool [execution block]" that were "scharp" and "hard" in "The iiii yere of kyng Richard." John Audelay's early fifteenth-century poem beginning "It is the best, crely and late, / Uche mon kepe his owne state" is an interesting poem in which the speaker urges others to stay in their own estate.

The poem of social commentary frequently takes the form of a satire. A well-known example is the satire against the blacksmiths, "Swarte-smekyd smethes smateryd wyth smoke," in which the speaker complains about the noise and fumes created by these men, whom he says "Dryve me to deth wyth den [din] of here dyntes [blows]." A very popular target for satire was the friar, whose corruption is pointed out in the lyric in which the narrator notes that though he has "yved now fourty yers," he has never seen "fatter men about the neres [kidneys] . . . then are these frers." A third frequent subject for satire was the role of women, as reflected in poems about the *querelle des femmes*, such as the *Notbrowne Mayde*, which debates the merits of women. Another type of social poem is the poem on the power of money. An example is the fourteenth-century lyric *Sir Peny*, which describes how "In erth there ys a lityll thyng / That reynes as a grete kyng." That little thing is "Sir Peny." The power of money is also illustrated by a *Harleian manuscript poem that relays the difficult life of the poor farmer who is forced to pay heavy taxes.

The *reverdie* is one of the genres borrowed from French sources for the later court poetry. *Reverdie* literally means "greening again" or song of spring; thus it is a lyric celebrating new life that comes with the return of spring. In some cases the *reverdie* occurs only as the opening for another type of poem. A well-known example of the *reverdie* is the opening lines of *Sumer Is I-Cumen In*.

The *pastourelle* is another secular genre that comes from French sources. This lyric takes the form of a dialogue in which a rural woman, usually a shepherdess, is wooed by an aristocratic man. The man is frequently a poet, who may be successful or unsuccessful in his suit. The dialogue may be broken off by the appearance of a male relative of the woman. As this genre developed, it contributed to the later Elizabethan pastoral lyric.

A similar genre from French sources is the *chanson d'aventure* (song of love-adventure). This lyric is usually a poem about knightly love in which the speaker travels into the country during the springtime and encounters a lady, with whom he carries on a wooing dialogue. An interesting example of this genre that uses readers' expectations to provide a surprise ending is *"Nou Sprinkes the Sprai."

The *alba* originated in the French vernacular verse of the twelfth century. The *alba*, or dawn song, is sung by a lover whose secret tryst with a beloved is interrupted by the rising of the sun, which signals the end of their meeting. As Gale Sigal pointed out, the word *alba* means "white" in the Old Provencal, which is associated with the brightness of dawn. The *alba*, unlike some of the other traditional French forms, provides an opportunity for a female speaker, although the poet is usually male. The first Middle English *alba* is found in Chaucer's longer narrative poem *Troylus and Criseyde*. According to Sigal, the *alba*'s characteristics are its theme of separation, its use of dialogue, a refrain containing the word *alba*, and the use of a watchman figure.

Most of the poets who wrote the various types of secular and religious lyrics remain anonymous. In some cases the anonymity is a result of loss of information about the writers, but more often the authors of the earlier lyrics remain unknown because these lyrics were not written in a culture that expected poetic expressions of an individual's emotions and ideas. In the early part of the period, most of the lyricists were friars or monks, but as the years progressed, more and more lay people, such as professional scriveners and minstrels, began writing.

The twelfth-century St. Godric (d. 1170) is the earliest known Middle English lyricist; at various times he was a merchant, religious pilgrim, and hermit near Durham. Three hymns are attributed to him, including the devotional *Sainte Marye Virgine*, which is addressed to the Virgin Mary, asking her to receive him, defend him, and cleanse him from sin so that he can be brought to God. Mary reportedly appeared to Godric and "taught him words and music." His second fragment of verse is a four-line hymn that came to him in a vision of his deceased sister. The third lyric, *Cantus Sancto Nicholao* is the result of a vision in which St. Nicholas appeared. Godric's lyrics are written in roughly four-stress lines.

Another early lyricist may have been King *Canute (d. 1035), whose *Song of Canute* was recorded by Thomas of Ely around 1167 in his *Liber Eliensis*. According to this source, the four lyric lines were composed by King Canute while listening to monks singing along the banks of the River Ouse. The lyric describes King Canute overhearing the monks' voices and ordering his knights to row nearer the land so that "here we thes muneches saeng."

From 60 to 90 percent of the thirteenth and early fourteenth-century lyrics were written by the Franciscan friars, sometimes as direct translations of Latin verse, at other times as devotionals or tools for preaching. The Franciscan movement developed in southern Europe in the late twelfth and early thirteenth centuries and focused on a devotional emphasis within an Augustinian theology. Middle English lyrics began to appear in significant numbers around 1240, approximately twenty years after the beginnings of the Franciscan friars in England, whose movements among the common folk would have exposed them to secular lyrics.

Some of the more well known friars during this period were Thomas of Hales (c. 1275), William Herebert (d. 1333), and John Grimestone (ca. 1372). Thomas of Hales's *Love Song* to Jesus (thirteenth century) is one of the first Middle English devotionals and combines the secular with the sacred through the image of Christ as a lover. This lyric, intended to be sung by a nun, praises virginity and love for Christ. The poem asks, in *Ubi sunt* format, "Hwer is Paris and Heleyne / That weren so bryht and feyre on bleo [appearance]?" Hale contrasts the mutability of secular love with the permanance and power of the love of Christ. Herebert's work survives in seventeen lyrics, most of which are paraphrases of Latin hymns. A fourteenth-century Franciscan, Herebert wrote seventeen hymn translations, and his "What ys he, thys lordling, that cometh vrom the vyht?" is a paraphrase of Isaiah 63:1-7. John Grimestone, a Norfolk Franciscan, compiled a preaching book around 1372 that which contains almost 250 lyric pieces. Preaching books, which were Latin prose manuals with alphabetical lists of sermon topics, frequently included both secular and religious lyrics interspersed with the prose entries. The number of English lyrics included in Grimestone's book is unusual for this period.

Richard *Rolle of Hampole (c. 1290-1349) was also a poet in the mystical tradition. Born in Yorkshire, Rolle was briefly a student at Oxford and then at nineteen became a hermit, continuing to travel for a while, and finally dying at Hampole. Rolle expressed his belief in *The Form of Living* (c. 1342) that it is sinful to "syng" and "lufe" secular songs; thus he wrote religious lyrics that focus on God's love and the crucifixion of Christ. Rolle expresses these ideas through his own mystical experience and through instructions for women in religious orders, such as his manual, *The Boke Maad of Rycharde Hampole to an Ankeresse*, intended for the nun Margaret Kirkby.

Geoffrey Chaucer (c. 1344-1400), although better known for his narrative poetry, was also a skillful lyric poet. Critical response to his lyric poetry has been negligible until the recent revival of interest in the last decade and a half. In his recent study of Chaucer's lyrics Jay Rudd argued that although Chaucer's earlier lyrics were more conventional, over time they became more individual expressions and merit reevaluation. Chaucer probably introduced ballades, roundels, and the rhyme-royal stanza into English. Only about twenty-two of his lyrics remain, including the well-known *To Rosemounde*, *Truth*, *Complaint to His Purse*, and *Lak of Stedfastnesse*, although there are at least twelve lyrical segments in his longer works, such as "Hyd, Absolon, Thy Gilte Tresses Clere" in the prologue to *The *Legend of Good Women*. Jay Rudd argued that a handful of Chaucer's poems "qualify him as one of the great lyric poets in the English language." Julia Boffey has recently noted that in addition to introducing the French forms, Chaucer also influenced the development of the Middle English lyric through his presentation of general situations, rhetorical strategies, and rhymes that were imitated by later lyric poets.

Thomas *Hoccleve wrote thirty-eight poems altogether, including both lyrics and longer poetic works, from 1402 to 1422. His lyrics cover a range of topics, from his experiences during his thirty-five years as a clerk in the Privy Seal office to humorous requests for money and hymns to the Virgin. The four lyrics for which he is particularly well known are *How to Die*, *Mother of God*, *The Letter of Cupid*, and *Prologue and a Miracle of the Blessed Virgin*. The satirical poem that begins "Of my lady well me rejoise I may!" turns upside down the conventions of female beauty in lines such as "Hir comly body shape as a footbal, / And she singeth full like a papejay." Hoccleve suffered from mental illness around 1416 but appears to have recovered over the next five years. Hoccleve's admiration for Chaucer is inscribed in the now famous lines "O Maister dere, and Fader reverent! / My Maister Chaucer, floure of eloquence."

John Lydgate (c. 1370-1450), once considered one of the most important fifteenth-century poets during his lifetime and for 150 years after his death, has suffered adverse criticism of his work and has only recently come under reappraisal. Born around Suffolk, he became a Benedictine monk and spent most of his life at the abbey of Bury Saint Edmunds. About 150,000 of his verse lines are still in existence. Some of his most effective are his poems on the Passion, which conjure up clear visual images of Christ's suffering, including *The Dolerous Pyte of Crystes Passioun*, a poem using the Christ/knight analogy. In this lyric Christ says, "I schal be your Trusty champioun." In a ballade Lydgate uses the *Ubi sunt* motif in a series of questions about famous historical figures, which ends each stanza with the line "All stand on chaunge as a midsomer rose."

John Audelay (early 1400s) wrote fifty-five extant poems, twenty-five of which are carols, in one manuscript dated 1426. Audelay was a blind priest in Shropshire, whose poems contain some personal references in their mention of his blindness and his name. His *O Ihesu Crist Hongyng on Cros* is an example of the lyrics on the passion, and his *Lady! Helpe, Jesu! Mercy* is an example of a poem about the fear of death. Most of his lyrics are penitential in nature and use a variety of meters and verse forms.

Charles d'Orleans (1394-1465) was French, the nephew of King Charles VI of France and a prisoner in England from 1415 to 1440 after his capture at Agincourt. He is well known for his ballades and rondels and for his *vers de société*. He wrote a series of love poems, including *For Dedy Liif, My Livy Deth I Wite*, a ballade, which explores the paradoxical nature of his "living death" as the result of the death of his love, and the humorous *My Ghostly Fader, I Me Confess*, which is written in the form of a confession based on a kiss he "stale" (stole) and now vows to "restore." He, like Chaucer and William Dunbar, is considered a court poet.

James Ryman (late 1400s) was a Franciscan who has been credited with writing 166 lyrics, some of which are Latin hymn translations and 119 of which are carols. Ryman is believed to have penned a quarter of all carols written up to 1550. Ryman's work covers a wide range from the folksy *Farewele! Advent, Christmas Is Come* (noted earlier for its complaint about the fish) to his serious lyrics on religious subjects.

Robert *Henryson (1420s or 1430s- c. 1505) is considered the most important of the "Scottish Chaucerians" (*see **Scottish Literature***) in the late fifteenth century. Little is known about his life, although his death is mentioned in William Dunbar's *Lament for the Makars*, and some city records indicate that he was a schoolmaster in Dunfermline's Benedictine abbey school. His name is attached to several lyrics, including the interesting *Robene and Makyne*, described as a "pastoral ballad" written in Middle Scots. He is also known for *The Moral Fables*, *The Testament of Cresseid*, and *Orpheus and Eurydice*.

William Dunbar (1465?-1550) was a well-known "Scottish Chaucerian" who wrote approximately eighty shorter poems, both religious and secular. Quite a few of his secular poems are based on his association with the court of the Scottish James IV, from whom he received a pension between 1500 and 1513. Dunbar received B.A. and M.A. degrees from the University of St. Andrews and around 1504 took religious orders. Among his most frequently anthologized lyrics are the aureate *Hale! Sterne Superne. Hale! In Eterne* and the allegorical *Done Is a Battell on the Dragon Blak!* Dunbar acknowledged Chaucer and Lydgate as his models. He is particularly known for his satires and allegories. Arthur K. Moore argued that Dunbar, as the last of the Middle English lyric poets, serves as a transition to the Renaissance lyricists.

As the preceding discussion makes apparent, the most well-known Middle English lyricists were men. The two best known Middle English women writers, *Julian of Norwich and Margery *Kempe, wrote in prose, and two other well-known medieval women writers, Christine de Pisan and Marie de France, wrote in French and had their works translated into English during this period. However, a recent study of Middle English women's writing by Alexandra Barratt argued that there were women lyricists during this period. Barratt discussed the fifteenth-century Juliana Berners, whose verse translation of *The Book of Hunting* is more practical than lyrical. More interestingly, in chapter 16 Barratt argued that there is good reason to believe that some anonymous fifteenth-century poems were written by women. In three cases poems were specifically ascribed to women: *A Hymn to Venus* is credited to Queen Elizabeth (wife of Edward IV), and two hymns to the Virgin are attributed to "an holy anchoress of Mansfield" and to Eleanor Percy, duchess of Buckingham. In addition to these attributions, there are other poems that Barratt felt may have been written by women because of their treatment of the topic and their tone, including two poems previously attributed to Chaucer, *The Assembly of Ladies* and *The *Floure and the Leaf.*

Middle English lyrics appear in a variety of places. Among the most common sources are the collections of sermons, the miscellanies, compilations of devotional materials, and books of hymns. These collections were compiled by scribes or friars who usually were not the authors of the lyrics. The most famous manuscript that includes Middle English lyrics is the British Library Harley manuscript (*see **Harley Lyrics***), which contains thirty-two lyrics, twenty-four of a religious nature and eight that are secular. The Harley manuscript, which includes lyrics (and prose) in English, French, and Latin, was copied at the Herefordshire priory between approximately 1250 and 1340. The anonymous lyrics are in several different dialects. To get a sense of what is contained in the Harley manuscript, see G. L. Brook's edition of *The Harley Lyrics* (Manchester, 1956) or N. R. Ker's *Facsimile of British Museum MS. Harley 2253* (London, 1965). Other important collections (of a religious nature) are found in John of Grimestone's preaching-book mentioned earlier and the late fourteenth-century Vernon Manuscript. Lyrics also appear in some of the mystery plays, such as the lullaby *Lulla, lulla, thow litel tine child* lyric that appears in the Coventry nativity play and poems in the Towneley shepherd and Nativity plays (*see **Drama**, **Medieval***) addressed to the Christ child. The drinking song of Noah's wife and her gossips in the Noah play is another popular example of a dramatic use of secular lyric.

Early critical response to the Middle English lyric was limited because the Middle English lyric was considered less sophisticated and worthy than its continental contemporaries. Among the earliest studies were Felix E. Schelling's *The English Lyric* (1913) and Edward Bliss Reed's *English Lyrical Poetry: From Its Origins to the Present Time* (1914). In the 1930s Carleton Brown's *English Lyrics of the XIIIth Century* and Richard L. Greene's *The Early English Carols* were among the first scholarly collections. *The Index of Middle English Verse*, compiled by Carleton Brown and R. H. Robbins (1943), provided a list of manuscripts, which has since been updated. Other important early collections include G. L. Brook's *The Harley Lyrics: The Middle English Lyrics of MS Harley 2253* (1948), Arthur K. Moore's *The Secular Lyric in Middle English*

(1951, reprinted 1970), and R. H. Robbins's *Secular Lyrics of the XIVth and XVth Centuries* (1952).

Other anthologies followed these early editions, including R. T. Davies' *Medieval English Lyrics: A Critical Anthology* (1964), Robert D. Stevick's *One Hundred Middle English Lyrics* (1964, revised and reissued in 1994), and Lewis and Nancy Owen's *Middle English Poetry: An Anthology* (1971). In 1982 George Pace and Alfred David edited the Variorum edition of Chaucer's *Minor Poems*.

Critical appreciation of the sacred Middle English lyric began to escalate after the publication of Stephen Manning's *Wisdom and Number: Toward a Critical Appraisal of the Middle English Religious Lyric* (1962). Other works that examine the lyric in its religious context include Rosemary Woolf's *The English Religious Lyric in the Middle Ages* (1968), Sarah Appleton Weber's *Theology and Poetry in the Middle English Lyric* (1969), Douglas Gray's *Themes and Images in the Medieval English Religious Lyric* (1972), David L. Jeffrey's *The Early English Lyric and Franciscan Spirituality* (1975), Patrick Diehl's *The Medieval European Religious Lyric: An Ars Poetica* (1985), and Siegfried Wenzel's *Preachers, Poets, and the Early English Lyric* (1986).

Other useful critical appraisals of the lyric appear in books and articles. Among the books are Raymond Oliver's *Poems without Names* (1970), Edmund Reiss's *The Art of the Middle English Lyric* (1972), Lois Ebin's edited collection of essays *Vernacular Poetics in the Middle Ages* (1984), Daniel J. Ransom's *Poets at Play: Irony and Parody in the Harley Lyrics* (1985), Douglas Gray's edited and completed version of J. A. W. Bennett's *Middle English Literature* (1986), Alasdair MacDonald's valuable introduction to the Middle English lyric in the *Companion to Early Middle English Literature* (1988), and Robert R. Edwards's *Ratio and Invention: A Study of Medieval Lyric and Narrative* (1989). Interesting articles include Rossell Hope Robbins' "The Middle English Court Love Lyric"(1980), John Scattergood's "Social and Political Issues in Chaucer: An Approach to Lak of Stedfastnesse" (*Chaucer Review*, vol. 21, no. 4), and John Stephens's "The Uses of Personae and the Art of Obliqueness in Some Chaucer Lyrics" (*Chaucer Review*, vol. 21, no. 3). For the most recent studies of the Middle English lyric, see the References below.

SELECTED BIBLIOGRAPHY

Barratt, Alexandra, ed. *Women's Writing in Middle English*. London and New York: Longman, 1992; Boffey, Julia. "The Reputation and Circulation of Chaucer's Lyrics in the Fifteenth Century." *Chaucer Review* 28:1 (1993), 23-39; Cornell, Christine. "'Purtreture' and 'Holsom Stories': John Lydgate's Accommodation of Image and Text in Three Religious Lyrics." *Florilegium* 10 (1988-91), 167-78; Figg, Kristen Mossler. *The Short Lyric Poems of Jean Froissart*. New York: Garland, 1994; Fries, Maureen. "(Almost) Without a Song: Criseyde and Lyric in Chaucer's *Troilus*." *Chaucer Yearbook* 1 (1992), 47-63; McClellan, William. "Radical Theology or Parody in a Marian Lyric of Ms Harley 2253." In *Voices in Translation: The Authority of "Olde Bookes" in Medieval Literature*. Deborah M. Sinnreich-Levi and Gale Sigal, eds. New

York: AMS, 1992, 157-68; Pickering, O. S. "Newly Discovered Secular Lyrics from Later Thirteenth-Century Cheshire." *Review of English Studies* 43 (1992), 157-80; Reiss, Edmund. "The Middle English Lyric." In *Old and Middle English Literature*. Dictionary of Literary Biography. Vol. 146. Eds. Jeffrey Helterman and Jerome Mitchell. Detroit: Gale, 1994. 392-99; Rudd, Jay. *"Many a Song and Many a Leccherous Lay": Tradition and Individuality in Chaucer's Lyric Poetry*. New York: Garland, 1992; Sigal, Gale. *Erotic Dawn-Songs of the Middle Ages: Voicing the Lyric Lady*. Gainesville: University Press of Florida, 1996; Stevick, Robert D., Ed. *One Hundred Middle English Lyrics*. Rev. Urbana: University of Illinois Press, 1994; Wimsatt, James. *Chaucer and His French Contemporaries: Natural Music in the Fourteenth Century*. Toronto: University Press of Toronto, 1991.

Sigrid King

M

MADRIGAL. The madrigal was an Italian literary and musical genre that began in the fourteenth century. At first the works were short *lyric poems, but they later became a type of arrangement of secular works, usually performed as solos. In their original form madrigals typically consisted of two strophes of three lines each, followed by the ritornello, a strophe of two lines. The strophe worked its way to England in the 1530s; by 1550 it evolved into its own unique style. The works developed into a single stanza of seven- or eleven-syllable lines with no set rhyme scheme, and the subject matter was usually love, inspired by *Petrarch's pastoral style. By the late sixteenth century the madrigal had become a vocal ensemble generally consisting of three to eight voices, sometimes accompanied by music. The songs could be lyric poetry, sonnets, sestinas, or other forms. As the genre evolved, the design of the works did also. Rather than simply putting the poem to music, as had been done in the earlier madrigals, the composers tried to place each work or phrase into an appropriate musical setting. This change led to great competition between madrigal composers; thus the genre changed greatly. Just as quickly as the madrigals expanded and grew, they burned out. The entire cycle of madrigals in England from its rise to its growth and decline occurred between 1520 and 1620.

SELECTED BIBLIOGRAPHY

Feldman, Martha. *City, Culture, and the Madrigal in Venice.* Berkeley: University of California Press, 1995; Godt, Irving. "A Systematic Classification for Madrigalism." *Ars Lyrica* 7 (1993), 75-81; Lincoln, Harry B. "Some Observations on Madrigal Settings of Petrarch's *'I' vo piangendo....*" *Mediaevelia* 12 (1989), 339-49.

Robert T. Lambdin

MAGELLAN, FERDINAND (Fernão de Magalhães) (1480-1521). The Spanish Crown directed Ferdinand Magellan to find a route to the Moluccas in 1519. He first touched South America at Permambuco, and his voyage became a coastal expedition until in 1520 he reached and passed through the straits that now bear his name. He continued northward along the coast, finally sailing northwestward on *Mare Pacificum*, the name he gave to the Pacific Ocean.

After months at sea he landed in the Landrone Islands and the Philippines, where he was killed by natives in the surf of Mindanao. Magellan's death in 1521 left it to Sebastian de Cano, commander of one of Magellan's vessels, to complete circumnavigation of the globe.

SELECTED BIBLIOGRAPHY

Joyner, Tim. *Magellan.* Camden, ME: International Marine, 1992; Noonan, John. *Ferdinand Magellan.* New York: Crestwood, 1993.

R. Churchill Curtis

MALORY, SIR THOMAS (c. 1408-1471). Sir Thomas Malory's *Le Morte D'Arthur* was the first coherent, abbreviated version of the *Arthurian legends. This work reduces the French Arthurian legends, which had by this point become rambling, separate stories about each particular character, into one text that clarifies an overall plot that includes all the known Arthurian figures. This last flowering of Arthurian legend in the literature of the Middle Ages was written in English in the late 1460s and published as a book by William *Caxton in 1485. All that is known of Malory is that he probably was a member of Parliament in 1445 and was imprisoned in 1451, where he wrote *Le Morte D'Arthur* and remained until his death.

Malory begins his text with the miraculous birth of Arthur, fruit of the adulterous union of the warlike Uther Pendragon and the chaste Igrayne. This is closely followed by the other important aspects of Arthur's early career: his coronation, his acquisition of the sword Excaliber from the Lady of the Lake, and his incestuous coupling with his sister Morgawse. Arthur attempts to cover this last mistake by ruthlessly drowning all the babies born around the same time (cf. Matthew 2:16). This brutality earns for Arthur the hatred of many powerful families, but does not kill the infant Mordred.

For some time Arthur escapes the repercussions of his guilt, as he wages triumphant campaigns against the Romans and the Saracens. By aiding her father, Lodegraunce, Arthur wins the fair Gwenyvere, who brings Uther's Round Table as her dowry. Arthur surrounds the table with knights of unmatched prowess, like Launcelot, Trystrame, and Galahad, who fight to remove evil from the world. All goes well for some time until the early seeds blossom into evil.

The final disintegration of the once-indomitable Order of the Round Table is caused, in the *Morte*, by many factors: Launcelot is Arthur's greatest knight and best friend, but he loves the King's wife, just as Trystrame loves La Beale Isode, wife of King Mark. The sainted Galahad is conceived when Launcelot is tricked into unfaithfulness to the Queen by Elayne; the bastard child becomes a knight so pure that the Holy Grail (the vessel used at the Last Supper and later to collect the blood of Christ as he hung on the cross) again visits earth because of Galahad's presence; thus begins a quest from which most of the knights do not return.   Simultaneously, Aggravayne and Gawayne succeed in a plot to trap Launcelot and Gwenyvere together.   When the knight arrives to save his lady, he accidentally kills the brothers of Aggravayne and Gawayne.   Gawayne demands vengeance from Arthur, his uncle, so they leave to wage war on Launcelot across the sea.   While Arthur is away, Mordred seizes the kingdom and the Queen.   Arthur returns to reprimand Mordred in a battle that begins through a mere accident when a soldier steps on a snake.   This war leaves only Arthur, Mordred, and Bedyvere standing.

Arthur kills Mordred, receives a mortal wound, and is taken away in a barge by mourning women in black hoods.   Bedyvere returns Excaleber to the lake and laments his lonely position.   Gwenyvere dies soon after as an abbess in the nunnery of Almysburye, and Launcelot, another newcomer to the monastic life, also dies shortly.

Malory greatly simplified the form for his English audience, dropping most of the magic and religious mysteries, while adding realism.   His method is a swift presentation of action that avoids complicated emotional analysis.   Whereas *Chrétien de Troyes excelled at psychological passages showing the inner life of a character, Malory relied upon showing rather than telling.   Many times there is a message, but it is rarely direct; one must decipher the carefully contrived layering of scenes.   In the *Morte* the characters are not interested in word puns, and there is much more direct conversation with few narrative interventions, so the dialogue must be assessed by the reader (LaFarge 227).

Malory did not tantalize, but seemed intent on clarifying the events for himself and his readers (Vinaver 1545).   The work can be viewed as composed of eight sections: the first two concentrate on Arthur's rise to power; the next three show him at his height; and the final three concentrate on the downfall of Camelot.   This configuration, according to D. S. Brewer, "makes sense in itself because it describes a general chronological progression, just like life, and is also comprehensible to medieval views of life.   Growth, flowering and decay; rise, supremacy and fall not only completely accord with normal experience, but can easily be imagined in such medieval terms as Fortune's wheel" (241).

Malory's work, with its frequent contradictions in detail and often confusing arrangement, is by no means perfect, but the story retains its beauty and dissolution, and most of Malory's embroidery is an improvement.   Much of what Malory discarded from French writers involved Merlin and Morgan le Fay, as the author was clearly concerned with the political ramifications of Arthur's decisions; possibly this interest in battle over magic, and especially the civil strife that ends Arthur's kingdom, reflects Malory's perception of the *Wars of the Roses (1455-1485), which were ravaging England as he wrote.   Malory was a knight himself, but apparently one uninterested in outmoded concepts of *courtly love; possibly for this reason he eliminated many of the love scenes between Launcelot and Gwenyvere, while concentrating on Launcelot as a Christian warrior.   Chrétien's *Lancelot* portrays this knight as the Queen's willing pawn who is often made to look foolish for his love.   Malory removed from Launcelot's character most aspects of the fawning courtly lover and substituted a warrior of great courage. Malory also increased Arthur's knightly prowess.

Arthur was not merely an English king, but a British one, so his name was used as a political tool by the Welsh Tudors from the ascension of Henry VII in 1485, the same year in which Caxton published the *Morte*. Caxton's preface claims Arthur's historicity as "the most renomed Crysten kyng . . . whyche ought moost to be remembred emonge us Englysshemen tofore Crysten kynges" (cxlii), but the evidence was too flimsy; the Tudors eventually chose *Alfred the Great for their hero, because his existence was indisputable and most of his actions had been carefully documented.

There are many theories suggesting different kings whom Malory may have intended Arthur to reflect. William Matthews believed that Malory wrote against *Edward III, "whose military successes, like Arthur's, had brought him within reach of the emperor's crown, but whose ambition combined with ill luck had resulted in a senseless and profitless campaign which had made him widely unpopular" (188). R. M. Lumianski found in the work a sympathy for Edward IV (882), while *The Arthurian Encyclopedia* (1986) noted that a passage near the end of *Morte* suggests that Malory sympathized with the ousted Lancastrian King Henry VI (Lacy 532).

By far the most comprehensive argument for the work as a parallel to other military triumphs and disasters is Eugene Vinaver's discussion of the idealized portrait of Arthur as a tribute to Henry V. Malory altered the section about Arthur and Emperor Lucius to make Arthur's expedition against the Romans resemble Henry V's triumphant campaign in France. Both kings follow the same route, appoint two leaders to rule while they are away, and are called rulers of two kingdoms. "Whether as a Lancastrian or as a follower of Warwick who had sworn allegiance to Henry VI while fighting his advisors and even resisted the Duke of York's attempt to assume the crown, Malory had every reason to remember Henry V as the model or the 'crowned knight'" (Vinaver xxxii).

D. S. Brewer agreed with Vinaver that Malory's work may be a tribute to Henry V, but added that it is more likely a tribute to Arthur himself and all that he stood for in the author's imagination. Brewer suggested that Malory postponed Arthur's fall so that the king can become established in greatness (239). It would seem likely also that Malory added this postponement, which allowed Arthur to be crowned emperor of Rome and rise to further glory, to elevate the tragedy, making the ultimate fall greater.

Malory's devotion to the chivalric past is evident, and he expressed scorn for the system's disintegration because "the people were soo new fangill" (1229; bk. 21, chap. 1). This is especially touching when we recall that Malory wrote in an age of great change--"when the art of printing, the new learning and the reformation were soon to sweep away all outgrowths of chivalric romance and devoted naive, primitive faith and religion" (Ven-Ten Bensel 154). There seems to have been a fifteenth-century reversion to the Middle Ages in several important, but mostly negative, aspects that Malory may have resented: "the *Lollard heresy was repressed, the real authority of Parliament declined, the Wars of the Roses restored the anarchy of feudalism" (MacCallum 89).

The source of Malory's chapter called "The Tale of the Sankgreall" uses the French Vulgate Quest for the outline of the Holy Grail: Malory did little to alter the basic material, but again his skill is shown in omitting selected expositions on the doctrines of grace and salvation. In the French version a multitude of hermits sermonize to various questing knights. Malory diminished the distinction between religious and secular *chivalry, making the distance less apparent between saintly Galahad and his more earthly father, Launcelot. The result is not always sound theology, but it does serve to integrate the Grail quest, a part of the work that had always seemed separate from the rest of the legend because of its intense moralizing.

Malory's conclusion, the aftermath of the battle between Arthur and Mordred, seems the most brilliant and majestic part of the *Morte*. Whereas violence and magic dominate early Arthurian tales, Malory's work is more concerned with feudal laws of loyalty and setting forth a more coherent definition of chivalry:

> At his greatest, in the final passages dealing with the last battle and death of Arthur, he seems to reflect in an enlarged form all the troubles of his own society, the ruin which civil strife had brought upon him and his kind. This is imaginatively seen in the dissolution of the Table Round, the bond and fellowship of knighthood. Conquest, like true and faithful love, belongs to the past: the first and last campaigns of Arthur represent for Malory a youthful hope of the past contrasted with a tragic present.
>
> (Bradbrook 395-96)

Without gratuitous moralizing, Malory expanded the nobility of Arthur and the enduring love of Launcelot and Gwenyvere for each other and the king. This devotion restores the story's unrelenting tragedy and adds a climax of befitting grandeur never before attained. The entire tale becomes a grim vision with relevance to any civilization, as Malory explores the forces, both internal and external, that ruin a kingdom.

While Launcelot does feel contrition for his sins when he confesses to a priest that he has "loved a quene unmesurabely and oute of measure longe" (897; bk. 13, chap 20), Malory does not blame this love, nor the love of Tristram and Isode, for the fall. Caxton asserted in his preface that Malory's work is moral in tone because it teaches readers "the noble actes of chyvalrye, the jentyl and vertuous dedes that somme knyghtes used in tho dayes, by whyche they came to honour, and how they that were vycious were punysshed and ofte put out to shame and rebuke" (cxlv). The consensus among critics, however, is that Malory's work is not intended to be didactic. Many note that the fall seems caused by conflicting loyalties: Launcelot owes allegiance to

Arthur, but loves Gwenyvere (Zesmer 109); Arthur admires Launcelot, but his ties of kinship with Gawain are stronger (Harrington 66); and as Arthur's illegitimate and unacknowledged son, Mordred feels that he owes the king no special loyalty (Kendrick 65).

This concern with loyalty seems explainable as a key aspect of chivalry. Most of the knights become disloyal because of their great ambitions, especially in the Grail quest and the backing of Mordred. It is understandable that the knights are untrue to Arthur and the chivalric code: "Since they cannot understand the meaning and purpose of the King's ideals, his followers fail to keep the vows of the high order of knighthood" (Ven-Ten Bensel 154). Beyond virtue, true chivalry depends upon blind obedience and loyalty to a cause--a rule of conduct that establishes order in times of disorder (Vinaver xxxiii). It is in times of struggle that chivalry is tested, and, as Malory clearly shows (possibly despite himself), it does not always work. Most of the knights are neither virtuous nor unambitious enough to follow the strict code. The Round Table fellowship fails, "and this was the fate of chivalry, because as a guiding principle, it was unequal to the problem which it undertook, and men soon saw that it merely professed to give the answer" (MacCallum 95-96). Arthur may have had the best of intentions, but he was surrounded by ordinary men of lesser standards. This is one of the main problems addressed in Tennyson's *Idylls of the King.*

SELECTED BIBLIOGRAPHY

Abbot, Reginald. "What Becomes a Legend Most? Fur in the Medieval Romance." *Dress* 21 (1994), 4-16; Barber, Richard, ed. *The Arthurian Legend.* London: Dorset, 1979; Bradbrook, M. C. "Malory and the Heroic Tradition." In *Arthur, King of Britain.* Richard Brengle, ed. New York: Prentice Hall, 1964. 392-95; Brewer, D. S. "the hoole booke." In *Middle English Survey.* Edward Vasta, ed.Notre Dame: University of Notre Dame Press, 1965. 233-58; Hares-Stryker, Carolyn. "Lily Maids and Watery Rests: Elaine of Astolat." *Victorian Literature and Culture* 22 (1994), 129-50; Harrington, David V. "The Conflicting Passions of Malory's 'Sir Gawain' and 'Sir Lancelot.'" *Arthurian Interpretations* 2 (1986), 64-69; Jones, W. Lewis. *King Arthur in History and Legend.* Cambridge: Cambridge University Press, 1911; Kendrick, Robert L. "The Administration of Justice in Malory's *Works.*" *Arthurian Interpretations* 1 (1987), 63-82; Lacy, Norris J., ed. *The Arthurian Encyclopedia.* New York: Beddick, 1986; LaFarge, Catherine. "Conversation in Malory's *Morte Darthur.*" *Medium Ævum* 55 (1984), 225-38; Lumiansky, R. M. "Sir Thomas Malory's *Le Morte Darthur,* 1947-87: Author, Title, Text." *Speculum* 62 (1987), 878-97; MacCallum, Sir Mungo William. *Tennyson's Idylls of the King" and Arthurian Story from the XVIth Century.* New York: Books for Libraries, 1971; Matthews, William. *The Tragedy of Arthur.* Berkeley: University of California Press, 1960; Morris, Rosemary. *The Character of King Arthur in Medieval Literature.* Totowa, NJ: Rowman and Littlefield, 1982; Tieken-Boon van Ostade, Ingrid. *The Two Versions of Malory's "Morte Darthur": Multiple Negation and the Editing of the Text.* Cambridge: Brewer, 1995; Ven-ten Bensel, Elise Francisca Wilhelmina Maria van der. *The Character of King Arthur in English Literature.* New York: Haskell House, 1966; Vinaver, Eugene, ed. *The Works of Thomas Malory.* 3 vols. continuously paged.

Oxford: Oxford University Press, 1987; Zesmer, David M. *Guide to English Literature: From "Beowulf" to Chaucer*. New York: Barnes, 1961.

Laura Cooner Lambdin

"MANCIPLE'S TALE, THE." "The Manciple's Tale" in Geoffrey *Chaucer's *Canterbury Tales* (c. 1387-1400) explains how crows became black. The source is Ovid's written version of an earlier folktale.

White crows are the norm, and an archer named Phebus has one who sings beautifully and speaks the English language. The crow tells Phebus that his wife was unfaithful to him while he was away from home. Using his skill in archery, Phebus kills his lover with one arrow; later he is so sorry about the murder that he breaks his bow. Phebus then turns on his tattletale crow; he pulls off the bird's feathers, turns him black, destroys his beautiful voice so that he no longer can sing sweetly or speak the human language, and gives him to the Devil. Ugly crows worldwide are now intended as a reminder against getting others in trouble.

SELECTED BIBLIOGRAPHY

Bush, Douglas. *English Poetry*. New York: Oxford University Press, 1963; Garbáty, Thomas J. *Medieval English Literature*. Toronto: Heath, 1984; Lambdin, Laura C., and Robert T. Lambdin, eds. *Chaucer's Pilgrims: An Historical Guide to the Pilgrims in the "Canterbury Tales."* Westport, CT: Greenwood Press. 1996; Patton, Celeste A. "False 'Rekennynges': Sharp Practice of Language in Chaucer's 'Manciple's Tale.'" *Philological Quarterly* 71:4 (Fall 1992), 399-417; Salter, Elizabeth. *Fourteenth-Century English Poetry*. Oxford: Clarendon Press, 1983.

Laura Cooner Lambdin

MANDEVILLE, SIR JOHN (?-1372). John Mandeville was born at St. Albans. He left England in 1322, traveled widely and took a new name in 1343 when he lived in Liège. A work composed in French about his travels was compiled between 1366 and 1371. Potential sources for the work include fourteenth century travel books. The work was quickly translated into Latin and English. It was an important influence on many English authors, including Geoffrey *Chaucer. It was the prototype of the travel books that would become so popular in the eighteenth century.

His most famous work is his *Travels of Sir John Mandeville*, a mid-fourteenth century text concerning the adventures of a fictitious knight--Sir John Mandeville (the name is taken from an actual knight under the reign of Edward II). The prologue calls for the reclaiming of the Promised Land by Christians, and so the work may be the result of the enormous interest that audiences had in the faraway lands and customs depicted in *chronicles of the *Crusades.

Mandeville's travels mirror that of a crusader as he goes from England to Constantinople to Jerusalem; he then continues his travels eastward to visit eventually Cathay (China), Persia (Iran), India, and the Isle of Java. The tale depicts the geography, superstitions, peoples, and customs Mandeville encounters. It contains few--if any--actual experiences of its author, and although unified under the persona of Mandeville, it is more a compilation from many sources than a tale of one man. One possible identity for the author of this work is Jean De Bourgogne, who in a deathed confession acknowledged writing Mandeville's adventures, but scholarship is divided on the authenticity of such a claim.

SELECTED BIBLIOGRAPHY

Burnett, Charles, and Patrick Gautier Dalche. "Attitudes towards Mongols in Medieval Literature: The XXII Kings of Gog and Magog from the Court of Frederick II to Jean de Mandeville." *Viator* 22 (1991), 153-67; Higgins, Iain. "Imagining Christendom from Jerusalem to Paradise: Asia in Mandeville's *Travels*." In *Discovering New Worlds: Essays on Medieval Exploration and Imagination*. Scott D. Westrem, ed. New York: Garland, 1991. 91-114; Mandeville, Sir John. *The Travels of Sir John Mandeville*. London: Macmillan, 1915; Westrum, Scott D. "Two Routes to Pleasant Instruction in Late Fourteenth Century Literature. In *The Work of Dissimilitude: Essays from the Sixth Citadel Conference on Medieval and Renaissance Literature*. David Allen and Robert A. White, eds. Newark: University of Delaware Press, 1992. 67-80.

Richard McDonald

MANNYNGE, ROBERT (c.1264-1340). Robert Mannynge was apparently from Brunne in Lincolnshire; all that is known of him is what he wrote about himself in the prologues to his two works, his verse *Chronicles of England* (1338) and *Handlynge Synne*. He became a member of the Gilbertine monastery after 1288. His works popularize religious and historical material. *Handlynge Synne*, composed around 1303, was an adaptation of William of Wadington's *Manuel des Pechez*, in which homilies are illustrated with legends and anecdotes. This compilation provides a vivid picture of his era. His *Chronicle* was based on Wace and Peter of Longtoft. It details English history through the death of *Edward I in 1307.

Handlynge Synne is a translation of the Anglo-French work *Manuel des Pechez*, composed around 1300. The English version of Mannyng is a collection of tales that serve as *exempla. Each of the Ten Commandments is given from one to three tales apiece. So too are discussed the *Seven Deadly Sins, the Seven Sacraments, the Twelve Requisites of Shrift, and the Twelve Graces of Shrift. Each of the stories contains a personal piece of social commentary, attacking such topics as dress, the evils of tournaments and miracle plays, and the problems of worldliness. Most stories are short and simple; in this way *Handlynge Synne* is one of the finest collections of exempla from this period.

SELECTED BIBLIOGRAPHY

Ho, Cynthia. "Dichotomize and Conquer: 'Womman Handlyng' in *Handlyng Synne*." *Philological Quarterly* 72:4 (Fall 1993), 383-401; Sullens, Idelle, ed. *Robert Mannyng of Brunne: "Handlyng Synne."* Binghamton, NY: State University of New York Press, 1983.

Richard McDonald

"MAN OF LAW'S TALE, THE." "The Man of Law's Tale" in Geoffrey *Chaucer's *Canterbury Tales* (c. 1387-1400) is told by a lawyer and written in rhyme-royal. The source of the tale is Nicholas *Trevet's *Anglo-Norman chronicle (c. 1335) and John Gower's version of the story in *Confessio Amantis* (1390). The daughter of the Roman Emperor, Constance, is courted by the Sultan of Syria, King Alla, who must become a Christian in order to win her hand. The Sultan's mother, Donegild, disapproves of the match and sets Constance adrift in a rudderless boat and kills all of the Christians at the wedding feast. Constance lands in Northumberland, where she rejects a lusty knight; as payment, the knight kills Hermengyld and frames Constance for the murder by putting the knife in her bed. Her innocence is proved by a miracle from God, so King Alla converts and marries Constance.

Alla leaves to oversee his realm, Constance has their baby Maurice, and Donegild sends Alla a message that the child is deformed because the mother is an elf. This ploy does not make Alla reject Constance, so Donegild forges a letter from the king to the constable demanding that Constance and the baby be set adrift upon the sea. Alla discovers his mother's treachery and has her killed as a traitor. Alla, Constance, and Maurice are reunited and reside peacefully in Northumberland.

SELECTED BIBLIOGRAPHY

Astell, Ann W. "Apostrophe, Prayer, and the Structure of Satire in the 'Man of Law's Tale.'" *Studies in the Age of Chaucer* 13 (1991), 81-97; Bush, Douglas. *English Poetry*. New York: Oxford University Press, 1963; Garbáty, Thomas J. *Medieval English Literature*. Toronto: Heath, 1984; Lambdin, Laura C., and Robert T. Lambdin, eds. *Chaucer's Pilgrims: An Historical Guide to the Pilgrims in the "Canterbury Tales."* Westport, CT: Greenwood Press, 1996; Schibanoff, Susan. "Worlds Apart: Orientalism, Antifeminism, and Heresy in Chaucer's 'Man of Law's Tale.'" *Exemplaria* 8:1 (Spring 1996), 59-96.

Laura Cooner Lambdin

MANUEL, JUAN. The nephew of *Alfonso X, el Sabio, this nobleman-adventurer is the first notable figure in the development of Spanish fiction. He is known for his efforts to translate and adapt the religious form of the *exempla sermons to fiction. Although a great deal of his writings have been lost, his masterpiece, *Libro del Conde Lucanor* (1323-35), seems to offer a very fair representation of his literary achievements. An early experimenter with prose style, Juan Manuel was the very first to use figurative language to any extent.

Libro del Conde Lucanor is a didactic work featuring a young count, Lucanor, seeking advice from his counselor, Patronio. Within this frame a series of stories then imparts moral and ethical guidance to the young man. Sources for the work include the Moorish and Christian moral exempla, the story of the *Crusades, particularly *Richard I, the Lionhearted, Aesop's fables, and writings of the church. Unlike Juan Ruiz, archbishop of Hito, Juan Manuel remains serious throughout his extant writings. No traces of humor, parody or irony are found.

SELECTED BIBLIOGRAPHY

Bloom. Leonard. "Chivalry as an Intellectual Ideal in Alfonso X, el Sabio, and Don Juan Manuel." In *The Western Pennsylvania Symposium on World Literatures, Selected Proceedings: 1974-1991, A Retrospective."* Greensburg, PA: Eadner, 1992, 71-79; de Looze, Laurence. "Subversion of Meaning in Part I of 'El Conde Lucanor.'" *Revista Canadiense de Estudios Hispanicos* 19:2 (Winter 1995), 341-55; Gerli, E. Michael and Harvey L. Sharrer, eds. *Hispanic Medieval Studies in Honor of Samuel G. Armistead.* Madison, WI: Hispanic Seminary of Medieval Studies, 1992; Lloyd, Paul M. "On Conducting Sociolinguistic Research in the Middle Ages." In E. Michael Gerli and Harvey L. Sharrer, eds. *Hispanic Medieval Studies in Honor of Samuel G. Armistead.* Madison: Hispanic Seminary of Medieval Studies, 1992; Whinnom, Keith. "Spanish Literary Historiography: Three Forms of Distortion." In Deyermond, *et al,* eds. *Medieval and Renaissance Spanish Literature: Selected Essays by Keith Whinnom.* Exeter, UK: University of Exeter Press, 1994, 96-113.

Rebecca Stephens

MAP, WALTER (c. 1140- c. 1209). Walter Map was a well-known medieval courtier and satirist. He was named the archdeacon of Oxford in the late twelfth century and a good companion to *Henry II. Before 1192 he composed *De Nugias Curialium* (The courtier's trifles), a collection of wit and satire. This collection also contains the *Dissuasio Valerii ad Rufinum de Non Ducenda Uxore*, a work that was originally thought to have been composed by St. *Augustine.

Walter Map was at one time thought to be the author who gave the Arthurian (*see Arthurian Legend*) cycle its religious and moral character. It was also believed that Map wrote a lost prose version of the Lancelot legend in which he noted that it was Lancelot's sin that prevented him from achieving the Grail Quest. Thus many erroneously believed that Map was one of the first authors to make the Arthur legend inseparable from the Grail legend.

SELECTED BIBLIOGRAPHY

Bychkov, Oleg. "The Use of the *De Officiis* in Walter Map's *De Nugis Curialium*." *Notes and Queries* 42 (240) 2 (June 1995), 157-59; Lawler, Traugott. "Medieval Annotation: The Example of the Commentaries on Walter Map's *Dissuasio Valerii*." In *Annotation and Its Texts*. Stephen Barney, ed. Oxford: Oxford University Press, 1991.

Robert T. Lambdin

MARTIANUS CAPELLA (c. 400- c. 440). Perhaps more popularly known as Marcian, Martianus Capella is best known as the author of the collection *De Nuptiis Philologiae et Mercurii*. The first two volumes of this nine-volume work discuss Mercury's courting of Philology. The collection's other seven volumes are encyclopedias devoted to each of the seven *liberal arts. The work remained a standard text into the English Renaissance. In literature Marcian is mentioned by Geoffrey *Chaucer in "The *Merchant's Tale" of the *Canterbury Tales* and also in *The *House of Fame*.

SELECTED BIBLIOGRAPHY

Bennett, Beth S. "The Rhetoric of Martianus Capella and Anselm de Besate in the Tradition of Menippean Satire." *Philosophy and Rhetoric* 24:2 (1991), 128-42; Parkes, M. B. "A Fragment of an Early Tenth-Century Anglo-Saxon Manuscript and Its Significance." *Anglo-Saxon England* 12 (1983), 129-40; Stahl, William Harris, Richard Johnson, and E. L. Burge, trans. *Martianus Capella and the Seven Liberal Arts. Vol. II: The Marriage of Philology and Mercury*. New York: Columbia University Press, 1977. Westra, H. J. "The Juxtaposition of the Ridiculous and the Sublime in Martianus Capella. *Florilegium* 3 (1981), 198-214.

Robert T. Lambdin

MASACCIO (1401-1428). Also known as Tommaso Guidi, the Italian artist Masaccio was far ahead of his time, and served as the precursor for the artistic rules that shaped the sixteenth century. His accentuation of contrast through the use of light enabled him to forgo the use of linear contours. Masaccio's work is characterized by the themes of nature and renewal. Art historians have utilized these traits to identify Masaccio's work, but many pieces are only doubtfully attributed to him. His extensive collaboration with Masolino also sheds uncertainty on the origins of many paintings of his time.

In 1422 Masaccio was commissioned to create a triptych at the Church of St. Giovenale; this work was painted in the Florentine tradition. Its most famous panel represented the *Madonna Enthroned with Saints and Two Adoring Angels*. His next work, in 1424, is entitled *Virgin and Child with St. Anne*. This painting depicts the Madonna and angels as "soft and graceful" forms and the Christ child and St. Anne in rougher figures. Masaccio was then commissioned to paint a polyptych in Pisa, the most celebrated part of which is entitled *Virgin and Child Enthroned*. Gradually the artist began to display the influence of *Donatello through his three-dimensional use of architecture in his works. This influence is evident in his most extensive work, the Branacci Chapel frescoes (1425). They include twelve panels depicting scenes such as Saint Peter in the act of baptism and the expulsion from the Garden of Eden. It is also interesting to note the psychological aspect of Masaccio's work, as he painted tenderly humanistic scenes in which the subjects seem to relate to each other in different situations.

SELECTED BIBLIOGRAPHY

Berti, Luciano. *Masaccio*. Firenze: Cantini, 1988; Gardner, Helen. *Gardner's Art through the Ages*. 6th ed. San Diego: Harcourt Brace Jovanovich, 1975; Spike, John T. *Masaccio*. New York: Abbeville, 1996.

Libby Bernardin

"MATTER OF BRITAIN, THE." The subject matters of medieval romances are drawn from common attributes of three types of romances gleaned from their definitions in Jean Bodel's thirteenth-century *Chanson des Saisnes*, where he divides the romances into three types: the "Matter of Britain," "*Matter of France," and "*Matter of Rome." To these, twentieth century critics added a fourth, "*Matter of England." The "Matter of Britain" romances are mainly concerned with *Arthurian romances. These works are semi-historical and usually concern material about Arthur and the knights of the Round Table. Major characters in these works include Lancelot, Guinevere, Sir Kay, Sir Galahad, and Tristram and Iseult. In this "Matter" are also included Breton *Lays, and Geoffrey *Chaucer's *"Franklin's Tale. "

SELECTED BIBLIOGRAPHY

Curtis, Jan. "Byzantium and the Matter of Britain: The Narrative Framework of Charles Williams's Later Arthurian Poems." *Quondam et Futurus* 2:1 (Spring 1992), 28-54; Jones, Sally Roberts. "Star Kings and Wizards: The Matter of Britain in the Twentieth Century." *New Welsh Review* 1:4 (1989), 5-9; Thompson, Raymond H. "Modern Visions and Revisions of the Matter of Britain." In *Approaches to Teaching Arthurian Tradition*. Maureen Fries and Jeanie Watson, eds. New York: Modern Language Association, 1992. 61-64.

Robert T. Lambdin

"MATTER OF ENGLAND, THE." "The Matter of England" draws its roots from the three "Matters" described by Jean Bodel in the thirteenth century. Twentieth century critics devised "The Matter of England" to distinguish *romances that were thematically concerned with English heroes from those associated with Arthur, or "The Matter of Britain." These works are usually semi-historical; among the most influential are *King Horn* and *Havelok the Dane*. The popularity of this type of literature is evidenced by the great number of extant manuscripts.

SELECTED BIBLIOGRAPHY

Frakes, Jerold C. "Metaphysical Structure as Narrative Structure in the Medieval Romance." *Neophilologus* 69:4 (1985), 481-89; Kohl, Stephan. "From Identity to Individualism: Heroes of Medieval Romance in Sixteenth-Century Literature." In *Anglistentag 1992 Stuttgart: Proceedings*. Hans Ulrich Seeber and Walter Gobel, eds. Tübingen: Niemeyer, 1993. 238-49; Lindahl, Carl. "The Oral Undertones of Late Medieval Romance." in *Oral Tradition in the Middle Ages*. W.F.H. Nicolaisen, ed. Binghampton, NY: Medieval and Renaissance Texts and Studies, 1995. 59-75.

Robert T. Lambdin

"MATTER OF FRANCE, THE." The term "The Matter of France" was established by Jean Bodel in the late thirteenth century concerning *romances that treat the legends of *Charlemagne. These are usually grouped into two classes, the Ferumbas class and the Otuel group. The Ferumbas group is concerned with incidents that are described in the French *chansons de geste*, such as the "Ferumbas" and the "Destruction of Rome." The Otuel group contains those romances about Otuel and Roland.

SELECTED BIBLIOGRAPHY

Frakes, Jerold C. "Metaphysical Structure as Narrative Structure in the Medieval Romance." *Neophilologus* 69:4 (1985), 481-89; Kohl, Stephan. "From Identity to Individualism: Heroes of Medieval Romance in Sixteenth-Century Literature." In *Anglistentag 1992 Stuttgart: Proceedings*. Hans Ulrich Seeber and Walter Gobel, eds. Tübingen: Niemeyer, 1993. 238-49; Lindahl, Carl. "The Oral Undertones of Late Medieval Romance." In *Oral Tradition in the Middle Ages*. W.F.H. Nicolaisen, ed. Binghamton, NY: Medieval and Renaissance Texts and Studies, 1995. 59-75.

Robert T. Lambdin

"MATTER OF ROME, THE." Jean Bodel, in his thirteenth-century work, noted "The Matter of Rome" to be a variety of *romances that concerned classical Rome or antiquity. Within this genre are included many tales about

Alexander the Great, such as *Alisaunder* and *Kyng Alexander*. Also included in this genre are stories about Ilium (Troy); among these are *Seege of Troy*, the oldest Troy romance in English. Finally, romances with subjects such as Thebes are classified as "Matters of Rome." John Lydgate's *Siege of Thebes* is an example.

SELECTED BIBLIOGRAPHY

Frakes, Jerold C. "Metaphysical Structure as Narrative Structure in the Medieval Romance." *Neophilologus* 69:4 (1985), 481-89; Kohl, Stephan. "From Identity to Individualism: Heroes of Medieval Romance in Sixteenth-Century Literature." In *Anglistentag 1992 Stuttgart: Proceedings*. Hans Ulrich Seeber and Walter Gobel, eds. Tübingen: Niemeyer, 1993. 238-49; Lindahl, Carl. "The Oral Undertones of Late Medieval Romance." In *Oral Tradition in the Middle Ages*. W.F.H. Nicolaisen, ed. Binghamton, NY: Medieval and Renaissance Texts and Studies, 1995. 59-75.

Robert T. Lambdin

"MELIBEE, TALE OF." The "Tale of Melibee" is told by the narrator of Geoffrey *Chaucer's *Canterbury Tales* (c. 1387-1400) after the host interrupts his rhyme of *"Sir Thopas." The didactic work is derived from a French adaptation of the Latin *Liber Consolationis et Consilii* by Albertanus of Brescia. In this long prose tale Melibee returns from work to find his daughter Sophie dead and his wife Prudence beaten. He knows that the crime has been committed by his three enemies and vows vengeance against them. Prudence persuades Melibee to forgive his enemies as God forgives trespasses.

SELECTED BIBLIOGRAPHY

Bush, Douglas. *English Poetry*. New York: Oxford University Press, 1963; Collette, Carolyn P. "Heeding the Counsel of Prudence: A Context for the Melibee." *Chaucer Review* 29:4 (1995), 416-33; Garbáty, Thomas J. *Medieval English Literature*. Toronto: Heath, 1984; Lambdin, Laura C., and Robert T. Lambdin, eds. *Chaucer's Pilgrims: An Historical Guide to the Pilgrims in the "Canterbury Tales."* Westport, CT: Greenwood Press, 1996.

Laura Cooner Lambdin

"MERCHANT'S TALE, THE." "The Merchant's Tale" from Geoffrey *Chaucer's *Canterbury Tales* (c. 1387-1400) is a humorous attack upon old men who marry young girls. January, an aged Lombard knight, weds May, an adolescent girl, despite the protests of his friends. Damyan, the knight's squire, becomes so enamored of May that he feels that this love will kill him. May visits his sickbed with promises to fulfill Damyan's desire. January is crippled by blindness and jealousy that make him cling ever more tightly to his young wife, who wants only to couple with his squire. Finally, May persuades January to take her to his private garden, where Damyan waits in a pear tree.

Pluto, the King of Fairyland, and Proserpina, his Queen, take an interest in the situation. While May and Damyan are fornicating in the pear tree, Pluto restores January's sight so that he may witness his wife's infidelity. January becomes very angry, but Proserpina gives May the presence of mind and glib tongue to convince her husband that his sight is still unclear. The old knight is made to believe that May was simply struggling with Damyan in order to help restore January's vision. January remains in a bad marriage, just as the storyteller, the Merchant, had earlier announced that his wife brought him only unhappiness.

SELECTED BIBLIOGRAPHY

Bush, Douglas. *English Poetry*. New York: Oxford University Press, 1963; Field, Rosalind. "'Superfluous Ribaldry': Spurious Lines in the 'Merchant's Tale.'" *Chaucer Review* 28:4 (1994), 353-67; Garbáty, Thomas J. *Medieval English Literature*. Toronto: Heath, 1984; Jost, Jean E. "May's Mismarriage of Youth and Elde: The Poetics of Sexual Desire in Chaucer's 'Merchant's Tale.'" In *Representations of the Feminine in the Middle Ages*. Bonnie Wheeler, ed. Dallas: Academia, 1993. 117-37; Lambdin, Laura C., and Robert T. Lambdin, eds. *Chaucer's Pilgrims: An Historical Guide to the Pilgrims in the "Canterbury Tales"*. Westport, CT: Greenwood Press, 1996; Salter, Elizabeth. *Fourteenth-Century English Poetry*. Oxford: Clarendon Press, 1983.

Laura Cooner Lambdin

"MILLER'S TALE, THE." One of the most popular of the pilgrims traveling together in Geoffrey *Chaucer's *Canterbury Tales* (c. 1387-1400) is Robyn the Miller. He is a coarse, big-boned, stout fellow who tells a bawdy tale full of raunchy humor. Such tales are known as *fabliaux (singular, fabliau), stories of low comedy.

In "The Miller's Tale" an old carpenter, John, jealously guards his young wife, Alison. Absolon, a foppish clerk flirts with Alison, who is uninterested in him because her attention is upon Nicholas, a scholar boarding in her home. John is persuaded that a flood is coming, so he hangs three bathtubs from the ceiling--one for himself, one for Alison, and one for Nicholas. John soon falls asleep in his tub, so Alison and Nicholas head down to the bedroom. As they are sporting in bed, the lovesick Absolon comes to the window begging Alison for a kiss. Alison sticks her buttocks out and Absolon kisses her there because he cannot see well in the dark.

Absolon is furious at having been tricked into kissing Alison in such a place, so he borrows a hot branding iron and returns to the bedroom window for revenge. He asks for another kiss, and this time Nicholas sticks out his buttocks. Absolon quickly applies the branding iron and burns Nicholas's backside. Nicholas screams so loudly in pain that he wakes John, who thinks that the flood has come. John cuts the cords holding up his tub, comes crashing to the ground, and wakes the townsfolk, who think that he is crazy. Curiously, Alison is the only character who emerges unscathed.

SELECTED BIBLIOGRAPHY

Bush, Douglas. *English Poetry*. New York, Oxford University Press, 1963; Garbáty, Thomas J. *Medieval English Literature*. Toronto: Heath, 1984; Lambdin, Laura C., and Robert T. Lambdin, eds. *Chaucer's Pilgrims: An Historical Guide to the Pilgrims in the "Canterbury Tales."* Westport, CT: Greenwood Press, 1996; Lamperis, Linda. "Bodies That Matter in the Court of Late Medieval England and in Chaucer's 'Miller's Tale.'" *Romanic Review* 86:2 (1995), 243-64; Malone, Edward A. "Doubting Thomas and John the Carpenter's Oaths in the 'Miller's Tale.'" *English Language Notes* 29:1 (September 1991), 15-17; Salter, Elizabeth. *Fourteenth-Century English Poetry*. Oxford: Clarendon Press, 1983.

Laura Cooner Lambdin

MINNESINGER. The minnesingers were the twelfth and thirteenth century *lyric poets of the German courts. They mostly performed the minnesongs or songs of love, although they also sang songs of religion and politics. Their poetry was greatly affected by the *Provençal troubadours; minnesingers often created great works in the tradition of *courtly love. Among the most famous minnesingers were the twelfth century Friedrich von Hausen and the thirteenth century *Walther von der Vogelweiden.

SELECTED BIBLIOGRAPHY

Riemer, Waldemar and Eugene Egert. "The Presentation and Function of Artistic Elements in Gottfried von Strassburg's 'Tristan.'" *Seminar* 30:2 (May 1994), 95-106; Thurlow, Peter. "Gottfried und Minnesang." *German Life and Letters* 48:3 (July 1995) 401-12.

Robert T. Lambdin

MINSTREL. Minstrels were musical entertainers or travelling poets of the late Middle Ages. They had their roots in the earlier tradition of the *gleemen or the *jongleurs. Minstrels were popular in the late thirteenth and fourteenth centuries and played an important part in the culture of their age. Typically, minstrels wandered from town to town, entertaining crowds by playing instruments, singing songs, reciting *romances, and delivering news. They were popular among all classes of society, from the masses to the clerics to the royalty.

Minstrels often composed original *lyrics, *ballads, legends, and romances. Thus they were not only musicians but also actors, journalists, and poets. A good example of a minstrel romance is *Havelok the Dane*. The minstrels were very popular during Geoffrey *Chaucer's time; however, their popularity and status declined in the fifteenth century. After the introduction of the printing press, they disappeared almost entirely.

SELECTED BIBLIOGRAPHY

Taylor, Andrew. "Fragmentation, Corruption, and Minstrel Narration: The Question of the Middle English Romances." *Yearbook of English Studies* 22 (1992), 38-62; Vasta, Edward. "Chaucer, Gower, and the Unknown Minstrel: The Literary Liberation of the Loathly Lady." *Exemplaria* 7:2 (Fall 19955), 395-418.

Robert T. Lambdin

MONGKE (?-1259), Mongol. Mongke was as great a general as were his predecessors, but he was foremost a reformer. He trimmed the excesses of the Mongol court, and under his rule commerce and trade flowered. As a military leader, he sent his brother Hulagu rampaging through western Asia. This campaign ended the Abbasid caliphate. Another brother, Kublai, led the Mongol assault against the last of the Chinese civilizations of the time, the Song Empire. While on a raid against Hezhou, Mongke fell ill and died. Although his successors held the empire together until 1368, its expansive days had passed.

SELECTED BIBLIOGRAPHY

Benson, Douglas S. *The Mongol Campaigns in Asia: A Summary of Mongolian Warfare with the Governments of Eastern and Western Asia in the 13th Century*. Chicago: The Author, 1991; Rashid al-Din Tabib. *The Successors of Ghengis Khan*. John Andrew Boyle, trans. New York: Columbia University Press, 1971.

R. Churchill Curtis

MONGOLIAN LITERATURE. The Mongolian Empire arose from the obscurity of the steppes in 1207 with the conquering of the Kirghiz and Oirat people by *Genghis Khan. The Mongols were a fierce people who, although they were nomads, banded into ails or aimaks--family units--that were tied to certain blocks of territory. They could move freely within that parcel, but were prohibited from crossing the boundaries into a territory belonging to another aimak.

Because the Mongols were nomads, their division into smaller units ruled by princes who were accountable to the khan meant that devotion to one's leader was prized above most other virtues. In a society spread out over such a large expanse of territory, complete adherence to and respect for the dictates of a centralized government was the only method for maintaining order within that society. There was no really effective method for policing such widely flung groups.

One of the other key elements in a nomadic society was, of course, transportation. The Mongolians prized their horses very highly because they were the only means for traveling with any rapidity across the vast steppes of Mongolia and the lands they conquered. Because the horse was revered for its utility, the heroes of Mongolian epics frequently consulted their horses on matters of importance and were sometimes even saved by their horses. The animals generally did all the hard work and sometimes even replaced their human masters as the heroes of the stories.

Prior to Genghis's rule history and teachings were transmitted orally around the campfires at night and sometimes on horseback during the frequent moves from location to location within a clan territory, but the Mongols had no court historians recording such information systematically. In fact, before Genghis they had no official alphabet and no real time for scholarship. Military orders and messages sent by messengers across long distances were not written down but were composed in alliterative rhyme, with the first letter of each of two or four lines being the same, so that the messenger could easily memorize the lines.

Mongolian poetic works were also frequently written in this alliterative rhyming style, likely for much the same reason. One of the more popular forms of entertainment was secular songs performed in a sort of amateur theater in one of the camp yards at night. The songs were woven around a story and formed a sort of operetta-like performance.

Once Genghis created his empire, however, a relatively peaceful era set in, and trade was conducted more often than warfare. It was during this period of settling that more of the Mongols began getting an education and learning how to read and write their own language and even the languages of neighboring peoples. Members of the nobility--the "Steppe Aristocrats"--began employing scribes to write official documents and put together written histories of the Mongol people as a whole, and some of the royal families had their family histories recorded in books that were considered both sacred and secret and were only to be seen by the eyes of the members of that family. As is true of many societies in which very few people can write, these books and anything written were considered almost to have magical powers and were regarded as something very akin to talismans. Most chapels and monasteries in Tibet had what was known as a Bungchang, a small room in which anything written was kept. In fact, clergy would frequently keep even incomplete manuscripts and fragments, such was the level of their reverence for anything written.

Just as medieval European scholars and clergy wrote official documents in Latin, the Mongolian scholars and clergy wrote their intellectual works in Tibetan instead of in the vernacular. The majority of educated Mongolians were the lamas, who knew Tibetan well, and sometimes even Sanskrit.

Political leaders like Genghis Khan were generally not book-smart, but knew enough about strategy to use the intellect of men who were educated when circumstances demanded. In fact, it was Genghis Khan who had the Mongols adopt the Uighur-Mongolian script so that they would have an alphabet. This was only replaced in 1294 when Kublai Khan commissioned the Tibetan monk Phagspa to devise an imperial script.

Unfortunately, in 1742 the Manchu Emperor Chien Ling ordered all books in possession of Mongolian families collected and brought to Peking. Accounts abound of instances in which, deliberately or inadvertently, valuable manuscripts were destroyed. The Uighur-Mongolian *The Golden Riddles of Genghis Khan* was just one of the many works that modern scholars only can access secondhand through accounts written by earlier scholars about the contents of such documents--accounts that are generally nothing more than tantalizing hints at the stories that have been lost.

At the beginning of the twentieth century the only known existing Mongolian work of literature was the historical chronicle of the Ordos prince Sagang Sechen, which was written in 1662. The *Chronicle of Sagang Sechen*, one of the many collections of stories and myths about Genghis Khan, was written to glorify the devotion of his vassals to the khan. One of the individual incidents that demonstrates this devotion is the reaction of Bogorchi to his master's overlooking him in doling out rewards. Bogorchi's wife pushes him to speak out against such ill treatment, but he tells her to hold her tongue. He reasons that Genghis is fair and honorable, so he will certainly give him reward for his unswerving loyalty in an appropriate way at an appropriate time. Genghis has been testing Bogorchi, and this answer earns him a sizeable award when it is related to the khan.

Early in the twentieth century, scholars began mounting serious searches throughout Mongolia for the hidden caches of manuscripts they believed had to exist somewhere. Most scholars by this time did not accept the theory that Chinese seizures of collections of Mongolian documents after the fall of the Mongolian Empire had been almost completely successful. Discoveries have been spotty at best, with finds being purely accidental a great deal of the time, but some expeditions have netted valuable manuscripts.

Fragments were all that were found of a Mongolian gloss on a manuscript of the *Bodhicaryavatara*, a Sanskrit work that provided instruction on how to live one's life in order to be reincarnated as a Bodhisattva. The work had been printed in 1312, and the translation had been done by a Tibetan who served the Mongol emperors, Chogsi Odser. However, this was one of the more important finds in a cache uncovered by an expedition in the desert near the Turfan depression.

Another item found in that excavation was a hymn to a lamaist deity, which had also been written by Chogsi Odser. Other items included fragments of letters from Mongol officials, religious writings, and scraps of documents. The ultimate importance of these findings was not only the contents of the documents themselves, but the discovery that there had been fourteenth-century Mongolian printed works.

Subsequent to this discovery, closer attention was paid to some documents that had been unearthed in 1902 and were assumed to be part of a large collection of notebooks containing financial data. As it turned out, the later pages in the notebook contained a large piece of a thirteenth-century Mongolian rendering of the epic of Alexander the Great. An original Mongolian Buddhist poem was also tacked on to the end of the manuscript.

A 1909 expedition to the ruins at Karakoto uncovered seventeen separate fourteenth-century Mongolian documents. Most were, again, fragments of letters or promissory notes or other official documents. One piece, however, consisted of thirty-four folios and gave directions for determining lucky and unlucky days. One of the smaller fragments was a fourteen-line rendering of one of Genghis Khan's rules for living.

Completely by chance, an agricultural worker came upon the grave of a Mongol soldier near the Volga. The body was clasping twenty-five scraps of birch bark, on which was written a poem that lamented the need for being so far from family and friends. It is the words of a young soldier out on campaign who wants nothing more than to be home with his mother and brothers and says nothing about love of country. The refrain anticipates the soldier's returning home quickly. Birch bark was commonly used by Mongolian commoners when they had nothing else on which to write.

Even the manuscripts that have come down to us basically intact and have been studied by scholars for a considerable number of years are still open to disagreements. For instance, *The Secret History of the Mongols* is generally believed to have been completed in the year 1240, but the reasoning for this is that it is known to have been completed in the year of the rat. Some scholars have made very convincing cases for the particular year of the rat in which this piece was completed being either earlier or later: it has variously been assigned to 1252, 1264, and 1228, though most scholars agree that 1240 is the most likely date.

Scholars are not even sure what language it was originally written in. Bits of it have been found in the Uighur-Mongolian script, so it was thought to have been composed in that, but others hold that the version written in the Sino-Mongolian script is the original. Still others contend that the first version was in the Phagspa script. Even the date of the first Chinese translation has been argued. It was first proposed that it was made sometime between 1368 and 1404, but other scholars have asserted that it was done in 1382. They were answered that it had to have been completed prior to that year, and then yet another scholar asserted that it was done in the year 1369. In 1934 Professor Ch'en Yuan put forth the theory that it must have been done between 1389 and 1398 because the devices used in the translation represent an improvement on the devices used in a manuscript compiled in 1382.

In any case, the *Secret History of the Mongols* is the oldest literary work written in Mongolian that has come down to modern scholars. Much of our knowledge of other works is secondhand, discovered through references made by later scholars or by travelers who brought back written summaries or descriptions of such works in their own languages. Palladius, who discovered the *Secret History* and translated it into Russian, concluded that this work was a compilation of fragments and borrowings from many different epic poems and stories and didactic literature and was assembled by more than one author.

Although the ostensible subject of this work is a history of Genghis Khan and his immediate family, scholars have noted that the real heroes seem to be the Steppe Aristocracy who are the leaders under Genghis Khan. There are some who believe that the attention paid to his knights takes away from the glory that should be accorded to the khan. However, as several scholars have pointed out, the emphasis on the power and skill of the knights reflects positively on the khan because his ability to rule such fabulous warriors makes him an even more remarkable leader. The reverence due to a leader who can inspire utter devotion in his followers and to the followers who are capable of unswerving devotion to duty and their lord is a common theme in early Mongolian literature.

The *Tarikh-i-Rashidi* of Mirza Haidar, like many of the surviving documents from medieval Mongolia, was written to preserve the memory of the Moghuls and their khans. It has been proposed that Mirza Haidar saw the power of the khans disintegrating as they intermarried with the races they conquered and adopted their customs. The infighting between the rulers and those who wished to take the throne from them led to a very quick turnover in rulers and to frequent shifting in boundaries of territories within the empire.

This particular manuscript is intended specifically to cover the story of the khans who separated from the main branch of the Chagatai, who were the ruling family in Transoxiana. The first part of the *Tarikh-i-Rashidi* is purely historical and was written in Kashmir in 1544 or 1545 and completed in 1546. The second part, written between 1546 and 1547, consists of personal reminiscences by the author about the princes, like Chagatai and Uzbeg, with whom he was acquainted.

Written in Persian, the *Tarikh-i-Rashidi* frequently lapses into verse, as do the majority of Mongolian prose works. Although it was intended to be an understandable, complete chronicle, the sentences are for the most part very long and complicated, meandering around the point and frequently failing entirely to come to any logical conclusion. The chronology is spotty, the figures and measurements are not stringently accurate, and the information is necessarily loose since it was passed straight to Mirza Haidar straight from oral tradition.

Rashid Ashid ad-Din, or Rashid al-Din, was a deputy to the vizier of the Mongol ruler of Persia, Ghazan, who ruled from 1295 to 1304. Born into a Jewish family in 1247, Rashid ad-Din was employed as a court physician to Khan Abaqua, the second Mongol ruler of Iran, who ruled from 1265 to 1281. Rashid ad-Din was eventually given by Ghazan, who was khan from 1295 to 1304, the task of compiling a history of the Mongol forefathers.

Ghazan's successor, Oljetu, who ruled from 1304 to 1316, had Rashid ad-Din complete the work under his auspices. To this end, the family history was repeated to him from the chronicle of the house, the *Altan Debter* or *Golden Book*, but because he was not a member of the family, he could not read it himself. That manuscript is now lost, but the book Rashid ad-Din compiled, the *Jami al-Tawarikh*, or *Complete Collection of Histories* has come down to us.

An early version, written between 1306 and 1307, consisted of three volumes, but the final version, completed in 1310, was comprised of four volumes. The first volume was a history of the Mongols from their beginning to the reign of Ghazan. The second volume, which began the part commissioned by Oljetu, was a general history of all the Eurasian people with whom the Mongols had come into contact, including the pre-Islamic kings of Persia, Muhammad, the caliphate up to 1250 when it was wiped out by the Mongols, the post-Muhammadan dynasties of Persia, Oghuz and his family, the Turks, the Chinese, the Jewish people, the Franks, and the Indians. Oljetu's biography up to the time of writing was originally at the beginning of the second volume.

The third volume was originally a geographical work containing descriptions of roads and postal routes included. The third volume of the later version contains the genealogies of the ruling houses of the Arab, Jewish, Mongolian, Frankish, and Chinese nations. The final version of the *Jami al-Tawarikh* was arranged thus: the first part of volume I is on the Turkish and Mongol tribes and the second contains the history of Genghis Khan and his ancestors, volume II covers the successors of Genghis Khan, and volume III covers the Il-Khans of Persia.

The World History of Rashid ad-Din was completed after the *Jami al-Tawarikh*, and was a collection of writings that were edited and translated into Persian. It was meant to cover the history of the prophet Muhammad and his companions, of China, of Hind and Sind, and of the children of Israel. It contains many pictures to illustrate its pages, but was left unfinished at Rashid ad-Din's death. The manuscript that survives today has many title pages that have no accompanying pieces, and the text is very patchy. The pictures are the only part that are really of use to scholars.

Many of the tales from medieval Mongolian literature (as well as the oral tradition) are about Genghis Khan, since he was the founder of the Mongolian Empire. One of the major works written about Genghis Khan is the *Secret History of the Mongols*, which was written around 1240 and is the oldest literary work that has come down to us in Mongolian. The *Secret History* is a series of epic stories strung together to present the partly mythical, partly factual history of the house of Genghis Khan.

The *Secret History* begins with a tracing of Genghis Khan's lineage that establishes his royal birthright, moves to a recounting of Alun Gua's miraculous conception and the birth of her three sons, and then switches back to tracing the family tree up to the birth of Genghis Khan and the death of Yesugei Bagatur. From there it moves into a series of stories about Genghis Khan, including several about his military and political activities. There are, of course, also some rather fantastic stories about the exploits of his knights: Uru'ut, Mangqut, Temujin, Joci Qasar, and Otcigin. The *Secret History* ends with the story of Genghis's death and the beginning of the rule of Ogedei.

Many experts feel that this is a compilation of the work of several authors who were either in Genghis's court or at least lived during the time of Genghis, rather than being a work by a single author. Scholars have noted that the heroes of this epic compilation appear to be Genghis's knights rather than the khan himself, and some feel that this detracts from the power of Genghis Khan. However, as scholars have noted, the fact that Genghis Khan could control a group of warriors with such fabulous powers only serves to cover him with greater glory, for to control them he must in some way be more powerful than them all.

The *Tale of Genghis's Two Runners* is an old Mongolian epic story about the khan that is mentioned frequently in various works written on the literature and folklore of the Mongolians. Scholars consider this tale of two brothers who were born from the mare Eremeg cagagci to be one of the best-written tales in the Genghis cult of epics

The two brothers were faithful servants to the khan and frequently rode out in the hunt. The younger brother eventually became insulted that they did not seem to garner much attention from the khan although they were strong and faithful. He persuaded his elder brother to run away from the khan to make him notice how valuable they were. The younger brother left, with the elder following reluctantly after a deep struggle with himself. The khan spent three years searching for the brothers, during which time the younger enjoyed his freedom, but the elder weakened from pining away for his khan and his mother.

After a time the younger brother became so worried about the health of his brother that he decided that they had to return to the khan so he would get well. There was a touching reunion between the master and his two foolish followers, ending with the khan riding the elder to a roundup and dedicating the younger one to a deity. It is from this incident that the practice of dedicating horses to deities ostensibly arose.

One of the minor pieces of literature that concern the Mongolian leader, Genghis Khan is the *Blue Book*, which was a compilation the khan had put together of his legal judgments. He began this practice of saving his edicts for posterity from 1206, which was the year he was elected khan. He ordered Shigis Hutuktu, one of his faithful followers, to keep this record in blue script on white paper.

Foreign scholars were frequently pressed into service by the Mongols. Kirakos of Ganjak (1201-1272) was an Armenian who was forced to serve the Mongols when he was captured in an invasion around 1241. His manuscript on the history of the Mongols, begun around the time he was captured, contains within it both a physical description of the invaders and a list of Mongolian words that he picked up. He also detailed the religious and social beliefs and customs of the Mongols, but one of the most striking features of his account is his rendition of the tale of Genghis's conception and birth. The tale of Alun

Gua, which also appears in the *Secret History*, is presented by Kirakos as having been told to him by one of the commanders, and this is the oldest manuscript in which this tale appears.

The *Yuan-shih*, the history of Mongolian rule of China, was written at the very end of the Mongol rule in that country. Emperor Shun-ti ordered the work compiled in 1343 at the instigation of project initiators and ministers Berke Buqa and Aruqtu and had it printed in 1345. The Bureau of Historiography appointed a group of Chinese, Jurchen, Tibetan, Turkish, Turkik-Mongolian, Muhammadan, Uighur, and Qarluq compilers, inspectors, and proofreaders. What makes this work different from most of the Mongolian histories is that while the previous works were mostly based on oral history, the *Yuan-shih* was written using the Chinese techniques of consulting written records to obtain pertinent factual material combined with the Mongolian flair for making a good story out of history.

The *Yuan-shih* is the history of three Chinese dynasties under Mongol rule, but what is unusual about this work is that it reflects more of the cultural traits of the conquered country than of the ruling empire. Many conquered peoples are forced to adopt the language, religion, and cultural customs of their conquerors, but since the Mongols had no real written language and very little education, they recognized that they could make use of the Chinese system that was already established. To that end, the Mongolian court had a bilingual administration, and documents that were not written in Chinese were frequently written in what has cleverly been dubbed "translationese Chinese," which was composed in Mongolian word order.

The History of the World Conqueror, written by Juvaini, breaks off in the reign of the Great Khan *Mongke, who ruled from 1251 to 1259. Juvaini served in the court of Il-Kahn Hulegu, the Mongol ruler of Baghdad. He was an eyewitness of some of the events he reported, having been present at the destruction of the headquarters of the Assassins at Alamut and the Mongol invasion of Khwarzim.

His purpose in writing the *History* was not only to record history for posterity, but also to justify the Mongolian rule. He recorded the events in his *History* and noted that after the successful sack of Bukhara, Genghis and his men had a huge drunken revel with the native dancing girls and then demanded tithes of the rich men of the town. Genghis then stood up, Juvaini reported, and told the townspeople that he and his forces were a punishment from God for the atrocities they had committed.

Juvaini began writing his history at Karakorum somewhere between May 1252 and September 1253. When he was appointed the governor of Baghdad in 1260, he had still not completed the *History* and must have given up on it, since it remained unfinished. The *History* reflects Juvaini's mastery of the Persian prose style through his use of word play and frequent lapses into moralizing or didacticism. He also periodically broke off into poetry, both his own and traditional verses.

SELECTED BIBLIOGRAPHY

Boyle, John Andrew. *The Mongol World Empire: 1260-1370*. London: Variorum Reprints, 1977; Chambers, James. *The Devil's Horsemen: The Mongol Invasion of Europe*. London: Weidenfeld and Nicolson, 1979; Cleaves, Francis Woodman. *The Secret History of the Mongols*. Vol 1. Cambridge, MA: Harvard University Press, 1982; Gray, Basil. *The World History of Rashid al-Din: A Study of the Royal Asiatic Society Manuscript*. London: Faber & Faber, 1978; Haidar, Mirza Muhammad. *A History of the Moghuls of Central Asia*. E. Denison Ross, trans. London: Curzon Press, 1972; Heissig, Walther. *A Lost Civilization: The Mongols Rediscovered*. London: Thames and Hudson, 1964; Hsiao, Ch'i-ch'ing. *The Military Establishment of the Yuan Dynasty*. Cambridge, MA: Harvard University Press, 1978; Juvaini. *The History of the World-Conqueror*. John Andrew Boyle, trans. 2 vols. Manchester: Manchester University Press, 1958; Lattimore, Owen. *Nomads and Commiasars: Mongolia Revisited*. New York: Oxford University Press, 1962. Pao, Kuo-Yi. *Studies on the Secret History of the Mongols*. Bloomington, IN: Indiana University Press, 1965; Poppe, Nicholas. *The Heroic Epic of the Khalkha Mongols*. J. Kreuger, D. Montgomery, and M. Walter, trs. Bloomington, IN: Mongolia Society, 1979. Rashid al-Din Tabib. *The Successors of Genghis Khan*. John Andrew Boyle, trans. New York: Columbia University Press, 1971.

Sara Parker

"MONK'S TALE, THE." In Geoffrey *Chaucer's *Canterbury Tales* (c. 1387-1400), "The Monk's Tale" is a series of seventeen tragedies recounted by the monk. Oddly, there is no didactic content or Christian message. The Monk seems horrified by any loss of riches or worldly treasures, making him appear shallow and hypocritical. The tragedies mostly come from the Bible, history and mythology and include the stories of Lucifer, Adam, Samson, Heracles, Nebuchadnezzar, Belshazzar, Nero, Alexander, and Julius Caesar. The Knight eventually interrupts the Monk's mournful recitation of historical tragedies.

SELECTED BIBLIOGRAPHY

Bush, Douglas. *English Poetry*. New York: Oxford University Press, 1963; DiMarco, Vincent. "Nero's Nets and Seneca's Veins: A New Source for the 'Monk's Tale.'" *Chaucer Review* 28:4 (1994), 384-92; Garbáty, Thomas J. *Medieval English Literature*. Toronto: Heath, 1984; Lambdin, Laura C., and Robert T. Lambdin, eds. *Chaucer's Pilgrims: An Historical Guide to the Pilgrims in the "Canterbury Tales."* Westport, CT: Greenwood Press, 1996.

Laura Cooner Lambdin

MORTE D'ARTHUR. See *Malory, Sir Thomas.*

MUM AND THE SOTHSEGGER. *Mum and the Sothsegger* is a fifteenth century alliterative poem composed in England. The work is a complaint aimed at the tumultuous reign of *Richard II at the same time that it delivers advice to Henry IV. The content of the entire poem is unknown, for only two sections of the original poem are extant. Unfortunately, there is a distinct gap between the two surviving sections of *Mum and the Sothsegger*.

The first section, found in a Cambridge manuscript, was originally titled *Richard the Redeless*. It is divided into a prologue and four sections or *passus*; in this way it is similar to William *Langland's *Piers the Plowman*. This led many early critics to falsely believe Langland to be the author. The second portion of thework, now located in the British Library, contains some 1,700 lines in a form oddly reminiscent of a mystery play (*see* **Drama**, **Medieval**). It contains allegorical characters, many of whom are unwilling to speak about the bad days in the reign of Richard II. The "Truth-teller" ("Sothsegger") of this poem is not believed by the other figures, even though he tells no lies; this is a blatant attack on Richard II's reign, where it appears that the spoken truth concerning the condition of the monarchy was unwelcome.

SELECTED BIBLIOGRAPHY

Barr, Helen. "The Treatment of Natural Law in 'Richard the Redeless' and 'Mum and the Sothsegger.'" *Leeds Studies in English* 23 (1992), 49-80; Wilcockson, Colin. "'Mum and the Sothsegger', Richard II, and Henry V." *Review of English Studies* 46:182 (May 1995), 219-24.

Robert T. Lambdin

N

NENNIUS (fl. 800s). Nennius's *Historia Brittonum* (History of the Britons) is the earliest extant historical source for the *Arthurian legend and for the legendary founder of Britain, Brutus--a story popularized by *Geoffrey of Monmouth. Nennius had numerous sources, including *Gildas, possibly *Bede, and local oral tradition. He wrote in the early 800s in the south of Wales, and his work covers the time from creation to 687, rather chaotically, ending almost 150 years before he wrote. His accounts of some incidents, like Arthur's twelve battles, are brief but suggestive of greater depths to stories he only hints at. He includes stories or legends of Brutus, Vortigen, St. Cuthbert, St. Patrick, and Arthur; mentions the Romans, Picts and Irish (*see Celtic Literature, Early*) as they contribute to British history; and includes information on British geography. His manuscript often includes the *Annales Cambriae* (Welsh *Annals from 447 to 954) at its end. (*See Chronicles and Annals.*)

SELECTED BIBLIOGRAPHY

Edwards, Thomas Charles. "The Arthur of History." in *The Arthur of the Welsh: Arthurian Legend in Medieval Welsh Literature*. Rachel Bramwich, *et al*, eds. Cardiff: University of Wales Press, 1991. 15-32; Nennius. *British History and the Welsh Annals*. John Morris, ed. and trans. Totowa, N.J.: Rowman and Littlefield, 1980; Smalley, Beryl. *Historians in the Middle Ages*. New York: Scribner's, 1974; Sterns, Indrikis. *The Greater Medieval Historians: An Interpretation and a Bibliography*. Lanham, MD: University Press of America, 1980; *The Works of Gildas and Nennius*. J. A. Giles, trans. London: J. Bohn, 1841.

Richard McDonald

"NOU SPRINKES THE SPRAI." The three-stanza Middle English secular *lyric "Nou Sprinkes the Sprai" is an example of the *chanson d'aventure* and is also in the form of a carol with a three-line burden. The narrative in the poem alternates between a female and a male speaker. Like most carols, this lyric begins with a burden that is then repeated after each stanza.

The opening burden is in the voice of a woman who states that now "sprinkes the sprai," meaning that nature is blooming, but she adds that she is so love sick she cannot sleep. The first stanza shifts into the voice of a male narrator who describes how, as he is riding out, he hears a young woman begin to sing. Her song begins with a curse, "The clot him clingge," which roughly means "may the earth/grave stick to/waste him." She goes on to exclaim how unhappy the person is who must always live in love-longing. The second stanza goes back to the male narrator, who calls the woman's song a "mirie note" and rides in her direction. He finds her in an arbor under a bough "with ioie inogh" and asks her why she sings. In the third stanza the young woman replies shortly that her beloved is untrue and "chaunges anewe." This final stanza ends with her statement that if she can contrive it, she will make him repent his treatment of her.

This lyric is particularly interesting for several reasons. First, the male speaker is a kind of "unreliable" narrator, a naíve narrator like the persona used in several of Geoffrey *Chaucer's works. The male speaker's happy mood and his insistence that the girl is a "mirie mai" misleads us in terms of her song. This expectation, as Edmund Reiss pointed out, creates an unexpected ending. In most lyrics of this genre the male and female speakers engage in a wooing dialogue, but here the poem ends with the maiden's grief and anger.

SELECTED BIBLIOGRAPHY

Barratt, Alexandra, ed. *Women's Writing in Middle English.* London and New York: Longman, 1992; Figg, Kristen Mossler. *The Short Lyric Poems of Jean Froissart.* New York: Garland, 1994; Pickering, O. S. "Newly Discovered Secular Lyrics from Later Thirteenth-Century Cheshire." *Review of English Studies* 43 (1992): 157-80; Reiss, Edmund. "The Middle English Lyric." In *Old and Middle English Literature. Dictionary of Literary Biography.* Vol. 146. Jeffrey Helterman and Jerome Mitchell, eds. Detroit: Gale, 1994. 392-99; Sigal, Gale. *Erotic Dawn-Songs of the Middle Ages: Voicing the Lyric Lady.* Gainesville: University Press of Florida, 1996; Stevick, Robert D., ed. *One Hundred Middle English Lyrics.* Rev. Urbana: University of Illinois Press, 1994.

Sigrid King

"NOW GOOTH SUNNE UNDER WODE." "Now Gooth Sunne under Wode," a twelfth-century example of the devotional *lyric, is attributed to St. Godric. The poem is a quatrain of four-stress lines rhyming *aabb*:

> Now gooth sunne under wode:
> Me reweth [pity], Marye, thy faire rode.
> Now gooth sunne under tree:
> Me reweth, Marye, thy sone and three.

The four lines of the poem are built around incremental repetition as the speaker addresses Mary. The first line describes the sun going down under the wood. In the second line the speaker expresses pity for Mary's fair "rode."

The poem moves from a general observation of the sun setting to the specific situation of Mary's loss: the sunset and the darkening wood, which Lewis Owen saw as meaning the figures of the Crucifixion to the poet. Like many other short lyric poems of this period, this seemingly simple work is made more complex by puns and wordplay. Edmund Reiss explained that "rode" means both countenance and cross. There are also puns on sun/son and wode/wood. Lewis and Nancy Owen noted that the darkening of the Virgin's face may be from the setting sun but also from her grief.

SELECTED BIBLIOGRAPHY

Owen, Lewis, and Nancy Owen, eds. *Middle English Poetry: An Anthology*. Indianapolis: Bobbs-Merrill, 1971; Pickering, O. S. "Newly Discovered Secular Lyrics from Later Thirteenth-Century Cheshire." *Review of English Studies* 43 (1992): 157-80; Reiss, Edmund. "The Middle English Lyric." In *Old and Middle English Literature*. Dictionary of Literary Biography. Vol. 146. Jeffrey Helterman and Jerome Mitchell, eds. Detroit: Gale, 1994. 392-399; Ruud, Jay. *"Many a Song and Many a Leccherous Lay": Tradition and Individuality in Chaucer's Lyric Poetry*. New York: Garland, 1992; Sigal, Gale. *Erotic Dawn-Songs of the Middle Ages: Voicing the Lyric Lady*. Gainesville: University Press of Florida, 1996; Stevick, Robert D., ed. *One Hundred Middle English Lyrics*. Rev. Urbana: University of Illinois Press, 1994.

Sigrid King

"NUN'S PRIEST'S TALE, THE." "The Nun's Priest's Tale," a *beast fable and mock heroic epic of Geoffrey *Chaucer's *Canterbury Tales* (c. 1387-1400), is one of the best known tales in the collection. It is both humorous and an instructive moral *exemplum. It was evidently a very popular tale in medieval England, as it appears in many manuscripts.

Chaunticleer the cock has a nightmare in which he dreams of being chased by a fox. When he expresses his horror to Pertelote, his favorite of his seven hens, she is disdainful of his fear and suggests that his dreams are caused by indigestion. The cock is angered enough to give Pertelote a sermon on the value of dreams. Don Russell, the fox, does indeed trick Chaunticleer into throwing back his head and closing his eyes to crow. The fox then seizes the cock and carries him off. Ultimately Chaunticleer tricks Don Russell into opening his mouth; the cock flies up into a tree and refuses to come down.

SELECTED BIBLIOGRAPHY

Bush, Douglas. *English Poetry*. New York: Oxford University Press, 1963; Fehrenbacher, Richard W. "'A Yeerd Enclosed Al Aboute': Literature as History in the

'Nun's Priest's Tale.'" *Chaucer Review* 29:2 (1994), 134-48; Furr, Grover C. Nominalism in the 'Nun's Priest's Tale: A Preliminary Study." In *Literary Nominalism and the Theory of Rereading Late Medieval Texts: A New Research Paradigm*. Richard J. Utz, ed. Lewiston, NY: Edwin Mellen, 1995. 135-46; Garbáty, Thomas J. *Medieval English Literature*. Toronto: Heath, 1984; Lambdin, Laura C., and Robert T. Lambdin, eds. *Chaucer's Pilgrims: An Historical Guide to the Pilgrims in the "Canterbury Tales."* Westport, CT: Greenwood Press, 1996; Nilsen, Don L. F. "Geoffrey Chaucer's Humor." *In Geardagum* 15 (1994), 77-84; Salter, Elizabeth. *Fourteenth-Century English Poetry*. Oxford: Clarendon Press, 1983.

Laura Cooner Lambdin

"NUT BROWN MAID." A fifteenth century English *ballad, "Nut Brown Maid" lauds a woman's constancy. It notes how the Nut Brown Maid is wooed by a knight who pretends that he has been banished. The knight, the son of an earl, pretends that he is a squire of low estate to test his beloved, the daughter of a baron. He alleges that he is fated to live his life as an outlaw forced into exile.

Every other stanza in the poem then presents extremely harsh images of the hardships that he will have to endure as a banished man. His beloved responds by stating her everlasting love for him; she will accompany him or die of a broken heart. The knight is exhilarated that his cherished lady has responded thus; she has validated her loyalty to him. After she has proven her love for him, the knight then reveals that he has not truly been banished and that he is in reality the son of a rich earl. The happy couple are then united and lead a life of grandeur.

This *lyric is a kind of cross between the ballad and the medieval *debate poems. The work resembles somewhat Walter's testing of Griselda in Geoffrey *Chaucer's *"Cleric's Tale." In this way it is reflective of the controversial question of whether women are as noble as men.

SELECTED BIBLIOGRAPHY

Morgan, Gwendolyn. *Medieval Balladry and the Courtly Tradition*. New York: Peter Lang, 1993; Morgan, Gwendolyn. *Medieval Ballads: Chivalry, Romance, and Everyday Life*. New York: Peter Lang, 1996; Oates, Joyce Carol. "The English and Scottish Traditional Ballads." *Southern Review* 15 (1979), 560-66; Pearsall, Derek. *Old and Middle English Poetry*. London; Routledge and Kegan Paul, 1977.

Robert T. Lambdin

O

OCKHAM, WILLIAM OF (c. 1285-1349). William of Ockham was a prominent English Franciscan *Scholastic philosopher and theologian. Born at Ockham in Surrey, he attended Oxford, where he penned a critique of the *Sentences* of *Peter Lombard.

Ockham's philosophy, greatly influenced by his mentor, John *Duns Scotus, resulted in the revival of a type of Nominalism, which maintained the difference between concrete realities and the abstraction of universals. Ockham's logical method was the foundation of an approach that relied upon the Thomistic combination of Aristotelian philosophy and Christian theology. In this approach Ockham felt that intellectual abstracts were not valid types of knowledge; reasoning must be built on proofs. This view became the precursor for theological skepticism, the idea that the existence of God is not susceptible to proof by human reason, but can be postulated only by intuition. These views landed Ockham in trouble with the papacy. The pope called on him to answer charges against his beliefs, which he was later forced to renounce, but his later writings continued his assault on papal policy. In his *Dialogues* (c. 1343) he attacked the temporal powers of the pope, asserting that a king had authority for civil matters. Ockham's *Razor* discusses his famous principle of using economy in logic, saying that assumptions used to explain phenomena should not be multiplied beyond what is needed.

SELECTED BIBLIOGRAPHY

Alanen, Lilli. "Descartes, Duns Scotus, and Ockham on Omnipotence and Possibility." *Franciscan Studies* 45 (1985), 157-88; Etzcorn, Girard J. "Ockham at a Provincial Chapter: 1323, Prelude to Abignon." *Archivum Franciscanum Historicum* 83:3 (July 1990), 557-76; Kennedy, Leonard A. "Early Fourteenth Century Franciscans and Divine Absolute Power." 50 (1990), 197-233; Klocker, Harry R. "Ockham and the Divine Freedom." *Franciscan Studies* 45 (1985), 245-61.

Robert T. Lambdin

OGHAM (OGAM). Ogham is the twenty-letter alphabet of the ancient British and Irish, used from about the fifth to the tenth centuries. The symbols are conjunctions of strokes for consonants and notches for vowels. This alphabet was purportedly invented by Ogam, mainly for use in inscriptions on wood and stone. This ancient alphabet became the choice of the druids, who maintained its use until their religion was usurped by Christianity and the language became Latinized.

SELECTED BIBLIOGRAPHY

McManus, Damian. *A Guide to Ogam.* Maynooth, Ireland: Sagart, 1991; Sims, William Patrick. "The Additional Letters of the Ogam Alphabet." *Cambridge Medieval Celtic Studies* 23 (Summer 1992), 29-75; Sims, William Patrick. "Some Problems in Deciphering the Early Irish Ogam Alphabet." *Transactions of the Philological Society* 91:2 (1993), 133-80.

Robert T. Lambdin

OGIER THE DANE. One of *Charlemagne's paladins, Ogier is a hero of French medieval *romances. His character may have been derived from Autgarius, originally one of Charlemagne's enemies, but later an ally. Traditionally, Ogier was a captive of Charlemagne's court, held as ransom for his father, Geoffrey of Dannemarch (Denmark). Ogier gained Charlemagne's favor for heroic deeds in Italy, but he killed the queen's nephew to avenge his son's death, and was therefore pursued, captured, and imprisoned. He was released to fight the Saracens in Spain and so came again into Charlemagne's favor. Eventually he was rewarded with the fills of Hainaut and Braburt.

     Another legend involves Ogier with Morgan le Fay, who brings him to Avalon when he is one hundred years old. She introduces him to King Arthur (*see* **Arthurian Legend**); Ogier becomes rejuvenated and ventures out to fight for France. She brings him back before he can fight a battle, keeping him virile until he is needed again.

SELECTED BIBLIOGRAPHY

Stablein, Patricia Harris. "Patterns of Textual Shift and the Alien Hero: 'Ogier the Dane' in the Europeanization of the French Epic." *Olifant* 12:1 (Spring 1987), 47-61; Wimsatt, James I. "Type Conceptions of the Good Knight in the French Arthurian Cycles, Malory, and Chaucer." In *Heroes and Heroines in Medieval English Literature.* Leo Carruthers, ed. Cambridge: Brewer, 1994, 137-48.

Robert T. Lambdin

OGODEI (1229-1241), Mongol Chingis. As his father's, *Genghis Khan's, chosen successor, Ogodei brought great administrative ability to the khanate. Far surpassed in bravery by his brother, Tolui, Ogodei was clearly the most brilliant of the four sons of Genghis. He soon demonstrated his abilities, marshalling his willful brothers under one banner. Under his leadership, the Mongols penetrated as far west as they were ever to do. They conquered both Russia and the Polish principalities in their victory at the Battle of Legnica in 1241.

Ogodei's first years were spent settling counter-claims of sovereignty in the Muslim Middle East, invading Korea, and, most important, completing the conquest of northern China. In 1236, when his army set out across the northern steppes for the West, Ogodei stayed behind to begin the construction of his new capital at Karakorum. This construction marked a significant cultural change, for the great khan was no longer a nomadic warrior but became a sedentary figure. A self-indulgent man who certainly possessed a fondness for alcohol, Ogodei enjoyed the pleasures of the capital and new palace while his armies stormed across the continent. Under the brilliant military leadership of his nephew Batu, the Mongols marched westward, smashing the forces of Christendom in Poland and Hungary. Only the death of Ogodei in 1241 saved Vienna.

SELECTED BIBLIOGRAPHY

Benson, Douglas S. *The Mongol Campaigns in Asia. A Summary of Mongolian Warfare with the Governments of Eastern and Western Asia in the 13th Century.* Chicago: The Author, 1991; Rashid al-Din Tabib. *The Successors of Ghengis Khan.* John Andrew Boyle, trans. New York: Columbia University Press, 1971.

R. Churchill Curtis

OLD ENGLISH POETRY. Just as we are indebted to Geoffrey *Chaucer's Middle English character sketches, our understanding of the *Anglo-Saxon era would be poorer and less accurate without examination of Old English poetry. As in the Old Testament Psalms with parallel construction (repetitive, contradictory, or incremental), the poetry of the era is essentially parallel and, unlike the Hebrew texts, alliterative. In many ways the balance of Anglo-Saxon verse resembles closely the balanced parallelism of Jonathan Swift and Alexander Pope and their early eighteenth century English verse.

Each Old English line is made up of two half-lines consisting of two accents each with variable numbers of unaccented syllables, and each half-line totaling at least four syllables, with the two halves bound together by consonantal alliteration. This can best be illustrated by *Judith*, an anonymous poem of the *Cynewulfian school:

Then a band of bold knights . . . busily gathered,
Keen men at the conflict; . . . with courage they stepped forth,
Bearing banners, . . . brave-hearted companions,

And fared to the fight, . . . forth in right order,
At the dawning of day; . . . dinned forth their shields
A loud-voiced alarm . . . Now listened in joy
The lankwold in the wood . . . and the wan raven,
Battle-hungry bird, . . . both knowing well
That the gallant people . . . would give them soon
A feast on the fated; . . . now flew on their track
The deadly devourer, . . . the dewy-winged eagle,
Singing his war song, . . . the swart-coated bird,
The horned of beak.
                        (199-211; trans. Faust & Thompson)

This passage superbly illustrates a number of the characteristics of Old English verse. The plethora of *alliterative consonants are obvious binders of the two half-lines. Perhaps because of the military flavor of the situation, such alliteration seemed more masculine to the later British romantic poets and especially to the British Proletarian poets (1929-1939). We note that like *Beowulf, the chief topic is battle and that in pagan poetry (meaning pagan with only a slight mingling of Christian themes as over against later Old English verse that was much more explicitly Christian, with only a few remnants of earlier beginnings) the role of fate is powerful: "A feast of the fated."

It is also clear that if war is glorified, it is also deplored. So the stanza that begins with knights, keen, courageous, brave-hearted, and heroic, ends with the delightful anticipation of birds and beasts of prey that they will soon turn to a feast that they have not run down and killed, but that men have killed for them. Thus the emphasis upon the world, now hungry but soon to be sated, the raven that profits from the battles of men, and the eagle as the one sure gainer and symbol of men's inability to live at peace.

The Anglo-Saxon technique standard of composite adjectives known as *kenning can be found in this passage, although it does not predominate. Generally it would be expressed of a king as ring-giver or bracelet-bestower, a queen as weaver of peace, or the sea as whale-path. These conventional descriptives were so general in usage that it might be claimed that The *Battle of Brunnanburgh obtains half of its diction and imagery from the common usage of earlier poems. This tendency has so continued to the present day that the brave-hearted example might as easily be taken from current writing. Among poets who used this technique extensively, we need only name Gerard Manley Hopkins in the Victorian era and Dylan Thomas in the modern era. In this same modern age war tends to be presented as a strange mixture of individual heroism, national catastrophe, and general humor. This last element seems largely lacking from Old English poetry. Finally, the dark vision of this verse might be expressed by Deor in his *Deor's Lament:

"His lifelong companions . . . were pain and sorrow."

SELECTED BIBLIOGRAPHY

Alexander, Michael. trans. *The Earliest English Poems: A Bilingual Edition.* Berkeley: University of California Press, 1970; Bragg, Lois. *The Lyric Speakers of Old English Poetry.* Rutherford, NJ: Fairleigh Dickinson University Press, 1991; Campbell, Jackson J., ed. *The Advent Lyrics of the Exeter Book.* Princeton: Princeton University Press, 1959; Conybeare, John Josias. *Illustrations of Anglo-Saxon Poetry.* William Daniel Conybeare, ed. New York: Haskell House, 1964; Doane, A. N. "The Ethnography of Scribal Writing and Anglo-Saxon Poetry: Scribe as Performer." *Oral Tradition* 9:2 (October 1994), 420-39; Dobbie, Elliott van Kirk. *The Anglo-Saxon Minor Poems.* New York: Columbia University Press. 1942; Gould, David. "A New Approach to Old English Meter Based upon an Analysis of Formulaic Language." *Neophilologus* 79:4 (October 1995), 653-69; Hamer, Richard. *A Choice of Anglo-Saxon Verse, Selected, with an Introduction and Parallel Verse Translation.* London: Faber, 1970; Hanning, Robert, and Joan Ferrante, trans. *The Lais of Marie de France.* New York: E. P. Dutton, 1978; Kaiser, Rolf. *Medieval English: An Old English and Middle English Anthology.* West Berlin: Markobrunner Str. 21, 1961; Kennedy, Charles. *An Anthology of Old English Poetry: Translated into Alliterative Verse.* New York: Oxford University Press, 1960; Kennedy, Charles. *Old English Elegies: Translated into Alliterative Verse with a Critical Introduction.* Princeton: Princeton University Press, 1936; Lehnert, Martin. *Poetry and Prose of the Anglo-Saxons.* Vol. 1: *Texts.* Halle: Veb Max Niemayer Verlag, 1960; Niles, John D. "Sign and Psyche in Old English Poetry." *American Journal of Semiotics* 9.4 (1992), 11-25; Spaeth, J. Duncan. *Old English Poetry: Translations into Alliterative Verse with Introduction and Notes.* New York: Gordian Press, 1967; Stanley, Eric G. "Heroic Women in Old English Literature." In *Heroes and Heroines in Medieval English Literature.* Leo Carruthers, ed. Cambridge: Brewer, 1994. 59-69.

Elton E. Smith

ORMULUM, THE. Orm, an Augustinian canon, is credited with writing *The Ormulum*, twelfth century Middle English poem that is a series of sermons with gospel text for each of thirty-two days. It is conceivable that the author originally planned to pen a sermon for each day of the year, but the text was never completed.

Additionally, Orm appears to have created his own type of spelling, for each short vowel is followed by a doubled consonant. *The Ormulum* is not the most exciting Middle English work, but it does provide the reader with a good idea of the thirteenth-century English vernacular.

SELECTED BIBLIOGRAPHY

Brink, Daniel. "The Variation between (th-) and (t-) in the *Ormulum*." In *On Germanic Linguistics: Issues and Methods.* Irmengard Rauch, Gerald F. Carr, and Robert L. Kyes, eds. Berlin: Mouton de Gruyter, 1992. 21-35; Kim, Myungsook. "On Lengthening in the Open Syllables of Middle English." *Lingua* 91:4 (December 1993), 261-77;

Morrison, Stephen. "New Sources or the *Ormulum*." *Neophilologus* 68:3 (July 1984), 444-50; Morrison, Stephen. "Orm's English Sources." *Archiv* 221:1 (1984), 54-64.

Robert T. Lambdin

OTTO OF FREISING (c. 1114-1158). Otto of Freising (Otto Frisigensis) is generally accepted as the greatest medieval German chronicler (*see* **Chronicles and Annals***)*. Born around 1114 to an Austrian of noble blood, Margrave Leopold III, Otto was able to study in Paris from 1128 to 1133. He was a member of the Cistercian order and became bishop of Freising in 1138. Even though he remained bishop of Freising his entire life, he accompanied Emperor Frederick Barbarossa I on many of his journeys. Otto even participated in the Second *Crusade, serving under his half-brother Emperor *Conrad III.

Otto's two principal historical works are *The History of Two Cities* and *The Deeds of Frederick Barbarossa*. *The History of Two Cities* is a universal history of the church and the secular world. Drawing on *Augustine's concept from *City of God* that the world was made up of citizens of two cities--one citizenry dedicated to pursuit of heavenly rewards, the other dedicated to earthly rewards--Otto created one of the most comprehensive histories to his day. He traced history from Creation up to 1147 and loosely adopted Augustine's attitudes toward living at the end of history. His work is comprised of eight volumes. The first three treat ancient biblical and pagan history. The next three concentrate on medieval history, drawing on numerous early sources from different locales, including *Jordanes and *Paul the Deacon. The seventh book focuses on the events of Otto's own day (1106-1146) and is comprised mostly of eyewitness accounts on Otto's part and from others. In contradistinction to Augustine, Otto found secular history to be of real importance to his work, but he firmly adopted Augustine's belief that the last age of man will be in heaven and depicted in his eighth and final volume what will happen on the Day of Judgement and the days that come thereafter.

In his *Deeds of Frederick* Otto began the story of Frederick Barbarossa, but died only a year after being requested to write the work. The text, even though it comprises only two of the numerous volumes Otto probably intended, is still the best account we have of Frederick and the rise of Frederick's family, the Hohenstaufens.

SELECTED BIBLIOGRAPHY

Brandt, William J. *The Shape of Medieval History*. New Haven: Yale University Press, 1966; Coleman, Joyce. "Talking of Chronicles: The Public Reading of History in Late Medieval England and France." *Cahiers de Littérature Orale* 36 (1994), 91-111; Eckhardt, Caroline D."The Merlin Figure in Middle English Chronicles." In *Comparative Studies of Merlin from the Vedas to C. G. Jung*. James Gollnick, ed. Lewiston, NY: Edwin Mellen, 1991. 21-39; Fines, John. *Who's Who in the Middle Ages*. New York: Barnes, 1970; Smalley, Beryl. *Historians in the Middle Ages*. New York:

Scribner's, 1974; Sterns, Indrikis. *The Greater Medieval Historians: An Interpretation and a Bibliography.* Lanham, MD: University Press of America, 1980.

Richard McDonald

OWL AND THE NIGHTINGALE, THE. The *Owl and the Nightingale* is an anonymous Middle English debate poem (*see* **Debate Poetry, Medieval European**) in octosyllabic couplets that was composed during the late twelfth or early thirteenth century (its Latin title is the *Altercacio inter Filomenam et Bubonem*). Authorship of the poem has been the subject of considerable scholarly conjecture; the two most likely possible authors are the Master Nicholas actually mentioned in the poem or the thirteenth-century poet John of Guildford (see the Wells, Atkins, or Grattan and Sykes editions of the poem for further information).

The poem, which was clearly generated by the intellectual climate of the so-called renaissance of the twelfth century, reflects the popularity of the debate tradition in medieval *lyric; the work is also indicative of the kind of learned discourse of the period that was seriously practiced and, because of the scholarly entrenchment of such discourse, was a fit subject for poetic parody. *The Owl and the Nightingale* is generally considered to be an outstanding example not only of avian debate literature but also of Middle English literature, employing sophisticated humor to examine serious rhetorical and philosophical concerns with the effective use of persuasive language as a practical tool of manipulation, and, more broadly, it serves as a satire of man's foolish behavior.

The narrator of the poem reports that while walking one summer day he overhears a contest between the two birds in which each claims superiority over the other. While this is the ostensible subject of the poem, in fact, each bird articulates specific religious and moral positions that are indeed the true substance of the debate.

Furthermore, the diction of the birds, the narrator's descriptions of them, and his reactions to and interpretations of the contest he witnesses are themselves essential aspects of the didactic and satiric content of the poem. The work is a complicated assessment of human contentiousness, the conflicting positions that occasion it, and the various verbal forms it can assume. *The Owl and the Nightingale* is clearly the work of a poet well versed in rhetoric and religion as well as poetry, and it stands as an excellent example of the kind of complex learned humor that would have been appreciated by an educated medieval audience.

SELECTED BIBLIOGRAPHY

Barratt, Alexandra. "Flying in the Face of Tradition: A New View of *The Owl and the Nightingale.*" *University of Toronto Quarterly* 56:4 (Summer 1987), 471-85; Boone, Laurel. "The Relationship between *The Owl and the Nightingale* and Marie de France's

Lais and Fables." *English Studies in Canada* 11:2 (June 1985), 157-77; Eadie, J. "The Authorship of *The Owl and the Nightingale*: A Reappraisal." *English Studies* 67:6 (December 1986), 471-77; Perryman, Judith C. "Lore, Life, and Logic in *The Owl and the Nightingale*." In *Companion to Early Middle English Literature*. N.H.G.E. Veldhoen and H. Aerston, eds. Amsterdam: VU University Press, 1995. 103-14; Potkay, Monica Brzezinski. "Natural Law in *The Owl and the Nightingale*." *Chaucer Review* 28:4 (1994), 368-83.

Nancy M. Reale

P

"PARDONER'S TALE, THE." The Pardoner of Geoffrey *Chaucer's *Canterbury Tales* (c. 1387-1400) recites a sermon against several of the *seven deadly sins, including gluttony, drunkenness, gambling, and swearing. Within his sermon the Pardoner includes an *exemplum that demonstrates the horrors of greed.

In "The Pardoner's Tale," after hearing a funeral bell toll, three drunken revelers vow to find and kill a man called Death who has done away with so many of their comrades. Up the road the three discover an old man who complains of being unable to die; this old man directs them to eight bushels of gold coins.

The gold inspires the three drunken young men to extreme avarice. One is sent to get wine from an inn which he poisons on the way back. While he is gone, the other two plot to kill him in a mock battle. After they kill him, they drink the poisoned wine and die also. The three men did indeed find Death, but were unable to destroy him.

SELECTED BIBLIOGRAPHY

Aspinall, Dana E. "'I Wol Thee Telle Al Plat': Poetic Influence and Chaucer's Pardoner." *University of Mississippi Studies* 11-12 (1993-95), 230-42; Bittering, Klaus. "'Goon A-Blakeberyed.'" *Neuphilologische Mitteilungen* 94:3-4 (1993), 279-86; Braswell, Mary Flowers. "Chaucer's Palimpsest: Judas Iscariot and the Pardoner's Tale." *Chaucer Review* 29:3 (1995), 303-10; Bush, Douglas. *English Poetry*. New York: Oxford University Press, 1963; Garbáty, Thomas J. *Medieval English Literature*. Toronto: Heath, 1984; Lambdin, Laura C., and Robert T. Lambdin, eds. *Chaucer's Pilgrims: An Historical Guide to the Pilgrims in the "Canterbury Tales."* Westport, CT: Greenwood Press, 1996; Salter, Elizabeth. *Fourteenth-Century English Poetry*. Oxford: Clarendon Press, 1983.

Laura Cooner Lumbdin

PARIS, MATTHEW (c. 1200-c. 1259). Matthew Paris is a historian to be ranked with *Bede and *William of Malmesbury, if only for the comprehensiveness of his work. He was born around 1200 and served as a

monk for St. Albans. He wrote, in Latin, a number of general histories of the
world that narrow and become more specific as he approaches his own time
period. His *Chronica Majora* is a monumental work covering history from
Creation to 1259 (the year of his death), and his *Historia Anglorum* chronicles
England from the Norman Conquest up to 1253.

Unlike many of the other medieval historians, Paris had unusually
diverse connections to court and was widely traveled--especially considering
that he was a Benedictine monk. He was probably friendly with Henry III and
had numerous acquaintances in London. These connections not only provided
him with stories of the goings-on at court, but made available to him court
letters and documents and the records of the royal exchequer. His work
contains the only known copy of the original Magna Carta. His history
encompasses Europe as well as England and grew increasingly comprehensive
and encyclopedic for the years covering his own lifetime. He was one of the
first to use marginal drawings to amuse the reader and marked his chronicles
with a symbolic code in the margin that called attention to important events in
that year, such as coronations or the deaths of bishops or noblemen. (His
drawings occasionally included snippets of dialog beside the character who
spoke them, similar to a modern cartoon.) In addition to including some
documents into his work itself, he compiled supplementary books of documents
relating to the events he portrayed.

Paris's work was derived from a number of sources, from which he
borrowed and amended at will, but the sheer breadth of his work would demand
such cannibalistic techniques--techniques that were especially common to
historians of the medieval period. He occasionally failed to understand the
importance of his sources or interrogate their veracity, but his historical output
is reminiscent of William of Malmesbury's. He wrote numerous historical
works including *Chronica Majora*; *Historia Anglorum*; *Liber Additamentorum*,
a book of additions to his *Chronica Majora*; *Vitae Offarum* (Lives of the
Offa's), a history of King Offa and his descendants, the legendary founders of
the St. Albans abbey; *Flores Historiarum*, (Flowers of History) compiled from
the *Chronica Majora;* and a number of saints' lives. His comprehensive and
prodigious writing and compiling make him one of the most significant of
medieval historians. (*See Chronicles and Annals.*)

SELECTED BIBLIOGRAPHY

Brandt, William J. *The Shape of Medieval History.* New Haven: Yale University Press,
1966; Gransden, Antonia. *Historical Writing in England c. 550 to c. 1307.* Ithaca:
Cornell University Press, 1974; Menache, Sophia. "Rewriting the History of the
Templars According to Matthew Paris." In *Cross Cultural Convergences in the Crusader
Period.* Michael Goodich, *et al,* eds. New York: Peter Lang, 1995. 183-213; Paris,
Matthew. *The Greater Chronicle.* J. A. Giles, trans. New York: AMS Press, 1968;
Smalley, Beryl. *Historians in the Middle Ages.* New York: Scribner's, 1974; Sterns,
Indrikis. *The Greater Medieval Historians: An Interpretation and a Bibliography.*
Lanham, MD: University Press of America, 1980; Townsend, David, and A. G. Rigg.

"Medieval Latin Poetic Anthologies, V: Matthew Paris' Anthology of Henry of Avranches (Cambridge University Library MS. Dd.11.78)." *Mediaeval Studies* 49 (1987), 352-90.

Richard McDonald

PARLIAMENT OF FOWLS, THE. See **Debate Poetry, Medieval European**.

PATIENCE. Patience is an alliterative poem found only in the famous Cotton Nero A X manuscript, which also contains **Sir Gawain and the Green Knight*, **Pearl*, and *Purity*, or **Cleanness*. The poem is a versified account of the Prophet Jonah that illustrates the nobility of an allegorical Patience. By presenting this trait in this manner, the poem cleverly demonstrates the need for practicing it. The poem is often humorous; it gleans its name from its opening word. While *Patience* is not considered to be the best work in the collection, it does function well as a companion piece to *Cleanness*.

SELECTED BIBLIOGRAPHY

Davis, Adam Brooke. "What the Poet of *Patience* Really Did to the Book of Jonah." *Viator* 22 (1991), 267-78; Finch, Casey, tran., Malcolm Andrew, and Ronald Waldron, eds. *The Complete Works of the "Pear" Poet.* Berkeley: University of California Press, 1993; Pohli, Carol Virginia. "Containment of Anger in the Medieval Poem, 'Patience.'" *English Language Notes* 29:1 (September 1991), 1-14.

Robert T. Lambdin

PAUL THE DEACON (c. 720-c. 799). Paul the Deacon (also called Paul the Lombard) wrote the *Historia Langobardorum* (History of the Lombards). Paul was probably born in the 720s and died in the 790s. He was most likely a monk in Pavia but may have first been a courtier there. In terms of historical merit Paul's work is the weakest of those of the barbarian historians, but it was very popular in its day, probably because of his portrayal of the Lombards as an extremely warlike race and his unabashed bias in his presentation of their origins and history. The unfinished work contains many lively stories of Lombard heroes. Beyond placing the various events in a crude chronological sequence, the *Historia* lacks unity, but Paul did comment on events and people that would have otherwise been lost to the world, and he is respected by modern historians for his faithful presentation of Lombard customs. As important as Paul the Deacon is because of his transcriptions, his efforts also illustrate the amount of historical evidence about other subjects that might have been lost to us forever.

SELECTED BIBLIOGRAPHY

Brandt, William J. *The Shape of Medieval History*. New Haven: Yale University Press, 1966; Goffart, Walter. *The Narrators of Barbarian History (A .D. 550-800)*. Princeton: Princeton University Press, 1988; Powell, Susan. "Lollards and Lombards: Late Medieval Bogeymen?" *Medium Ævum* 59:1 (1990), 133-39; Smalley, Beryl. *Historians in the Middle Ages*. New York: Scribner's, 1974; Sterns, Indrikis. *The Greater Medieval Historians: An Interpretation and a Bibliography*. Lanham, MD: University Press of America, 1980.

Richard McDonald

PEARL. *Pearl* is an alliterative poem of some 1,200 lines that is found only in the famous Cotton Nero A X manuscript in the British Library; this famous manuscript also contains *Purity*, *Patience*, and *Sir Gawain and the Green Knight*. An *elegy, *Pearl* was composed sometime around 1370. It is arranged in 101 octosyllabic-line stanzas grouped in every instance but one into bunches of 5 stanzas (section 15 contains 6 stanzas) related by a quasi-refrain at the end of each stanza. This portion of the final line becomes a part of the first line of the next stanza.

In *Pearl* the poet is wandering about on an August morning, a departure from the typical April or May morning of traditional *dream visions. He enters an arbor where he searches for his pretty little pearl that has slipped from his grasp. His search is in vain, as sleep overtakes him, allowing for his wondrous vision. He dreams that he is in an idyllic land of fields, woods, and cliffs; through this runs a river. The dreamer attempts to ford the river, but his crossing is interrupted by a maiden on the other side. She is dressed in a white robe and adorned with pearls. On her head is a crown. The dreamer recognizes her as his lost Pearl.

He is surprised to find that she is now a queen, since she had only been on earth only a couple of years before her demise. He asks how this could be, and she responds that all are queens and brides of the Lamb. She then demonstrates a homiletic explanation for this statement by telling the parable of the vineyard and answers the perplexed dreamer's questions before revealing New Jerusalem to him. Hundreds of thousands of pearls pass into the city, led by the Lamb. The poet becomes enraptured by the sight of his Pearl entering the sacred city and strives to join her. As he ventures again into the river, the dreamer awakens in the arbor; he feels both sorrow and joy, for he knows that his Pearl is in God's care.

The poem ends with the narrator giving thanks for the hope he has been provided. *Pearl* is a dream vision of immense mystical and devotional pathos that embodies the Augustinian dogma that grace will result in heavenly reward. The poem relies upon the *Roman de la Rose* and the Apocalyptic vision of New Jerusalem as its sources.

SELECTED BIBLIOGRAPHY

Blanch, Robert J., and Julian N. Wasserman. *From "Pearl" to "Gawain": "Forme" to "Fynisment."* Gainesville: University Press of Florida, 1995; Bowers, John M. *"Pearl* in Its Royal Setting: Ricardian Poetry Revisited." *Studies in the Age of Chaucer* 17 (1995), 111-55; Bowers, John M. "The Politics of *Pearl.*" *Exemplaria* 7:2 (Fall 1995), 419-41; Reichardt, Paul F. "Sir Israel Gollancz and the Editorial History of the *Pearl* Manuscript." *Papers on Language and Literature* 31:2 (Spring 1995), 145-63.

Rebecca Chalmers

PEASANTS' REVOLT. "The Peasants' Revolt" refers to the 1381 uprising of commoners from Essex and Kent in Britain. The conflict was brought about as a direct result of the tyranny of *John of Gaunt's deeds toward these people. Taxes had been raised for the third time in four years, and the people had finally had enough; when agents of the king attempted to collect, they were confronted by a mob. News of this attack spread quickly. In London an armed mob attacked John's home, Savoy Palace, and burned it to the ground. The revolt escalated so quickly that the young *Richard II called for peace, saying that he would accede to some of the rebels' demands.

However, the leader of the revolt, Wat *Tyler of Kent, was murdered by the lord mayor of London, William Walworth, as Tyler rode peacefully to enact a treaty with Richard. Following Tyler's death, the rebels were quickly scattered, and John of Gaunt fiercely repressed them. The revolt is important in literature because it became the basis for works by many authors, especially with regard to the desire of the common workers to end the repressive feudalism. Among these was John Ball, a preacher who was later condemned to death. Critics believe that William *Langland added a portion of *Piers Plowman* as a response to the revolt, and the insurrection is also mentioned in Geoffrey *Chaucer's *Canterbury Tales.*

SELECTED BIBLIOGRAPHY

Crane, Susan. "The Writing Lesson of 1381." In *Chaucer's England: Literature in Historical Context.* Barbara Hanawalt, ed. Minneapolis: University of Minnesota Press, 1992, 201-21; Hudson, Anne. *"Piers Plowman* and the Peasants' Revolt: A Problem Revisited." *Yearbook of Langland Studies* 8 (1995), 85-106; Justice, Steven. *Writing and Rebellion: England in 1381.* Berkeley: University of California Press, 1994; Rampton, Martha. "The Peasants' Revolt of 1381 and the Written Word." *Comitatus* 24 (1993), 45-60; Russell, J. Stephen. "Is London Burning? A Chaucerian Allusion to the Rising of 1381." *Chaucer Review* 30:1 (1995), 107-09.

Robert T. Lambdin

PECOCK, REGINALD (1395-1460). Reginald Pecock was a Welsh cleric whose many literary works reflect the development of the English vernacular. Around 1440 Pecock composed *The Donet*, a work that provided an introduction to many of the supposed "truths" of Christianity. This work was composed in the form of a dialogue between a father and his son. Pecock then composed many treatises that he hoped would furnish rules for living a good religious life.

Perhaps Pecock's most important work was *The Repressor of Over Much Blaming of the Clergy*, in which he strove to defend Catholicism against the tenets of the *Lollards. The work begins as a general overview of the problems with Lollard dogma and then attacks specific flaws in the notions raised by the Lollards, such as the use of images in the church or the notion of whether the clergy should own property. This belief may have been controversial, but he did not stop there. Pecock went on to push his notion that the church should not brand the Wycliffites as heretics; rather, it should reach out to them. This served to isolate Pecock, who was called before the archbishop of Canterbury. In 1458 he was forced to resign his position and recant his opinions. He was assigned to Thorney Abbey, where he remained in seclusion until his death in 1461.

SELECTED BIBLIOGRAPHY

Brockwell, Charles W., Jr. "The Historical Career of Bishop Reginald Pecock: The 'Poor Scholeris Myrrour' or a Case Study in Famous Obscurity." *Harvard Theological Review* 74:2 (April 1981), 177-207; Swanton, Michael. *English Literature before Chaucer*. New York: Longman, 1987.

Robert T. Lambdin

PELAGIAN. The Pelagians were adherents to the doctrine of Pelagius, a British monk who lived sometime in the fourth or fifth century. Pelagius denied the doctrine of original sin and believed in the freedom of the will. His dogmas proved so controversial that they were disputed by many on the Continent, especially by St. *Augustine. In 418, Pelagius was condemned by Pope Zosimus.

The basis of the controversy falls in the idea that the Pelagians maintained that Adam's fall did not involve nor condemn all in the future. In essence, people could not be held responsible for the acts of those who preceded them. The Pelagians also determined that the human will was inherently good, even if it was not helped by divine grace. Therefore, the Pelagians may have felt that it was unfair to condemn all who had not converted to Christianity before their deaths, such as Plato and *Aristotle. This idea was held strongly by many, and the tenet did not fade quickly even after the pope's condemnation. Indeed, this sect remained active until 529, when the Augustinian ideal, that only God can give grace, was accepted by the Council of Orange. In the Middle Ages there was something of a revival of Pelagian thought. The mainstays of this ideology were condemned by Thomas Bradwardine who labeled them "New Pelagians," and the movement soon dissipated.

SELECTED BIBLIOGRAPHY

Dumville, David. "Late-Seventh- or Eighth-Century Evidence for the British Transmission of Pelagius." *Cambridge Medieval Celtic Studies* 10 (Winter 1985), 39-52; Forthomme, Nicholson M. "Pelage et Alcuin." *Etudes Classiques* 59:1 (Jan 1991), 43-51; Rees, B. R. ed. and trans. *The Letters of Pelagius and His Followers.* Rochester, NY: Boydell, 1991.

Robert T. Lambdin

PERCEVAL. Although *Chrétien de Troyes wrote only about a third of *Perceval,* we recognize the mark of his greatness in this tale of a country lad who grows up to quest for the Holy Grail, a vessel given great spiritual and mystical significance. In this *romance the themes are religious love, holy responses and unholy failing. The work was apparently left unfinished by Chrétien because of his death. That Chrétien's writing is often odd and full of inconsistencies and unmotivated responses is obvious to any reader; yet the scholar of medieval literature recognizes the subtle psychological motivations at play and Chrétien's laudably innovative techniques.

SELECTED BIBLIOGRAPHY

Bruckner, Matilda Tamaryn. "The Poetics of Continuation in Medieval French Romance: From Chrétien's 'Conte du Graal' to the 'Perceval' Continuations." *French Forum* 18:2 (May 1993), 133-49; Guerin, M. Victoria. *The Fall of Kings and Princes: Structure and Destruction in Arthurian Tragedy.* Stanford: Stanford University Press. 1995; Hindman, Sandra. "King Arthur, His Knights, and the French Aristocracy in Picardy." *Yale French Studies* 1991, 114-33; Zemel, Roel. "The New and Old Perceval: Guillaume's 'Fergus' and Chrétien's 'Conte du Graal.'" *Bibliographical Bulletin of the International Arthurian Society* 46 (1994), 423-42.

Laura Cooner Lambdin

PETERBOROUGH CHRONICLE, THE. The *Peterborough Chronicle* is a portion of the Laud manuscript of the *Anglo-Saxon Chronicle* (*see **Chronicles and Annals**). The only portion of the *Anglo-Saxon Chronicle* believed to have been composed after 1080, *The Peterborough Chronicle* is a key element of English Literature because it provides clear evidence of the shift from Old to Middle English. Perhaps because it dates from between 1120 and 1154, as compared to the other earlier components, the *Peterborough Chronicle* is clearly the most developed portion of the *Anglo-Saxon Chronicle.*

SELECTED BIBLIOGRAPHY

Dekeyser, Xavier. "Relative Markers in the *Peterborough Chronicle*." *Folia* 7:1 (1987), 93-105; Kniezsa, Veronika. "Accents and Digraphs in the *Peterborough Chronicle*." *Studia Anglica Posnaniensia* 21(1988), 15-23; Schipper, William. "A Ghost Word in the *Peterborough Chronicle*." *Notes and Queries* 38 (236) 2 (June 1991), 154.

Robert T. Lambdin

PETER LOMBARD (c. 1100-1164). Peter Lombard was an Italian theologian. He studied Aristotelian philosophy under Peter *Abelard. This would have a profound influence upon his life. Around 1150 Lombard composed the *Sententiarum libri quatuor*, or the *Four Books of Sentences*. These were four books in which Lombard collated a collection of the philosophies of the early church fathers concerning the topics of the nature of God, Creation, Redemption, and the sacraments. In these works Lombard quoted, when possible, the early church authorities' opinions concerning doctrinal questions. The work is a novelty because Lombard then cited other church officials to answer these opinions.

The seminal text of this collection was the fourth volume, which pertained to the nature of the sacraments. The work was so important that in the thirteenth century any aspiring scholar who wished to become noted as a theological authority was required to study, analyze, and then write a commentary on this work.

SELECTED BIBLIOGRAPHY

Colish, Marcia. "From Sacra Pagina to Theologia: Peter Lombard as Exegete of Romans." *Medieval Perspectives* 6 (1991), 1-19; Colish, Marcia. "Psalterium Scholasticorum: Peter Lombard and the Emergence of the Scholastic Psalms Exegesis." *Speculum* 67:3 (July 1992), 531-48.

Robert T. Lambdin

PETER THE HERMIT (c. 1050-1115). Also known as Peter of Amiens and Pietro l'Ermita, Peter was a French monk who was one of the instigators of the First *Crusade (1096-99). He preached widely and enthusiastically in favor of this endeavor. In 1096 he actually led a portion of the crusade to Asia Minor. He is remembered by Tasso in his *Gerusalemme Liberata;* in this work Peter advises and urges the Christians to take action against the infidels.

SELECTED BIBLIOGRAPHY

Bull, Marcus Graham. *Knightly Piety and the Lay Response to the First Crusade: The Limousin and Gascony, c. 970-c. 1130.* Oxford: Clarendon Press, 1993; Chazon, Robert. *In the Year 1096: the First Crusade and the Jews.* Philadelphia: Jewish Publication Society, 1996.

Robert T. Lambdin

PETRARCH (1304-1374). Petrarch, or Francesco Petrarca, was born in Arezzo, but he spent much of his youth in Avignon and Carpentras. He studied law at Bologna, but his interests fell mainly into Latin and Greek Literature and writing. His renown as a scholar and poet was such that he was crowned at Rome in 1341 with the laurel, a ceremony that had not been performed since ancient times. He spent the latter part of his life wandering from city to city. He was friends with Giovanni *Boccaccio and was very interested in the revival of classical learning. It was his dedication to this resolve that made him the founder of Renaissance humanism. He earned his designation as the first "modern man" because of his many attributes that set him apart from his contemporaries. He loved nature dearly, as is evidenced by his descriptions and feats of mountain climbing. He also was frank in his resorting to meditation over psychological conflicts. Unlike many of his peers, he preferred Plato to *Aristotle, but he is most renowned for his humanistic treatment of his love, Laura. His adoration of his beloved transcended the hyperbolic conventions of the courtly tradition.

Petrarch was also a prolific correspondent, and many of his letters survive. Additionally, he composed works in Latin, such as *De viris illustribus* (On illustrious men), and epic poems, such as his *Africa*, which features Scipio Africanus as its hero. He also wrote the dialogue *Secretum*, which takes the form of a debate. In the *Secretum*, Petrarch reveals his love of Laura and the laurel (fame), which conflict with his spiritual feelings. His writings also include many treatises, some eclogues, and even a guide book to the Holy Land.

But his most important works are his Italian poems, collected in a *canzione*, or songbook. This folio, often called the *Rime* or *Rime sparse* ("Scattered lyrics"), includes sonnets, *canzoni, *sestine, hallate* and *madrigals. Editors later broke this work into two sections, *In vita di Madonna Laura* (During the life of my lady Laura) and *In morte di Madonna Laura* (After the death of my Lady Laura). It is not believed that Laura was a real woman, yet Petrarch presents her image in a way much more realistic than the conventional ladies of the *Provençal troubadours or in the literature of *courtly love. Indeed, she is even more ethereal than the *donna angelica* (angelic ladies) found throughout the poems of this time, seen especially in *Dante's Beatrice.

Some of Petrarch's poems were addressed to friends, while others were penned for contemporary patrons and concerned current affairs. Other works are even religious; however, the most dominant theme in Petrarch's work is Laura. He created in her a woman whose beauty and actions captivated the poet, causing him both joy and remorse, for a relationship with her was unworkable. Petrarch achieved this conflict by recording in the works explicit psychological details formalized in figurative language and other literary devices. When Laura died, the poet found no relief in the grief that replaced his previous despair. This resulted in a more spiritual tone that borders on consolation. This collection of works became the source and the inspiration for an entire movement called European Petrarchism that dominated poetry for centuries.

Petrarch's other vernacular work is the *Trionfi*, which was inspired by Dante and composed in *terza rima*. This composition allegorically describes the procession of Love, Chastity, Death, Fame, Time, and Eternity and contains both historical and literary persons as examples. Included in this work again is Laura. Petrarch was still revising this piece when he died in 1374.

Petrarch's influence became nearly universal. Geoffrey *Chaucer used Petrarch's translation of the Latin Griselda story of the *Decameron* as an inspiration for his *"Cleric's Tale" in the *Canterbury Tales*. Chaucer also derived a portion of *Troylus and Criseyde* from a piece of Petrarch's *Rime*. English Petrarchism became extremely strong, as seen in the works of Sir Thomas Wyatt and Henry Howard Surrey in the sixteenth century. Petrarch's influence continued until the nineteenth century. In the English Renaissance the *Trionfi* was also an important source for authors such as Henry Parker and Percy Bysshe Shelley.

The humanistic ideas of Petrarch, carried forth by his younger devotees, far outweighed all other influences as humanism developed in Italy. His lyric poetry's influence on later lyrics has been even greater. Although Chaucer's use of Petrarchism was the beginning of the Italian's influence in foreign lands, it continued into Spain and Dalmatia in the fifteenth century and moved to France and heavily into England by the sixteenth. Many of the poems were set to music by Italians, French, and Germans. Among the great composers to use Petrarchan themes were Dufay and Liszt.

SELECTED BIBLIOGRAPHY

Asher, Lyell. "Petrarch at the Peak of Fame." *PMLA* 108:5 (October 1993), 1050-63; Kennedy, William J. *Authorizing Petrarch.* Ithaca: Cornell University Press, 1994; Quillen, Carol E. "A Tradition Invented: Petrarch, Augustine, and the Language of Humanism." *Journal of the History of Ideas* 53:2 (April-June 1992), 179-207; Stock, Brian. "Reading, Writing, and the Self: Petrarch and His Forerunners." *New Literary History* 26:4 (Fall 1995), 717-30.

Robert T. Lambdin

PHILIP II (1165-1223) Capetian, king of France (1179-1223). Because he was thrust into the role of monarch early, Philip had no time for education. He was a cold and calculating realist and became one of the outstanding figures of his time. Philip was the consolidator and creator of the organized state. He built the early stages of Paris, paved many of the streets and built its wall, and began the Louvre. Establishing and maintaining a six-year alliance with King *Henry II of England, Philip was able to defeat both Artois and the counts of Champagne, adding both Artois and Vermandois to his own lands.

Public opinion affected Philip greatly; he was one of the first French leaders who appeared to pay any attention to what his subjects thought. Philip's ability to be affected by public opinion probably best explains his joining King *Richard and Frederick Barbarossa on the Third* Crusade. However, their quarrel during the crusade led to Philip's return to France and, eventually, intrigue against Richard and final defeat for the French. These events restored Angevin power in northern France. Public pressure was also instrumental in the re-establishment of Philip's marriage to Ingeborg of Denmark.

After Richard's death Philip and King *John struggled over the lands of the Angevin line north of the Loire, with Philip gaining control. Since he desired to be master of the North, Philip turned from war and statecraft, pitting the barons against each other and using his position as protector of the church to weaken them further. He sought the support of the towns and the rich as a balance to the feudal position of the barons. Philip systematized both the royal finances, the regular extraction of feudal aids and obligations due the Crown, and the collection of customs, tolls, and fees. This in no way can be thought of as having established a modern tax system, however. Philip also established a permanent army.

SELECTED BIBLIOGRAPHY

Belloc, Hilaire. *Miniatures of French History*. Peru, IL: Sherwood Sugden, 1990; Poly, Jean-Pierre. *The Feudal Transformation: 900-1200*. New York: Holmes & Meyer, 1990.

R. Churchill Curtis

PHILIP IV (1268-1314) Capetian, king of France (1285-1314). Philip IV the Fair is the king who finally brought the church under royal domination. Between 1296 and 1303 Philip IV became embroiled in a conflict with Pope Boniface VIII, who claimed papal supremacy. In 1296 Boniface issued a bull that forbade secular taxation upon the clergy without papal consent. Philip retorted by restricting papal trade in precious metals and mounting a strong propaganda campaign. Boniface, engaged in pressing matters elsewhere, had no choice and annulled the bull the following year. Boniface died and was followed in 1305 by Clement V, a Frenchman. Pope Clement, lingering in France after his election, reluctantly had to accept French royal domination. He took up residence at Avignon, thus beginning the Babylonian—or Avignonese Captivity—of the papacy. This "captivity" lasted from 1309 to 1376, during which time Clement was forced to quash the bulls of Boniface and to support the suppression of the Knights Templars by Philip.

SELECTED BIBLIOGRAPHY

Belloc, Hilaire. *Miniatures of French History.* Peru, IL: Sherwood Sugden, 1990; Poly, Jean-Pierre. *The Feudal Transformation: 900-1200.* New York: Holmes & Meyer, 1990.

R. Churchill Curtis

"PHYSICIAN'S TALE, THE." "The Physician's Tale" told by the doctor-pilgrim of Geoffrey *Chaucer's *Canterbury Tales* (c. 1387-1400) is taken from Livy, but is most like the version of it to be found in the thirteenth century *Romance of the Rose.*

The sweet, beautiful, and obedient Virginia is told by her father Virginius that he must kill her or she will be dishonored by the amorous Appius, the judge in town. Virginia prefers that her father kill her rather than that she be shared with Appius, so Virginius cuts off her head. Appius sentences Virginius to hang for this deed, but the townsfolk revolt. Appius kills himself instead.

SELECTED BIBLIOGRAPHY

Bush, Douglas. *English Poetry.* New York: Oxford University Press, 1963; Garbáty, Thomas J. *Medieval English Literature.* Toronto: Heath, 1984; Harley, Marta Powell. "Last Things First in Chaucer's 'Physician's Tale': Final Judgement and the Worm of Conscience." *Journal of English and Germanic Philology* 91:1 (January 1992), 1-16; Hirsch, John C. "Modern Times: The Discourse of the 'Physician's Tale.'" *Chaucer Review* 27:4 (1993), 387-95; Lambdin, Laura C., and Robert T. Lambdin, eds. *Chaucer's Pilgrims: An Historical Guide to the Pilgrims in the "Canterbury Tales."* Westport, CT: Greenwood Press, 1996; Salter, Elizabeth. *Fourteenth-Century English Poetry.* Oxford: Clarendon Press, 1983.

Laura Cooner Lambdin

PIERO DELLA FRANCESCA (1426-1492). Piero della Francesca was a master painter of linear perspective, incorporating a mathematical precision in his works. A skilled geometrician, he introduced the triangle as a compositional device. He is also known for innovations such as the art of projecting shadows and his use of oil paints, a new medium for colors. His extremely personal style results in easy attribution of his works. One of his earlier undertakings was the frescoes of Saint Egidio in Florence. Shortly after, Pope Nicholas V commissioned two frescoes in the Vatican. Francesca was frequently commissioned to create altar pieces and banners for churches around Italy.

Another major work was his cycle of frescoes illustrating the Legend of the Cross in the Church of San Francesco. These frescoes are distinguished by their "harmony of color" and the contrast of light and shade. *Flagellation* is a well-known panel in this series. *The Apotheosis* can be seen at the Uffizi; it exemplifies Francesca's theme of man at the center of nature--the glorification of man. The artist wrote a treatise on perspective and measurement entitled *De prospectivo pingendi*, and this fascination is displayed in such works as the St. Jerome panel of the Rimini fresco. He encompasses the architecture of the church into all his frescoes; it serves as a complement to the paintings. In his later years Francesca was somewhat influenced by the Flemish school--his works embodied more freedom and gentleness and were slightly asymmetrical.

SELECTED BIBLIOGRAPHY

Gardner, Helen. *Gardner's Art through the Ages.* 6th ed. San Diego: Harcourt Brace Jovanovich, 1975; Lavin, Marilyn Aronberg. *Piero della Francesca.* New York: Abrams, 1992; Lavin, Marvin. *Piero della Francesca: San Francesco, Arezzo.* New York: Braziller, 1994; Lightbown, R. W. *Piero della Francesca.* New York: Abbeville, 1992.

Libby Bernardin

POLO, MARCO (1254?-1324?), **MAFFEO, AND NICCOLÒ.** Maffeo and Niccolò Polo were Venetian traders in the Black Sea area and Central Asia from 1255 to 1266. They managed to reach China and returned in 1269 to Acre. Their efforts proved profitable and they set out once again in 1271, accompanied by Marco, Niccolò's teen-aged son.

This march was extraordinary, stretching from Mosal to Kastgas, then across the Gobi Desert to Karakorum, the new Mongol capital built by *Ogodei. Ogodei was so impressed by the travelers that he made them part of his personal service. For more than fifteen years the Europeans explored all parts of the empire—Chochin, China, India, and Burma—finally returning to Europe by sea. The members of the Polo expeditions gained new insights into space, navigation, and distance.

Perhaps the Polos would have remained locally famous but internationally unknown had not Marco Polo dictated *A Book of Experiences* in 1297. This "travelogue" became immediately popular and spread their fame widely. There are recent studies that suggest that this book—and perhaps the entire part played by Marco—was a fabrication, but almost no significant historian gives credence to this claim. Today the exploits of the Polos remains extraordinary deeds.

SELECTED BIBLIOGRAPHY

Noonan, John. *Marco Polo*. New York: Crestwood House, 1993; Stefoff, Rebecca. *Marco Polo and the Medieval Explorers*. New York: Chelsea House, 1992.

                                                                                        R. Churchill Curtis

PONCE DE LEON, JUAN (1460-1521). One of the greatest Spanish explorers, Juan Ponce de Leon was given a royal patent in 1521 by Philip II to colonize the lands of the Florida peninsula. He wandered around the North Atlantic coast for months searching for the legendary Fountain of Youth; however he found only disease and pestilence, which ruined his chance at success. His efforts are associated with Spain's claim to this area and the subsequent establishment of St. Augustine.

SELECTED BIBLIOGRAPHY

Devereux, Anthony Q. *Ponce de Leon, King Ferdinand, and the Fountain of Youth*. Spartanburg, SC: Reprint Press, 1993; Faber, Harold. *The Discoverers of America*. New York: Scribner, 1992.

                                                                                        R. Churchill Curtis

"PRIORESS'S TALE, THE." The most seemingly anti-Semitic of the stories told by Geoffrey *Chaucer's pilgrims in the *Canterbury Tales*, (c. 1387-1400), "The Prioress's Tale" concerns a schoolboy who is murdered in a Jewish ghetto. The Virgin Mary pities the boy's mother, who cannot find her child, and so allows him to sing despite his slashed throat. When the boy's body is discovered, an abbot removes a grain that Mary had lain on his tongue to allow his song, and thus the holy martyr is able to pass from this world. The Jews who murdered the boy are hung.

At 238 lines, this poem is the shortest completed story in the *Canterbury Tales*. The prioress, Madame Eglentine, has such seemingly courtly manners that the content of her tale has always puzzled critics; it may be the case that Chaucer was satirizing the bigotry sometimes evident in the attitudes of those of her class.

SELECTED BIBLIOGRAPHY

Bush, Douglas. *English Poetry*. New York: Oxford University Press, 1963; Garbáty, Thomas J. *Medieval English Literature*. Toronto: Heath, 1984; Lambdin, Laura C., and Robert T. Lambdin, eds. *Chaucer's Pilgrims: An Historical Guide to the Pilgrims in the "Canterbury Tales."* Westport, CT: Greenwood Press, 1996; Pigg, Daniel. "Refiguring Martyrdom: Chaucer's Prioress and Her Tale." *Chaucer Review* 29:1 (1994), 65-73; Rex,

Richard. *"The Sins of Madame Eglentyne" and Other Essays on Chaucer*. Newark: University of Delaware Press, 1995; Rudat, Wolfgang E. H. "Gender-Crossing in the 'Prioress' Tale': Chaucer's Satire on Theological Anti-Semitism?" *Cithara* 33:2 (May 1994), 11-17; Salter, Elizabeth. *Fourteenth-Century English Poetry*. Oxford: Clarendon Press, 1983.

Laura Cooner Lambdin

PROVENÇAL. Provençal was the language of Provence in southern France in the Middle Ages; it was adopted by the troubadours as their official literary language. After the demise of the influence of the troubadours, the language nearly faded away; however, today a small number of people still speak the language, which has been renamed Occitan. The Provençal literature of the troubadours was usually *lyric poetry. While this constituted a great deal of their canon, troubadours also gained reputations for their compositions of *courtly love songs. These works spread throughout the Continent and were great influences on the poems of *Petrarch and his followers.

SELECTED BIBLIOGRAPHY

Carruthers, J. "The 'Passé Surcomposé Regional': Towards a Definition of Its Function in Contemporary Spoken French." *Journal of French Language Studies* 4:2 (September 1994), 171-90.

Robert T. Lambdin

PROVERBS OF ALFRED, THE. The *Proverbs of Alfred* from around 1150 survives only in a manuscript copied sometime in the thirteenth century. The poem is initially anecdotal concerning *Alfred's life. It then moves on to a series of thirty-five sayings or proverbs, which the author credits to Alfred. These adages gained great fame in the Middle Ages and influenced a great deal of literature. Each of these witticisms begins with the common phrase "Thus quath Alfred." It is doubtful that Alfred is actually responsible for any of the proverbs; it became common, almost cliché, for poets to ascribe any proverbs or witty sayings of dubious authority to Alfred. Perhaps the greatest example of the ongoing influence of *The Proverbs of Alfred* is seen in the classic Middle English *debate poem, *The *Owl and the Nightingale*.

SELECTED BIBLIOGRAPHY

Bitterling, Klaus. "The 'Proverbs of Alfred' and the Middle English Dictionary." *Neuphilologische Mitteilungen* 84:3 (1983), 344-46; Crépin, André. "Mentalités anglaises au temps d'Henri II Plantagenet d'après les 'Proverbs of Alfred.'" *Cahiers de Civilisation Médiévale* 37:1-2 (January-June 1994), 48-60.

Robert T. Lambdin

PRUDENTIUS (348-c. 410). The medieval Spanish Christian Latin poet Prudentius is renowned as a hymn writer. Ironically, the work most associated with him is probably the *Psychomachia* or *The Battle for the Soul of Man*, a work that has nothing to do with music. Written around 405, the *Psychomachia* had a great influence upon both medieval and Renaissance England. The theme of Man's battle for his soul is found throughout the literature of these times, especially in the Middle English moralities and other works, such as the *debate poem "The Dispute between the Body and the Soul."

SELECTED BIBLIOGRAPHY

References: Kimminich, Eva. "The Way of Vice and Virtue: A Medieval Psychology." *Comparative Drama* 25:1 (Spring 1991), 77-86; Lewis, C. S. *The Allegory of Love.* 1936. Oxford: Oxford University Press, 1977; Orchard, Andy. "Conspicuous Heroism: Abraham, Prudentius, and the Old English Verse 'Genesis.'" In *Heroes and Heroines in Medieval English Literature*. Leo Carruthers, ed. Cambridge: Brewer, 1994. 45-58; Weiland, Gernot R. "The Anglo-Saxon Manuscripts of Prudentius's *Psychomachia.*" *Anglo-Saxon England* 16 (1987), 213-31.

Robert T. Lambdin

PTOLEMY (2nd century A. D.). An Alexandrian astronomer and geographer, Ptolemy (whose full Latin name was Claudius Ptolemaeus) is best known for his *Almagest,* which described a new system of astronomy that was accepted until the sixteenth century. This "Ptolemaic System" posited that the sun, planets, and stars revolve around the earth. The movements of these bodies were plotted by an arrangement of epicycles, small circles with their centers on the circumference of a larger one. When one of these bodies was seen moving out of its path, it was assumed that it was simply entering a new series of epicycles. The system was ideal for the church; it had only to add epicycles to the bodies to make the system seem cogent. However, this made the entire philosophy extremely complicated. When Copernicus posited his heliocentric theory in 1530, the idea of a man-centered universe easily usurped it.

In its prime Ptolemy's system was combined with *Aristotle's popular notion of natural philosophy, which posited nature as orderly, hierarchical, and teleological. In this regard, Ptolemaic astronomy formed the core of medieval world practice when suitably adapted to Christianity.

SELECTED BIBLIOGRAPHY

Dilke, Oswald A., and Margaret S. Dilke. "The Adjustment of Ptolemaic Atlases to Feature the New World." In *European Images of the Americas and the Classical Tradition I*. Wolfgang Haase and Meyer Reinhold, eds. Berlin: de Gruyter, 1994, 117-34; Tolmacheva, Marina. "Ptolemaic Influence on Medieval Arab Geography: The Case

Study of East Africa." In *Discovering New Worlds: Essays On Medieval Exploration and Imagination*. Scott D. Westrem, ed. New York: Garland, 1991. 125-41; van Helden, Albert. "The Dimensions of the Discarded Image: Cosmography in the High Middle Ages." In *Mapping the Cosmos*. Jane Chance and R. O. Wells, eds. Houston: Rice University Press, 1985. 65-75.

Robert T. Lambdin

Q

QUADRIVIUM. The term "quadrivium" refers to a more advanced grouping of four of the seven *liberal arts: arithmetic, geometry, astronomy, and music. These, when considered next to the *trivium of grammar, rhetoric, and logic, were considered to be of a higher order. *Martianus Capella is usually credited with originating the grouping of the quadrivium in the early fifth century. Later *Boethius abetted the acceptance of this division when he defended the split in his *On the Art and Discipline of the Liberal Arts*. The quadrivium remained important for several centuries; it reached its apex in the eleventh and twelfth centuries before it lost favor in the thirteenth century. Continental scholars rejected the division, which then became associated with Oxford. Critics see this as the completion of the rift between the academics of the Continent and those of Britain. To them, this demonstrated a lack of interest in the material sciences.

SELECTED BIBLIOGRAPHY

Burnett, Charles. "Adelard, Music, and the Quadrivium." In *Adelard of Bath: An English Scientist and Arabist of the Early Twelfth Century*. Charles Burnett, ed. London: University of London, 1987. 69-86; Hart, Thomas Elwood. "The Quadrivium and Chrétien's Theory of Composition: Some Conjunctures and Conjectures." *Symposium* 35:1 (Spring 1981), 57-86; Stahl, William Harris, trans. *Martianus Capella and the Seven Liberal Arts, Volume I: The Quadrivium of Martianus Capella: Latin Traditions in the Mathematical Sciences 50 B. C.-A. D. 1250; With a Study of the Allegory and the Verbal Disciplines*. New York: Columbia University Press, 1991; White, Alison. "Boethius in the Medieval Quadrivium." In *Boethius: His Life, Thought, and Influence*. Margaret Gibson, ed. Oxford: Blackwell, 1981.

Robert T. Lambdin

QUEM QUAERITIS TROPE. A text in the medieval Easter liturgy, the *Quem quaeritis trope* is named for the Latin question "Whom seek Ye?" It is a dialogue between the women and the angel at the opening of Jesus' empty tomb. Sometime in the eleventh century this trope began to be acted out during the matins service. It began as a brief scene and gradually expanded with priests, nuns, and choirboys playing the parts. From this simple beginning sprouted medieval *drama.

SELECTED BIBLIOGRAPHY

Brockett, Clyde W. "Reconstructing an Ascension Drama from Aural and Visual Art: A Methodological Approach." *Fifteenth Century Studies* 13:213 (1988), 195-209; Gibson, James M. "*Quem Queritis in Presepe*: Christmas Drama or Christmas Liturgy?" In *Drama in the Middle Ages: Comparative and Critical Essays*. Clifford Davidson and John H. Stroupe, eds. New York: AMS Press, 1990, 106-28; Kobialka, Michal. "The *Quem Quaeritis*: Theater History Displacement." *Theater History Studies* 8 (1988), 35-51; Wright, Stephen K. "St. Erkenwald and *Quem Quaeritis*: A Reconsideration." *English Language Notes* 31:3 (Mar 1994), 29-35.

Robert T. Lambdin

R

"REEVE'S TALE, THE." "The Reeve's Tale," a *fabliau, is one of Geoffrey *Chaucer's *Canterbury Tales* (c. 1387-1400). Oswald the Reeve tells the tale in answer to "The *Miller's Tale," which had insulted carpenters. (Oswald is a carpenter and a Reeve.) At both the beginning and end of his tale Oswald explains his intention to requite the Miller. In the tale a Miller is cuckolded when two young clerks have sexual relations with his wife and his daughter.

Simkin the Miller is well known for stealing large portions of the grain brought to his mill. Two students from Oxford, John and Alan, have personally brought the grain from their college to watch over it and stop the Miller's thievery. John and Alan intend never to let the grain from their sight, but Simkin lets their horse run loose so they must chase it. When the young scholars return with their horse, it is late, so Simkin, who has stolen more grain than ever while the students were gone, offers to let them sleep in the room where he sleeps with his wife, beautiful daughter and infant. Hoping to recoup some of their losses, John and Alan decide to have some sport with the wife and daughter. John moves the infant's cradle and tricks the wife into his bed. Alan gets into bed with the daughter, who tells him where to find their stolen grain. Intending to wake John and tell him about the grain, Alan mistakenly wakes Simkin because of the misplaced cradle. A fight follows, but Alan and John escape with their grain.

SELECTED BIBLIOGRAPHY

Bush, Douglas. *English Poetry.* New York: Oxford University Press, 1963; Garbáty, Thomas J. *Medieval English Literature.* Toronto: Heath, 1984; Justman, Stewart. "The 'Reeve's Tale' and the Honor of Men." *Studies in Short Fiction* 32:1 (Winter 1995), 21-27; Lambdin, Laura C., and Robert T. Lambdin, eds. *Chaucer's Pilgrims: An Historical Guide to the Pilgrims in the "Canterbury Tales."* Westport, CT: Greenwood Press, 1996; Salter, Elizabeth. *Fourteenth-Century English Poetry.* Oxford: Clarendon Press, 1983; Woods, William. "The Logic of Deprivation in Chaucer's 'Reeve's Tale.'" *Chaucer Review* 30:2 (1995), 150-63.

Laura Cooner Lambdin

REYNARD THE FOX. A popular medieval *beast fable, *Reynard the Fox* is found in French, Flemish, and German literature. The premise of the text is a sardonic look at contemporary life, done by endowing animals with human personality. The plot concerns the struggle for power between Reynard, a sly fox, and the physically stronger wolf, Isengrim. In the editions the sly fox usually defeats the brute strength of the wolf. Additionally, Reynard outwits characters such as the lion, King Noble; the bear, Sir Bruin; the cat, Tibert; and the cock, Chanticleer.

These cyclical episodes were derived from numerous animal fables that circulated in Europe, including Aesop's fables and Marie de France's *Ysopet.* For two centuries, from the twelfth to the fourteenth, the tales were presented in numerous forms; constant additions and deletions were the norm. By the fifteenth century the humor and satire were replaced by works which were more didactic. The texts were often glossed so that the significance of the characters and events was explained. These expressed purposes included satires of power struggles, such as those between the church, the barons, and the king. Portions of the tale were known in England, but William *Caxton's translation in 1481 was the thorough adaptation of the work in English. Before this edition the tale was referred to as *Vox and the Wolf.* Geoffrey *Chaucer's *"Nun's Priest's Tale" relies heavily upon this beast fable.

SELECTED BIBLIOGRAPHY

Bellon, Roger. "Trickery as an Element of the Character of Renart." *Forum for Modern Language Studies* 22:1 (January 1986), 34-52; Bidard, Josseline. "Reynard the Fox as Anti-Hero." In *Heroes and Heroines in Medieval English Literature.* Leo Carruthers, ed. Cambridge: Brewer, 1994. 119-23;

Robert T. Lambdin

RHYMING POEM, THE. The *Rhyming Poem* is found in the Exeter Book and is noted for its rhyme scheme, wherein the final words in each half-line rhyme. This technique is found mainly in Old English poetry. The poem concerns the variances that occur in life. As an example, the poem contrasts the mischances of a discredited king against his many accomplishments. This pseudo-*Boethian lament was also common in Old English *elegies.

SELECTED BIBLIOGRAPHY

Earl, James W. "Hisperic Style in the Old English 'Rhyming Poem.'" *PMLA* 102:2 (March 1987), 187-96; Wentersdorf, Karl P. "The Old English 'Rhyming Poem': A Ruler's Lament." *Studies in Philology* 82:3 (Summer 1985), 265-94.

Robert T. Lambdin

RICHARD I Coeur de Lion (1157-1199) king of England (1189-1199). The greatest of all of the knights-errant, Richard spent less than one year of his entire reign in England, visiting his realm only twice and then only to raise money for his continental ventures. Taxation was heavy. The government remained in the hands of ministers trained largely by *Henry II, but there appeared a tendency toward a common antipathy of barons and people toward the Crown. Richard, having taken the Cross in 1188, went on the Third *Crusade with Frederick Barbarossa and *Philip II, his most dangerous foes. On his return trip, Duke Leopold of Austria captured Richard and turned him over to his emperor, Henry VI, who held Richard for a staggering ransom. Both John and Philip bid for the prisoner, but Richard was finally able to pay his own ransom, partially from taxes levied upon the English people. This Third Crusade gave Englishmen their first taste of eastern adventure, but drew few participants.

The domestic situation included a series of anti-Semitic outbreaks. The king's peace was maintained at home by the rise, once again, of the fortunes of the archbishop of Canterbury and the help of a rising middle class in both the towns and shires. Charters were granted to towns, and the knights of the shires were called upon to assume a share of county business. Knights (elected by the local gentry) served as coroners and called the local juries. This period also produced the first merchant guild in 1193.

SELECTED BIBLIOGRAPHY

Bridge, Anthony. *Richard the Lionheart*. New York: Evans, 1990; Edwards, Cyril. "The Magnanimous Sex-Object: Richard the Lionheart in Medieval German Lyric." In *Courtly Literature: Culture and Context*. Keith Busby and Erik Kooper, eds. Amsterdam: Benjamins, 1990. 159-77; Finlayson, John. "Richard, Coer de Lyon: Romance, History, or Something in Between?" *Studies in Philology* 87:2 (Spring 1990), 156-80.

R. Churchill Curtis

RICHARD II (1367-1400) Lancaster, king of England (1377-1399). Richard II, son of the Black Prince, was a minor at his ascendancy. *John of Gaunt dominated the council that ruled until Richard became King without regency in 1380. During the period when Richard's rule was not fully accepted, the *Peasants' Revolt occurred. This lamentable happening was caused largely by landlords' insistence upon a return to older forms of tenure and land rents. The peasants burned manors, records of tenure, and other items, and finally marched on London.

The Tower was seized and Archbishop Sudbury was murdered. Richard met with the rebels and, through subterfuge, completely disarmed them. He granted manumission and sent them home. As soon as the rebels had dispersed, Richard tore up the charters to which he had agreed and recanted manumission. What he had started, however—the dissolution of serfdom— could not be stopped, and the condition slowly disappeared.

Richard also collided with the Church and Parliament. Richard wished to persecute the *Lollards, a sect led by John *Wycliffe, but Parliament would not support the action. The schism with Parliament took place over a demand from that body for financial accounting. Richard reacted with an unsuccessful invasion of Scotland, usurious taxation, and a reign of terror that undermined support for the king. He was forced to abdicate in 1399. Thrown into the Tower, Richard died the following year. (There are many claims that he was murdered.) His abdication brought the election of Henry IV of the House of Lancaster.

SELECTED BIBLIOGRAPHY

Bowers, John M. "Chaste Marriage: Fashion and Texts at the Court of Richard II." *Pacific Coast Philology* 30:1 (1995), 15-26; Budra, Paul. "Writing the Tragic Self: Richard II's Sad Stories." *Renaissance and Reformation* 18:4 (Fall 1994), 5-15; Hille, Ordelle E., and Gardiner Stilwell. " A Conduct Book for Richard II." *Philological Quarterly* 73:3 (Summer 1994), 317-28.

R. Churchill Curtis

RICHARD COEUR DE LION. A fourteenth century verse *romance, *Richard Coeur de Lion* is often associated with two other romances from this period, *Of Arthour and of Merlin* and *King Alisaunder*. In the work the poet notes that *Richard* is based on a French original, but the poem is decidedly not pro-French; indeed, the work demonstrates clear disdain for Philip, the French king.

Richard describes the humiliation of the Saracens in the Third *Crusade. The poem concludes abruptly with both sides agreeing to a two year truce. In the work Richard is presented in highly romantic terms, appearing anonymously in different sections as a Red Knight and as a White Knight. His emblems, including a black raven, a red hound, and a white dove, all have didactic Christian significance and relate to the crusade he is about to undertake. Curiously, Richard's mother *Eleanor of Aquitaine is missing from the poem. Also, Richard is married to an Eastern princess in an elaborate ceremony.

SELECTED BIBLIOGRAPHY

Clemente, Linda M. *Literary Objets d'Art: Ekphrasis in Medieval French Romance, 1150-1210.* New York: Peter Lang, 1992; Kelly, Douglas. *Medieval French Romance.* New York: Twayne, 1993.

Robert T. Lambdin

RICHARD THE REDELESS. See *Mum and the Sothsegger*

RIDDLES. The use of playful language in *Anglo-Saxon riddles is clearly related to the use of the exact Latin form in *charms and magic. Indeed, many seem to have been translated from Latin, with no evidence of claim and authorship. The total number extant of ninety is minus about twelve that have been lost. Some are true folk-riddles; others were taken from learned literary authors. Actually more descriptive than the epic form, they reveal the ordinary rural life of medieval England as nothing else. Humor seems almost entirely lacking from the great battle epics, and even in the riddle it takes the form of intellectual exercises rather than jokes. Nevertheless, a riddle is still the mind at play.

The first riddle of the collection clearly refers to the wind: "Who sends me traveling? I rage with a savage sound; I set houses on fire, I fell trees, I stir waves and bear commerce--What am I called?" The second riddle is entitled "A Storm." The diction and balanced cadence suggest that this, along with "The Wind," may be two parts of a threefold riddle clearly written by a literary master.

> Tell me, wise man,
> Who was it that drew me. . . from the depth of the ocean
> When the streams again. . . became still and quiet,
> Who before had forced me. . . in fury to rage?

"Storm III" once again raises the question of the identity of the Master of wind and wave:

>   anguish arises,
> Terror of mind. . . to the tribes of men,
> Distress in the strongholds, . . . when the stalking goblins,
> The pale ghosts shoot. . . with their sharp weapons.
> The fool alone fears not. . . their fatal spears;
> But he perishes too. . . if the true God send
> Straight from above. . . in streams of rain,
> Whizzing and whistling. . . the whirlwind's arrow,
> The flying death.

All three of the first riddles display great dramatic intensity, command of evocative language, and superb construction. Riddle XV, on the other hand, can only be the work of rural observation and long close acquaintance with the larger, stronger digging creatures. In great detail "The Badger" speaks of color and fur, of care for her young, terror of dogs, and willingness to bare her own breast to the foe in order to protect her family. Two lines, 28 and 29, have raised the contention that instead of a badger this may be a porcupine:

> If I reach, in my rage . . . through the roof of my hill

And deal my deadly . . . darts of battle.

A long and involved riddle, XXVI, probably written by a cleric, describes a codex or manuscript of a Bible. An animal is killed, the skin is prepared for writing, and the letters are black, decorated with crimson and gold. The identifying lines are 16 and 17:

All the works of wisdom . . . spread wide the fame
Of the Sovereign of nations! . . . Read me not as a penance!

While it is clear that these exercises were mainly exercises of the mind, they also functioned as intellectual games. Perhaps this explains why so many riddles were copied and passed on,

SELECTED BIBLIOGRAPHY

Lapidge, Michael. "Stoic Cosmology and the Source of the First English Riddle." *Anglia* 112: 1 (1994), 1-25; McCarthy, Marcella. "A Solution to 'Riddle 72' in the Exeter Book." *Review of English Studies* 44:174 (May 1993), 204-10.

Elton E. Smith

ROBERT OF GLOUCESTER (fl. 1260-1300). Robert of Gloucester was a metrical chronicler who is assumed have written a *chronicle of England that covers Britain from its roots in the Fall of Troy to Henry III's reign in 1272. It is obvious that the chronicler was aided by others in his compilation of the text. The *Chronicle* is probably a condensation from other sources, including *Geoffrey of Monmouth. The work is important because it presents the English language in its transition stage before Geoffrey *Chaucer.

SELECTED BIBLIOGRAPHY

Eckhardt, Caroline D. "The Merlin Figure in Middle English Chronicles." In *Comparative Studies of Merlin from the Vedas to C. G. Jung.* James Gollnick, ed. Lewiston, NY: Edwin Mellen, 1991. 21-39; Gellrich, Jesse M. *Discourse and Dominion in the Fourteenth Century.* Princeton: Princeton University Press, 1995; Vollrath, Hanna. "Oral Models of Perception in Eleventh-Century Chronicles." In *Vox Intexta: Orality and Textuality in the Middle Ages.* Alger Nicholas Doane and Carol Braun Pasternak, eds. Madison: University of Wisconsin Press, 1991. 102-11.

Robert T. Lambdin

ROBIN HOOD. A legendary English outlaw and popular hero, Robin Hood is best known through a cycle of *ballads. It is believed that Robin was born in

Locksley, Nottinghamshire, around 1160. It has also been alleged that Robin was the outlawed Robert Fitz-Ooth, earl of Huntingdon, in disguise.

Robin lived in the forest; this was either by choice or because he was outlawed. His chief residence was Sherwood Forest. Medieval ballads teem with anecdotes of his courage and skills in both combat and archery. He was famed also for his generosity and popularity. The legends note that he robbed the rich and gave his contraband to the poor. His chivalric magnanimity and his attitude concerning the protection of women and children were also legendary. Tradition notes that Robin was bled to death by the prioress of Kirkley. He had gone to her during his old age to be bled, and she let him die.

Almost as notorious as Robin are his companions, his "merry men," including Little John, Friar Tuck, Will Scarlet, and Allan-a-Dale, and his love, Maid Marian. One tradition notes that Robin and Little John were defeated with Simon de Montfort at the Battle of Evesham. Because of his popularity, Robin became a stock character in May Day festivals. He was first mentioned in English literature in a 1377 edition of *Piers the Plowman*. He is the hero of a ballad series of some 450 four line stanzas, "A Lytell Geste of Robyn Hode" (1510).

SELECTED BIBLIOGRAPHY

Anderson, Eric R. "Game and Reality in Medieval English Outlaw Narratives." *Aethlon* 8:2 (Spring 1991), 73-88; Ayton, Andrew. "Military Service and the Development of the Robin Hood Legend in the Fourteenth Century." *Nottingham Medieval Studies* 36 (1992), 126-47; Drabble, Margaret, ed. *The Oxford Companion to English Literature*. 5th ed. Oxford: Oxford University Press, 1985; Hanawalt, Barbara. "Ballads and Bandits: Fourteenth-Century Outlaws and the Robin Hood Poems." In *Chaucer's England: Literature in Historical Context*. Barabara Hanawalt, ed. Minneapolis: University of Minnesota Press, 1992. 154-75; Knight, Stephen. "Robin Hood and the Royal Restoration." *Critical Survey* 5:3 (1993), 298-312.

Robert T. Lambdin

ROLLE, RICHARD, OF HAMPOLE (c. 1290-1349). Richard Rolle was one of Britain's first prominent devotional mystics. He was probably born at Thornton-le Dale in North Yorkshire around the turn of the thirteenth century. He attended Oxford for a few terms, but at age nineteen he quit, moved to Hampole, and adopted the life of a hermit.

Rolle lived near a Cistercian nunnery; it was there that he met Margaret Kirkeby. He addressed many of his writings to her. Rolle alsois known to have composed a number of epigrams, commentaries, and minor poems. The topics of his work included the soul's approach to a mystic state through its ablution of worldliness. This, according to Rolle, was accomplished only through meditation, prayer, and the acceptance of God.

Rolle's texts emphasized an individual spiritual existence, a concept in direct opposition to the teachings of traditional religion. Ironically, he gained his greatest repute as the author of *The Pricke of Consciousness*, a didactic poem divided into seven books; the aim of this compilation was to push the reader into doing only good things. Yet Rolle is probably not the author. Regardless, the *Pricke* is considered by many to be the last great religious poem before William *Langland's *Piers the Plowman.*

SELECTED BIBLIOGRAPHY

Austell, Anne. "Feminine Figurae in the Writings of Richard Rolle: A Register of Growth." *Mystics Quarterly* 15:3 (September 1983), 117-24; Hargreaves, Henry. "'Lessouns of Dirige': A Rolle Text Discovered." *Neuphilologische Mitteilungen* 91:3 (1990), 311-19; Moyes, Malcolm Robert. *Richard Rolle's "Expositio super Novem Lectiones Mortuorum": An Introduction and Contribution towards a Critical Edition.* Salzburg: Institut für Anglistik und Amerikanistik, 1988; Renevy, Denis. "Encoding and Decoding: Metaphorical Discourse of Love in Richard Rolle's Commentary on the First Verses of the Song of Songs." *Medieval Translator* 4 (1994), 200-17; Riehle, Wolfgang. "The Authorship of 'The Prick of Conscience' Reconsidered." *Anglia* 111:1 (1993), 1-18.

Robert T. Lambdin

ROMANCE. The cliché of the knight rescuing the damsel in distress characterizes the medieval romance. Romances are found in French, English, and German medieval literature. They include characters who are concerned with social rank, *chivalry, and adventure; the tales usually exhibit elements of the fantastic. The fighting is not premeditated, but light-hearted and impulsive. The hero of the medieval romance usually sets out on a quest, during which he encounters various unrelated adventures that compose the narrative. A narrator relates the tale in verse or prose--the prose form distinguishes later romances. Medieval English romances reached the peak of popularity in the fourteenth century; their decline was speeded in the next two centuries by the Renaissance humanists. It is useful to group Middle English romances by subject matter, representing four classes.

The *"Matter of England" tales are based on the Germanic, and probably the most famous example is *Richard Coeur de Lion* (c. 1350). The *"Matter of France" tales include *The Song of Roland* (fifteenth century) and are marked by their relevance to the reigns of *Charlemagne and William of Orange. The third group, the *"Matter of Rome," relates legends of Alexander the Great and also legends of Thebes and Troy. Geoffrey *Chaucer's *Troilus and Criseyde* provides an example of this classification. The *"Matter of Britain" is probably the most well-known group, centering around *Arthurian legend and including such works as *Sir Gawain and the Green Knight* (fourteenth century) and Thomas *Malory's *Le Morte D'arthur* (fifteenth century). Middle English romances generally demonstrate less refinement than their French counterparts, but also borrow the alliterative and couplet verse forms from the French.

SELECTED BIBLIOGRAPHY

Abbott, Reginald. "What Becomes a Legend Most? Fur in the Medieval Romance." *Dress* 21 (1994), 4-16; Berthelot, Anne."The Romance as Conjointure of Brief Narratives." *L'Esprit Créateur* 33:4 (Winter 1993), 51-60; Clemente, Linda M. *Literary Objets d'Art: Ekphrasis in Medieval French Literature, 1150-1210.* New York: Peter Lang, 1992; Frakes, Jerold C. "Metaphysical Structure as Narrative Structure in the Medieval Romance." *Neophilologus* 69:4 (1985), 481-89; Kelly, Douglas. *Medieval French Romance.* New York: Twayne, 1993; Kennedy, Elspeth. "The Narrative Techniques Used to Give Arthurian Romance a 'Historical' Flavour." in *Conjunctures.* Keith Busby and Norris Lacy, eds. Amsterdam: Radopi, 1994. 219-33; Lindahl, Carl. "The Oral Undertones of Late Medieval Romance." In *Oral Tradition in the Middle Ages.* W.F.H. Nicolaisen, ed. Binghampton, NY: Medieval and Renaissance Texts and Studies, 1995. 59-75; Nolan, Barbara. *Chaucer and the Tradition of "Roman Antique."* Cambridge: Cambridge University Press, 1992; Rockwell, Paul Vincent. *Rewriting Resemblance in Medieval French Romance: "C'est n'est pas un graal."* New York: Garland, 1995; Spivack, Charlotte, and Roberta Lynne Staples. *The Company of Camelot: Arthurian Characters in Romance and Fantasy.* Westport, CT: Greenwood Press, 1994.

Anna Shealy

ROMAUNT OF THE ROSE, THE. Three fragments of the Middle English poem *The Romaunt of the Rose* exist; critics are relatively sure that at least portions of two of these were composed by Geoffrey *Chaucer. The work, an English version of the *Roman de la Rose,* encompasses about one-third of the content of the original French work, which was started about 1225 by Guillaume de Lorris and completed some fifty years later by Jean de Meun. The English version consists of three parts.

In this *dream vision a lover attempts to pick the rose of love from an immaculate garden. Failing to do so, he receives advice from several allegorical figures, including Idleness, Mirth, and Disdain. Perhaps because the French source differs so greatly in content because of its dual-authorship, Chaucer's version is a difficult text. De Lorris strove to create a catalog of *courtly love that was serious and overtly romantic. De Meun in his emendations and additions was much more sardonic and cynical toward women. Thus Chaucer's work becomes comedic as it presents these two conflicting sides.

SELECTED BIBLIOGRAPHY

Eckhardt, Caroline D. "The Art of Translation in *The Romaunt of the Rose.*" *Studies in the Age of Chaucer* 6 (1984), 41-63; Levey, David. "'Courtly Love' and the Middle

English *Romaunt of the Rose.*" *Unisa English Studies* 25:2 (September 1987), 1-6; Oizumi, Akio. and Kunihiro Miki, eds. *A Complete Concordance to the Works of Geoffrey Chaucer.* Vol. IX, *A Concordance to "The Romaunt of the Rose."* Hildesheim: Olms-Weidmann, 1991; Smith, Meret. "Literary Loanwords from Old French in *The Romaunt of the Rose.*" *Chaucer Review* 17:1 (Summer 1982), 89-93.

Robert T. Lambdin

"RUIN, THE." "The Ruin" is a haunting Old English poem located in the *Exeter Book. Although a mere forty-five lines in length, the poem paints an eerie scene of a city in Britain, probably Bath, left wasted and in ruins. It contains a series of wistful laments in a place where lichen is eating through the remnants and towers lie crumbling. "The Ruin" stands by itself in Old English poetry because it is concerned with a place, and not a person.

SELECTED BIBLIOGRAPHY

Morgan. Gwendolyn. "Introduction: 'The Ruin.'" *Northwest Review* 29:3 (1991), 106-08; Renoir, Alain. "The Old English 'Ruin': Contrastive Structure and Affective Impact." In *The Old English Elegies: New Essays in Criticism and Research.* Martin Green, ed. Rutherford, NJ: Fairleigh Dickinson University Press, 1983. 148-73.

Robert T. Lambdin

RUSSIAN LITERATURE, OLD. Much like the literary traditions of European countries, Old Russian literature began in forms primarily historical or ecclesiastical and shows significant linguistic development in a relatively compressed time frame. The oldest dated writings in Russian are not original creations; they are Old Slavonian church manuscripts that were recopied into Russian. Similar copying was done of Byzantine and Greek originals a bit later. Actual Old Russian literature, particularly when compared to New Russian Literature, is primarily didactic in tone, as is most early medieval literature. In Russia such ideological concerns were influenced by Byzantine literature.

One fascinating element of Old Russian literature is a complete lack of typical genre distinctions between prose and poetry or between narrative and drama. A prayer, a heroic epic, and a sermon may all contain elements of both prose and poetry, depending upon the writing style that the author feels will make his art form more moving or appealing in each section. The writing is always careful and well planned from the introduction to the conclusion.

The literature of Old Russia can be divided into two distinct periods based upon the two major centers of Russian cultural life. The first was that of Kiev, until about 1200, when the Moscow period began. The distinctions between Kievan and Muscovite literature can sometimes seem artificial, and the two, of course, are very similar during the intermediate period. However, there are some significant stylistic differences.

Kievan literature is mostly uniform and owes much of its foundation to Scandinavian invaders--and the efficient military system the Scandinavians taught to the exploited Slavic population. Certain short *sagas show this influence in their rigid and terse styles. The Scandinavian saga style was also incorporated into the Slavic concern with maintaining a record of their separate history; hence one notes the highly anecdotal elements of the Old Russian historical *chronicles.

The Byzantine emphasis upon Christianity was by far the greatest influence upon old Kievan literature and society, making both fairly disciplined and concerned with encouraging the highest moral standards. Ideals of saintliness and asceticism flowered in an abundance of hagiographic writing. Enormous piety was expected of a saint, and martyrdom was usually appreciated as well. *Hagiography remained popular until the time of Peter the Great (1672-1725). Pious heroes were usually pragmatic and realistic in the writing of Kiev, although later "funny saints" and "fools in Christ" were added for amusing diversions from an overwhelming loftiness.

As one might expect, martyrdom among royalty was of great interest. Short biographies from Nestor's *Chronicle* (c. 1116) discuss two Russian princes who endured and nearly revelled in martyrdom. This demonstrates a particularly early Russian appreciation for a mixture of pathos and Christianity. Supplications and sermons gave Old Russian literature much of its lyricism.

Hilarion, appointed metropolitan of Kiev in 1051, wrote sermons with much emphasis upon saints and the saintly qualities of royalty. His writing is primarily allegorical and based upon the Scriptures. Cyril of Turov (c. 1130-1182) was a great poet whose work reflects the next stage in Old Russian lyricism. His poetry mixes homiletic qualities with an appreciation for nature and the changing seasons. Cyril's poems lack the spontaneous overflow of emotion evident in early Slavic folksongs because they are intended to reflect Byzantine hymns. Serapion of Vladimir (d. 1275) was among the final Old Kievan homiletic writers; his *Sermon of the Merciless Heathens* is an apocalyptic view of the ruination of Kiev by infidels who invade as divine punishment for the sins of the nation.

As the feudal system increased and the decentralization of power occurred, so grew anxiety about the fate of towns during the feudal wars. This is brilliantly reflected in *The Igor Tale* (1187), a beautiful poetic epic. Lyricism, hagiography, and annalism combined to produce Old Russian epic-heroic narrative literature. The lyricism of *The Igor Tale* differs from the more emotional *Narrative of Batu Khan's Invasion of R'azan* (1237).

When political life recentralized in Moscow, there developed Muscovite hagiography, which dropped the simplicity and veracity of Old Kievan hagiography in favor of more fictional accounts. The artistic expression of a glorious, young Moscow was more flowering and expository. Epiphanius the Wise (d. 1420) wrote several overembroidered biographies: *Life of St. Stefan of Perm* (1397), *Life of St. Sergius of Radonez* (1417), and probably the *Life and Death of Great Prince Dimitris* (early fifteenth century).

Required reading of all literate Muscovites was Nestor-Iskander's *Tale of the Taking of Constantinople*, which showed the increasing concern with current events; it was written shortly after the conquest of Constantinople by the Moslems under the Turkish sultan Muhammed II in 1453. This writing introduced a new twist in the literature that ultimately became revisionist historiography.

By the end of the reign of *Ivan IV the Terrible (1533-1584), Russian literature and language had undergone a complete change from its early simplicity. It became full of ornamental speeches, complicated syntax, and sophisticated phrases. The favorite theme changed from the glorification of a saint to the exaltation of a tsar. Also gone were any democratic tendencies in favor of presenting a powerful aristocrat who would quickly suppress any dissenters. The emphasis was upon economic wealth and most traces of asceticism were eliminated. The new partnership between the church and the tsar was clearly grounded in the rewards of this world rather than the spiritualism of the next. This emphasis upon riches and might could not have been more different from the piety of the Old Kievan hagiography.

SELECTED BIBLIOGRAPHY

Ledkovsky, Marina, Charlotte Rosenthal, and Mary Zirin, eds. *Dictionary of Russian Women Writers*. Westport, CT: Greenwood Press, 1994; May, Rachel. *The Translator in the Text: On Reading Russian Literature in English*. Evanston, IL: Northwestern University Press, 1994; Nemec Ignashev, Dianne. *Women and Writing in Russia and the USSR: A Bibliography of English Language Sources*. New York: Garland, 1992; Pearson, Irene. "Images of Saintliness in Medieval Russian Literature." In *From Dante to Solzhenitsyn: Essays on Christianity and Literature*. Robert M. Yule, ed. Wellington: Victoria University of Wellington, 1978. 35-54.

Laura Cooner Lambdin

S

SAGA. The sagas, in a strict sense, are stories of the medieval period of Iceland and other Scandinavian countries that recorded the legendary and historical accounts of heroic adventures, especially as the tales relate to members of specific families. These were long, narrative epics indigenous to Norway, Iceland, and Ireland. The earliest Icelandic sagas were composed in prose, in much the same manner as Irish epics and *romances. The word "saga" is derived from the old Norse word for "story," and a great bulk of this material remains extant. Sagas were generally divided into three types: family, kings, and heroic. The greatest amount of these works, written later than the prose works, are composed as poems

The family sagas, or *Aettirsogur*, are among the most numerous of sagas that survive today. These works usually come from Scandinavian roots and often deal with the miraculous migrations and settling of these peoples into different regions. This type also includes works that relate the adventures found in Viking expeditions to Europe, Britain, and even the New World. Other popular topics included feuds among individuals, families, and clans, as well as disputes about property and, most important, reputation.

The family sagas, like the kings' sagas, are noted for their seemingly detached objectivity. The observer of many of these works seems to be someone not involved directly with either side of the dispute. Traditionally, it was believed that the family sagas were somewhat historical, drawn from oral renditions of an earlier era. This may be true in some instances, but today most of these works are regarded more as historical fiction, with added deeds and exploits to heighten the fame of those involved.

Among the best known sagas is *Njáls Saga*, a narrative devoted to the deeds of Gunnarr. He is a worthy hero who weds Hallgerðr, a woman who does not share his upright character. She is directly responsible, through a series of amoral character errors, for a series of feuds and conflicts that result in Gunnarr's death. Additionally, his friend, Njál, a sage individual and a lawyer, is burned to death. Yet because he loves peace, Njál dies with no ill will toward the evil Hallgerðr; instead, he accepts death with a Christian stoicism. This work serves to illustrate typical elements of the sagas, including the thematic growth of social stability and awareness. Sagas also depend upon intense psychological investigations of the roles emotions play in the development of character. It is the examination of emotional traits that the characters must be aware of before they can grow to understand their function in life.

The other types of sagas demonstrate a variety of other themes. The *Eyrbyggja Saga* is a great example of the scrutiny of the rigid communities that had recently developed. The works of this genre did not depend upon the supernatural elements found in previous works. Indeed, the *Laxdale Saga* tells of a tragic love triad and its political implications. At the same time, the *Grettis Saga* recounts the life of a notorious outlaw, Grettir the Strong; this work is noted as perhaps the best example of a true saga. This work is highly suggestive of the story of *Beowulf*.

The *Heimskringla* of *Snorri Sturluson acts in much the same way as the medieval *chronicles in its treatment of the kings of Norway. Sagas continued to be composed until the late thirteenth century. However, these later sagas are the exceptions rather than the rule because it is likely that most of the accounts of the sagas occurred between 930 and 1050. They existed in oral form first and then were transcribed several hundred years later.

SELECTED BIBLIOGRAPHY

Byock, Jesse L. "Choices of Honor: Telling Saga Feud, Thattr, and the Fundamental Oral Progression." *Oral Tradition* 10:1 (March 1995), 166-80; Finlay, Alison. "Skalds, Troubadours, and Sagas." *Saga Book* 24:2-3 (1995), 105-53;; Mundal, Els. "Women and Old Norse Narrative." In *Contexts of Pre-Novel Narrative: The European Tradition*. Roy Eriksen, ed. Berlin: Mouton de Gruyter, 1994. 135-51; Olason, Vesteinn. "The Marvelous North and Authorial Presence in the Icelandic 'Fornaldarsaga.'" In *Contexts of Pre-Novel Narrative: The European Tradition*. Roy Eriksen, ed. Berlin: Mouton de Gruyter, 1994. 101-34.

Robert T. Lambdin

SAWLES WARDE. *Sawles Warde*, or *The Safeguarding of the Soul*, is an *allegory found only in the three manuscripts of the works known as the *Katherine Group. It is probably a twelfth-century translation of part of Hugh of St. Victor's *De Anima*. The text presents a morality on the body as the dwelling place of the most precious treasure imaginable, the soul. The work then recounts the difficulties of protecting the soul from the vices. This, according to the text, can be accomplished only through management of Wit and through the assiduity of the Four Cardinal Virtues. The work is important because it provides an early example of the allegorical morality castle, a technique also found in *The *Castle of Perseverance*.

SELECTED BIBLIOGRAPHY

Breeze, Andrew. "Welsh Cais 'Sergeant' and 'Sawles Warde.'" *Notes and Queries* 40 (238): 3 (September 1993), 297-303; Eggebroten, Anne. "'Sawles Warde': A Retelling of *De Anima* for a Female Audience." *Mediaevalia* 10 (1988), 27-47. Millett, Bella. "Hali Meihad, 'Sawles Warde,' and the Continuity of English Prose." In *Five Hundred Years of Words and Sounds*. Eric Gerald Stanley and Douglas Gray, eds. Totowa, NJ: Brewer, 1983. 100-08.

Robert T. Lambdin

SCHOLASTICISM. Scholasticism refers to the school of thought prevalent from the twelfth to fifteenth centuries. Scholastics attempted to confirm the doctrines of Christianity through the logical deductive method of reasoning developed by *Aristotle. Some of the problems that the Scholastics examined were the nature of God and the scope of the infinite. Peter *Abelard, *Bernard of Clairvaux, and *Anselm were the most notable figures of the "first era" of Scholasticism during the twelfth century.

The second era (thirteenth century), known as the "golden era" of Scholasticism, included Thomas *Aquinas and John *Duns Scotus, whose divergences divided Scholastic thinkers into two groups, the "Thomists" and the "Scotists." After this great period scholasticism began to experience a decline, and the arguments grew relatively petty and insignificant. Roger *Bacon's introduction of inductive methods of reasoning replaced the deductive logic of scholasticism, speeding the end of the Scholastic age.

SELECTED BIBLIOGRAPHY

Kinney, Daniel. "In the Wake of Thomas More: Juan Luis Vives." *Moreana* 18:70 (June 1981), 67-72; Rummel, Erika. "*Et cum theolgoia bella poeta gerit*: The Conflict between Humanists and Scholastics Revisited." *The Sixteenth Century Journal* 23:4 (Winter 1992), 713-26.

Anna Shealy

SCHOOLMEN. "Schoolmen" refers to a collection of scholars and writers from the eleventh to the fifteenth century who attempted to accommodate the tenets of *Aristotle to those of the church fathers. They were usually teachers of theology or philosophy who felt that the inclusion of the classical thoughts in tandem with those of the early Christians were of import in a fair teaching of the curriculum. They were astounded that the tenets of the pagan Aristotle could apply so well to church dogma. Indeed his teachings would be used for centuries to come and continues to be a vital part of current theology. The movement evidently became quite popular, for the slate of Schoolmen is rather impressive; it includes Peter *Abelard, Thomas *Aquinas, John *Duns Scotus, and Albertus Magnus. The schoolmen each made their marks in the philosophy and teachings of this period.

SELECTED BIBLIOGRAPHY

Drabble, Margaret, ed. *The Oxford Companion to English Literature.* 5th ed. Oxford: Oxford University Press, 1985; Swanton, Michael. *English Literature before Chaucer.* New York: Longman. 1987.

Robert T. Lambdin

SCOGAN, HENRY (c. 1360-1407). Henry Scogan was the tutor to the sons of Henry IV. Today only one extant work is ascribed to Scogan, his "Morale Balade." However, it is commonly believed that he was an acquaintance of Geoffrey *Chaucer and that Chaucer most likely dedicated his 1393 poem "Lenvoy" to him.

SELECTED BIBLIOGRAPHY

Halmundsson, May Newman. "Chaucer's Circle: Henry Scogan and His Friends." *Medievalia et Humanistica* 10 (1981), 129-39; Swanton, Michael. *English Literature before Chaucer.* New York: Longman, 1987.

Robert T. Lambdin

SCOP. Similar to the *gleemen, a scop was a kind of *Anglo-Saxon court poet. Although he probably traveled around from court to court, his place in the king's retinue was comparable to that of the Welsh *bard or the Irish fili. Scops were composers as well as reciters; their themes were mainly heroic, extolling the accomplishments of the early Germanic people. Later, biblical themes were employed. Scops were also probably expected to eulogize their patrons. Thus they compare well with and have often been referred to as the precursors to the poet laureate.

SELECTED BIBLIOGRAPHY

Brown, Ray. "The Begging Scop and the Generous King in 'Widsith.'" *Neophilologus* 73:2 (April 1989), 281-92; Opland, Jeff. "Scop and Imbongi III: The Exploitation of Tradition." *Pacific Quarterly* 8:4 (1984), 44-59.

Robert T. Lambdin

SCOTT, MICHÆL (c. 1160-1235). Philosopher and astrologer, Michæl Scott was born probably in Durham, of Scottish border ancestry. He was educated in the universities of Oxford, Paris, and Padua, where he studied philosophy and natural magic. Scott spent much of his life in Europe and translated, under the patronage of Emperor Frederick II, *Aristotle's *De animalibus* and *De caelo.*

His own writings include studies of astrology, alchemy, and medicine, embodying the medieval beliefs of physiognomy, the natural magic akin to Celtic belief in the object-soul, or the ascription of human qualities to plants, objects, and animals, and alchemical concept of planetary influence on metals. He was one of the earliest philosophers who would be labeled a sorcerer and magician; his work was revived later in the Renaissance by philosophers such as Giovanni Picos della Mirandola. In Renaissance England, Scotland, and other parts of Europe, philosophers revived classical hermetic texts during the Neo-Platonic movement. Michæl Scott was later mentioned in *Dante's *Inferno, "The Lay of the Last Minstrel" by Sir Walter Scott, and *The Three Perils of Man* by James Hogg.

SELECTED BIBLIOGRAPHY

Barrow, G.W.S. *Bruce and the Community of the Realm of Scotland.* Berkeley: University of California Press, 1965; Bold, Alan Norman. *Scotland: A Literary Guide.* London: Routledge, 1989; McKenna, Stephen R., ed. *Selected Essays on Scottish Language and Literature.* Lewiston, NY: Edwin Mellen Press, 1992.

J. Scott Plaster

SCOTTISH LITERATURE. The literary tradition of Scotland arose later than that in England due to a number of factors such as the lack of a unifying national political identity, but the wealth of the region's oral traditions and the influence of literature of other languages lent its early makars many themes and forms with which to experiment. Not much of early middle Scots survives, and when we hear William *Dunbar's roll call of poets in his "Lament of the Makars," we feel regret that the work of so many poets has been lost. Though the nation's early oral origins in the Celtic Highlands are generally disregarded in favor of the much later Anglo emergence, it is perhaps the Celtic roots of the Scottish character that distinguish it from southern English and help to make the early Scots literature unique, though its creators employed and imitated English methods and techniques.

Therefore when we begin our discussion of the emergence of the first language we can call true English in the speech of the Lowland Scots, we do so with the understanding that it is not that far removed from the Highland customs and belief, always prevalent, never suppressed in its nation or its literature. To say that there was no literature in Scotland until the emergence of literary forms in the thirteenth and fourteenth centuries would be to ignore the tremendous oral culture that suffused the daily life of the Celts, the earliest songs, *ballads, and tales of legendary heroes. When the Lowlands of Scotland became largely *Anglo-Norman, the incoming language assimilated the older Celtic traditions, and was infused with the supernatural and magical pagan beliefs. It is from these oral traditions that the ballads arose, however they were composed, from the *minstrels and Gaelic bards, the haunting echoes of which occur especially among the group of ballads collected by Walter Scott, Bishop Percy, and later Francis Child. Romances such as *Sir Orfeo also survived from the Middle Ages, including Tristram, the work of the first named Scots author *Thomas of Ercceldoune, or Thomas the Rhymer.

The first sustained written literature of early Scotland arose when the Wars for Independence offered a political, unifying purpose. Works such as John *Barbour's The *Bruce (1375) and *Blind Harry's (Henry the Minstrel's) The Wallace (c. 1460) depicted the early patriots of the movement, instilling patriotism and helping to shape the national Scottish character. The Heroes, *Robert the Bruce (King Robert I), and William *Wallace, embodied the Scottish ideals of bravery and resistance as they led their men into battles pitted against armies many times their size. Fighting for Freedom and Right, the legendary figures were immortalized in Barbour's and Harry's poetry, which recorded historical fact, more or less, while contributing the first significant literary works of an emerging nation.

Barbour was among a group of poets of the fourteenth and fifteenth centuries known as the Scottish Makars and sometimes called the Scottish Chaucerians because of the similarity of some of their work to *Chaucer's. The group also included Robert *Henryson, William Dunbar, Gavin Douglas, Blind Harry, and James I. Although they employed similar stanza forms such as the rhyme-royal, they brought their own language and tumbling *alliterative verse to the genres and used the medium to comment on their own native Scotland. From Dunbar's statement about the mutability of human existence in his Testament of Cresseid to Henryson's skillful use of the *beast fable to make social and human commentary, the Scottish Makars were no mere imitators, but skillful creators of original literature about a unique nation. A careful study of the group's work shows them more indebted to their French and classical sources than to Chaucer.

This early Scottish poetry, when compared to the aereate continental verse of Chaucer and his contemporaries, does not prove to be identical, and it should not be. The character of the middle Scots is seemingly always present, no matter what form it takes. In The Tretis of Dunbar, we are struck with the life of his language, and we conclude that he owes no great debt to Chaucer for succeeding in peopling his poetry with three characters as colorful as the Wife of Bath. Later, in the political and religious satire of Sir David *Lindsay, we are glad that he did not cloak his candid, ribald language in an allegorical shroud, but rather entertains us in the vernacular and idiom of his audience.

The literature of the middle Scots evolved from oral traditions later than in the South and was enriched, rather than hampered, by its later development. Its poets helped shape a uniquely Scottish character in an era when its people were struggling to retain an identity and to gain independence from a powerful England. Resolute in their fight to remain free, the warriors, with their Celtic will and independence, did not lose what made them distinct from their neighbors. In the same way, its literature did not lose its own character; despite the use of continental forms and genres, the Scottish Makars remained distinct artists, contributing works that survive as testaments to their will and nation.

Although they employed techniques, forms, and themes similar to those of Chaucer, to dismiss them as merely derivative and unimportant would be a mistake. The Scottish Chaucerians, most notably Henryson and Dunbar, contributed works of alliterative verse in rhymed stanzaic form. This use of alliterative verse lasted longer in Scotland than in England, and of the rhymed form, the combined 4,000 lines of Scots are more than double what has been preserved from their southern neighbors. Alliterative verse, using words with the same initial consonant in the same line or lines, is valuable for study of the medieval period because of the wealth of vocabulary that was incorporated in order to pack as many words with the same initial consonant in lines as possible. The Scottish alliterative poets often used rare words and words of French or Scandinavian origin, though much of the vocabulary would have been familiar to their audience. The tumbling verse, as it was called by King James I, was at its most extreme in the burlesque alliteration of Henryson in works such as "Sum practysis of medicine," in which he satirized those of supposed medical knowledge.

As a makar, Dunbar clearly distinguishes himself from his model in works such as *The Tretis of the Tua Marritt emem and the Wedo*, akin to Chaucer's "The *Merchant's Tale" and portrait of the Wife of Bath. Yet in Dunbar's poem, instead of one outspoken and shameless character, he includes three who let their hair down, drink wine, and candidly discuss the trials of marriage.

Of equal merit are original works of Robert Henryson. His *Testament of Cresseid* stands as a dramatic sequel to Chaucer's *Troylus and Criseyde* and is considered the finest narrative tragedy of medieval and Renaissance Scottish literature. Henryson's *Moral Fables*, a set of thirteen beast fables with multiple *moralitates*, illuminate aspects of human nature and extol the virtues of patience and prudence. The Scottish Makars, though perhaps indebted to their model, have a place as makars in their own right, exploring the same genres and stanza forms, but in the middle Scots, and providing social, political, and human commentary about their own native clime.

The Bruce, composed in 1375 by poet-historian John Barbour (1316?-1396), is the truest national epic of early Scotland. A poem of 13,550 lines of octosyllabic couplets, it is the first major work written in the language of the Lowland Scots and helped to carve and shape the character and temper of that region. Barbour chronicled with reasonable historical accuracy the ascension of Robert the Bruce (Robert I) to the Scottish throne during the nation's tumultuous war of liberation from England. The historical verse narrative follows the Scottish patriot from his ascension in 1306 until his death in 1329. Of even more importance than the work's literary virtue was Barbour's political purpose of reinvigorating the patriotism of previous generations in a time when the state of the nation was perilous. Robert the Bruce, the hero of the work, is dramatized as a model of courage, valor, and moral and physical strength, but above all, a defender of freedom and independence.

As far as historical accuracy is concerned, Barbour was careful and deliberate, but without leeching his narrative of interest and artistic effect. Of the few errors that have been attributed to him, the ones that are rightly so are minor or justifiable, such as the sequencing of some events and the exclusion of some other historical figures of the period, notably William Wallace. Barbour's piece is valuable for purely historical reasons because it is the only source for several key facts about the life of the title character. Judging from his detailed depictions, it is probable that he also had experience from eyewitness accounts. Many of the events of the poem actually happened during Barbour's lifetime, while the rest were likely composed from extensive collections of oral histories and detailed chronicles.

In an episodic rather than thorough or comprehensive fashion, Barbour traced in twenty books the trials of Robert the Bruce, his friend James Douglas, his brother Edward, and his nephew Randolph. As the poem opens, Bruce has refused an offer of titular kingship as vassal to *Edward I of England, determined instead to claim his rightful rule of an independent Scotland. Barbour carefully characterized his hero through detailed episodes and the reiteration of his virtues. Choosing freedom over an empty title, Bruce is outlawed, and after his small army is defeated, they are forced to seek refuge in the mountains and hills. His wife and daughter, whom he had hidden in a castle, are captured and imprisoned. Bruce gains gradual support when others witness his bravery and prowess in battle as he leads sieges of castles, including the recapture of Kildrummy Castle, where he rescues his wife and daughter. During the years of war England sees its king die and his son Edward II take command. The biggest victory for Bruce was at the battle of Bannockburn, which is recounted in one of the poem's most memorable passages. Crowned in 1306, Robert Bruce continued to wage war and rid his land of the English. He eventually succeeded, sacking the few remaining English castles, including the one at Stirling. A truce in the war called for by the Pope did not yet declare Scotland an independent land, so Bruce did not resign his campaign and continued to siege. When he died at age fifty, Robert the Bruce was finally king of an independent Scotland.

The Bruce laid a solid foundation for future literature of the Scottish Lowlands, marking a departure from earlier unrhymed alliterative verse and a beginning of continental rhymed forms. As a national work, Barbour's piece is important historically and as a contribution that helped shape the nation's character. As a work of literature, The Bruce is unparalleled as a commemoration of Scottish chivalry and patriotism. The work is not quite as unified or dignified as an epic, and the rhyme is more regular and correct than musical. The plot structure is not as intricate as that of great epic works. As a history, it does not observe the same veracity a modern historian would insist upon. But overall, the work's value as a cultural contribution, a political affirmation, a historical preservation, and a stirring work of literature is unmistakable.

SELECTED BIBLIOGRAPHY

Barrow, G.W.S. Bruce and the Community of the Realm of Scotland. Berkeley: University of California Press. 1965; Bold, Alan Norman. Scotland: A Literary Guide. London:

Routledge, 1989; Ebin, Lois A. "John Barbour's *Bruce*: Poetry, History, and Propaganda." *Studies in Scottish Literature* 9 (April 1972): 218-42; Greentree, Rosemary. *Reader, Teller, and Teacher: The Narrator of Robert Henryson's Moral Fables*. New York: Peter Lang, 1993; Mainster, Phoebe A. "How to Make a Hero: Barbour's Recipe: Reshaping History as Romance." *Michigan Academician* 20 (Spring 1988): 225-38; McKenna, Stephen R. *Selected Essays on Scottish Language and Literature*. Lewiston, NY: Edwin Mellen Press, 1992; Trace, Jacqueline. "The Supernatural Element in Barbour's *Bruce*." *Massachusetts Studies in English* 1 (Spring 1968): 55-65.

J. Scott Plaster

"SEAFARER, THE." An *Old English poem from the *Exeter Book, "The Seafarer" is part of a small group of poems often labeled *elegies, although the fitness of this label has been much debated. The narrator describes life as a seafarer, suffering through stormy weather and loneliness, but also feeling the yearning to travel. From there the poem modulates into a meditation on life. Drawing upon traditional Christian ideas that equate life with a pilgrimage to the heavenly country, seafaring stands allegorically for the journey through life that all people make. A seafarer ought not to become distracted by enjoyment of the material world. As the narrator says at the poem's end, "uton we hycgan hwær we ham agen, / ond þonne geþencan hu we þider cumen," (let us consider where we have a home and then think how we may come thither).

Ambiguous language, textual corruption, and the apparent division of the poem into two halves, one descriptive, the other didactic, have made "The Seafarer" a subject of sustained critical controversy. Early in this century many editors considered the overtly religious conclusion a late addition and printed the poem without it (this is the reason Ezra Pound's famous translation lacks the concluding lines), but the conclusion is now generally seen as a logical continuation of the seafaring motif. Although the two poems are separated in the manuscript, "The Seafarer" is often read as forming a kind of diptych with "The *Wanderer," also found in the Exeter Book. Both present images of exile, of estrangement from worldly society. In "The Seafarer" this exile results from a voluntary decision, an ascetic desire to engage in a pilgrimage.

SELECTED BIBLIOGRAPHY

Conde-Silvestre, Juan C., comp. "'The Wanderer' and 'The Seafarer': A Bibliography, 1971-1991." *SELIM: Journal of the Spanish Society for Medieval English Language and Literature* 2 (1992), 170-86; Jacobs, Nicolas. "Syntactical Connections and Logical Disconnection: The Case of 'The Seafarer.'" *Medium Ævum* 58:1 (1989), 105-13; Orton, Peter. "The Form and Structure of 'The Seafarer.'" *Studia Neophililogica* 63: 1 (1991), 37-55.

Karl Hagen

"SECOND NUN'S TALE, THE." "The Second Nun's Tale" is a hagiographic story included in Geoffrey *Chaucer's *Canterbury Tales* (c. 1387-1400); the reference to the *Life of St. Cecilia* indicates this tale was written before 1387. The tale also contains borrowings from Dante. Written in rhyme-royal, it is an adaptation of an older tale from Latin sources of the martyr St. Cecilia, who was both Roman nobility and a Christian.

Cecilia converts her bridegroom Valerian and his brother Tiburtius, and together they perform many miracles and conversions. When the three refuse Almachius's demand that they make sacrifices to Jupiter, Almachius murders them all. Cecilia manages to continue her work converting others to Christianity for three days after she has been killed; finally she leaves her earthly body and is buried by St. Urban.

SELECTED BIBLIOGRAPHY

Bush, Douglas. *English Poetry*. New York, Oxford University Press, 1963; Fields, Peter. "Chaucer's Cecile as Christian-Humanist Disputer of the Sacred." *In Geardagum* 15 (1994), 29-39; Garbáty, Thomas J. *Medieval English Literature*. Toronto: Heath, 1984; Jankowski, Eileen S. "Reception of Chaucer's 'Second Nun's Tale': Osbern Bokenham's 'Lyf of S. Cycyle.'" *Chaucer Review* 30:3 (1996), 306-18; Johnson, Lynn Staley. "Chaucer's Tale of the Second Nun and the Strategies of Dissent." *Studies in Philology* 89:3 (Summer 1992), 314-33; Lambdin, Laura C., and Robert T. Lambdin, eds. *Chaucer's Pilgrims: An Historical Guide to the Pilgrims in the "Canterbury Tales."* Westport, CT: Greenwood, 1996; Salter, Elizabeth. *Fourteenth-Century English Poetry*. Oxford: Clarendon Press, 1983.

Laura Cooner Lambdin

SECOND SHEPHERD'S PLAY, THE. *The Second Shepherd's Play,* written around 1425, is considered the preeminent achievement of the *Wakefield Master (*see **Drama, Medieval**). The play is composed in the playwright's characteristic nine line stanza and his typically colloquial language. Although it is a part of the Towneley cycle, more than any other mystery play, it has developed an individualized reputation for excellence. The play is anthologized more often than any other medieval drama. In fact, despite its rather singular nature, it has become representative of cycle plays in general. The play is admired for its lively humor, its vivid characterizations (particularly those of Mak the sheep stealer and his testy wife Gill), and its bitter social protests. The play successfully combines a farcical story of sheep stealing with an enactment of the Nativity, thus creating one of the most unusual Christmas narratives in literature. These components make *The Second Shepherd's Play* a timeless production.

The Second Shepherd's Play begins with a group of three shepherds-- Coll, Gib, and Daw--who complain of the weather and of social injustice. The first laments social inequity, the second marriage, and the third labor relations.

They collectively construct an image of a world in need of redemption. The entrance of the notorious sheep stealer Mak alerts the Shepherds to the peril of their flocks, and despite their efforts to avoid theft by making Mak sleep between them, they lose an ewe to the villain. When the shepherds discover the misdeed, they search Mak's house for their missing property; however, Mak and his cantankerous wife Gill have disguised the sheep as their infant child and hidden him in a cradle. The fraud might have been successful had the shepherds not decided to present Mak's child with gifts as a reconciliation for their seemingly unfounded suspicions. When they discover the hoax, they punish the perpetrator by tossing him in a blanket, a relatively mild penalty in a society that would hang a man for stealing sheep. In the final scenes of the play the shepherds, lying in the field, are summoned to Christ's nativity, where they present the infant God with gifts that are more characteristic of fifteenth century England than of ancient Judea--a tennis ball, a bough of cherries, and a bird.

The majority of the scholarship on *The Second Shepherd's Play* has sought to elucidate the numerous parallels between the sheep stealing subplot and the Nativity. Of course, the farcical episode is a parody of the Nativity, with Mak, Gill, and the sheep a demonic inversion of Jesus, Mary and Joseph. Moreover, the shepherds' gifts to the sheep are a burlesque of their later presentations to the Christ child, and one can hardly escape the allusion within the subplot to Christ as the Lamb of God. The greatest achievement of *The Second Shepherd's Play* is the way in which the playwright has managed to make the Christmas story more immediate and consequently more powerful for his audience by placing it in a contemporary setting, by making the gifts to the infant Christ items characteristic of their own environment and, therefore, more clearly representative of their own desire to celebrate the Incarnation. By making the shepherds' complaints reminiscent of contemporary social ills, the playwright emphasizes the immediacy of redemption for the English people, thus bridging the fifteen hundred year gap between their faith and the Incarnation.

SELECTED BIBLIOGRAPHY

Fiondella, Maris G. "Derrida, Typology, and the *Second Shepherd's Play*. The Theatrical Production of Christian Metaphysics." *Exemplaria* 6:2 (Fall 1994), 429-58; Helterman, J. *Symbolic Action in the Plays of the Wakefield Master*. Athens: University of Georgia Press, 1981; Irace, Kathleen. "Mak's 'Sothren Tothe': A Philological and Critical Study of the Dialect Joke in the *Second Shepherd's Play*." *Comitatus* 21 (1990), 38-51.

James Keller

SEVEN DEADLY SINS. Thomas *Aquinas authoritatively discussed the seven deadly sins, or vices most responsible for the downfall of man. His list included anger, covetousness, envy, gluttony, lust, pride, and sloth. Aquinas noted that these vices were not distinguished by themselves as deadly, but became so by their potential for causing other sins. Of these, Aquinas felt that pride was the worst. These seven items became the basis for many of the moralities of England.

SELECTED BIBLIOGRAPHY

Conley, John. "The Garbing in *Everyman* of the Seven Deadly Sins Specified in Elckerlijc." *Notes and Queries* 39(237):2 (July 1991), 159-60; Evans, Deanna Delmar. "Dunbar's 'Tretis': The Seven Deadly Sins in Carnivalesque Disguise." *Neophilologus* 73:1 (January 1989), 130-41; Norman, Joanne E. "Sources for the Grotesque in William Dunbar's 'Dance of the Sevin Deidly Synnis.'" *Scottish Studies* 29 (1989), 55-75; O'Gorman, Richard. "A Middle French Prayer to the Virgin against the Seven Deadly Sins: Text of Copenhagen, MS Gl. kgl. Saml. 3447." *Manuscripta* 35:2 (July 1991), 138-45.

Robert T. Lambdin

SEVEN SAGES OF ROME. *The Seven Sages of Rome* is a fourteenth century collection of *romance compiled from Oriental originals, including the *Book of Sidibad*. The work has a definite framework wherein Emperor Diocletian hires seven sages to teach his son. This process is interrupted when Diocletian's wife, the boy's stepmother, grows jealous of the lad. She makes a false claim to Diocletian that his son tried to seduce her. The emperor gives his son a chance to refute the charge, but he has been placed under a spell by the wicked woman and is unable to speak for seven days. Because of his silence, he is sentenced to death. Every night the stepmother has told Diocletian a tale, each of which concerns the perilous relationships between fathers and sons. Each morning one of the seven sages hired to instruct the lad tells a tale to refute the former; the theme of these tales is the danger of trusting women. Thus Diocletian is alternately persuaded to and then dissuaded from killing his son. The sages with their actions stall the execution long enough for the spell to wear off, and after seven days he is able to speak. He exposes the treachery of his stepmother, and Diocletian orders that she be burned at the stake. The format of the work is effective because all of the stories are *exempla about the dialectic concerning who is more loyal, the son or the wife. The stories were immensely popular; Geoffrey *Chaucer in his fragmented "The Squire's Tale" uses a variation of a portion of this collection. It is this exotic appeal that made *The Seven Sages of Rome* such a popular romance of the medieval period.

SELECTED BIBLIOGRAPHY

Ho, Cynthia. "Framed Progyny: The Medieval Descendants of Shaharizad." *Medieval Perspectives* 7 (1992), 91-107; Runte, Hans. "From the Vernacular to Latin and Back: The Case of 'The Seven Sages of Rome.'" In *Medieval Translators and Their Craft.*

Jeanette Beer, ed. Kalamazoo: Medieval Institute, 1989. 93-133; Runte, Hans, R., J. Keith Wikaley, and Anthony J. Farrell, eds. *The "Seven Sages of Rome" and "The Bok of Sinbad."* New York: Garland Press, 1984; Speer, Mary B. "Recycling the 'Seven Sages of Rome.'" *Zeitschrift für Romanische Philologie* 99:3 (1983), 288-303; Wikeley, J. Keith. *Italian Versions of the "Seven Sages of Rome": A Guide to Editions and Secondary Literature.* Edmonton: University of Alberta Press. 1990.

Robert T. Lambdin

"SHIPMAN'S TALE, THE." "The Shipman's Tale" is *fabliau is told by the shipman to the pilgrims of Geoffrey *Chaucer's *Canterbury Tales* (c. 1387-1400). The plot is a common one in such tales: a man buys sex from a woman with money he has borrowed from her husband. When the husband asks for repayment, the lover says that he paid the wife.

A rich merchant has a beautiful wife whom his cousin John, a monk, desires. Before the merchant leaves town on business, the wife complains to the monk that she must pay some bills for expensive dresses, but that her husband is stingy. John asks the husband for a loan, gives the money to the wife, and enjoys her sexual favors while the merchant is away. When the husband returns, John says that he has repaid the loan to the wife. When her husband asks for the money, the wife pretends that she thought it was meant as a gift to the monk and offers to repay her husband in bed.

SELECTED BIBLIOGRAPHY

Bush, Douglas. *English Poetry.* New York: Oxford University Press, 1963; Garbáty, Thomas J. *Medieval English Literature.* Toronto: Heath, 1984; Lambdin, Laura C., and Robert T. Lambdin, eds. *Chaucer's Pilgrims: An Historical Guide to the Pilgrims in the "Canterbury Tales."* Westport, CT: Greenwood Press, 1996; Salter, Elizabeth. *Fourteenth-Century English Poetry.* Oxford: Clarendon Press, 1983; Thormann, Janet. "The Circulation of Desire in the 'Shipman's Tale.'" *Literature and Psychology* 39:3 (1993), 1-15; Winnick, R. H. "'Luke 12' and Chaucer's 'Shipman's Tale.'" *Chaucer Review* 30:2 (1995), 164-90.

Laura Cooner Lambdin

SHIRLEY, JOHN (c. 1366-1456). John Shirley gained fame as a bibliophile and an antiquarian. He became important in the study of medieval literature because he was among the first to ascribe to Geoffrey *Chaucer many of his shorter poems, including "Of Mars" and "The Complaint of Venus." Unfortunately, he also erroneously ascribed several works, including Sir John*Clanvowe's *The Cuckoo and the Nightingale,* Thomas *Hoccleve's *The Letter of Cupid,* and Thomas *Usk's *The Testament of Love,* to Chaucer. The life of John Shirley is somewhat sketchy. It is considered true that he was a traveler who took great pleasure in translating works from French and Latin into the vernacular. In this way, many early works were saved and translated, thus allowing a greater audience to discover their content.

SELECTED BIBLIOGRAPHY

Bold, Alan Norman. *Scotland: A Literary Guide.* London: Routledge, 1989; Lerer, Seth. "British Library MS *Harley* 78 and the Manuscripts of John Shirley." *Notes and Queries* 37(235):4 (December 1990), 400-03.

Robert T. Lambdin

SIC ET NON. Sic et Non is a compilation of theological arguments ("Yes and No") by Peter *Abelard. The work is notable as being an extremely impartial listing of arguments, both pro and con, about the main doctrinal questions of the Middle Ages. It is unique because it presents no attempts to offer or to derive conclusions in answer to the questions.

SELECTED BIBLIOGRAPHY

Bowden, John. *Who's Who in Theology from the First Century to the Present.* New York: Crossroad , 1992; Slaymaker, William E. "Freedom: *Sic et Non*: The Case of Katz und Maus." *Germanic Notes* 13:2 (1982), 22-24.

Anna Shealy

SIETE PARTIDAS. The historical document *Siete Partidas* was commissioned by *Alfonso X, el Sabio (1221-1284), king of Castile (1221-1284). The work seeks to codify the legal system of Castile, although it was not put into practice completely until a century later. The seven parts of the document correspond to the seven letters in Alfonso's name. They include the Christian religion and ecclesiastical code; the monarchy and its relationships with all other social classes and positions; justice and its administration; marriage and friendship; contracts, loans, and purchases; wills and inheritances; and crimes and punishments. In addition to establishing and clarifying legal codes, the work also chronicles the social history of the time, with discourses upon customs, morals, values, and even popular entertainments. The *Siete Partidas* is a seminal legal work; it was consulted by the writers of the United States Constitution, and it is respected for its accuracy and comprehensiveness as a legislative work.

SELECTED BIBLIOGRAPHY

Chandler, Richard, and Kessel Schwartz. *A New History of Spanish Literature.* Baton Rouge: Louisiana State University Press, 1961; Deyermond, Alan, W. F. Hunter, and

Joseph T. Snow, eds. *Medieval and Renaissance Spanish Literature: Selected Essays by Keith Whinnom*. Exeter, UK: University of Exeter Press, 1994; Deyermond, Alan, and Jeremy Lawrance. *Letters and Society in Fifteenth-Century Spain*. London: Dolphin Book Co., 1993; Deyermond, A. D., *A Literary History of Spain: The Middle Ages*. London: Ernest Benn, 1971; Green, Otis H. *Spain and the Western Tradition: The Castilian Mind in Literature from "El Cid" to "Calderón."* Vol. 1. Madison: University of Wisconsin Press, 1963; Lloyd, Paul M. "On Conducting Sociolinguistic Research in the Middle Ages." In *Hispanic Medieval Studies in Honor of Samuel G. Armistead*. E. Michael Gerli and Harvey L. Sharrer, eds. Madison: Hispanic Seminary of Medieval Studies, 1992; Northup, George Tyler. *An Introduction to Spanish Literature*. Chicago: University of Chicago Press, 1965.

Rebecca Stephens

SIR DEGARÉ. The *Breton Lay begins with a very powerful ruler in England, an undefeated man. This ruler had only one child--a daughter he loved dearly, though her birth cost him his wife and her mother. When the girl came of age, suitable suitors from all over sought her hand; however, the ruler refused to give her to any one unless that person could unseat him from his horse. Every year on the anniversary of the queen's death, the ruler would ride with his daughter to the abbey where the queen was buried to say a mass. On one of these treks the daughter and her damsels were separated from the group, heading west when they should have gone south. They wandered into a thick forest, sat down, and cried until they fell asleep under a hawthorn tree--all but the daughter, who goes about gathering flowers and listening to the birds sing. She wanders so far that she loses sight of her women, when "a jolly knight" (82) appears. He tells her not to fear; he is an honorable knight, and he has loved her for many years. Then he rapes her, informs her that she will soon bear a son, gives her his sword with which he will identify his son when he returns, and disappears as quickly as he came. Weeping, she finds her way back to her maidens and wakes them, and they head on their way.

Before long, her predicament forces her to confide in one of her servants, who helps her keep her secret. At the appropriate time a boy is born. In a cradle with the baby she puts gold, silver, and a pair of gloves, and she hangs a letter about his neck asking that whoever finds him take care of him until he is ten years old. The servant carries the baby to a hermitage, where a holy man christens him Degaré; then he sends the boy to live with his married sister and her husband. When the boy is ten years old, they send him back to the hermit, who teaches him over the next ten years. By the time Degaré is twenty, he is a very competent clerk and a good fighter. Seeing this, the hermit gives Degaré all that remains from his mother's bequest and tells him the story of his arrival, and Degaré sets off to find his kin, carrying only a stout oak staff for protection. He soon puts the staff to use, rescuing an earl from a dragon's attack. In return, the earl knights him, and Degaré goes on his way with a knave and a steed given him by the nobleman.

During his journey he comes across people who have gathered because the king has decreed that any person bold enough to joust with the king would marry his daughter and inherit the kingdom. Degaré decides to accept the challenge because he has nothing to lose. After they make several passes at each other, the king's horse rears and he falls. The king is embarrassed and the daughter is distressed that she must wed this person of unknown heritage, but a bargain is a bargain. However, the narrator quickly reveals that Degaré's bride-to-be was his mother, and the characters themselves soon learn the truth also. She gives him the only clue about his father (the sword), and the next morning Degaré rides off with his knave in search of the mysterious person. Riding west through a thick forest, they come across a castle that stands wide open. The castle is inhabited by a beautiful lady with whom Degaré falls in love. She reveals that her father was a baron who left her his only heir without spouse to protect her. A stout giant who has fallen in love with her has slain all the men in the kingdom except her dwarf; she, however, does not love the giant. Degaré promises to help her; in return, she promises to give herself and her land to him.

Degaré slays the giant but refuses to settle down; he feels that he first must adventure into another land for twelve months. So she gives him gold, silver, and fresh armor and with many tears sends him on his way. Riding farther west, into a forest, he meets "a jolly knight" (901) who challenges his presence there. Degaré responds that he is merely seeking battle, to which the knight replies he has found his "pere" (pun on peer and the French for father *père*). The narrator informs us that the son is riding against the father, yet neither knows the other. They fight on horse, they fight on foot, they break many lances, and finally the son draws his pointless sword, which the father recognizes. The father reveals the truth; then they travel back to England together. The father weds the mother, and the son weds the lady, thereby bringing an end to the adventure.

This is a tale purporting to tell how far a knight would fare to seek adventure. It is also, as John Finlayson has reminded us, the tale of a person who barely manages to avoid "the two fatal errors of Oedipus--patricide and marriage with his mother" (357). The line "Will ye hear what man he was" (8) is comparable to a teaser commercial for the evening's movie of the week, perhaps as a wandering minstrel tries to draw in an attentive audience who will pay him well for his talents. According to G. V. Smithers, however, the story is a little inept--too many twists are packed into the story, with the hero first having to battle his grandfather to discover his mother, then battle his father to reunite the father with the mother. The plot is also complicated by two recognition-tokens (when one usually suffices)--a pair of gloves that magically only fit the mother and a sword.

SELECTED BIBLIOGRAPHY

Colopy, Cheryl. "'Sir Degaré': A Fairy Tale Oedipus." *Pacific Coast Philology* 17:1 (November 1982), 31-39; Jacobs, Nicolas. "The Lost Conclusion of the Auchinleck 'Sir

Degarre.'" *Notes and Queries* 37(235):2 (June 1990), 154-58; Jacobs, Nicolas. "The Process of Scribal Substitution and Redaction: A Study of the Cambridge Fragment of 'Sir Degarre.'" *Medium Ævum* 53:1 (1984), 26-48.

Peggy Huey

SIR FERUMBAS. A Middle English *romance related to the French *Charlemagne romances *Fierabras* and the *Destruction of Rome, Sir Ferumbas* is a well developed example of "The *Matter of France." The romance relates the capture of Rome and the holy relics by Ferumbas, the sultan of Babylon's son. The Saracen giant battles a character named Oliver; they later become friends. Ferumbus and his sister, Floripas, are converted to Christianity. The two remain friends with Roland, Oliver, and Charlemagne. Floripas eventually marries Guy of Burgundy. This story is the same as that of *The Sowdone of Babylon*, a late fourteenth-century version of a French romance that is no longer extant.

SELECTED BIBLIOGRAPHY

Burlin, Robert. "Middle English Romance: The Structure of Genre." *Chaucer Review* 30:1 (1995), 1-14; Speed, Diane, ed. *Medieval Romance I.* Durham: Durham Medieval Texts, 1993; Speed, Diane, ed. *Medieval Romance II.* Durham: Durham Medieval Texts, 1993.

Robert T. Lambdin

SIR GAWAIN AND THE GREEN KNIGHT (c. 1370). The *romance *Sir Gawain and the Green Knight* is perhaps the most famous of the literature of the *Arthurian legends. It is composed in *alliterative verse, and each stanza contains a bob and wheel. The poem, composed by an unknown called the *Pearl*-Poet or the *Gawain* Poet, appears in a manuscript of the Cotton Collection in the British Library. The poem is accompanied in the manuscripts by the poems *Pearl*, *Purity* (or *Cleanness*), and *Patience. Sir Gawain and the Green Knight* concerns the ordeals of the ideal knight, Sir Gawain. The action in the romance centers upon two major themes: the beheading game with the green knight and Gawain's temptation to adultery. The mysticism of the tale make it appealing to a wide range of audiences.

The work begins during New Year's festivities at Arthur's court. Arthur announces that he is bored and wishes to be amazed. A green knight on horseback bursts into the castle and challenges any of Arthur's men to chop off his head. To this he adds a codicil--whosoever opts to behead him must go to the green knight's chapel in one calendar year so that he may requite the blow. While most of Arthur's knights cringe at this challenge, his nephew, Sir Gawain, defends his uncle's honor by accepting the offer. Gawain successfully beheads the giant, who, much to the chagrin of the court, calmly picks up his severed head and leaves, telling Gawain that he will see him in twelve months.

The ensuing year passes quickly, and Gawain sets off in search of the green chapel, where the giant is to requite his chop. After a long, brutal journey Gawain happens across a magnificent castle where he is welcomed by Lord Bercilak, his beautiful wife, and an ugly old hag. Bercilak suggests to Gawain that they play an exchange-of-gifts game: each day Bercilak will go hunting and, at the end of the day will give to Gawain all that he bags in exchange for all that the knight "wins" at the castle while his host is away.

On the first two days Gawain is tempted amorously by Bercilak's beautiful wife. The first day the knight opts to cop a single kiss from the lady and two on the second. As per his contract with Bercilak, each night he exchanges the kisses he received for the hoard of animals slain by his host during his hunts. On the third day Gawain accepts from his hostess a green sash or girdle. She convinces him that it is magical and will protect Gawain from the giant's blade; all that he has to do is wear it. When Bercilak returns from the third day's hunt, the two again trade their goods. However, Gawain neglects to inform his host about accepting the sash. He has violated his contract.

The next day Gawain leaves the castle and readies for his meeting with the giant green knight. Gawain first gives confession and then enters the giant's lair. As he approaches, he hears an ominous sound: it is the green knight sharpening his huge blade. Gawain is fearful, but he prepares to receive his blow. The giant rises, tells Gawain not to flinch, and feigns the first two strikes. These are symbolic of Gawain's forthrightness with Bercilak on the first two nights. The third blow from the green knight nicks Gawain's neck, leaving him with a permanent reminder of his indiscretion.

The green knight then becomes Bercilak. It was he all along who was playing with the knight. He had put his wife up to the scandalous game as a means of embarrassing Arthur's court. It is here that the audience is told that the ugly hag who lives with Bercilak is also his beautiful wife, Morgan le Fay. Gawain returns to Camelot a marked man. He has all of his knights wear green sashes to remind themselves that they are not perfect. Thus *Sir Gawain and the Green Knight* ends with a rather dogmatic homily.

SELECTED BIBLIOGRAPHY

Blanch, Robert J. and Julian J. Wasserman. "The Current State of *Sir Gawain and the Green Knight* Criticism." *The Chaucer Review* 27:4 (1993), 401-12; Kang, Ji-Soo. "The Green Girdle and the Narrative Circularity in *Sir Gawain and the Green Knight*." *Journal of English Language and Literature* 41:4 (Winter 1995), 927-45; Narin, Elisa Marie. "'Þat on . . . Þat Oþer': Rhetorical Descriptio and Morgan la Fay in *Sir Gawain and the Green Knight*." *Pacific Coast Philology* 23:1-2 (1988), 60-66; Weiss, Victoria L. "The Play World and the Real World: Chivalry in *Sir Gawain and the Green Knight*. *Philological Quarterly* 72:4 (Fall 1993), 403-18.

Robert T. Lambdin

SIR GOWTHER. In the *Breton Lay *Sir Gowther,* there was a fiend who was able to sleep with women, begetting Merlin and more. This particular tale is about how such a child was begotten, causing much woe for his mother.

An Austrian duke weds a beautiful noble lady, but for seven years they are unable to have any children. The duke decides that they must part because he needs a child to inherit his lands. In distress from this news, the lady goes walking in their chestnut orchard, where she encounters and makes love with someone who appears to be her spouse. After their coupling, however, he appears as himself, informing her that she is with child--a child who will be a wild youth. Hurrying back to her chamber, she convinces her spouse that an angel has told her that she will conceive the heir he desires this night. Nine months later she delivers a child that they christen "Goughthere" (or Gowther). The ravenous child slays nine wet-nurses before he is a year old. He grows up quickly, becoming the best sword fighter in the land. When the duke dies, the duchess flees to a stronghold with several persons who were loyal to her. The new duke becomes famous (or infamous) for destroying all religious persons he meets, as well as anyone else who does not do his bidding.

One day when he is out hunting, he comes upon a nunnery. When the nuns come to greet him, he destroys all of them. Then he goes on a rampage until an old earl comments that he must be the offspring of a fiend to be doing so many evil things. Enraged, Gowther rides to his mother's castle and insists that she tell him the truth about his father. Chastened by the truth, he sets off for Rome to be shriven by the pope. As penance, the pope decrees that he must wander the land without speaking a word, getting his meat from a hound's mouth, until all his sins have been forgiven. His wanderings take him to the castle inhabited by the emperor of Almayn (Germany), who allows him shelter there. The emperor's beautiful daughter falls in love with the handsome stranger (who cannot say a word, according to his penance, but loves her in return). One day the sultan of Persia sends for the daughter's hand in marriage; the emperor, however, rejects the heathen's offer, so the sultan comes with his army and they battle.

Gowther asks God to send him armor, a shield, and a horse so he can ride in defense of the lord who has been kind to him. When the equipment immediately arrives (with a black horse), he joins the fray, defeats the Saracens and then returns to his humble position in the household. The next day the sultan's messenger informs them that the sultan will avenge his defeat because reinforcements have arrived. Gowther again is magically equipped (this time with a blood-red horse) and again defeats the Saracens soundly. While the rest of the court is reveling, an exhausted Gowther goes to bed and thinks upon his sins and saving his soul. The following morning the sultan's messenger issues a new challenge--more reinforcements have arrived; this time Gowther faces them on a milky white steed. Although Gowther fights quite smartly, the sultan manages to capture the emperor temporarily; Gowther slays the sultan, but is himself severely injured in the process, causing much distress for the daughter, who swoons, falls out of her tower, and nearly breaks her neck. The pope comes from Rome to inform Gowther that he is now a child of God, the daughter comes out of her coma, she and Gowther wed, and they return to Ostryche (Austria) where he atones for the evil-doings of his childhood by founding several abbeys.

This tale begins with a demon begetting the hero with a noble woman, clearly tying in the Celtic motif. However, because the father is the devil himself, not a mere fairy, the tale serves a higher purpose to show God's grace. The tale also provides a warning against entering into liaisons with otherworldly creatures; even though this one eventually turns out wellin the end, it is not without much travail on the hero's part.

SELECTED BIBLIOGRAPHY

Bradstock, E. M. "'Sir Gowther': Secular Hagiography or Hagiographical Romance or Neither?" *Journal of the Australasian Universities Language and Literature Association* 59 (May 1983), 26-47; Robson, Margaret. "Animal Magic: Moral Regeneration in 'Sir Gowther.'" *Yearbook of English Studies* 22 (1992), 140-53; Shaner, Mary E. "Instruction and Delight: Medieval Romances as Children's Literature." *Poetics Today* 13:1 (Spring 1992), 5-15.

Peggy Huey

SIR ISUMBRAS. *Sir Isumbras* is a verse *romance of some eight hundred lines that originated in the Northeast Midlands of England sometime before 1320. The theme of this work is based upon the tenets of St. Eustace, who believed that man is tried by fate. In the romance, Isumbras is a man who seemingly has it all, for he is rich, strong, and handsome. Unfortunately, he is too aware of his essence for he is also guilty of two sins: pride and arrogance. God sends to Isumbras a bird that offers him two choices: he may suffer either in his youth or in his old age.

Isumbras selects youth and promptly loses everything he had. He is no longer wealthy, handsome, or powerful. For a full twenty-one years Isumbras endures the wrath of the evil Saracens. However, he braves his lot very well. After these years of torment an angel appears to Isumbras, telling him that he is forgiven for his sins. With this, Isumbras's wealth is restored and he is again affluent. He lives his life better knowing now how fortunate he is. This theme of a character's torment and perseverance is found in many of the fourteenth century English romances.

SELECTED BIBLIOGRAPHY

Reichl, Karl. "Syntax and Style in *Sir Isumbras*." In *Language and Civilization: A Concentrated Profusion of Essays and Studies in Honor of Otto Hietsch*. Claudia Blank, ed. New York: Peter Lang, 1992. 183-203; Shaner, Mary E. "Instruction and Delight: Medieval Romances as Children's Literature." *Poetics Today* 13:1 (Spring 1992), 5-15;

Thompson, Anne B. "Jaussian Expectation and the Production of Medieval Narrative: The Case of 'St. Eustace' and *Sir Isumbras.*" *Exemplaria* 5:2 (Fall 1993), 387-407.

Robert T. Lambdin

SIR LAUNFAL. In the Breton *lay *Sir Launfal* by Thomas Chestre, Arthur (*see Arthurian Legend*) and his knights are at Carlisle. With the group is a young bachelor, Sir Launfal, a very generous person, one who has been Arthur's faithful steward for ten years. The plot thickens one Whitsuntide when Arthur marries Guenivere, the daughter of King Ryan of Ireland, who for some reason dislikes Launfal and snubs him at her wedding. Being the noble knight he is, Launfal fabricates an excuse to leave the court. He moves to the town of Carloun, where, continuing his lavish lifestyle, he becomes destitute before a year has passed. One day Launfal rides west into the forest, stopping to rest in the shade of a tree. As he is sitting there feeling sorry for himself, two well-dressed maidens approach. Dame Tryamour, the daughter of the king of the fairies, has sent them to invite him for a visit. He graciously accompanies them further into the forest to a magnificent Saracen pavilion topped by a gem-studded eagle more elaborate than anything owned by either Alexander or Arthur. Tryamour declares her love for Launfal, promising to make him rich if he forsakes all other women for her. He accepts her offer; however, he must never tell anyone about her or he will lose her love. He returns to Carloun to receive her presents, and the lords of Carloun host a tournament in his name at which he defeats many Welsh knights. Afterwards he hosts a feast that lasts a fortnight, while Dame Tryamour visits him every night.

Jealous of Launfal's fame and prowess, a knight from Lombardy, Sir Valentine, challenges Launfal to a joust for the honor of Launfal's lady. Launfal accepts the challenge, sails to Lombardy, and slays Valentine. This angers the Lombardy lords, who swear to kill Launfal; however, he draws his sword and slays them first, then returns to Britain. Arthur hears of Launfal's fame and sends for him to reinstate him as steward of the hall. During the associated feast which lasts forty days, the queen decides to dance with Launfal because he is the fairest bachelor without a spouse, and she has decided that she loves him and has loved him for the past seven years. Because of his promise to Tryamour, however, he rejects her love. She, of course, plots revenge, telling Arthur lies that lead him to order Launfal's slaying. A court of his peers insists that he bring his beloved to court to prove his claim of her worth, or he will be hanged as a thief. Launfal has a year and a fortnight to return with his love. When that day comes, Launfal, of course, cannot present his lady to the court because she has deserted him as she swore she would if he ever spoke of her. Therefore, the king condemns him, insisting that the sentence be completed. Just as they are about to kill Launfal, a lone damsel arrives, announces that she has come to prove Launfal's innocence, and goes on to do so. Launfal leaps on his horse and rides away with her to the land of the fairies.

This tale, which is based on Marie de France's *Lanval*, ends with the assertion "Thomas Chestre made this tale" (1039), the only one of the eight basic tales standardly classified as "Breton lays" that is ascribed to a particular author (except for Geoffrey *Chaucer's *"Franklin's Tale," generally considered an imitation of the form). It is part of a group classified as "tail-rhyme romances," which poets primarily created for less educated audiences such as those found in the market square or the courtyard of an inn instead of the sophisticated audiences of the courts for whom Marie designed *Lanval* (Bliss 1). The tail-rhyme is the pattern most suitable for public recitation because its simple, strongly-marked rhythm enables both the reciter and the listener to retain the narrative thread more easily. *Launfal* is apparently a conflation of three works: along with *Lanval*, the primary source is the Middle English romance (also based upon *Lanval*) *Sir Landevale*, with additional passages from *Graelent*, an anonymous Breton (as in Old French) lay (Bliss 2). The poem itself only survives in one early-fifteenth-century manuscript, Cotton Caligula A II, found in the British Library. The romances *Octavian* and **Libeaus Desconsus* appear before and after the poem, with similarities in style and language that suggest a common authorship of the three.

While there seems to be an implicit connection between Launfal and some of the legends associated with Lancelot (for example, Guenivere first dislikes Launfal, then decides she loves him), in the tale Launcelot du Lake is specifically mentioned in line 910 in terms of an assignment given him by Arthur; therefore, the characters must not be the same person.

SELECTED BIBLIOGRAPHY

Bliss, A. J., ed. "Introduction." *Sir Launfal.* New York: Barnes and Noble, 1960. 1-52; Bolton, W.F. *The Penguin History of Literature: The Middle Ages.* London: Penguin, 1993; Bullock-Davies, Constance. "The Form of the Breton Lay." *Medium Ævum* 42 (1973), 19-31; Donovan, Mortimer J. *The Breton Lays: A Guide to Varieties.* Notre Dame: University of Notre Dame Press, 1969; Gibbs, A. C., ed. "Introduction." *Middle English Romances.* Evanston: Northwestern University Press, 1966. 1-25; Glenn, Jonathan A. "'Sir Launfal' and the Horse Goddess." *Medieval Perspectives* 7(1992), 64-77; Ker, W. P. *Epic and Romance.* 1908. New York: Dover, 1957; Loomis, Laura Hibbard. *Medieval Romance in England.* 2nd ed. New York: B. Franklin, 1960; O'Brien, Timothy D. "The 'Readerly' Sir Launfal." *Parergon* 8:1 (June 1990), 33-45; Rickert, Edith. *Early English Romances in Verse: Done into Modern English by Edith Rickert: Romances of Love.* New York: Cooper Square, 1966; Rumble, Thomas C. *The Breton Lays in Middle English.* Detroit: Wayne State University Press, 1965; Smithers, G. V. "Story-Patterns in Some Breton Lays." *Medium Ævum* 22.2 (1953), 61-92.

Peggy Huey

SIR ORFEO (KING ORFEW). *Sir Orfeo* is a Breton *lay in which Orfeo (or Orfew) is a ruler of Thrace who loves to play the harp; in fact, he is considered the best harpist in the world. His spouse, Heurodis (or Meroudys), is the fairest beauty in all the kingdom. One May morning the queen goes into her garden with two of her servants and falls asleep under a tree. When she awakes several hours later, in a panic she tears her robes and scratches her face. Orfeo comes running, only to have her inform him that she must go away. It seems that while she slept, a monarch spirited her away to show her his castles and then ordered her to be under the same tree the next day to go dwell with him forever. He warned her that any attempts to thwart his plans would result in her being torn limb from limb and carried away all the same. Orfeo is distraught. The next day he and his soldiers keep guard, but the fairies carry the queen away from under their noses. Orfeo turns control of his kingdom over to his steward and goes into the wilderness to dwell with the beasts for ten years. The only thing he carries with him is his harp, which he periodically plays to the delight of all the birds and beasts.

Occasionally he catches sight of the monarch of the fairies or some of the knights; then one day he spies a group of women who are out hawking. He recognizes Heurodis as one of these individuals, and follows them when they ride back into a rock to a fair country three miles into the rock. Going up to the elaborate castle in the middle of this land, Orfeo offers to play his harp for the lord of the manor, who is surprised to see him, as no one has ever before voluntarily visited this kingdom. After Orfeo charms them with his music, the lord offers him payment; Orfeo asks for the person asleep under the tree (who is really Heurodis). The lord has to keep his word, so Orfeo and his love return to the surface, then journey back to Thrace. Once there, he decides that he needs to test the loyalty of his steward, who has been tending to the kingdom for the past ten years. Leaving the queen in a safe place, Orfeo takes his harp and goes into town. As he plays for the court, the steward recognizes the harp and asks how the wandering minstrel came by it. Orfeo's response is that he had found it next to a person torn to pieces by the lions and wolves. This information distresses the steward to the point that he swoons, proving his loyalty to Orfeo. The ruler reveals himself and sends for his queen, and they all live happily ever after.

This variation on the classical story of Orpheus and Eurydice (known to the Middle Ages through the work of Ovid's *Metamorphoses*, Virgil's *Georgics*, and *Boethius's *Consolation of Philosophy* as translated by King *Alfred) differs from the sources with its happy ending. This version is grounded in the Celtic folk-belief that at the moment of death people are snatched from this world by the fairies, who spirit them away to a splendorous land from which they occasionally can be brought back (Walter *Map's *De Nugis Curialium* iv.8, a late-twelfth-century story, offers an example of this occurrence and may provide a Celtic source for the *Orfeo* poet). The poet transforms here the dark underworld of the classical versions into a bright fairy kingdom more indicative of a sun-god than of Hades, complete with a medieval king and court; also, instead of dying, the queen is abducted while sleeping, which allows for the happy ending after she is rescued. In addition, Orfeo's inconsolable grief transforms into a ten-year self-exile from society until finally, the magic of Orfeo's harping apparently counters the magic of the otherworld to enable the queen's rescue.

Sir Orfeo begins with an introduction almost identical to that of the **Lay Le Freine*; both works align themselves with "the Britons [who] made these lays" (line 16 in Rickert). The basic outline of the story is remarkably parallel, creating a unified work. After a fifty-six line prologue, the story moves from the loss of Heurodis to the loss of Orfeo's kingdom because of his grief. The loss sequence is followed by Orfeo's experiences in the fairy kingdom, during which he regains Heurodis, and the work culminates in his experiences back in the human world, during which he regains his kingdom (Severs 199). The entire experience emphasizes the importance of loyalty and fidelity: first in Orfeo's allegiance to Heurodis, then the the steward's allegiance to Orfeo. The world depicted in this lay definitely exemplifies, as A.V.C. Schmidt and Nicolas Jacobs explained, "lofty idealism and noble conduct" in the face of all the suffering the main character undergoes (28).

The appearance of this poem in the same manuscript as *Lay Le Freine* (the Auchinleck manuscript. of the mid-fourteenth century), as well as the similarity of a number of phrases in the two poems, suggests that a single author or translator produced them. **Sir Degaré* also appears in this manuscript, but there are no special connections between that poem and *Sir Orfeo* beyond those associated with the basic poetic form. *Sir Orfeo* contains most of the qualities traditionally associated with the lay, to the point that critics such as W. P. Ker, Laura Hibbard Loomis, and John Finlayson consider it the paradigm of the form.

SELECTED BIBLIOGRAPHY

Clark, Rosalind. "*Sir Orfeo*: The Otherworld vs. Faithful Human Love." In *Proceedings of the Medieval Association of the Midwest.* Mel Storm, ed. Emporia KS: Emporia State University, 1993. 71-80; Connelly, William J. "The Affirmation of Love and Loyalty in *Sir Orfeo*." *Medieval Perspectives* 7 (1992), 34-43; Cook, Robert. "Chaucer's 'Franklin's Tale' and *Sir Orfeo*." *Neuphilologische Mitteilungen* 95:3 (1994), 333-36; Finlayson, John. "The Form of the Middle English *Lay*." *Chaucer Review* 19 (1985): 352-368; Ker, W. P. *Epic and Romance.* 1908. New York: Dover, 1957; Kooper, Erik. "The Twofold Harmony of the Middle English *Sir Orfeo*." In *Companion to Middle English Literature.* N. H. G. E. Veldhoen, ed. Amsterdam: VU University Press, 1995. 115-32; Loomis, Laura Hibbard. *Medieval Romance in England.* 2nd ed. New York: B. Franklin, 1960; McGillivray, Murray. *Memorization in the Transmission of the Middle English Romances.* New York: Garland, 1990; Schmidt, A. V. C., and Nicolas Jacobs, eds. "The Breton Lays and Sir Orfeo." *Medieval English Romances: Part One.* New York: Holmes and Meier, 1980. 21-33; Severs, J. Burke. "The Antecedents of Sir Orfeo." In *Studies in Medieval Literature: In Honor of Professor Albert Croll Baugh.* MacEdward Leach, ed. Philadelphia: University of Pennsylvania Press, 1961. 187-207.

Peggy Huey

SIR PATRICK SPENS. The longevity of *Sir Patrick Spens* is such that it was revived in contemporary British popular song some five hundred years after its composition. It probably dates from the late thirteenth or early fourteenth century if it refers, as is generally believed, to the death of the "Maid of Norway" in 1290. Generally, *ballads recording actual events are composed shortly after the occurrence; and this ballad, aside from bearing a close correspondence to historical fact, is also remarkably accurate in its mention in longer versions of the song of weekdays, holidays, the duration of the trip, and the phases of the moon. However, while the story line is historical, no satisfactory identification of a real Patrick Spens has ever been made.

Sir Patrick Spens relates the Scottish king's decision to send a ship across the North Sea to Norway at a particularly dangerous time of the year for sailing. At the encouragement of a knight of his court, he places the vessel in charge of Sir Patrick Spens. Spens, however, receives the news with foreboding, since he knows that the voyage must be almost sure death, and suspects a deliberate plot to destroy him. He nonetheless orders the ship to be made ready, much to the dismay of his shipmen, who observe warnings of an imminent storm. The ship, of course, sinks, drowning all aboard. The ballad closes with references to both the doomed lords and their ladies waiting at home. Those regarding the nobles are near comic observations on their hats floating on the surface of the water and of the drowned knights lying at Sir Patrick's feet on the ocean bottom in a parody of medieval fealty. The treatment of the ladies awaiting their return is equally sardonic, observing that they will be fanning themselves and combing their hair for a long time before they see the ship's return.

Aside from studies of the relationship of *Sir Patrick Spens* to historical fact, the most thorough analyses of the poem are found in Moore and Morgan. Moore observed the artistic contrast between the sedentary court denizens (the king and his nobles are seen sitting, drinking, and idly musing, while the ladies wait, stand, and sit while fanning themselves) and the active nature of the hero (who walks, makes the ship ready, and sails) and concluded that this underscores an implicit value judgment in the ballad. Morgan followed Moore in this, but concluded that the poem is consistently sardonic and imbued with the class jealousy of the commoners not only with regard to the court versus the country but also in the treatment of the ladies and the drowned lords. The ballad certainly is bitter and is typical in its association of aristocratic behavior with treachery and of chivalric duty with stupidity and disaster.

SELECTED BIBLIOGRAPHY

Battersby, James L. "The Character of 'Sir Patrick Spens.'" *Hypotheses* 9 (Spring 1994), 10-13; Moore, Richard. "'Sir Patrick Spens.'" *Explicator* 37:3 (Spring 1979), 6-7; Morgan, Gwendolyn. *Medieval Balladry and the Courtly Tradition.* New York: Peter Lang, 1993, Morgan, Gwendolyn. *Medieval Ballads: Chivalry, Romance, and Everyday Life.* New York: Peter Lang, 1996; Ryan, William M. "Formula and Tragic Irony in 'Sir

Patrick Spens.'" *Southern Folklore Quarterly* 44 (1980), 73-83; Watson, Walter. "'Sir Patrick Spens.'" *Hypotheses* 7 (Fall 1993), 2-4.

Gwendolyn Morgan

"SIR THOPAS" (c. 1387-1400). "Sir Thopas" was apparently intended as a parody of long, exaggerated romances often told by traveling *minstrels. In the *Canterbury Tales*, the pilgrim *Chaucer tells the story in which Sir Thopas, a Flanders knight, quests in search of an elf queen to love, but he is hindered by Oliphant, a stone throwing giant. The knight is without his armor and must return home for battle with the giant. At this point in the long-winded and dull narrative, Harry Bailley, host of the Tabard Inn and judge of the pilgrims' tales, interrupts and asks Chaucer to stop his poor tale.

SELECTED BIBLIOGRAPHY

Berry, Craig A. "Borrowed Armor/Free Grace: The Quest for Authority in *The Faerie Queen* and Chaucer's 'Tale of Sir Thopas.'" *Studies in Philology* 91:2 (Spring 1994), 136-66; Bush, Douglas. *English Poetry*. New York: Oxford University Press, 1963; Dailender, Celia R. "The 'Thopas'-'Melibee' Sequence and the Defeat of Antifeminism." *Chaucer Review* 29:1 (1994), 26-39; Garbáty, Thomas J. *Medieval English Literature*. Toronto: Heath, 1984; Tschann, Judith. "The Layout of 'Sir Thopas' in the Ellesmere, Hengwrt, Cambridge Dd. 4.24, and Cambridge Gg. 4.27 Manuscripts." *Chaucer Review* 20:1 (1985), 1-13; Salter, Elizabeth. *Fourteenth-Century English Poetry*. Oxford: Clarendon Press, 1983.

Laura Cooner Lambdin

SKALDIC VERSE. Skalds were the *minstrels or court poets of Scandinavia who flourished from the late ninth to the eleventh centuries. Skaldic verse is a very artistic type of Old Norse poetry. Poetry of this genre is usually marked by intricate meter, alliteration, and diction. Works of this nature are usually constructed in a format called the "dróttkvaett." Each strophe contains eight six-syllable lines; the lines are alliterated on stressed syllables in the even lines and the odd lines contain two alternating syllables in stressed positions. Additionally, the odd lines contain half-rhymes. The diction of these works is full of *kennings and far reaching metaphors.

Bragi Boddason is the first known Skaldic poet. The form then caught on and was very popular for the next two hundred years. A popular type of Skaldic poetry was that which memorialized heroes and actions. These poems usually concerned the Norse chieftains' actions. These verses might have disappeared had it not been for the composers of the *sagas, who saw fit to include these works in their kings' and family sagas.

SELECTED BIBLIOGRAPHY

Frank, Roberta. "Skaldic Verse and the Date of *Beowulf.*" In *The Dating of "Beowulf."* Colin Chase, ed. Toronto: University of Toronto Press, 1981. 123-39; Poole, R. G. "The Cooperative Principle in Medieval Interpretations of Skaldic Verse, Snorri Sturluson, Thjodolfr Arnorsson, and Eyvindr Skaldaspillir." *Journal of English and Germanic Philology* 87 (January 1988), 159-78.

Robert T. Lambdin

SKELTON, JOHN (c. 1460-1529). John Skelton was an English poet and churchman born in Norfolkshire. He became legendary for his sarcasm and practical jokes. At Oxford and Cambridge and at the court in London he showed wit and earnestness. He had become honorary laureate and tutor to Prince Henry (later *Henry VIII) by his early thirties. He was loyal to the church and was ordained in 1498, but many of his poems are satires directed against English clerical abuses. He attacked Colin Clout and Cardinal Wolsey, in particular, for their clerical abuses. Skelton was fearful of Wolsey and spent his last six years in sanctuary at Westminster Abbey, where he died on June 21, 1529.

Skelton translated ancient authors in a prose style that was an unsuccessful compromise with classical style, but his unique verse style, described as "Skeltonic," was freely adapted from the works of the wits of the Middle Ages. He used lines only two or three accents in length and repeated the same rhyme for as many as nine consecutive lines. In "Philip Sparrow" he imparted a mock daintiness about mourning a dead bird, and in "The Tunning of Elinor Rumming" he heaped up images at a fast, ludicrous pace. The peculiarities of Skelton's work prevented it from influencing later poets, but Skelton remains one of the few readable English poets to write during the two hundred years that separated *Chaucer and Spenser.

SELECTED BIBLIOGRAPHY

Kezar, Dennis Dean. "'The Fall of a Sparrow': Skelton's Fictive Text and the Manufacture of Fame." *Renaissance Papers* 1995, 15-32; Scattergood, John. "Skelton's 'Magnyfycence' and the Tudor Royal Household." *Medieval English Theatre* 15 (1993), 21-48; Stevens, Mark "John Skelton's Inflated Reputation as an Enricher of English Vocabulary." *Language Quarterly* 30:1 (Winter-Spring 1992), 20-27.

Rebecca Chalmers

SNORRI STURLUSON (c. 1178-1241). The author of the famous Old Norse work the *Heimskringla*, Snorri Sturluson was a leading Icelandic historian of his day. The *Heimskringla* is similar to the *chronicles of Middle English, as it recounts the kings of Norway from primordial days until 1177. Because this work also contains a good collection of Old Norse *sagas and poems, it is a seminal text, assuring Snorri's place in of Old Icelandic literature.

Snorri's personal life illustrates the highs and lows of an ambitious man. He was an insider in the royal court, a position that allowed him to become a first hand observer of the political machine of his time. He was astute enough to convey his observations into his works, such as the *Prose *Edda* and the biography of a Viking poet, the *Egils Saga*. However, having ear with those in charge can also be fateful; in 1241 Snorri was assassinated on order of Norway's King Hakon.

SELECTED BIBLIOGRAPHY

Andersson, Theodore M. "The Politics of Snorri Sturlusson." *Journal of English and Germanic Philology* 93:1 (January 1994), 55-78; Durrenberger, Paul, and Bob Quinlan. "The Structure of the Prose *Edda*." *Arv: Nordic Yearbook of Folklore* 41 (1985), 65-76; Poole, R. G. "The Cooperative Principle in Medieval Interpretations of Skaldic Verse, Snorri Sturluson, Thjodolfr Arnorsson, and Eyvindr Skaldaspillir." *Journal of English and Germanic Philology* 87 (Jan 1988), 159-78;

Robert T. Lambdin

SOMNIUM SCIPIONIS (DREAM OF SCIPIO). The *Somnium Scipionis* is the final tale in Cicero's *De Republica* and survives in its complete form only through chance. While *De Republica* survives only in fragments, Macrobius in the fourth century found the dream portion of Cicero's work to his liking. He added a Neoplatonic commentary on the work, thus making this section of Cicero's text more appealing to medieval thinkers. It differs from the traditional explication of love because the *Somnium* is blatantly unsympathetic to love. In the work the young Scipio dreams that he espies his grandfather, who shows the lad where those who follow virtue will reside for eternity. This abode, located in a portion of the Milky Way, is designed especially for those who become celebrated because of their efforts to serve their countries. It is conceivable that the *Somnium* may have been instrumental in *Petrarch's adaptation of Scipio Africanus as the hero in *Africai*. Also, the work may have influenced Geoffrey *Chaucer, who relies upon a poetical summary of the *Somnium* in a portion of his *Parliament of Fowls* (*See *Debate Poetry, Medieval European*).

SELECTED BIBLIOGRAPHY

Arthur, Ross G. "Chaucer's Use of the 'Dream of Scipio' in *The Parliament of Fowls*." *American Benedictine Review* 38:1 (March 1987), 29-49; Peden, Alison M. "Macrobius and Medieval Dream Literature." *Medium Ævum* 54:1 (March 1985), 59-73.

Robert T. Lambdin

SORDELLO (c. 1200-c. 1270). Sordello was an Italian troubadour who wrote in the +Provençal style. Sordello became a very important author of medieval literature because his love poetry was a vital part of the growth of this genre in Italy; thus, the works of France and Italy may be merged from similar sources. The works of Sordello cannot be grouped into a solitary theme, for he composed conventional didactic works as well as complaints. His *Serventese* was written on the death of his patron, Blacatz. However, it is in *Dante's *Purgatorio* that Sordello truly gains his fame. He resides in the Ante-Purgatory; given this limited freedom, he leads Dante and Virgil on a portion of their trip. In *Purgatorio* vii he guides the pair to the valley of the kings before taking his leave. It is believed that Dante included him in this volume because of Sordello's fervent lament over Blacatz's death.

SELECTED BIBLIOGRAPHY

Carcaleanu, Eleonora. "Dante, Sordello, Statiu: Tripticul apoteozei lui Virgiliu in *Divina commedia*." *Analele Stiintifice ale Universitatii* 26 (1980), 71-77; Carruthers, J. "The 'Passé Surcomposé Regional': Towards a Definition of Its Function in Contemporary Spoken French." *Journal of French Language Studies* 4:2 (September 1994), 171-90.

Robert T. Lambdin

SPECULUM MEDITANTIS. *Speculum Meditantis*, a Norman-French poem by John Gower, composed around 1378, is also known as *Speculum Hominis* or *Mirour de l'omme*. It consists of about thirty-thousand lines in twelve-line stanzas. This didactic work describes the contest for men's souls between the seven vices; here, the fight rages between the offspring sired by Satan and the seven virtues, with their offspring by Reason. This work gives a detailed examination of both sides of men in all classes of life. It ends by determining that all men are corrupt and must turn to the Virgin Mary for mercy and aid. Truly the *Speculum Meditantis* is one of the great homiletic works of the medieval period.

SELECTED BIBLIOGRAPHY

Olsen, Alexandra Hennessey. "In Defense of Diomede: 'Moral Gower' and *Troilus and Criseyde*." *In Geardagum* 8 (1987), 1-12; Owen, Charles A. Jr. "Notes on Gower's Prosody." *Chaucer Review* 28:4 (1994), 405-13.

Robert T. Lambdin

SQUIRE OF LOW DEGREE, THE. *The Squire of Low Degree* is a metrical *romance from fifteenth-century Britain. Often viewed as a rather insignificant tale, it is the story of a lower class squire's seemingly unattainable love for the king of Hungary's daughter. The squire initially proclaims his love to her, but she defers answering him until the lad has made a name for himself as a knight. As luck would have it, one of the king's stewards sees this tryst and reports his findings to his liege. The king is horrified and has the young man imprisoned. This makes his daughter disconsolate, and nothing the king does will cheer her. Thus the king relents and releases the squire, who immediately departs for adventure and to achieve glory. Much to the delight of the princess, his achievements make him worthy enough for her, and the couple are wed.

The story from this romance survives only in a sixteenth century printing by W. Copland, for no total manuscript of this work is extant. *Wynkyn de Worde published one of the fragments in 1520. The work itself is of value because of its clear descriptions of foods, drinks, and general mannerisms of late medieval England.

SELECTED BIBLIOGRAPHY

Diehl, Huston. "'For No Theves Shall Come Thereto': Symbolic Detail in 'The Squyr of Lowe Degree.'" *American Benedictine Review* 32:2 (1981), 140-55; Hudson, Harriet E. "Construction of Class, Family, and Gender in Some Middle English Popular Romances." In *Class and Gender in Early English Literature*. Britton Harwood and Gillian Overing, eds. Bloomington: Indiana University Press, 1994. 76-94; Rivers, Bryan. "The Focus of Satire in 'The Squire of Low Degree.'" *English Studies in Canada* 7:4 (December 1981), 379-87; Spearing, A. C. "Secrecy, Listening, and Telling in 'The Squyr of Lowe Degre.'" *Journal of Medieval and Renaissance Studies* 20:2 (Fall 1990). 273-92; Tigges, Wim. "Romance and Parody." in *Companion to Middle English Romance*. Henk Aertson and Alasdair McDonald, eds. Amsterdam: VU University Press, 1990. 129-51.

Robert T. Lambdin

"SQUIRE'S TALE, THE."   One of the stories in Geoffrey *Chaucer's *Canterbury Tales* (c. 1387-1400), "The Squire's Tale" is unfinished and is told by a young man who is a squire accompanying his father, the knight, on a pilgrimage to the shrine of St. Thomas *Becket in Canterbury Cathedral. The squire begins to tell an incoherent *romance about the Tartar King Cambus, who is given a brass horse, a mirror, a ring, and a sword. The king's daughter Canacee wears the ring, which allows her to understand a falcon who complains of being abandoned by a tercelet. The squire promises to tell of Cambuscan's adventures with the magical gifts and of Canacee's suitors, but the tale is incomplete. In the *Faerie Queene* Spenser finished the tale for Chaucer.

SELECTED BIBLIOGRAPHY

Bush, Douglas. *English Poetry*. New York, Oxford University Press, 1963; Garbáty, Thomas J. *Medieval English Literature*. Toronto: Heath, 1984; Lambdin, Laura C., and Robert T. Lambdin, eds. *Chaucer's Pilgrims: An Historical Guide to the Pilgrims in the*

"Canterbury Tales." Westport, CT: Greenwood Press. 1996; Owen, Charles A. Jr. "The Falcon Complaint in the 'Squire's Tale.'" In *Rebels and Rivals: The Contestive Spirit in the "Canterbury Tales."* Susanna Grier Fein *et al*, eds. Kalamazoo: Medieval Institute, 1991. 173-88; Salter, Elizabeth. *Fourteenth-Century English Poetry.* Oxford: Clarendon Press, 1983; Seymour, M. C. "Some Satiric Pointers in the 'Squire's Tale.'" *English Studies* 70:4 (1989), 311-14; Sharon-Zisser, Shirley. "The 'Squire's Tale' and the Limits of Non-Mimetic Poetry." *Chaucer Review* 26:4 (1992), 377-94.

Laura Cooner Lambdin

"SUMER IS ICUMEN IN." Written some time between 1230 and 1240, the poem "Sumer Is Icumen In" was for many years considered the first "real" *lyric. The poem is in the form of a *rondel and appears, along with music and Latin directions for voice, in a thirteenth-century commonplace book written by the Reading Abbey monks. This example of the reverdie lyric (or "song of spring") has two stanzas and a two-line refrain. The form alternates between three- and four-stress lines with rhymes *abcbb abcbbbb bb.*

In the first stanza spring is celebrated in the images of seed, flower, and leaf, and the cuckoo, a symbol for new life, is urged to sing. The second stanza focuses on animal life, as the ewe bleats after her lamb, the cow lows after her calf, the bullock leaps, and the buck "verteth." The cuckoo is again joyfully urged to sing and never stop. After the second stanza the refrain comes in: "Sing, cuccu, nu! Sing, cuccu! / Sing, cuccu! Sing, cuccu, nu [now]!"

In this poem the focus is clearly on the growth and vitality of nature. Edmund Reiss said that "icumen" is a past participle, meaning that summer has already arrived and the poet is celebrating its effects, which are presented in a series of present tenses "punctuated by imperatives," with "simple and rustic details." Lewis and Nancy Owen described this poem as a round with musical notations, designed for four voices accompanied by two additional voices. This is one of the finest examples of true lyric poetry to come from the medieval period.

SELECTED BIBLIOGRAPHY

Obst, Wolfgang. "'Sumer is Icumen in'. . . A Contradiction?" *M&L* 64:3-4 (July-Oct 1983), 151-61; Owen, Lewis, and Nancy Owen, eds. *Middle English Poetry: An Anthology.* Indianapolis: Bobbs-Merrill, 1971; Reiss, Edmund. *The Art of the Middle English Lyric: Essays in Criticism.* Athens: University of Georgia Press, 1972; Sigal, Gale. *Erotic Dawn-Songs of the Middle Ages: Voicing the Lyric Lady.* Gainesville: University Press of Florida, 1996; Stevick, Robert D., ed. *One Hundred Middle English Lyrics.* Rev. Urbana: University of Illinois Press, 1994.

Sigrid King

SUMMA THEOLOGICA. St. Thomas *Aquinas composed the *Summa Theologica*, his major philosophical treatise, sometime between 1265 and 1274; the full title is *Summa Totius Theologiae*. The work, noted as a summary of all theology, is still recognized by the Catholic Church as the doctrinal basis for all of its teachings.

The *Summa* applies the methodology of Aristotelian logic to problems of Christian doctrine. It systematizes and quotes from both classical and early Christian thinkers. Aquinas stresses the importance of logical argument in matters of reason, but also notes the supremacy of revelation through scriptural and church pronouncements on matters dealing with faith.

The *Summa* is composed in three sections. The first elaborates upon the existence and nature of God and his universe. The second treats virtues and vices from both the practical viewpoint of society and the theoretical aspect; this creates a type of moral philosophy. The third section discusses the role of Jesus and the sacraments in the soul's salvation. Aquinas died before the third section was complete. His student Reginald of Piperno completed the work, based upon his understanding of Aquinas's design.

SELECTED BIBLIOGRAPHY

Campbell, Neil. "Aquinas' Reasons for the Aesthetic Irrelevance of Tastes and Smells." *British Journal of Aesthetics* 36:2 (April 1966), 166-76; Ward, Ian. "Natural Law and Reason in the Philosophies of Maimonides and St. Thomas Aquinas." *Durham University Journal* 86:55 (1) (January 1994), 21-32.

Robert T. Lambdin

"SUMMONER'S TALE, THE." "The Summoner's Tale" is a scatological story in Geoffrey *Chaucer's *Canterbury Tales* (c. 1387-1400) seems specifically designed to highlight the Summoner's moral bankruptcy although it is intended as an attack on the Friar. A sick man named Thomas is bedridden and angry at a local friar's constant attempts to exhort money from him in the most greedy and insensitive way imaginable. Thomas tells the friar that a special gift awaits him if he will reach under the bed covers. The friar greedily puts his hand under the sheets, and Thomas rewards him by breaking wind. The friar is made to promise that according to the rules of his order, he will distribute the gift equally among his fellow friars. When the friar complains to the lord of the village about this poor treatment, he gets no sympathy. The lord and his family pretend to hold a serious scholarly discussion about how best to equally divide the noise and odor of the fart among the friars in the area.

SELECTED BIBLIOGRAPHY

Bush, Douglas. *English Poetry*. New York: Oxford University Press, 1963; Cox, Catherine S. "'Grope Wel Bihynde': The Subversive Erotics of Chaucer's Summoner."

Exemplaria 7:1 (Spring 1995), 145-77; Garbáty, Thomas J. *Medieval English Literature.* Toronto: Heath, 1984; Hasenfratz, Robert. "The Science of Flatulence: Possible Sources for the 'Summoner's Tale.'" *Chaucer Review* 30:3 (1996), 241-61; Lambdin, Laura C., and Robert T. Lambdin, eds. *Chaucer's Pilgrims: An Historical Guide to the Pilgrims in the "Canterbury Tales."* Westport, CT: Greenwood Press. 1996; Pulsiano, Phillip. "The Twelve-spoked Wheel of the 'Summoner's Tale.'" *Chaucer Review* 29:4 (1995), 382-89; Salter, Elizabeth. *Fourteenth-Century English poetry.* Oxford: Clarendon Press, 1983.

Laura Cooner Lambdin

SWORD DANCE. The sword dance was performed as an allegory of the death and resurrection of the year. The dance contained several stock characters, including a fool and "Bessy," a man who dressed as a woman. A standard theme of the dance saw an armed mob surround one of these characters; they first harried their prey before they metaphorically slew him. The characters came to be introduced audibly with rhymed speeches; thus the sword dance is considered one of the earliest influences upon the later mummers' play.

SELECTED BIBLIOGRAPHY

Gregson, Keith. "A Cumbrian Sword Dance." *English Dance and Song* 42:2 (1980), 9; Hayden, Bryan. "The Bedlington Sword Dance." *English Dance and Song* 41:1 (1979), 5-7; Renwick, Roger de V. "The Mummers' Play and the Old Wives Tale." *Journal of American Folklore* 94:374 (October-December 1981), 433-455.

Robert T. Lambdin

T

TAILLEFER (d.1066). As recorded by *Henry of Huntingdon, Taillefer was a *minstrel who accompanied the army of *William the Conqueror. It is said that before he was slain at the Battle of Hastings, he led the invading army, encouraging the men with his songs about *Charlemagne and Roland. It is not clear whether Taillefer recited the *Chanson de Roland* or presented another version of the legend.

SELECTED BIBLIOGRAPHY

Ailes, Marianne. "French Studies: Early Medieval." *Year's Work in Modern Language Studies* 54 (1992), 49-67; Benton, John F. *Culture, Power, and Personality in Medieval France.* London: Hambledon Press, 1991; Mason, Germaine, *A Concise Survey of French Literature.* New York: Greenwood Press, 1969; Speer, Mary B. "Old French Literature." In *Scholarly Editing: A Guide to Research.* D. C. Greetham, ed. New York: Modern Language Association of America, 1995.

Robert T. Lambdin

TALIESIN. Taliesin is believed to have been a Welsh *bard, although there is no tangible evidence that he ever truly existed. He is first alluded to in the *Saxon Genealogies* of the *Historia Brittonum,* composed in the late seventh century. It was noted that Taliesin was among the first bards with supernatural powers; in his case, legends reported that Taliesin could foretell the future and cause inadequate poets to be struck dumb. While many works and poems were ascribed to him, it is doubtful that he composed them, especially considering his questionable existence. Even *The Book of Taliesin,* a fourteenth-century work, is a collection of poems composed by several authors. Nevertheless, he gained such a reputation that a town was named after him; Taliesin was established in Cardiganshire near the spot where rumor had it that the poet was buried.

SELECTED BIBLIOGRAPHY

Breeze, Andrew. "Master John of St. David's, a New Twelfth-Century Poet." *BBCS* 40 (1993), 73-82; Conran, Tony. "The Ballad and Taliesin." *Cambrian Medieval Celtic Studies* 28 (Winter 1994), 1-24; Jacobs, Nicolas. "The Old English Heroic Tradition in Light of Welsh Evidence." *Cambridge Medieval Celtic Studies* 2 (Winter 1981), 9-20; McDiarmid, Matthew P. "Brett and Pict: Taliesin and Aneirin in Early Scotland." In

Selected Essays on Scottish Language and Literature. Steven R. McKenna, ed. Lewiston, NY: Edwin Mellen, 1992. 1-12; Wood, Juliette. "Virgil and Taliesin: The Concept of Magician in Medieval Folklore." *Folklore* 94:1 (1983), 91-104.

Robert T. Lambdin

TESEIDA, IL (1339?-1341). An early epic poem written by Giovanni *Boccaccio during the end of his tenure at Naples, *Il Teseida* was possibly completed or revised after his return to Florence in 1341. Continuing in the tradition of the **Filocolo* and **Filostrato*, this work reflects a growing concern on Boccaccio's part about the relationship of fortune to human aspirations for love. The work, whose plot is drawn from the *Thebaid* of Statius and from the unknown author of the *Roman de Thèbes*, is written in *ottava rima* in twelve books and relates the adventures of two close Theban friends, Palemones and Arcita, who fight for the love of the beautiful young Emilia, sister to Queen Hippolita, consort of Theseus, in an elaborate tournament in which an entire catalog of Greek heroes participate. Arcita wins in Pyrrhic fashion; he dies shortly after from his wounds. Theseus, duke of Athens, then gives Emilia's hand to Palemones; the last part of the narrative is devoted to the nuptial celebrations and the sexual prowess and happiness of the groom. This work inspired, in its turn, Geoffrey *Chaucer's *"Knight's Tale."

The epic is filled with mythological references and demonstrates yet again Boccaccio's wide reading practice that continued throughout his life. Scholars have noted a fair number of anachronisms to his epic setting, but the work is nevertheless filled with epic speeches, talk of war, and military adventures. Of equal interest to scholars, perhaps, is the fact that Boccaccio considered this poem worthy of complex and complete glossing and annotations that he provided in footnotes and commentary, possibly after he returned to Florence. Most of the glosses explain the relationship of the metaphorical function of mythography to the historicized narrative. Mars, Venus, and other references are all carefully explained in this commentary. The auto-exegesis is particularly interesting because of its addition of learned explication to popular poetry, prefiguring in a certain sense his encyclopedic masterpiece, the **Genealogy of the Gentile Gods*. Much of the allegorical and didactic imagery contained in the poem is thereby reinforced and emphasized in the commentary. The character development in this work, however, is not as authentic as that of *Filostrato*. Emilia's character, in particular, is flat and conventional and lacks the vigor and appeal of Cressida. Her sensual presence is certainly a powerful one in the poem, but the reader's overall impression of her is negative: as Bergin pointed out, "Boccaccio is careful to assure us that she is not moved by love but merely by that vanity that dwells in every woman's heart." Boccaccio's cynical portrait of her may in fact have been parodic as his interest in the conventional courtly characterization wanes and his attention turned to different approaches.

At any rate, scholars tend to find this poem less interesting than either *Filostrato* or the **Decameron*.

SELECTED BIBLIOGRAPHY

Bergin, Thomas. *Boccaccio.* New York: Viking Press, 1981; Branca, Vittore. *Boccaccio: The Man and His Works.* R. Monges, trans. and Dennis McAuliffe, ed. New York: New York University Press, 1976; Havely, Nigel. *Chaucer's Boccaccio.* Cambridge: D. S. Brewer, 1992; Hollander, Robert. *Boccaccio's Two Venuses.* New York: Columbia University Press, 1977; Kirkham, Victoria. *The Sign of Reason in Boccaccio's Fiction.* Florence: Olschki, 1993; Martinez, Ronald L. "Before the *Teseida*: Statius and Dante in Boccaccio's Epic." *Studi sul Boccaccio* 20 (1991-92), 205-19; Scherer, Margaret Roseman. *The Legends of Troy in Art and Literature.* New York: Phaidon, 1963; Smarr, Janet M. *Boccaccio and Fiammetta.* Urbana: University of Illinois Press, 1985; Wetherbee, Winthrop. "History and Romance in Boccaccio's *Teseida*." *Studi sul Boccaccio* 20 (1991-1992), 173-84.

Theresa Kennedy

THOMAS À KEMPIS (1380-1471). Thomas à Kempis was a German Augustinian monk and author. He entered the monastery of Mt. St. Agnes in 1407 and remained there the rest of his life. He is noted as one of the Christian mystics. His most important work is probably *De Imitatione Christi* or The Imitation of Christ which caught on all over the Continent and was translated from Latin into various vernaculars. This work consists of four books that trace in great detail the lengthy progress of the soul from its innate wickedness to Christian perfection. This, to Kempis, occurred in a series of steps wherein the soul moves from an entity detached from everything to one in union with God. The sheer simplicity of the work concerning its universal dogma made it a popular text in religious instruction.

SELECTED BIBLIOGRAPHY

Armstrong, Elizabeth Psakis. "Womanly Men and Manly Women in Thomas À Kempis and St. Theresa." In *Vox Mystica: Essays on Medieval Mysticism.* Anne Clark Bartlett, et al, eds. Cambridge MA: D. S. Brewer, 1995. 107-15; Williams, Gerhild Scholz. "On Finding Words: Witchcraft and the Discourses of Dissidence and Discovery." In *The Graph of Sex and the German Text: Gendered Culture in Early Medieval Germany.* Lynne Tatlock, ed. Amsterdam: Rodopi, 1994. 45-66.

Robert T. Lambdin

THOMAS OF ERCELDOUNE (c. 1220-1297). Thomas the Rhymer, or Thomas Learmont, was a poet and seer who lived at Erceldoune in Berwickshire. Because he was said to have predicted, among other events, the death of Alexander III, the

Battle of Bannockburn, and the accession of James VI to the throne, he was sometimes known as "True Thomas" and said to have the same powers as Merlin. The *romance of *Sir Tristrem* is generally attributed to Thomas; if this is correct, the work makes him the earliest named poet of Scotland. The oldest known manuscript was discovered in the Advocates' Library, probably "Englishized" by its transcribers, but still particularly Scottish. The origins of the tale are uncertain, though there is a Tristan in French and German tales, and writers of France, Italy, Spain, and Germany have represented him as one of the knights of the Round Table. The *Tristrem* attributed to Thomas the Rhymer employs the bob-and-wheel stanza and moderate alliteration.

Thomas the Rhymer was also the subject of a romance in the fifteenth century, but probably the most intriguing work is the *ballad he figures in, *Thomas Rhymer* (Child no. 37). In the ballad he receives his gift of prophecy from the Queen of the Færies in a journey to the Other World. A beautiful "lady bright" comes riding on a horse as Thomas sits on a riverbank. She entices him to join her, promising to show him wonders that he has never seen. She shows him three roads, one the thorny, narrow path to heaven, the other the broad path to hell, and the third, which they follow, the road to Elfyn ("elfland"). In Elfyn the road leads to a garden where the beautiful lady plucks an apple from a tree, gives it to him, and thusly instills in him the power to tell the truth, or the gift of prophecy.

The *Ballad of Thomas Rhymer* is one of the supernatural ballads, along with others like *Lady Isabella and the Elf Knight, The Carpenter's Wife*, and *Tam Lin*, and it is rich in the Celtic folklore of the Scottish highlands. The oldest of the ballads collected by Harvard professor Francis Child in the late 1800, this group of ballads have a magical allure that most of the others do not possess. *Thomas Rhymer* is, of the group, almost unique in that no harm comes to the human character. The supernatural element survived in ballads and tales of primarily Scottish and Irish origin in tinges that resound with ancient Celtic belief.

SELECTED BIBLIOGRAPHY

Lupack, Alan, ed. *Lancelot of the Laik and Sir Tristram*. Kalamazoo: Medieval Institute, 1994; McIntosh, Angus. "'Sir Tritrem': An English or a Scottish Poem?" In *In Other Words*. Mackenzie J. Lachlan and Richard Todd, eds. Dordrecht: Foris, 1989, 85-95.

J. Scott Plaster

THREE RAVENS, THE and **THE TWA CORBIES.** *The Three Ravens* and *The Twa Corbies* are *ballad analogues that offer a remarkably concise comparison between the visions of the medieval aristocracy and the common people. The earliest complete version of *The Three Ravens* comes from Thomas Ravenscroft's *Melismata* (1611), but fragments of it are found in a manuscript of the high Middle Ages. *The Twa Corbies*, on the other hand, was not recorded in writing until the eighteenth century, but despite early speculation that it is a late, cynical literary reworking of the *Ravens*, it is now generally conceded a medieval origin. Indeed, an argument as to which of the two is earlier has occupied scholars of the ballad for several decades. Moreover, it is *The Twa Corbies* that now appears to be a genuine popular product, while *The Three Ravens* bears the hallmarks of an aristocratic literary ballad.

Both ballads center on a conversation between ravens about where they will find dinner. One observes that a recently slain knight lies nearby. In the *Ravens*, however, the knight's hawk and hounds guard the body from scavengers until his true love, metamorphosed into a pregnant doe, can bury him appropriately. The lady then dies of heartbreak, and the ballad concludes with the optimistic exclamation that all gentlemen should be granted such loyal companions. In *The Twa Corbies*, on the other hand, no such obstacles exist for the carrion birds. Indeed, the hawk has flown off to catch wild fowl, the hound has gone to find another party with which to hunt, and the lady has remarried. There is even the suggestion that the knight has been ignobly murdered and that his beloved was complicit in the crime. The corbies are able to pick out the knight's eyes, eat his flesh, and take his hair as thatching material. The body is left to the elements with nobody the wiser.

SELECTED BIBLIOGRAPHY

Chandran, K. Narayana. "'The Three Ravens' and Ash Wednesday II." *Central Institute of English and Foreign Languages Bulletin* 4:1-2 (June-December 1991), 124-26; Morgan, Gwendolyn. *Medieval Balladry and the Courtly Tradition*. New York: Peter Lang, 1993; Morgan, Gwendolyn. *Medieval Ballads: Chivalry, Romance, and Everyday Life*. New York: Peter Lang, 1996.

Gwendolyn Morgan

THRUSH AND THE NIGHTINGALE, THE. *The Thrush and the Nightingale*, composed during the second half of the thirteenth century, is a Middle English avian *debate poem by an anonymous author who may have been writing with knowledge of the earlier, more accomplished *The *Owl and the Nightingale* (some scholars believe that *The Thrush and the Nightingale* may be a translation of an Old French poem). The principal subject of the later debate, argued by the two eponymous birds, is the relative worth of women. The poem is written in tail-rhyme in a simple style that boasts little descriptive or connective detail; after a brief introduction there is unadorned alternation of the voices of the two birds until the debate is concluded.

The nightingale has a long literary association with love, and here it is the Nightingale who serves as the proponent for women, saying that they are valuable because they offer comfort to men. The Thrush, however, contends that women are by nature deceitful, providing examples of men who were harmed by women, among them Adam, Constantine, and Samson. The

Nightingale counters with the example of the Virgin Mary, the Thrush reverses his position, and the debate abruptly ends.

While this poem lacks the literary and rhetorical sophistication of *The Owl and the Nightingale*, it does serve as a good example of medieval avian debate and of the debates about the worth of women that were relatively common during the Middle Ages; indeed, it can be considered a good reflection of the kind of misogyny often in evidence in medieval literature. The poem offers a religious resolution to the debate presented, but it is clear that this is a pro forma conclusion rather than a serious religious statement; indeed, despite the obvious gravity of the issue involved, the poem can most profitably be viewed as a somewhat clumsy attempt at a humorous treatment of a common theme in an established literary genre. For the Middle English text of the poem, critical, linguistic, and bibliographical notes on it, and manuscript information, the reader is referred to John W. Conlee, *Middle English Debate Poetry: A Critical Anthology*; this work also includes other Middle English poems in which nightingales appear as disputants.

SELECTED BIBLIOGRAPHY

Conlee, John W., ed. *Middle English Debate Poetry: A Critical Anthology*. East Lansing: Colleagues Press, 1991; Conlee, John W. *"The Owl and the Nightingale* and Latin Debate Tradition." *Comparatist* 4 (1980); Star, Jonathan, and Shahram Shiva, trans. *A Garden beyond Paradise: The Mystical Poetry of Rumi*. New York: Bantam, 1992.

Nancy M. Reale

TRIVET, NICHOLAS (1258-c. 1334). Nicholas Trivet was born in 1258 to a family that owned land in Norfolk and Somerset. His father was most likely a knight in the service of the king. Nicholas became a Dominican at Oxford sometime before 1297. He taught there for a short while and then traveled to Paris to study at the university. In 1314 he returned to Oxford to teach. He wrote numerous materials, including a wide variety of university disputations, many biblical commentaries, and several histories. Within his lifetime he achieved an international reputation. His three main historical works are *Historia ab orbe Condito ad Christi Nativitatem* (History from the Creation of the World to the Birth of Christ); a *chronicle of *Anglo-Norman history from creation to 1285; and the *Annales Sex Regum Angliae* (Annals of Six English Kings--from Stephen to Edward I). Trivet's *Historia* and Anglo-Norman chronicle are not published; his history from Creation to the birth of Christ chronicles world history, but is of little historical value. The Anglo-Norman chronicle is of note because it was highly popular in its day and provides a source text for Geoffrey *Chaucer's *"Man of Law's Tale"--the tale of Constance.

In his *Annales* Trivet uses numerous written sources for the earliest time periods, but relied more and more on firsthand information as events approached contemporary times. His treatment of history was patriotic, often presenting events in their most positive light for the monarchy, but he included transcriptions of a number of important documents into his work, including the only known copies of correspondence between Edward I and Boniface VIII. In addition, Trivet included information about his order (the Dominicans) and some of their history in England. Some of his most memorable writing is the intimate depictions, gained from eyewitnesses accounts, of Henry III and Edward I. Trivet was one of the few members of a mendicant order to achieve literary popularity during the thirteenth century, and this was probably due to his interest in intimate description and amusing anecdotes.

SELECTED BIBLIOGRAPHY

Correale, Robert M. "Chaucer's The 'Friar's Tale', Lines 1511-12, and *Les Chronicles* of Nicholas Trevet." *Notes and Queries* 25(233):3 (September 1988), 296-98; Gransden, Antonia. *Historical Writing in England II: c. 1307 to Early Sixteenth Century.* Ithaca: Cornell University Press, 1982; Lord, Mary Louise. "Virgil's *Eclogues*, Nicholas Trevet, and the Harmony of the Spheres." *Mediaeval Studies* 54 (1992), 186-273; Smalley, Beryl. *Historians in the Middle Ages.* New York: Scribner's, 1974.

Richard McDonald

TRIVIUM. The trivium was a division of the seven *liberal arts that included the three elements of grammar, rhetoric, and logic. The trivium was obviously more methodological and therefore was easily distinguished from the mathematically inclined *quadrivium. This distinction reached its peak in eleventh and twelfth century Chartres and became a seminal influence in the thinking of authors such as *John of Salisbury. By the twelfth century logic was of such great import that the trivium was altered to include its former parts along with the new sub-orders of logic and dialectic. Precise debate became the cornerstone of thirteenth century thought; thus the subjects of grammar and rhetoric were considered passé. Massive debates ensued concerning the nature of not only the trivium but also the whole of the seven liberal arts; the declining nature of this portion resulted in the word "trivial" as a disparaging description of something.

SELECTED BIBLIOGRAPHY

Hernadi, Paul. "Coverage and Discovery: The Case for Detrivializing the Trivium." *ADE* Bulletin 89 (Spring 1988), 38-40; Klifman, Harm. "Dutch Language Study and the Trivium: Motives and Elaborations." *Historiographia Linguistica* 15:1-2 (1988), 63-83.

Robert T. Lambdin

TROILUS AND CRISEYDE. *Troilus and Criseyde* was originally considered Geoffrey *Chaucer's most important work. In Caroline Spurgeon's *Five Hundred Years of Chaucer Criticism and Allusion*, originally published in three volumes, there are before 1700 twice as many references to *Troilus* as to the *Canterbury Tales*, and three times as many as to the *"General Prologue." This is because in the Middle Ages *courtly love, always secret and adulterous, was the most popular subject for secular literature. Courtly love was a culture marker that distinguished the gentle from the churl. Giovanni *Boccaccio's *Filostrato*, Chaucer's principal source for his poem, is not a celebration of courtly love. It is much more like a *fabliau. Criseyde accepts Troilo as her lover voluntarily and promptly. Chaucer replaced this realistic behavior with elaborate arrangements to preserve Criseyde's good name--the meeting at Deiphebus's house in Book II, the consummation in Book III, the elaborate complaints in Book IV, and Troilus's refusal to come to her assistance in Book V. All of the poetic psychologizing about the motives and reactions of the principals in Chaucer's poem presents an epitome of the courtly ideal. The love "complaint" was the principal *lyric form in the Middle Ages. Until the Puritan revolution of 1642, courtiers were expected to appreciate and write about the sentiment, the secretiveness, and the frustration of love. After the Puritan revolution literary taste began to turn to realism and satire, which led to the emergence of the novel. With this development in taste, the *Canterbury Tales* replaced *Troilus* as Chaucer's most important work, a position it has occupied ever since.

Troilus must have been completed shortly after Chaucer lost his controllership of customs in 1386 and had more time for his writing. At III.624-25 there is a reference to the conjunction of the moon, Saturn, and Jupiter in the zodiacal sign of Cancer that occurred in May 1385 for the first time in six hundred years. Chaucer's interest in astronomy, evidenced by his *Treatise on the Astrolabe* and *Equatorie of the Planets*, would account for his including this astronomical event in a poem that he was currently working on.

The transitional nature of *Troilus* in the development of Chaucer's art is reflected by the critical discussion of its genre. Is it the first English novel, or a sophisticated medieval *romance, or a genuine tragedy? The five-book structure of the poem suggests the five-act structure of an Elizabethan play. Shakespeare recognized the dramatic potential by adapting it as his *Troilus and Cressida*, but he moved back toward Boccaccio's fabliau version by depicting Criseyde as dissolute. Chaucer was much more sympathetic with her situation. Abandoned unprotected by her traitor father in war-torn Troy and then bundled off to the Greeks by the heartless city fathers, she had reason to be fearful. Criseyde's sexual arousal and her trepidations about losing her reputation and independence, when set against her confident handling of Pandarus and Troilus, give Chaucer's poem a depth that the story does not have in Boccaccio or Shakespeare. There is a thorough analysis of the conflicting critical interpretations in Alice R. Kaminsky, *Chaucer's "Troilus and Criseyde" and the Critics* (1980).

The effect of *Troilus* results not only from the quality of the narrative but from the quality of the verse. The rhyme royal stanzas in which it is expressed are Chaucer's most impressive poetry. The prosody changes as the story develops. The lines and stanzas in the first two books are much more lively than the subdued tone of the last two. Book III shows the variety to best advantage. When Pandarus lectures Troilus on the sin of boasting he is diffuse (and knows it, III. 295), but the verse is firm and rhetorical. When Troilus replies (III. 360), he is nearly incoherent. The stanzas run together until III.386 when he recovers his poise. The tone becomes sonorous as Criseyde reflects on the unstableness of temporal joy (III.813), but the meter picks up again when Troilus swoons (III. 1093). The variations in tone and rhythm reflect the quality of the actions as accurately as movie music, and the variations in the manuscripts show Chaucer adjusting and polishing as he went along.

For a thousand years the myth of descent from Aeneas was a sacred literary tradition throughout Europe. Virgil's *Aeneid* began the tradition, and it was continued by Frankish and Burgundian chroniclers. *Geoffrey of Monmouth introduced the tradition that the founder of Britain was Brutus, great-grandson of Aeneas, who founded his capital, New Troy, on the banks of the Thames. The most popular medieval account of the Trojan war was the *Roman de Troie* of Benoît de Sainte Maure. Benoît evidently invented the story of Troilus and Briseida (note the B) on the Trojan side to match the traditional story of Achilles and Polyxena on the Greek side, but his version begins with Briseida's departure from Troy and concentrates on the wooing of Diomede. Most of his long poem (23,126 lines) is devoted to the siege and combats of the war itself. From this account, transmitted through the Latin of Guido delle Collone, Boccaccio abstracted the love story of Troilo and Criseyde (note the C) in his *Filostrato* to memorialize (as he said) his unhappy love affair with Maria d'Aquino. The development of the English versions of the Troy story has been traced by C. David Benson, *The History of Troy in Middle English Litgerature* (1980). For text and bibliography to 1987 see John Fisher's edition of *The Complete Poetry and Prose of Geoffrey Chaucer*. There is an annual annotated bibliography in *Studies in the Age of Chaucer*.

SELECTED BIBLIOGRAPHY

Borch, Marianne. "Poet and Person: Writing the Reader in *Troilus*." *Chaucer Review* 30:3 (1996), 215-28; Farell, Thomas J. "The Fyn of the *Troilus*." In *Subjects on the World's Stage: Essays on British Literature in the Middle Ages and Renaissance*. David Allen and Robert A. White, eds. Newark: University of Delaware Press, 1995, 38-53; Fisher, John H. *The Complete Poetry and Prose of Geoffrey Chaucer*. 2nd ed. New York: Holt, Rinehart, and Winston, 1988; Hardman, Phillipa. "Chaucer's Articulation of the Narrative in *Troilus*: The Manuscript Evidence." *Chaucer Review* 30:2 (1995), 111-33; Hewett-Smith, Kathleen M. "Transcript and Error in the Text of *Troilus*." *Studies in the Age of Chaucer* 13(1991), 99-119; Spurgeon, Catherine Frances Eleanor. *Five Hundred Years of Chaucer Criticism and Allusion, 1357-1900*. New York: Russell, 1960. Stanbury, Sarah. "The Voyeur and the Private Life in *Troilus and Criseyde*." *Studies in* the Age of Chaucer 13 (1991), 141-58; Storm, Melvin. "The Intertextual Cresseida: Chaucer's Henryson or Henryson's Chaucer?" *Studies in Scottish Literature* 28 (1993), 105-22.

John H. Fisher

TROUVÈRES. The term "trouvères" applies to the group or school of poets of northern France in the twelfth and thirteenth centuries. They were influenced by the works of the troubadours of Southern France, and their works were mostly *lyrics pertaining to love. However, they also composed *chansons de geste* as well as chivalric *romances. Trouvères were usually professional entertainers, similar to the *jogleurs; some trouvères were also clerics. Additionally, after courtly society developed and the lyric fell from favor, these types of verse became fashionable and were composed by feudal lords.

Among the most famous trouvères was the *clerc* *Chrétien de Troyes, who composed some of the earliest known *Arthurian romances. Other noted trouvères included Conon de Bethune, whose forte was songs about the *Crusades, and Bernart de Ventadorn who attended the court of *Eleanor of Aquitaine, the granddaughter of Guilhelm IX, the first known troubadour. The poetry reached its height around 1200, most notably in the work of Gâce Brulé. After this period the desire for this poetry diminished, and the composition of these poems decreased also.

SELECTED BIBLIOGRAPHY

Doss-Quinby, Egal. *The Lyrics of the Trouvères: A Research Guide (1970-1990)*. New York: Garland Press, 1994; Topsfield, Leslie. "Troubadours and Trouvères." in *European Writers: The Middle Ages and the Renaissance, I; Prudentius to Medieval Drama*. William Jackson, ed. New York: Scribner's, 1983. 161-84.

Robert T. Lambdin

TYLER, WAT (d. 1381). Wat Tyler was the leader of the *Peasants' Revolt in Britain in 1381. With Jack Straw, Tyler led the peasants of Kent and Essex to London. The peasants demanded an abolition of serfdom, the poll tax, and all restrictions on labor and trade. They sacked Canterbury and several buildings in London, causing *Richard II to accede to Tyler's demands. Richard met with Tyler at Smithfield and even began having papers drawn up to sate the peasants.

However, Tyler was not content and foolishly delivered a new set of demands the next day. The lord mayor of London, William Walworth, took offense at these extreme demands and killed Tyler. In 1382 Parliament revoked Richard's concessions. This insurrection is mentioned one time in Geoffrey *Chaucer's *Canterbury Tales*, and John Gower described the revolt in his *Vox Clamantis*.

SELECTED BIBLIOGRAPHY

Hudson, Anne. "*Piers Plowman* and the Peasants' Revolt: A Problem Revisited." *Yearbook of Langland Studies* 8 (1985), 85-106; Justice, Steven. *Writing and Rebellion: England in 1381.* Berkeley: University of California Press, 1994; Rampton, Martha. "The Peasants' Revolt of 1381 and the Written Word." *Comitatus* 24 (1993), 45-60; Russell, J. Stephen. "Is London Burning? A Chaucerian Allusion to the Rising of 1381." *Chauce rReview* 30:1 (1995), 107-09.

Robert T. Lambdin

TYNDALE, WILLIAM (c. 1495-1536). William Tyndale was an English Protestant preacher who is best known for his translation of the Bible from Latin into the vernacular. In 1522 Tyndale began translating the Scriptures. After relocating to Hamburg, he began printing his edition of the New Testament in 1525. However, when he attempted to distribute the work in England, the bishops denounced it, and the copies were ordered destroyed. This crushed Tyndale, who moved back to the Continent and worked as a pamphleteer.

Tyndale later found himself in a dispute with Sir Thomas More after the publication of Tyndale's tract *An Answere unto Sir Thomas Mores Dialoge.* More was so irate that he saw to Tyndale's arrest for heresy. In 1535 Tyndale was imprisoned at Vilvorde; he was convicted and sentenced to death. Despite the intervention of many, including Thomas Cromwell, Tyndale was strangled and burned at the stake. He did leave his legacy, though. His version of the Bible is very accurately translated, and he thus brought the Scriptures to a multitude who previously had been unable to truly grasp their meaning.

SELECTED BIBLIOGRAPHY

Auski, Peter. "'Waxing Soft and Melting': William Tyndale and the Prose of Regeneration." *English Renaissance Prose Newsletter* 2:1 (1988), 1-21, Daniell, David. *William Tyndale: A Biography.* New Haven: Yale University Press. 1994; Dick, John A., and Anne Richardson, eds. *William Tyndale and the Law.* Kirksville, MO: Sixteenth Century Journal Publishers, 1994; Richardson, Anne. "Tyndale's Quarrel with Erasmus: A Chapter in the History of the English Reformation." *Fides et Historia* 25:3 (Fall 1993), 46-65; Zecher, Henry. "The Bible Translation that Rocked the World." *Notes on Translations* 7:2 (1993), 12-15.

Robert T. Lambdin

U

UBI SUNT. The Latin term *Ubi sunt* refers to laments in Old and Middle English poetry that eerily posit the question "Where are they?" Found in such Old English poems as **Beowulf* and "The Wanderer," the works usually concern the narrator's realization of the mutability of the world. In later poetry of the Middle Ages the *Ubi sunt* becomes equated with *lyric poetry. Its popularity is evidenced in the great amounts of French poetry that evolved, especially the poems of of Francois *Villon.

SELECTED BIBLIOGRAPHY

Cunningham, J. S. "'Where are They?' The After-Life of a Figure of Speech." *Proceedings of the British Academy*. 65 (1979), 369-94; Garde, Judith. "Sapentia, Ubi Sunt, and the Heroic Ideal in *Beowulf*." *Studia Neophilologica* 66:2 (1994), 159-73; Matsuda, Takami. "The *Ubi sunt* Passages in Middle English Literature." *Studies in English Literature* 59 (1983), 65-81.

Robert T. Lambdin

ULFILAS (311-381). Ulfilas or Wulfila was the bishop of the Visigoths, consecrated in 341 who translated the Bible from Greek into his vernacular, Gothic. To do such a task, Ulfilas supposedly created an alphabet. Thus Ulfilas was the originator of a task that missionaries have continued to the present, that of converting the spoken dialect into writing so that those not familiar with a particular language may receive the Word of God. Today only fragments of the text survive; the best found in the Codex Argentus at Uppsala. Philologically these pieces are of great value, for they give a clear demonstration of the German language as it changed in the Middle Ages.

SELECTED BIBLIOGRAPHY

Ebbinghaus, E. A. "Some Remarks on the Life of Bishop Wulfila." *General Linguistics* 32:2-3 (1992), 95-104; Ebbinghaus, E. A. "'Ulfila(s)' or 'Wulfila?'" *Historische Sprachforschung Solidus Historical Linguistics* 104:2(1991), 236-38. Greiner, Paul. "Tempted by Original Syntax: Luther, Wulfila, and the Greek New Testament." In *On*

Germanic Linguistics: Issues and Methods. Irmengard Rausch, et al., eds. Berlin: Mouton de Gruyter, 1992, 97-107; Lendinara, Patricia. "Wulfila as the Inventor of the Gothic Alphabet: The Tradition in Late Antiquity and the Middle Ages." *General Linguistics* 32:4 (1992), 217-25.

Robert T. Lambdin

ULSTER CYCLE, THE. See Celtic Literature.

USK, THOMAS (d.1388). Thomas Usk was the undersheriff of London who was executed in 1388. He is the author of *The Testament of Love*, which was one-time erroneously attributed to Geoffrey *Chaucer. This allegorical prose piece may have been composed by the condemned Usk, who was in prison for his support of *John of Gaunt, in an attempt to gain his freedom. The work, a kind of variation of a *Boethian lament, calls upon "Margaret of virtu" to pity him. Some have dated the work to 1385, but this appears to be too early, for *The Testament of Love* draws from *Troilus and Criseyde*, which dates after this time.

SELECTED BIBLIOGRAPHY

Burnley, J. D. "Chaucer, Usk, and Geoffrey of Vinsauf." *Neophilologus* 69:2 (April 1985), 284-93; Lewis, Lucy. "Langland's 'Tree of Charity' and Usk's 'Wexing Tree.'" *Notes and Queries* 42(240):4 (December 1995), 429-33; Reiss, Edmund. "The Idea of Love in Usk's 'Testament of Love.'" *Mediaevalia* 6 (1980), 261-77; Stokes, Myra, and John Scattergood. "Travelling in November: Sir Gawain, Thomas Usk, Charles of Orleans, and the De Re Militari." *Medium Ævum* 53:1 (1984), 78-82, 83; Strohm, Paul. "Politics and Poetics: Usk and Chaucer in the 1380s." In *Literary Practice and Social Change in Britain, 1380-1530.* Lee Patterson, ed. Berkeley: University of California Press, 1990. 83-112.

Robert T. Lambdin

V

VALENTINE AND ORSON. The title characters of the medieval French *romance *Valentine and Orson* are the sons of Bellisant, the sister of King Pepin. Bellisant weds Alexander, the emperor of Constantinople. An archbishop opposed to the union accuses her of unfaithfulness, and she is banished. Her children are left orphans; Orson is spirited away by a bear and raised in the wild, while Valentine is raised by his uncle and eventually becomes a knight. Quite by chance, Valentine happens across Orson in the wild. Before they know who each other in, Valentine has to tame Orson. Once this is accomplished, the two are united in great adventures. Among these are their capture and imprisonment by Clerimond, the sister of the giant Ferrages. They are rescued by the giant's messenger, Pucolet, a dwarf. It is after this event that the brothers realize who they are and are reunited.

SELECTED BIBLIOGRAPHY

Kelly, Douglas. *Medieval French Literature*. New York: Twayne, 1993; McCracken, Peggy. "The Queen's Secret: Adultery and Political Structure in the Feudal Courts of Old French Romance." *Romanic Review* 86:2 (March 1995), 289-306; Rockwell, Paul Vincent. *Rewriting Resemblance in Medieval French Romance*. New York: Garland, 1995.

Robert T. Lambdin

VERCELLI BOOK, THE. Composed before 1000, *The Vercelli Book*, an Old English manuscript made in England, is now possessed by the Vercelli chapter in northern Italy. The manuscript contains prose sermons and some of the most well known *Old English poems. These include The *Dream of the Rood, *Andreas*, and two of the four poems signed by and therefore attributed to *Cynewulf, including *Elene* and *The Fates of the Apostles*.

SELECTED BIBLIOGRAPHY

O'Carragain, Eamonn. "How did the *Vercelli* Collector Interpret 'The Dream of the Rood'?" *Occasional Papers in Linguistics and Language Learning* 62:2 (April 1981),

97-109; Scragg, D. G. "The Compilation of the *Vercelli Book*." In *Anglo-Saxon Manuscripts: Basic Readings*. Mary Richards, ed. New York: Garland, 1994. 317-43; Vickey, John R. "A Source and an Allusion in *Vercelli* 'Homily XIV' (Folio 77V, Lines 1-17." *Neophilologus* 75:4 (October 1991), 612-18.

Robert T. Lambdin

VESPUCCI, AMERIGO (1451-1512). Although Amerigo Vespucci was born in Florence, he was an agent of the Medici, the leading Italian banking firm, and resided in Seville.   Apparently influenced by the example of Columbus, Vespucci claimed an earlier voyage in 1497-98, but scholars doubt this. Underwritten by the Medici, Vespucci made a joint expedition with Alonso de Ojeda from May 1499 to June 1500, touching the shores of French Guiana and discovering the mouths of the Amazon.   They returned to Spain by way of Español, an island in the Caribbean, in 1500.

The following year Vespucci set out on his own in the service of Portugal. It is this voyage that is commonly said to have established Portugal's claim to Brazil. Accounts of Vespucci's travels, claiming the discovery of a New World, were published as *Paesi*.   In 1507 the geographer Martin Waldseemüller applied the term *America* to South America.

SELECTED BIBLIOGRAPHY

Arciniegas, German. *Amerigo y e Nuevo Mundo*. Madrid: Alianza Editorial, 1990; Vespucci, Amerigo. *Letters from a New World*. David Jacobson, trans. New York: Marsilio, 1992.

R. Churchill Curtis

VICE, THE. The vice is a stock character in medieval *drama. He was usually a fool or an idiot in the *interludes; however, by the later moralities he became the figure, other than Satan, most associated with evil. The character seems to have been derived from figures found in the mysteries and moralities including "The Vices" and the *"Seven Deadly Sins."

SELECTED BIBLIOGRAPHY

Bauer, Matthias. "Count Malvolio, Machevill, and Vice." *Connotations* 1:3 (November 1991), 224-43; Bronson, Larry. "Chaucer's Pandarus: 'Jolly Good Fellow' or 'Reverend Vice?'" *Ball State University Forum* 24:4 (Autumn 1983), 34-41; Muir, Lynette. *The Biblical Drama of Medieval Europe*. Cambridge: Cambridge University Press, 1995.

Robert T. Lambdin

VILLEHARDOUIN, GEOFFREY DE (c. 1150-1213). Geoffrey de Villehardouin was born into an affluent French family and later became marshal of Champagne. He also participated in the Fourth *Crusade; his personal accounts are contained in his *Conquête de Constantinople*, considered to be among the first great French prose works. The book recounts events from 1202 to the capture of Constantinople in 1203. Villehardouin's work details events that caused the Crusades to stray from their religious objectives. Their seemingly pious intent became an aggressive secular pursuit of power. Constantinople's fall led to dissension among the allies as they argued what their next step should be; conspiracies ran rampant. This discord was only settled when the lands in question were divided.

SELECTED BIBLIOGRAPHY

Buda, Milada. "Early Historical Narrative and the Dynamics of Textual Reference." *Romanic Review* 80:1 (January 1989), 1-17; Pickard Peter. "Blaise de Vigenere's Translation of Villehardouin." *Zeitschrift für Französische Sprache und Literatur* 91 (1981), 1-40.

Robert T. Lambdin

VILLON, FRANÇOIS (1431-after 1463). French poet François Villon is considered to rank among the finest authors of the late Middle Ages. His name was originally François de Montcorbier or François de Loges. He took the name of the patron who adopted him around 1438. Villon was a great student; he received his master of arts from the Sorbonne in 1452, before his twenty-first birthday.

Villon was also involved in the shadier side of life; he often brawled, and in 1455 he killed a priest. From then on, he was repeatedly under arrest, sentenced to prison, exiled, or running from the law. In 1456 he wrote his *Petit Testament*, a series of *lays that parodied the legal style. *Petit Testament* explained that he was leaving Paris because of a broken heart; he was actually probably fleeing arrest, and he bequeathed useless items and possessions to his friends and enemies.

In 1461 he composed *Grand Testament*. This poem, some two thousand lines long made him famous; unlike *Petit Testament*, this work is more melancholy and pathetic, although some sections are bitterly humorous. The *Grand Testament* is a self-effacing view of his life as a beggar and thief, but it serves to criticize and deride the vanity of all human life. The work includes *ballads and *rondeaux*, including the "Ballade des dames du temps jadis," which was later translated by Dante Gabriel Rossetti as "The Ballad of Dead Ladies." Also included is the work he addressed as a request for his mother to pray for him, "Ballade pur prier Nostre Dame."

In 1462 he was at the scene of another murder and was sentenced to be hanged. He was thus inspired to write his own epitaph, the "Ballade des Pendus," "The Ballad of the Hanged Men." In this work he denounces justice enforced by men and appeals for divine intervention. In 1463 Villon's friends successfully had the sentence commuted to ten years of banishment. After this Villon disappeared, and nothing more was ever known of him. His poems were not printed and released until 1489.

Villon remained rather unknown until the nineteenth century, when he became romanticized as a rogue, a sympathetic outlaw. His works were translated by noted authors such as Rossetti and Algernon Swinburne; his ballad were extremely popular. In 1928 Bertolt Brecht adopted some of these ballads for the lyrics of his *Threepenny Opera*. J. H. Huntley made a fictitious Villon the hero of his 1901 *If I Were King*, a work adapted by Rudolf Friml in his 1925 operetta *The Vagabond King*.

SELECTED BIBLIOGRAPHY

Dale, Peter, trans. *François Villon: Selected Poems*. London: Penguin, 1978; Deltcheva, Romiana, and Eduard Vlasov. "'The Goëthe Syndrome': Villon and Rabelais as Ideological Figures in Mandelstam and Bakhtin." *Canadian Review of Comparative Literature* 21:4 (1994), 577-96; Peckham, Robert D. "The Current State of Villon Studies." *Fifteenth Century Studies* 20 (1993), 247-57; Regalado, Nancy Freeman. "Gathering the Works: The 'Oeuvres de Villon' and the Intergeneric Passage of the Medieval French Lyric into Single-Author Collections." *L'Esprit Createur* 33:4 (Winter 1993), 87-100; Sargent-Baur, Barbara N., ed. and trans. *François Villon: Complete Poems*. Toronto: University of Toronto Press, 1994.

Anna Shealy

VITALIS, ORDERIC (1075-1142). Orderic Vitalis, although he lived in Normandy, devoted much of his attention to *Anglo-Saxon history. Orderic's main contribution to history was his *Ecclesiastical History of England and Normandy*, and his topic is as reminiscent of *Bede as is his title. He probably began the thirteen-volume Latin work at the order of the abbot of St. Evroul, where he was a monk and had lived since the age of ten. He was born at Atcham near Shrewsbury in England in 1075 to aristocratic parents who felt that he would best be served by a life in the Church. He thought of himself as English, although he lived almost his entire life in Normandy.

Volumes III-VI and volumes VIII-XIII follow a consecutive development and contain the history of Normandy and England up to the Norman Invasion. Book VII recounts French and English history from 688 to 1087 and reveals some of Orderic's sympathy for the Anglo-Saxons. Book I features the history of the church from Creation to Christ, and Book II recounts the lives of the apostles and popes. Like numerous other historians, Orderic tended to moralize history and explained his exclusion of the Greeks and

Romans from his history on the grounds that pagans did not deserve to have their deeds recorded for posterity.

He was able to travel occasionally in England and often included descriptions of English locales in his text. He blended both secular and ecclesiastical history into his volumes, although he favored church history and showed open disgust for the antics of courtiers. His work, though dependent on many sources, brings in enough of his own beliefs and devotion to God to be unique. He openly admitted that writing history was difficult for him, but he felt that history was morally edifying to his audience and continued writing into his sixty seventh year.

SELECTED BIBLIOGRAPHY

Chibnall, Marjorie. "Anglo-French Relations in the Work of Orderic Vitalis." In *Documenting the Past*. J. S. Hamilton and Patricia Bradley, eds. Wolfeboro: Boydell, 1989; Chibnall, Marjorie. "Orderic Vitalis on Castles." In *Studies in Medieval History Presented to R. Allen Brown*. Bill Christopher, et al, eds. Wolfeboro: Boydell, 1989; Chibnall, Marjorie. *The World of Orderic Vitalis*. Oxford: Clarendon, 1984; Gransden, Antonia. *Historical Writing in England c.550 to c.1307*. Ithaca: Cornell University Press, 1974; Smalley, Beryl. *Historians in the Middle Ages*. New York: Scribner's, 1974; Sterns, Indrikis. *The Greater Medieval Historians: An Interpretation and a Bibliography*. Lanham, MD: University Press of America, 1980.

Richard McDonald

VOLSUNGA SAGA. A Scandinavian prose cycle of legends, the *Volsunga *Saga* goes back to the West Germanic heroic lais (*see* **Lays**); these are also the base of the *Nibelungenlied* (*see* **German Literature**). The saga is also a main source of Wagner's cycle *Der Ring des Nibelunges*, despite the fact that some names and details differ.

The saga is named after Volsung, the grandson of Odin and the father of Sigmund. Siegfried, the hero, is Sigmund's son. Siegfried kills Fafnir, the dragon, the guardian of a treasure of gold and a magic ring; both of these carry the curse of their original owner, from whom the god Loki forcibly took them. Siegfried then begins his travels, taking the cursed treasure, accompanied by Grani, the magic horse given to him by Odin.

Siegfried awakens Brunhild, a sleeping Valkyrie maiden, and they become engaged; however, he leaves her in search of adventure. Siegfried becomes the comrade of three sons of a Rhine king and their sister Gudrun. They conspire to give Siegfried a magic potion that will make him forget Brunhild. It is then arranged that he will marry Gudrun if he helps one of the king's sons, Gunthar, win the hand of Brunhild.

Brunhild has surrounded herself with a circle of fire that a prospective suitor must cross; her assumption is that only Siegfried could do this. Siegfried rides through the circle and then takes the shape of Gunthar, winning Brunhild's promise of marriage. He reverts to his own shape, and a double marriage occurs.

However, later, during an argument, Gudrun tells Brunhild of the deception. Brunhild becomes so enraged that she has Siegfried killed, even though she is still in love with him. Brunhild then kills herself. Gudrun then marries Atli, king of the Huns, who vows to gain the cursed treasures, which are now with Gudrun's brothers. They sink the gold in the Rhine and die in battle, refusing to the end to reveal where the gold is hidden. Gudrun then avenges them by killing Atli and the sons she has borne him.

SELECTED BIBLIOGRAPHY

Albano, Robert A. "The Role of Women in Anglo-Saxon Culture: Hildebruth in *Beowulf* and as a Curious Counterpart in the *Volsunga Saga.*" *English Language Notes* 32:1 (1994), 1-10; Anderson, George K. trans. *The Saga of the Volsungs: Together with Excerpts from the "Nornageststhattr" and Three Chapters from the "Prose Edda."* Newark: University of Delaware Press, 1982; Byock, Jesse L., trans. *The Saga of the Volsungs: The Norse Epic of Sigurd the Dragon Slayer.* Berkeley: University of California Press, 1990.

Robert T. Lambdin

VOX CLAMANTIS (c.1382-1354). John Gower composed the *Vox Clamantis* (The voice of one crying) as a *dream allegory that describes the *Peasants' Revolt and Wat *Tyler's murder in 1381. In the work Gower establishes his premise that all classes of men are of corrupt nature. The work displays a three-tiered classification of society: the clerk, soldier, and plowman. In the end the poem is of value because of its exposure of social corruption and its attack upon contemporary manners.

SELECTED BIBLIOGRAPHY

Juby, W. H. "'A Theves Dede': A Case of Chaucer's Borrowing from Gower." *ANQ* 1:4 (October 1988), 123-25; Olsson, Kurt. "John Gower's *Vox Clamantis* and the Medieval Idea of Place." *Studies in Philology* 84:2 (Spring 1987), 134-58; Pearsall, Derek. "Interpretive Models for the Peasants' Revolt." In *Hermeneutics and Medieval Culture.* Patrick Gallacher, ed. Albany: State University of New York Press, 1989. 63-70.

Robert T. Lambdin

VULGATE, THE. St. *Jerome was commissioned by Pope Damasus (366-84) to compose this late version of the Bible. The work derives its name from the Latin "vulgatus," made public or common; Jerome began the work in 382, using Greek and Hebrew sources. Jerome's text was used in the first printed Bible, the Mazarin Bible. The work became the authorized Latin text of the Roman Catholic Church, and Pope Clement VIII (1592-1605) had this work revised into the Clementine text.

SELECTED BIBLIOGRAPHY

Barr, Jane. "The Vulgate 'Genesis' and St. Jerome's Attitude to Women." In *Equally in God's Image: Women in the Middle Ages*. Julia Bolton Holloway, Constance S. Wright, and Joan Bechtold, eds. New York: Peter Lang, 1990. 122-28; McQuaig, William. "The Tridentine Ruling on the Vulgate and Ecclesiastical Censorship in the 1580s." *Renaissance and Reformation* 18:3 (Summer 1994), 43-55; Thompson, John J. "Literary Associations of an Anonymous Middle English Paraphrase of Vulgate Psalm L." *Medium Ævum* 57:1 (1988), 38-55.

Robert T. Lambdin

VULGATE CYCLE, THE. The Vulgate Cycle is a group of Arthurian *romances (*see Arthurian Legend*) written in French prose. This collection was composed sometime around 1230 and contains the three romances that constitute the prose *Lancelot*: *Lancelot*, the *Queste del Saint Graal*, and *Mort Artu*. Besides these great romances, the olio also contains the *Estoire del Saint Graal* and *Merlin*, obviously both concerned with the Arthurian legend. The cycle is valuable because it became extremely popular, working its way from the continent to Britain. There it was an influence on *Geoffrey of Monmouth's rendition of the Arthurian legends. Further, Thomas *Malory relied heavily upon this version in his construction and accounts of Arthur and Camelot in the *Morte D'Arthur*.

SELECTED BIBLIOGRAPHY

Burns, E. Jane. *Arthurian Fictions: Rereading the "Vulgate Cycle."* Columbus: Ohio State University Press for Miami University, 1985; Burns, E. Jane. "'La Voie de la voix': The Aesthetics of Indirection in the *Vulgate Cycle* I *The Legacy of Chrétien de Troyes*, Norris J. Lacy, Douglas Kelly, and Keith Busby, eds. Amsterdam. Rodopi, 1988. 151-67; Saycell, K. J. "Romance and Mysticism: Saint Bernard and the Thirteenth Century Arthurian Vulgate Cycle." *Unisa* 29:1 (Apr 1991), 1-7.

Robert T. Lambdin

W

WAKEFIELD MASTER. The individual known only as the Wakefield Master is credited with authoring and/or revising several plays within the Towneley Cycle (See **Drama**). He is an unknown cleric whose dramatic skills far exceeded those of his contemporaries. His best-known work is the most often anthologized play within the whole of medieval drama, The *Second Shepherd's Play*. Other plays attributed to the pen of the Wakefield Master are the following: *Noah, The First Shepherd's Play, Herod the Great,* and *The Buffeting*. Portions of other plays bear the signs of the Wakefield Master's authorship; these include four stanzas within *The Conspiracy*, approximately twenty-two stanzas within the *Scourging*, one stanza in both *The Crucifixion* and *The Pilgrims*, nine stanzas within *The Dicing*, and approximately forty stanzas within *The Judgement*. Of course, his influence on these latter plays is entirely speculative.

The Wakefield Master's authorship is determined by techniques largely unique to him within medieval drama. Chief among these is the use of a nine-line stanza. His plays also demonstrate a highly developed sense of the comic. *The Second Shepherd's Play,* for instance, focuses on the comic machinations of a group of rascals and yet is ostensibly a Nativity play. Another feature of the Wakefield Master's technique is the inclusion of social satire. In the aforementioned play the three shepherds begin by alluding to various social ills, including the conflicts between the classes, between husband and wife, and between employers and employees. Two final features that identify the Wakefield Master's work are his use of colloquial diction and his references to events and locations in and around the town of Wakefield.

SELECTED BIBLIOGRAPHY

Helterman, J. *Symbolic Action in the Plays of the Wakefield Master*. Athens, GA: University of Georgia Press, 1981; Meredith, Peter. "The Towneley Cycle." In *The Cambridge Companion to Medieval English Theatre*. Ed. Richard Beadle. Cambridge: Cambridge University Press, 1994. 134-62.

James Keller

WALDHERE. *Waldhere* is an *Old English epic heroic verse probably from the eighth century. Among many continental variants, the best-known is the Latin poem *Waltharius* by Ekkehard of St. Gall, from the first half of the tenth century. Its "happy ending" makes it notable in an age of tragic climaxes.

Alphere, king of Aquitaine, has a son, Waltharius, who is betrothed to Hiltgund, daughter of Herericus, king of Burgundy. But when Attila, king of the Huns, invades, he takes both children as hostages, as well as much treasure. Likewise, seeing that there is no hope of resistance, the king of the Franks voluntarily sends as hostage a youth of noble birth named Hagano. Both boys win renown as Attila's warriors, but Hagano escapes, leaving Waltharius to become Attila's chief general. Upon his return from a victorious campaign, Waltharius gives the customary feast to the king and his court, but when all their guests are deep in drunken sleep, Waltharius and Hiltgund flee, taking with them much gold. Crossing the Rhine near Worms, they are besieged in a Vosges cave by Guntharius, king of the Franks, Hagano, and eleven soldiers. Waltharius offers half the gold as an equivalent division, but Guntharius demands all the gold plus Hiltgund and their horses. In righteous rage Waltharius slays all eleven of the soldiers, but Hagano and Guntharius lie in wait and fall upon them when they venture out of the cave. All three of the main contestants are maimed, but Waltharius is able to escape and finally seal the earlier betrothal with marriage to Hiltgund.

Two fragments remain of the original manuscript, A and B, both in the Copenhagen Royal Library. In A, Hiltgund warns Waltharius not to rush into battle: "I am burdened / With fear that too fiercely . . . to the fight thou shalt rush." She urges him to remember that God will protect him and the wonderful sword, Miming, the handiwork of Weland.

In B, Guntharius boasts of wielding an even better sword sent by Theodoric to Widia, son of Weland. The fragment ends with the assurance that "the holy Lord" will grant victory to the combatant who in "his earlier work . . . has earned the reward."

SELECTED BIBLIOGRAPHY

Andersson, Theodore M. "The Speeches in the 'Waldere' Fragments." In *De Gustibus*. John Miles Foley and J. Chris Womack, eds. New York: Garland, 1992. 21-29; Dickins, B. *Runic and Heroic Poems of the Old Teutonic Peoples.* Cambridge: Cambridge University Press, 1915; Garde, Judith N. *Old English Poetry in Medieval Christian Perspective: A Doctrinal Approach.* Cambridge: Brewer, 1995; Hill, Joyce, ed. *Old English Minor Heroic Poems.* Durham, Eng.: Department of English Language and Medieval Literature, 1983; Pasternack, Carol Braun. *The Textuality of Old English Poetry.* Cambridge: Cambridge University Press, 1995.

Elton E. Smith

WALLACE, SIR WILLIAM (c. 1270 -1305). A Scottish patriot who was the subject of poet *Blind Harry's (*see* ***Henry the Minstrel***) *The Wallace*, William Wallace has been heralded by as much acclaim as virtually any hero, has been remembered in popular songs, and has become a part of the national temperament of the Scotland that he fought to make free. The son of Sir Malcolm Wallace, knight of Elderslie, and his wife, the daughter of Sir Raynauld Crawford, sheriff of Ayr, he was born during the reign of Alexander III. His Scotland had fallen under English rule during the reign of *Edward I, whose soldiers were left to garrison the Scots castles and towns.

Wallace raised a small band of loyal men who raided the English convoys and foraging parties. Joining forces with Sir Andrew de Moray, they defeated the English army at Stirling Bridge in 1297 and later captured Berwick in raids upon northern England. Wallace became the recognized leader of the Scottish resistance and was knighted and named Guardian of Scotland by John Balliol. As leader, Wallace lost the support of many of the dissenting Scots lords and was severely outnumbered twice when Edward raised armies of thousands with archers and cavalry to quell the Scottish Problem. In an early version of the scorched earth policy, Wallace and his men retreated and took the goods of the fields and the livestock with them.

In the battle at Falkirk Wallace was betrayed and lost part of his force when in the heat of battle the leader of a large part of the army marched off the field, leaving Wallace to retreat and flee from the English. Realizing his situation, Wallace left for France to attempt to gain support. Not getting it, he returned to Scotland in 1303 and continued to lead a small band of men in raids against the English. After a series of victories against the English, Wallace was betrayed by a servant, captured, and brought to London. Accused of treason, he was condemned to death, hanged, and drawn and quartered in 1305. His head was placed on a pole on London Bridge.

Wallace was revered as a national hero. Many of the facts that are known about his life are preserved in *The Wallace* written by the poet Blind Harry in about 1460. Composed nearly a hundred years after *Barbour's work, it was meant to be a companion to *The *Bruce*. Wallace's life was supposedly also detailed in Arnold Blair's Latin *Life of Wallace*, although that work has not survived. Harry's work is occasionally entertaining, but often equally tedious. Given to exaggeration, even more so than Barbour in his sketch of a hero, Harry leads Wallace southward almost to the gates of London in his physical exploits of battle. Though lacking sight, he had an eye for detail in his descriptions.

Written in a form reminiscent of Geoffrey *Chaucer and William *Dunbar, *The Wallace* sustains the form for its eleven books of some 12,000 lines. Although not generally included in the group known as the Scottish Chaucerians or Makars (*see* ***Scottish Literature***), poet Harry does seem to have used Chaucer's verse as a model, though by no means did he rival it. Choosing the romantic rather than the historical approach to preserving his hero Wallace, Harry appropriately depicts the hero in the larger-than-life proportions that the figure acquired in the eyes of his Scottish nation. William Wallace, the figure of Blind

Harry's poem, though he lost his life, was victorious in the legends of his nation because he never ceased to fight for the freedom of his Scotland, no matter what the cost.

SELECTED BIBLIOGRAPHY

Goldstein, R. James. "Blind Harry's Myth of Blood: The Ideological Closure of the *Wallace.*" *Studies in Scottish Literature* 25 (1990), 70-82; Harward, V. "Harrys *Wallace* and Chaucer's *Troilus and Criseyde.*" *Studies in Scottish Literature* 10 (1972), 48-50; Schofeld, W. H. *Mythical Bards and the Life of William Wallace.* Cambridge: Harvard University Press, 1920; Walsh, Elizabeth. "Harry's *Wallace*: The Evolution of a Hero." *Scottish Literary Journal* 11:1 (May 1984), 5-19.

J. Scott Plaster

WALTHER VON DER VOGELWEIDE (c. 1170-1230). Walther von der Vogelweide, a German *minnesinger is among the most renowned of the medieval *lyric poets. He was attached to the Viennese court, but he left to become a wandering *minstrel. He is noted for breaking from the conventions of traditional love poetry, twisting this tradition by making his poems vehicles for his religious and political opinions. He continued to do this even though he risked falling into disfavor with his patrons. The German national song "Deutschland, Deutschland über alles" is an adaptation of one of Walther's patriotic lyrics. In the 1845 opera *Tännhauser*, Wagner included a Walther character who appears as a contestant in a singing tournament.

SELECTED BIBLIOGRAPHY

Ebbinghaus, Ernst A. "Walther von der Vogelweide 18, 1-14; *Festschrift* for Frank Banta." In *Semper Idem et Novus.* Francis G. Gentry, ed. Cöppingen: Kümmerle, 1988. 187-91; Heinen, Hubert. "When Palor Pales: Reflections on Epigonality in Late 13th-Century Minnesongs." *Medieval Perspectives* 4-5 (1989-90), 53-68; McMahon, James V. *The Music of Early Minnesang.* Columbia, SC: Camden House, 1990; Wenzel, Horst. "Walther von der Vogelweide, Jesus Christ, and Jeff Wall: The Portrait of the Author in European Tradition." *SiM* 3:3-4 (Winter-Spring 1991), 453-66.

Robert T. Lambdin

"WANDERER, THE." "The Wanderer" is one of the so-called *Old English *elegies from the *Exeter Book. The poem is largely in the voice of an *eardstapa* ("earth-stepper") who relates his state of exile. His lord is dead, and he is separated from family, friends, and home. Even sleep, in which he might dream of joy and security in the lord's hall, proves burdensome, for upon awakening the contrast with the state of exile makes the sorrow even sharper.

The speaker then considers how the wise man will realize that everything on earth is transitory, everything falls eventually to ruin. The poem ends with the conclusion that contemplation of the transitory world ought to lead one to put one's trust in heaven, the only place where the immutable can be found.

Interpretation of the poem has varied depending on which parts of the poem are assigned to the wanderer's direct discourse and which to the narrator (the manuscript does not indicate speech with punctuation). If the final remarks about turning one's mind to God are in the narrator's voice, then the wanderer is left in a meditation of sorrow, without realizing the hope of Christian salvation. It seems equally plausible, however, to assign these words to the wanderer, which reinforces the poem's general movement from sorrow to wisdom. Like "The *Seafarer," "The Wanderer" employs the theme of exile, but rather than a voluntary journey, the exile here seems a permanent state of human existence.

SELECTED BIBLIOGRAPHY

Conde-Silvestre, Juan C., comp. 'The Wanderer' and 'The Seafarer': A Bibliography 1971-1991." *SELIM: Journal of the Spanish Society for Medieval English Language and Literature* 2 (1992), 170-86; Galloway, Andrew. "Dream Theory in 'The Dream of the Rood' and 'The Wanderer.'" *Review of English Studies* 45:180 (November 1994), 475-85; Green, Martin. "Man, Time, and Apocalypse in 'The Wanderer,' 'The Seafarer,' and *Beowulf.*" In *Old English Shorter Poems: Basic Readings.* Katherine O'Brien O'Keeffe, ed. New York: Garland, 1994. 281-302; Shippey, T. A. "'The Wanderer' and 'The Seafarer' as Wisdom Poetry." in *Companion to Old English Poetry.* Henk Aerston and Jolf H. Bremmer, Jr., eds. Amsterdam: Vrije University Press, 1994. 145-58.

Karl Hagen

WARS OF THE ROSES (1455-1485). The so-called "Wars of the Roses" were a series of encounters between members of the British House of York and the House of Lancaster. The skirmishes contested who was the rightful heir to the throne of England. The wars are named such because of the roses that were the emblems of the feuding houses: white for York and red for Lancaster. The factions were united in 1485 after Henry Tudor, earl of Richmond and a Lancastrian, defeated the Yorkist Richard III at the Battle of Bosworth Field. Henry was proclaimed King Henry VII and married Elizabeth of York, the daughter of Edward IV. This united the families and brought the dispute to an end.

SELECTED BIBLIOGRAPHY

Murph, Roxane C., comp. *The Wars of the Roses in Fiction: An Annotated Bibliography, 1440-1994.* Westport, CT: Greenwood Press, 1994; Ross, Charles. "Rumour, Propaganda, and Popular Opinion during the Wars of the Roses." In *Patronage, the*

Crown, and the Provinces in Later Medieval England. Ralph A. Griffiths, ed. Highlands, NJ: Sutton, 1981. 15-32.

Robert T. Lambdin

WELSH LITERATURE. Far fewer early works survive in Wales than in Ireland, and whereas Irish literature preserves a large number of prose narratives but relatively few poems, in Wales the situation is reversed. While poetry of many kinds flourished in Wales throughout the Middle Ages--from the poems of *Taliesin and Aneirin near the end of sixth century to the late medieval poetry of Dafydd ap Gwilym near the end of the fourteenth--only a small number of prose works survive. Those that do represent several different narrative genres, suggesting that many more works of each kind once probably existed. Also testifying to the existence of such stories is the *Welsh Triads*, a poem consisting of an extensive catalog of allusions to characters and events that must have been well-known to medieval audiences from oral tradition.

The early literature of Wales, like that of Ireland (*see* **Celtic Literature, Early**), was transmitted orally for many hundreds of years before some of it was written down during the later centuries of the Middle Ages. The earliest Welsh poets are Taliesin and Aneirin, and while their poems were not recorded until long after their original composition, scholars are confident in dating their elegies, battle poems, and heroic lays to the late sixth and early seventh centuries. About a dozen poems, written between 575 and 585, are attributed to Taliesin. His earliest poem eulogizes Cynan Garwy, the king of Powys in Wales, but most of his poems celebrate members of the ruling dynasty of Rheged, an area in southwestern Scotland. Taliesin's most highly-regarded poem is his elegy on Owain ab Urien of Rheged. His battle poems, "The Battle of Gwên Ystrad" and "The Battle of Argoed Llwyfain," contain descriptions of warfare similar to those occurring in other heroic works.

The Welsh battle poem of greatest renown, however, is Aneirin's "The Gododdin," which celebrates the heroic defeat of the northern British forces by the Saxons at Catterick. The title of the poem refers to the British kingdom of Gododdin, which stretched from Edinburgh southward to the River Tyne, encompassing much of present-day Northumberland. The poem relates how Mynddawd of Gododdin wined and dined three hundred crack British warriors for a year before leading them down the old Roman road to Catterick (in modern-day Yorkshire), where they engaged the Saxons. In the great battle that took place there the British forces were virtually annihilated. Aneirin praises the bravery of the fallen heroes in a series of stanzas arranged in "runs," where each stanza begins with repeated verses, giving them an almost incantational quality:

> Men went to Catraeth, embattled, with a cry,
> A host of horsemen in brown armour carrying shields,
> Spear-shafts held aloft with sharp points,

And shining mail-shirts and swords . . . .

Men went to Catraeth with the dawn,
Their ardour shortened their lives.
Before their hair turned grey, death came to them.

"The Gododdin" contains a passing reference to King Arthur (see **Arthurian Legend**), and if it is not a later addition, as some scholars suspect, it would be the earliest recorded reference to the legendary figure. The Black Book of Carmarthen also contains several poems and fragments (e.g., "The Stanzas of the Graves") that allude to the Arthurian legend. Perhaps the most intriguing early Welsh poem, however, is "The Spoils of Annwfyn" from the Book of Taliesin. This fragmentary poem describes a raid upon the Otherworld in which the men of Britain, led by Arthur, attempt to free a prisoner or attempt to retrieve a cauldron of rebirth (or of poetic inspiration?)--or possibly all of these things. It is not clear whether the mission succeeded, but it is clear that from the three ships that assailed Annwfyn, only seven men returned.

Although medieval Welsh literature does not possess large groups of interconnected tales like those in the Irish Cycles, the eleven tales of *The Mabinogion* are roughly similar. The first four tales, known as the Four Branches of the Mabinogi, provide a Welsh counterpart to the Irish Mythological Cycle, for these tales are constructed from an assortment of mythological incidents. Perhaps corresponding somewhat to the tales of the Ulster Cycle is *"Kulhwch and Olwen," a Welsh tale that combines a great many narrative elements, popular, traditional, and mythological; this story also appears to be the earliest surviving Arthurian tale of the Middle Ages. Corresponding to the Kings Cycle are the two pseudo-historical works of *The Mabinogion*, "The Dream of Maxen" and "Lludd and Llevelys," which are sometimes called "Brutian" tales because of their points of connection to *Geoffrey of Monmouth's *Historia Regum Brittaniae*. "The Dream of Rhonabwy" is like none of the others but appears to be a piece of Arthurian satire that humorously plays off the splendors of Arthur's court against the coarser realities of medieval life. The remaining tales in *The Mabinogion*--the courtly romances "Owein," "Peredur," and "Gereint and Enid"--find closer parallels in *French literature than in Irish literature, and each of them has a direct counterpart in one of the *romances of *Chrétien de Troyes.

The first four tales of *The Mabinogion* are probably the work of a single author-redactor of the late eleventh century, a man who wove a complex narrative tapestry out of mythological materials he did not fully understand and into which he inserted story elements common in international folklore. Among the narrative elements and motifs in the Four Branches deriving from Celtic mythological tradition are the Waste Land theme, a raid conducted by mortals into the Otherworld, and the involvement of a human in an Otherworldly conflict. The Four Branches of the Mabinogi may be the fossilized remains of a cycle of tales concerning Pryderi, who is also called Mabon. It is from the name Mabon that the term "Mabinogi" derives, meaning stories about the family of the divine Mabon.

"Pwyll," the First Branch of *The Mabinogion*, focuses on Pwyll and Rhiannon, the parents of Pryderi, and describes events leading up to Pryderi's birth and childhood. In the opening section of the story, which has similarities to the Irish tale "The Wasting Sickness of Cü Chulainn," Pwyll must atone for a breach of courtesy by spending a year and a day in the Otherworld and by doing battle there against an enemy of Arawn, the king of Annwfyn. In the second section Pwyll is rewarded for his good service to Arawn by the appearance of the beautiful horse-woman Rhiannon. Pwyll and Rhiannon plan to be married, but before they can be, Pwyll unwittingly commits another blunder, this time in the form of a rash promise. As a result, he nearly loses Rhiannon to a rival; but in the end, by following Rhiannon's wise advice, Pwyll is able to win her back. In the third section of "Pwyll" Rhiannon bears Pwyll a son, but the boy mysteriously vanishes and Rhiannon is accused of killing him. On May Eve the boy re-appears in a remote area to an ordinary couple. They raise the lad as their own son, but eventually the foster father notices the boy's resemblance to Pwyll and realizes that he must be the king's lost child. The boy is reunited with his true parents, and Rhiannon's innocence is established. Following Pwyll's death, Pryderi becomes ruler of the seven cantrevs of Dyved.

The most complex tale in *The Mabinogion* is "Kulhwch and Olwen," which describes how Arthur's nephew Kulhwch was able to win the hand of Olwen, the giant's daughter. Blended together in this remarkable story are many narrative elements and motifs from Celtic folklore. In addition to myths of the seasons and regeneration myths, the story contains such well-known devices as the jealous stepmother, the fair unknown, the request for a boon, the undertaking of a series of impossible tasks, advice from the oldest animals, assistance from the helpful animals, a raid upon the Otherworld, and the pursuit of a havoc-wreaking beast. "Kulhwch and Olwen" also possesses wide-ranging tonal qualities, including passages of brutal realism and delicate lyricism, displays of rhetorical virtuosity, and many humorous and whimsical observations and situations. King Arthur plays only a supporting role in the tale, but he is the central figure in an extended episode in which he and his men pursue the terrible boar Twrch Trwyth across the hills and valleys of western Britain.

"Peredur Son of Evrawg," one of the three courtly romances in *The Mabinogion*, is a close analogue to *Chrétien de Troyes's *Perceval. Both Chrétien's Perceval and *The Mabinogion*'s Peredur are naïve Welsh lads who emerge from their sheltered forest upbringings and quickly take their place among King Arthur's finest knights. Peredur and Perceval are the original Grail knights in Arthurian literature (pre-dating Galahad), and their stories are the earliest ones to merge the themes of the Maimed King and the Waste Land with the Grail theme. The relationship between "Peredur" and Chrétien's *Perceval* has never been determined, though it is possible that they stem from a common source. Because "Peredur" is a good deal less polished and courtly, it may provide a better reflection of the original narrative material.

The final Welsh story to be mentioned here is "The Tale of Gwion Bach." While this story was not recorded prior to the sixteenth century, it is undoubtedly an old one. It tells how Gwion Bach came to acquire the drops of poetic inspiration and how he was chased by the witch Ceridwen, who finally caught him and swallowed him, with the result that he was reborn as Taliesin. The story then concerns Taliesin, relating how he came to the court of Maelgwn of Gwynedd as a youth of thirteen and confounded the king's *bards, thereby rescuing his master Elphin--whose hapless actions are recounted in the nineteenth century in Thomas Love Peacock's novel *The Misfortunes of Elphin*.

During the twelfth and thirteenth centuries Wales produced a group of poets called the Poets of the Princes. Some sixty of them are known by name, and Hywel ab Owain Gwynedd (c. 1140-1170) is considered one of the best. The Poets of the Princes were trained over long periods of time, and their poems reflect a large number of formal conventions including extensive alliteration, internal rhyming, and a variety of metrical patterns. The most remarkable development during this period was the creation of a complex metrical system known as *cynghanedd*. *Cynghanedd* is somewhat similar to *Anglo-Saxon *alliterative verse, though a good deal more complicated. For our purposes, let it suffice to say that *cynghanedd*, under the organizing direction of the main stresses within a line of verse, involves a pattern of different consonant sounds that are repeated in a strict order throughout a line of verse.

The greatest Welsh poet of the Middle Ages is Dafydd ap Gwilym, who lived and wrote in Wales about the same time that Geoffrey *Chaucer was living and writing in London. Like Chaucer, he was influenced by literary developments on the Continent and yet remained a remarkably original poet. He possessed a delightful sense of irony and a genius for satire, and he wrote in a variety of forms and styles. Dafydd wrote about nature ("A Celebration of Summer") and about love ("The Mist"), and he wrote serious meditative poems such as "The Ruin." His love of comic narrative is reflected in "In a Tavern," a poem squarely in the *fabliau* tradition. In this short verse-tale the speaker attempts to seduce a serving girl after the tavern's customers have retired to their beds. But he is thwarted by a series of mishaps involving the banging and clanging of kitchen utensils, the barking of dogs, and the intervention of three vulgar Englishmen who try to beat him up. By the end of his harrowing experience, the narrator is just grateful to have survived his ordeal in one piece.

Although little is known about many of the authors of early Celtic literary works, that is not the case for several early Celts of historical significance. One such figure is the early Irish leader Brian Borumha (A. D. 926-1014), who achieved for Ireland many of the things that *Alfred the Great had achieved in England a century earlier. In 976 Brian assumed the kingship of Munster, and in the following decades he attempted to bring the other provincial kings of Ireland under his control. In 1005 Brian finally achieved supremacy over the other Irish provinces and was invested at Armagh as *Imperator Scotorum*. After having united Ireland under his rule, Brian encouraged his countrymen to restore the churches ravaged by the Vikings and to revive learning and the arts. He also forced Ireland's Viking settlers into restricted areas close to the seaports. But in 1014 the Vikings, led by Sihtric of Dublin, rose up against the Irish. Brian and his

Munstermen, with support from one of his oldest enemies, Malachy of Tara, engaged the Vikings at the Battle of Clontarf. There Brian and several other Irish leaders fell, yet the Irish were victorious. Sihtric retained possession of the area around Dublin, but most of the surviving Vikings departed from Ireland, never to return.

Two pairs of men--Llywelyn the Great and his grandson Llywelyn ap Gryfudd in Wales, and William *Wallace and Robert the Bruce in Scotland-- emerged as prominent nationalistic figures during the thirteenth and early fourteenth centuries. Llywelyn the Great ruled over Gwynedd from 1194 to 1240. In the early decades of the thirteenth century he participated in the baronial revolt against England's King *John, and in 1218 he forced the English regency to accept the Peace of Worcester, giving him control over much of North and South Wales. Llywelyn's expansionist designs in Wales were continued by his grandson, Llywelyn ap Gruffydd, who in 1258 bestowed upon himself the title Prince of Wales. However, the younger Llywelyn's refusal to do homage to *Edward I of England provoked England's invasion of Wales during the 1270s and 1280s. When Llywelyn ap Gruffydd was killed in 1282, Welsh dreams of independence died with him--at least for the time being.

After quashing the Welsh rebellion, Edward I turned his attentions to Scotland. Things came to a head when John Balliol, whom Edward had invested as King of Scotland, refused to assist Edward in his war against *Philip IV, the Fair, of France and instead forged his own alliance with France. Edward quickly forced Balliol to abdicate and then annexed Scotland to England as a "forfeited fief." Adding insult to injury, the English took possession of the Stone of Scone-- on which Scottish kings had been crowned since ancient times--and removed it to Westminster Abbey. It was then that William Wallace, the son of a lesser Scottish nobleman, rallied his countrymen. Wallace led his war party in a series of successful guerrilla raids upon their English overlords. Determined to put down this upstart, Edward himself led the English army to Scotland. The English met the Scots at Falkirk, and the Scots, led by Wallace, were soundly defeated. But they continued to fight on, and Wallace's execution in 1305 only fanned the flames of Scottish nationalism.

Scotland's cause was taken up by Robert the Bruce, a Scottish nobleman whose early career had been marked by duplicity and treachery. In 1306 Robert went to Glasgow, where he received absolution for his sins; shortly thereafter he received the Scottish crown at Scone. Upon the death of Edward I in 1307, Robert's task became easier, for Edward's son Edward II had little ability in military matters. In 1314 at Bannockburn, Robert the Bruce led the Scots in their crushing defeat of the English and in so doing won the hearts of his people. He is celebrated in several medieval poems, including John Barbour's *The Bruce*, written in the Middle Scots dialect of English. William Wallace is celebrated in the poem *The Wallace*, written by the Scottish poet Blind Harry (Henry the Minstrel).

The Christianized Celts also produced several notable churchmen, including John Scotus Erigena, one of the great intellectuals of the earlier Middle

Ages. Born in Ireland early in the ninth century, John rose to prominence as the head of the palace school of Charles the Bald in France. In 851 he produced the book *On Predestination*, in which he denied the existence of evil. When his work was condemned as heretical, John remained undaunted. He created additional controversy when he declared that the communion Host was not God's body but only a symbol of it. When his long-time protector Charles the Bald died in 877, John Scotus Erigena was forced to leave France. At the invitation of King Alfred, he took up a teaching position at Malmesbury in England, where he remained until his death. Two centuries later the English historian *William of Malmesbury wrote that John Scotus Erigena was stabbed by his own students "because he tried to make them think."

In the second quarter of the twelfth century the English churchman Geoffrey of Monmouth produced one of the most important literary works of the twelfth century, *Historia Regum Brittaniae*. Written in Latin, this work not only describes the founding of Britain by the legendary Brutus but also contains the first extensive literary account of the life of King Arthur. Geoffrey was born in Monmouth, a town on the Welsh Marches, and his work reflects his familiarity with Wales and a particular fondness for the ancient city of Caerleon. Geoffrey claimed to be translating "an ancient British book"--that is, one written in Welsh-- at the request of Walter, the Archdeacon of Oxford. That claim has long been doubted, yet there can be little doubt that his work contains much legendary material that stems from early Celtic tradition. Geoffrey's work is also the first to associate King Arthur with the legendary Merlin.

*Giraldus Cambrensis, or Gerald the Welshman, was born about 1146 at Manorbier, Pembrokeshire. His father was William de Barri, one of the great Norman lords of South Wales, but his grandmother had been Welsh. Gerald prepared for a career in the church, studying first at St. Peter's Abbey in Gloucester and then at the University of Paris. After returning to his native land, he accompanied Prince John to Ireland in 1184, during *Henry II's conquest of Ireland. From that experience he wrote the *Topography of Ireland* and the *History of the Conquest of Ireland*. Later Gerald wrote *A Description of Wales* and *A Journey through Wales*, describing his experiences as he accompanied the archbishop of Canterbury through Wales in an attempt to enlist support for the Crusades. Gerald's life-long aspiration was to become the bishop of St. David's, but he died in 1223 without achieving his dream.

Walter *Map, born about 1135, was a senior contemporary of Gerald's. Like Gerald, he was part English and part Welsh, and he too studied first at St. Peter's Abbey in Gloucester and then in Paris. Throughout his adult life Map was closely connected to the court of Henry II. He served as the king's justice in Wales and the West Midlands and became chancellor of Lincoln and finally archdeacon of Oxford. After his death in 1209 or 1210, Map's name was attached to a large group of satiric poems, though scholars now limit his authorship to a few Latin poems and the long work *De Nugis Curialium* (Courtiers' trifles), which contains a wide array of tales, anecdotes, and satiric attacks. Map's keenest satire was directed at monasticism and specifically the Cistercians. His other satiric target was marriage, which he bitterly ridiculed in the widely ciculated *Epistola Valerii ad Rufinum* (The letter of Valerius to Rufinus) contained in part IV of the *De Nugis*. But the *De Nugis* is most notable for reflecting Map's great love of stories about supernatural phenomena. There are stories about fairy lovers, stories about strange knights who appear at tournaments and then suddenly vanish, and one about an ancient British king who makes a brief visit to the Celtic Otherworld only to find on his return to the mortal realm that hundreds of years have passed.

SELECTED BIBLIOGRAPHY

Jarman, A. O. H. and Gwilym Rees Hughes, *A Guide to Welsh Literature.* Vol. I. Swansea: C. Davis, 1976; Parry, Thomas. *A History of Welsh Literature.* Trans. By H. I. Bell, Oxford: Clarendon Press, 1955; Rees, Alwyn, and Brinley Rees. *Celtic Heritage.* London: Thomas and Hudson, 1961.

John Conlee

WEYDEN, ROGIER VAN DER (c. 1400-1464). A Flemish painter who joined the workshop of Robert Campin in 1427, Rogier van der Weyden added a new spiritual quality to works of his time. His fluid and dynamic compositions stress human action and drama, but are religious in theme. His paintings express a yearning to share in the passion of Christ.

        Some of his earlier works are influenced by Campin and Jan van Eyck, yet unlike his mentors he placed the figures and action onto a shallow stage to focus the observers' attention and to impose a disciplined structure. *Descent from the Cross* is considered by some to be his finest religious work. *Francisco d'Este* and *Madonna and Child With Four Saints* bear the arms of the Medici family, indicating that the painter may have worked for Italian patrons, though some critics discount that he visited Rome in 1450. He gained international fame and influenced painters not only in Flanders, but throughout Europe.

SELECTED BIBLIOGRAPHY

Campbell, Lorne. *Van der Weyden.* New York: Harper and Row, 1980; Davies, Martin. *Rogier van der Weyden: An Essay with a Critical Catalogue of Paintings Assigned to Him and to Robert Campin.* New York: Phaidon, 1972; Gardner, Helen. *Gardner's Art Through The Ages.* 6th Edition. San Diego: Harcourt Brace Jovanovich, 1975.

Libby Bernardin

WIDSITH. *Widsith* is an epic heroic Old English poem of the late sixth or early seventh century. The title character's very name, Widsith (Faraway) suggests that this is not so much the autobiography of a single man as the story of the ideal *scop or *minstrel who not only lists the mead-halls in which he has sung and the gifts that were given to him, but also sets up a geography and chronology impossible for a single man. Even if lines 75 and 82-84 are interpolated, it strains the bounds of possibility to hear of the tribes among whom he traveled: Caesar and the Romans, Israelites, Assyrians, Egyptians, and so on. Thus, although the genealogy may be taken as genuine (ll. 1-5), and the list of great tribal chieftains (ll. 10-49) may include some he actually met, there are still such anomalies as Alexander the Great and Attila the Hun: So when he makes the claim "So forth I fared . . . in foreign lands All over the earth" he is merging actual contemporary rulers along with a list of the great he would have cherished meeting--rather like imaginary conversations with the mighty dead. He also makes a surprising claim for the viewpoint of the pagan epic: "Of evil and good There I made trial." We are accustomed to the chest-beating of heroes mighty in battle, but scarcely to a census of those who are evil and those who are good. When he does travel among warring factions, he makes the appreciative comment: "These warriors were not . . . the worst of comrades" (125). In the tradition of excessive praise, he modestly describes his songs sung in harmony with harp accompaniment: "They never had heard . . . a nobler song." Line 94 of *Widsith* marks a return from imagined heroes and tribes to his actual home and tribal chieftain and his wife:

> . . . when I came to my home,
> To my beloved prince, . . . the lord of the Myrgings,
> Who gave me the land . . . that was left by my father;
> And Ealhhild then also . . . another ring gave me,
> Queen of the doughty anew, . . . the daughter of Eadwine.
> Her praise has passed . . . to all parts of the world ,
> Wherever in song . . . I sought to tell
> Where I knew under heavens . . . the noblest of queens,
> Golden-adorned, . . . giving forth treasures.

The poet is perfectly justified in claiming that his song has immortalized his queen, for without the epic, what would we know about Ealhhild, Eadwine, and indeed the Myrgings themselves? Back home again, among old friends and familiar faces, he draws two summaries from his long wandering. Having weighed the balances of good and evil, he decides for the lords:

> So I ever have found . . . as I fared among men
> That in all the land . . . most beloved is he
> To whom God giveth . . . a goodly kingdom
> To hold as long . . . as he liveth here.

This is the temporal blessing that can come to a lord. What of the minstrels who wander, sing, and evaluate what they experience?

> Thus wandering widely . . . through many lands,

> Express their needs . . . and speak their thanks.
> Ever south and north . . . some one thye meet
> Skillful in song . . . who scatters gifts,
> To further his fame . . . before his chieftains,
> To do deeds of honor, . . . till all shall depart,
> Light and life together: . . . lasting praise he gains,
> And has under heaven . . . the highest honor.

The minstrel indeed receives rich gifts, but has it in his powers of song to give the even richer gift of immortality.

SELECTED BIBLIOGRAPHY

Bliss, Alan. "The Aviones and 'Widsith' 26a." *Anglo-Saxon England* 14 (1985), 97-106; Brown, Ray. "The Begging Scop and the Generous King in 'Widseth.'" *Neophilologus* 73:2 (April 1989), 281-92; Chambers, R. W. *Widsith: A Study in Old English Heroic Legend.* New York: Russell and Russell, 1970; Conybeare, John Josias. *Illustrations of Anglo-Saxon Poetry.* New York: Haskell House, 1964; Fry, Donald K. "Two Voices in 'Widsith.'" *Mediaevalia* 6 (1980), 37-56; Hill, Joyce. "Widsid and the Tenth Century." In *Old English Shorter Poems: Basic Readings.* Katherine O'Brien O'Keeffe, ed. New York: Garland, 1994. 319-33; Jacobs, Nicolas. "The Old English Heroic Tradition in Light of Welsh Evidence." *Cambridge Medieval Celtic Studies* 2 (Winter 1981), 9-20; Rallman, David A. "'Widsith' as an Anglo-Saxon Defense of Poetry." *Neophilologus* 66:3 (July 1982), 431-39.

Elton E. Smith

"WIFE OF BATH'S TALE, THE." "The Wife of Bath's Tale" story from Geoffrey *Chaucer's *Canterbury Tales* (c. 1387-1400) is an *exemplum answering the question "What do women most want?" A knight is given a year and a day to discover the answer to this question because he raped a young maiden; if he cannot answer correctly, he will be killed at King Arthur's court (*see* **Arthurian Legend**). When the time has elapsed, the knight returns none the wiser for his traveling and questioning. Just as he despairs, a group of dancing maidens capture his attention. The dancers all disappear, leaving only an old hag.

The hag promises to give the knight the correct answer if he will vow to do whatever she asks. They go to court and he answers as the hag tells him that women most desire to have sovereignty over their husbands. All of the women in court agree that this is true, so the hag demands that the knight marry her.

The knight is horrified at the thought of sharing a marriage bed with a foul witch, so she offers him a choice: She can be ugly and faithful or beautiful and unfaithful. The knight asks the hag to make the choice, which clearly indicates that he has learned his lesson. She rewards him by being both beautiful and faithful.

SELECTED BIBLIOGRAPHY

Bush, Douglas. *English Poetry.* New York, Oxford University Press, 1963; Garbáty, Thomas J. *Medieval English Literature.* Toronto: Heath, 1984; Lambdin, Laura C., and Robert T. Lambdin, eds. *Chaucer's Pilgrims: An Historical Guide to the Pilgrims in the "Canterbury Tales."* Westport, CT: Greenwood Press, 1996.

Laura Cooner Lambdin

WILLIAM I (THE CONQUERER) (1027-1087) Norman, king of England (1066-1087). William, a Norman leader, won the Battle of Hastings (October 14, 1066) against Harold, English king and earl of Wessex. This victory brought about almost immediate collapse of the English cause in the south, speedy submission, acceptance of William, and William's coronation. In the north William put down "the great rising of Morca and Edwin" by 1069. In that same year William led a terrible "harrying of the north" as a warning. He depopulated a strip of the northern English countryside from York to Durham and ended all opposition. By 1070 William had brought the rest of England under his rule. He built garrison castles in the problem areas with the use of forced labor.

William reduced all opposition militarily, then confiscated all lands of those in rebellion. Theoretically, every bit of land in England then belonged to the king; in fact, only the great estates changed hands and were assigned to the followers of William based upon Norman tenure. The king retained about one-sixth of the land for himself, but less than one-half of the land went to the Normans. Except on the border, the earldoms, reduced in size became honorific; few compact holdings survived. Great tenants-in-chief and numerous other lesser tenants emerged. A direct oath (the Oath of Salisbury) was required of all vassals. Construction of castles (except on the borders) became a matter of royal license, and coinage became a royal monopoly. Private war was prohibited; Anglo-Saxon shires and hundreds were continued for administrative purposes.

When London was granted a charter, local custom was guaranteed. Also, the monarchy established a royal council, the Great Council (*curia regis*), which met infrequently (three meetings per year were required). This replaced the Anglo-Saxon Witan.

The church was allowed to retain its lands. Pope Alexander II had blessed William's conquest; William instituted the much needed Cluniac reforms. Older bishops were replaced by zealous Norman reformers. *Lanfranc, a new archbishop of Canterbury, carried through widespread reform. He enforced celibacy, reorganized monastic chapters, established new school disciplines, and founded numerous monastic orders. Episcopal jurisdiction was separated from lay jurisdiction. The bishops were given their own courts, which was a decisive step in the foundation of common law as an independent force. William drew his chief administrators from the church. Without royal approval, no papal bull or brief nor papal legate might be received. The king retained a veto on all decrees.

Dangelt, shire farms, judicial fines, and the usual feudal revenues were all made non-feudal revenue. The great Domesday survey occurred when royal commissioners on circuit collected an oath from the citizens of the counties and villages giving full information as to size, resources, and present and past ownership of every piece of land. Arranged by counties, the *Domesday Book gave a unique record as a basis for taxation and administration.

SELECTED BIBLIOGRAPHY

Douglas, David Charles. *William the Conqueror: The Norman Impact upon England.* London: Methuen, 1977; Houts, Elisabeth M. C. van. "Camden, Cotton, and the Chronicles of the Norman Conquest of England." *British History Journal* 18:2 (Autumn 1992), 148-62; Townsend, David. "Anglo-Latin Hagiography and the Latin Transition." *Exemplaria* 3:2 (Fall 1991), 385-433.

R. Churchill Curtis

WILLIAM OF MALMESBURY (1095-1143). William of Malmesbury was a monk at the Abbey of Malmesbury in Wiltshire. He was born in 1095 and had one parent of Norman and one of English descent. Early in life he devoted himself to the Abbey of Malmesbury and worked under the abbot in the abbey library, later becoming the abbey librarian. He was the greatest scholar the abbey ever produced, and his familiarity with the resources of the library allowed him to be a student of varied interests, studying the Scriptures, *hagiography, theology, the classics, canon law, and history. It would seem that William could have written on any number of subjects, but he chose primarily to devote his writing to history in Latin. He was the first monk since *Bede to produce numerous historical texts and wrote one of the earliest secular histories of England, his *Gesta Regum.*

One of the most interesting elements of William's work is that he revised his works a number of times. In some cases we have early and later copies of the same work and can see what influenced his revisions. His earlier work is more trusting of dubious sources and more likely to embellish and elaborate on stories and fantastic legends. His later revisions are in a leaner style that attempts to achieve greater factual accuracy. He revised his *Gesta Regum* twice and his history of the church, *Gesta Pontificum*, once. Additionally he wrote *The Life of Saint *Dunstan* and a history of Glastonbury Abbey. He was working on his *Historia Novella,* a chronicle of factual events in the style of the **Anglo-Saxon Chronicle,* up until his death.

William recognized Bede as the only professional historian of Britain prior to his time and found the *Anglo-Saxon Chronicle* too crude for his liking, but he used both sources to create his histories, which include many lively, if sometimes uncredible, stories. He acknowledged many of his sources in a manner similar to Bede's and found every variety of history worthy of his attention, writing hagiography, secular and ecclesiastical histories, and a biography of King Edward, now lost, during his career. His extensive writing and rewriting and his mature attention to accuracy make him the premiere historian of his century. (*See **Chronicles and Annals.***)

SELECTED BIBLIOGRAPHY

Gransden, Antonia. *Historical Writing in England c. 550 to c. 1307.* Ithaca: Cornell University Press, 1974; Smalley, Beryl. *Historians in the Middle Ages.* New York: Scribner's, 1974; Sterns, Indrikis. *The Greater Medieval Historians: An Interpretation and a Bibliography.* Lanham, MD: University Press of America, 1980; William of Malmesbury. *William of Malmesbury's Chronicle of the Kings of England: From the Earliest Period to the Reign of King Stephen,* New York: AMS Press, 1968. Wright, Neil. "William of Malmesbury and Latin Poetry: Further Evidence of a Benedictine Reading." *Revue Benedictine* 101:1 (1991), 122-53.

Richard McDonald

WILLIAM OF PALERNE. *William of Palerne* is among the first English *romances of the fourteenth century *alliterative revival. The work is based upon the twelfth century French *Roman de Guillaume de Palerne* and was evidently composed under the patronage of Humphrey de Bohun. The romance is not among the best of this genre, but it does contain many interesting traits. In the work William is the prince of Apulia, whose uncle tries to poison him. William is saved from this evil intent by a Spanish prince who has been turned into a werewolf by his evil stepmother. Thus this is one of the first instances that demonstrates the medieval belief in werewolves, or lycanthropy. William, saved from sure death, eventually marries Melior, the daughter of the Roman emperor, with whom he has been deeply smitten. William then departs for Spain, where he slays the king. This action breaks the spell upon the Spanish prince, and they all live productive lives.

SELECTED BIBLIOGRAPHY

Barron, W. R. J. "Alliterative Romance and the French Tradition." in *Middle English Alliterative Poetry and Its Literary Background: Seven Essays.* David Lawton, ed. Cambridge: Brewer, 1982. 70-87; Kooper, Erik. "Grace: The Healing Herb in 'William of Palerne.'" *Leeds Studies in English* 15 (1984), 83-93; Morgan, Hubert E. "'William of Palerne' and 'Alaflekks' Saga." *Florilegium* 6 (1984), 137-58.

Richard McDonald

"WULF AND EADWACER." "Wulf and Eadwacer" is an enigmatic nineteen line Old English poem that is one of the *elegies from the *Exeter Book. In this poem the speaker is a woman who wishes to see her exiled lover, Wulf. The work is a puzzle because the narrator appears to taunt someone named Eadwacer. Thus, while the poem's theme appears to be the separation of lovers, the poem may simply be a venting of frustration on behalf of the author.

SELECTED BIBLIOGRAPHY

Aertsen, Henk. "'Wulf and Eadwacer': A Woman's 'Cri de Cour'--For Whom, For What?" In *Companion to Old English Poetry*. Henk Aersten, ed. Amsterdam: Vrije University Press, 1994. 119-44; Baker, Peter S. "The Ambiguity of 'Wulf and Eadwacer.'" In *Old English Shorter Poems*.Katherine O'Brien O'Keeffe, ed. New York: Garland, 1994. 409-26; Hough, Carole A. "'Wulf and Eadwacer': A Note on Ungelic." *American Notes and Queries* 8:3 (Summer 1995), 3-6; Pulsiano, Phillip and Kirsten Wolf. "The 'Hwelp' in 'Wulf and Eadwacer.'" *English Language Notes* 28:3 (Mar 1991), 1-9.

Robert T. Lambdin

WULFSTAN (d. 1023). Wulfstan was bishop of London in 996, bishop of Worcester and archbishop of York from 1002. Wulfstan, who often used the Latin pen-name *Lupus*, was extremely active in the political life of early eleventh-century England. He served as an advisor to kings Æthelred and Cnut, helping to draft legislation for both. Among Wulfstan's surviving literary output are twenty-one sermons, the *Canons of Edgar*, aimed at reforming the secular clergy, and the *Institutes of Polity*, a work of political theory. Wulfstan often used the work of his contemporary Ælfric as source material, but inevitably shapes it to his own unique and highly recognizable style. Wulfstan avoids metaphors and similes, frequently relying on parallelism, alliteration, and rhyme, with his prose arranged in short rhythmic clauses that often seem to resemble Old English verse forms.

His best-known work, the *Sermo Lupi ad Anglos* (Sermon of Wolf to the English), is characteristic of both his style and his pastoral concerns. It was delivered in the midst of a period of severe Danish attacks, which Wulfstan sees as symptomatic of the world approaching its end: "Beloved men, know what is true: this world is in haste, and it nears the end, and thus it is continually worse in the world as things go on; and so it must greatly worsen because of the people's sins before the Antichrist's coming, and indeed it will then be terrible and grim widely throughout the world." The Danish ravages are interpreted as divine punishment for English sins, particularly disloyalty to both the Church and the country.

SELECTED BIBLIOGRAPHY

Cummings, Michael. "A Systemic Functional Approach to the Thematic Structure of the Old English Clause." In *On Subject and Theme: A Discourse Functional Perspective.* Ruqaiya Hasan and Peter H. Fries, ed. Amsterdam: Benjamins, 1995. 275-316; Morrison, Stephen. "A Reminiscence of Wulfstan in the Twelfth Century." *Neuphilologische Mitteilungen* 96:3 (1995), 229-34; Odenstedt, Bengt. "Who Was Wulfstan? A New Theory of 'Othere's and Wulfstan's Voyages.'" *Studia Neophilologica* 66:29 (1994), 147-57.

Karl Hagen

WYCLIFFE, JOHN (c. 1330-1384?). John Wycliffe is best known today for his influence on the translation of the Bible into the vernacular. In his own time he was recognized both as an outstanding teacher at Oxford and as the spokesman for the anti-clerical cause. When he was called upon by *John of Gaunt and others to defend England against papal taxation and the appointment of English benefices to non-Englishmen, he had already produced an impressive body of philosophical/religious writing that was challenging but within the orthodoxy characteristic of a university. His progression toward heresy was fueled by political controversy and personal problems.

At first he sought to provide his employers with a theological basis for their desire to out-maneuver the church hierarchy. When his work brought strong ecclesiastical censure and many of his patrons deserted him, he fought on with increasing harshness and strikes at central Catholic dogma. Though several attempts were made by the church to silence him, he had not been excommunicated when he died on December 31, 1384, so he was buried in consecrated ground. Two decades later he was judged a heretic; still later, in 1428, his bones were burned and thrown into a stream.

The treatise *On the Incarnation of the Word*, completed about 1370, was his last non-polemic work; praised as a significant religious writing, it ironically foreshadowed his role as a reformer, the term he attached to the purpose of this divine intrusion into history. *Protestation*, which was prepared as his defense at the inconclusive trial at Lambeth, is little more than a string of biblical texts. This emphasis on the authority of Scripture is the conviction that led to Bible translations. *On the Truth of Holy Scripture* (1378) is a hastily assembled defense of the literal inspiration of the Bible, arguing against the need of official interpretations. To exalt the authority of the Bible was half his reforming purpose; the other half was to decrease the authority of the church.

On the Church (1378) attacks the inaccurate definitions of "the church" as the clergy or the community of believers. Rather, the church is made up of those predestined by God to receive salvation, the Augustinian (*see Augustine, St.*) doctrine of predestination. Wycliffe argued that since no man can know for sure that he is one of the elect, even the pope may not be and therefore should not be a trusted authority. Furthermore, it was useless to pray for the dead, or the living, since the fate of each person had already been determined by God when the world was created.

In *On the Office of the King* Wycliffe considered the relative importance of church and state. He concluded that since the pope is the vicar of Christ, representing the humanity of God, and the king is the vicar of God, representing the divinity of God, the king should take precedence over the pope. Furthermore, the clergy should live as the Levites did, on just tithes and offerings.

By 1379 Wycliffe was ready to turn his attention to a central Catholic doctrine, the mystery of the Eucharist. In *On the Power of the Pope* he pointed out that transubstantiation did not become doctrine until the reign of Pope *Innocent III (1198-1216). In *On the Eucharist* he insisted that common sense reasoned that the "very presence" of the body of Christ was symbolic and that the effectiveness of its blessing depended upon the spiritual receptiveness of the communicant receiving it. The orthodox teaching encouraged a kind of idolatry and a dangerous exaltation of the office of the priesthood. The trilogy *On Simony, On Apostasy,* and *On Blasphemy*, published in 1381-82, presents an uncompromising denunciation of every grade of the church hierarchy. *Trialogue* takes the extreme Protestant position that the test of all ecclesiastical authority was whether or not the specific situation was found in the Gospels.

While there is no record that Wycliffe ever wrote anything in English, it is known that he preached in English, and his work encouraged those who would put into practice his belief that the Bible was the ultimate authority, understandable to any sincere reader, to begin the long and painful road to the translation of the Scriptures into hundreds of vernaculars. Although he was not a systematic theologian, his wide range of subjects and his teaching skills served later generations with reasons and resources for true reformation.

SELECTED BIBLIOGRAPHY

Hudson, Anne. "The Mouse in the Pyx: Popular Heresy and the Eucharist." *Trivium* 26 (1991), 40-53; Hudson, Anne. *"Piers Plowman* and the Peasants' Revolt:" A Problem Revisited." *Yearbook of Langland Studies* 8 (1995), 85-106; Kenny, Anthony, ed. *Wyclif in His Times.* Oxford: Oxford University Press, 1986; Lindberg, Conrad. "From Jerome to Wyclif: An Experiment in Translation: The First Prologue." *Studia Neophilologica* 63:2 (1991), 143-45; McFarlane, K. B. *John Wycliffe and the Beginnings of English Nonconformity.* London: English Universities Press at Saint Paul's House, 1953; Trevelyan, George Macaulay. *England in the Age of Wycliffe.* London: Longmans Green and Co., 1972.

Esther Smith

WYNKYN DE WORDE (d. 1535). Wynkyn de Worde was the chief assistant to William *Caxton, whom he had met in Cologne. Upon Caxton's death in 1491, Wynkyn took over Caxton's printing business, which he ran until his death in 1535. One of Wynkyn's biggest moves was his relocation of the operation to Fleet Street. Soon Fleet Street was a thriving locale for a myriad of presses. Wynkyn's publications were apparently in great demand, as his catalogs from 1490 to1535 show great numbers of volumes being published.

SELECTED BIBLIOGRAPHY

Aronoff, Mark. "The Orthographic System of an Early English Printer: Wynkyn de Worde." *Folia* 8:1-2 (1989), 65-97; Meale, Carol M. "Caxton, de Worde, and the Publication of Romance in Later Medieval England." *Library* 14:4 (December 1992), 283-98; Mukai, Tyuoshi. "Wynkyn de Worde's treatment of Stephen Hawe's 'Exemple of Vertu.'" *Studies in Medieval Language and Literature* 5 (1990), 57-74.

Robert T. Lambdin

WYNNERE AND WASTOUR. *Wynnere and Wastour* is an alliterative dream *debate poem composed around 1350. The poem is datable to this time because it discusses economic problems noted in other works and compilations. The poem begins as a *dream vision in which the narrator relates seeing two armies preparing for battle on a plain. *Edward III observes the two sides and then sends his son the Black Prince to deter the sides from battle. At the prince's behest the two leaders present their stances to him. One side, "Wynnere," is the master of wealth through thrift in society. This army is joined by the pope and friars in support of this cause. The foe, "Wastour," is the immoderate spender, the metaphor of extravagance; he has been joined by the nobility and their soldiers. Obviously a sort of class war is brewing.

Edward's judgment speech is incomplete. He seems to be working as an arbiter and advises the parties to simply live their lives, not the lives of others. He sends Wastour to London as a means of stimulating the economy, while Wynnere is directed to the affluent courts of the cardinals and the pope. This economic study compares well with William *Langland's *Piers the Plowman* because of its concerns for the less fortunate and its sermonizing against the rich.

SELECTED BIBLIOGRAPHY

Scattergood, John. "'Winner and Waster' and the Mid-Fourteenth Century Economy." In *The Writer as Witness: Literature as Historical Evidence*. Tom Dunne, ed. Cork: Cork University Press, 1987. 39-57; Trigg, Stephanie. "The Rhetoric of Excess in 'Winner and Waster.'" *Yearbook of Langland Studies* 3 (1989), 91-108.

Robert T. Lambdin

WYNTOUN, ANDREW OF (c. 1350-1425). Around 1420 Andrew of Wyntoun composed the *Orygynale Cronykil*. This work is a metrical history (*see Chronicles and Annals*) of Scotland from its early times to the reign of James I. Andrew also included in his work stories that would be important to William Shakespeare in his composition of *Macbeth*. The *Cronykil* also contains most of the information about the life and works of John *Barbour. Andrew Wyntoun was a serious writer who pioneered the novel idea that his work was "original" because it started at the beginning of Scotland's history. The *Cronykil* was well known, but it was not published until 1795.

SELECTED BIBLIOGRAPHY

Goldstein, R. James. "'For He Wald Vsurpe Na Fame': Andrew of Wyntoun's Use of the Modesty Topos and Literary Culture in Early Fifteenth Century Scotland." *Studies in Scottish Literature* 25 (1990), 100-20; Wilson, Grace G. "Andrew of Wyntoun: More than Just 'That Dreich Clerk.'" *Scotia* 10 (1986), 1-14.

Robert T. Lambdin

WYRD. "Wyrd" is the Old English word for "fate." In *Anglo-Saxon England the concept of fate manifests itself mainly in a hero's willingness to test it by matching his courage against heavy odds. Usually it was believed that fate would eventually decree the death of the hero; however, the hero's courage in the face of seemingly insurmountable odds could defer this ending. It is noted in *Beowulf* that fate could save an undoomed man whose courage was good. However, once fate had decreed a man's doom, it was beyond courage's ability to save him.

SELECTED BIBLIOGRAPHY

Lochrie, Karma. "Wyrd and the Limits of Human Understanding: A Thematic Sequence in the Exeter Book." *Journal of English and Germanic Philology* 85:3 (1985), 323-31; Major, C. Tidmarsh. "A Christian Wyrd: Syncretism in *Beowulf*." *English Language Notes* 32:3 (Mar 1995), 1-10.

Robert T. Lambdin

XIMENES, FRANCISCO (1436-1517). Francisco Ximenes was a Spanish cardinal who printed the Complutensian Polyglot Bible. He also established the University of Alcala. While these are fine achievements, Ximenes gained notoriety as the instigator of one of the more diabolical acts of the Middle Ages: ho personally condemned volumes of Arabic written works as pagan. He had these works destroyed; thus innumerable works were forever lost.

SELECTED BIBLIOGRAPHY

Bowden, John. *Who's Who in Theology: From the First Century to the Present*. New York: Crossland, 1992.

Robert T. Lambdin

Y

YVAIN. A French *romance composed by *Chrétien de Troyes, *Yvain* is a more consciously composed and classically structured work about marital, rather than adulterous, love. The story is really the opposite of the *Erec et Enide* tale. Yvain wins Laudine's love, but neglects her to accompany Gauvain on a quest. Laudine promises to wait for a year, but Yvain does not return in time, so she no longer loves him. Yvain goes mad, constantly devising new ways to make Laudine love him and failing in his attempts to renew her affection. Yvain is attended by a dutiful lion, is cured of his madness, and serves as rescuer of unfortunate ladies. He saves a damsel named Lunete who is able to convince Laudine to reconcile with Yvain.

SELECTED BIBLIOGRAPHY

Busby, Kieth. "Chrétien de Troyes English'd." *Neophilologus* 71:4 (October 1987), 596-613; Florence, Melanie J. "Description as Intertextual Reference: Chrétien's 'Yvain' and Hartmann's 'Iwein.'" *Forum for Modern Language Studies* 29:1 (January 1993), 1-17; Matthews, David. "Reading the Woman Reading: Culture and Commodity in Chrétien's *Pesme* Adventure Episode." *Forum for Modern Language Studies* 30:2 (April 1994), 113-23;

Laura Cooner Lambdin

YWAIN AND GAWAIN. *Ywain and Gawain* is a fourteenth century *romance of which only one manuscript exists. The poem itself concerns more the deeds of Ywain, although Gawain does have a decent role. *Ywain and Gawain* is a variation of *Chrétien de Troyes's *Yvain*, although at four thousand lines of rhyming couplets, the English version is some three thousand lines shorter than the French. Additionally, the English version suppresses many of the French romance's themes, especially a good portion of Chrétien's commentary on *courtly love.

In the romance Ywain slays a knight who is able to control the weather and then marries the slain man's widow. Gawain then convinces Ywain to venture off with him, leaving his new wife behind. This does not sit entirely well with the woman, but she is powerless to stop the two. Gawain and Ywain have the usual romantic assortment of adventures which climax in the two heroes unknowingly doing battle against each other. Before they can be injured, each recognizes the other, and they are reunited. Gawain then helps Ywain reconcile with his wife.

SELECTED BIBLIOGRAPHY

Faris, David E. "The Art of Adventure in the Middle English Romance: 'Ywain and Gawain' and 'Eger and Grime.'" *Studia Neophilologica* 53:1 (1981), 91-100.

Robert T. Lambdin

Z

ZANZIS. This is an obscure reference to a writer whose name may actually have been "Zauzis." The reference to Zanzis by Geoffrey *Chaucer, in *Troilus and Criseyde*, may have resulted from his misinterpretation of one of Giovanni *Boccaccio's works. Others posit that Chaucer meant the Athenian painter Zeuxis, whom Cicero says attempted to assemble the finest features of a number of women in order to re-create a likeness of Helen. Others find neither explanation convincing, but offer no other explanation.

SELECTED BIBLIOGRAPHY

Bênet's Readers's Encyclopedia. 1948. 3rd ed. NY: Harpers, 1987. Drabble, Margaret, ed. *The Oxford Companion to English Literature.* 5th ed. Oxford: Oxford, University Press, 1985. Swanton, Michael. *English Literature before Chaucer.* NY: Longman, 1987.

Robert T. Lambdin

Selected Bibliography

Aers, David, ed. *Medieval Literature: Criticism, Ideology, and History.* New York: St. Martin's, 1986.

Allen, David, and Robert A. White, eds. *Subjects on the World's Stage: Essays on British Literature of the Middle Ages and the Renaissance.* Newark: University of Delaware Press, 1995.

Archibald, Elizabeth. "Incest in Medieval Literature and Society." *Forum for Modern Language Studies* 25:1 (January 1989), 1-15.

Daneke, Joost. "Transference Figures in Medieval Literature: The Madonna of Guibert de Nogent." In *Fathers and Mothers in Literature.* Henk Hillenaar and Walter Schonau, eds. Amsterdam: Rodopi, 1994. 89-101.

Bartlett, Anne Clark, *et al.*, eds. *Vox Mystica: Essays on Medieval Mysticism in Honor of Professor Valerie M. Lagorio.* Cambridge: Brewer, 1995.

Baswell, Christopher. *Virgil in Medieval England: Figuring the Aeneid from the Twelfth Century to Chaucer.* Cambridge: Cambridge University Press, 1995.

Bekker-Nielsen, Hans, et al, eds. *Hagiography and Medieval Literature: A Symposium.* Odense: Odense University Press, 1981.

Beer, Jeanette M. A. *Narrative Conventions of Truth in the Middle Ages.* Geneve: Dros, 1981.

Benton, Janetta Rebold. *The Medieval Menagerie: Animals in the Art of the Middle Ages.* New York: Abbeville, 1992.

Betts, Gavin, ed. *Three Medieval Greek Romances.* New York: Garland, 1995.

Blamires, Alcuin. *Woman Defamed and Woman Defended: An Anthology of Medieval Texts.* Oxford: Clarendon Press, 1992.

Bloch, R. Howard, and Stephen G. Nichols. *Medievalism and the Modernist Temper.* Baltimore: Johns Hopkins University Press, 1996.

Boitani, Piero, and Anna Torti, eds. *Mediaevalitas: Reading the Middle Ages.* Cambridge: Brewer, 1996.

Boland, Margaret M. "The Poet as Architect in Medieval Literature." *Tamkang Journal* 24 (April 1986), 405-16.

Bowie, Linda Julian. "'All's Fowl in Love and War': Birds in Medieval Literature." *Furman Studies* 30 (December 1984), 1-17.

Brewer, Derek. "The Place of Medieval Literature in English Studies." In *Actes du Congres de Poitiers.* Société des Anglicistes de l'Enseignement Superieur, ed. Paris: Didier, 1984. 679-94.

Brook, Leslie C. "French Studies: Late Medieval Literature." *Year's Work in Modern Language Studies* 54 (1992), 68-78.

Brown, Cynthia J. *Poets, Patrons, and Printers: Crisis of Authority in Late Medieval France*. Ithaca: Cornell University Press, 1995.

Brown, Russell E. "Pregnancy in Classical and Medieval Literature." *Neophilologus* 75:3 (July 1991), 321-26.

Brownlee, Kevin, and Walter Stephens, eds. *Discourses of Authority in Medieval and Renaissance Literature*. Hanover: Published for Dartmouth College by University Press of New England, 1989.

Brownlee, Marina S., Kevin Brownlee, and Stephen G. Nichols, eds. *The New Medievalism*. Baltimore: Johns Hopkins University Press, 1991.

Bruzelius, Caroline, and Jill Meredith, eds. *The Brummer Collection of Medieval Art*. Durham: Duke University Press, 1991.

Bumke, Joachim. *Courtly Culture: Literature and Society in the High Middle Ages*.Thomas Dunlap, trans.Berkeley: University of California Press, 1991.

Bunson, Matthew. *Encyclopedia of the Middle Ages*. New York: Facts on File, 1995.

Burnett, Charles, and Patrick Gautier Dalche. "Attitudes towards the Mongols in Medieval Literature: The XXII Kings of Gog and Magog from the Court of Frederick II to Jean de Mandeville." *Viator* 22 (1991), 153-67.

Burrow, J. A. *Essays on Medieval Literature*. Oxford: Clarendon Press, 1984.

Busby, Keith, ed. *The Arthurian Yearbook, II*. New York, Garland, 1992.

Busby, Keith, and Norris J. Lacy, eds. *Conjunctures*. Amsterdam: Rodopi, 1994.

Cachey, Theodore J. Jr., ed. *Dante Now: Current Trends in Dante Studies*. Notre Dame: University of Notre Dame Press, 1995.

Carruthers, Leo, ed. *Heroes and Heroines in Medieval English Literature*. Cambridge: Brewer, 1994.

Chance, Jane, ed. *Gender and Text in the Later Middle Ages*. Gainesville: University Press of Florida, 1996.

Chinca, Mark, et al, eds. "Displacement and Recognition: A Special Issue on Medieval Literature." *Paragraph* 13:2 (July 1990).

Classen, Albrecht, ed. *Canon and Canon Transgression in Medieval German Literature*. Goppingen: Kummerle, 1993.

-----. "Women in Medieval Literature and Life: Their Role and Appearance: Pedagogical Perspectives in Medieval Studies." *Michigan Germanic Studies* 14:1 (1988), 1-15.

-----. *Women as Protagonists and Poets in the German Middle Ages: An Anthology of Feminist Approaches to Middle High German Literature*. Goppingen: Kumerle, 1991.

Copeland, Rita, ed. *Criticism and Dissent in the Middle Ages*. Cambridge: Cambridge University Press, 1996.

Curtius, Ernst Robert. *European Literature and the Latin Middle Ages*. Princeton: Princeton University Press, 1990.

Daichman, Graciela S. *Wayward Nuns in Medieval Literature*. Syracuse: Syracuse University Press, 1986.

Davidson, Clifford, and John H. Stroupe, eds. *Drama in the Middle Ages: Comparative and Critical Essays: Second Series*. New York: AMS Press, 1990.

Davidson, Linda Kay, and Maryjane Dunn-Wood. *Pilgrimage in the Middle Ages: A Research Guide*. New York: Garland, 1993.

Dean, James M. and Christian K. Zacher, eds. *The Idea of Medieval Litrerature: New Essays on Chaucer and Medieval Culture in Honor of Donald R. Howard*. Newark: University of Delaware Press, 1992.

Delany, Sheila. "Anatomy of the Resisting Reader: Some Implications of Resistance to Sexual Wordplay in Medieval Literature." *Exemplaria* 4:1 (Spring 1992), 7-34.

Dinzelbacher, Peter. "The Way to the Other World in Medieval Literature and Art." *Folklore* 97:1 (1986), 70-87.

Doane, Alger Nicholson, and Carol Braun Pasternack, eds. *Vox Intexta: Orality and Textuality in the Middle Ages.* Madison: University of Wisconsin Press, 1991.

Donnelly, Dorothy F., ed. *"The City of God": A Collection of Critical Essays.* New York: Peter Lang, 1995.

Doob, Penelope B. R. "Late Medieval Literature: Ricardian Poetry." In *Approaches to Teaching Sir Gawain and the Green Knight.* Miriam Youngerman Miller and Jane Chance, eds. New York: Modern Language Association of America, 1986.

Ebin, Lois, ed. *Vernacular Poetics in the Middle Ages.* Kalamazoo: Medieval Institution Publications, 1984.

Ellis, Roger, and Ruthe Evans, eds. *The Medieval Translator 4.* Binghamton, NY: Medieval & Renaissance Texts & Studies. 1994.

Emmerson, Richard Kenneth. "The Prophetic, the Apocalyptic, and the Study of Medieval Literature." in *Poetic Prophecy in Western Literature.* Jan Wojcik and Raymond-Jean Frontain, eds. Rutherford; London: Fairleigh-Dickinson University Press, 1984.

Emmerson, Richard K., and Bernard McGinn, eds. *The Apocalypse in the Middle Ages.* Ithaca: Cornell University Press, 1992.

Fajardo-Acosta, Fidel, eds. *The Influence of the Classical World on Medieval Literature, Architecture, Music, and Culture.* Lewiston, NY: Edwin Mellen, 1992.

Ferrante, Joan. "The Court in Medieval Literature: The Center of the Problem." In *The Medieval Court in Europe.* Edward E. Haymes, ed. Munich: Fink, 1986.

Finke, Laurie A., and Martin B. Shichtman, eds. *Medieval Texts and Contemporary Readers.* Ithaca: Cornell University Press, 1987.

Flores, Angel, ed. *An Anthology of Medieval Lyrics.* New York: Modern Library, 1962.

Ford, Boris. *The Age of Chaucer.* Baltimore: Penguin Books, 1969.

Ford, Terence, and Andrew Green, eds. *The Pierpont Morgan Library: Medieval and Renaissance Manuscripts.* New York: Research Center for Musical Iconography, City University of New York, 1988.

Forni, Pier Massimo. *Adventures in Speech: Rhetoric and Narration in Boccaccio's Decameron.* Philadelphia: University of Pennsylvania Press, 1996.

Fraker, Charles F. *The Libro de Alexandre: Medieval Epic and Silver latin.* Chapel Hill: University of North Carolina Press, 1993.

Ganim, John M. "Medieval Literature as Monster: The Grotesque before and after Bakhtin." *Exemplaria* 7:1 (Spring 1995), 27-40.

Goebel, Ulrich. and David Lee, eds. *Interpreting Texts from the Middle Ages: The Ring of Words in Medieval Literature.* Lewiston, NY: Edwin Mellen, 1993.

Gould, Rita Slaght. "Saints, Shrews, and Scapegoats: Misalliances in Medieval Literature." In *The Aching Heart: Family Violence in Life and Literature.* Sara Munson Deats and Lagretta Tallent Lenker, eds. New York: Plenum, 1991.

Graybill, Robert V., et al, eds. *Teaching the Middle Ages, III.* Warrensburg, MO: Ralph, 1989.

Grotans, Anna A., and David W. Porter, eds. *The St. Gall Tractate: A Medieval Guide to Rhetorical Syntax.* Columbia, SC: Camden House, 1995.

Gumbrecht, Hans Ulrich. "Strangeness as a Requirement for Topicality: Medieval Literature and Reception Theory." *L'Esprit Créateur* 21:2 (1981), 5-12.

Hasty, Will, and James Hardy, eds. *German Writers and Works of the Early Middle Ages, 800-1170*. Detroit: Gale Research, 1995.

-----. *German Writers and Works of the High Middle Ages 1170-1280*. Detroit: Gale, 1994.

Haycock, Marged."Welsh Studies:Early and Medieval Literature." *Year's Work in Modern Language Studies* 54 (1992), 578-87.

Holloway, Julia Bolton, et al, eds. *Equally in God's Image: Women in the Middle Ages*. New York: Peter Lang, 1990.

Hotchkiss, Valerie R. "Gender Transgression and the Abandoned Wife in Medieval Literature." In *Gender Rhetorics: Postures of Dominance and Submission in History*. Richard C. Trexler, ed. Binghamton, NY: Center for Medieval and Renaissance Texts and Studies, 1994. 207-18.

Jackson, W. H., ed. *Knighthood in Medieval Literature*. Woodbridge, Erng: Brewer, 1981.

Jager, Eric. *The Tempter's Voice: Language and the Fall in Medieval Literature*. Ithaca: Cornell University Press, 1993.

Jerbashian, E. M. "The Tradition of the Armenian Medieval Literature and H. Toumanian." *Patma-Banasirakan Handes* 2:133 (1991), 23-35.

Kahane, H., and Kahane, R. "Justinian's Credo in Western Medieval Literature." *Byzantinische Zeitschrift* 84-85:1 (1991-92), 37-42.

Keenan, Hugh. "Typology and English Medieval Literature." In *Typology and Medieval English Literature*. Hugh Keenan, ed. New York: AMS Press, 1992. 169-81.

Keller, Barbara G. *The Middle Ages Reconsidered: Attitudes in France from the Eighteenth Century through the Romantic Movement*. New York: Peter Lang, 1994.

Kelly, Henry Ansgar. *Ideas and Forms of Tragedy from Aristotle to the Middle Ages*. Cambridge: Cambridge University Press, 1993.

-----. "The Varieties of Love in Medieval Literature according to Gaston Paris." *Romance Philology* 40:3 (February 1987), 301-27.

Kibler, William W., et al. *Medieval France: An Encyclopedia*. New York: Garland, 1995.

Kieckhefer, Richard. *Magic in the Middle Ages*. Cambridge: Cambridge University Press, 1989.

Knox, Dilwyn. *Ironia: Medieval and Renaissance Ideas on Irony*. New York: Brill, 1989.

Kooper, Erik. "Multiple Births and Multiple Disasters: Twins in Medieval Literature; Medieval Studies in Honor of Douglas Kelly." In *Conjunctures: Medieval Studies in Honor of Douglas Kelly*. Keith Busby and Norris Lacy, eds. Amsterdam: Rodopi, 1994. 253-69.

Kramer, Dewey Weiss. "A Neglected Source of Medieval Literature: The Rule of St. Benedict and the Memento Mori." *American Benedictine Review* 43:2 (June 1992), 109-30.

Kristjansson, Jonas. *Eddas and Sagas: Iceland's Medieval Literature*. Peter Foote, trans. Reykjavik: Hid Islenska Bokmenntafelag, 1988.

Krstovic, Jelena O., ed. *Classical and Medieval Literature Criticism V: Excerpts from Criticism of the Works of World Authors from Classical Antiquity through the Fourteenth Century, from the First Appraisals to Current Evaluations*. Detroit: Gale, 1991.

Kruger, Steven F. *Dreaming in the Middle Ages*. Cambridge: Cambridge University Press, 1992.

Lacy, Norris J., ed. *Medieval Arthurian Literature: A Guide to Recent Research* New York: Garland, 1996.

Law, Vivian, ed. *History of Linguistic Thought in the Early Middle Ages.* Amsterdam: Benjamins, 1993.

Levy, Bernard S., ed. *The Bible in the Middle Ages.* Binghamton, NY: Medieval and Renaissance Texts and Studies, 1992.

Lomperis, Linda. and Sarah Stanbury, eds. *Feminist Approaches to the Body in Medieval Literature.* Philadelphia: University of Pennsylvania Press, 1993.

Marx, C. W. *The Devil's Rights and the Redemption in the Literature of Medieval England.* Cambridge: Brewer, 1995.

Masters, Bernardette A. "The Distribution, Destruction, and Dislocation of Authority in Medieval Literature and Its Modern Derivatives." *Romanic Review* 82:3 (May 1991), 270-85.

McGlathery, James M., ed. *Music and German Literature: Their Relationship since the Middle Ages.* Columbia, SC: Camden House, 1992.

Mermier, Guy, ed. *Contemporary Readings of Medieval Literature.* Ann Arbor: Department of Romance Languages, University of Michigan, 1989.

Miller, Gordon L. *The Way of the English Mystics: An Anthology and Guide for Pilgrims.* Ridgefield, CT: Morehouse, 1996.

Millett, Bella, ed. *"Ancrene Wisse," the Katherine Group, and the Wooing Group.* Cambridge: Brewer, 1996.

Murphy, Michael. "Vows, Boasts and Taunts, and the Role of Women in Some Medieval Literature." *English Studies* 66:2 (April 1985), 105-12.

Nichols, Fred J., ed . and trans. *An Anthology of Neo-Latin Poetry.* New Haven: Yale University Press, 1979.

Nicolaisen, W. F. H., ed. *Oral Tradition in the Middle Ages.* Binghamton, NY: Medieval and Renaissance Texts and Studies, 1995.

Noble, Thomas F. X., and Thomas Head, eds. *Soldiers of Christ: Saints and Saints' Lives from Late Antiquity and the Early Middle Ages.* University Park: Pennsylvania State University Press, 1995.

Nolan, Edward Peter. *Now through a Glass Darkly: Specular Images of Being and Knowing from Virgil to Chaucer.* Ann Arbor: University of Michigan Press, 1990.

Olson, Paul A. *The Journey to Wisdom: Self-Education in Patristic and Medieval Literature.* Lincoln: University of Nebraska Press, 1995.

Orchard, Andy. *Pride and Prodigies: Studies in the Monsters of the Beowulf-Manuscript.* Cambridge: Brewer, 1995.

Paden, William D., ed. *The Future of the Middle Ages: Medieval Literature in the 1990s.* Gainesville: University Press of Florida, 1994.

Pagis, Dan. *Hebrew Poetry of the Middle Ages and the Renaissance.* Berkeley: University of California Press, 1991.

Payer, Pierre J. *The Bridling of Desire: Views of Sex in the Later Middle Ages.* Toronto: University of Toronto Press, 1993.

Pearsall, Derek. "Medieval Literature in Historical Context." *Review* 4 (1982), 171-77.

Petrucci, Armando. *Writers and Readers in Medieval Italy: Studies in the History of Written Culture.* Charles M. Radding, ed and trans. New Haven: Yale University Press, 1995.

Pfeffer, Wendy. *The Change of Philomel: The Nightingale in Medieval Literature.* New York: Peter Lang, 1985.

Poupard, Dennis, et al. eds. *Classical and Medieval Literature Criticism, I: Excerpts from Critical Works of World Authors from Classical Antiquity through the Fourteenth Century, from First Appraisals to Current Evaluations.* Detroit: Gale, 1988.

Quinn, William A. "The Garland Library of Medieval Literature." *Translation Review* 19 (1986), 3-9.

Rigney, Ann, and Douwe Fokkema, eds. *Cultural Participation: Trends since the Middle Ages.* Amsterdam: Benjamins, 1993.

Ross, Leslie. *Text, Image, Message: Saints in Medieval Manuscript Illustrations.* Westport, CT: Greenwood Press, 1994.

Russell, J. Stephen, ed. and intro., and Julian Wasserman, afterword. *Allegoresis: The Craft of Allegory in Medieval Literature.* New York: Garland, 1988.

Sampson, Rodney. *Early Romance Texts: An Anthology.* Cambridge: Cambridge University Press, 1980.

Saunders, Corinne J. *The Forest of Medieval Romance: Avernus, Broceliande, Arden.* Cambridge: Brewer, 1993.

Scaglione, Aldo D. *Knights at Court: Courtliness, Chivalry, and Courtesy from Ottonian Germany to the Italian Renaissance.* Berkeley: University of California Press, 1991.

Senior, W. A. "Medieval Literature and Modern Fantasy: Toward a Common Metaphysic." *Journal of the Fantastic in the Arts* 3:3 (1994), 32-49.

Shichtman, Martin B. "Medieval Literature and Contemporary Critical Theory: A Symposium." *Philological Quarterly* 67:4 (Fall 1988), 403-80.

Sidwell, Keith. *Reading Medieval Latin.* Cambridge: Cambridge University Press, 1995.

Solterer, Helen. *The Master and Minerva: Disputing Women in Medieval French Culture.* Berkeley: University of California Press, 1995.

Spearman, R. Michael, and John Higgitt, eds. *The Age of Migrating Ideas: Early Medieval Art in Northern Britain and Ireland.* Dover, NH: Sutton, 1993.

Specht, Henrik. "The Beautiful, the Handsome, and the Ugly: Some Aspects of the Art of Character Portrayal in Medieval Literature." *Studia Neophilologica* 56:2 (1984), 129-46.

Speed, Diane, ed. *Medieval English Romances I.* Durham, Eng.: Durham Medieval Texts, 1993.

-----. *Medieval English Romances II.* Durham, Eng.: Durham Medieval Texts, 1993.

Stokes, Myra, and T. L. Burton, eds. *Medieval Literature and Antiquities: Studies in Honor of Basil Cottle.* Cambridge: Brewer, 1987.

Stone, Gregory B. *The Death of the Troubadour: The Late Medieval Resistance to the Renaissance.* Philadelphia: University of Pennsylvania Press, 1994.

Sullivan, C. W., III, ed. *The Mabinogi: A Book of Essays.* New York: Garland, 1996.

Switten, Margaret L. *Music and Poetry in the Middle Ages: A Guide to Research on French and Occitan Song, 1100-1400.* New York: Garland, 1995.

Taylor, Robert A., et al. *The Centre and Its Compass: Studies in Medieval Literature in Honor of Professor John Leyerle.* Kalamazoo: Medieval Institution Publications, 1993.

Terry, Patricia, trans. *The Honeysuckle and the Hazel Tree: Medieval Stories of Men and Women.* Berkeley: University of California Press, 1995.

Thomas, Patrick A. "The Split Double Vision: The Erotic Tradition of Medieval Literature." *Neohelicon* 15:1 (1988), 187-206.

Thompson, B. Russell, Mercedes Vaquero, and Carlos Alberto Vega. "Spanish Studies: Medieval Literature." *Year's Work in Modern Language Studies.* 54(1992), 299-320.

Tkacz, Catherine Brown. "The Bible in Medieval Literature: A Bibliographic Essay on Basic and New Sources." *Religion and Literature* 19:1 (Spring 1987), 63-76.

Torrini-Roblin, Gloria. "Gomen and Gab: Two Models for Play in Medieval Literature." *Romance Philology* 38:1 (August 1984), 32-40.

Traversa, Vincenzo, ed. *The Laude in the Middle Ages.* New York: Peter Lang, 1994.

Trexler, Richard C., comp. *Gender Rhetorics: Postures of Dominance and Submission in History.* Binghamton, NY: Medieval and Renaissance Texts and Studies, 1994.

Troyan, Scott D. *Textual Decorum: A Rhetoric of Attitudes in Medieval Literature.* New York: Garland, 1994.

Utz, Richard J., ed. *Literary Nominalism and the Theory of Rereading Late Medieval Texts: A New Research Paradigm.* Lewiston, NY: Edwin Mellen Press, 1995.

Van Engen, John, ed. *The Past and Future of Medieval Studies.* Notre Dame: University of Notre Dame Press, 1994.

Vaquero, Mercedes, and Alan Deyermond, eds. *Studies on Medieval Spanish Literature in Honor of Charles F. Fraker.* Madison: Hispanic Seminary of Medieval Studies, 1995.

Wailes, Stephen L. *Medieval Allegories of Jesus' Parables.* Berkeley: University of California Press, 1987.

Watanabe-O'Kelly, Helen. *The Cambridge History of German Literature.* Cambridge: Cambridge University Press, 1997.

Waterhouse, Ruth, and John Stephens. "The Backward Look: Retrospectivity in Medieval Literature." *Southern Review* 16:3 (Nov 1983), 356-73.

Welliver, Edith. "Lessing's Approach to Medieval Literature." *Lessing Yearbook Jahrbuch* 17 (1985), 121-32.

Wells, David A. "German Studies: Medieval Literature." *Year's Work in Modern Language Studies.* 54 (1992), 648-98.

Wenzel, Siegfried. *Macaronic Sermons: Bilingualism and Preaching in Late-Medieval England.* Ann Arbor: University of Michigan Press, 1994.

Wheeler, Bonnie, ed. *Representations of the Feminine in the Middle Ages.* Dallas: Academia, 1993.

Wilhelm, James J, ed. *Lyrics of the Middle Ages.* New York: Garland, 1990.

Williams, David. *Deformed Discourse: The Function of the Monster in Mediaeval Thought and Literature.* Montreal: McGill-Queen's University Press, 1996.

Windeatt, Barry. *English Mystics of the Middle Ages.* Cambridge: Cambridge University Press, 1994.

Wolterbeek, Marc. *Comic Tales of the Middle Ages: An Anthology and Commentary.* New York: Greenwood Press, 1991.

Wright, Roger, ed. *Latin and the Romance Languages in the Early Middle Ages.* London: Routledge, 1991.

Zak, Nancy C. *The Portrayal of the Heroine in Chrétien de Troyes's Erec et Enide, Gottfried von Strassburg's Tristan, and Flamenca.* Göppingen: Kümmerle, 1983.

Ziolkowski, Jan. "Avatars of Ugliness in Medieval Literature." *Modern Language Review* 79:1 (January 1984), 1-20.

-----. "Saints in Invocations and Oaths in Medieval Literature." *Journal of English and Germanic Philology* 87 (April 1988), 179-92.

Index

About the Contributors

Libby Bernardin teaches English Composition in the Transition Year program at the University of South Carolina. She has published several poems and a novel, *The Stealing*. She is currently working on her second novel.

Rebecca Chalmers completed her master of fines arts in creative writing at the University of South Carolina. Besides medieval literature, her literary interests include poetry, particularly contemporary poetry.

John Conlee is an associate professor of English at the College of William and Mary. He has published extensively in Old and Middle English literature, especially debate poetry.

R. Churchill Curtis teaches history in the Transition Year program in the College of Hospitality, Retail and Sport Management at the University of South Carolina--Columbia. His interests lie mainly in the Civil War, a subject in which he enjoys a national reputation.

Miriam Davis is an assistant professor of history at Delta State University. She studied on a Fulbright in England, receiving her M.A. in medieval archaeology from the University of York. She earned her Ph.D. in medieval history from the University of California at Santa Barbara. Her main interests lie in combining the history and archaeology of medieval England to gain a better understanding of the period.

Silvia R. Fiore is a professor of English at the University of South Florida. She has published extensively on Boccaccio, Dante, and Machiavelli, including *Niccolò Machiavelli* (1982).

John H. Fisher is professor emeritus of the University of Tennessee and one of the foremost Chaucerian scholars. His extensive publication list includes an edition of Chaucer's works, as well as numerous critical volumes on them. He has published *The Emergence of Standard English* (1996).

Karl Hagen is a graduate student at the University of California, Los Angeles. He is currently completing his dissertation on the use and reception of medieval sermons, and has published on Middle English metrics. He also contributed to *Chaucer's Pilgrims* (Greenwood Press, 1996).

Peggy Huey most recently taught English at the University of Alabama. Among her other interests are Chaucer, the *Gawain* poet, and John Mandeville.

James Keller is associate professor of English at the Mississippi University for Women. He has published extensively on such authors as O'Neill, Nashe, Chaucer, and Marlowe.

Theresa Kennedy is currently teaching at Mary Washington College. Her interests include Italian medieval and Renaissance literature, especially Boccaccio and Petrarch.

Sigrid King teaches English at Carlow College. She has had work published in *Black American Literature*. Besides medieval literature, her interests include the English Renaissance, American Literature, and literary theory.

Laura Cooner Lambdin is now an independent researcher and author following ten years of teaching literature and composition at the university level. She has published several articles and books concerning medieval and Victorian literary topics.

Robert T. Lambdin teaches English in the Transition Year Program at the University of South Carolina. He has several publications on Chaucer and is the co-editor with his wife, Laura Cooner Lambdin of *Chaucer's Pilgrims* (Greenwood Press, 1996). His other interests include Aztec and Incan literature.

Richard McDonald is an assistant professor at Utah Valley State University. He has published a variety of articles and chapters concerning Old and Middle English literature.

Gwendolyn Morgan is an associate professor of medieval and British literature at Montana State University. She is the author of several books, including *Medieval Ballads: Chivalry, Romance, and Everyday Life* (1996). In addition she has composed numerous articles on the explications and translations of Anglo-Saxon poetry.

Sara Parker completed her doctoral work at the University of South Carolina-- Columbia. She has published works on Tacitus and William Morris. In addition to her medieval work, she is finishing a book on Wilkie Collins.

J. Scott Plaster is an independent scholar with interests in medieval and American Literature, particularly Appalachian literature.

Nancy M. Reale is a master teacher and coordinator of humanities in the General Studies Program at New York University. She is principally interested in the manner in which inherited texts are redefined and reinterpreted by successive authors.

Anna Shealy is a graduate student at the University of South Carolina. Besides her interest in medieval literature, she also enjoys studying twentieth-century American literature, especially the works of William Faulkner.

Elton E. Smith is a Distinguished Professor of English at the University of South Florida. His large catalog of publications includes many works on Victorian poets and authors, especially *The Two Voices of Tennyson*.

Esther Smith is a retired English professor and the author of many articles and books, including literary criticism, fiction, and poetry.

Rebecca Stephens is an assistant professor of English at Meredith College. Aside from medieval literature, her other interests include Virginia Woolf and Toni Morrison.

ISBN 0-313-30054-2

90000>

EAN

9 780313 300547

HARDCOVER BAR CODE